Barcelona

timeout.com/Barcelona

Published by Time Out Guides Ltd, a wholly owned subsidiary of Time Out Group Ltd.
Time Out and the Time Out logo are trademarks of Time Out Group Ltd.

© **Time Out Group Ltd 2008**
Previous editions 1996, 1998, 2000, 2001, 2002, 2003, 2004, 2005, 2006, 2007.

10 9 8 7 6 5 4 3 2 1

This edition first published in Great Britain in 2008 by Ebury Publishing
A Random House Group Company
20 Vauxhall Bridge Road, London SW1V 2SA

Random House Australia Pty Limited 20 Alfred Street, Milsons Point, Sydney, New South Wales 2061, Australia
Random House New Zealand Limited 18 Poland Road, Glenfield, Auckland 10, New Zealand
Random House South Africa (Pty) Limited Isle of Houghton, Corner Boundary
Road & Carse O'Gowrie, Houghton 2198, South Africa

Random House UK Limited Reg. No. 954009

For further distribution details, see www.timeout.com

ISBN 978-1-84670-070-5

A CIP catalogue record for this book is available from the British Library

Printed and bound by Firmengruppe APPL, aprinta druck, Wemding, Germany

The Random House Group Limited supports The Forest Stewardship Council (FSC), the leading international forest
certification organisation. All our titles that are printed on Greenpeace approved FSC certified paper carry the FSC
logo. Our paper procurement policy can be found at http://www.rbooks.co.uk/environment

Time Out Guides Limited
Universal House
251 Tottenham Court Road
London W1T 7AB
Tel + 44 (0)20 7813 3000
Fax + 44 (0)20 7813 6001
Email guides@timeout.com
www.timeout.com

Editorial

Editor Edoardo Albert
Consultant Editor Sally Davies
Copy Editor John Shandy Watson
Listings Editors Alex Phillips, Roberto Rama,
  Dylan Simanowitz
Proofreader Patrick Mulkern
Indexer Tom Lamont

Managing Director Peter Fiennes
Financial Director Gareth Garner
Editorial Director Ruth Jarvis
Deputy Series Editor Dominic Earle
Editorial Manager Holly Pick
Assistant Management Accountant Ija Krasnikova

Design

Art Director Scott Moore
Art Editor Pinelope Kourmouzoglou
Senior Designer Henry Elphick
Graphic Designer Gemma Doyle
Junior Graphic Designer Kei Ishimaru
Digital Imaging Simon Foster
Ad Make-up Jodi Sher

Picture Desk

Picture Editor Jael Marschner
Deputy Picture Editor Katie Morris
Picture Researcher Helen McFarland
Picture Desk Assistant Troy Bailey

Advertising

Sales Director Mark Phillips
International Advertising Manager Kasimir Berger
International Sales Consultant Ross Canadé
International Sales Executive Charlie Sokol
Advertising Sales (Barcelona) Creative Media Group
Advertising Assistant Kate Staddon

Marketing

Group Marketing Director John Luck
Marketing Manager Yvonne Poon
Sales and Marketing Director North America Lisa Levinson

Production

Group Production Director Mark Lamond
Production Manager Brendan McKeown
Production Coordinator Caroline Bradford
Production Controller Susan Whittaker

Time Out Group

Chairman Tony Elliott
Financial Director Richard Waterlow
Group General Manager/Director Nichola Coulthard
Time Out Magazine Ltd MD Richard Waterlow
Time Out Communications Ltd MD David Pepper
Time Out International MD Cathy Runciman
Group Art Director John Oakey
Group IT Director Simon Chappell

Contributors

Introduction Edoardo Albert. **Saint alive series** Edoardo Albert. **History** Nick Rider, Sally Davies. **Barcelona Today** William Truini (*Model B Barcelona; New cops on the block* Stephen Burgen). **Architecture** Nick Rider, Sally Davies (*Not-so-green spaces* Stephen Burgen). **God's Builder** Austen Ivereigh (*Holding the lingua* Stephen Burgen). **Where to Stay** Annie Bennett (*The best hotels* Alex Phillips; *The hotel on the hill* Tara Stevens; *Suites you, sir* Alice Ross). **Sightseeing** Sally Davies, Nadia Feddo, Nick Mead, John O'Donovan (*Coming to a stand still* Nadia Feddo; *Big trouble in little China* Stephen Burgen; *Page burner* Stephen Burgen; *La Real thing* Edoardo Albert; *Garden art* Sally Davies). **Restaurants** Sally Davies. **Cafés, Tapas & Bars** Sally Davies; *additional reviews* Kirsten Foster. **Shops & Services** Kirsten Foster (*Where to shop* Alice Ross; *Greed is green* Alex Phillips). **Festivals & Events** Nadia Feddo. **Children** Nadia Feddo. **Film** Jonathan Bennett (*City in lights* Nadia Feddo). **Galleries** Alex Phillips. **Gay & Lesbian** Dylan Simanowitz, Roberto Rama. **Music & Nightlife** Michael Kessler, Patrick Welch (*Jazz it up* Stephen Burgen). **Performing Arts** Classical Music & Opera Dani Campi, Alice Ross; *Theatre & Dance* Stephen Burgen (*Windmill of the grind* Nadia Feddo). **Sport & Fitness** Dani Campi; Daniel Aubrey (*More than a club* Peterjon Cresswell). **Trips Out of Town** Sally Davies, Tara Stevens. **Directory** Alex Phillips (*On yer bike* Nadia Feddo).

Maps john@jsgraphics.co.uk.

Photography by Elan Fleisher, except: page 12 AISA; page 15 Index/The Bridgeman Art Library; page 18 akg-images; page 20 AA World Travel Library/Alamy; page 23 Hulton-Deutsch Collection/Corbis; page 48 akg-images/ullstein bild; page 61 Karl Blackwell; page 88 Olivia Rutherford; page 141 The Bridgeman Art Library; page 173 Greg Gladman; page 209 Marta Casas; page 223 Turespaña; page 224 Natalie Pecht; page 244 Nazario; page 273 www.fcbarcelona.cat

Illustrations by Dave McKean

The Editor would like to thank Sally Davies, Alex Phillips, John Shandy Watson and Daniel Aubrey, and all contributors to previous editions of *Time Out Barcelona*, whose work forms the basis for parts of this book.

Contents

Introduction

Barcelona emerged from its decades-long hibernation during the Franco years determined to establish itself as a city apart. It had been down that road before, in the 19th and early 20th centuries, when great exhibitions announced the city to the world as it staked its claim to a status it had known in medieval times as one of the Mediterranean's great trading centres. This time the exhibit was sport and the result the triumphant 1992 Olympics. Barcelona was back.

But what do you do for an encore? In the run up to the Olympics Barcelona had performed one of the great urban transformations of modern times, turning itself around to face the sea. The finest architects and planners from around the world were invited to contribute and most were eager to fill the gaps created when the ugly high-rise blocks thrown up during the Franco years were torn down. But these architects and designers were not just making buildings and parks, they were creating a concept of a city for a new world. That the idea worked, though, was in large part due to the people of Barcelona rather than the foreign consultants. For them, the city was already special as the place where the heart of Catalan nationalism beat most strongly, a nationalism that had already taken extraordinary shape a century before in the architectural legacies of Modernista architects like Lluís Domènech i Montaner, Josep Puig i Cadafalch and, of course, Antoni Gaudí.

The concept created, it seemed like the whole world bought into it: in poll after poll Barcelona was voted the city best loved by visitors. And come they did, in ever-increasing numbers, until the city council began to worry about the devaluation of the Barcelona brand. Even this city of consummate cool could only stand so many drunken stag and hen parties. As an increasing number of residents began to feel their city was being taken away from them the council acted, removing late-night licences, acting against drunkenness and even instituting quality controls on the acts lining La Rambla. Was Barcelona in danger of becoming a victim of its own success?

That's not how the authorities see it. More prestigious projects are in the pipeline, including the reinvention of Las Arenas bullring as a futuristic shopping and leisure centre by Lord Rogers, and Jean Nouvel's new park in Poblenou. But can a city exist on design alone? Gaudí, the presiding genius of the city, would have said no, and it is his example that shows another side to the city. For the architect was both a radical innovator, yet a man deeply rooted in the spiritual and cultural traditions of his homeland. For him there was no radical scission between old and new, but rather a creative interpenetration of the two, each casting new light on the other. Thus his vision of Catalonia is different from the secular one presented by most of the agencies selling Barcelona to the world, and in this edition of the guide we highlight the ideas and work of the great architect. In 'God's Builder' we look at the progress he is making towards sanctification, as the Vatican investigates claims that he should be declared a saint, while in the 'Saint alive' series we highlight some of the people who inspire a different vision for the future of Catalonia and its magnificent capital city.

ABOUT TIME OUT CITY GUIDES

This is the 11th edition of *Time Out Barcelona*, one of an expanding series of Time Out guides produced by the people behind the successful listings magazines in London, New York and Chicago. Our guides are all written by resident experts who have striven to provide you with all the most up-to-date information you'll need to explore the city or read up on its background, whether you're a local or a first-time visitor.

THE LIE OF THE LAND

We have divided the city into areas – simplified for convenience from the full complexity of Barcelona's geography – and the relevant area name is given with each venue listed in this guide. We've also included addresses, phone numbers and websites. Wherever possible, a map reference is provided for venues listed; the maps can be found at the back of the book. For further orientation information, *see p82*.

ESSENTIAL INFORMATION

For all the practical information you might need for visiting Barcelona – including visa and customs information, details of local transport, a listing of emergency numbers, information on local weather and a selection of useful websites – turn to the Directory at the back of this guide. It begins on page 301.

THE LOWDOWN ON THE LISTINGS

We have tried to make this book as easy to use as possible. Addresses, phone numbers, bus information, opening times and admission prices are all included in the listings. However, businesses can change their arrangements at any time. Before you go out of your way, we'd strongly advise you to phone ahead to check opening times and other particulars. While every effort and care has been made to ensure the accuracy of the information contained in this guide, the publishers cannot accept responsibility for any errors it may contain.

LANGUAGE

Barcelona is a bilingual city; street signs, tourist information and menus can be in either Catalan or Spanish, and this is reflected in the guide. We have tried to use whichever is more commonly used or appropriate in each case.

PRICES AND PAYMENT

We have listed prices in euros (€) throughout and we have noted where venues such as shops, hotels, restaurants and theatres accept the following credit cards: American Express (AmEx), Diners Club (DC), MasterCard (MC) and Visa (V). Many will also accept travellers' cheques, and/or other cards such as Carte Blanche. The prices we've listed in this guide should be treated as guidelines only, not gospel.

Advertisers

We would like to stress that no establishment has been included in this guide because it has advertised in any of our publications and no payment of any kind has influenced any review. The opinions given in this book are those of Time Out writers and entirely independent.

If prices vary wildly from those we've quoted, ask whether there's a good reason for the difference. If not, go elsewhere. Then please let us know. We aim to give the best and most up-to-date advice, so we want to know if you've been badly treated or overcharged.

TELEPHONE NUMBERS

It is necessary to dial provincial area codes with all numbers in Spain, even for local calls. Hence all normal Barcelona numbers begin 93, whether you're calling from inside or outside the city. From abroad, you must dial 34 (the international dialling code for Spain) followed by the number given in this book, including the initial 93. For more information on telephones, *see p320*.

MAPS

The map section includes a map of the entire region around Barcelona for planning trips out of town and maps of the local rail and metro networks, plus overviews of the greater Barcelona area and its neigbourhoods. We have included detailed street maps of the Eixample, the Raval, Born, Sant Pere and other districts, as well as a large-scale map of the Old City. There is also a comprehensive street index. The maps start on page 335 and pinpoint the specific locations of hotels (❶), restaurants (❶) and cafés and bars (❶).

LET US KNOW WHAT YOU THINK

We hope you enjoy the *Time Out Barcelona Guide*, and we'd like to know what you think of it. We welcome tips for places that you consider we should include in future editions and take note of your criticism of our choices. You can email us at guides@timeout.com.

There is an online version of this book, along with guides to over 100 international cities, at **www.timeout.com**.

L'AUDITORI

TRAM Línia T4 (Auditori / Teatre Nacional)

METRO Línia 1 (Marina) · Línia 2 (Monumental)

BUS Línies 6, 7, 10, 56, 62, B21, B25 · **NIGHT BUSES**: N0, N2, N3, N7, N11

TRAIN Línia 1,3,4,7 (Arc de Triomf)

BICING Estació c. Padilla, 151

Photo: © Martí E. Berenguer

DIAGONAL

In Context

Torre Agbar. *See p140.*

History

Live free(ish) or decline.

As city histories go, Barcelona's has always been on the uneven side. Economic disaster has followed boom as desperate times have followed peaceful ones, partly thanks to Catalonia's precarious fortunes as a political entity – sometimes an independent, powerful nation and, indeed, once a world power; sometimes an embattled subdivision of a larger entity. While cultural, political and social diversity flourish in today's Barcelona, it has not always been that way. For long periods of its history, the city was the victim of attempts by governments in Madrid to absorb an unwilling Catalonia within a unified Spanish state. Under several leaders, notably Philip V in the 17th century and Franco in the 20th century, these attempts resulted in a policy aimed at stamping out any vestige of Catalan culture or independence. However, the region has always re-emerged from such persecutions stronger, more vibrant and with a heightened desire to show the world its distinctive character, both socially as well as culturally.

IN THE BEGINNING

The Romans founded Barcelona in about 15 BC on the Mons Taber, a small hill between two streams that provided a good view of the Mediterranean and which today is crowned by a cathedral. At the time, the plain around it was sparsely inhabited by the Laetani, an agrarian Iberian people who produced grain and honey, and gathered oysters. Then called Barcino, the town was smaller than Tarraco (Tarragona), which was the capital of the Roman province of Hispania Citerior, but it had the only harbour between there and Narbonne.

Like virtually every other Roman new town in Europe, Barcino was originally a fortified rectangle with a crossroads at its centre (which is where the Plaça Sant Jaume is today). It was also a decidedly unimportant provincial town, but the rich plain provided it with a produce garden, and the sea nearby gave it an incipient maritime trade. It acquired a Jewish community soon after its foundation and became associated with Christian martyrs, most particularly Santa

Eulàlia (see p88 **Saint alive**), Barcelona's first patron saint. Eulàlia was supposedly executed at the end of the third century via a series of revolting tortures that included being rolled naked in a sealed barrel full of glass shards down the alley now called Baixada ('Descent') de Santa Eulàlia.

The people of Barcino accepted Christianity in 312, at a time when the Roman empire was facing a growing threat of invasion by the tribes milling around its borders. In response to the barbarian threat, the town's rough defences were replaced with massive stone walls in the fourth century, many sections of which can still be seen today. It was these ramparts that ensured Barcelona's continuity, making the stronghold desirable to later warlords.

Nonetheless, defences like these could not prevent the empire's disintegration. In 415, Barcelona, as it became known, briefly became capital of the kingdom of the Visigoths, under their chieftain Ataülf. They soon moved on southwards to extend their control over the whole of the Iberian peninsula, and for the next 400 years the town was a neglected backwater. The Muslims swept across the peninsula after 711, crushing Goth resistance; they made little attempt to settle Catalonia, but much of the Christian population retreated into the Pyrenees, the first Catalan heartland.

Then, at the end of the eighth century, the Franks drove south, against the Muslims, from across the mountains. In 801, Charlemagne's son, Louis the Pious, took Barcelona and made it a bastion of the Marca Hispanica (Spanish March), which was the southern buffer of his father's empire. This gave Catalonia a trans-Pyrenean influence entirely different from that of the other Christian states in Spain; equally, it is for this reason that the closest relative of the Catalan language is Provençal, not Castilian.

'Catalonia was independent and the Counts of Barcelona free to forge its destiny.'

When the Frankish princes returned to their main business further north, loyal counts were left behind to rule sections of the Catalan lands. At the end of the ninth century, Count Guifré el Pilós (Wilfred 'the Hairy'; photo p15) managed to gain control over several of these Catalan counties from his base in Ripoll. By uniting them under his rule, he laid the basis for a future Catalan state, founding the dynasty of the Counts of Barcelona, which reigned in an unbroken line until 1410. His successors made Barcelona their capital, thereby setting the seal on the city's future.

As a founding patriarch, Wilfred is the stuff of legends, not least of which is that he was the creator of the Catalan flag. The story goes that he was fighting the Saracens alongside his lord, the Frankish emperor, when he was severely wounded. In recognition of Wilfred's heroism, the emperor dipped his fingers into his friend's blood and ran them down the count's golden shield; thus, the Quatre Barres, four bars of red on a yellow background, also known as La Senyera. Recorded facts make this story highly unlikely, but whatever its origins, the four-stripe symbol was first recorded on the tomb of Count Ramon Berenguer II from 1082, making it the oldest national flag in Europe. What is not known is exactly in what way Wilfred was so notably hairy.

In 985, a century after Wilfred, a Muslim army attacked and sacked Barcelona. The hirsute count's great-grandson, Count Borrell II, requested aid from his theoretical feudal lord, the Frankish king. He received no reply, and so repudiated all Frankish sovereignty over Catalonia. From then on, although the name was not yet in use, Catalonia was effectively independent, and the Counts of Barcelona were free to forge its destiny.

CONFIDENT GROWTH

In the first century of the new millennium, Catalonia was consolidated as a political entity, and entered an age of cultural richness. This was the great era of Catalan Romanesque art, with the building of the magnificent monasteries and the churches of northern Catalonia, such as Sant Pere de Rodes near Figueres, and the painting of the glorious murals now housed in the Museu Nacional on Montjuïc. There was also a flowering of scholarship, reflecting Catalan contacts with northern Europe and with Islamic and Carolingian cultures. In Barcelona, shipbuilding and trade in grain and wine grew, and a new trade developed in textiles. The city expanded both inside its old Roman walls and outside them, with vilanoves (new towns) appearing at Sant Pere and La Ribera.

Catalonia also gained more territory from the Muslims to the south, beyond the Penedès, and – either through marriage or with Arab booty – in what is now southern France. The most significant marriage, however, occurred in 1137, when Ramon Berenguer IV (1131-62) wed Petronella, who was heir to the throne of Aragon. In the long term, the marriage bound Catalonia into Iberia. The uniting of the two dynasties created a powerful entity known as the Crown of Aragon: each element retained its separate institutions, and was ruled by monarchs known as the Count-Kings. Since

Aragon was already a kingdom, it was given precedence, and its name was often used to refer to the state, but the language used in the court was Catalan and the centre of government remained in Barcelona.

Ramon Berenguer IV also extended Catalan territory to its current frontiers in the Ebro valley. At the beginning of the next century, however, the dynasty lost virtually all its land north of the Pyrenees to France, when Count-King Pere I 'the Catholic' was killed at the Battle of Muret in 1213. This proved a blessing. In future years, the Catalan-Aragonese state became oriented towards the Mediterranean and the south, and was able to embark on two centuries of imperialism that would be equalled in vigour only by Barcelona's burgeoning commercial enterprise.

EMPIRE BUILDING

Pere I's successor was the most expansionist of the Count-Kings. Jaume I 'the Conqueror' (1213-76) abandoned any idea of further adventures in Provence and joined the campaign against the Muslims to the south, taking Mallorca in 1229, Ibiza in 1235 and, at greater cost, Valencia in 1238 (he made the last of these another separate kingdom, the third part of the Crown of Aragon). Barcelona became the centre of an empire that spanned the Mediterranean.

The city grew tremendously. In the middle of the 13th century, Jaume I ordered the building of a second wall along the line of La Rambla, encircling the area between there and the modern Parc de la Ciutadella, thus bringing La Ribera and the other *vilanoves* within the city. In 1274, he also gave Barcelona a form of self-government: the Consell de Cent, a council of 100 chosen citizens, an institution that would last for more than 400 years. In Catalonia as a whole, royal powers were strictly limited by a parliament, the Corts, with a permanent standing committee known as the Generalitat.

The Count-Kings commanded a powerful fleet and a mercenary army centred on the Almogàvers, irregular warriors who had been hardened in the endless battles against the Muslims on the Catalan frontier. The Almogàvers were themselves feared equally by Christians and Muslims, as they travelled the Mediterranean conquering and plundering in the name of God and the Crown of Aragon.

In 1282, Pere II 'the Great' sent his armies into Sicily; Catalan domination over the island would last for nearly 150 years. The Catalan empire reached its greatest strength under Jaume II 'the Just' (1291-1327). Corsica (1323) and Sardinia (1324) were added to the Crown of Aragon, although the latter would never submit and became a constant focus of revolt.

THE GOLDEN AGE

The Crown of Aragon was often at war with Arab rulers, but its capital flourished through commerce with every part of the Mediterranean, both Christian and Muslim. Catalan ships also sailed into the Atlantic, to England and Flanders, their ventures actively supported by the Count-Kings and burghers of Barcelona and regulated by the first-ever code of maritime law, known as the *Llibre del Consolat de Mar* (written in 1258-72). By the late 13th century, around 130 consulates ringed the Mediterranean, all engaged in a complex system of trade.

Not surprisingly, this age of power and prestige was also the great era of building in medieval Barcelona. The Count-Kings' imperial conquests may have been ephemeral, but their talent for permanence in building can still be seen today. Between 1290 and 1340, the construction of most of Barcelona's best-known Gothic buildings was initiated. Religious edifices such as the cathedral, Santa Maria del Mar and Santa Maria del Pi were matched by civil buildings such as the Saló de Tinell and the Llotja, the old market and the stock exchange. As a result, Barcelona contains the most important collection of historic Gothic civil architecture anywhere in Europe.

The ships of the Catalan navy were built in the monumental Drassanes (shipyards), begun by Pere II and completed under Pere III, in 1378. In 1359, Pere III also built the third, final city wall along the line of the modern Paral·lel, Ronda Sant Pau and Ronda Sant Antoni. This gave the Old City of Barcelona its definitive shape. La Ribera, 'the waterfront', was the centre of trade and industry in the 14th century city. Just inland, the Carrer Montcada was where newly enriched merchants displayed their wealth in opulent Gothic palaces. All around were the workers of the various craft guilds, grouped together in their own streets.

The Catalan Golden Age was also an era of cultural greatness. Catalonia was one of the first areas in Europe to use its vernacular language, as well as Latin, in written form and as a language of culture.

The oldest written texts in Catalan are the *Homílies d'Organyà*, 12th-century translations from the Bible. The court and the aristocracy seem to have attained an unusual level of literacy very early: Jaume I even wrote an autobiography, the *Llibre dels Feits*, or 'Book of Deeds', in which he recounted his achievements.

Incipient Catalan literature was given a vital thrust by Ramon Llull (1235-1316, *see p140* **Saint alive**). After a debauched youth, he experienced a series of religious visions and became the first man in post-Roman Europe to write philosophy in a vernacular language.

Steeped in Arabic and Hebrew writings, Llull brought together Christian, Islamic, Jewish and classical ideas, and wrote a vast amount on other subjects too, from theories of chivalry to poetry and visionary tales, in doing so creating Catalan as a literary language. Catalan translations were undertaken from Greek and Latin. Chroniclers such as Ramon Muntaner recorded the exploits of Count-Kings and Almogàvers; in 1490, in the twilight of the Golden Age, the Valencian Joanot Martorell published *Tirant lo Blanc*, a bawdy adventure widely considered the first European novel.

REVOLT AND COLLAPSE

The prosperity of the medieval period did not last. The Count-Kings had overextended Barcelona's resources, and overinvested in far-off ports. By 1400, the effort to maintain their conquests, especially Sardinia, had exhausted the spirit and the coffers of the Catalan imperialist drive. The Black Death, which arrived in the 1340s, also had a devastating impact on Catalonia, intensifying the bitterness of social conflicts between the aristocracy, the merchants, the peasants and the urban poor.

In 1410, Martí I 'the Humane' died without an heir, bringing to an end the line of counts of Barcelona, unbroken since Wilfred 'the Hairy'. The Crown of Aragon was passed to a member of a Castilian noble family, the Trastámaras: Fernando de Antequera (1410-16). In the 1460s, the effects of war and catastrophic famine led to a sudden collapse into violent and destructive civil war and peasant revolt. The population was depleted to such an extent that Barcelona would not regain the numbers it had had in 1400 (40,000) until the 18th century.

In 1469, an important union for Spain initiated a woeful period in Barcelona's history; dubbed by some Catalan historians the *Decadència*, it eventually led to the end of Catalonia as a separate entity. In that year, Ferdinand of Aragon (1479-1516) married Isabella of Castile (1476-1504), thereby uniting the different Spanish kingdoms, even though they would retain their separate institutions for another two centuries.

EAST OF EDEN

As Catalonia's fortunes had declined, so those of Castile to the west had risen. In 1492, Granada, the last Muslim foothold in Spain, was conquered; Isabella decreed the expulsion of all Jews from Castile and Aragon; and, most famously, Columbus discovered America.

The Catalan flag is drawn in Wilfred the Hairy's blood. *See p13.*

It was Castile's seafaring orientation towards the Atlantic, as opposed to the Mediterranean, that confirmed Catalonia's decline. The discovery of the New World was a disaster for Catalan commerce: trade shifted away from the Mediterranean, and Catalans were barred from participating in the exploitation of the new empire until the 1770s. The weight of Castile within the monarchy was increased, and it soon became the clear seat of government.

In 1516, the Spanish crown passed to the House of Habsburg, in the shape of Ferdinand and Isabella's grandson, Holy Roman Emperor Charles V. His son, Philip II of Spain, established Madrid as the capital of all his dominions in 1561. Catalonia was managed by viceroys, and the power of its institutions was restricted, with a down-at-heel aristocracy and a meagre cultural life, although at least Barcelona does appear at the end of Cervantes' *Don Quixote* (and Madrid doesn't; *photo p18*).

GRIM REAPERS

While Castilian Spain went through its Golden Century, Catalonia was left on the margins. However, worse was to come in the following century with the two national revolts, both heroic defeats that have since acquired a central role in Catalan mythology.

The problem for the Spanish monarchy was that Castile was an absolute monarchy and thus could be taxed at will, but in the former Aragonese territories, and especially Catalonia, royal authority kept coming up against a mass of local rights and privileges. As the Habsburgs' empire became entrenched in wars and expenses that not even American gold could meet, the Count-Duke of Olivares, the formidable great minister of King Philip IV (1621-65), resolved to extract more money and troops from the non-Castilian dominions of the Crown. The Catalans, however, felt they were taxed enough already.

In 1640, a mass of peasants, later dubbed Els Segadors (the Reapers), gathered on La Rambla in Barcelona, outside the Porta Ferrissa (Iron Gate) in the second wall. The peasants rioted against royal authority, surged into the city and murdered the viceroy, the Marquès de Santa Coloma. This began the general uprising known as the Guerra dels Segadors, or the 'Reapers' War'. The authorities of the Generalitat, led by its president Pau Claris, were fearful of the violence of the poor; lacking the confidence to declare Catalonia independent, they appealed for protection from Louis XIII of France. French armies, however, were unable to defend Catalonia adequately, and in 1652 a destitute Barcelona capitulated to the equally exhausted army of Philip IV. In 1659, France and Spain

made peace with a treaty that gave the Catalan territory of Roussillon, around Perpignan, to France. After the revolt, Philip IV and his ministers were magnanimous, allowing the Catalans to retain what was left of their institutions despite their disloyalty.

THE REIGN IN SPAIN

Fifty years later, came the second of the great national rebellions, this one being the War of the Spanish Succession. In 1700, Charles II of Spain died without an heir, and Castile accepted the grandson of Louis XIV of France, Philip of Anjou, as King Philip V of Spain (1700-46). However, the alternative candidate, Archduke Charles of Austria, promised that he would restore the traditional rights of the former Aragonese territories, and won their allegiance as a result. He also had the support, in his fight against France, of Britain, Holland and Austria.

But Catalonia had backed the wrong horse. In 1713, Britain and the Dutch made a separate peace with France and withdrew their aid, leaving the Catalans stranded, with no possibility of victory. After a 13-month siege in which every citizen was called to arms, Barcelona fell to the French and Spanish armies on 11 September 1714. The most heroic defeat of all, the date marked the most decisive political reverse in Barcelona's history, and is now commemorated as Catalan National Day, the Diada. Some of Barcelona's resisters were buried next to the church of Santa Maria del Mar in the Born, in the Fossar de les Moreres (Mulberry Graveyard), now a memorial.

In 1715, Philip V issued his decree of Nova Planta, abolishing all the remaining separate institutions of the Crown of Aragon and so, in effect, creating 'Spain' as a single, unitary state. Large-scale 'Castilianisation' of the country was initiated, and Castilian replaced the Catalan language in all official documents. In Barcelona, extra measures were taken to keep the city under control. The crumbling medieval walls and the castle on Montjuïc were refurbished with new ramparts, and a massive new citadel was built on the eastern side of the Old City, where the Parc de la Ciutadella is today. To make space, thousands were expelled from La Ribera and forcibly rehoused in the Barceloneta, Barcelona's first-ever planned housing scheme, with its barrack-like street plan unmistakably provided by French military engineers. The citadel became the most hated symbol of the city's subordination.

URBAN RENAISSANCE

Politically subjugated and without a significant native ruling class, Catalonia nevertheless revived in the 18th century. Shipping picked up, and Barcelona started a booming export trade

Don Quixote. *See p17.*

to the New World in wines and spirits from Catalan vineyards, and textiles, wool and silk. In 1780, a merchant called Erasme de Gómina opened Barcelona's first true factory, a hand-powered weaving mill in C/Riera Alta with 800 workers. In the next decade, Catalan trade with Spanish America quadrupled; Barcelona's population had grown from 30,000 in 1720 to around 100,000 by the end of the 18th century.

The prosperity was reflected in a new wave of building in the city. Neo-classical mansions appeared, notably on C/Ample and La Rambla, but the greatest transformation was La Rambla itself. Until the 1770s, it had been a dusty, dry riverbed where country people came to sell their produce, lined on the Raval side mostly with giant religious houses and on the other with Jaume I's second wall. In 1775, the Captain-General, the Marqués de la Mina, embarked on an ambitious scheme to demolish the wall and turn the Rambla into a paved promenade. Beyond the Rambla, the previously semi-rural Raval was swiftly becoming densely populated.

Barcelona's expansion was briefly slowed by the French invasion of 1808. Napoleon sought to appeal to Catalans by offering them national recognition within his empire, but was met with curiously little response. After six years of turmoil, Barcelona's growing business class resumed its many projects in 1814, with the restoration of the Bourbon monarchy in the shape of Ferdinand VII (1808-33).

GETTING UP STEAM

Ferdinand VII attempted to reinstate the absolute monarchy of his youth and reimpose his authority over Spain's American colonies, but he failed. On his death he was succeeded by his three-year-old daughter Isabella II (1833-68), but the throne was also claimed by his brother Carlos, who was backed by the country's most reactionary sectors.

To defend Isabella's rights, the Regent, Ferdinand's widow Queen María Cristina, was obliged to seek the support of liberals, and so granted a very limited form of constitution. Thus began Spain's Carlist Wars, which had a powerful impact in conservative rural Catalonia, where Don Carlos's faction won a considerable following, in part because of its support for traditional local rights and customs.

While this struggle went on, a liberal-minded local administration in Barcelona, freed from subordination to the military, was able to engage in city planning, opening up the soon-to-be fashionable C/Ferran and Plaça Sant Jaume in the 1820s and later adding the Plaça Reial. A change came in 1836, when the government in Madrid decreed the Desamortización (or the 'disentailment') of Spain's monasteries. In

Barcelona, where convents and religious houses still took up great sections of the Raval and the Rambla, a huge area was freed for development. The Rambla took on the appearance it roughly retains today, while the Raval filled up with tenements and textile mills several storeys high.

'Oda a la Pàtria is credited with initiating the rebirth of Catalan culture.'

In 1832, the first steam-driven factory in Spain was built on C/Tallers, sparking resistance from hand-spinners and weavers. Most of the city's factories were still relatively small, however, and the Catalan manufacturers were aware that they were at a disadvantage in competing with the industries of Britain and other countries to the north. Complicating matters further, they didn't even have the city to themselves. Not only did the anti-industrial Carlists threaten from the countryside, but Barcelona soon became a centre of radical ideas. Its people were notably rebellious, and liberal, republican, free-thinking and even utopian socialist groups proliferated between sporadic bursts of repression. (In 1842, a liberal revolt, the Jamancia, took over Barcelona, and barricades went up around the city. This would be the last occasion on which Barcelona was bombarded from the castle on Montjuïc, as the army struggled to regain control.)

By this time, the Catalan language had been relegated to secondary status, spoken in every street but rarely written or used in cultured discourse. Then, in 1833, Bonaventura Carles Aribau published his *Oda a la Pàtria*, a romantic eulogy in Catalan of the country, its language and its past. The poem had an extraordinary impact and is still traditionally credited with initiating the Renaixença ('rebirth') of Catalan heritage and culture. The year 1848 was a high point for Barcelona and Catalonia, with the inauguration of the first railway in Spain, from Barcelona to Mataró, and the opening of the Liceu opera house.

SETTING AN EIXAMPLE

The optimism of Barcelona's new middle class was counterpointed by two persistent obstacles: the weakness of the Spanish economy as a whole, and the instability of their own society, which was reflected in atrocious labour relations. No consideration was given to the manpower behind the industrial surge: the underpaid, overworked men, women and children who lived in appalling conditions in high-rise slums within the cramped city. In 1855, the first general strike took place in

Saint alive St George

What do William Shakespeare, Miguel de Cervantes and St George have in common? They all died on or near 23 April, with the master dramaturge and literary don arranging well-nigh simultaneous exits in 1616. Of course, we're slightly less certain about the exact date of St George's death – the more sceptical among historians doubting the fact of his birth let alone the time of his passing – but that has not stopped the enterprising Catalans from amalgamating the feast of their patron saint with the celebrations of the two literary lions. La Diada de Sant Jordi (St George's Day) had been associated since medieval times with lovers, the paramours giving gifts of roses, but in the 1920s the writer Vicent Clavel Andrés proposed marking the birth of Cervantes as a book day. A little tweaking saw the date changed to 23 April in 1930 and since then the Dia del Llibre has gone from strength to strength, with Unesco declaring, in 1995, that 23 April should be World Book and Copyright Day.

Thus this most adaptable and travelled of saints makes his way into the 21st century world of supra-national organisations and officially endorsed culture. George has come a long way from the little town in Cappadocia

where he was, possibly, born. Of course, there is no historical source for where he came from, nor for the idea that he was a Roman soldier, and not even that he was martyred. But then, there aren't that many historical sources at all for obscure third-century soldiers. What we do have, however, are traces of a man whose mark in history has been all but obscured by later legends. His cult spread rapidly through the eastern Roman empire and by 494 he was cautiously canonised by Pope Gelasius I as one of those 'whose names are justly reverenced among men, but whose acts are known only to God'.

Nature abhors a vacuum and the religious mind dislikes a blank canvas, so the story of St George soon began to be filled in. The oldest traditions state that he was a soldier who refused to abjure his religion despite the orders of the Emperor Diocletian, and was beheaded. George's sufferings soon underwent inflation, taking in poison drinks, being cut into pieces, molten lead and being sawn in two. If some of these sufferings sound a trifle, well, terminal, don't worry since George was restored to life three times before finally expiring. Pope Gelasius, while accepting George's sanctity, was somewhat more sceptical about his invulnerability and forbade the promulgation of these legends.

The cult of St George really took off with the Crusades. Those knights that survived brought the Cappadocian home with them, and in the 13th century the best seller of the age, Jacobus de Voragine's Golden Legend, featured a new twist to the tale: dragon killing. George became the emblem of the courtly, chivalric culture of medieval Europe, the ideal to be attempted by the rowdy, licentious but essentially pious nobility and a hero to the peasantry who took every advantage of clerically sanctioned days off. Since St George offered protection to those travelling by sea port cities like Barcelona adopted him as patron. The saint duly reciprocated. According to Jaume I, George helped the Catalans conquer the city of Mallorca, and the soldier saint played his part in the long Reconquista.

Despite the assaults of modern scholars, St George's recent move into the literary realm suggests that the old warhorse still has some legs on him. This is one old soldier who positively relishes new tricks.

Barcelona. Inaugurating a long cycle of conflict, the Captain-General, Zapatero, refused to permit any workers' organisations to function, and bloodily suppressed all resistance.

One response to the city's problems that had almost universal support in Barcelona was the demolition of the city walls, which had imposed a stifling restriction on its growth. For years, however, the Spanish state refused to relinquish its hold on the city. To find space, larger factories were established in villages around Barcelona, such as Sants and Poblenou, and in 1854 permission finally came for the demolition of the citadel and the walls. The work began with enthusiastic popular participation, crowds of volunteers joining in at weekends. Barcelona at last broke out of the space it had occupied since the 14th century and spread outwards into its new *eixample* (extension), to a controversial new plan by Ildefons Cerdà.

In 1868, Isabella II, once a symbol of liberalism, was overthrown by a progressive revolt. During the six years of upheaval that followed, power in Madrid would be held by the provisional government, a constitutional monarchy under an Italian prince and later a federal republic. However, workers were free to organise; in 1868, Giuseppe Fanelli brought the first anarchist ideas, and two years later, the first Spanish workers' congress took place in Barcelona. The radical forces were divided between many squabbling factions, while the established classes of society felt increasingly threatened and called for the restoration of order. The Republic proclaimed in 1873 was unable to establish its authority, and succumbed to a military coup less than a year later.

THE MIDAS TOUCH

In 1874, the Bourbon dynasty, in the person of Alfonso XII, son of Isabella II, was restored to the Spanish throne. Workers' organisations were again suppressed. The middle classes, however, felt their confidence renewed. The 1870s saw a frenzied boom in stock speculation, known as the *febre d'or* (gold fever), and the real take-off of building in the Eixample. From the 1880s, Modernisme became the preferred style of the new district, the perfect expression of the confidence and impetus of the industrial class. The first modern Catalanist political movement was founded by Valentí Almirall.

Barcelona felt it needed to show the world all that it had achieved, and that it was more than just a 'second city'. In 1885, a promoter named Eugenio Serrano de Casanova proposed to the city council the holding of an international exhibition, such as had been held successfully in London, Paris and Vienna. Serrano was a highly dubious character who eventually made

off with large amounts of public funds, but by the time this became clear, the city fathers had fully committed themselves to the event.

The Universal Exhibition of 1888 was used as a pretext for the final conversion of the Ciutadella into a park. Giant efforts had to be made to get everything ready in time, a feat that led the mayor, Francesc Rius i Taulet, to exclaim that 'the Catalan people are the yankees of Europe'. The first of Barcelona's three great efforts to demonstrate its status to the world, the 1888 Exhibition signified the consecration of the Modernista style, as well as the end of provincial, dowdy Barcelona and its establishment as a modern-day city on the international map.

THE CITY OF THE NEW CENTURY

The 1888 Exhibition left Barcelona with huge debts, a new look and lots of reasons to believe in itself as a paradigm of progress. The Catalan Renaixença continued, and acquired a more political tone. In 1892, the Bases de Manresa, a draft plan for Catalan autonomy, were drawn up. Middle-class opinion gradually became more sympathetic to political Catalanism.

A truly decisive moment came in 1898, when the underlying weakness of the Spanish state was made plain over the superficial prosperity of the first years of the Bourbon restoration. It was then that Spain was forced into a short war with the United States, in which it lost its remaining empire in Cuba, the Philippines and Puerto Rico. Industrialists were horrified at losing the lucrative Cuban market, and despaired of the ability of the state ever to reform itself. Many swung behind a conservative nationalist movement: the Lliga Regionalista (Regionalist League), founded in 1901 and led by Enric Prat de la Riba and the politician-financier Francesc Cambó, promised both national revival and modern, efficient government.

At the same time, however, Barcelona continued to grow, fuelling Catalanist optimism. In 1897, the city incorporated most of its satellite communities, reaching a population of over half a million, and in 1907 it initiated the 'internal reform' of the Old City by creating the Via Laietana, which cut right through it.

Catalan letters were thriving. The Institut d'Estudis Catalans (Institute of Catalan Studies) was founded in 1906, and Pompeu Fabra set out to create the first Catalan dictionary. Above all, Barcelona had a vibrant artistic community, centred on Modernisme, which consisted of great architects and established painters such as Rusiñol and Casas, but also the many penniless bohemians who gathered round them, among them a young Picasso.

The bohemians were drawn to the increasingly wild nightlife of the Raval, where cabarets, bars and brothels multiplied at the end of the 19th century. Located around the cabarets, though, were the very poorest of the working classes, for whom conditions had only continued to decline; Barcelona had some of the worst cases of overcrowding and the highest mortality rates in Europe. Local philanthropists called for something to be done, but Barcelona was more associated with revolutionary politics and violence than with peaceful social reform. Rebellion among the working classes pre-dated the arrival of anarchism; in the 19th century, the Catholic Church was the frequent target of the mobs, protesting against its collusion with the authorities and the control it exercised over the day-to-day life of the poorer classes.

In 1893, more than 20 people were killed in a series of anarchist terrorist attacks, which included the notorious throwing of a bomb into the wealthy audience at the Liceu. The perpetrators acted alone, but the authorities seized the opportunity to round up the usual suspects for questioning – mainly local anarchists and radicals. Several of them, known as the 'Martyrs of Montjuïc', were later tortured and executed in the castle above the city. One retaliation came in 1906, when a Catalan anarchist tried to kill King Alfonso XIII on his wedding day.

Anarchism was still only in a fledgling stage among workers in the 1900s. However, rebellious attitudes, along with growing republican sentiment and a fierce hatred of the Catholic Church, united the underclasses and led them to take to the barricades. The Setmana Tràgica (Tragic Week) of 1909 began as a protest against the conscription of troops for the colonial war in Morocco, but degenerated into a general riot, with the destruction of churches by excited mobs. Suspected culprits were summarily executed, as was the anarchist educationalist Francesc Ferrer, who was accused of 'moral responsibility' even though he wasn't even in Barcelona at the time.

These events dented the optimism of the Catalanists of the Lliga. However, in 1914 they secured from Madrid the Mancomunitat, or administrative union, of the four Catalan provinces, the first joint government of any kind in Catalonia in 200 years. Its first president was Prat de la Riba, who would be succeeded on his death in 1917 by the architect Puig i Cadafalch. However, the Lliga's plans for an orderly Catalonia were to be obstructed by a further surge in social tensions.

CHAMPAGNE AND SOCIALISTS

Spain's neutral status during World War I gave a huge boost to the Spanish, and especially Catalan, economy. Exports soared as Catalonia's manufacturers made millions supplying uniforms to the French army. Barcelona's industry was at last able to diversify from textiles into engineering, chemicals and other more modern sectors.

Barcelona also became a place of refuge for anyone in Europe who wanted to avoid the war. Its refugee community included artists Sonia and Robert Delaunay, Francis Picabia, Marie Laurencin and Albert Gleizes, but the city was also a bolt-hole for all kinds of low-life from around the continent. The Raval area was soon dubbed the Barrio Chino (Chinatown), identifying it as an area of sin and perdition. Some of the regular patrons of the lavish new cabarets were industrialists; many of the war profits were spent immediately in conspicuous consumption. The war also set off massive inflation, driving people from rural Spain into the big cities. Barcelona doubled in size in 20 years to become the largest city in Spain, and also the fulcrum of Spanish politics. Workers' wages, meanwhile, had lost half their real value.

The chief channel of protest in Barcelona was the anarchist workers' union, the Confederación Nacional del Trabajo (CNT), constituted in 1910, which gained half a million members in Catalonia by 1919. The CNT and the socialist Union General de Trabajadores (UGT) launched a joint general strike in 1917, roughly co-ordinated with a campaign by the Lliga and other liberal politicians for political reform. However, the politicians soon withdrew at the prospect of serious social unrest. Inflation continued to intensify, and in 1919 Barcelona was paralysed for more than two months by a CNT general strike over union recognition. Employers refused to recognise the CNT, and the most intransigent among them hired gunmen to get rid of union leaders. Union activists replied in kind, and virtual guerrilla warfare developed between the CNT, the employers and the state. More than 800 people were killed on the city's streets over five years.

In 1923, in response both to the chaos in the city and a crisis in the war in Morocco, the Captain-General of Barcelona, Miguel Primo de Rivera, staged a coup and established a military dictatorship under King Alfonso XIII. The CNT was already exhausted, and it was suppressed. Conservative Catalanists, longing for an end to disorder and the revolutionary threat, initially supported the coup, but were rewarded by the abolition of the Mancomunitat and a vindictive campaign by the Primo regime against the Catalan language and national symbols. This, however, achieved the opposite of the desired effect, helping to radicalise and popularise Catalan nationalism. After the terrible struggles of the previous years, the

General Francisco Franco. *See p26.*

1920s were actually a time of notable prosperity for many in Barcelona, as some of the wealth recently accumulated filtered through the economy. It was also, though, a highly politicised society, in which new magazines and forums for discussion – despite the restrictions of the dictatorship – found a ready audience.

A prime motor of Barcelona's prosperity in the 1920s was the International Exhibition of 1929. It had been proposed by Cambó and Catalan business groups, but Primo de Rivera saw that it could also serve as a propaganda event for his regime. A huge number of public projects were undertaken, including the post office in Via Laietana, the Estació de França and Barcelona's first metro line, from Plaça Catalunya to Plaça d'Espanya. Thousands of migrant workers came from southern Spain to build them, many living in decrepit housing or shanty towns on the city fringes. By 1930, Barcelona was very different from the place it had been in 1910; it contained more than a million people, and its urban sprawl had crossed into neighbouring towns.

For the Exhibition itself, Montjuïc and Plaça d'Espanya were redeveloped, with grand halls by Puig i Cadafalch and other local architects in the style of the Catalan neo-classical movement Noucentisme, a backward-looking reaction to the excesses of Modernisme. They contrasted strikingly, though, with the German pavilion by Ludwig Mies van der Rohe (the Pavelló Barcelona, *photo p26*), which emphatically announced the trend towards rationalism.

Walk on Roman remains

Duration: 45 minutes.

The Roman settlement of Barcino has had an unappreciated impact on the two millennia of life that followed its beginnings. Many of Barcelona's most familiar streets – C/Hospital, even Passeig de Gràcia – follow the line of Roman roads, and the best way to get an idea of the Roman town is to walk the line of its walls. Along the way sit all kinds of Roman remains, poking out from where they were reused or constructed over by medieval builders and those who followed them.

A good place to start a walk is at **C/Paradís**, between the cathedral and Plaça Sant Jaume, where a round millstone is set into the paving to mark what was believed to be the precise centre of the Mons Taber. It's here that you'll find the remains of the **Temple Romà d'Augusti** (*see p95*). Where C/Paradís meets the Plaça Sant Jaume was where Barcino's two main thoroughfares once met; the road

on the left, **C/Llibreteria**, began life as the **Cardus Maximus**, the main road to Rome. Just off this road is the Plaça del Rei and the extraordinary **Museu d'Història de la Ciutat**, below which is the largest underground excavation of a Roman site in Europe.

Rejoining C/Llibreteria, turn left at **C/Tapineria** to reach **Plaça Ramon Berenguer el Gran** and the largest surviving stretch of ancient wall, incorporated into the medieval Palau Reial. Continue along Tapineria, where you'll find many sections of Roman building, to **Avda de la Catedral**. The massive twin-drum gate on C/Bisbe, while often retouched, has not changed in its basic shape, at least at the base, since it was the main gate of the Roman town. To its left you can see fragments of an aqueduct, and at its front Joan Brossa's bronze letters, spelling out 'Barcino'. If you take a detour up C/Capellans to **C/Duran i Bas**, you can see another four arches of an aqueduct; heading left and straight over the Avda Portal de l'Àngel is the Roman necropolis in **Plaça Vila de Madrid**, with the tombs clearly visible. In accordance with Roman custom, these had to be outside the city walls.

Returning to the cathedral, turn right into **C/Palla**. A little way along sits a large chunk of Roman wall, only discovered in the 1980s when a building was demolished. C/Palla runs into **C/Banys Nous**; at no.16 sits a centre for disabled children, inside which is a piece of

THE REPUBLIC SUPPRESSED

Despite the Exhibition's success, Primo de Rivera resigned in January 1930, exhausted. The king appointed another soldier, General Berenguer, as prime minister, with the mission of restoring stability. The dictatorship, though, had fatally discredited the old regime, and a protest movement spread across Catalonia against the monarchy. In early 1931, Berenguer called local elections as a first step towards a restoration of constitutional rule. The outcome was a complete surprise, for republicans were elected in all of Spain's cities. Ecstatic crowds poured into the streets, and Alfonso XIII abdicated. The Second Spanish Republic was proclaimed on 14 April 1931.

The Republic arrived amid real euphoria, especially in Catalonia, where it was associated with hopes for both social change and national reaffirmation. The clear winner of the elections

in the country were the Esquerra Republicana, a leftist Catalanist group led by Francesc Macià. A raffish figure, Macià was one of the first politicians in Spain to win genuine affection from ordinary people. He declared Catalonia to be an independent republic within an Iberian federation of states, but later agreed to accept autonomy within the Spanish Republic.

The Generalitat was re-established as a government that would, potentially, acquire wide powers. All aspects of Catalan culture were then in expansion, and a popular press in Catalan achieved a wide readership. Barcelona was also a small but notable centre of the avant-garde. Miró and Dalí had already made their mark in painting; under the Republic, the Amics de l'Art Nou (ADLAN, Friends of New Art) group worked to promote contemporary art, while the GATCPAC architectural collective sought to bring rationalist architecture to the city.

wall with a relief of legs and feet (phone ahead for a viewing time; 93 318 14 81). At no.4 is **La Granja** (*see p176*), a lovely old café with yet another stretch of Roman wall at the back; beyond this is the junction with **C/Call**, the other end of the *cardus*, and so the opposite side of the Roman town from Llibreteria-Tapineria. The staff of the clothes wholesalers at C/Call 1 are also used to people wandering in to examine their piece of Roman tower. Carry on across C/Ferran and down **C/Avinyó**, the next continuation of the perimeter. Two sides of the cave-like dining room at the back of **El Gallo Kiriko**, the Pakistani restaurant at no.19, are actually formed by portions of the Roman wall.

From **C/Milans**, turn left on to **C/Gignás**. Near the junction with **C/Regomir** are remains of the fourth sea gate of the town, which would have faced the beach, and the Roman shipyard. Take a detour up C/Regomir to visit one of the most important relics of Barcino, the **Pati Llimona** (*see p91*); then, continue walking up **C/Correu Vell**, where there are more fragments of wall, to reach one of the most impressive relics of Roman Barcelona in the small, shady **Plaça Traginers**: a Roman tower and one corner of the ancient wall, in a remarkable state of preservation despite having had a medieval house built on top of it. Finally, turn up **C/Sots-Tinent Navarro**, which boasts a massive stretch of Roman rampart, to end the walk at Plaça de l'Àngel.

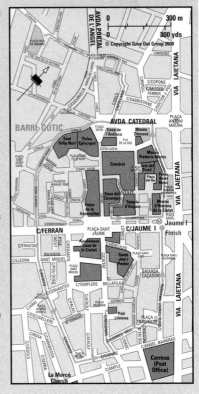

In Madrid, the Republic's first government was a coalition of republicans and socialists led by Manuel Azaña, its overriding goal to modernise Spanish society through liberal-democratic reforms. However, as social tensions intensified, the coalition collapsed, and a conservative republican party, with support from the traditional Spanish right, secured power shortly after new elections in 1933. For Catalonia, the prospect of a return to right-wing rule prompted fears that it would immediately abrogate the Generalitat's hard-won powers. On 6 October 1934, while a general strike was launched against the central government in Asturias and some other parts of Spain, Lluís Companys, leader of the Generalitat since Macià's death the previous year, declared Catalonia independent. But the 'uprising' turned out to be something of a farce: the Generalitat had no means of resisting the army, and the new 'Catalan Republic' was rapidly suppressed. The Generalitat was thus suspended and its leaders were imprisoned.

Over the following year, fascism seemed to become a real threat for the left, as political positions became polarised. Then, in February 1936, elections were won by the Popular Front of the left across the country. The Generalitat was reinstated, and in Catalonia the next few months were peaceful. In the rest of Spain, though, tensions were close to bursting point; right-wing politicians, refusing to accept the loss of power, talked openly of the need for the military to intervene. In July, the 1929 stadium on Montjuïc was to be the site of the Popular Olympics, a leftist alternative to the 1936 Olympics in Nazi Germany. On 18 July, the day of the Games' inauguration, army generals launched a coup against the Republic and its left-wing governments, expecting no resistance.

UP IN ARMS

In Barcelona, militants from the unions and leftist parties, on alert for weeks, poured into the streets to oppose the troops in fierce fighting. Over the course of 19 July, the military were worn down, and they surrendered in the Hotel Colón on Plaça Catalunya (by the corner with Passeig de Gràcia, the site of which is now occupied by the Radio Nacional de España building). Opinions have always differed as to who could claim most credit for this victory: workers' militants have claimed it was the 'people in arms' who defeated the army, while others stress the importance of the police remaining loyal to the Generalitat throughout the struggle. A likely answer is that they actually encouraged each other.

Tension released, the city was taken over by the revolution. Militias of the CNT, different Marxist parties and other left-wing factions marched off to Aragon, led by streetfighters such as the anarchists Durruti and García Oliver, to continue the battle. The army rising had failed in Spain's major cities but won footholds in Castile, Aragon and the south, although in the heady atmosphere of Barcelona in July 1936 it was often assumed that their resistance could not last and that victory was near inevitable.

Far from the front, Barcelona was the chief centre of the revolution in republican Spain, the only truly proletarian city. Its middle class avoided the streets, where, as George Orwell recorded in his *Homage to Catalonia*, everyone you saw wore workers' clothing. Barcelona became a magnet for leftists from around the world, drawing writers André Malraux, Ernest Hemingway and Octavio Paz. All kinds of industries and public services were collectivised, including cinemas, the phone system and food distribution. Ad hoc 'control patrols' of the revolutionary militias roamed the streets supposedly checking for suspected right-wing agents and sometimes carrying out summary executions, a practice that was condemned by many leftist leaders.

The alliance between the different left-wing groups was unstable and riddled with tensions, though. The communists, who had some extra leverage because the Soviet Union was the only country prepared to give the Spanish Republic arms, demanded the integration of these loosely organised militias into a conventional army under a strong central authority. The following months saw continual political infighting between the discontented CNT, the radical Marxist party Partit Obrer d'Unificació

Pavelló Barcelona. *See p23.*

appreciated – with heavy raids throughout 1938, especially by Italian bombers based in Mallorca. The Basque Country and Asturias had already fallen to Franco, and in March 1938 his troops reached the Mediterranean near Castellón, cutting the main republican zone in two. The Republic had one last throw of the dice, in the Battle of the Ebro in the summer of 1938, when for months the Popular Army struggled to retake control of the river. After that, the Republic was exhausted. Barcelona fell to the Francoist army on 26 January 1939. Half a million refugees fled to France, to be interned in barbed-wire camps along the beaches.

THE FRANCO YEARS

In Catalonia, the Franco regime was iron-fisted and especially vengeful. Thousands of Catalan republicans and leftists were executed, among them Generalitat president Lluís Companys; exile and deportation were the fate of thousands more. Publishing, teaching and any other public cultural expression in Catalan, including even speaking it in the street, were prohibited, and every Catalanist monument in the city was dismantled. All independent political activity was suspended, and the entire political and cultural development of the country during the previous century and a half was brought to a drastic and abrupt halt.

The epic nature of the Spanish Civil War is known worldwide; more present in the collective memory of Barcelona, though, is the long *posguerra* or post-war period, which lasted for nearly two decades after 1939. During those years, the city was impoverished, and, as a result, food and electricity were rationed; Barcelona would not regain its prior standard of living until the mid 1950s. Nevertheless, migrants in flight from the still more brutal poverty of the south started to flow into the city, occupying precarious shanty towns around Montjuïc and other areas in the outskirts. Reconstruction work on the nearly 2,000 buildings destroyed by bombing was slow, and the regime built little during its first few years other than monumental showpieces and the vulgarly ornate basilica on top of Tibidabo, which was said to have been erected to expiate Barcelona's 'sinful' role during the war.

Some underground political movements were able to operate: the anarchist Sabaté brothers carried on their own small-scale urban guerrilla campaign, and 1951 saw the last gasp of the pre-war labour movement in a general tram strike. Some Catalan high culture was tolerated, and the young Antoni Tàpies held his first exhibition in 1949. For many people, though, the only remaining focus of any collective excitement was Barcelona football club, which

Marxista (POUM) and the communists. Co-operation broke down totally in May 1937, when republican and communist troops seized the telephone building in Plaça Catalunya (on the corner of Portal de l'Àngel) from a CNT committee, sparking off the confused war-within-the-civil-war witnessed by Orwell from the roof of the Teatre Poliorama. A temporary agreement was patched up, but shortly afterwards the POUM was banned, and the CNT excluded from power. A new republican central government was formed under Dr Juan Negrín, a socialist allied to the communists.

After that, the war gradually became more of a conventional conflict. This did little, however, to improve the Republic's position, for the nationalists under General Francisco Franco (*photo p23*) and their German and Italian allies had been continually gaining ground throughout it all. Madrid was under siege, and the capital of the Republic was moved to Valencia, and then to Barcelona, in November 1937.

Catalonia received thousands of refugees, as food shortages and the lack of armaments ground down morale. Barcelona also had the sad distinction of being the first major city in Europe to be subjected to sustained intensive bombing – to an extent that has rarely been took on an extraordinary importance at this time, above all in its twice-yearly meetings with the 'team of the regime', Real Madrid.

As a fascist survivor, the Franco regime was subject to a UN embargo after World War II. Years of international isolation and attempted self-sufficiency came to an end in 1953, when the USA and the Vatican saw to it that this anti-communist state was at least partially re-admitted to the western fold. Even a limited opening to the outside world meant that foreign money finally began to enter the country, and the regime relaxed some control over its population. In 1959, the Plan de Estabilización ('Stabilisation Plan'), drawn up by Catholic technocrats of the Opus Dei, brought Spain definitively within the western economy, throwing its doors wide open to tourism and foreign investment. After years of austerity, tourist income at last brought the Europe-wide 1960s boom to Spain and set off change at an extraordinarily fast pace.

'After years of austerity, tourist income brought the Europe-wide 1960s boom to Spain and set off change at an extraordinarily fast pace.'

Two years earlier, in 1957, José María de Porcioles was appointed mayor of Barcelona, a post he would retain until 1973. Porcioles has since been regarded as the personification of the damage that was inflicted on the city by the Franco regime during its 1960s boom; he was also accused of covering Barcelona with drab high-rises and road schemes without any concern for the city's character. Sadly, many very valuable historic buildings, such as the grand cafés of the Plaça Catalunya, were torn down to make way for terribly bland modern business blocks, and minimal attention was paid to collective amenities.

After the years of repression and the years of development, 1966 marked the beginning of what became known as *tardofranquisme*, 'late Francoism'. Having made its opening to the outside world, the regime was losing its grip, and labour, youth and student movements began to emerge from beneath the shroud of repression. Nevertheless, the Franco regime never hesitated to show its strength. Strikes and demonstrations were dealt with savagely, and just months before the dictator's death, the last person to be executed in Spain by the traditional method of the garrotte, a Catalan anarchist named Puig Antich, went to his death in Barcelona. In 1973, however, Franco's closest

follower, Admiral Carrero Blanco, was killed by a bomb planted by the Basque terrorist group ETA, leaving no one to guard over the core values of the regime. Change was in the air.

GENERALISIMO TO GENERALITAT

When Franco died on 20 November 1975, the people of Barcelona celebrated; by evening, there was not a bottle of cava left in the city. But no one knew quite what would happen next. The Bourbon monarchy was restored under King Juan Carlos, but his intentions were not clear. In 1976, he charged a little-known Francoist bureaucrat, Adolfo Suárez, prime minister, with the task of leading the country to democracy.

The first years of Spain's 'transition' were difficult. Nationalist and other demonstrations continued to be repressed by the police with considerable brutality, and far-right groups threatened less open violence. However, political parties were legalised, and June 1977 saw the first democratic elections since 1936. They were won across Spain by Suárez's own new party, the Union de Centro Democratico (UCD), and in Catalonia by a mixture of socialists, communists and nationalists.

It was, again, not clear how Suárez expected to deal with the huge demands of Catalonia, but shortly after the elections he surprised everyone by going to visit the president of the Generalitat in exile, veteran pre-Civil War politician Josep Tarradellas. His office was the only institution of the old Republic to be so recognised, perhaps because Suárez astutely identified in the old man a fellow conservative. Tarradellas was invited to return as provisional president of a restored Generalitat, and he arrived amid huge crowds in October 1977.

The following year, the first free council elections since 1936 were held in Barcelona. They were won by the Socialist Party, with Narcís Serra appointed as mayor. The Socialist Party has retained control of the council ever since. In 1980, elections to the restored Generalitat were won by Jordi Pujol and his party, Convergència i Unió, which held power for the next 23 years.

CITY OF DESIGN

Inseparable from the restoration of democracy was a complete change in the city's atmosphere after 1975. New freedoms – in culture, sexuality and work – were explored, and newly released energies expressed in a multitude of ways. Barcelona soon began to look different too, as the inherent dowdiness of the Franco years was swept away by a new Catalan style for the new Catalonia: postmodern, high-tech, punkish, comic strip, minimalist and tautly fashionable. For a time, street culture was highly politicised,

Key events

c15 BC Barcino founded by Roman soldiers.
cAD 350 Roman stone city walls built.
415 Barcelona briefly capital of the Visigoths.
719 Muslims attack and seize Barcelona.
801 Barcelona taken by the Franks.
985 Muslims sack Barcelona; Count Borrell II renounces Frankish sovereignty.
1035-76 Count Ramon Berenguer I of Barcelona extends his possessions into southern France.
1137 Count Ramon Berenguer IV marries Petronella of Aragon, uniting the two states in the Crown of Aragon.
1213 Pere I is killed and virtually all his lands north of the Pyrenees are seized by France.
1229 Jaume I conquers Mallorca, then Ibiza (1235) and Valencia (1238); second city wall built in Barcelona.
1274 Consell de Cent, municipal government of Barcelona, established.
1282 Pere II conquers Sicily.
1298 Gothic cathedral begun. Population of city c40,000.
1323-34 Conquest of Corsica and Sardinia.
1347-48 Black Death cuts population by half.
1462-72 Catalan civil war.
1479 Ferdinand II inherits Crown of Aragon, and with his wife Isabella unites the Spanish kingdoms.
1492 Final expulsion of Jews, and discovery of America.
1522 Catalans refused permission to trade in America.
1640 Catalan national revolt, the Guerra dels Segadors.
1652 Barcelona falls to Spanish army.
1702 War of Spanish Succession begins.
1714 Barcelona falls to Franco-Spanish army after siege.
1715 Nova Planta decree abolishes Catalan institutions; new ramparts and citadel built around Barcelona. Population 33,000.
1808-13 French occupation.
1814 Restoration of Ferdinand VII.
1833 Aribau publishes *Oda a la Pàtria*, beginning of Catalan cultural renaissance. Carlist wars begin.
1836-37 Dissolution of Barcelona monasteries.
1842-44 Barcelona bombarded for the last time from Montjuïc, to quell Jamancia revolt.
1854 Demolition of Barcelona city walls.
1855 First general strike is suppressed.
1859 Cerdà plan for the Eixample approved.

1868 September: revolution overthrows Isabella II. November: first anarchist meetings held in Barcelona.
1873 First Spanish Republic.
1874 Bourbon monarchy restored under Alfonso XII.
1882 Work begins on the Sagrada Família.
1888 Barcelona Universal Exhibition.
1899 FC Barcelona founded; electric trams introduced to the city.
1900 Population of Barcelona 537,354.
1909 Setmana Tràgica, anti-church and anti-army riots.
1910 CNT anarchist workers' union founded.
1921 First Barcelona metro line opened.
1923 Primo de Rivera establishes dictatorship in Spain.
1929 Barcelona International Exhibition.
1930 Population 1,005,565. Fall of Primo de Rivera.
1931 14 April: Second Spanish Republic.
1934 October: Generalitat attempts revolt against new right-wing government in Madrid, and is then suspended.
1936 February: Popular Front wins Spanish elections; Catalan Generalitat restored. 19 July: military uprising against left-wing government is defeated in Barcelona.
1937 May: fighting within the republican camp in Barcelona.
1939 26 January: Barcelona taken by Franco's army.
1959 Stabilisation Plan opens up the Spanish economy.
1975 20 November: Franco dies.
1977 First democratic general elections in Spain since 1936; provisional Catalan Generalitat re-established.
1978 First democratic local elections in Barcelona won by Socialists.
1980 Generalitat fully re-established under Jordi Pujol.
1982 Pasqual Maragall becomes mayor.
1992 Olympics Games held in Barcelona.
1996 Partido Popular wins Spanish elections.
1997 Joan Clos replaces Maragall as mayor.
2003 Coalition of left-wing parties wins control of Generalitat.
2004 PSOE (Socialist Party) wins the Spanish elections.
2006 Jordi Hereu replaces Joan Clos as mayor.
2006 Maragall stands down, José Montilla becomes President of the Generalitat.

but simultaneously it was also increasingly hedonistic. In the 1980s, design mania struck the city, a product of unbottled energies and the rebirth of Barcelona's artistic, artisan and architectural traditions.

This emphasis on a slick, fresh style first began underground, but it was soon taken up by public authorities and, above all, the Ajuntament, as a part of its drive to reverse the policies of the regime. The technocrats in the city administration began to 'recover' the city from its neglected state, and in doing so enlisted the elite of the Catalan intellectual and artistic community in their support. No one epitomises this more than Oriol Bohigas, the architect and writer who was long the city's head of culture and chief planner. A programme of urban renewal was initiated, beginning with the open spaces, public art and low-level initiatives, such as the campaign in which hundreds of historic façades were given an overdue facelift.

This ambitious approach to urban problems acquired much greater focus after Barcelona's bid to host the 1992 Olympic Games was accepted, in 1986. The Games were to be Barcelona's third great effort to cast aside suggestions of second-city status and show the world its wares. The exhibitions of 1888 and 1929 had seen developments in the Ciutadella and on and around Montjuïc; the Olympics provided an opening for work on a citywide

scale. Taking advantage of the public and private investment the Games would attract, Barcelona planned an all-new orientation of itself towards the sea, in a programme of urban renovation of a scope unseen in Europe since the years of reconstruction after World War II.

Inseparable from all this was Pasqual Maragall, mayor of Barcelona from 1982 to 1997, a tireless 'Mr Barcelona' who appeared in every possible forum to expound his vision of the role of cities, and intervened personally to set the guidelines for projects or secure the participation of major international architects. In the process, Barcelona, a byword for modern blight only a few years before, was turned into a reference point in urban affairs.

ENDGAMES

The Games were held in July and August 1992 and hailed as an outstanding success. Barcelona and Catalonia rode out Spain's post-1992 recession better than any other part of the country. The Ajuntament announced still more large-scale projects, such as the jazzing up of the old Port and the Raval. Pasqual Maragall, however, was to stand down amid general surprise in 1997, and went on to become the Socialist candidate for President of the Generalitat in the 1999 elections. He would not succeed until 2003, when he enjoyed a muted triumph in the regional elections, which saw gains for the previously fringe left-wing parties: the 'eco-communists' of the ICV and, above all, Esquerra Republicana (ERC), with whom the PSC was forced to form a left-wing coalition. The ERC is directly descended from the old Esquerra of the 1930s, and it all but doubled its vote, so that in some areas as much as one-fifth of voters supported a party that, at least theoretically, is in favour of total or partial Catalan independence, and that rejects the Spanish monarchy.

Maragall took control of the Generalitat in return for a commitment to push strongly for a new Autonomy Statute. In this he was mostly successful, but after a series of political gaffes stepped down for the elections in November 2006, and in his place the PSC chose as candidate Andalucía-born José Montilla. Those elections also failed to bring home an absolute winner; further negotiations resulted in the same tripartite coalition as in the previous election, therefore giving the presidency to Montilla, the first ever non-Catalan president of the Generalitat. Over at City Hall, meanwhile, Maragall had been replaced with smooth-talking Joan Clos. His successor, Jordi Hereu, brought the Socialist Party to another (slim) victory in the local elections of May 2007, having also formed a coalition with the ICV, though not, this time, with Esquerra.

Barcelona Today

Boom time continues for the Catalan capital.

In May of 2007, the Catalan socialists (PSC) won municipal elections yet again, extending their reign in Barcelona to nearly three decades. Looking at their record, it can't be said they've done a bad job. The PSC can justifiably claim responsibility for having transformed the city from a gritty, post-industrial backwater into one of the world's most attractive urban centres. But the years in power have begun to show.

Turnout for the 2007 elections was abysmally low. The winner, incumbent mayor Jordi Hereu, had been handpicked eight months before the election by his predecessor, Joan Clos. Despite serving as stand-in mayor, however, the chubby, nondescript Hereu (whose surname means 'heir' in Catalan) was met by more than one blank look as he campaigned around town. When the socialists won, it was certainly not through having fielded the more brilliant candidate. Rather, the win pointed to what may well be Barcelona's most serious problem: the absence of significant political opposition in the city.

Oddly absent from the election debates, for example, was any real criticism of the city government's role in a series of ambitious real estate schemes around town. The most glaring of these is of course the Fòrum 2004 area, which

emptied hundreds of millions of euros from municipal coffers and quite literally paved the way for the construction of Barcelona's own scaled-down version of Miami Beach. All this would be fine if it weren't for the fact that the two rundown shoreline neighbourhoods on either side of the Fòrum area, Barceloneta and La Mina, have been begging the Ajuntament (City Hall) for years for improvements to their deteriorating neighbourhoods.

It's no coincidence that developers are concentrating on the former working class neighbourhoods and industrial zones, such as the Raval, Barceloneta, Poblenou, the Zona Franca and the Fòrum area. The simple truth is, Barcelona's days as a working man's city have long since vanished. Traditional industries, such as textiles and automobile manufacturing are now mostly located out of town, or have disappeared altogether. The decline of urban-based industry led to the deterioration of central, working class neighbourhoods, which now find themselves in a tug-of-war between tourists and a growing wave of immigrants from around the world. Former industrial zones, meanwhile, are being refitted with high-tech office space and luxury residences.

CULTURE CLASH

When contrarians to City Hall's handling of things do appear, they are more likely to crop up outside the official machinery of politics. Such is the case with the culture-based initiative led by actress Simona Levi and her Conservas theatre group. Mining widespread, unrepresented discontent among young people who are unable to find affordable housing in pricey Barcelona, Levi has presented her popular, tech-savvy *Realidades Avanzadas* ('Advanced Realities'), in which the present order of things is overthrown in absurd political theatre. Another notable figure on the scene is comedian/activist Leo Bassi, who set up his very own 'BassiBus', a satirical take on the Bus Turistic (*see p84*), which, instead of visiting the usual tourist attractions, tours areas of particularly brazen real estate speculation.

Culture has made its official debut in politics, meanwhile, in the form of the recently created Ciutadans de Catalunya party, the initiative of a host of prominent cultural figures, such as actor/playwright Albert Boadella and writer Félix de Azúa. The party has gained surprising support for its vision of a more relaxed, non-nationalistic, bilingual Catalonia, in opposition to the current official one in which Catalan identity and language are imposed in schools (Catalan is the sole official language in public schools), business (by law, shop signs must be in Catalan) and culture. In recent Catalan national elections, Ciutadans won an unexpected three seats in the Catalan Parliament.

In a corner of the world where language and cultural identity are such delicate issues, the appearance of Ciutadans has stirred up strong emotions. Incensed Catalan nationalists, for example, claim that the upstart party is really just a camouflaged, subversive vehicle engineered by centralists in Madrid to undermine the hard-won resurgence of the Catalan language in daily life. Local newspaper reports revealing that the new party's young president, Albert Rivera, had previously been associated with the Spanish Partido Popular (PP) certainly hasn't calmed the debate. Despite its success in the Catalan national elections, Ciutadans failed to win any representation in the May 2007 Barcelona municipal elections.

THE TRAP OF TOURISM

While Catalonia continues to fight to maintain its identity, Barcelona's enduring success on the tourist circuit has brought with it its own flood of erosive influences. Out-of-towners spend upwards to nine million euros a day in the city, enticing more and more businesses (and sometimes, as in the case of the Born, whole neighbourhoods) to cater to short-term visitors. Where once it had been common for *barcelonins* to take their Sunday stroll along La Rambla, hordes of sightseers from around the world have now mostly replaced them. Tourism has also aggravated the city's housing shortage, as thousands of flats have been converted into short-term holiday rentals.

The city continues to exert strong powers of attraction on Europe's young, hip set, despite rising competition from Valencia and Madrid. Members of this crowd cite Barcelona's reputation as a 'party town', along with its general coolness in everything from clothes to food to design to music and back to clothes, as compelling reasons to live here for a spell. City Hall has put something of a damper on this party image by instituting a wide range of *incivisme* laws aimed at curbing uncivil behaviour, such as drinking alcohol or urinating in the street, with hefty fines for offenders. A city-wide clampdown on live music in bars without the requisite permits has also had a sobering effect on the nightlife scene.

INTO THE FUTURE

Pumped up by tourism and its glowing international reputation, the city's economy continues to boom. In fact, despite the loss of most of its traditional industries and its current reputation as a party town, the European Cities Monitor currently ranks Barcelona as Europe's fifth most attractive city for business.

'Intel has set up its only research lab outside the USA in Barcelona.'

One of the keys to this apparent contradiction lies in the efforts of a discreet, but immensely effective semi-public body, the Consorci de la Zona Franca. Originally created to manage the Zona Franca, a duty-free area and 600-hectare industrial zone stretching along the Delta de Llobregat between the port and the airport, the Consorci has outgrown its function as rent collector to the companies installed in the Zona Franca and is now one of the city's driving economic forces. To provide a glimpse of the Consorci's muscle, the institution has committed over 700 million euros to different projects in Barcelona and around Catalonia for the period 2006-09. Most of this money is being spent on transforming Barcelona into what the Consorci's president, Manuel Royes, likes to term a 'city of knowledge'.

The idea is straightforward enough. Using its semi-public status, the Consorci acquires or appropriates real estate in the city and then funnels wads of capital towards building new, state-of-the-art facilities to retool Barcelona for the so-called 'knowledge economy', the blossoming worldwide economy based on advances in high-tech, knowledge-based areas. Notable among these facilities are the €100-million PRBB biomedical research centre (unmistakeable for its large semi-circle, cell-like shape) located in Barceloneta near the Hotel Arts, currently housing some 80 international research teams; and the Nexus I and II buildings on the Universitat Politècnica de Catalunya's campus, home to Europe's most powerful supercomputer, the MareNostrum. The gamble appears to be paying off, as the city has attracted some of the world's most important high-tech companies, such as Intel, the giant chipmaker, which has set up its only research lab outside the USA in Nexus II.

It's hard to argue with the merits of these endeavours, as they bring to Barcelona's economy a much-needed counterweight to its reliance on tourism. Indeed, just about the only criticism the Consorci has received has come from stray artists forced out of their

Model B Barcelona

Many residents feel that, ever since the success of the 1992 Olympics and the resulting tourist boom, the city council has viewed Barcelona primarily as a commodity to be marketed rather than a place to live. This disenchantment hit a peak with the much trumpeted Forum of International Cultures in 2004, which, by any yardstick, was a hugely expensive failure. Another problem is that the eight million visitors flock to a small part of the city, principally the Old City and the Gaudí buildings. The pressure of tourism has led Barcelona residents to avoid La Rambla between April and October, and increasingly they have abandoned the bars and restaurants of the Old City to the visitors.

Throughout the past 15 years, the so-called 'Barcelona model' has been hailed as a template for urban regeneration, with its mix of public and private finance, renovation of historic centres, daring new developments and a policy of reducing population density by replacing housing with large public buildings, such as the MACBA. Even Lisbon, whose shabby charm is reminiscent of pre-Olympics Barcelona, has invited the city's mayor, Jordi Hereu, to discuss how the model might be applied there.

But has the model run its course? Yes, says Jordi Borja, one of the planners who devised the city's renewal: '*Barcelonins* feel they have been dispossessed of their city, a city that, ten years earlier, they felt was theirs more than ever.' Yes, says the architect Josep Montaner, citing the city authorities' obsession with mounting huge public events instead of focusing on its citizens' needs, and the pressure of tourism (eight million in 2007). And Robert Hughes, art historian and author of a fine history of the city, says it has become 'both overcrowded and too preoccupied with its image'.

And yet the city never tires of dreaming up gimmicks to attract visitors: the Year of Gaudí, the Year of Dalí, the Year of Gastronomy. It has also dedicated itself to the lucrative conference trade, building more facilities and thus pushing up the demand for hotels to host the thousands of delegates who, in turn, make it harder for tourists to find a bed, increasing the demand for hotels. There are two sides to every coin: the conferences bring in free-spending visitors but they have also fuelled the demand for prostitutes. Likewise cheap flights bring in the weekenders, but then the city has to deal with loutish stag parties.

Tourism puts any city at risk of becoming a parody of itself: London with its royalty and Beefeaters, Paris with its chic and rusty roués. Barcelona has it all: great climate, beautiful architecture, excellent food and its own city beach. But it risks becoming a victim of its own success, a town drowning in tourists.

post-industrial factory studios in places like Poblenou, or squatters' collectives, such as Miles de Viviendas, which clamour for more affordable housing. Whether in response or not, the Consorci has recently begun building 500 socially protected flats for young people, as well as the construction of an entirely new, 2,000 flat neighbourhood on the grounds of the former Sant Andreu military barracks. The organisation has even jumped on the global warming bandwagon and plans to build a research centre for renewable energies.

City Hall, too, continues to make a fanfare about its plans for creating a 'sustainable' city, instituting such measures as obligatory solar panels to heat water on all new buildings, and introducing a public bike share service, Bicing (*see p310* **On yer bike**). Watch this space: if any city in the world can make green the new black, this is the one.

New cops on the block

Once they've run up the flag, one of the first things small nations demand is their own police force. Catalonia, autonomous though not independent, is no exception, and since 1983 the local force, the Mossos d'Esquadra ('squad lads'), has been gradually taking over the duties of the Guardia Civil and Policia Nacional. The only other autonomous area to have its own force is the Basque Country, where the local Ertzaintza has been deployed since 1982.

The Mossos have a long history, coming into existence early in the 18th century as a sort of people's militia during the War of Spanish Succession. During the Civil War, they took the Republican side and so, inevitably, were dissolved under the victorious Franco regime. A small group was reinstated in 1950 but the modern Mossos are the product of post-transition, democratic Spain. Although they have wide powers, organised crime and terrorism remain within the brief of the Guardia Civil and Policia Nacional.

Although the process of replacing former forces began in 1994, the Mossos were not deployed in Barcelona until 2005, where, thanks to the black paramilitary uniforms and raffish berets of the mobile brigades, they quickly became gay icons. This was only the first of a number of unintended results. Soon there were complaints about racism, harassment of young immigrants and the use of excessive force.

However, 2007 will surely go down as their *annus horribilis*, as the force was rocked by a series of scandals. A concealed camera revealed two suspects being beaten up in the Les Corts police station; five Mossos were suspended from duty pending charges. Shortly after, at the same station, female officers were filmed stripping, handcuffing and beating a young Russian woman whose main offence appeared to be that she was drunk. Days later, a Mosso was charged with manslaughter after he shot dead a young schizophrenic who had threatened him with a pickaxe.

Then came the revelation that members of the force had armed themselves with a non-regulation martial arts weapon, the *kubotan*; they were filmed using it against a squatters' demonstration. A day later, Sergio Carmona died in police custody as he tried to escape from a Mossos patrol car in Badalona. The police account says that he kicked out the car window and though, handcuffed, climbed on to the roof. He died of head injuries after the driver braked sharply. As a result two Mossos face charges of negligence.

The Mossos reaction to this bad press was to stage a demonstration in defence of their 'professional dignity' and to demand the resignation of Joan Saura, the Catalan government minister who approved the secret cameras at Les Corts. Professional dignity aside, the events of 2007 suggest that the Mossos still have a lot to learn about public relations.

Sant Pau del Camp. *See p36.*

Architecture

Quite simply, some of the best buildings in the world.

A recent exhibition on new Spanish architecture at New York's MoMA caused no little pride in the country of its focus. It was, however, to kick-start a heated debate over Barcelona's architectural prowess. Criticism came from two directions: on the one hand, it was claimed that Barcelona is becoming an urban-design theme park, its chronic housing shortage glossed over while millions of euros are spent on big-name architects and flashy landmark buildings; and on the other hand, that this would be all very well if the architects in question were at least local.

There are more than 5,000 trained architects in Barcelona – a remarkable figure, given an overall population of 1.5 million – and yet, with the notable exception of the late Enric Miralles, recent big names to be commissioned are all from elsewhere: Jean Nouvel, Zaha Hadid, Herzog and de Meuron, and Barcelona stalwart Lord Rogers. This sits uneasily with those who take pride in the use of grand architectural projects as a means of expressing a local identity, and yet Spain has looked beyond its borders for artistic and architectural talent since Moorish times. Where Catalonia particularly succeeds, since Gaudí's day and even earlier, is in having the vision and courage to commission new buildings that at the time have seemed ambitious and, often, outlandish.

Architecture is sometimes regarded as Catalonia's greatest contribution to the history of art. Indeed, there are few cities in the world that boast as many examples of architectural flair as Barcelona; no fewer than nine of its buildings have now been designated as UNESCO World Heritage Sites. Catalan craftsmen have been famed since the Middle Ages for their use of fine materials and skilled finishings, and Catalan architects have been both artists and innovators: traditional Catalan brick vaulting techniques were the basis of visionary structural innovations that allowed later architects to span larger spaces and build higher structures. Contemporary Catalan architects have inherited the international prestige of their forebears; the work of artists such as Ricardo Bofill, Oriol Bohigas and Enric Miralles can be seen in a number of major cities around the world, although you won't find much in Barcelona itself.

Unlike many European cities, Barcelona has never rested on its architectural laurels or tried to preserve its old buildings as relics. Contemporary buildings are often daringly constructed alongside or even within old ones, and a mix of old and new is a prime characteristic of some of the most successful recent projects seen in Barcelona, which all goes to create a thoroughly modern city firmly rooted in its architectural heritage. The importance of architecture is also reflected in public attitudes: Barcelona's citizens take a keen interest in their buildings. A range of architectural guides, some in English, is available and informative leaflets on building styles are also provided (in English) at the city's tourist offices.

ROMAN TO GOTHIC

The Roman citadel of Barcino was founded on the hill of Mons Taber, just behind the cathedral, which to this day remains the religious and civic heart of the city. It left an important legacy in the fourth-century city wall, fragments of which are visible at many points around the Old City. Barcelona's next occupiers, the Visigoths, left little, although a trio of fine Visigothic churches survives in nearby Terrassa. When the Catalan state began to form under the counts of Barcelona from the ninth century its dominant architecture was massive, simple Romanesque. In the Pyrenean valleys there are hundreds of fine Romanesque buildings, notably at Sant Pere de Rodes, Ripoll, Sant Joan de les Abadesses and Besalú. There is, however, little in Barcelona. On the right-hand side of the cathedral, if you are looking at the main façade, is the 13th-century chapel of Santa Llúcia, which is incorporated into the later building; tucked away near Plaça Catalunya is the church of Santa Anna; and in La Ribera sits the Capella d'en Marcús, a tiny travellers' chapel. The city's greatest Romanesque monument, however, is the beautifully plain 12th-century church and cloister of **Sant Pau del Camp** (*photo p35*), built as part of a larger monastery.

By the 13th century, Barcelona was the capital of a trading empire and was growing rapidly. The settlements – called *ravals* or *vilanoves* – that had sprung up outside the Roman walls were brought within the city by the building of Jaume I's second set of walls, which extended west to La Rambla. This commercial growth and political eminence formed the background to the great flowering of Catalan Gothic, which saw the construction of many of the city's most important civic and religious buildings. The cathedral was begun in 1298, in place of an 11th-century building. Work

began on the **Ajuntament** (Casa de la Ciutat) and **Palau de la Generalitat** – later subject to extensive alteration – in 1372 and 1403 respectively. Major additions were made to the Palau Reial of the Catalan-Aragonese kings, especially the Saló del Tinell of 1359-62. The great hall of the **Llotja** (Stock Exchange) was built between 1380 and 1392. Many of Barcelona's finest buildings were begun or completed in these years, in the midst of the crisis that followed the Black Death.

Catalan Gothic has characteristics that distinguish it from northern, classic Gothic. It is simpler, and gives more prominence to solid, plain walls between towers and columns, rather than the empty spaces between intricate flying buttresses that were trademarks of the great French cathedrals. This means that the Catalan buildings appear much more massive. In façades, as much emphasis is given to horizontals as to verticals; octagonal towers end in cornices and flat roofs, not spires. Decorative intricacies are mainly confined to windows, portals, arches and gargoyles. Many churches have no aisles but only a single nave, the classic example of this being the beautiful **Santa Maria del Pi** in Plaça del Pi, built between 1322 and 1453. This style has, ever since, provided the historic benchmark for Catalan architecture. It is simple and robust, yet elegant and practical. Innovative, sophisticated techniques were developed: the use of transverse arches supporting timber roofs allowed the spanning of great halls uninterrupted by columns, a system used in the **Saló del Tinell**. Designed by Pere III's court architect Guillem Carbonell, it has some of the largest pure masonry arches in Europe, the elegance and sheer scale of which give the space tremendous splendour. The **Drassanes**, built from 1378 as the royal shipyards (and now the Museu Marítim), is really just a very beautiful shed, but its enormous parallel aisles make this one of the most imposing spaces in the city.

La Ribera, the Vilanova del Mar, was the commercial centre of the city, and gained the magnificent masterpiece of Catalan Gothic, **Santa Maria del Mar**, built from 1329 to 1384. Its superb proportions are based on a series of squares imposed on one another, with three aisles of almost equal height. The interior is quite staggering in its austerity.

The architecture of medieval Barcelona, at least that of its noble and merchant residences, can be seen at its best along Carrer Montcada, next to Santa Maria. Built by the city's merchant elite at the height of its confidence and wealth, this line of buildings conforms to a very Mediterranean style of urban palace and makes maximum use of space. A plain exterior

Santa Maria del Mar.

faces the street, with heavy doors opening into an imposing patio, on one side of which a grand external staircase leads to the main rooms on the first floor (*planta noble*), which often have elegant open loggias.

MARKING TIME

By the beginning of the 16th century, political and economic decline meant that there were far fewer patrons for new buildings in the city. A good deal was built in the next 300 years, but rarely in any distinctively Catalan style; as a result, these structures have often been disregarded. In the 1550s, the **Palau del Lloctinent** was built for the royal viceroys on one side of Plaça del Rei, while in 1596 the present main façade was added to the Generalitat, in an Italian Renaissance style.

The Church also built lavishly around this time. Of the Baroque convents and churches along La Rambla, the Betlem (1680-1729), at the corner of C/Carme, is the most important survivor. Later Baroque churches include **Sant Felip Neri** (1721-52) and **La Mercè** (1765-75). Another addition, after the siege of Barcelona in 1714, was new military architecture, since the city was encased in ramparts and fortresses. Examples remaining include the Castell de Montjuïc, the buildings in the Ciutadella, and the Barceloneta.

A more positive 18th-century alteration was the conversion of La Rambla into a paved promenade, a project that began in 1775 with the demolition of Jaume I's second wall. Neo-classical palaces were built alongside: **La Virreina** and the **Palau Moja** (at the corner of C/Portaferrisa) both date from the 1770s. Also from that time, but in a less classical style, is the **Gremial dels Velers** (Candlemakers' Guild) at Via Laietana 50, with its two-coloured stucco decoration.

However, it wasn't until the closure of the monasteries in the 1820s and '30s that major rebuilding on La Rambla could begin. Most of the first constructions that replaced them were still in international, neo-classical styles. The site that is now the **Mercat de la Boqueria** was first remodelled in 1836-40 as Plaça Sant Josep to a design by Francesc Daniel Molina, based on the English Regency style of John Nash. That project is buried beneath the 1870s market building, but its Doric colonnade can still be detected. Molina also designed the **Plaça Reial**, begun in 1848. Other fine examples from the same era are the colonnaded Porxos d'en Xifré, blocks built in 1836 opposite the Llotja on Passeig Isabel II, by the Port Vell.

BIRTH OF THE MODERN CITY

In the 1850s, Barcelona was able to expand physically, with the demolition of the walls, and psychologically, with economic expansion and the cultural reawakening of the Catalan Renaixença. And, from the off, one could see in

Palau de la Música Catalana. *See p43.*

operation one of the characteristics of modern Barcelona: audacious planning. The city would eventually spread outwards and be connected up to Gràcia and other outlying towns through the great grid of the **Eixample**, designed by Ildefons Cerdà (1815-75). An engineer by trade, Cerdà was a radical influenced by utopian socialist ideas, and concerned with the poor condition of workers' housing in the Old City.

With its love of straight lines and grids, Cerdà's plan was closely related to the visionary rationalist ideas of its time, as was the idea of placing two of its main avenues along a geographic parallel and a meridian. Cerdà's central aim was to alleviate overpopulation while encouraging social equality by using quadrangular blocks of a standard size, with strict building controls to ensure they were built only on two sides, to a limited height, and with a garden. Each district would be of 20 blocks, with all community necessities. In the event, however, this idealised use of space was rarely achieved, private developers regarding Cerdà's restrictions as pointless interference. Buildings exceeded planned heights, and all the blocks from Plaça Catalunya to the Diagonal were enclosed. Even the planned gardens failed to withstand the onslaught of construction.

However, the development of the Eixample did see the refinement of a specific type of building: the apartment block, with giant flats on the principal floor (first above the ground), often with large glassed-in galleries for the drawing room, and small flats above. In time, the interplay between the Eixample's straight lines and the disorderly tangle of the older city became an essential part of the city's identity.

MODERNISME

Art nouveau was without doubt the leading influence in the decorative arts in Europe and the US between 1890 and 1914. In Barcelona, its influence merged with the cultural and political movement of the Catalan Renaixença to produce what became known as Modernisme (used here in Catalan to avoid confusion with 'modernism' in English, which refers to 20th-century functional styles).

For all of Catalonia's traditions in building and the arts, no style is as synonymous with it as Modernisme. This is in part due to the huge modern popularity of its most famous practitioner, Antoni Gaudí, and to its mix of decoration, eccentric unpredictability, dedicated craftsmanship and practicality. Modernisme can also be seen as matching certain archetypes of Catalan character, as a passionately nationalist expression that made use of Catalan traditions of design and craftwork. Artists strove to revalue the best of Catalan art,

showing interest in the Romanesque and Gothic of the Catalan Golden Age; Domènech i Montaner, for example, combined iron-frame construction with distinctive brick Catalan styles from the Middle Ages, regarding them as an 'expression of the Catalan earth'.

'Modernisme was an artistic movement in the fullest sense of the word.'

All art nouveau had a tendency to look at both the past and future, combining a love of decoration with new industrial techniques and materials; so it was in Catalonia. Even as they constructed a nostalgic vision of the Catalan motherland, Modernista architects plunged into experiments with new technology. Encouraged by wealthy patrons, they designed works made of iron and glass, introduced electricity, water and gas piping to building plans, were the first to tile bathroom and kitchen walls, made a point of allowing extensive natural light and fresh air into all rooms, and toyed with the most advanced, revolutionary expressionism.

Catalan Modernista creativity was at its peak from 1888 to 1908. The Eixample is the style's display case, with the greatest concentration of art nouveau in Europe, but Modernista buildings can be found in innumerable other

Pavelló Barcelona. *See p43.*

locations: in streets behind the Avda Paral·lel and villas on Tibidabo, in shop interiors and dark hallways, in country town halls and in the cava cellars of the Penedès.

International interest in Gaudí often eclipses the fact that there were many other remarkable architects and designers working at that time. Indeed, Modernisme was much more than an architectural style: the movement also included painters such as Ramon Casas, Santiago Rusiñol and Isidre Nonell, sculptors such as Josep Llimona, Miquel Blay and Eusebi Arnau, and furniture-makers like the superb Mallorcan Gaspar Homar. Much more than any other form of art nouveau, it extended into literature, thought and music, marking a whole generation of Catalan writers, poets, composers and philosophers. Although it was in architecture that it found its most splendid expression, Modernisme was an artistic movement in the fullest sense of the word, and, in Catalonia, it took on a nationalistic element.

Seen as the genius of the Modernista movement, Antoni Gaudí i Cornet was really a one-off, an unclassifiable figure. His work was a product of the social and cultural context of the time, but also of his own unique perception of the world, together with a deep patriotic devotion to anything Catalan.

Gaudí worked first as assistant to Josep Fontseré in the 1870s on the building of the **Parc de la Ciutadella**; the gates and fountain are attributed to him. Around the same time he also designed the lamp-posts in the Plaça Reial, but his first major commission was for **Casa Vicens** in Gràcia, built between 1883 and 1888. An orientalist fantasy, the building is structurally quite conventional, but Gaudí's use of surface material already stands out in the neo-Moorish decoration, multicoloured tiling and superbly elaborate ironwork on the gates. Gaudí's **Col·legi de les Teresianes** convent school (1888-89) is more restrained, but the clarity and fluidity of the building, with its simple finishes and use of light, are very appealing.

In 1878, Gaudí met Eusebi Güell, heir to one of the largest industrial fortunes in Catalonia. The pair shared ideas on religion, philanthropy and the socially redemptive role of architecture, and Gaudí produced several buildings for Güell. Among them were **Palau Güell** (1886-88), an impressive, historicist building that established his reputation, and the crypt at **Colònia Güell** outside Barcelona, one of his most structurally experimental and surprising buildings.

In 1883, Gaudí became involved in the design of the **Sagrada Família**, begun the previous year. He would eventually devote himself to it entirely. Gaudí was profoundly religious; part

of his obsession with the building came from a belief that it would help redeem Barcelona from the sins of secularism and the modern era (some Catalan Catholics have long campaigned for him to be made a saint, *see pp46-49*). From 1908 until his death in 1926, he worked on no other projects, often sleeping on site, a shabby, white-haired hermit, producing visionary ideas that his assistants had to interpret into drawings (on show in the museum alongside).

The Sagrada Família became the testing ground for Gaudí's ideas on structure and form, although he would live to see the completion of only the crypt, apse and Nativity façade, with its representation of 30 species of plants. As his work matured, he abandoned historicism and developed free-flowing, sinuous expressionist forms. His boyhood interest in nature began to take over from more architectural references, and what had previously provided external decorative motifs became the inspiration for the actual structure of his buildings.

In his greatest years, Gaudí combined other commissions with his cathedral; **La Pedrera**, which he began in 1905, was his most complete project. The building has an aquatic feel about it: the balconies resemble seaweed, and the undulating façade is reminiscent of the sea, or rocks washed by it. Interior patios are in blues and greens, and the roof resembles an imaginary landscape inhabited by mysterious figures. The **Casa Batlló**, on the other side of Passeig de Gràcia, was an existing building that Gaudí remodelled in 1905-07; the roof looks like a reptilian creature perched high above the street. The symbolism of the façade is the source of endless speculation. Some link it to the myth of St George and the dragon; others maintain it is a celebration of carnival, with its harlequin-hat roof, wrought-iron balcony 'masks' and cascading, confetti-like tiles. This last element was an essential contribution of Josep Maria Jujol, who many believe was even more skilled than his master as a mosaicist.

Gaudí's fascination with natural forms found full expression in the **Park Güell** (1900-14), where he blurred the distinction between natural and artificial forms in a series of colonnades winding up the hill. These paths lead up to the large central terrace projecting over a hall; a forest of distorted Doric columns planned as the marketplace for Güell's proposed 'garden city'. The terrace benches are covered in some of the finest examples of *trencadís* (broken mosaic work), again mostly by Jujol.

Modernista architecture received a vital, decisive boost around the turn of the 19th century from the Universal Exhibition of 1888. The most important buildings for the show were planned by the famed Lluís Domènech i

Not-so-green spaces

Having lived long within its walls, Barcelona is not a city of parks. The Parc de la Ciutadella was created little more than a century ago and, until the 1992 Olympics, you had to go up to Gaudí's Park Güell, Montjuïc or Tibidabo to get some air. Since 1992, the opening up of the beach promenade along the seafront has fulfilled the function performed by New York's Central Park or London's Royal parks.

In recent years, however, two new parks have been created in the former northern industrial zone of Poblenou and the triangle that lies beyond it between Avda Diagonal and the sea that has become known as Diagonal Mar. Internationally renowned architects have been commissioned – with budgets that match their fame – to create these parks. The first, **Parc Diagonal Mar**, the work of Catalan architect Enric Miralles (Scottish Parliament) opened in 2002. The second, the **Parc Central del Poblenou**, which is due to open in late 2007, has been designed by the French architect Jean Nouvel (Institut du Monde Arabe).

Miralles' park, which cost €35 million (or €1 million an acre), was a central part of the redevelopment plan for the Diagonal Mar area, which adjoins La Mina, one of the poorest and most blighted *barris* of Barcelona. Along with the park, the people of La Mina now also have a Hilton and other five-star hotels. So, not much use there. But they do, at least, have the park. Or do they?

Well, not really, at least not if we agree that in a park, it's the feet that do the talking. Few people use it, with the locals not warming to Miralles' undulating landscape and trademark structures. There is water, though the public does not have access, and a lot of art, though few trees. The children's play area iwould be improved enormously by the addition of old-fashioned swings and slides. Even the former mayor Joan Clos condemned it as 'an urban planning disaster' while the international organisation Project for Public Spaces added it to its 'Hall of Shame' saying it was 'designed by lawyers, a place where no spontaneous, unforeseen event can ever happen. It's a classic case of design run amok, where creating a place for human use was merely an afterthought.'

Nouvel's Poblenou project was already taking flak before it opened. His plans include giant plants, an island, a cratered lunar landscape and a perfumed garden, all enclosed within bougainvillea-clad concrete walls. Both he and Miralles have been denounced as 'exclusive' for creating their parks within walls. Mayeb the parks need time to develop their identity. On the other hand, perhaps architects, always so eager to make a 'statement', are not best suited to creating the sort of spaces where people will want to go for a snog or a stroll, to kick a ball or read the paper while their children play.

And a few more trees would be nice.

Montaner (1850-1923), who was then far more prominent than Gaudí as a propagandist for Modernisme in all its forms, and much more of a classic Modernista architect. Domènech was one of the first Modernista architects to develop the idea of the 'total work', working closely with large teams of craftsmen and designers on every aspect of a building. Not in vain was he dubbed 'the great orchestra conductor' by his many admirers.

Most of the Exhibition buildings no longer exist, but one that does is the **Castell dels Tres Dragons** in the Ciutadella park, designed as the Exhibition restaurant and now the Museu de Zoologia. It already demonstrated many key features of Modernista style: the use of structural ironwork allowed greater freedom in the creation of openings, arches and windows; and plain brick, instead of the stucco usually applied to most buildings, was used in an exuberantly decorative manner.

Domènech's greatest creations are the **Hospital de Sant Pau**, built as small 'pavilions' within a garden to avoid the usual effect of a monolithic hospital, and the fabulous **Palau de la Música Catalana** (*photo p38*), an extraordinary display of outrageous decoration. He also left quite a few impressive constructions in Reus, near Tarragona, notably the ornate mansions **Casa Navàs** and **Casa Rull**, as well as the spectacular pavilions of the **Institut Pere Mata**, a psychiatric hospital and forerunner of the Hospital de Sant Pau.

'The Pavelló Barcelona's impact was extraordinary.'

Third in the trio of leading Modernista architects was Josep Puig i Cadafalch (1867-1957), who showed a neo-Gothic influence in such buildings as the **Casa de les Punxes** (or the 'House of Spikes', officially the Casa Terrades) in the Diagonal, combined with many traditional Catalan touches. Nearby on Passeig de Sant Joan, at no.108, is another of his masterpieces: the **Casa Macaya**, its inner courtyard inspired by the medieval palaces of C/Montcada. Puig was responsible for some of the best industrial architecture of the time, an area in which Modernisme excelled: the Fundació La Caixa's cultural centre recently moved from Casa Macaya to another of Puig i Cadafalch's striking creations, the **Fàbrica Casaramona** at Montjuïc, built as a textile mill; outside Barcelona he designed the extraordinary **Caves Codorníu** wine cellars. Undoubtedly his best-known work, however, is the **Casa Amatller**, between Domènech's

Casa **Lleó Morera** and Gaudí's Casa Batlló in the Manzana de la Discòrdia.

The style caught on with extraordinary vigour all over Catalonia, and some of the most engaging architects are not very well known internationally. Impressive apartment blocks and mansions were built in the Eixample by Joan Rubió i Bellver (**Casa Golferichs**, Gran Via 491), Salvador Valeri (**Casa Comalat**, Avda Diagonal 442) and Josep Vilaseca. North of Barcelona is La Garriga, where MJ Raspall built exuberant summer houses for the rich and fashionable families of the time; there are also some dainty Modernista residences in coast towns, such as Canet and Arenys de Mar. Some of the finest Modernista industrial architecture is in Terrassa, designed by the municipal architect Lluís Moncunill (1868-1931), while another local architect, Cèsar Martinell, built co-operative cellars that are true 'wine cathedrals' in Falset, Gandesa and many other towns in southern Catalonia.

THE 20TH CENTURY

By the 1910s, Modernisme had become too extreme for Barcelona's middle classes; Gaudí's later buildings, indeed, were met with derision. The new 'proper' style for Catalan architecture was Noucentisme, which stressed the importance of classical proportions. However, it failed to produce anything of much note: the main buildings that survive are those of the 1929 Exhibition, Barcelona's next 'big event' that served as the excuse for the bizarre, neo-Baroque **Palau Nacional**. The Exhibition also brought the city one of the most important buildings of the century: Ludwig Mies van der Rohe's German Pavilion, the **Pavelló Barcelona** (*photo p39*), rebuilt near its original location in 1986. Its impact at the time was extraordinary; even today, it seems modern in its challenge to the conventional ideas of space.

Mies van der Rohe had a strong influence on the main new trend in Catalan architecture of the 1930s, which, reacting against Modernisme and nearly all earlier Catalan styles, was quite emphatically functionalist. Its leading figures were Josep Lluís Sert and the GATCPAC collective (Group of Catalan Architects and Technicians for the Progress of Contemporary Architecture), who struggled to introduce the ideas of Le Corbusier and of the International Style to local developers. Under the Republic, Sert built a sanatorium off C/Tallers and the Casa Bloc, a workers' housing project at Passeig Torres i Bages 91-105 in Sant Andreu. In collaboration with Le Corbusier, GATCPAC also produced a plan for the radical redesign of the whole of Barcelona as a 'functional city', the Pla Macià of 1933-34; drawings for the scheme

Las Arenas.

present a Barcelona that looks more like a Soviet-era new town in Siberia, and few regret that it never got off the drawing board. In 1937, Sert also built the Spanish Republic's pavilion for that year's Paris Exhibition, since rebuilt in Barcelona as the **Pavelló de la República** in the Vall d'Hebron. His finest work, however, came much later in the shape of the **Fundació Joan Miró**, built in the 1970s after he had spent many years in exile in the United States.

BARCELONA'S NEW STYLE

The Franco years had an enormous impact on the city. As the economy expanded at breakneck pace in the 1960s, Barcelona received a massive influx of migrants, in a context of unchecked property speculation and minimal planning controls; the city became ringed by a chaotic mass of high-rise suburbs. Another legacy of the era are some ostentatiously tall office blocks, especially on the Diagonal and around Plaça Francesc Macià.

When a democratic city administration took over the reins at the end of the 1970s, there was a lot to be done. A generation of architects had been chafing at Francoist restrictions for years. However, the tone set early on, above all by Barcelona's chief planner Oriol Bohigas – who has continued to design individual buildings as part of the MBM partnership with Josep Martorell and David Mackay – was one of 'architectural realism', with a powerful combination of imagination and practicality.

Budgets were limited, so the public's hard-earned funds initially were to be concentrated not on buildings but on the gaps between them: public spaces, a string of fresh, modern parks and squares, many of which were to incorporate original artwork. From this quiet beginning, Barcelona placed itself at the forefront of international urban design.

Barcelona's renewal programme took on a far more ambitious shape with the award of the 1992 Olympics, helped by a booming economy in the late 1980s. The third and most spectacular of the city's great events, the Barcelona Games were intended to be stylish and innovative, but most of all they were designed to provide a focus for a sweeping renovation of the city, with emblematic new buildings and infrastructure projects linked by clear strategic planning.

The three main Olympic sites – Vila Olímpica, Montjuïc and Vall d'Hebron – are quite different. The Vila Olímpica had the most comprehensive masterplan: drawn up by Bohigas and MBM themselves, it sought to extend Cerdà's grid down to the seafront.

The main project on Montjuïc was to be the transformation of the 1929 stadium, but there is also Arata Isozaki's Palau Sant Jordi and its space-frame roof. Vall d'Hebron is the least successful of the three sites, but Esteve Bonell's Velòdrom is one of the finest (and earliest) of the sports buildings, built in 1984 before the Olympic bid had even succeeded.

Fish.

Not content with all the projects completed by 1992, the city continued to expand through the '90s. Post-1992, the main focus of activity shifted to the Raval and the Port Vell (old port), and then more recently to the Diagonal Mar area in the north of the city. Many of the striking buildings here are by local architects, among them Helio Piñón and Albert Viaplana. Their work combines fluid, elegant lines with a strikingly modern use of materials, from the controversial 1983 **Plaça dels Països Catalans** through transformations of historic buildings such as the Casa de la Caritat, now the **Centre de Cultura Contemporània**, and all-new projects like **Maremàgnum** in the port.

Other contributions to post-Olympic Barcelona were made by foreign architects: notable examples include Richard Meier's bold white **MACBA**, Norman Foster's **Torre de Collserola** and Frank Gehry's **Fish**. Recently, two venerable buildings have been remodelled in the service of the city's residents: the last stage of Gae Aulenti's interior redesign of the Palau Nacional on Montjuïc has been finished after 14 years to create the expanded **Museu Nacional d'Art de Catalunya**, and the **CosmoCaixa** building in Tibidabo, which again converts a 19th-century hospice into a spectacular exhibition space, this time as home to the new science museum. Also undergoing a major facelift, the Mudéjar-style arches of **Las Arenas** bullring are being converted by Richard Rogers into a shopping and leisure centre.

In the 21st century, architectural projects are becoming increasingly circumscribed by commercial imperatives, sometimes causing tensions between the traditions of Barcelona urban architecture, the needs of a city of this size and the globalisation of commerce. The huge changes to the cityscape linked to the Fòrum Universal de les Cultures 2004 are a particluar case in point. The area at the mouth of the Besòs river, near where Avda Diagonal meets the sea, was transformed for the occasion, most notably by the construction of a triangular building, the **Edifici Fòrum**, designed by Herzog and de Meuron of Tate Modern fame. Nearby, Enric Miralles, best known for the Scottish Parliament building, created a fiercely modern and rather soulless park, the Parc Diagonal Mar (*see p42* **Not-so-green spaces**).

Whether this fourth stage in the re-imagining of the city can be linked to those outbursts of Barcelona's architectural creativity in the service of urban planning is debatable. While the value of many of these buildings is unquestionable, some see the dark hand of big business behind the latest developments and dismiss the new expansions connected to the Fòrum as more about making money than art. On the other hand, others defend this new, pragmatic approach to remodelling the city as another example of Barcelona's 1,000-year-old capacity to reinvent itself in the search to create a city that is both beautiful to look at and comfortable to live in.

La Pedrera (Casa Milà).

God's Builder

Gaudíte.

Genius, prophet, visionary – all these are words used of Antoni Gaudí. But was he also a 'saint'?

According to a dedicated group of Catholics in Barcelona, who have persuaded the Vatican to take the possibility seriously, the answer is an emphatic *sí*. The 'Cause' for Gaudí's canonisation – as applications for sainthood are known – is already well advanced: Rome is studying the assembled evidence, and the Association for the Beatification of Antoni Gaudí say the first stage on the path to sainthood – declaring him 'blessed' – is likely to be reached in a matter of years.

If so, it will be a first: despite its centuries of sponsoring great art and music, no professional artist has ever been declared a saint by the Catholic Church. (There was the 'blessed' Fra Angelico, but he was a friar who painted rather than a professional painter.) If Gaudí is eventually canonised then Barcelona's

great architect will have broken the mould not just of architecture but of holiness too.

The move is not without its critics, especially those who belong to that branch of Catalan nationalism with a secular vision of Catalonia. Gaudí, an artistic genius of international fame and a hero of Catalan nationalism, belongs, they say, to the whole of humanity; and they resent what they see as the Church's attempt to muscle in and claim him for itself. Among the critics is Josep Maria Subirachs, one of the sculptors working to complete the Sagrada Família. 'Everyone of different religions, different beliefs, comes here to see his work,' he says. 'He should be left as he is.'

But the Association – formed in 1992 by two architects, his biographer, a priest (who has since died) and a Japanese sculptor who converted to Catholicism while working on the Sagrada Família – insists that to acknowledge the importance of Gaudí's faith to his art in no way diminishes his universal importance or appeal. One of the association's founders, Josep Maria Tarragona, author of one of the most respected books on Gaudí, says knowing that he was a Catholic mystic gives the interpretative keys for understanding his art. 'That doesn't mean a non-Christian cannot understand Gaudí,' he says. 'But you cannot separate the man and his work from his faith.'

If the idea of Gaudí as saint seems strange, says Tarragona, it may be because we are accustomed to the iconic image of the artist as tortured, alienated and anarchic; the notion of an architect as both a radical modernist and a deeply prayerful, pious man therefore 'breaks the template'. That makes him doubly attractive to the Catholic Church: Gaudí's canonisation would help other professional, working people understand that they too can be holy.

The Cause was encouraged by one of the architect's admirers, Pope John Paul II, who was fascinated to discover Gaudí as an 'ordinary layman' rather than a monk or priest. In 2000 – by canonisation standards, the speed of light – he gave the go-ahead (technically, a *nihil obstat*) for the process to begin; three years later a 1,000-page dossier was lodged in Rome. Over the next years, theologians will examine evidence of Gaudí's 'heroic virtues'. For Gaudí to be declared 'blessed' – the first stage towards sainthood – the Association needs to provide proof of a miracle: someone who has been cured in a scientifically inexplicable manner after praying to Gaudí. A number have stepped forward with tales of cures, but none so far has been sufficiently miraculous to make the grade.

But the Association has already succeeded in putting the spotlight on a dimension of Gaudí and his work that has been often overlooked in the rush to declare him a modernist icon. Gaudí's conversion at the age of about 31 to a life of austerity and prayer was dramatic, and his art flowed from his relationship with God. All his works, Gaudí would later say, 'come from the Great Book of Nature'; his task was that of 'collaboration with the Creator'.

Gaudí knew that nature had none of the abstract geometry associated with conventional architecture. 'God's shapes' were fibrous – wood, bone, muscle – and formed by gravity. But Gaudí also observed that forms in nature served a function. If an architect looked for that same function in his work, he could arrive at beauty, whereas if he sought beauty, he would reach only abstraction. Gaudí's major works – La Pedrera, Park Güell and not least the

Holding the lingua

Catalans do like to talk about the *fet diferencial* (that which sets them apart – from the Spanish, of course) and cite a range of social and culinary customs. However, the real difference is language, and the degree to which this lies at the heart of their cultural identity became clear when Catalonia was invited to be the 'guest of honour' at the 2007 Frankfurt Book Fair.

Although it was Catalan culture that was invited, Frankfurt is a book fair and so the argument centred on what is and is not Catalan literature, to the point that the Catalan parliament took it upon itself to rule that the Catalan language is 'the only identifier' of Catalan literature. That might seem to settle the matter, were it not for the fact that some of the best known 'Spanish' writers, both within Spain and internationally, happen to be Catalans who write in the more widely read of their two languages, Spanish.

The ruling that defines Catalan literature as that written in Catalan excludes Carlos Ruiz Zafón (*The Shadow of the Wind*), the bestselling 'Spanish' author since Cervantes.

Out, too, goes Javier Cercas (*Soldiers of Salamis*), Eduardo Mendoza (*City of Marvels*), Maruja Torres, Terenci Moix, Juan Goytisolo, Juan Marsé (*Lizards' Tails*) and Manuel Vázquez Montalbán (creator of the gourmet-detective Pepe Carvalho), all Catalans, all of whom write or wrote in Spanish.

Were the Catalans shooting themselves in the foot by excluding their best-known authors? Not at all, argued Albert Sánchez-Piñol, whose *Pell Freda* (Cold Skin) was an international bestseller. To him it is quite simple. 'The French are clear about it: it's French literature if it's written in French. If someone lives in your country for 30 years but writes in Arabic, then it's Arabic literature. There's nothing to argue about.'

But critics argued that the Catalans should have followed the example of the founder of Catalan literature, Ramon Llull (*see p140* **Saint alive**), of whom it was said, 'He spoke a dozen languages, among them Latin, Hebrew, Arabic, French, Spanish and Catalan and, when someone spoke, they say, he always answered in their language.'

Sagrada Família – are initially upsetting, because they are more like nature than like architecture. Yet this is what makes his work both captivating and timeless.

Few could have predicted the path Gaudí's life would later take. He was by far the city's best architect – and its most expensive. In his twenties he was a wealthy dandy, dressing extravagantly and giving orders to his workmen without getting down from his horse-drawn carriage. Like Picasso and Dalí after him, Gaudí 'was conscious of his brilliance', says Tarragona. 'He knew that western architecture had come so far, and he was way ahead of it.'

This was a recipe for the kind of egotism which befell Picasso and Dalí in their lifetimes. But fate, or God, stepped in: the young man was knocked sideways when Pepita Moreu, a beautiful, wealthy lady who fascinated Gaudí, refused his offer of marriage. A second woman to whom he proposed chose a convent life instead. Gaudí fell back on his faith. He shed his wealth, and adopted the life of a pauper and mystic. The vital moment came in 1883, when, in his early thirties, Gaudí took over the plans for the Sagrada Família: here, he believed, was the task that God had given him for the rest of his life. Every day thereafter, he worked on the Sagrada Família, read the Bible, attended Mass, and said the Rosary. He lived alone, rarely travelling, writing little (although he was a great talker), and reading almost exclusively from spiritual texts.

'Life is love, and love is sacrifice. Sacrifice is the only really fruitful thing' – Gaudí.

Yet Gaudí was no hermit. He appeared in 3,000 Barcelona newspaper and journal articles in his lifetime – an average of twice a week. A Catalan nationalist, he was arrested under the dictatorship of Primo de Rivera (1922-31) for refusing to speak Castilian. He belonged to the League of Our Lady of Montserrat, a Catholic nationalist organisation that advocated a pluralistic, democratic Catalonia (as opposed to the integrists or Carlists, who spurned both Madrid and Rome). And he was active in a Catholic group of artists, the Cercle Artístic de Sant Lluc, headed by a figure vital to his conversion, Bishop Torras i Bages.

The joy of artistic creation was so immense, so overwhelming Gaudí believed, that if the artist did not respond through fasting and poverty, he would be 'over-compensated'. His asceticism could be extreme: people recall him

nibbling lettuce leaves dipped in milk. One Lent, in 1894, Gaudí had to be told to eat by his spiritual director after a radical fast left him at death's door. 'Life is love, and love is sacrifice,' the architect used to say. 'Sacrifice is the only really fruitful thing.' Hence the Sagrada Família, which he conceived as an 'expiation' for the sins of the world.

A craftsman by training, Gaudí was demanding of his workers, but endlessly kind. The site of the Sagrada Família was at the time located in one of the city's poorest *barris*, where he was loved and respected as an *obrerista* – one who identified with the working classes. They returned the compliment, protecting 'their' Sagrada Família from the anticlerical mobs who torched Barcelona's churches in 1909. After Gaudí's death in 1936, the studio containing his designs and models for the church went up in flames during the next bout of anticlerical fury; yet alone among the tombs at the Sagrada Famila, Gaudí's was spared from desecration.

Saints are not made of plaster; becoming holy is about struggling with vices and faults. Gaudí could be blunt and impatient with people who did not see things as immediately and clearly as he did. And his battle with his temper was lifelong. 'I have always fought, and I have always succeeded,' he told his spiritual director shortly before his death, 'except in one thing: in the struggle against my bad temper. This I have not been able to overcome.'

Those backing the Cause believe that while plenty of artists have been touched by divine inspiration in their work, few exhibited the intimate personal relationship with God that Gaudí did. Unlike other artists who so often burned out or died young, Gaudí's greatness increased with age, as his life became ever more ordered towards prayer. 'Mozart could write the *Coronation Mass* without having a devout life,' says Tarragona. 'God gave him the grace, as of course he did with Michelangelo in the creation of the *Pietà* or the Sistine Chapel. But in Gaudí we get both divine inspiration and a personal life proper to a mystic.'

Gaudí himself was in no doubt who he was working for. When people clucked that the Sagrada Família would never be finished in his lifetime 'God's architect' would just shrug. 'My client,' he would answer, 'is not in a hurry.'

Run over by a no.30 tram on his way to evening prayer in 1926, Gaudí was mistaken for a beggar and taken to the city's pauper hospital. When his friends found him there the next day, he refused to budge: he had always wanted to leave this world poor, he said. And he did, two days later, aged 74, mourned by a city which hailed him as an artistic genius – and a saint.

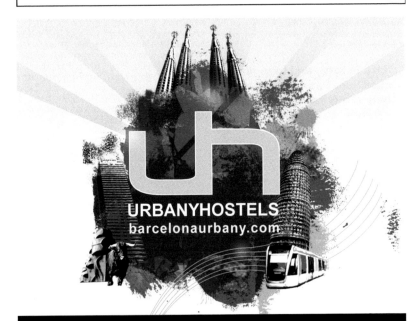

Where to Stay

H1898. *See p55*.

Where to Stay

Barna's best beds.

New hotels have been springing up over the last few years, and the trend shows no sign of slowing down. While this has certainly made it easier to find accommodation in a city with year-round high occupancy, there remains a real dearth of more modest hotels that offer fewer frills but provide all the facilities most travellers need.

The glut of top-end accommodation means that hotels are continually revising their rates according to demand and, at off-peak times, when there are fewer business travellers, offer rooms at heavily reduced prices. Be sure to check online for preferential rates.

There is now quite a good range of boutique hotels, but again, they are mostly at the upper end of the scale. If you look hard enough, however, there is plenty of charm at the budget end, as many *hostales* are situated in fabulous old buildings with elaborate doorways, grand staircases and beautiful tiled floors. A new generation of hoteliers is transforming old-fashioned, gloomy *hostales* into bright, friendly establishments with en-suite bathrooms, internet access and other modern essentials.

Booking in advance is strongly advised, at least in those places where it's possible: many of the cheaper hotels won't accept reservations. Hotels often require you to guarantee your booking with credit-card details or a deposit; whether or not you've provided either, it's always worth calling a few days before your arrival to reconfirm the booking (get it in writing if you can; many readers have reported problems) and to check the cancellation policy. Often you will lose at least the first night.

To be sure of getting a room with natural light or a view, ask for an outside room (*habitació/habitación exterior*), which will usually face the street. Many of Barcelona's buildings are built around a central patio or airshaft, and the inside rooms (*habitació/habitación interior*) around them can be quite gloomy, albeit quieter. However, in some cases, these inward-facing rooms look on to large, open-air patios or gardens, which have the benefit of being quiet and having a view.

> ❶ Green numbers given in this chapter correspond to the location of each hotel on the street maps. *See pp338-345.*

Hotels of two-star quality and more (listed under Expensive and Mid range) have air-conditioning as standard. Air-con is increasingly common even in no-frills places, however, and around half the *hostales* in the Budget listings are equipped with it.

The law now prohibits smoking in communal areas in hotels. As a result, some hotels have banned smoking altogether, and many have the majority of floors/rooms as non-smoking.

Theft is a problem, especially in lower-end establishments, but occasionally also in luxury ones. If you're sleeping cheap, you might want to travel with a padlock to lock your door, or at least lock up your bags. As a rule of thumb, check to see if youth-hostel rooms have lockers if you're sharing with other people. Use hotel safes where possible.

STAR RATINGS AND PRICES

Accommodation in Catalonia is divided into two official categories: hotels (H) and *pensiones* (P). To be a hotel (star-rated one to five), a place must have en-suite bathrooms in every room. Ratings are based on physical attributes rather than levels of service; often the only difference between a three- and a four-star hotel is the presence of a meeting room. *Pensiones*, usually cheaper and often family-run, are star-rated one or two, and are not required to have en-suite bathrooms (though many do). Some *pensiones* are called *hostales*, but, confusingly, are not youth hostels; those are known as *albergues*.

For a double room, expect to pay €50-€75 for a budget *pensión*, €80-€180 for a mid-range spot and €200 upwards for a top-of-the-range hotel. However, prices vary depending on the time of year; always check for special deals. All bills are subject to seven per cent IVA (value added tax) on top of the basic price; this is not normally included in the advertised rates, but we have factored it into the prices we have given. Breakfast is not included unless stated.

Booking agencies

Barcelona Hotel Association

Via Laietana 47, 1°, 2ª, Barri Gòtic (93 301 62 40/ www.barcelonahotels.es). Metro Urquinaona. **Open** *Sept-June 9am-6pm Mon-Fri; July, Aug 8.30am-2.30pm Mon-Fri.* **Map** p344 D3.

The website of this hoteliers' organisation lists 264 hotels and apartments in all categories, and there

Party like it's **H1898**. *See p55.*

are also special offers and last-minute rates available. Credit card details must usually be given to secure a reservation online, but your account will not be debited until you finally check out of the hotel. Reservations cannot be made in the office, although information can be provided here.

Barcelona On-Line

Gran Via de les Corts Catalanes 662, Eixample (93 343 79 93/www.barcelona-on-line.es). Metro Passeig de Gràcia. **Open** 9am-7pm Mon-Fri; 9am-2pm Sat. **Map** p342 G8.

This is a highly professional agency where you can book hostel, hotel rooms and private apartments online, on the phone or at the above office. Staff are multilingual and the service is free, but, depending on the hotel, there can be a fee if you cancel less than 48 hours before arrival. You'll also need to make a prepayment for apartment reservations.

Viajes Iberia

Plaça de Sants 12, Eixample (93 431 90 00/ www.viajesiberia.com). Metro Plaça de Sants. **Open** 8.30am-1.30pm, 4.30-7.30pm Mon-Fri; 10am-1.30pm Sat. **Credit** AmEx, DC, MC, V. **Map** p338 A7.

This agency can book a room at many of Barcelona's hotels and some *pensiones*. The reservation fee varies, and you will need to pay a deposit. **Other locations** throughout the city.

Barri Gòtic & La Rambla

La Rambla is flanked by hotels ranging from no frills to luxury, but the totally touristy environment – not to mention the noise – may prove a bit much for some people. The medieval labyrinth of the Gòtic conceals some cheaper alternatives, but bear in mind that old buildings can often be grotty rather than charming.

Expensive

H10 Racó del Pi

C/Pi 7 (93 342 61 90/www.h10hotels.es). Metro Liceu. **Rates** €181-€230 double. **Rooms** 37. **Credit** AmEx, DC, MC, V. **Map** p344 C4 ❶

Part of the H10 chain, the Racó del Pi offers spacious rooms with parquet floors, handsome terracotta-tiled bathrooms and an elegant glass conservatory on the ground floor. It can be a bargain out of season. Check the website for details.
Bar. Disabled-adapted room. Internet (free wireless). No-smoking floors (2). TV.
Other locations H10 Catalunya Plaza, Plaça Catalunya 7, Eixample (93 317 71 71); and throughout the city.

H1898

La Rambla 109 (93 552 95 52/www.nnhotels.es). Metro Catalunya or Liceu. **Rates** €181-€490 double. **Rooms** 169. **Credit** AmEx, DC, MC, V. **Map** p344 B3 ❷

A dapper new luxury hotel in a 19th-century building – the former Philippine Tobacco Company headquarters – H1898 is right on La Rambla. Rooms are subject to Henley Regatta-type colour schemes; one floor is all perky green-and-white stripes, another is red and white, and so on. The more expensive rooms have generous wooden-decked terraces, while some of the suites have private plunge pools. *Photo p53. Bar (2). Business centre. Disabled-adapted rooms (6). Gym. Internet (free wireless). No-smoking floors (5). Parking (€23/day). Pool (outdoor/indoor). Restaurant. Room service. Spa. TV (pay movies).*

Hotel Colón

Avda Catedral 7 (93 301 14 04/www.hotelcolon.es). Metro Jaume I. **Rates** €155-€240 double. **Rooms** 145. **Credit** AmEx, DC, MC, V. **Map** p344 D4 ❸

If you have had it up to here with minimalism, stay at this stalwart of the Barcelona hotel scene and sink into a chintzy armchair that actually looks like a chair rather than an artwork. With thick carpets and walls bedecked in bright floral prints, the Colón is all about making guests feel comfortable. The great location, on the square in front of the cathedral, is best enjoyed in one of the rooms that overlook the magnificent Gothic edifice, some of which have balconies.

The best Hotels

For romantic weekends

For the decadent, lounge in luxury in **Hotel Neri** (*see p56*) a former 18th-century palace. If originality is your thing, head for the extravagant **Casa Fuster** (*see p73*). Book ahead for one of the five design rooms, each of which is unique in in its own way; breakfast is served throughout the day. For tranquillity, head uptown to the chic neighbourhood of San Gervasi where **Petit Hotel** (*see p75*) is cute and neat with the added benefit of an ample breakfast. Budget lovers should try **Hostal Girona** (*see p71*) and laze on the ample patio.

For families

For hotel-phobes who suffer from flashbacks of *The Shining*, seek the personal touch at friendly **Hostal San Remo** (*see p73*). Families book ahead for one of six large rooms at **Pensió 2000** (*see p61*) or centrally located studios and apartments are both available at **Citadines** (*see p75*). For winter wanderers, **Hosteria Grau** (*see p65*) has an open fireplace, charming communal areas and six apartments for rent.

For a breath of fresh air

For those intent on relaxation at any cost, the lofty spa on the 42nd and 43rd floor of **Hotel Arts** (*see p65*) is ideal and the beach is just outside, should you care to descend. Similarly swish, Spaciomm at **Hotel Omm** (*see p69*) offers the very latest in ancient eastern relaxation techniques. If views are your thing, there's a panoramic one from the rooftop pool of **Gran Hotel La Florida** (*see p75*). **Hotel Petit Palace Opera Garden** (*see p56*) combines centrality with tranquillity. Smoke free zones – yes, the restaurant too – include **Hotel Colón** (*see p55*) near the cathedral.

For something special

Cool customers stay at quirky **Casa Camper** (*see p63*). For those who thrive in the thick of it all, **Hotel Cram** (*see p68*) has the look and feel of a nightclub to get and keep you in the mood, plus the added bonus of a top notch restaurant where you can recharge your batteries.

For simplicity

Sleep, shower and go? **Abba Rambla Hotel** (*see p63*) is one of the better and most central options. **Hostal La Palmera** (*see p65*) is just behind La Boqueria market, but is surprisingly quiet. For impulsive arrivals, the mid-priced **Hotel Nuevo Triunfo** (*see p67*) is good and central. For hostellers, **Barcelona Mar Youth Hostel** (*see p78*) has another branch, reachable by metro, if more central options are full.

Bar. Disabled-adapted rooms (3). Internet (free high-speed in rooms). No-smoking hotel. Restaurant. Room service. TV: pay movies.
Other locations Hotel Regencia Colón, C/Sacristans 13, Barri Gòtic (93 318 98 58).

Hotel Le Meridien Barcelona

La Rambla 111 (93 318 62 00/www.barcelona. lemeridien.com). Metro Liceu. **Rates** €430-€480 double. **Rooms** 233. **Credit** AmEx, DC, MC, V. **Map** p344 B3
Le Meridien is a great place to stay if you'd like to mix up your stay in Barcelona with a little celebrity spotting. The stars, being used to attention, are attracted by the lure of its ultra-luxurious suites. The hotel has revamped its genteel image with wood floors and leather furnishings, along with Egyptian cotton bed-linen, rain showers and plasma-screen TVs. Despite its size, it manages to retain an air of intimacy thanks to helpful, friendly staff. All rooms are soundproofed, and the best look out over La Rambla.
Bar. Disabled-adapted rooms (4). Gym. Internet (high-speed in rooms). No-smoking floors (8). Parking (€20-€25/day). Restaurant. Room service. TV.

Hotel Neri

C/Sant Sever 5 (93 304 06 55/www.hotelneri.com). Metro Jaume I. **Rates** €280.20-€347 double. **Rooms** 22. **Credit** AmEx, DC, MC, V. **Map** p345 C5
A sumptuous, sensual boutique hotel, ideal for a romantic weekend, located in a former 18th-century palace. The lobby, which teams flagstone floors and wooden beams with funky designer fixtures, red velvet and lashings of gold leaf, gives a taste of what's to come in the 22 rooms, where the neutral tones, natural materials and rustic finishes (untreated wood and unpolished marble) stand in stylish contrast with bolts of lavish satins and velvets, sharp design and high-tech perks (hi-fis, plasma-screen TVs).

Bar. Disabled-adapted room. Internet (wireless). No-smoking rooms (10). Restaurant. Room service. TV: pay movies.

Hotel Petit Palace Opera Garden

C/Boqueria 10 (93 302 00 92/www.hthoteles.com). Metro Liceu. **Rates** €140-€320 double. **Rooms** 61. **Credit** AmEx, DC, MC, V. **Map** p345 B5
A private mansion was completely gutted to create this new minimalist haven on a busy street just off La Rambla. The 61 rooms are white and futuristic, with a different zingy colour on each floor and opera scores printed on the walls above the beds. Lamps and chairs lend a 1960s air, so pack your kinky boots and groovy flares to enjoy your stay to the full. Some bathrooms have massage showers, others jacuzzi baths. Only breakfast is served in the chic dining room. There's a little-known public street garden at the back: a real luxury in this densely packed area.
Bar. Disabled-adapted rooms (2). Internet (free wireless). No-smoking floors (6). Room service. TV.

Mid range

Duc de la Victòria

C/Duc de la Victòria 15 (93 270 34 10/www.nh-hotels.com). Metro Catalunya. **Rates** €115-€190 double. **Rooms** 156. **Credit** AmEx, DC, MC, V. **Map** p344 C3/4
The trusty NH chain has high standards of comfort and service, and this good-value downtown branch is no exception. The 156 rooms, with blue-and-beige colour scheme, may be unexciting, but the superior quality beds ensure you get a good night's sleep. A stone's throw from La Rambla.
Disabled-adapted rooms (3). Internet (free high-speed in rooms). No-smoking floors (4). Restaurant (lunch; dinner Mon-Fri only). Room service. TV (pay movies).

Grand Hotel Central. *See p59.*

Hostal Jardí

*Plaça Sant Josep Oriol 1 (93 301 59 00). Metro
Liceu.* **Rates** €86-€98 double. **Rooms** 44. **Credit**
AmEx, DC, MC, V. **Map** p345 B5 ⑧
A victim of its own success, the Jardí now requires
you to book three months in advance. There is a
rather institutional feel about both rooms and lobby,
but the location is excellent, overlooking a pretty
square. It is only really worth staying here if you get
one of the best rooms with a balcony from which to
enjoy the view. Apart from the frugal furnishings,
some rooms are dark, but all have en-suite bathrooms, and the place is sparkling clean.
No-smoking hotel. TV.

Hotel Nouvel

*C/Santa Anna 20 (93 301 82 74/www.hotel
nouvel.com). Metro Catalunya.* **Rates** (incl
breakfast) €170-€220 double. **Rooms** 54.
Credit MC, V. **Map** p344 C3 ⑨
Opened in 1917, the Nouvel has bags of old-world
charm. Guestrooms don't quite live up to the lobby,
which features carriage lanterns, an ornate ceiling
and curved wooden fittings. But they are airy, comfortable and decorated in a neutral classic style, with
spacious, well-equipped bathrooms.
No-smoking rooms (7). Restaurant. TV.

Hotel Oriente

*La Rambla 45 (93 302 25 58/www.husa.es). Metro
Liceu.* **Rates** €150-€225 double. **Rooms** 140.
Credit AmEx, DC, MC, V. **Map** p345 A6 ⑩
It was Barcelona's first-ever 'grand hotel', opening
in 1842, but the Oriente had been getting increasingly shabby until a recent renovation brightened
things up considerably. All the bedrooms now have
pale wood floors, minimalist design and sleek electrical gadgetry, in striking contrast to the ritzy ball-
room and dining room. Sadly, no amount of

renovation can do away with the noise leaking up
from La Rambla; if you happen to be a light sleeper
we highly recommended that you ask for a room at
the back of the hotel, or pack earplugs.
*Bar (Mar-Oct only). Internet (€2/hr shared terminal).
TV.*

Budget

Hostal Fontanella

*Via Laietana 71, 2° (93 317 59 43/www.hostal
fontanella.com). Metro Urquinaona.* **Rates** €59-€80
double. **Rooms** 11. **Credit** AmEx, DC, MC, V.
Map p344 D2 ⑪
The splendid Modernista lift lends a somewhat
unjustified aura of grandeur to this 11-room *hostal*,
where Laura Ashley devotees will feel totally at
home amid the chintz, lace and dried flowers. The
downside of the Fontanella's central location – on
the thoroughfare bordering the Born, the Barri Gòtic
and the Eixample – is that outward-facing rooms are
abuzz with the sound of busy traffic. However, it's
a clean and comfortable place to stay, and double-
glazing has recently been installed, making the outdoors somewhat less present indoors.
TV.

Hostal Lausanne

*Portal de l'Àngel 24, 1° 1ª (93 302 11 39/
www.hostallausanne.com). Metro Catalunya.*
Rates €50-€65 double. **Rooms** 17. **No credit
cards. Map** p344 C3 ⑫
Situated on one of downtown's busiest shopping
streets, this *hostal* occupies the first floor of an
impressive building. Unlike some *hostales*, the place
feels spacious, with light pouring in from both ends
of the building. Of the 17 basic rooms, four have en-
suite bathrooms and some have balconies. It may be
a bit dated, but it's a friendly and safe place, with a
fun backpacker vibe. The street is quiet at night.
Internet (free shared terminal). TV room.
Other locations Hostal Europa, C/Boqueria 18,
Barri Gòtic (93 318 76 20).

Hostal Noya

*La Rambla 133, 1° (93 301 48 31). Metro
Catalunya.* **Rates** €36-€42 double. **Rooms** 15.
No credit cards. Map p344 B2/3 ⑬
Cheap and cheerful, the Noya is run by the smiling,
helpful Feli, who is always on hand to welcome you
as you get your breath back after lugging your bags
up three flights of stairs. Rooms are basic but some
have balconies looking out on to La Rambla and there
are handsome old tiles on the floor. The lone bathroom is weathered and worn, and it can get busy since
it's shared between 15 rooms (there is a separate WC),
but all bedrooms do have their own washbasins.
Other locations Pensión Bienestar, C/Quintana 3,
Barri Gòtic (93 318 72 83).

Hostal Rembrandt

*C/Portaferrissa 23, pral (tel 93 318 10 11/www.
hostalrembrandt.com). Metro Liceu.* **Rates** €50-€65
double. **Rooms** 27. **Credit** MC, V. **Map** p344 C4 ⑭

A charming 27-room *hostal*: fairly stylish (for the price) with lots of wood panelling, soft lighting and a lift. An added bonus is the pretty interior courtyard, which makes for a pleasant chill-out zone/eating area. Rooms out front can be a little noisy, but the passing stream of humanity means you will never be bored. The same people also rent out apartments on nearby C/Canuda (€75-€150 for two people, minimum three night stay).
Internet (€3/hr shared terminal).

Hotel Toledano
La Rambla 138, 4° (93 301 08 72/www.hoteltoledano. com). Metro Catalunya. **Rates** €64 double. **Rooms** 17. **Credit** AmEx, DC, MC, V. **Map** p344 B3 ⓰
All 17 rooms in this kitsch hotel are spotless and some have air-conditioning, but whether you end up with acres of space or just up from a broom cupboard is a lottery. Some rooms have balconies overlooking La Rambla, while others provide a glimpse of the cathedral. Service is friendly, and – rather unusually for this category – there is free wireless internet in the rooms as well as shared terminals. A book-exchange system is another nice touch. There are 12 more basic rooms in the *pensión* upstairs (same number). Booking is essential.
Internet (free shared terminal, free wireless in rooms). TV room.

Pensió Alamar
C/Comtessa de Sobradiel 1, 1° 2ª (93 302 50 12/ www.pensioalamar.com). Metro Jaume I or Liceu. **Rates** €36-€45 double. **Rooms** 12. **Credit** AmEx, DC, MC, V. **Map** p345 C6 ⓰
A basic, but tasteful family-run *hostal*. Beds are new and excellent quality, with crisp cotton sheets, and windows are double-glazed to keep noise to a minimum. The downside is the 12 rooms share two bathrooms. There are good discounts for longer stays, and larger rooms for families. Single travellers are made very welcome, with no supplement for occupying a double room. Guests can make their own meals in a well-equipped kitchen and do their laundry. More suitable for those looking for a quiet, homely atmosphere than clubbers.
TV room.

Pensión Hostal Mari-Luz
C/Palau 4 (tel 93 317 34 63/www.pensionmari luz.com). Metro Jaume I or Liceu. **Rates** €35-€52 double; €16-€20/person 4-6-person rooms. **Rooms** 14. **Credit** AmEx, DC, MC, V. **Map** p345 C6 ⓰
The entrance and staircase of this 18th-century stone building are certainly imposing, but the downside is that you then have to climb several flights of stairs to reach the Mari-Luz. Catch your breath, though, and you'll find the effort is well worth it, for the smiling service and friendly atmosphere. Stripped wood doors and old floor tiles add character to the 14 otherwise plain but quiet rooms, some of which face a plant-filled inner courtyard. There are dorms as well as double and triple rooms.
Other locations Pensión Fernando, C/Ferran 31, Barri Gòtic (93 301 79 93).

Residencia Victòria
C/Comtal 9, 1° 1ª (93 318 07 60/93 317 45 97/ www.residenciavictoria.com). Metro Catalunya. **Rates** €40-€44 double. **Rooms** 28. **Credit** MC, V. **Map** p344 C3 ⓰
This spacious and peaceful *pensión* is located on the second floor (no lift). Rooms are basic, clean and light, all with sinks but no en-suite bathrooms. Extras include communal cooking and washing facilities, and a cute outdoor terrace. Friendly service keeps people coming back, so book in advance.
TV room.

Born & Sant Pere
New hotels are cropping up in revamped old buildings in these medieval areas. The Born in particular is an established cool zone, with many restaurants, bars and boutiques.

Expensive

Grand Hotel Central
Via Laietana 30 (93 295 79 00/www.grandhotel central.com). Metro Jaume I. **Rates** €175-€370 double. **Rooms** 147. **Credit** AmEx, DC, MC, V. **Map** p345 D5 ⓰
The Grand Hotel Central is another of the recent wave of Barcelona hotels to adhere to the unwritten but tyrannical design protocol that grey is the new black. The Central's shadowy, Hitchcockian corridors open up on to sleekly appointed rooms that come with flat-screen TVs, DVD players and Molton Brown toiletries. But the real charm of the hotel lies up above, on its roof. Here you can sip a cocktail and admire the fabulous views while floating comfortably in the vertiginous infinity pool. *Photo p56.*
Bar. Business centre. Disabled-adapted rooms (4). Gym. Internet (free wireless). No-smoking floors (4). Parking (€25/day). Pool (outdoor). Restaurant. Room service. TV.

Mid range

Banys Orientals
C/Argenteria 37 (93 268 84 60/www.hotel banysorientals.com). Metro Jaume I. **Rates** €105 double. **Rooms** 56. **Credit** AmEx, DC, MC, V. **Map** p345 D6 ⓰
Banys Orientals is one of the best deals to be found in Barcelona. It exudes cool, from its location at the heart of the Born to the stylish shades-of-grey minimalism of its rooms, and nice touches such as complimentary mineral water on the landings. The main debit is the small size of some of the double rooms.
Disabled-adapted room. Internet (free shared terminals). No-smoking floors (2). Restaurant. TV.

Chic&basic
C/Princesa 50 (93 295 46 52/www.chicandbasic. com). Metro Arc de Triomf or Jaume I. **Rates** €118-€193 double. **Rooms** 31. **Credit** AmEx, DC, MC, V. **Map** p345 F5 ⓰

The hotel on the hill

The **AC Miramar** (*see p67*) may be the hottest hotel in town, but the plans to develop the palace on Montjuïc into a hotel were greeted with outrage in Barcelona. For a start, there was the bastardisation of the building itself, a villa built for the 1929 International Exhibition, which many citizens felt should have been preserved for posterity. The second bone of contention was the rumour that the work would disturb the medieval Jewish burial grounds that are believed to be on the mountain. Regardless, one sympathetic restoration later and the results are impressive.

On arrival, local architect Oscar Tusquet's champagne-coloured marble lobby gives a suitably lofty air to the place, enhanced by a stairwell built to resemble the ramparts of a castle. The austerity of the architecture is softened by leather sofas and a chandelier inspired by the Sagrada Familia, dripping crystal-like diamonds on a red carpet. A casual lounge area that serves also as a cocktail bar, gives on to an ample terrace with views over a richly scented orange patio.

So what of the rooms? While the smallest may not that big, they are at the top of the building, and have large private terraces with a hot tub. Some of the larger deluxe rooms and suites do not, so be sure to specify a sea view and a terrace. The advantage of the more expensive rooms is that many have Lavasca egg-shaped baths: something to bear in mind for romantic winter weekends.

A monochrome space-age theatrical vibe reigns supreme here: if you've ever dreamed of entering your room through a shimmering curtain of transparent plastic twirls, as if you were walking into a waterfall, then welcome home. The building retains its original grand staircase, now attractively furnished with oversized chairs and sofas. A chill-out room contains tea- and coffee-making facilities, a fridge and a microwave, as well as sofas and pouffes. *Bar. Disabled-adapted room. Gym. Internet (wireless). No-smoking hotel (except restaurant). Restaurant. TV.*

Ciutat Barcelona

C/Princesa 35 (93 269 74 75/www.ciutatbarcelona. com). Metro Jaume I. **Rates** €107-€170 double. **Rooms** 78. **Credit** AmEx, DC, MC, V. **Map** p345 E5 ㉒

The Ciutat Barcelona opened in 2006 and has gone over big on the colour co-ordination – even the plastic cups in the bathrooms match the red, blue or green colour-scheme of the rooms. Retro shapes prevail in the stylish furnishings and decoration, but rooms are small. There is a great roof terrace with a plunge pool. The Colors restaurant on the ground floor is popular with non-guests. *Disabled-adapted rooms (4). Internet (free high-speed in rooms, free wireless in communal areas). No-smoking floors (4). Pool (outdoor). Restaurant. Room service. TV: cable.*

Budget

Hostal Orleans

Avda Marquès de l'Argentera 13, 1º (93 319 73 82/ www.hostalorleans.com). Metro Barceloneta. **Rates** €55-€60 double. **Rooms** 27. **Credit** AmEx, DC, MC, V. **Map** p345 F7 ㉓

It may look a bit grungy when viewed from the street, but inside the Orleans is surprisingly luxurious for a *hostal*, with comfortable, refurbished rooms and en-suite bathrooms that would not look out of place several categories up the hotel scale. The spacious quadruple rooms are a positive steal for groups. It's set in a good location for those wanting to sample Born nightlife and is right by Estació de França, where the airport trains arrive and depart. *TV.*

Pensió 2000

C/Sant Pere Més Alt 6, 1º (93 310 74 66/www. pensio2000.com). Metro Urquinaona. **Rates** €59-€75 double. **Rooms** 6. **Credit** AmEx, MC, V. **Map** p344 D3 ㉔

Pensió 2000 is a good-value pension located in a fine old building across from the Palau de la Música Catalana. Only two of the rooms are en suite, but the shared facilities are kept clean. The large rooms make it suitable for holidaying families. *Photo p63.*

Raval

The Raval is the edgy neighbour of the Barri Gòtic, but recent regeneration means it's also the coolest *barri* for bars and restaurants, with a lively multicultural vibe.

Expensive

Casa Camper

C/Elisabets 11 (93 342 62 80/www.casacamper.com). Metro Catalunya. **Rates** (incl breakfast & snack) €225-€264 double. **Rooms** 25. **Credit** AmEx, DC, MC, V. **Map** p344 A3 ❷

Devised by the Mallorcan footwear giant, this is a holistic concept-fest of a boutique hotel, designed by Ferran Amat, although the stark rooms won't be to all tastes. There is nothing as naff as a minibar, but you can help yourself to free snacks and refreshments in the café whenever the fancy takes you. Specially designed bicycles are available for rent at €17.40/4hrs or €23.20/day.
Bar. Business centre. Disabled-adapted room. Internet (free wireless). No-smoking hotel. TV: pay movies, DVD.

Hotel Silken Ambassador Ramblas

C/Pintor Fortuny 13 (93 342 61 80/www.hotelessilken.com). Metro Catalunya. **Rates** €290-€360 double. **Rooms** 105. **Credit** AmEx, DC, MC, V. **Map** p344 B3 ❷

The Ambassador features a heady blend of water features, gold paint and smoked glass, a glittering colossus of a chandelier and a free-standing Modernista bar that dominates the lounge area. Rooms are straightforward with no scary designer features, and there's also a pool and jacuzzi on the rooftop.
Bar. Disabled-adapted rooms (4). Gym. Internet (free wireless, free shared terminal). No-smoking floors (4). Parking (€21/day). Pool (outdoor). Restaurant. Room service. TV: pay movies.

Mid range

Abba Rambla Hotel

C/Rambla del Raval 4 (93 505 54 00/www.abba hoteles.com). Metro Liceu or Sant Antoni. **Rates** €125-€268 double. **Rooms** 49. **Credit** AmEx, MC, V. **Map** p342 E10 ❷

The Abba Rambla is a comfortable and friendly base, although rooms are a bit bland. More stylish are the ground-floor lounge and breakfast bar, where you eat perched on high stools.
Disabled-adapted room. Internet (free shared terminal, free wireless). No-smoking floors (3).

Hostal Gat Raval

C/Joaquín Costa 44, 2º (93 481 66 70/www.gat accommodation.com). Metro Universitat. **Rates** €73-€82 double. **Rooms** 25. **Credit** AmEx, MC, V. **Map** p342 E9 ❷

Gat Raval embodies everything that 21st-century budget accommodation should be: smart, clean and funky, with bright rooms each boasting a work by a local artist. Some rooms have balconies while others have views of the MACBA. The only downsides are that nearly all the bathrooms are communal (though they are very clean) and there is no lift. Laptops for hire at €6.50/hr.
Internet (€6.50/hr wireless). No-smoking hostal. TV.

Pensió 2000: an ideal place for families to stay. *See p61.*

Hostal Gat Xino

C/Hospital 155 (93 324 88 33/www.gat accommodation.com). Metro Sant Antoni. **Rates** (incl breakfast) €81-€95 double. **Rooms** 35. **Credit** AmEx, MC, V. **Map** p342 E10 ㉙

The 'Gats' are pioneers of a new way to stay: inexpensive, modern places that combine the polish of a boutique hotel with the practicality and price of a B&B. This is the second to open, and it has a bright breakfast room complete with apple-green polka-dot walls, a patio and a roof terrace with black beanbags on which to chill out. There's more bright green to be found in the bedrooms (all of which are en suite), with good beds, crisp white linen, flat-screen TVs and backlit panels of Raval scenes. The best rooms have small terraces of their own.

Hostal-Residencia Ramos

C/Hospital 36 (93 302 07 23/www.hostalramos.com). Metro Liceu. **Rates** €65-€73 double. **Rooms** 23. **Credit** MC, V. **Map** p345 A5 ㉚

This family-run *hostal* offers one of the best deals in the Raval. There's no air-conditioning, but plenty of windows and balconies keep the place cool – although then you have to contend with the street noise. Rooms (all en suite) are basic and vary in size, but are light and airy. The best have balconies looking on to the *plaça*, where there is usually an interesting mixture of the Raval's multicultural communities and newer, super-cool inhabitants to keep you amused.
Internet (free wireless). TV.

Bar. Internet (€6.50/hr shared terminal or wireless). No-smoking hostal. TV.

Hotel Arts.

Hotel España

C/Sant Pau 9-11 (93 318 17 58/www.hotel espanya.com). Metro Liceu. **Rates** (incl breakfast) €90-€148 double. **Rooms** 83. **Credit** AmEx, DC, MC, V. **Map** p345 A5 ③①

The lower floors at this Modernista landmark were designed by Domènech i Montaner in 1902. The main restaurant is decorated with floral tiling and elaborate woodwork, while the larger dining room beyond it features dreamy murals of mermaids by Ramon Casas, and the bar boasts a sculpted marble fireplace. After all this grandeur, the bedrooms are unexciting but have been considerably improved in recent years. All are en suite, and the nicest ones open on to a bright interior patio.
Disabled-adapted rooms (2). Internet (€5/hr shared terminal). Restaurant. TV.

Hotel Mesón Castilla

C/Valldonzella 5 (93 318 21 82/www.mesoncastilla. com). Metro Universitat. **Rates** (incl breakfast) €139-€155 double. **Rooms** 57. **Credit** AmEx, DC, MC, V. **Map** p344 A2 ③②

If you want a change from modern design, check into this chocolate-box hotel, which opened in 1952. Before then, it belonged to an aristocratic Catalan family. Public areas are full of antiques and artworks, while the rooms are all decorated with hand-painted furniture from Olot in northern Catalunya, with tiled floors. The best have terraces, with a delightful plant-packed one off the breakfast room.
Parking (€20.80/day). TV.

Hotel Principal

C/Junta de Comerç 8 (93 318 89 74/www.hotel principal.es). Metro Liceu. **Rates** €75-€170 double. **Rooms** 112. **Credit** AmEx, DC, MC, V. **Map** p345 A5 ③③

The Principal offers good value for money outside peak periods, when rates rise sharply. The family-run hotel has flat-screen TVs, original artworks and marble bathrooms, some with massage showers. Guests can relax on loungers on the roof, where there is also a suite with a private terrace. The buffet breakfast is served in a pleasant, light room. The street can be a bit seedy.
Disabled-adapted rooms (4). Internet (free wireless, free shared terminal). No-smoking floors (2). TV.

Hotel Sant Agustí

Plaça Sant Agustí 3 (93 318 16 58/www.hotelsa. com). Metro Liceu. **Rates** (incl breakfast) €110-€164 double. **Rooms** 82. **Credit** AmEx, DC, MC, V. **Map** p345 A5 ③④

With its sandstone walls and huge, arched windows that look out on to the *plaça*, not to mention the pink-marble lobby filled with forest-green furniture, this imposing hotel is the oldest in Barcelona. Previously the convent of St Augustine, it was converted into a hotel in 1840. Rooms are spacious and comfortable, but there's no soundproofing. Good buffet breakfast.
Bar. Disabled-adapted rooms (2). Internet (free shared terminal, free wireless in communal areas). Restaurant (dinner only). TV.

Budget

Hostal La Palmera

C/Jerusalem 30 (93 317 09 97/hostallapalmera @terra.es). Metro Liceu. **Rates** (incl breakfast) €54-€59 double. **Rooms** 20. **Credit** MC, V. **Map** p344 A4 ③⑤

With a great location behind La Boqueria market, this well-run, basic *hostal* is a short stagger from some of Raval's funkiest bars, but is surprisingly quiet at night. The decor is unremarkable, but the rooms are light, airy and spotless, most have en-suite bathrooms and some have balconies overlooking the market.
Other locations Hostal Bertolin, C/Carme 116, 1°, Raval (93 329 06 47/reservations 93 317 09 97).

Hosteria Grau

C/Ramelleres 27 (93 301 81 35/fax 93 317 68 25/ www.hostalgrau.com). Metro Catalunya. **Rates** €69-€85 double. €93-€170 apartment. **Rooms** 19. **Credit** AmEx, DC, MC, V. **Map** p344 B2 ③⑥

This charming, family-run *hostal* oozes character, with a tiled spiral staircase and fabulous 1970s-style communal areas, including a funky café next door. The open fireplace is a luxury if you visit in the winter. Rooms are basic, comfortable and fairly quiet. There are also six apartments available on the top floor. A popular choice, so book well in advance.
Bar. Internet (free shared terminal). TV room.

Barceloneta & the Ports

Hotels are springing up along Barcelona's waterfront, particularly in the stretch between the Hotel Arts and the Fòrum, north of the city centre. These are mostly aimed at business travellers, so rates fall at weekends and during holiday periods. Staying in this area is a good idea if you want to spend more time on the beach than sightseeing.

Expensive

Hotel Arts

C/Marina 19-21 (93 221 10 00/www.ritzcarlton. com). Metro Ciutadella-Vila Olímpica. **Rates** €390-€813 double; €508-€1,926 suite; €1,284-€2,568 apartment; €10,700 royal suite. **Credit** AmEx, DC, MC, V. **Map** p343 K12 ③⑦
See p79 **Suites you, sir.**
Bar. Business centre. Disabled-adapted rooms (4). Gym. Internet (free high-speed, free wireless). No-smoking floors (20). Parking (€37.50/day). Pool (outdoor). Restaurants (4). Room service. Spa. TV: DVD.

Hotel Duquesa de Cardona

Passeig Colom 12 (93 268 90 90/www.hduquesa decardona.com). Metro Drassanes or Jaume I. **Rates** €181-€300 double. **Rooms** 41. **Credit** AmEx, DC, MC, V. **Map** p345 C7 ③⑧

This elegantly restored 16th-century palace retains lots of its original palatial features and is furnished

with natural materials – wood, leather, silk and stone – that are complemented by a soft colour scheme that reflects the paintwork. The cosy bedrooms make it the ideal hotel for a romantic stay, particularly the deluxe rooms and junior suites on the higher floors that have views out across the harbour. The beach is a ten-minute walk away, but guests can sunbathe on the decked roof terrace and then cool off afterwards in the mosaic-tiled plunge pool. The arcaded hotel restaurant serves a menu of modern Catalan dishes.
Business centre. Disabled-adapted room. Internet (free high-speed). No-smoking floors (1). Pool (outdoor). Restaurant. Room service. TV.

Hotel Medinaceli
Plaça del Duc de Medinaceli 8 (93 481 77 25/www. gargallo-hotels.com). Metro Drassanes. **Rates** €155 double. **Rooms** 44. **Credit** AmEx, DC, MC, V. **Map** p345 B8 ⑱
The 44 rooms in this restored palace near the harbour are done out in soothing rusty shades. Some of the bathrooms have jacuzzi baths, while others come with massage showers. Repro versions of the sofa Dalí created inspired by Mae West's lips decorate the lobby, to match the crimson velvet thrones in the first-floor courtyard.
Bar. Disabled-adapted room. Internet (€12/24hrs wireless). TV.

Budget

Hostal Poblenou
C/Taulat 30, pral (93 221 26 01/www.hostal poblenou.com). Metro Poblenou. **Rates** (incl breakfast) €75 double. **Rooms** 7. **Credit** MC, V.
Poblenou is a delightful *hostal* in an elegant restored building that offers a lot more than you would expect for the money. The five rooms are all light and airy, with their own bathrooms, and breakfast is served on a sunny terrace. There is wireless internet as well as a shared terminal, and guests can help themselves to tea, coffee and mineral water at no extra cost. The owner, Mercedes, is on hand to provide any help or information you might need during your stay. Situated a few minutes' walk from the beach in Poblenou, this hotel is a good way to get an authentic experience of Barcelona away from the tourist hordes, with the centre a metro ride away.
Internet (free shared terminal, free wireless). No-smoking rooms (5). TV.

Montjuïc & Poble Sec

Away from the concentration of tourists but within reasonable walking distance of La Rambla, Poble Sec is a proper neighbourhood, squashed in between Montjuïc mountain and the Avda Paral·lel. It is a good choice if you are planning on visiting some of the museums and attractions on Montjuïc, and also if your interests lie rather with the bars and restaurants of the Raval.

Expensive

AC Miramar
Plaza Carlos Ibáñez 3, Passeig de Miramar (93 281 16 00/www.ac-hotels.com). Metro Paral·lel. **Rates** €250-€350. **Rooms** 75. **Credit** AmEx, DC, MC, V. **Map** p342 D12 ⑩
See p61 **The hotel on the hill.**

Mid range

Hotel Nuevo Triunfo
C/Cabanes 34 (93 442 59 33/www.hotelnuevo triunfo.net). Metro Paral·lel. **Rates** €103-€144 double. **Rooms** 40. **Credit** MC, V. **Map** p342 E11 ㊶
With 40 fresh, bright and spotless rooms, the Hotel Nuevo Triunfo is located in a peaceful street at the foot of Montjuïc. Rooms are bland but comfortable enough, and the four most desirable – two of which are singles – counteract the austerity of the sparse, modern fittings with their charming plant-filled terraces. A good place to try when central places are full.
Disabled-adapted room. Internet (€3/hr shared terminal). No-smoking floors (4). TV.

Budget

Hostal BCN Port
Avda Paral·lel 15, entl (93 324 95 00/www.hostal bcnport.com). Metro Drassanes or Paral·lel. **Rates** €74-€85 double. **Rooms** 29. **Credit** MC, V. **Map** p342 E12 ㊷
A smart new *hostal* near the ferry port, the BCN Port has rooms that are furnished in a chic contemporary style with not a hint of the kitsch decor prevalent in more traditional budget places. All the 29 rooms have en-suite bathrooms, as well as televisions and air-conditioning. Check the website for discounts.
Internet (free wireless). No-smoking rooms (25). TV.

Eixample

Uptown and upmarket, the broad avenues forming the vast grid of streets of the Eixample district contain dozens of architectural gems, interspersed with boutiques and bars. As well as some of Barcelona's most fashionable hotels, there are some great budget options hidden away in Modernista buildings too.

Expensive

Hotel Axel
C/Aribau 33 (93 323 93 93/www.axelhotels.com). Metro Universitat. **Rates** €188-€210 double. **Rooms** 66. **Credit** AmEx, DC, MC, V. **Map** p342 F8 ㊸
Housed in a Modernista building, with multicoloured tiles in the lobby and bright rooms with bleached floors, the Axel is a cornerstone of the Gaixample, as the area around the hotel is known. The good-looking (of course) staff sport T-shirts with the logo 'heterofriendly', and certainly everyone is

made welcome at this funky boutique hotel. King-size beds come as standard, as does free mineral water from fridges in the corridors. 'Superior' rooms have stained-glass gallery balconies and hydro-massage bathtubs. The Sky Bar on the rooftop is where it all happens, with a little pool, jacuzzi, sun deck, sauna and steam room. Non-guests are welcome to frequent the bar and roof terrace, where club nights are held, so there is always a bit of a buzz going on.

Bar. Business centre. Disabled-adapted rooms (2). Gym. Internet (free wireless). No-smoking floors (5). Pool (outdoor). Restaurant. Room service. Sauna. TV.

Hotel Catalonia Ramblas

C/Pelai 28 (93 316 84 00/www.hoteles-catalonia.es). Metro Catalunya. **Rates** €205-€227 double. **Rooms** 221. **Credit** AmEx, DC, MC, V. **Map** p344 B1 ⓐ

The former building of *La Vanguardia* newspaper has been so thoroughly revamped for its new role as a hotel that little more than the pretty green-and-white Modernista façade remains of the original structure, which was designed in 1903 by Josep Majó Ribas. Wood laminate is used throughout the lobby, corridors and rooms, giving the place a rather wardrobey feel, apart from on the vast open space of the ground floor. A staircase at the rear takes you out to a pleasant pool and sun deck, which, along with the handy location and the excellent service typical of this chain, make this new hotel a good practical option, despite the blandness of the decor.

Bar (2). Business centre. Disabled-adapted rooms (4). Gym. Internet (free wireless). No-smoking floors (8). Pool (outdoor). Restaurants (2). Room service. Spa. TV: cable.

Hotel Claris

C/Pau Claris 150 (93 487 62 62/www.derbyhotels. com). Metro Passeig de Gràcia. **Rates** €161-€375 double. **Rooms** 120. **Credit** AmEx, DC, MC, V. **Map** p340 G7 ⓐ

Antiques and contemporary design merge behind the neo-classical exterior of the Claris, which contains the largest private collection of Egyptian art in Spain. Some bedrooms are on the small side, while others are duplex, but all have Chesterfield sofas and plenty of art. Warhol prints liven up the fashionable East 47 restaurant. The rooftop pool is just about big enough to swim in, with plenty of loungers, and a cocktail bar and DJ.

Business centre. Disabled-adapted rooms (2). Gym. Internet (free wireless). No-smoking floors (4). Parking (€20/day). Pool (outdoor). Restaurant. Room service. TV.

Hotel Condes de Barcelona

Passeig de Gràcia 73-75 (93 445 00 00/www. condesdebarcelona.com). Metro Passeig de Gràcia. **Rates** €190-€370 double. **Rooms** 235. **Credit** AmEx, DC, MC, V. **Map** p340 G7 ⓐ

Renowned for its good service, the family-owned Condes is made up of two buildings that face each other on C/Mallorca at the intersection of Passeig de Gràcia. The building on the north side occupies a

19th-century palace and has a plunge pool on the roof, where the terrace offers evening dining and jazz. In the newer building, rooms on the seventh floor have terraces and a bird's-eye view of La Pedrera. Lodgings range from comfortable standard rooms to themed studios that boast extras such as jacuzzis. Both offer 'romantic weekend' packages, including champagne, theatre tickets, gourmet lunch boxes and airport transfers.

Bar. Disabled-adapted rooms (2). Gym. Internet (free high-speed, free wireless). No-smoking floors (3). Parking (€17.40/day). Pool (outdoor). Restaurant. Room service. TV: pay movies.

Hotel Cram

C/Aribau 54 (93 216 77 00/www.hotelcram.com). Metro Universitat. **Rates** €140-€225 double. **Rooms** 67. **Credit** AmEx, DC, MC, V. **Map** p342 F8 ⓐ

A pretty corner building dating back to 1892, with a salmon-pink façade, now has a startling contemporary interior. The subtly lit red-and-black lobby makes you feel you are entering a nightclub, and indeed, there is the now-inevitable chill-out lounge with oversized cushions in tones of burnished gold and burgundy on the ground floor. Most of the 67 rooms have balconies, while suites have private sun decks. Some rooms have semicircular shower booths, others jacuzzi tubs. Breakfast is served on the roof terrace, where there is a black-tiled small pool and bar. The first floor houses Michelin-starred restaurant Gaig (*see p164*).

Bars (2). Disabled-adapted rooms (2). Internet (free wireless). No smoking floors (5). Parking (€17/day). Pool (outdoor). Restaurant. Room service. TV.

Hotel Granados 83

C/Enric Granados 83 (93 492 96 70/www.derby hotels.com). Metro Diagonal. **Rates** €107-€375 double. **Rooms** 77. **Credit** AmEx, DC, MC, V. **Map** p340 F7 ⓐ

The original ironwork structure of this former hospital lends an unexpectedly industrial feel to the Granados 83. The 77 rooms, with brickwork walls, include duplex and triplex versions, some with their own terraces and plunge pools. For mortals in the standard rooms, there is a rooftop pool and sun deck.

Bar (2). Business centre. Disabled-adapted rooms (2). Internet (free high-speed). No-smoking hotel. Parking (€18.50/day). Pool (outdoor). Restaurant. Room service. TV.

Hotel Jazz

C/Pelai 3 (93 552 96 96/www.nnhotels.com). Metro Catalunya. **Rates** €172-€315 double. **Rooms** 108. **Credit** AmEx, DC, MC, V. **Map** p344 A1 ⓐ

Rooms at the Hotel Jazz are super-stylish in calming tones of, naturally, grey, beige and black, softened with parquet floors and spiced up with dapper pinstripe cushions and splashes of funky colour. The beds are larger than usual for hotels, and the bathrooms feature cool, polished black tiles. A rooftop pool and sun deck top things off.

Bar. Business centre. Disabled-adapted rooms (4). Internet (free shared terminals, free wireless in rooms). No-smoking hotel. Pool (outdoor). TV.
Other locations Hotel Barcelona Universal Avda Paral·lel 76-78, Poble Sec (93 567 74 47); and throughout the city.

Hotel Majestic

Passeig de Gràcia 68 (93 488 17 17/www.hotel majestic.es). Metro Passeig de Gràcia. **Rates** €350-€420 double; €1,600-€3,900 apartment. **Rooms** 303. **Credit** AmEx, DC, MC, V. **Map** p340 G7 ⑤⓪
See p79 **Suites you, sir.**
Bars (2). Business centre. Disabled-adapted rooms (4). Gym. Internet (€6/hr wireless). No-smoking floors (7). Parking (€23.50/day). Pool (outdoor). Restaurant. Room service. TV: pay movies.

Hotel Omm

C/Rosselló 265 (93 445 40 00/www.hotelomm.es). Metro Diagonal. **Rates** €246-€310 double. **Rooms** 91. **Credit** AmEx, DC, MC, V. **Map** p340 G6 ⑤①
See p79 **Suites you, sir.**
Bar. Disabled-adapted rooms (2). Gym. Internet (free high-speed, free wireless). No-smoking floors (4). Pool (outdoor). Restaurant. Room service. TV.

Hotel Pulitzer

C/Bergara 8 (93 481 67 67/www.hotelpulitzer.es). Metro Catalunya. **Rates** €165-€300 double. **Rooms** 91. **Credit** AmEx, DC, MC, V. **Map** p344 B2 ⑤②
Just off Plaça de Catalunya, the Pulitzer has become a popular place to meet before a night out. A discreet

façade reveals an impressive lobby that's stuffed with comfortable white leather sofas, a reading area overflowing with glossy picture books and a swanky bar and restaurant. The rooftop terrace is a fabulous spot for a cocktail, with squishy loungers, scented candles and tropical plants, and views across the city. The rooms themselves are not big, but they are sumptuously decorated with cool grey marble, fat fluffy pillows and kinky leather trim.
Bar. Disabled-adapted rooms (5). Internet (free wireless). No-smoking floors (4). Restaurant. Room service. TV.

Prestige Paseo de Gràcia

Passeig de Gràcia 62 (93 272 41 80/www.prestige hotels.com). Metro Passeig de Gràcia. **Rates** €250-€350 double. **Rooms** 45. **Credit** AmEx, DC, MC, V. **Map** p340 G7 ⑤③
Perfectly situated for just about everything, this sublime boutique hotel was created by architect Josep Juanpere, who took a 1930s building and revamped it with funky oriental-inspired minimalist design and Japanese gardens. The rooms are equipped with B&O TVs, intelligent lighting systems, free minibars and even umbrellas. Outside their rooms, the hotel's guests hang out in the cool Zeroom lounge-bar-library, where expert concierges (of the funky rather than fusty variety) are constantly on hand to help you get the most out of your stay in Barcelona. If you can't bear to leave, you can even buy a copy of one of the designer fixtures to take home. *Photo p70.*

Clarify your view of Egyptian art at **Hotel Claris**.

Stay in the heart of things at **Prestige Paseo de Gràcia**. *See p69.*

Bar. Disabled-adapted room. Internet (free wireless).
No-smoking floors (5). Room service. TV.
Other locations Prestige Congress, Pedrosa B 9-11,
Hospitalet de Llobregat (93 267 18 00).

Mid range

Hostal d'Uxelles

Gran Via de les Corts Catalanes 688, pral (93 265
25 60/www.hoteluxelles.com). Metro Tetuán. **Rates**
€90-€104 double. **Rooms** 21. **Credit** AmEx, MC, V.
Map p343 H8 ❸

A pretty, tastefully decorated *hostal*, with friendly
staff, which is a delightful place to stay and a bargain
to boot. The angels above reception are a hint of
what's to come: Modernista tiles, cream walls with
gilt-framed mirrors, antique furnishings and bright,
Andaluz-tiled bathrooms (all en suite). The best
rooms have plant-filled balconies with tables and
chairs, where you can have breakfast.
No-smoking rooms (16). Room service. TV.
Other locations Hostal d'Uxelles, 2 Gran Via de les
Corts Catalanes 667, entl 2ª, Eixample (93 265 25 60).

Hostal Palacios

Rambla Catalunya 27, 1º (93 301 30 79/www.hostal
palacios.com). Metro Catalunya. **Rates** €81-€150
double. **Rooms** 11. **Credit** AmEx, DC, MC, V.
Map p342 F8 ❸

Situated in a sumptuous Modernista building, the
11 rooms at the Palacios are well equipped and decorated in a tasteful classical style, with good bathrooms, air-con, digital TV and internet connection.
Rates may seem high for a *hostal*, but the standard
of the rooms (particularly the larger ones), together
with the location, make the Palacios good value.
Internet (free shared terminal, €6/hr wireless). TV.

Hotel Astoria

C/Paris 203 (93 209 83 11/www.derbyhotels.es).
Metro Diagonal. **Rates** €120-€200 double.
Rooms 114. **Credit** AmEx, DC, MC, V.
Map p340 F6 ❸

With its art deco restaurant and dramatic lobby with
a domed, stuccoed ceiling adorned with frescoes of
dolphins, the Astoria successfully combines classic
charm with designer features. The 114 rooms have
been stylishly revamped, though vintage features
have been preserved. The bar, with its marble floors,
chandeliers and Chesterfield sofas, is the perfect setting for a pre-dinner cocktail, and there is a sauna
and rooftop swimming pool too. *Photo p77.*
Bar. Gym. Internet (free wireless). No-smoking floors
(6). Parking (€23.55/day). Pool (outdoor). Restaurant
(lunch only). Room service. TV.

Market Hotel

Passatge Sant Antoni Abat 10 (93 325 12 05/
www.markethotel.com.es). Metro Sant Antoni.
Rates (incl breakfast) €96-€110 double. **Rooms** 47.
Credit AmEx, MC, V. **Map** p342 D9 ❸

The people who brought us the wildly successful
Quinze Nits chain of restaurants have gone on to
apply their low-budget, high-design approach to this
new hotel, single-handedly filling what was a gaping €60-€100 hole in the accommodation price range
in the process. The monochrome rooms, though not
huge, are comfortable and stylish for the reasonable
price charged and downstairs is a handsome and
keenly priced restaurant that is typical of the group.
What's more, the nearby Mercat Sant Antoni is
closed for two years, thus ensuring you won't be
woken at dawn by shouting stallholders.
Disabled-adapted rooms (2). Internet (free wireless).
Restaurant. TV.

Hostal Palacios: Modernista building, modest cost.

the5rooms

*C/Pau Claris 72 (93 342 78 80/www.thefiverooms.
com). Metro Catalunya or Urquinaona.* **Rates** (incl
breakfast) €155-€185 double. **Rooms** 5. **Credit** MC,
V. **Map** p344 D1 ⓽
The5rooms is a chic and comfortable B&B in a
handsome building, where the delightful Jessica
Delgado makes every effort to make guests feel at
home. Books and magazines are dotted around the
stylish sitting areas and bedrooms, and breakfast is
served at any time of day. Jessica is also a useful
source of information on the city. Book in advance.
*Internet (free wireless). No-smoking hotel.
Restaurant. Room service. TV.*

Budget

Hostal Central Barcelona

*C/Diputació 346, pral 2ª (93 245 19 81/www.
hostalcentralbarcelona.com). Metro Tetuán.* **Rates**
€61-€78 double. **Rooms** 20. **Credit** DC, MC, V.
Map p343 J8 ⓾
Lodging at the Central, spread across two floors of
an old Modernista building, is like staying in a rambling flat rather than a *hostal*. Rooms have original
tiling and high ceilings, but are kitted out with air-
conditioning and double glazing. Most have en-suite
facilities, but the modern glass-brick cubicles in
some eat up bedroom space. Clean and friendly, this
is a bargain for budget travellers and is a metro ride
away from most sights.
No-smoking hostal.

Hostal Centro

*C/Balmes 83, 1º 2ª (93 323 30 88/www.hostal-
centro.net). Metro Passeig de Gràcia.* **Rates** €47-€65
double. **Rooms** 12. **Credit** MC, V. **Map** p340 F7 ⓺⓿
Housed in a Modernista building with a lift and original tiled floors, most of the rooms at this *hostal* are
surprisingly spacious, with en-suite bathrooms (the
cheaper rooms have shared bathrooms). The best
have views out on to C/Balmes or the patio at the
rear. With internet access and hot and cold drinks'
machines, this is a basic, but practical, place to stay.
Internet (free wireless).

Hostal Eden

*C/Balmes 55, pral 1ª (93 452 66 20/www.hostal
eden.net). Metro Passeig de Gràcia.* **Rates** €57-€70
double. **Rooms** 30. **Credit** AmEx, MC, V.
Map p340 F8 ⓺⓵
Located on three floors of a Modernista building, this
warm and relaxed *hostal* with friendly, helpful staff
offers free internet access and has a sunny patio with
a shower for you to cool off. The best rooms have
marble bathrooms with corner baths, and nos.114
and 115, at the rear, are quiet and have large windows overlooking the patio.
*Internet (free shared terminals). No-smoking rooms
(8). TV.*

Hostal Girona

*C/Girona 24, 1º 1ª (93 265 02 59/www.hostal
girona.com). Metro Urquinaona.* **Rates** €65-€70
double. **Rooms** 26. **Credit** DC, MC, V.
Map p344 F1 ⓺⓶
A gem of a *hostal,* filled with antiques, chandeliers
and oriental rugs. The rooms may be on the simple
side, but they all have charm to spare, with tall windows, pretty paintwork (gilt detail on the ceiling
roses) and tiled floors. It's worth splashing out on
rooms in the refurbished wing, with en-suite bathrooms, although the rooms in the older wing are
good too, and some have en-suite showers. Brighter,

Friendly Rentals

BARCELONA
MADRID
SAN SEBASTIAN
VALENCIA
MALLORCA
SANTANDER
SITGES
GRANADA
SEVILLE
LISBON

Friendly Rentals offers more than 600 vacation and corporate apartments in Barcelona, Madrid, San Sebastian, Valencia, Mallorca, Santander, Sitges, Granada, Seville and Lisbon. Our apartments have vanguard designer decoration and are located in the best areas.

Check our web page www.friendlyrentals.com

outward-facing rooms have small balconies overlooking C/Girona or bigger balconies on to a huge and quiet patio. Gorgeous and good value. *TV.*

Hostal Goya

C/Pau Claris 74, 1º (93 302 25 65/www.hostal goya.com). Metro Urquinaona. **Rates** €78-€102 double. **Rooms** 19. **Credit** MC, V. **Map** p344 D1 ③
Why can't all *hostales* be like this? Located in a typical Eixample building with fabulous tiled floors, the bedrooms are done out in chocolates and creams, with comfy beds, chunky duvets and cushions; the bathrooms are equally luxurious. The best rooms either give on to the street or the terrace at the back. The Goya is excellent value for money and a real gem of a place to stay. What's more, guests leaving the city in the evening after a busy final few hours sightseeing can still use a bathroom to shower and change before they go. That's service.
No-smoking hostal. TV room.

Hostal San Remo

C/Ausiàs Marc 19, 1º 2ª (93 302 19 89/www. hostalsanremo.com). Metro Urquinaona. **Rates** €64-€68 double. **Rooms** 7. **Credit** MC, V. **Map** p344 E2 ④
Staying in this bright, neat and peaceful apartment feels a bit like staying with an amenable relative. The friendly owner Rosa and her fluffy white dog live on site and take good care of their guests. All seven of the rooms have air-conditioning, blue-and-white striped bedspreads and modern wooden furniture; five out of seven have en-suite bathrooms, and most of them have a little balcony and double glazing. A good place to stay.
No-smoking hostal. TV.

Residencia Australia

Ronda Universitat 11, 4º 1ª (93 317 41 77/ www.residenciaustralia.com). Metro Universitat. **Rates** €52-€79 double. **Rooms** 4. **Credit** MC, V. **Map** p344 B1 ⑤
Maria, the owner of Residencia Australia, fled Franco's Spain to Australia in the 1950s and only returned after the Generalissimo's death to carry on the family business and open this small, friendly, home-from-home *pensión*. There are just four cute rooms (one en suite); all are cosy, clean and simply furnished. There's a minimum two-night stay. The family also has two apartments nearby that can be booked if rooms are full.
Internet (free shared terminal). TV.

Gràcia

One of Barcelona's most charismatic *barris*, Gràcia is just off the beaten tourist track, which only adds to its allure. Its narrow streets and leafy squares have a villagey feel to them, but there are also plenty of decent restaurants, shops and nightlife available. What's more, it's only a short metro ride to the centre.

Expensive

Casa Fuster

Passeig de Gràcia 132 (93 255 30 00/www. hotelcasafuster.com). Metro Diagonal. **Rates** €430-€455 double. **Rooms** 96. **Credit** AmEx, DC, MC, V.
Map p340 G6 ⑥
See p79 **Suites you, sir.** *Photo p75.*
Bar. Business centre. Disabled-adapted rooms (5). Gym. Internet (free high-speed, free wireless). No-smoking floors (3). Pool (outdoor). Restaurant. Room service. TV: pay movies.

Mid range

Hotel Confort

Travessera de Gràcia 72 (93 238 68 28/www. mediumhoteles.com). Metro Diagonal or Fontana. **Rates** €97-€192 double. **Rooms** 36. **Credit** AmEx, DC, MC, V. **Map** p340 F5 ⑦
The Confort is light years ahead of other similar establishments, with 36 simple but smart, modern bedrooms with curvy, light wood furnishings and gleaming marble bathrooms. All the rooms get lots of light, thanks to several interior patios. There's a bright dining room and lounge, with a large leafy terrace that makes a lovely setting for a sunny summer breakfast or a cool drink on a balmy night. Although the hotel is just off the tourist track, most sights are within walking distance and there are plenty of restaurants in the vicinity.
Disabled-adapted room. Internet (free wireless). TV.
Other locations Hotel Monegal, C/Pelai 62, Eixample (93 302 65 66); and throughout the city.

Budget

Hostal H.M.B.

C/Bonavista 21, 1º (93 368 20 13/www.hostal hmb.com). Metro Diagonal. **Rates** €70-€78 double. **Rooms** 13. **Credit** MC, V. **Map** p340 G6 ⑧
An excellent addition to Barcelona's budget hotel scene, the HMB opened in 2006 and it feels every bit as crisp, clean and airy as you might hope. Situated on the first floor with a lift, it has 13 rooms, which have high ceilings and are tastefully decorated in tones of blue and green with wood floors, flat-screen TVs and good lighting. All have private marble bathrooms with good showers. Bright contemporary artwork adorns the lobby and corridors.
Internet (free wireless). TV.

Sants

Although Plaça d'Espanya and Parc Joan Miró do have their charms, the only real reason to stay in Sants is to be on hand to catch an early train. Rates drop at weekends and other off-peak business seasons, but it can be difficult to find a place to stay when there's a big convention in town. It's a ten- to 15-minute metro ride to town.

Budget

Hostal Sofía

Avda Roma 1-3, entl (93 419 50 40). Metro Sants Estació. **Rates** €40-€60 double. **Rooms** 17. **Credit** DC, MC, V. **Map** p339 C7

The 17 basic rooms of Hostal Sofía, situated just across the busy roundabout from the city's main station, are a very sound budget option if an early train or quick stopover forces you to spend the night in the city. Some rooms have en-suite bathrooms. As the *hostal* is on the first floor and traffic is fierce, outward-facing rooms are usually very noisy.
TV (some rooms).

Zona Alta

Perhaps not ideal for a first visit to Barcelona, but staying in the city's more uptown neighbourhoods is not a bad idea if you've done the tourist trail on your previous trips. In the Zona Alta you'll get a taste of what Barcelona life is like in a chic residential area.

Expensive

Gran Hotel La Florida

Carretera de Vallvidrera al Tibidabo 83-93 (93 259 30 00/www.hotellaflorida.com). **Rates** €230-€280 double. **Rooms** 74. **Credit** AmEx, DC, MC, V.

From 1925 to the 1950s, this was Barcelona's grandest hotel, frequented by royalty and stars such as Ernest Hemingway and James Stewart. It has lavish suites designed by artists including Rebecca Horn, private terraces and gardens, a five-star restaurant, a summer outdoor nightclub, and a luxury spa. Perched on Tibidabo, La Florida offers bracing walks in the hills and breathtaking 360-degree views, which culminate in a jaw-dropping infinity pool (with a heated indoor part for winter dips). It calls itself an 'urban resort' and is indeed a good choice if you want to relax in opulent style and spend most evenings in the hotel. Bear in mind that getting a cab from town at night can be tricky: there's a free shuttle service but it only runs until 8pm in summer and earlier in winter (though this may change). Check the website for discounts. *Photo p78.*
Bar. Business centre. Disabled-adapted rooms (2). Gym. Internet (free wireless). No-smoking floors (5). Parking (€19.30/day). Pool (outdoor/indoor). Restaurants (2). Room service. Spa. TV: pay movies.

Mid range

Petit Hotel

C/Laforja 67, 1º 2ª (93 202 36 63/www.petit-hotel.net). FGC Muntaner. **Rates** €86-€105 double. **Rooms** 4. **Credit** MC, V. **Map** p340 E5

This charming and convivial B&B has four neat, fresh-feeling bedrooms set around the comfortable and softly lit lounge. Although only two of the rooms are en suite, the others have large, immaculate mod-

Casa Fuster. *See p73.*

ern bathrooms located just outside. The owners, Rosa and Leo, are happy to chat to guests and provide information on the city. Breakfast, which is better than in many hotels, is served 8.30am-1.30pm.
Internet (€4/hr shared terminal). TV.

Apartment hotels

Citadines

La Rambla 122, Barri Gòtic (93 270 11 11/ www.citadines.com). Metro Catalunya. **Rates** €139-€185 1-2 person studio; €220-€280 1-4 person apartment; €20-€30 cleaning. **Rooms** 131. **Credit** AmEx, DC, MC, V. **Map** p344 B3

An apartment block on La Rambla, Citadines offers 115 smartly renovated studios and 16 one-bedroom apartments (all sleep four). It's ideal for longer business trips, groups or families, in an extremely handy location. One weekly clean is included in the price; there's an option to pay extra for the daily cleaning service. Breakfast (€13) is served in a cafeteria on the first floor, which looks out over La Rambla.
Disabled-adapted rooms (6). Parking (€21/day). TV.

Hispanos Siete Suiza

C/Sicilia 255, Eixample (93 208 20 51/www.hispanos7suiza.com). Metro Sagrada Familia. **Rates** (apartments, incl breakfast) €175-€250 1-2 people; €205-€236 3 people; €230-€290 4 people; €390-520 up to 6 people. **Apartments** 19. **Credit** AmEx, DC, MC, V. **Map** p341 J7

Lovers of vintage automobiles will get a real kick out of the Hispanos Siete Suiza, named after the seven lovingly restored pre-war motors that take up much of the lobby. The 19 elegant and spacious apartments each have a kitchen and sitting area decked out with parquet floors, a terrace and two bedrooms. Decor is classical and inoffensive, with no designer trickery. All profits go to the cancer research foundation that runs the hotel. The complex also has a good restaurant called La Cupola. (Rates rise considerably during holidays.)
Bar. Disabled-adapted room. Internet (free high-speed). Parking (€23/day). Restaurant. Room service. TV.

Apartment & room rentals

Short-term room and apartment rental is a rapidly expanding market. People who have visited the city several times, or want to spend longer than a few days, are increasingly opting for self-catering accommodation rather than hotels. Some companies rent out their own apartments, while others act as intermediaries between apartment owners and visitors, taking a cut of the rents.

When renting, it pays to use a little common sense. Check the small print (payment methods, deposits, cancellation fees, etc) and exactly what is included (cleaning, towels and so on) before booking. Note that apartments offered for rental tend to be very small.

In addition to the companies listed below, the following offer apartments: www.rentthesun.com, www.inside-bcn.com, www.oh-barcelona.com, www.rentaflatinbarcelona.com, www.

friendlyrentals.com, www.1st-barcelona.com, www.apartmentsbcn.net, www.flatsbydays.com, and the gay-operated www.outlet4spain.com. In addition, www.habitservei.com can also help to find rooms in shared flats.

Barcelona-Home

C/Viladomat 89-95 Ent. 3 (93 423 34 73/www.barcelona-home.com). **Open** 10am-2pm, 3.30-7pm Mon-Fri. **Rates** vary. **No credit cards.** **Map** p339 D9.
A reputable company staffed by knowledgeable young people, Barcelona-Home aims to sort out accommodation problems and provide other services including guided tours, airport transfers, language courses and whatever else clients might need. Apartment rental prices are surprisingly reasonable considering the level of service, and the website is a great starting point for information on Barcelona.

Loquo

www.loquo.com.
The holiday rentals section of this website has listings by individuals rather than companies, often at lower rates than agencies. People use the site to advertise their flats if they are going away on holiday and want to sublet, for example, although most are more formal arrangements. Bear in mind that postings can accentuate the positive, so double-check details.

Youth hostels

See p318 Study for reliable student and youth services, and agencies and websites that can take telephone and online reservations for hostels and apartments.

The best of old and new at **Hotel Astoria**. *See p70.*

Alberg Mare de Déu de Montserrat

Passeig de la Mare de Déu del Coll 41-51, Gràcia (93 210 51 51/93 483 83 63/www.tujuca.com). Metro Vallcarca. **Open** *Reception* 8am-3pm, 4.30-11pm daily. **Rates** (incl breakfast) €16-€20 under-25s; €20-€24 over-25s; €2/per person/stay sheets. **Credit** DC, MC, V.

Located in a magnificent building north of the centre, this 214-bed hostel boasts an architectural edge, with many original features, including Modernista tilework, whimsical plaster carvings and stained-glass windows, not to mention the beautiful gardens. IYHF cards are not obligatory (available here for €6), but beds cost €2 extra without one.
Disabled-adapted room. Internet (€3/hr shared terminals). No-smoking hostel. Parking (free). Restaurant. TV room.

Barcelona Mar Youth Hostel

C/Sant Pau 80, Raval (93 324 85 30/www.barcelona mar.com). Metro Paral·lel. **Open** 24hrs daily. **Rates** (incl breakfast) €18-€28; €2.50 per person/stay sheets. **Credit** AmEx, DC, MC, V. **Map** p342 E11 73

The no-nonsense Barcelona Mar Youth Hostel, with its pleasant communal areas, sparkling washrooms and handy on-site facilities is cheap as chips. There are no individual rooms, only dorms neatly stacked with bunk beds (150 in total), but in a token nod to privacy, there are areas that can be curtained off.

Gran Hotel La Florida. *See p75.*

Disabled-adapted room. Internet (free shared terminal). Laundry. Lockers (free). No-smoking hostel. TV room.
Other locations Alfonso XIII 28, Badalona (93 399 14 20/www.barcelonadream.net).

Center Ramblas Youth Hostel

C/Hospital 63, Raval (93 412 40 69/www.center-ramblas.com). Metro Liceu. **Open** 24hrs daily. **Rates** (incl breakfast) €16-€20 under-25s; €19.55-€25 over-25s, €2-€3 per person/stay sheets & towels. **No credit cards.** **Map** p344 A4 74

This super-friendly hostel has 201 beds in all, in dorms that sleep three to ten. Facilities include free internet access, a communal fridge, microwave, safes and individual lockers for each guest. It's a good place to make friends, but beds sell out fast, so reserve your space at least two weeks in advance.
Disabled-adapted room. Internet (free shared terminal). Lockers (free). No-smoking hostel. TV room.

Centric Point

Passeig de Gràcia 33, Eixample (93 215 65 38/ www.centricpointhostel.com/www.equity-point.com). Metro Passeig de Gràcia. **Open** 24hrs daily. **Rates** (incl breakfast) €19-€34 per person dormitory; €45-€55 per person twins; single use €90. €2 per person/night sheets/blankets/towels. **Credit** DC, MC, V. **Map** p340 G8 75

The newest addition to the Equity Point group goes considerably upmarket, with more than 400 beds in an impressive Modernista building in one of the swankiest locations in the city. There are doubles and dorms, mostly with en-suite facilities. There is free internet access, satellite TV and breakfast. Lots of information on Barcelona is available.
Disabled-adapted rooms (2). Internet (free wireless). Lockers (free). No-smoking hostel. TV room.

Gothic Point

C/Vigatans 5, Born (93 268 78 08/www.gothicpoint. com). Metro Jaume I. **Open** 24hrs daily. **Rates** (incl breakfast) €19.50-€23 per person; €45 per person twins; single use €55. €2 per person/night sheets/blankets/towels. **Credit** DC, MC, V. **Map** p345 D6 76

Belonging to the same group as Centric Point, this friendly 154-bed hostel has a faintly Asian feel. Dorms (six to 14 beds) are a bit cramped, and although an undersheet and pillowcase are provided, anything else must be rented. There are washing machines and dryers, a microwave and fridge. Beach bums might prefer to stay at Sea Point on the seafront.
Disabled-adapted room. Internet (free shared terminal). Lockers (€1.50). No-smoking hostel. TV room.
Other locations Sea Point, Plaça del Mar 1-4, Barceloneta (93 224 70 75/www.seapointhostel.com); La Ciutat Albergue Residencia, Alegre de Dalt 66, Zona Alta (93 213 03 00/http://laciutat.nnhotels.es).

Itaca Alberg-Hostel

C/Ripoll 21, Barri Gòtic (93 301 97 51/www. itacahostel.com). Metro Catalunya or Urquinaona. **Open** *Reception* 7am-4am daily. **Rates** (incl sheets) €18-€24 dormitory; €55-€60 twin. **Credit** MC, V. **Map** p344 D4 77

Suites you, sir

As you'd expect from a city with panache, Barcelona has plenty of pricey, upmarket places to stay. However, if money is no issue and you're after ridiculous levels of service, here are some truly special options.

Casa Fuster

The Modernista building, which stands imposingly at one end of Passeig de Gracia, is a century old but has recently been extravagantly refurbished. Its sleek rooms are more restrained in style than the stately lobby and exterior, with Modernista touches but a soothing, modern feel. The most luxurious suites boast features such as large carved-stone balconies overlooking Passeig de Gracia and its designer boutiques, as well as enormous bathrooms complete with spa baths, and impressive lounges with plump couches and full-height windows. *See p73.*

Hotel Majestic

The Majestic pulls out all the stops for its biggest-spending guests, offering perks like a pillow menu, a round-the-clock butler service, daily servings of champagne and canapés, and a complimentary convertible car. Its enormous penthouses are places of jaw-dropping luxury, with jacuzzis on their private terraces, hydromassage tubs in the bathrooms, and flat-screen TVs and Bang & Olufsen hi-fis scattered liberally through the bedrooms and lounges. The rooms themselves have been decorated with billionaire sybarites in mind: think mahogany tones, sumptuous velvety fabrics and designer fittings at every turn. *See p69.*

Hotel Omm

For contemporary, understated elegance, head for the thickly carpeted, barely lit corridors of Hotel Omm. Designed by Barcelona-based duo Sandra Tarruella and Isabel L'opez and owned by local restaurant titans Tragaluz, its suites are pretty small by local standards but full of neat, stylish touches. The chic furnishings are in studiedly neutral tones and interesting textures, including a pared-down, modern take on the four-poster bed, and unfussy but plush sofas and armchairs. The emphasis is on comfortable minimalism; guests in the most exclusive suites also get complimentary access to the hotel's luxurious, hushed spa baths, as well as the rooftop terrace, bar and mini-pool. *See p69.*

Hotel Arts

For LA-style glamour and a view of the Mediterranean, look no further than the Hotel Arts, which was built for the Olympics and has been housing supermodels and tycoons in style ever since. Towards the top of the tower are several floors of massive, ultra-plush apartments, where niceties such as welcome massages, a luggage unpacking service, and 24-hour butler service are lavished on high-rolling clients, in addition to complimentary Mini Coopers for the duration of the visit. Decor is slick, sunny and modern, with furniture by Catalan designer Jaume Tressera; little details like a private entrance for the publicity-shy are designed with the VIP visitor in mind. *See p65.*

Although right in the centre of the city, this is a laid-back place where you can recharge your batteries in peace. On a quiet street a stone's throw from the cathedral, it has a homely atmosphere that is highlighted by its swirling murals, squishy sofas and lobby music; there's also a communal kitchen, a breakfast room and shelves of books and games. Its 33 beds are in five cheerful and airy dorms, all with balconies. The bathrooms are clean.
Dining room. Internet (€1.60/hr shared terminal). Kitchen. Lockers (free). No-smoking hostel.

Campsites

For more information on campsites, get the *Catalunya Campings* or the *Campsites Close to Barcelona* books or log on to www.camping total.org or www.barcelonaturisme.com.

Camping Masnou

Carretera N2, km 633, El Masnou (93 555 15 03/ www.campingmasnou.com). **Open** *Reception* Oct-May 9am-noon, 3-7pm daily. June-Sept 8am-10pm daily. *Campsite* 7am-11.30pm daily. **Rates** €6.50/person; €4.50 1-10s; free under-1s; €6.50 car/caravan; €5 electricity. **Credit** MC, V.
Along with the tents there's space for camper vans, a swimming pool, a restaurant and a bar.

Tres Estrellas

Carretera C-31, km 186.2, Gavà (93 633 06 37/ www.camping3estrellas.com). **Open** *Reception* mid Mar-mid Oct 9am-9pm daily. *Campsite* 24hrs daily. Closed mid Oct-mid Mar. **Rates** €5.75-€6.89/person; €4.25-€4.57 3-10s; free under-3s; €7.41-€7.84 car/caravan; €4.81 electricity. **Credit** MC, V.
The campsite is by the beach, 12km (8 miles) from Barcelona. There's a regular bus service into town.

DISCOVER A UNIQUE MUSEUM IN BARCELONA

One Museum, 1,000 years of art
From the best romanesque art collection in Europe to *modernisme* and the avant-garde

Museu Nacional d'Art de Catalunya

Palau Nacional - Parc de Montjuïc - Barcelona   www.mnac.cat

Tuesday to Saturday: 10 am - 7 pm
Sunday and holidays: 10 am - 2.30 pm
Audioguide in seven languages
Children and seniors free
Free parking for buses
Panoramic views of Barcelona

M^NAC

Sightseeing

Features

Casa Vicens. *See p133*.

Introduction

The city starts here.

The evocative beauty of the Old City is so alluring that many visitors remain willing captives to its labyrinthine streets, entranced by the atmosphere and wealth of ancient buildings. It's a shame to miss out on the rest of the city, however, such as the architecural glories of the Eixample, the hills of Montjuïc and Tibidabo, and the new Fòrum district, which has emerged from the ashes of a post-industrial wasteland.

AN OVERVIEW

Barcelona, like any other city, is defined by its geography but in this case the definition is precise: sea, hills and rivers constrain its area. The city squeezes into the remaining available space, a dense and sometimes confusing tangle of streets and houses. To make things easier for the visitor, in this guide we have divided Barcelona into a number of defined districts that are shown on the Barcelona overview map on page 336 and the locator maps at the beginning of each sightseeing chapter. Every venue we list, be it restaurant, shop or tourist attraction, is placed within one of these areas. Either headings within the chapter will indicate which district is being dealt with, or the specific address will include the area within it. For example: C/Pelai 18, Raval is in Raval.

As to the areas themselves, we begin the Sightseeing section with the **Barri Gòtic** (Gothic Quarter, *see pp85-96*), the medieval heart of the city. The boundaries to this ancient quarter are the pedestrian boulevard La Rambla, the transport hub of Plaça de Catalunya, and Via Laietana.

Crossing Via Laietana brings you to **Born & Sant Pere** (*see pp97-103*). These old commercial districts are given a green boundary by the Parc de la Ciutadella, with the heavy traffic using the Ronda Sant Pere marking the division between Old City and the Eixample ('Extension').

Crossing La Rambla from the Barri Gòtic plunges the visitor into the **Raval** (*see pp104-109*), once notorious and still an edgier part of town than many of Barcelona's sometimes over-designed districts.

Once Barcelona turned its back on the sea, cut off by a railway line and put off by toxic waste dumped into the water. All that changed with the 1992 Olympics and today **Barceloneta & the Ports** (*see pp110-115*) offer a marine respite to city dwellers. To find the big blue the basic idea is to head downhill: Barcelona slopes gently down to the shore.

The hills of **Montjuïc** (*see pp117-124*) offer a welcome escape from the heat and crowds of the city, and some of the city's best galleries and museums too.

It's easy to tell when you've left the Old City and entered the **Eixample** (*see pp125-132*): narrow, labyrinthine streets and alleys become broad, traffic clogged, geometrically precise roads. Barcelona's extension encloses much of the old, stretching from Montjuïc, around Raval and the Barri Gòtic, to finally finish as Sant Pere's cap. It's here that you'll find most of the city's Modernisme masterpieces.

Beyond lie **Gràcia & Other Districts** (*see pp133-143*), which include once independent towns swallowed up as Barcelona has spread; despite this you'll find each area retains a distinct and separate identity.

One other piece of advice: bag snatchers and pickpockets are quite common. Don't carry unnecessary valuables and beware anyone trying to clean something off your shoulder or sell you a posy. Those wanting to swap a coin for one from your country are also wont to empty out your wallet.

GETTING AROUND

The Old City is compact and can be crossed on foot in about 20 minutes. The metro (*see p304*) is quick and serves most areas. Buses (*see p304*) reach the parts not covered by the metro and run through the night.

A fun way to get around (and to head to the beach) is to hire a Trixi rickshaw (www.trixi.com). Running 11am-8pm, March to November, and costing €10 per half-hour, they can be hailed on the street, or by calling 93 310 13 79.

Discount schemes

As well as the discount schemes described below, a ticket on the Bus Turistic (*see p84*) also includes a book of coupons valid for admittance to many of the city's museums and attractions.

Articket

The Articket (€20) is, as the name suggests, a useful investment for anyone aiming to see a significant number of Barcelona's museums and galleries. It gives free entry to seven major museums and art galleries (one visit is allowed to each venue over a period of six months): Fundació Miró (*see p121*), MACBA (*see p107*), the MNAC (*see p122*), La Pedrera (*see p130*), the Fundació Tàpies (*see p127*), the CCCB (*see p107*) and the Museu Picasso (*see p99*). The ticket is available from participating venues, as well as at tourist offices (*see p322*), via www.telentrada.com or www.barcelonaturisme.com, and at branches of Caixa Catalunya.

Barcelona Card

Rates *2 days* €24; €20 reductions. *3 days* €29; €25 reductions. *4 days* €33; €27 reductions. *5 days* €36; €31 reductions.

This pass allows two to five days of unlimited transport on the metro and buses, as well as discounts on the airport bus and cable cars, and reduced entry to a wide variety of museums and attractions, along with discounts at dozens of restaurants, bars and shops. The Barcelona Card is sold at the airport, tourist offices (*see p322*), L'Aquàrium (*see p227*), Casa Batlló (*see p127*), the Monument a Colom (*see p112*), Estació de Sants railway station, Estació Nord bus station, at branches of El Corte Inglés (*see p193*) and on the tourist office website (www.barcelonaturisme.com), which also offers a 10% discount.

Two days in Barcelona

If you must fill two photo albums when you get home, here's how.

DAY ONE

Start with a stroll down **La Rambla**. From there, cut into the **Plaça Reial**, admire Gaudí's lamp-posts and from there head to the heart of the **Barri Gòtic** and the **cathedral**. Crossing the Via Laietana takes you to the **Palau de la Música Catalana**, with its extraordinary interior. From here head down into the Born proper, and perhaps tuck into some lunchtime tapas outside the majestic **Santa Maria del Mar**. From here it's a skip and a hop to the **Museu Picasso**. If you've any energy left, wander down to the **Port Vell**, **Barceloneta** and the **beach**, with its seafront restaurants.

DAY TWO

Head up the **Passeig de Gràcia** to admire the masterpieces of the **Manzana de la Discòrdia**. Further up is Gaudí's **La Pedrera**, with its Modernista apartment and strange and beautiful roofscape. You'll have to backtrack slightly to catch a direct metro to Gaudí's most legendary work, the **Sagrada Família**. The Avda Gaudí has several good places for you to grab a *bocadillo*, after which you could drop into the astonishing **Hospital Sant Pau**. From here hop in a cab (or on a tourist bus) to the beautiful colours of Gaudí's **Park Güell**. The 24 bus will get you back in time for dinner.

Tours

By bike

Barcelona by Bicycle
Un Cotxe Menys, C/Esparteria 3, Born (93 268 21 05/www.bicicletabarcelona.com). Metro Barceloneta. **Open** 10am-7pm Mon-Sat; 10am-2pm Sun (call ahead for bike hire outside these times). **Tours** 11am daily. *Apr-Sept* 11am, 4.30pm Mon, Fri-Sun. **Rates** *Tours* €22 incl guide & bike rental. **Hire** €5 1hr; €11 half-day; €15 1 day; €65 1wk. **No credit cards.** **Map** p345 E7.

Individuals or small groups simply meet in Plaça Sant Jaume for a three-hour English-speaking tour. Booking is required for a tailor-made tour, which departs from C/Esparteria 3. Bike hire is available.

Fat Tire Bike Tours
C/Escudellers 48 (93 301 36 12/www.fattirebiketours barcelona.com). Metro Drassanes. **Tours** *Mar-mid Apr, mid Sept-mid Dec* 11am daily. *Mid Apr-mid May* 11am, 4pm. *Mid May-mid Sept* 11am, 4pm, 7pm daily. **Rates** *Tours* €22. **Hire** €7 3hrs; €10 6hrs. **No credit cards. Map** p345 C6.

Booking isn't necessary, although there are discounts for pre-arranged groups. Tours meet in Plaça Sant Jaume and last over four hours, taking in the Old City, Sagrada Família, Ciutadella park and the beach.

By bus

Barcelona Tours
93 317 64 54/www.barcelonatours.es. **Tours** *Nov-May* 9am-8pm daily; approx every 15-20mins; *June-Oct* 9am-8pm daily; approx every 8-10mins. **Tickets** *1 day* €20; €13 reductions. *2 days* €24; €16 reductions. Free under-4s. Available on board bus. **No credit cards.**

A decent recorded commentary on the sights, via headphones, and fewer passengers are the advantages to these bright orange buses. The disadvantages are that tours are not as frequent as those of rival Bus Turístic, and there are no discounts offered to attractions. In the Old City a logical place to start is outside the Hard Rock Café in Plaça Catalunya. It takes around three hours to cover the large tour circuit which includes La Pedrera, Sagrada Família, Park Güell and Nou Camp.

Bus Turístic
93 285 38 32/www.tmb.net. **Tours** *Apr-Oct* 9am-9pm daily; approx every 6-10mins. *Nov-Mar* 9am-7pm daily; approx every 30mins. **Tickets** *1 day* €19; €11 reductions. *2 days* €23; €15 reductions. Free under-4s. Available from tourist offices or on board bus. **No credit cards.**

Bus Turístic (white and blue, with colourful images of the sights) runs three circular routes: the northern (red) route passes La Pedrera, Sagrada Família, Park Güell, the tram stop to Tibidabo and Pedralbes; the southern (blue) route takes in Montjuïc, Port Vell, Vila Olímpica and the Barri Gòtic; the new green route goes to Poblenou and the Fòrum. Tickets are valid for all routes and ticket holders get discount vouchers for a range of attractions; tickets from tourist offices or on the bus.

On foot

The Travel Bar (C/Boqueria 27, 93 342 52 52) organises pub/club crawls on Tuesday, Thursday and Saturday at 9.30pm for €15.

Barcelona Walking Tours
807 117 222/www.barcelonaturisme.com. **Tours** (in English) *Gothic* 10am daily. *Picasso* 10.30am Tue-Sun. *Modernisme* 4pm Fri, Sat. *Gourmet* 11am Fri, Sat. **Tickets** *Gothic, Modernisme* €9.50; €4 reductions. *Picasso, Gourmet* (reservations are essential) €12; €6 reductions. **No credit cards. Map** p344 C2.

Run by the city council, these popular walking tours now have four itineraries. The Gourmet tour includes 13 stops in the city's emblematic cafés, food shops and markets. The Gothic tour concentrates on the history and buildings of the Old City, while the Picasso visits the artist's haunts and ends with a visit to the Picasso Museum (entry is included in the price). The Modernisme tour is a circuit of the 'Golden Square' in the Eixample, taking in Gaudí's Casa Batlló and La Pedrera. Tours take 90mins to 2hrs, excluding the museum trip. All tours start in the underground tourist office in Plaça Catalunya.

My Favourite Things
Mobile 637 265 405/www.myft.net.

Outings (€26) that include peeks into the hidden nooks of the city, sailing trips along the seafront, walking tours for families with children, and salsa or flamenco lessons. Phone or log on for details.

Ruta del Disseny
www.rutadisseny.com.

Not a route, but a guide to the city's 100 best-designed buildings, as chosen by experts such as Oriol Bohigas and Javier Mariscal. It's divided into four categories: drink, food, shopping and architecture, and also has nine well-chosen itineraries. The guidebook (containing a map) is available at bookshops, the Plaça Catalunya tourist office (*see p322*) and the Hospital Sant Pau (*see p128*) or there is a comprehensive website.

Ruta del Modernisme
93 317 76 52/www.rutadelmodernisme.com. **Rates** €12.

Not so much a route as a guidebook to 115 Modernista buildings both in Barcelona and 13 other Catalan towns, and ones that ties in with the small red circles you can see set in to pavements. It's available at the Plaça Catalunya tourist office (*see p322*), the Hospital Sant Pau (*see p128*) and the Pavellons Güell (*see p138*). There's a suggested one-day itinerary, a list of the 30 most important Modernista buildings, and one of the most beautiful old shops. Profits go towards helping building conservation.

Barri Gòtic

Barna central.

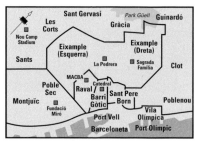

Maps pp344-345

Some visitors to Barcelona never venture beyond the Gothic Quarter and it's easy to see why. There are few more atmospheric places in the world and, since much of the area has been pedestrianised, the narrow streets are perfect for a leisurely walk, taking in Roman ruins, medieval palaces and Gothic churches.

For the last 2,000 years, the heart of the city has been Plaça Sant Jaume, set on the gentle hill of Mons Taber where the original Roman camp once stood. At the crossroads of the streets of C/Call, C/Bisbe and C/Ciutat, dominating the forum, was the **Temple of Augustus**, four columns of which can still be seen in C/Pietat. The square now hosts the municipal government (**Ajuntament**) and the Catalan regional government (**Palau de la Generalitat**) buildings, which stand opposite each other. They have not always done so: the square was only opened up in 1824, when a church was demolished. Soon after, the stolid neo-classical façade was added to the Ajuntament.

The façade of the Generalitat (1598-1602), on the other hand, is one of the few Renaissance buildings in the city. This architectural dearth can be explained by a terrible series of wars that lasted from about 1460 until 1715. The greater extent of both buildings, however, was built in the early 15th century. Both buildings' original main entrances – that of the Generalitat (1416-18) being particularly noteworthy – open on to what was once the *decumanus maximus* at the side.

On this street is what must be one of the most photographed features of the Barri Gòtic, the neo-Gothic Pont dels Sospirs (Bridge of Sighs) across C/Bisbe from the Generalitat. It's a pastiche from 1928, when the idea of the area

as a 'Gothic Quarter' took off. Other alterations from the same period include the decorations on the Casa dels Canonges (a former set of canons' residences, and now Generalitat offices), on the other side of the bridge. A little further down C/Bisbe is the Plaça Garriga i Bachs, with Josep Llimona's bronze monument to the martyrs of 1809, dedicated to the *barcelonins* who rose up against Napoleon and were executed.

In C/Santa Llúcia, in front of the **cathedral**, is Casa de l'Ardiaca; originally a 15th-century residence for the archdeacon (*ardiaca*), it has a superb tiled patio. The huge square at the foot of the steps leading up to the cathedral is Plaça Nova, which houses an antiques market every Thursday (*see p196*) and is a traditional venue for festivals, music concerts and *sardana* dancing (*see p218*). At ground level, on the south-east corner of the square is *Barcino*, a visual poem by Joan Brossa installed in 1994, referring to the ancient name for Barcelona, which was supposedly named by the Carthaginians after Hannibal's father, Hamil Barca. Directly above is the Roman aqueduct; the final archway of the city's two aqueducts dating from the first century AD is preserved inside the tower that defended the north-eastern side of the gate; one of these has been externally rebuilt. Fast forward two millennia to the opposite side of Plaça Nova, dominated by one of the first high-rise blocks in the city, the Col·legi d'Arquitectes (Architects' Association). It's mainly of interest for its graffiti-style sand-blasted triptych of Catalan folk scenes, designed by Picasso while in self-imposed exile in the 1950s and executed by Norwegian artist Carl Nesjar. Behind its atypical style is a story that when Picasso heard that Miró was also being considered, he responded dismissively that he could easily 'do a Miró'. The middle section depicts the *gegants* (giant figures who lead processions at popular festivals) and figures holding palm branches; the left-hand section (on C/Arcs) symbolises the joy of life, while the right-hand section (on C/Capellans) depicts the Catalan flag. There are also two interior friezes depicting a *sardana* dance and a wall of arches.

In front of the cathedral, on the right as you come out, is the **Museu Diocesà**, housing religious art; around the side of the cathedral, meanwhile, is the little-visited but fascinating

Ready for take off?

Choose one of the coolest scooters in town and discover the fantastic city of Barcelona for yourself. Feel different from a tourist! Drive yourself or book one of our guided tours.
MotoLoco Barcelona · Phone +34 932 213 452 · www.motoloco.es

rent a scooter – feel the city like a local.

Catedral. *See p89.*

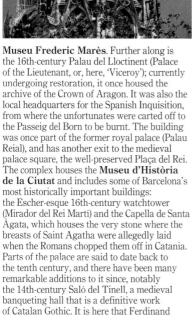

Museu Frederic Marès. Further along is the 16th-century Palau del Lloctinent (Palace of the Lieutenant, or, here, 'Viceroy'); currently undergoing restoration, it once housed the archive of the Crown of Aragon. It was also the local headquarters for the Spanish Inquisition, from where the unfortunates were carted off to the Passeig del Born to be burnt. The building was once part of the former royal palace (Palau Reial), and has another exit to the medieval palace square, the well-preserved Plaça del Rei. The complex houses the **Museu d'Història de la Ciutat** and includes some of Barcelona's most historically important buildings: the Escher-esque 16th-century watchtower (Mirador del Rei Martí) and the Capella de Santa Àgata, which houses the very stone where the breasts of Saint Agatha were allegedly laid when the Romans chopped them off in Catania. Parts of the palace are said to date back to the tenth century, and there have been many remarkable additions to it since, notably the 14th-century Saló del Tinell, a medieval banqueting hall that is a definitive work of Catalan Gothic. It is here that Ferdinand and Isabella are said to have received Columbus on his return from America.

The narrow streets centred on C/Call once housed a rich Jewish ghetto (*call*). At the corner of C/Sant Domènec del Call and C/Marlet is the medieval **synagogue**, now restored and open to the public. At C/Marlet No.1 is a 12th-century inscription from a long-demolished house. Hebrew inscriptions can be seen on stones in the eastern wall of the Plaça Sant Iu, across from the cathedral, and at ankle level in the south-west corner of the Plaça del Rei.

Near the centre of the *call* is the beautiful little Plaça Sant Felip Neri and its fine Baroque church, whose damaged façade is the result of an Italian bombing raid during the Civil War. More than 200 people were killed, many of them refugee children on a Sunday outing. This square is another 20th-century invention; the shoemakers' guild building (now housing the **Museu del Calçat**) was moved here in 1943 to make way for the Avda de la Catedral, while the nearby tinkers' guild was moved earlier last century, when Via Laietana was driven through the district. Close by are the attractive Plaça del Pi and Plaça Sant Josep Oriol, where there are great pavement bars and artisanal weekend markets. The squares are separated by Santa Maria del Pi, one of Barcelona's most distinguished Gothic churches, with a magnificent rose window and spacious single nave. Opposite is the 17th-century neo-classical retailers' guild-hall, with its colourful 18th-century sgraffiti.

Despite the expansion of Barcelona into the Eixample, the old centre has remained a hub of cultural, social and political life. In C/Montsió, a narrow street off Portal de l'Àngel, is the Els Quatre Gats café (*see p176*), legendary haunt

Saint alive St Eulàlia

Faith. Nonsense, say Catalans, hanging on to Laia, as she is known, for all they are worth. Besides, our little saint suffered much more than yours. Eulàlia of Méribel was merely tortured with hooks and burnt alive; Eulàlia of Barcelona really suffered. In 303, the brave girl went to Barcelona's governor, Dacian, to tell him off for his cruelty to the city's Christians. Since Dacian's orders came straight from the Emperor Diocletian he rapidly sized up the relative advantages of clemency for the Christians or doing what

The Romans were not an imaginative people save in one important area: pain. A culture that had turned sadism into both public spectacle and, for some imperial families, private sport, really let themselves go when it came to devising new and interesting ways of putting people to death. Crucifixion was, of course, the old standby, easily carried out by any Tom, Dick or Horace, but for a properly painful end the Romans really let their fancies fly. Thus the gruesome tortures meted on 13-year-old Eulàlia are, to some degree, support for the historicity of her end.

Some historians insist that St Eulàlia of Barcelona and St Eulàlia of Méribel are the same person on the spurious grounds that there can't really have been two 13-year-old virgins with the same name martyred for the

the emperor said, and sentenced Eulàlia to as many tortures as she had years. These included being whipped; torn with hooks; rolled down what is today the Baixada de Santa Eulàlia in a barrel filled with nails and glass; having hot oil poured on her wounds; being put in a flea-filled box; having her breasts cut off; and, the appropriate final punishment, crucifixion. Legend has it that Eulàlia suffered all these torments in silence. What is not disputable is that Dacian may have miscalculated the percentages. Today, Eulàlia is the co-patron saint of Barcelona, with her feast day on 12 February, and she is particularly revered as an intercessor for children, while Dacian is a forgotten functionary of a failed imperial persecution.

of Picasso and other artists and bohemians, in a wonderful Modernista building designed by Puig i Cadafalch. Between C/Portaferrissa and Plaça del Pi is C/Petritxol, one of the most charming streets of the Barri Gòtic, known for its traditional *granges* offering coffee and cakes, and also housing the Sala Parés (*see p238*), the city's oldest art gallery; Rusiñol, Casas and the young Picasso all exhibited here. On the other side of C/Portaferrissa, heading up C/Bot, is the newly done-up Plaça Vila de Madrid, where there are the excavated remains of a Roman necropolis and a rare expanse of city-centre grass. Between here and the Plaça Catalunya is the marvellous little Romanesque Església de Santa Anna, begun in 1141 and containing an exquisite 14th-century cloister.

Back on the seaward side of the Barri Gòtic, if you walk from Plaça Sant Jaume up C/Ciutat, to the left of the Ajuntament, and turn down

the narrow alley of C/Hércules, you'll come to Plaça Sant Just, a fascinating old square with a recently restored Gothic water fountain from 1367, and the Església de Sants Just i Pastor, built in the 14th century on the site of a chapel founded by Charlemagne's son Louis the Pious, and now looking rather unloved inside.

The once wealthy area between here and the port became more run-down throughout the 20th century. It has a different atmosphere from the northern part of the Barri Gòtic: shabbier and with less prosperous shops. The city authorities made huge efforts to change this, particularly in the 1990s, when new squares were opened up: Plaça George Orwell on C/Escudellers, known as the 'Plaça del Trippy' by the youthful crowd that hangs out there and the subject of much heated debate when CCTV was recently introduced (the irony of which was lost on no one), and Plaça Joaquim

Xirau, off La Rambla. Another tactic was the siting of parts of the Universitat Pompeu Fabra on the lower Rambla. Just above is the area's heart: Plaça Reial (*photo p96*), known for its bars, cheap backpacker hostels and rather scuzzy atmosphere at night. It's still a popular spot for a drink or an outdoor meal (provided you don't mind the odd drunk and are prepared to keep an eye on your bags). An addition from the 1840s, the *plaça* has the Tres Gràcies fountain in the centre and lamp-posts designed by the young Gaudí. It's the only work he ever did for the city council.

The grand porticoes of a number of the buildings around the Església de La Mercè, once the merchants' mansions, stand as testament to the former wealth of the area before the building of the Eixample. The Plaça de la Mercè itself was only created in 1982, with the destruction of the houses that used to stand here; the 19th-century fountain was moved here from the port. There is also a dwindling number of lively *tascas* (small traditional tapas bars) on C/Mercè. Beyond C/Ample and the Mercè, you emerge from narrow alleys or the pretty Plaça Duc de Medinaceli on to the Passeig de Colom, where a few shipping offices and ships' chandlers still recall the atmosphere of decades gone by. Monolithic on Passeig de Colom is the

Capitania General, the army headquarters, whose façade has the dubious distinction of being the one construction in Barcelona that is directly attributable to the dictatorship of Primo de Rivera.

Ajuntament (City Hall)
Plaça Sant Jaume (93 402 70 00/special visits 93 402 73 64/www.bcn.cat). Metro Jaume I or Liceu. **Open** *Office* 8.30am-2.30pm Mon-Fri. *Visits* 10.30am-1.30pm Sun. **Admission** free. **Map** p345 C6.
Around the left-hand corner of the city hall's rather dull 18th-century neo-classical façade is the old entrance in a wonderfully flamboyant 15th-century Catalan Gothic façade. Inside, the centrepiece and oldest part, is the famous Saló de Cent, where the Consell de Cent (Council of One Hundred) ruled the city between 1372 and 1714. The Saló de Cròniques is filled with Josep Maria Sert's immense black-and-gold mural (1928), depicting the early 14th-century Catalan campaign in Byzantium and Greece under the command of Roger de Flor. Full of art and sculptures by the great Catalan masters from Clarà to Subirachs, the interior of the city hall is open for guided tours (in different languages) on Sundays.

Catedral
Pla de la Seu (93 342 82 60/www.catedralbcn.org). Metro Jaume I. **Open** *Combined ticket* 12.30-5pm daily. *Church* 8am-12.30pm, 5-7.30pm Mon-Fri; 8am-12.30pm, 5-6pm Sat; 8am-12.30pm, 5-6pm Sun.

Sightseeing

Museu Frederic Marès: an unusual repository of art and objects. *See p92.*

BARCEL⊗NA M⊗DERNISME R⊗UT

New Guided Visits !!

Domènech i Montaner's **Hospital de Sant P**
Daily visits in English at 10'15 and 12'15 am

Domènech i Montaner's **Palau Montaner**
Visits in English every Saturday at 10'30 am

...and **Gaudí's Pavellons Güell**
Friday through Monday at 10'15 and 12'15 am

More information at 933 177 652 and www.rutadelmodernisme.com

 Ajuntament de Barcelona   Institut del Paisatge Urbà
i la Qualitat de Vida

Cloister 9am-12.30pm, 5-7pm daily. *Museum* 10am-1pm, 5.15-7pm daily. **Admission** *Combined ticket* €5. *Church & cloister* free. *Museum* €1. *Lift to roof* €2. *Choir* €2. **No credit cards**. **Map** p345 C5/D5.
The present-day cathedral is the third church to stand on this site. The first was a three-naved basilica that was destroyed by Al-Mansur in 985, the remains of which can be seen in the Museu d'Història de la Ciutat (*see p92*); of the second Romanesque building, only two doors and the chapel of Santa Llúcia to the right of the main façade remain. Construction on the Gothic cathedral began in 1298 but went at a pace that makes the Sagrada Família project look snappy; the work on the neo-Gothic façade remained unfinished until the end of the 19th century, being completed by the architects Josep Oriol Mestres and August Font i Carreras, who took inspiration from a 15th-century drawing by Mestre Carli. It is a cavernous and slightly forbidding place, but contains many images, paintings and sculptures and an intricately carved choir built in the 1390s. The cathedral museum, which is in the 17th-century chapterhouse, displays paintings and sculptures, including works by Gothic masters Jaume Huguet, Bernat Martorell and Bartolomé Bermejo. Santa Eulàlia, patron saint of Barcelona, lies in the dramatically lit crypt in an alabaster tomb carved with scenes from her martyrdom. To one side, there's a lift to the roof; take it for a magnificent view of the Old City. The glorious light-filled cloister is famous for its fierce geese and half-erased floor engravings, marking which guild paid for which side chapel: scissors for the tailors, shoes for the cobblers and so on. A combined ticket (*visita especial*) has a special timetable intended to keep tourists and worshippers from bothering one another. During the afternoons, ticketholders have the run of the cloister, church, choir and lift, and can enter some chapels and take photos (normally prohibited). *Photos p87.*

Centre Cívic Pati Llimona

C/Regomir 3 (93 268 47 00). Metro Jaume I.
Open 10am-2pm, 4-9pm Mon-Fri; 10am-2pm, 4-8pm Sat. *Exhibitions* 10am-2pm, 4-9pm Mon-Fri; 10am-2pm, 4-8pm Sat. Closed Aug. **Admission** free. **Map** p345 C6.
Centre Cívic Pati Llimona incorporates part of a round tower that dates from the first Roman settlement with later Roman baths and a 15th-century residence. The excavated foundations of the tower are visible from behind glass from the street. The building is now used as a civic centre and is open to the public, staging frequent photography exhibitions.

Museu del Calçat (Shoe Museum)

Plaça Sant Felip Neri 5 (93 301 45 33). Metro Jaume I. **Open** 11am-2pm Tue-Sun. **Admission** €2.50; free under-7s. **No credit cards**. **Map** p345 C5.
Housed in what was once part of the medieval shoe-makers' guild, this quirky little footwear museum details the cobbler's craft from Roman sandals to '70s platform boots. The earlier examples are reproductions, although those from the 17th century to the present day are originals, including swagged musketeers' boots and delicately hand-painted 18th-century party shoes. There is also a section devoted to celebrity footwear, including shoes belonging to cellist Pau Casals and the first Catalan boot to reach the summit of Everest, worn by Carles Vallès in 1985. Another highlight is the enormous pair of shoes made for the statue of Columbus (*see p112*), which are, according to Guinness, the biggest in the world.

Sightseeing

Palau de la Generalitat. *See p92.*

Museu Diocesà

*Avda de la Catedral 4 (93 315 22 13). Metro
Jaume I.* **Open** 10am-2pm, 5-8pm Tue-Sat; 11am-2pm
Sun. **Admission** €6; €3 reductions; free under-7s.
Credit (shop only) MC, V. **Map** p344 D4.

A hotchpotch of religious art punctuated with exhibitions on unrelated themes, Barcelona's Diocesan
Museum is worth a visit for a gander at its 14th-
century alabaster virgins, altarpieces by Bernat
Martorell and wonderful Romanesque murals. The
building itself is also interesting, and includes the
Pia Almoina, a former almshouse, stuck on to a
Renaissance canon's residence, which in turn was
built inside a Roman tower.

Museu Frederic Marès

*Plaça Sant Iu 5-6 (93 310 58 00/www.museumares.
bcn.cat). Metro Jaume I.* **Open** 10am-7pm Tue-Sat;
10am-3pm Sun. **Admission** €3; €1.50 reductions;
free under-16s. Free 3-7pm Wed, 1st Sun of mth.
Guided tours noon Sun. **Credit** (shop only)
AmEx, MC, V. **Map** p345 D5.

Barcelona's most celebrated pack rat, Frederic
Marès (1893-1991) managed to fill a whole palace
with his obsessive hoardings after he cut a deal
with the Ajuntament: he would donate his extraordinary collections to the city, if, in return, the city
would find an appropriate building in which to
house both them and him. The result is one of the
city's most varied and intriguing museums, where
the kaleidoscope of objects reflects Marès' widely

ranging interests in travel and sculpture and also his
indulgently tolerated kleptomania as he 'borrowed'
many items from his wealthy friends.

The ground floor of the museum contains an array
of Romanesque crucifixes, virgins and saints, while
the first floor takes sculpture right up to the 20th
century. The basement contains the remains from
ecclesiastical buildings that date back to Roman
times: capitals, tombs, gargoyles, stone window
frames and entire church portals, exquisitely carved.
On the second floor is the Gentleman's Room, which
is stuffed to the gunwales with walking sticks, key
fobs, smoking equipment, matchboxes and opera
glasses, while the charming Ladies' Room contains
more feminine items such as fans, sewing scissors,
nutcrackers and perfume flasks. Also on the second
floor is a room devoted to photography, and Marès'
study and library, now filled with sculptures (many
of them his own). Note: the museum used to close
floors down on different days of the week; all floors
are now open. *Photos p89.*

Museu d'Història de la Ciutat

*Plaça del Rei 1 (93 315 11 11/www.museuhistoria.
bcn.cat). Metro Jaume I.* **Open** *June-Sept* 10am-8pm
Tue-Sat; 10am-3pm Sun. *Oct-May* 10am-2pm,
4-7pm Tue-Sat; 10am-3pm Sun. **Guided tours** by
appointment. **Admission** *Permanent exhibitions*
€5; €2.50 reductions; free under-16s. *Temporary
exhibitions* varies. Both free 4-8pm 1st Sat of mth.
No credit cards. **Map** p345 D5.

The City History Museum had a chance beginning.
Stretching from the Plaça del Rei to the cathedral
are 4,000sq m of subterranean Roman excavations,
including streets, villas and storage vats for oil and
wine, which were discovered by accident in the late
1920s when a whole swathe of the Gothic Quarter
was upended to make way for the central avenue
of Via Laietana. The excavations continued until
1960; today, the underground labyrinth is accessed
via the Casa Padellàs, a merchant's palace dating
from 1498, which was laboriously moved from its
original location in C/Mercaders for the construction of Via Laietana. Admission allows access to the
Capella de Santa Àgata – with its 15th-century
altarpiece by Jaume Huguet, one of the greatest
Catalan painters in medieval times – and the Saló
del Tinell, at least when there's no temporary exhibition. This majestic room (1370) began life as the
seat of the Catalan parliament and was converted
in the 18th century into a Baroque church, which
was dismantled in 1934. The Rei Martí watchtower
is still closed to the public while it awaits reinforce-
ment. Tickets for the museum are also valid for the
monastery at Pedralbes (*see p139*) and the Museu
Verdaguer (*see p137*).

Palau de la Generalitat

*Plaça Sant Jaume (93 402 46 17/www.gencat.net).
Metro Jaume I or Liceu.* **Guided tours** every
30mins approx 10.30am-1pm 2nd & 4th Sun of
mth; Fri-Sun by appointment. **Admission** free.
Map p345 C5.

La Rambla. See p95.

Coming to a stand still

Of all the jobs in the world, standing still in the sweltering heat under a thick layer of greasepaint in a rubber costume is not one of the best. Despite the hardship involved, there were so many human statues working on La Rambla that the Ajuntament felt compelled to cull the numbers. The plan was to reduce the overcrowding that often brought pedestrian traffic to a standstill, but also to get rid of the lowlier specimens who were often little more than panhandlers shuffling about in costume.

Councillors promised to 'root out those who are not up to standard', although it was never clear how they planned to judge artistic quality. Instead the Ajuntament simply introduced new regulations in January 2007 that effectively halved the number of statues. The rules specify that a statue must wear home-made costumes and make-up, not masks or shop-bought outfits. Further rules prohibit statues from using street furniture as props; they cannot oblige the public to pay nor request a minimum fee to pose for a photo; they must avoid all expressions of violence and must not use any animals.

Curiously enough, there is no say on whether the statues must actually remain motionless. Indeed, many seem to be in almost constant motion: a ringletted Jesus blesses passers by; the businessman on the toilet strains extra hard and doffs his bowler hat, and the devil frightens off the children. After a bout of increasingly off-the-wall figures, the new rules have also brought about a renaissance of the more traditional statues of metallic-effect soldiers, angels and ladies with parasols. In a surreal about-turn, German artist Christain Jankowsky recently cast bronze statues of three of the most emblematic figures on La Rambla: Che Guevara, the Roman gladiator and Dalí's 'La Mujer del Escritorio Antropomortico' ('Woman with Drawers'), with open drawers extruding from her dress. To the confusion of passers by, he then posed his works on La Rambla.

Surreal experiments aside, the statues are now limited to just 20 spots clustered around C/Bonsuccés, C/Portaferrissa, the Liceu and C/Nou de la Rambla, the aim being to avoid clogging the narrowest parts of La Rambla, which can become impassable when crowds stop to take photos. Those deemed unworthy of the 'statue' label are banished to the purgatory of La Rambla de Santa Mònica down by the Columbus monument, with the breakdancers, acrobats and tango couples.

Spanish Courses for all levels all year round. Range of accommodatio[n] and social activities.

She'd left [...]

Past Perfec[t]

TEFL Courses for teachers including CELTA, DELTA, Young Learners and on-line distance learning.

Plaza de Catalunya

Plaza Urquinaona

Fontanella

Trafalge[r]

ih

IH BARCELONA
C/Trafalgar 14,
08010 Barcelona
932 684 511
study@bcn.ihes.com
www.ihes.com

Like the Ajuntament, the Palau de la Generalitat has a Gothic side entrance that opens out on to C/Bisbe, with a beautiful relief of St George (Sant Jordi), patron saint of Catalonia, made by Pere Johan in 1418. Inside the building, the finest features are the first-floor Pati de Tarongers ('Orange Tree Patio'), which was to become the model for many patios in Barcelona, and the magnificent chapel of Sant Jordi of 1432-34, which is the masterpiece of Catalan architect Marc Safont. The Generalitat is traditionally open to the public on Sant Jordi (St George's Day, 23 April), when its patios are spectacularly decorated with red roses. But be aware that queues are huge. It normally also opens on 11 September (Catalan National Day) and 24 September (La Mercè). *Photo p91.*

Sinagoga Shlomo Ben Adret

C/Marlet 5 (93 317 07 90/www.calldebarcelona.org). Metro Jaume I or Liceu. **Open** 11am-6pm Mon-Fri; 11am-3pm Sat-Sun. **Admission** €2. **Map** p345 C5.
It's only in the last few years that historians have come to agree that the small basement in the building at C/Marlet No.5 was the synagogue of the main call. The front of the building, slightly skewing the street, fulfils religious requirements by which the façade has to face Jerusalem; the two windows at knee height allow light to enter from that direction.

Temple Romà d'Augusti

C/Paradís 10 (93 315 11 11). Metro Jaume I. **Open** 10am-8pm Tue-Sat 10am-3pm Sun. **Admission** free. **Map** p345 D5.
The Temple Romà d'Augusti is housed in the Centre Excursionista de Catalunya (a hiking club): four fluted Corinthian columns that formed the rear corner of the Temple of Augustus, built in the first century BC as the hub of the town's forum. Opening hours can vary, so it's a good idea to call ahead before making a special trip.

La Rambla

This mile-long boulevard is one of the most famous promenades in the world. The identikit souvenir shops, pickpockets and surging crowds of tourists have driven away many of the locals who used to come here to play chess or have political debates, but despite a fall in fortunes, it remains the first port of call for visitors to the city. The multitude of human statues, fortune-tellers, card sharps, puppeteers, dancers and musicians might be infuriating to anyone late for work, but for those with a seat at a pavement café, it's not far short of pure theatre. Be warned that pickpockets are not the only thieves operating here – unless you are happy to pay €15 for a stein of diluted cola you should avoid the terrace bars and restaurants along La Rambla, although the council is trying to smarten it up (*see p93* **Coming to a stand still**).

The name derives from *ramla*, an Arabic word for sand; originally, this was a seasonal riverbed, running along the western edge of the 13th-century city. From the Middle Ages to the Baroque era, many churches and convents were built along here, some of which have given their names to sections of it: as one descends from Plaça Catalunya, it is successively called Rambla de Canaletes, Rambla dels Estudis (or dels Ocells), Rambla de Sant Josep (or de les Flors), Rambla dels Caputxins and Rambla de Santa Mònica. For this reason, many people refer to it in the plural, as Les Rambles.

La Rambla also served as the meeting ground for city and country dwellers, for on the far side of these church buildings lay the still scarcely built-up Raval, 'the city outside the walls', and rural Catalonia. At the fountain on the corner with C/Portaferrissa, colourful tiles depict the city gateway that once stood here (*porta ferrissa* means 'iron gate'). The space by the gates became a natural marketplace; from these beginnings sprang La Boqueria (*see p206*), now the largest market in Europe.

La Rambla took on its recognisable present form between approximately 1770 and 1860. The second city wall came down in 1775, and La Rambla was paved and turned into a boulevard. But the avenue only acquired its definitive shape after the closure of the monasteries in the 1830s, which made swathes of land available for new building. No longer on the city's edge, La Rambla became a wide path through Barcelona's heart.

As well as having five names, La Rambla is divided into territories. The first part – at the top, by Plaça Catalunya – has long belonged, by unwritten agreement, to groups of men perpetually engaged in a *tertulia*, a classic Iberian half-conversation, half-argument about anything from politics to football. The Font de Canaletes drinking fountain is beside them; if you drink from it, goes the legend, you'll return to Barcelona. Here too is where Barça fans converge in order to celebrate their increasingly frequent triumphs.

Next comes perhaps the best-loved section of the boulevard, which is known as Rambla de les Flors because of its line of magnificent flower stalls, which are open into the night. To the right is the **Palau de la Virreina** exhibition and cultural information centre (*see p96*), and the superb Boqueria market. A little further is the Pla de l'Os (or Pla de la Boqueria), which is the centrepoint of La Rambla, with a pavement mosaic created in 1976 by Joan Miró. On the left, where more streets run off into the Barri Gòtic, is the extraordinary Bruno Quadros building (1883), with umbrellas on the wall and a Chinese dragon protruding over the street.

Plaça Reial. *See p89.*

The lower half of La Rambla is initially more restrained, flowing between the sober façade of the Liceu opera house (*see p263*) and the more fin-de-siècle (architecturally and atmospherically) Cafè de l'Opera (*see p175*), which is Barcelona's second most famous café after the Zurich. On the right is C/Nou de la Rambla (where you'll find Gaudí's neo-Gothic Palau Güell, which is closed to the public until at least 2010; *see p109*); the promenade then widens into the Rambla de Santa Mònica. The area has long been popular among prostitutes; clean-up efforts have reduced their visibility and renovations (including the 1980s addition of an arts centre, the **Centre d'Art Santa Mònica**) have done much to dilute the seediness of the area, but single males walking at night can expect to be approached. Across the street are the unintentionally hilarious Museu de Cera (Wax Museum; *see p227*) and, at weekends, many stalls selling bric-a-brac and craftwork. Then it's just a short skip and a hop to the port, and the Monument a Colom Columbus column (*see p112*).

Centre d'Art Santa Mònica

La Rambla 7 (93 316 28 10/www.cultura.gencat. net/casm). Metro Drassanes. **Open** 11am-8pm Tue-Sat; 11am-3pm Sun. **Admission** free. **Map** p345 A7.
The cloister and tower of the convent of Santa Mònica (1626) were turned into this exhibition space in 1988, with recent alterations allowing for more space. Each year, there are around 20 shows from local and international artists and photographers.

Museu de l'Eròtica

La Rambla 96 bis (93 318 98 65/www.erotica-museum. com). Metro Liceu. **Open** *June-Sept* 10am-10pm daily. *Oct-May* 10am-9pm daily. **Admission** €7.50; €6.50 reductions. **Credit** AmEx, MC, V. **Map** p344 B4.
Mostly visited by stags and hens in search of a cheap thrill, the Erotic Museum is anything but. Expect plenty of filler in the form of airbrushed paintings of the maidens-and-serpents school, with the odd fascinating item such as studded chastity belts or a Victorian walking stick topped with an ivory vagina; some genuine rarities include Japanese drawings, 19th-century engravings by German Peter Fendi and compelling photos of brothels in the city's Barrio Chino in the decadent 1930s. Other curiosities include S&M apparatus and simulated erotic phone lines illustrating the 'sensuality of the voice', but the Eròtica is something of an embarrassment for a district with such connoisseurship of the bawdy.

Palau de la Virreina

La Rambla 99 (93 301 77 75/www.bcn.cat/cultura). Metro Liceu. **Open** 11am-2pm, 4-8.30pm Tue-Fri; 11am-8.30pm Sat; 11am-3pm Sun. **Admission** €3.50; €1.75 reductions; free under-16s. **No credit cards.** **Map** p344 B4.
This classical palace, with Baroque features, takes its name from the widow of an unpopular former viceroy of Peru, who commissioned it and lived in it after its completion in the 1770s. The Virreina houses the city cultural department, has information on events and shows, and also strong programming in its two distinct exhibition spaces. Upstairs is dedicated to one-off exhibitions, with the smaller downstairs gallery focused on historical and contemporary photography.

Born & Sant Pere

Born again.

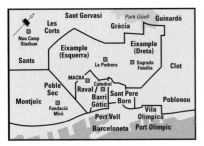

Maps pp344-345

The Born has been the commercial hub of Barcelona since medieval times but these days it has been, well, not so much reborn as rebranded. Now the money is spent on designer clothes and haircuts rather than fruit and vegetables, with the food stores around the old market being turned into fashionable bars and restaurants. It's all immaculately turned out. The neighbouring area of Sant Pere is not quite so well groomed but it's catching up fast, in particular around the Santa Caterina market.

Both districts together are still sometimes referred to as La Ribera ('the waterfront'), a name that recalls the time before permanent quays were built, when the shoreline reached much further inland and the area was contained within the 13th-century wall.

From the north-east, the grand gateway to the area is the **Arc de Triomf**, an imposing, red-brick arch built by Josep Vilaseca as the entrance for the 1888 Universal Exhibition. On the west side, the Josep Reynés sculptures adorning the arch represent Barcelona hosting visitors to the Exhibition, while the Josep Llimona sculptures on the east side depict prizes being awarded to the Exhibition's most outstanding contributors.

La Ribera is demarcated to the east by the **Parc de la Ciutadella** and to the west by Via Laietana, both products of historic acts of urban vandalism. The first came after the 1714 siege, when the victors, acting on the orders of Philip V, destroyed 1,000 houses, hospitals and monasteries to construct the fortress of the Ciutadella (citadel). The second occurred when the Via Laietana was struck through the district in 1907, in line with the theory of 'ventilating' unsanitary city districts by driving wide avenues

through them; it is now a traffic-choked canyon. In 2008, work is due to start on turning over some of Via Laietana's car lanes to pedestrians.

Within La Ribera, Sant Pere and the Born are divided by C/Princesa – also made more pedestrian-friendly in 2006 with wider pavements and seating – running between the Parc de la Ciutadella and the Plaça de l'Àngel (once called the Plaça del Blat, or 'wheat square'), the former commercial and popular heart of the city where all grain was traded. The area north of C/Princesa is centred around the monastery of Sant Pere de les Puelles, which still stands, if greatly altered, in Plaça de Sant Pere. For centuries, this was Barcelona's main centre of textile production; to this day, streets such as Sant Pere Més Baix and Sant Pere Més Alt contain many textile wholesalers and retailers.

The area may be medieval in origin, but its finest monument is one of the most extraordinary works of Modernisme – the **Palau de la Música Catalana**, facing

Fascinating. **Museu Picasso**. *See p99.*

Big trouble in little China

Chinese immigration to Barcelona began in the late 1990s and the current population stands at about 12,000, a tiny fraction of the 300,000 immigrants who have settled in the city since 2000. However, the concentration of Chinese in one small area of the city and in the clothing industry has brought them disproportionate attention. In 1999, they ran about 40 businesses. By the start of 2007 this had risen to close to 200, all situated in the area between Trafalgar, Diputació, Bruc and Nápols streets.

No one disputes that the Chinese community is hard-working and friendly. Furthermore, most of them are young and there is a good gender balance (compare this with Pakistani immigrants, close to 90 per cent of whom are male). They are self-sufficient and demand little from social services. But this very self-sufficiency is held against them as they are accused of resisting integration and of turning the area into a Chinese ghetto. The other complaint is that, because they are prepared to pay over the odds, they are pushing up house prices and that local shops are closing and being replaced by faceless wholesale clothing outlets, thus undermining the life and character of the *barri*.

In response to these complaints, the city council suspended the issue of licences to new businesses of any type in the area while they worked out a plan that would ensure 'diversity', although given that one study revealed that 35 per cent of the businesses in C/Trafalgar were unlicensed anyway, this may have little impact. Things came a head in May 2007 when a local butchers was bought out by Chinese interests. A group of residents called for a demonstration against the proliferation of Chinese businesses in the area. The Chinese wisely decided to close for the day, but in the event the march was cancelled in the face of strong opposition from the city council and the chamber of commerce. The organisers denied the march was racially motivated.

Much of the problem derives from the fact that, as wholesalers, the Chinese have little daily contact with local residents. When they have been here a little longer, Chinese commerce will diversify to include restaurants and other outlets. The advent of a real Chinatown would be a welcome addition to the Barcelona scene.

C/Sant Pere Més Alt. Less noticed on the same street is a curious feature, the Passatge de les Manufactures, a 19th-century arcade between C/Sant Pere Més Alt and C/Ortigosa.

Sant Pere has been renovated, with the gradual opening up of a continuation of the Avda Francesc Cambó, which now swings around to meet with C/Allada-Vermell, a wide street that was formed when a block was demolished in 1994. The district's market, **Mercat de Santa Caterina**, is one of Barcelona's oldest, and has been rebuilt to a design by the late Enric Miralles (who also famously designed the Scottish Parliament); remains of the medieval Convent de Santa Caterina are shown below glass at one end. Another convent located nearby is the Convent de Sant Agustí, which is now a civic centre, on C/Comerç. The entrance contains *Deuce Coop*, a magical 'light sculpture' by James Turrell,

which was commissioned by the Ajuntament in the 1980s and is turned on after dark.

Where C/Carders meets C/Montcada is the Plaçeta d'en Marcús, with a small chapel, the 12th-century Capella d'en Marcús, built as part of an inn. It was founded by Bernat Marcús, who is said to have organised Europe's first postal service, the *correus volants* ('flying runners'). This chapel, then outside the city wall, was where his riders set off from for the north, and it also provided a refuge for them and other travellers who arrived after the city gates had closed for the night.

From this tiny square, C/Montcada, one of the unmissable streets of old Barcelona, leads into the Born. The street takes its name from the Montcada dynasty, who served the counts of Barcelona for generations, finally becoming the leading power in the land in the mid 11th century. A medieval Fifth Avenue, it is lined with a succession of merchants' mansions, the greatest of which house a variety of museums, including the **Museu Tèxtil**, the **Museu Barbier-Mueller d'Art Precolombí** and, above all, the **Museu Picasso**. In 1148, land ceded to Guillem Ramon de Montcada became the site for the construction of this street, where the opulence of the many merchant-princes of the time is still very visible. The streets nearby were filled with workshops supplying anything the inhabitants needed, and these trades are commemorated in the names of many of the streets, *see p102* **Walk on**.

'Born' originally meant 'joust' or 'list', and in the Middle Ages, and for many centuries thereafter, the neighbourhood's main artery, the Passeig del Born, was the centre for the city's festivals, processions, tournaments, carnivals and the burning of heretics by the Inquisition. At one end of the square is the old Born market, which is a magnificent 1870s wrought-iron structure and used to be Barcelona's main wholesale food market. It closed in the 1970s, and the market was transferred elsewhere. Plans to turn the structure into a library were thwarted by the discovery of perfectly preserved medieval remains. The foundations of buildings razed by Philip V's troops were found to contain hundreds of objects, some domestic and some, like rusty bombs, suggesting the traumas of the period. A viewing platform, with useful diagrams and notes, has been erected on C/Fusina and ultimately the remains will be incorporated into a cultural centre and museum, although progress is painfully slow.

At the other end of the Passeig from the market stands the greatest of all Catalan Gothic buildings, the spectacular basilica of **Santa Maria del Mar**. On one side of it, a funnel-shaped red-brick square was opened in 1989 on the site where it is believed the last defenders of the city were executed after Barcelona fell to the Spanish army in 1714. Called the Fossar de les Moreres ('Mulberry Graveyard'), the square is inscribed with patriotic poetry, and nationalist demonstrations converge here every year on Catalan National Day, 11 September. The 'eternal flame' sculpture is a more recent, and less popular, addition.

From here, narrow streets lead to the Plaça de les Olles, or the grand Pla del Palau and another symbol of La Ribera, **La Llotja** (the 'exchange'). Its neo-classical outer shell was added in the 18th century, but its core is a superb 1380s Gothic hall, sadly closed to the public, save for occasional functions organised through the Chamber of Commerce. Until the exchange moved to the Passeig de Gràcia in 1994, this was the oldest continuously functioning stock exchange in Europe.

Museu Barbier-Mueller d'Art Precolombí

C/Montcada 14 (93 310 45 16/www.barbier-mueller.ch). Metro Jaume I. **Open** 11am-7pm Tue-Fri; 10am-7pm Sat; 10am-3pm Sun. **Admission** €3; €1.50 reductions; free under-16s. Free 1st Sun of mth. **Credit** (shop only) AmEx, MC, V. **Map** p345 E6.
Located in the 15th-century Palau Nadal, this world-class collection of pre-Columbian art was ceded to Barcelona in 1996 by the Barbier-Mueller Museum in Geneva. The Barcelona holdings focus solely on the Americas, representing most of the styles from the ancient cultures of Meso-America, Andean America and the Amazon region. Dramatically spotlit in black rooms, the frequently changing selection of masks, textiles, jewellery and sculpture includes pieces dating from as far back as the second millennium BC running through to the early 16th century (showing just how loosely the term 'pre-Columbian' can be used).

Museu de Ciències Naturals de la Ciutadella

Passeig Picasso, Parc de la Ciutadella (93 319 69 12/ www.bcn.cat/museuciencies). Metro Arc de Triomf. **Open** 10am-6.30pm Tue-Sat; 10am-2.30pm Sun. **Admission** *All exhibitions & Jardí Botànic* €5; €3.50 reductions. *Museums only* €3.50; €2 reductions. *Temporary exhibitions* €3.50; €2 reductions. Free under-12s. Free 1st Sun of mth. **No credit cards**. **Map** p343 H11.
Now more than 125 years old, the Natural History Museum comprises the zoology and geology museums in the Parc de la Ciutadella. Both suffer from old-school presentation: dusty glass cases that are filled with moth-eaten stuffed animals and serried rows of rocks. However, the zoology museum is redeemed by its location in the Castell dels Tres Dragons, which was built by Domènech i Montaner as the café-restaurant for the 1888 Universal Exhibition, and by its interesting temporary exhibitions. For children aged three to 12, Dragó-DRAGONET offers a series of free activities with hands-on exploration of the animal world. The geology part, housed in the Museu Martorell, is for aficionados only, with a dry display of minerals, painstakingly classified, alongside explanations of geological phenomena found in Catalonia. More interesting is the selection from the museum's collection of 300,000 fossils, many found locally. A combined ticket also grants entrance to the Jardí Botànic on Montjuïc (*see p121*).

Museu Picasso

C/Montcada 15-23 (93 256 30 00/www.museupicasso. bcn.cat). Metro Jaume I. **Open** (last ticket 30mins before closing) 10am-8pm Tue-Sun. **Admission** *Permanent collection only* €6; €4 reductions. *With temporary exhibition* €8.50; €5.50 reductions; free under-16s. Free (museum only) 1st Sun of mth. **Credit** (shop only) AmEx, MC, V. **Map** p345 E6.
When it opened in 1963, the museum dedicated to Barcelona's favourite adopted son was housed in the Palau Aguilar; the permanent collection of some 3,500

Sightseeing

pieces now spreads across five adjoining palaces, two of which are devoted to temporary exhibitions.

The museum is the second most visited in the city after, you guessed it, the one at the Nou Camp, but waiting in the queue you might not believe it. Rather than being an overview of the artist's work, the Museu Picasso is a record of the vital formative years that the young Picasso spent nearby at La Llotja art school (where his father taught), and later hanging out with Catalonia's fin-de-siècle avant-garde. Those looking for hits like *Les Demoiselles d'Avignon* (1907) and the first Cubist paintings from the time (many of them done in Catalonia), as well as his collage and sculpture, will be disappointed. The founding of the museum is down to a key figure in Picasso's life, his friend and secretary Jaume Sabartés, who donated his own collection for the purpose. Tribute is paid with a room dedicated to Picasso's portraits of him (best known is the Blue Period painting of Sabartés wearing a white ruff), and Sabartés's own doodlings. The seamless presentation of Picasso's development from 1890 to 1904, from deft pre-adolescent portraits to sketchy landscapes to the intense innovations of his Blue Period, is unbeatable, then it leaps to a gallery of mature Cubist paintings from 1917. The pièce de résistance is the complete series of 58 canvases based on Velázquez's famous *Las Meninas*, donated by Picasso himself after the death of Sabartés, and now stretching through the Great Hall. The display later ends with linocuts, engravings and a wonderful collection of ceramics that were donated by Picasso's widow. Temporary exhibitions are often fascinating. *Photo p97.*

Museu Tèxtil

C/Montcada 12 (93 319 76 03/www.museutextil. bcn.cat). Metro Jaume I. **Open** 10am-6pm Tue-Sat; 10am-3pm Sun. **Admission** Combined admission with Museu de les Arts Decoratives & Museu de Ceràmica €3.50; €2 reductions; free under-16s. Free 1st Sun of mth. **Credit** (shop only) AmEx, DC, MC, V. **Map** p345 E6.

Housed in adjoining palaces, the extensive Textile Museum is divided into three main sections: textiles, liturgical vestments, tapestry and rugs; clothing and accessories; and the city's lace and embroidery collection. The permanent exhibition provides a chronological tour of this branch of the history of art and technology, from its oldest piece, a man's Coptic tunic from a seventh-century tomb, through to Karl Lagerfeld. Among curiosities, such as the world's largest collection of kids' skin gloves and an 18th-century bridal gown in black figured silk, the real highlight is the fashion collection – from Baroque to 20th century – that Manuel Rocamora donated in the 1960s; this is one of the finest of its type anywhere in the world. Recent important donations include more than 100 pieces by Spanish designer Cristóbal Balenciaga. The museum shop is a great place to pick up presents, and there's a wonderful café outside in the courtyard. At some unspecified date in the future, the collection will move to the new Museu de Disseny (Design Museum) in the Plaça de les Glòries.

Museu de la Xocolata

C/Comerç 36 (93 268 78 78/http://pastisseria.cat/ ct/PortadaMuseu). Metro Jaume I. **Open** 10am-7pm Mon, Wed-Sat; 10am-3pm Sun. **Admission** €3.90; €3.40 reductions; free under-7s. **Credit** MC, V. **Map** p345 F5.

The best-smelling museum in town draws chocholics of all ages to its collection of *mones* (chocolate sculptures); made by Barcelona's master pastissers for the Easter competition, the *mones* range from multicoloured models of Gaudí's Casa Batlló to extravagant scenes of Don Quixote tilting at windmills. Inevitably, this is not a collection that ages well: photos have replaced most of the older sculptures, and those that are not in glass cases bear the ravages of hands-on appreciation from the museum's smaller visitors. A brief history of chocolate is pepped up with audio-visual displays and the odd touch-screen computer, but the busiest area is the cookery workshop, with classes for all ages and levels. That, and the irresistible chocolate shop.

Palau de la Música Catalana

C/Sant Francesc de Paula 2 (93 295 72 00/www. palaumusica.org). Metro Urquinaona. **Open** Box office 10am-9pm Mon-Sat. Guided tours 10am-3.30pm daily. **Admission** €9; €8 reductions. **Credit** (minimum €20) MC, V. **Map** p344 D3.

Possibly the wildest, most extreme expression of Modernisme ever built, the façade of Domènech i Montaner's concert hall, with its bare brick, busts

Parc de la Ciutadella. *See p102.*

Walk on Medieval trading

Duration: 45 minutes.

From **Plaça de l'Àngel**, site of the Plaça del Blat, the grain market, cross Via Laietana to **C/Bòria**, a name that probably means 'outskirts' or 'suburbs', since it was outside the original city. C/Bòria continues into the evocative little **Plaça de la Llana**, the old centre of wool (*llana*) trading in the city, which is now an animated meeting place for the Dominican Republic community. Alleys to the left were associated with food trades: **C/Mercaders** ('traders', probably in grain), **C/Oli** ('olive oil') just off it, and **C/Semoleres**, where semolina was made. To the right on Bòria is **C/Pou de la Cadena** ('well with a chain'), a reminder that water was essential for textile working.

After Plaça de la Llana, the Roman road's name becomes **C/Corders** ('rope-makers') and then **C/Carders** ('carders' or combers of wool). Where the name changes there is a tiny square, Placeta Marcús, with an even smaller Romanesque chapel, the **Capella d'en Marcús**, built in the early 12th century.

If you carry on a little way along C/Carders (keeping an eye out for pickpockets and bag-snatchers, who tend to favour this area), you arrive at the **Plaça Sant Agustí Vell**, where the architecture can be dated as far back as the Middle Ages. Just off it, **C/Basses de Sant Pere** leads away to the left, where you'll find a 14th-century house.

Retrace your steps down C/Carders, then turn left into **C/Blanqueria** ('bleaching'). Here wool was washed before being spun. At **C/Assaonadors** ('tanners'), turn right. At the end of this street, behind the Marcús chapel, is a statue of John the Baptist, patron saint of the tanners' guild.

Now you are at the top of **C/Montcada**, one of Barcelona's great museum centres and a beautiful street in itself. The first of the line of medieval merchants' palaces you reach after crossing C/Princesa is the **Palau Berenguer d'Aguilar**, home of the **Museu Picasso**, which has also taken over four more palaces. Opposite is one of the finest and largest palaces, the **Palau dels Marquesos de Lliò**, now the **Museu Tèxtil**, with a fine café. Further down to the right is the milliners' street, **C/Sombrerers**; opposite it is Barcelona's narrowest street, **C/Mosques** ('flies'), not even wide enough for an adult to lie across, and now closed off with an iron gate because too many people were urinating in it at night. C/Montcada ends at **Passeig del Born**, a hub of the city's trading for 400 years.

and mosaic friezes representing Catalan musical traditions and composers, is impressive enough, but it is surpassed by the building's staggering interior. A great deal of money has been spent to improve the acoustics, but visitors don't really come here to feast their ears: the eyes have it. Decoration erupts everywhere: the ceiling centrepiece is of multicoloured stained glass; 18 half-mosaic, half-relief figures representing the musical Muses appear out of the back of the stage; and on one side, massive Wagnerian valkyries ride out to accompany a bust of Beethoven. By the 1980s, the Palau was bursting under the pressure of the musical activity going on inside it, and an extension and renovation project by Oscar Tusquets that spanned more than 20 years involved the demolition of the ugly church next door to make way for the extension of the façade, a subterranean concert hall and a new entrance. Rather than try to compete with the existing façade, the new part has subtler, organic motifs.

Guided tours are available in English, Catalan or Spanish every 30 minutes or so. Be sure to ask questions, particularly if there's something you really want to know – the guides are very knowledgeable, but unless they're drawn out by visitors they tend to concentrate mainly on the triumphs of the renovation. If you have a chance, an even better way to see the hall is by catching a concert (*see p263*). This year is the centenary of the building.

Parc de la Ciutadella

Passeig Picasso (no phone). Metro Arc de Triomf or Barceloneta. **Open** 10am-sunset daily. **Map** p343 H11/J11.

Named after the hated Bourbon citadel – the largest in Europe – that occupied this site from 1716 to 1869, this elegant park came into being after the anti-Bourbon revolution of 1868, when General Prim announced that the area could be reclaimed for public use. The garrison fort was gleefully pulled down and pleasure gardens built to host the 1888 Universal Exhibition; Domènech i Montaner's Castell de Tres Dragons at the entrance served as the cafeteria, while the Arc de Triomf to the north formed the main entrance. Prim is honoured with an equestrian statue at the southern end.

Although half the land is taken up by the city zoo, the park is still surprisingly extensive and contains a host of attractions, including the Natural History Museum, a boating lake and more than 30 pieces of

Turn left, and on the left is C/**Flassaders** ('blanket makers'), and to the right C/**Rec**, the old irrigation canal. Go down Rec to turn right into C/**Esparteria**, where *espart* (hemp) was woven. Turnings off it include C/**Calders**, where smelting furnaces were found, and C/**Formatgeria**, for cheese. After that is C/**Vidrieria**, where glass was stored and sold. Esparteria runs into C/Ases, which crosses C/**Malcuinat** ('badly cooked'). Turn left into C/**Espaseria** ('sword-making') to emerge out of ancient alleys on to the open space of Pla del Palau. Turn right, and then right again into C/**Canvis Vells** ('old exchange'). There's a tiny street to the left, C/**Panses**, that has an archway above it, with an ancient stone carving of a face over the second floor. This face indicated the location of a legalised brothel.

At the end of Canvis Vells is **Plaça Santa Maria** and the parish church, **Santa Maria del**

Mar. On the left-hand side is C/**Abaixadors** ('unloaders'), where porters used to unload their goods; from the square, C/**Argenteria** ('silverware') will lead back to Plaça de l'Àngel.

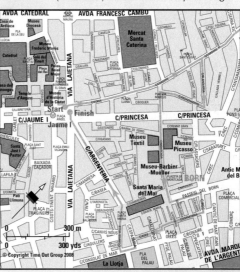

imaginative statuary. The giant mammoth statue, which can be found at the far side of the boating lake, is a huge hit with kids, as is the trio of prancing deer, dedicated to Walt Disney, by the old zoo entrance in the south-eastern corner. Also worth seeking out is the Cascade, an ornamental fountain on which Gaudí worked as assistant to Josep Fontseré, the architect of the park. On the old parade ground in the middle of a small pond is one of the most striking sculptures of Catalan Modernisme: *El Desconsol* (Grief) by Josep Llimona. Also not to be missed are Fontseré's slatted wooden *Umbracle* (literally, 'shade house'), which provides a pocket of tropical forest within the city, and the elegant *Hivernacle* ('winter garden') that was designed by Josep Amargós in 1884. *Photo p101.*

Santa Maria del Mar

Plaça de Santa Maria (93 310 23 90). Metro Jaume I. **Open** 9am-1.30pm, 4.30-8pm Mon-Sat; 10am-1.30pm, 4.30-8pm Sun. **Admission** free. **Map** p345 E6.
Possibly the most perfect surviving example of the Catalan Gothic style, this graceful basilica stands out for its characteristic horizontal lines, large bare surfaces, square buttresses and flat-topped octagonal

towers. Its superb unity of style is down to the fact that it was built relatively quickly, with construction taking just 55 years (1329-1384). Named after Mary in her role as patroness of sailors, it was built on the site of a small church known as Santa Maria del Arenys (sand), for its position close to the sea. In the broad, single-nave interior, two rows of perfectly proportioned columns soar up to fan vaults, creating an atmosphere of space around the light-flooded altar. There's also superb stained glass, especially the great 15th-century rose window above the main door. The original window, built only slightly earlier, fell down during an earthquake, killing 25 people. The incongruous modern window at the other end was a 1997 addition, belatedly celebrating the Olympics.

It's perhaps thanks to the group of anti-clerical anarchists who set this magnificent church ablaze for 11 days in 1936 that its superb features can be appreciated – without the wooden Baroque altar and chapel furniture that clutter so many Spanish churches, the simplicity of its lines can emerge. On Saturdays, the basilica is in great demand for weddings, and its acoustics make it a popular venue for concerts; particularly stirring are the Requiem mass at Easter and Handel's *Messiah* at Christmas.

Raval

One of the most ethnically diverse places in Europe.

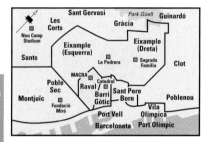

Sant Gervasi — Park Güell — Guinardó
Les Corts — Gràcia
Nou Camp Stadium
Sants — Eixample (Esquerra) — Eixample (Dreta)
La Pedrera — Sagrada Família — Clot
MACBA — Catedral
Poble Sec — Raval / — Sant Pere — Poblenou
Montjuïc — Barri Gòtic — Born
Fundació Miró — Vila Olímpica
Port Vell — Port Olímpic
Barceloneta

Map p342

The Raval lay for a long time outside the city walls and even now, with the ramparts long since demolished, it retains the air of an area set apart from the rest of the city. There are streets here that the brand-conscious city council would definitely prefer visitors not to see, although these are the streets that the Raval's own poster boy, Jean Genet, chronicled in *The Thief's Journal*. The fact that Genet was a thieving 1920s rent boy who revelled in the area's intoxicating mix of absinthe bars, seedy theatres, brothels, anarchist groups and doss-houses should give you an idea of what to expect. But much has changed over the last 80 years and, while the forces of gentrification have not yet succeeded in remaking the Raval, the recent wave of immigration has changed the character of the neighbourhood forever. Although the old red-light district still retains its traditional population of prostitutes, transsexuals, drug addicts and poor labourers, in 2006 more than half the *barri*'s residents were from outside Spain, the majority being from Pakistan and Ecuador. The Raval is one of the most ethnically diverse places in Europe; shop signs are in a babel of languages and advertise everything from halal meat to Bollywood videos and cheap phonecalls home to South America. Another assault on the Raval's traditional character is being led by students and artists, attracted by the new faculty buildings and old industrial spaces respectively. But – with an estimated 70 per cent of the incoming population under 35 – the Raval has lost none of its addiction to night-time activities.

Despite the signs of gentrification, be warned that the Raval has not lost its associations with crime and sleaze. So visitors should still take care, particularly after dark in the area down towards the port. That said, as long as you exercise the usual precautions such as staying off badly lit side streets and not conspicuously flaunting your new digital camera, the Raval can make for Barcelona's most exhilarating wander.

Ever on the margins, Raval (*arrabal* in Spanish) is a generic word adapted from the Arabic *ar-rabad*, meaning 'outside the walls'. When a defensive wall was built down the north side of La Rambla in the 13th century, the area now sandwiched between Avda Paral·lel and La Rambla was a sparsely populated green belt of garden plots. Over the centuries, the land was to absorb functional spillover from the city in the form of monasteries, churches, religious hospitals, prisons and virtually any noxious industry that citizens didn't want on their doorstep. When industrialisation arrived in the 18th century, the area became Barcelona's working-class district.

This was also the part of town where the most land was available; more emerged after the government dissolved the monasteries in 1836, and early industries, mainly the textile mills, took the space. Some of the bleak buildings known as *cases-fàbriques* (residential factories) can still be seen here; among them is the Can Ricart textile factory on C/Sant Oleguer, now converted into a swimming pool and sports centre that opened to the public in July 2006, which connects to the existing sports centre on C/Sant Pau.

Workers lived in crowded slums devoid of ventilation or running water, and malnutrition, TB, scrofula and typhus kept the average life expectancy to 40 years. It's no coincidence that the city's sanatoriums, orphanages and hospitals were based here. Then known to most people as the Quinto, or 'Fifth District', the area was also where the underclasses forged the centre of revolutionary Barcelona, a breeding ground for anarchists and other radicals. Innumerable riots and revolts began here; entire streets became no-go areas after dark.

Heroin's arrival in the late 1970s caused extra problems; the semi-tolerated petty criminality became more threatening and affected the tourist trade. Spurred on by the approaching 1992 Olympics, the authorities made a clean sweep of the Lower Raval. Whole blocks with associations to drugs or prostitution were demolished, and many of the displaced families were transferred to housing estates on the edge of town, out of sight and out of mind.

A sports centre, a new police station and office blocks were constructed, and some streets were pedestrianised. But the most dramatic plan was to create a *'Raval obert al cel'* ('Raval open to the sky'), the most tangible result of which is the sweeping, palm-lined Rambla del Raval. Completed in 2000, it's a continuation of the Avda Drassanes, an earlier attempt to open up the Raval in the 1960s. Nearly five blocks vanished in its wake, and more fell, some very grudgingly indeed, to provide land for the current grand project: L'Illa de la Rambla del Raval (also known as the Illa Robador), a mega-complex halfway up the new rambla that will contain a hotel, offices, protected housing, shops and the Filmoteca. Construction began in 2004; the underground parking and some of the housing are now complete – the first residents occupied the apartments in July 2006, and work has now begun on the star of the show, a luxury ten-storey hotel owned by the Barceló chain and designed by Pere Puig that should provide the area with a glittering new landmark.

Efforts to bring life to the rambla include licences for new clubs and bars, Botero's deliciously bulging *Gat* (Cat) sculpture and an ethnic weekend street market. The market's multicultural nature reflects the number of immigrants living in the Raval, originally attracted by the lower cost of housing. The facelift has raised the prices, though, and as the immigrants, often young men sleeping ten to a room, are squeezed out, a wealthier community of arty western expats and university students has moved in, scattering the area with galleries, boutiques and cafés. C/Doctor Dou is now packed with galleries, C/Ferlandina is packed with boho cafés, and the old industrial spaces along C/Riereta now serve as studios to more than 40 artists.

Upper Raval

The Upper Raval is doing its best to shed its unsavoury association with the louche Lower Raval. In recent years, many late-night bars, galleries and restaurants have opened, and the addition of the four-star Casa Camper design hotel has placed the area as the pretender to the Born's crown of desirability. The smartest streets are in the north-west of the area, between C/Carme and Plaça Catalunya. However, don't go thinking that you'll find some gentrified area with all its old poverty and desperation confined to sharply defined enclaves: the Raval still has an edge, and it can cut.

From La Rambla, signposts for the MACBA carefully guide visitors along the gentrified 'tourist corridors' of C/Tallers and C/Bonsuccès to a bourgeois bohemian's playground of cafés, galleries and boutiques. The centre of the Upper

Sk8 over to **MACBA** for some sick art. *See p107.*

Sightseeing

Raval is the Plaça dels Àngels, where the 16th-century Convent dels Àngels houses both the FAD design institute and a gigantic almshouse, the Casa de la Caritat, converted into a cultural complex housing the **MACBA** and the **CCCB**. When the clean, high-culture MACBA opened in 1995, it seemed to embody everything the Raval was not, and it was initially mocked as an isolated and isolating social experiment. But, over the years, the square has become unofficial home to the city's skateboarders and the surrounding streets have filled with restaurants and boutiques. In 2006, after seven years of building work, the university faculties of philosophy, geography and history finally opened opposite the entrance to the CCCB, and thousands of students are now changing the character of the place.

Below here C/Hospital and C/Carme meet at the Plaça Pedró, where the tiny Romanesque chapel (and ex-lepers' hospital) of Sant Llàtzer sits. From La Rambla, the area is accessed

Page burner

Like New York, Barcelona has long appealed to writers as the setting for their books. The city is the only identifiable place in Cervantes' *Don Quixote* and ever since writers have been using it as the backdrop for their stories. The Old City holds a particular attraction, above all the area on the southern side of La Rambla known as the Raval.

It was in the seedy streets of the lower half of the Raval that Jean Genet set much of his autobiography, *The Thief's Journal*. Here, too, fellow Frenchman Pieyre de Mandiargues set *La Marge*, his novel about the Barcelona demi-monde. The book was later filmed as *The Streetwalker*, starring Silvia Kristel of *Emmanuelle* fame. Both Genet and De Mandiargues have squares in the Raval named for them, on either side of C/Nou de la Rambla. The Plaça Pieyre de De Mandiargues is, fittingly, lined with prostitutes.

Claude Simon's civil war novel *La Palace* was set there and in other parts of the Old City. Simon won the 1985 Nobel prize for literature but the city has not seen fit to name a square in his honour.

As well as attracting writers from outside, the Raval is a breeding ground for Catalan literary talent. The best known and most widely translated is Manuel Vázquez Montalbán, whose left-wing, food-loving detective Pepe Carvalho helped put the Raval on the literary map. Many of his Carvalho books are available in English. Less well known outside Spain are some of the Raval's other literary sons and daughters, such as Terenci Moix (*La Torre de los Vicios Capitales*), who spent much of his adult life in London, and the novelist Maruja Torres, who is also a columnist for *El País* newspaper.

If these have not had much impact outside the Spanish-speaking world, the same cannot be said of Carlos Ruiz Zafón, whose *The*

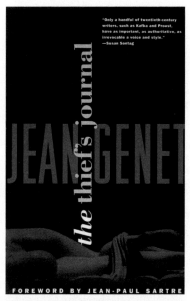

"Only a handful of twentieth-century writers, such as Kafka and Proust, have as important, as authoritative, as irrevocable a voice and style."
—Susan Sontag

JEAN GENET
the thief's journal
FOREWORD BY JEAN-PAUL SARTRE

Shadow of the Wind is a bestseller in a dozen languages, making Zafón the most successful Spanish author since Cervantes.

Tourists with a literary bent can follow in their favourite writer's or character's footsteps thanks to the Consortium of Barcelona Libraries. The organisation has organised literary walks over recent years which have been collected in *Walks Through Literary Barcelona* by Sergio Vila-Sanjuán and Sergi Dora. There are also walks organised by the CCCB, though the commentary is usually only available in Catalan. See www.bcn.es/biblioteques/pagstot/activitats/itineraris/html or www.cccb.org for more information.

along either street or through the Boqueria market, itself the site of the Sant Josep monastery until the sale of church lands led to its destruction in the 1830s. Behind the Boqueria is the **Antic Hospital de la Santa Creu**, which took in the city's sick from the 15th century until 1926; it now houses Catalonia's main library and the headquarters of the Institute of Catalan Studies; and **La Capella**, an attractive exhibition space. C/Carme is capped at the Rambla end by the 18th-century Església de Betlem (Bethlehem) with its serpentine pillars and geometrically patterned façade. Its name features on many shop signs nearby; older residents still refer to this part of the Raval as Betlem.

Antic Hospital de la Santa Creu & La Capella

C/Carme 47-C/Hospital 56 (no phone). Metro Liceu. **Open** 9am-8pm Mon-Fri; 9am-2pm Sat. *La Capella* (93 442 71 71) noon-2pm, 4-8pm Tue-Sat; 11am-2pm Sun. **Admission** free. **Map** p344 A4.

This was one of Europe's earliest medical centres. There was a hospital on the site as early as 1024, but in the 15th century it expanded to centralise all the city's hospitals and sanatoriums (with the exception of the Santa Margarida leper colony, which remained outside the city walls). By the 1920s, it was hopelessly overstretched, and its medical facilities were moved uptown to the Hospital Sant Pau. One of the last patients was Gaudí, who died here in 1926; it was also where Picasso painted one of his first important pictures, *Dead Woman* (1903).

The buildings remain some of the most majestic in the city, combining a 15th-century Gothic core with Baroque and classical additions. They're now given over to cultural institutions, among them the Massana Arts School, Catalonia's main library (and the second largest in Spain), the Institute of Catalan Studies and the Royal Academy of Medicine. Highlights include a neo-classical lecture theatre complete with revolving marble dissection table (open 10am-2pm Mon-Fri), and the entrance hall of the Casa de Convalescència, tiled with lovely Baroque ceramic murals telling the story of Sant Pau (St Paul); one features an artery-squirting decapitation scene. La Capella, the hospital chapel, was rescued from a sad fate as a warehouse and sensitively converted to an exhibition space for contemporary art. The beautifully shady colonnaded courtyard is a popular spot for reading or eating lunch.

CCCB (Centre de Cultura Contemporània de Barcelona)

C/Montalegre 5 (93 306 41 00/www.cccb.org). Metro Catalunya. **Open** *Mid June-mid Sept* 11am-8pm Tue-Sat; 11am-3pm Sun. *Mid Sept-mid June* 11am-2pm, 4-8pm Tue, Thur, Fri; 11am-8pm Wed, Sat; 11am-7pm Sun. **Admission** *1 exhibition* €4.40; €3.30 reductions & Wed. *2 exhibitions* €6; €5.50 reductions & Wed. Free under-16s. **Credit** MC, V. **Map** p344 A2.

Spain's largest cultural centre was opened in 1994 at the Casa de la Caritat, a former almshouse, built in 1802 on the site of a medieval monastery. The massive façade and part of the courtyard remain from the original building; the rest was rebuilt in dramatic contrast, all tilting glass and steel, by architects Piñón and Viaplana, known for the Maremàgnum shopping centre (*see p193*). As a centre for contemporary culture, the CCCB tends to pick up whatever falls through the cracks elsewhere: a slew of film cycles and multimedia presentations, and various flamenco, literary, music and dance festivals (*see pp218-225* Festivals & Events). The CCCB's exhibitions tend to favour production values over content, but there are occasional gems. *Photo p109.*

MACBA (Museu d'Art Contemporani de Barcelona)

Plaça dels Àngels 1 (93 412 08 10/www.macba.es). Metro Catalunya. **Open** *June-Sept* 11am-8pm Mon, Wed-Fri; 10am-8pm Sat; 10am-3pm Sun. *Oct-May* 11am-7.30pm Mon, Wed-Fri; 10am-8pm Sat; 10am-3pm Sun. **Guided tours** (Catalan/Spanish) 6pm Wed, Sat; noon Sun. **Admission** *Museum* €4; €3 reductions. *Museum & temporary exhibitions* €7.50; €6 reductions. *Temporary exhibitions* €6; €4.50 reductions. **Credit** MC, V. **Map** p344 A2.

No work of art inside the MACBA can quite live up to the wow factor of Richard Meier's cool iceberg of a museum set in the skateboarder plains of the Plaça dels Àngels. Even some of the best sculptures are on the outside: *La Ola* (The Wave) a curving bronze behemoth by Jorge Oteiza, and the monochrome mural *Barcelona*, by Eduardo Chillida. Since it opened in 1995, the place has fattened up its holdings considerably, but the shows are often heavily political in concept and occasionally radical to the point of inaccessibility. If you can't or won't see the socio-political implications of, say, a roomful of beach balls, the MACBA may leave you cold.

For 2008 shows include a retrospective of artist Francesc Torres (June-Sept) and, the big one, the 'Universal Archive' (Sept-Jan 2009).

The exhibits cover the last 50 years or so; although there's no permanent collection as such, some of these works are usually on display. The earlier pieces are strong on artists such as Antonio Saura and Tàpies (of whom director Manuel Borja Villel is an ardent fan), who were members of the Dau-al-Set, a group of radical writers and painters, much influenced by Miró, who kickstarted the Catalan art movement after the post-Civil War years of cultural apathy. Jean Dubuffet and Basque sculptors Jorge Oteiza and Eduardo Chillida also feature. Works from the last 40 years are more global, with the likes of Joseph Beuys, Jean-Michel Basquiat, AR Penck and photographer Jeff Wall; the contemporary Spanish collection includes Catalan painting (Ferran Garcia Sevilla, Miquel Barceló) and sculpture (Sergi Aguilar, Susana Solano). Every Thursday and Friday from May to September, the MACBA stays open until midnight (€3 after 8pm) and offers guided tours of the exhibitions (at 8.30pm and 10pm). *Photo p105.*

CASUAL FOOD FOR CASUAL PEOPLE

SANDWICH&FRIENDS®
CASUALFOOD

Chic and modern restaurants with the greatest sandwiches in Barcelona. They also serve fresh salads, desserts and ice creams. The sophisticated interior of the restaurant is designed by Cesc Pons, and all the stores have a spectacular mural designed by the famous international artist, Jordi Labanda.

Opening hours: Sun-Wed 9:30am-1am, Thurs-Sat 9:30am-2:30am. Kitchen open all day.
Sandwich&Friends locations:

CITY CENTRE
Rambla Catalunya 5
Tel. 93 342 73 76

RAVAL
C/Hospital 102-104
Tel. 93 329 82 77

BORN
Passeig del Born 27
Tel. 93 310 07 86

UPPER SIDE
Madrazo 15
Tel. 93 415 66 54

EIXAMPLE
Aribau 179
Tel. 93 200 45 95

www.**sandwichandfriends**.com

Lower Raval

The lower half of the Raval, from C/Hospital downwards, is generally referred to as the Barrio Chino (translated into Catalan as 'Barri Xino' or simply 'el Xino'). The nickname was coined in the 1920s by a journalist likening the neighbourhood to San Francisco's Chinatown, and referred to its underworld feel rather than to any Chinese population. In those days, drifters filled the bars and there were cheap hostels along streets such as Nou de la Rambla, alongside high-class cabarets and brothels for the rich and cheap porn pits for the poor. A glimpse of the old sleaze can still be found in bars such as Bar Pastis and Marsella (also known as the 'absinthe bar', *see p186*). A small and appropriately seedy square is named after Jean Genet, whose novel *The Thief's Journal* (1949) describes his days as a Xino rent boy and beggar in the 1920s and '30s.

Just beneath C/Hospital in the Plaça Sant Agustí lies one of the Raval's more arresting pieces of architecture, the unfinished 18th-century Església de Sant Agustí (no.2, 93 318 62 31, mass Mon-Fri 7pm; noon, 1pm & 7pm Sat, noon, 1pm, 6pm & 7pm Sun). The stone beams and jags protruding from its left flank (on C/Arc de Sant Agustí) and the undecorated sections of the Baroque façade show how suddenly work stopped when funding ran out. Inside, the Capella de Santa Rita is packed out on her feast day, 22 May; Rita is the patron saint of lost causes and it is to her that the unhappy and unrequited bring their red roses to be blessed.

C/Nou de la Rambla, the area's main street, is home to Gaudí's first major project: **Palau Güell** at no.3. Begun in 1886, it was built for Gaudí's patron, Eusebi Güell. A fortress-like edifice shoehorned into a narrow six-storey sliver, it was an extension of Güell's parents' house (now a hotel) on La Rambla; it's closed for renovation until 2010. Nearby, in C/Sant Pau, is a Modernista landmark, Domènech i Montaner's Hotel España, and at the end of the same street sits the Romanesque church of **Sant Pau del Camp**. Iberian remains dating to 200 BC have been found next to the building, marking it as one of the oldest parts of the city. At the lower end of the area were the Drassanes (shipyards), now home to the Museu Marítim (*see p112*). Along the Avda Paral·lel side of this Gothic building lies the only large remaining section of Barcelona's 14th-century city wall.

Sant Pau del Camp

C/Sant Pau 101 (93 441 00 01). Metro Paral·lel. **Open** *Visits* 10am-1.30pm, 5-8pm Mon-Fri. *Mass* 8pm Sat; noon Sun. **Admission** *Visits* €2; €1 reductions. *Mass* free. **No credit cards. Map** p342 E11.
The name, St Paul in the Field, reflects a time when the Raval was still countryside. In fact, this little Romanesque church is over 1,000 years old; the date carved on its most prestigious headstone – that of Count Guifré II Borell, son of Wilfred the Hairy and inheritor of all Barcelona and Girona – is AD 912.

The church's impressive façade includes sculptures of fantastical flora and fauna along with human grotesques. The tiny cloister is another highlight with its extraordinary Visigoth capitals, triple-lobed arches and central fountain.

CCCB. See p107.

Sightseeing

Barceloneta & the Ports

Shore leave.

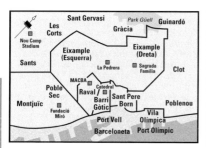

Maps p114 & pp342-343

Maps p114 & pp342-343

Port Vell

A visitor to Barcelona before the Olympics might have been excused for missing the fact that this is a city by the sea. Any water-bound tourist would have had to struggle past the container port, brave crosing a busy motorway and railroad yards, not to mention making it through an area crawling with thieves, prostitutes and all manner of lowlifes. Turning

Barcelona around to face the sea was one of the most drastic urban renewal projects the city has ever undertaken, and the area – rechristened Port Vell ('Old Port') – has changed beyond recognition, attracting more than 18 million visitors a year. The clean-up has extended to the whole seven kilometres (four miles) of city seashore, which is now a virtually continuous strip of modern construction bristling with new docks, marinas, hotels, cruise ships and ferry harbours and leisure areas such as Diagonal Mar ending out at the Edifici Fòrum (*see p142*), with its giant swimming area.

Barcelona has always had a natural harbour, sheltered by the protective mass of the mountain of Montjuïc, but the first wharves were not built until the Middle Ages, when Barcelona was on its way to being the dominant power in the western Mediterranean. The immense Drassanes Reials (Royal Shipyards) are among the world's finest surviving pieces of civilian Gothic architecture; they now house the **Museu Marítim** and bear witness to the sovereignty of the Catalan navy as the city became a military centre and the hub of trading routes

Port Vell: The 'Old Port' is Barcelona's new playground.

between Africa and the rest of Europe. The city's power was dealt a blow when Christopher Columbus sailed westwards and found what he thought was the East; soon the Atlantic became the important trade route and Barcelona went into recession. Prosperity returned in the 19th century, when the city became the base for the Spanish industrial revolution.

Despite putting the city out of business, Columbus was commemorated in 1888 with the **Monument a Colom**, a statue inspired by Nelson's Column, complete with eight majestic lions. Consistent with the great discoverer's errant sense of direction, his finger is not pointing west to the Americas, but eastwards, to Mallorca. A cynic might suggest that he is pointing in bemusement at the World Trade Center, a ship-shaped construction built on a jetty and housing offices, a posh hotel and a tower for the **Transbordador Aeri** cable car. Or he could be pointing at the Moll d'Espanya ('wharf of Spain'), an artificial island linked to land by the Rambla de Mar footbridge. The island is home to the Maremàgnum shopping mall (*see p193*), an IMAX cinema (*see p236*) and L'Aquàrium (*see p227*).

Take a lift through the centre of Columbus's column to check out the view from the top, or jump aboard the cable car (*transbordador aeri*). Below, both the **catamaran** and the **Golondrinas** pleasure boats begin their excursions out to sea. To the right, beyond the busy ferry and cruise ports, is the grandly named Porta d'Europa, the longest drawbridge in Europe, which curtains off the vast container port. Big as it is, plans are under way to enlarge the container port by diverting the mouth of the River Llobregat a mile or so to the south, doubling port area in size by 2050. Andreu Alfaro's enormous *Onas* (Waves) greatly cheers up the gridlocked roundabout of Plaça de la Carbonera, where a grim basin of coal marks where the steamboats once refuelled.

To the left of Columbus is the refurbished Moll de la Fusta ('Wood Wharf') boulevard, built after the city sea walls were demolished in 1878. The wooden pergolas, one of which is topped by Javier Mariscal's popular fibreglass *Gamba* (Prawn), are all that remain of some ill-fated restaurants and clubs, while traffic noise and congestion has been greatly reduced by passing the coastal motorway underneath the boulevard. Just over the grassy slopes is the *Ictineo II*, a replica of the world's first combustion-powered submarine which was created by Narcís Monturiol and launched from Barcelona port in 1862. Roy Lichtenstein's *Barcelona Head* signposts the marina, with more than 450 moorings for leisure boats, and the Palau de Mar, a warehouse which

has had the standard developer's makeover into offices and eating spaces, and the **Museu d'Història de Catalunya**.

Catamaran Orsom
Portal de la Pau, Port de Barcelona (93 441 05 37/ www.barcelona-orsom.com). Metro Drassanes. **Sailings** (approx 1hr 20mins-call to confirm times) *Mar-Oct* noon-8pm. **Tickets** €12/€14.50; €6-€9.50 reductions. **No credit cards. Map** p342 F12.
Departing from the jetty just by the Monument a Colom, this 23m (75ft) catamaran is the largest in Barcelona; it chugs up to 80 seafarers round the Nova Bocana harbour area, before unfurling its sails and peacefully gliding across the bay. There are 8pm jazz cruises from June to September or, if you don't want to fight for the trampoline sun deck, the catamaran can also be chartered for private trips.

Las Golondrinas
Moll de Drassanes (93 442 31 06/www.las golondrinas.com). Metro Drassanes. **Sailings** *Drassanes to breakwater & return* (35mins) Jan-Mar, Nov, Dec 11am-2pm Mon-Fri; 11.45am-7pm Sat, Sun. Apr-June, Oct 11am-6pm Mon-Fri; 11.45am-7pm Sat, Sun. July-Sept 11.45am-7.30pm daily. *Drassanes to Port Fòrum & return* (1hr 30mins) Jan-Mar, Nov, Dec 11.30am, 1.30pm Mon-Fri; 11.30am, 1.30pm, 4.30pm Sat, Sun. Apr-June, Oct 11.30am, 1.30pm, 4.30pm Mon-Fri; 11.30am, 1.30pm, 4.30pm, 6.30pm Sat, Sun. July-Sept 11.30am, 1.30pm, 4.30pm, 6.30pm, 8.30pm daily. **Tickets** *Drassanes to breakwater & return* €5; free under-4s. *Drassanes to Port Fòrum & return* €10.50; €7.50 reductions; free under-4s. **Credit** MC, V. **Map** p342 F12.

Monument a Colom. *See p112.*

For more than 115 years, the 'swallow boats' have chugged around the harbour, giving passengers a bosun's-eye view of Barcelona's rapidly changing seascape out as far as the Port Fòrum. The fleet is made up of three double-decker pleasure boats and two glass-bottomed catamarans, moored next to the Orsom catamaran (*see p111*). Boats leave around every 40 minutes for the shorter trip.

Monument a Colom

Plaça Portal de la Pau (93 302 52 24). Metro Drassanes. **Open** 9am-8pm daily. **Admission** €2.30; €1.50 reductions; free under-4s. **No credit cards.** **Map** p342 F12.

Located where La Rambla meets the port, the Monument a Colom was designed for the Universal Exhibition of 1888. It's hard to believe from ground level, but Colom (Catalan for Columbus) himself is actually 7m (23ft) high; his famous white barnet comes courtesy of the city pigeons. A tiny lift takes you up inside the column to a circular bay for a panoramic view of the city and port. Claustrophobes and vertigo sufferers should stay away; the slight sway can be unnerving. *Photo p111.*

Museu d'Història de Catalunya

Plaça Pau Vila 3 (93 225 47 00/www.mhcat.net). Metro Barceloneta. **Open** 10am-7pm Tue, Thur-Sat; 10am-8pm Wed; 10am-2.30pm Sun. **Admission** €3; €2.10 reductions; free under-7s. Free to all 1st Sun of mth. **Credit** (shop only) MC, V. **Map** p342 G12/F12.

Museu d'Història de Catalunya.

The Catalan History Museum spans the Paleolithic era right up to Jordi Pujol's proclamation as President of the Generalitat in 1980 and offers a virtual chronology of the region's past revealed through two floors of text, photos, film, animated models and reproductions of everything from a medieval shoemaker's shop to a 1960s bar. Hands-on activities such as trying to lift a knight's armour or irrigating lettuces with a Moorish water wheel add a little pzazz to the rather dry early history; to exit the exhibition, visitors walk over a huge 3D map of Catalonia. Every section has a decent introduction in English, but the reception desk will lend a copy of the in-depth English-language museum guide free of charge. The excellent temporary exhibitions, often collections of photos and posters, typically examine recent aspects of regional history. The museum occupies a stylishly converted 19th-century port warehouse, and the views from the rooftop café terrace are unbeatable.

Museu Marítim

Avda de les Drassanes (93 342 99 20/www. museumaritimbarcelona.com). Metro Drassanes. **Open** 10am-7pm daily. **Admission** €6.50; €3.25 reductions; free under-7s. *Temporary exhibitions* vary. *Combined ticket with Las Golondrinas* (35mins) €9.20; €7-€5.50 reductions; free under-4s. **Credit** MC, V. **Map** p342 F12.

A full-scale replica of Don Juan de Austria's royal galley is the mainstay of the collection at the Museu Marítim, complete with a ghostly crew of galley slaves projected on to the rowing banks. The original ship was built in these very same shipyards, one of the finest examples of civil Gothic architecture in Spain and a monument to Barcelona's importance in Mediterranean naval history. With the aid of an audio guide, the maps, nautical instruments, multimedia displays and models show you how shipbuilding and navigation techniques have developed over the years. Admission also covers the Santa Eulàlia schooner docked in the Moll de la Fusta. *See p115* **La Real thing.**

Transbordador Aeri

Torre de Sant Sebastià, Barceloneta (93 441 48 20). Metro Barceloneta. **Open** *Mid June-mid Sept* 11am-8pm daily. *Mid Sept-mid June* 10.45am-7pm daily. **Tickets** €9 single; €12.50 return; free under-6s. **No credit cards.** **Map** p342 E12/F13/G13.

Designed as part of the 1929 Expo, these rather battered old cable cars run between the Sant Sebastià tower at the very far end of Passeig Joan de Borbó to the Jaume I tower in front of the World Trade Center; the final leg ends at the Miramar lookout point on Montjuïc. The towers are accessed by lifts.

Barceloneta

Once a working-class neighbourhood dependent on fishing and heavy industry, this triangular spit of land is now a prime slice of seafront real estate where many of the famously tiny

Beach life. *See p114.*

Sightseeing

apartments are being converted into short-stay holiday flats. But Barceloneta has not completely lost its charm; the interior of this cramped and chaotic neighbourhood (hidden behind the restaurant-lined boulevard of Passeig Joan de Borbó) is a real slice of old Barcelona.

Barceloneta had a turbulent birth. When the old maritime *barri* of La Ribera was demolished in 1714 to make way for the citadel (*see p102*), thousands were left homeless. It was not until 1753 that the new district of Barceloneta was created; the homeless refugees had had to make do with makeshift slums on the beach for nearly 40 years. Military engineer Prosper Verboom maximised the potential of the triangle of reclaimed marshland with narrow rows of cheap worker housing set around a parade ground (now the market square). The two-storey houses became home to fishermen, sailors and dock workers, and soon became so overcrowded that they were split in half and later quartered. These famous *quarts de casa* typically measured no more than 30 square metres (323 square feet), had no running water until the 1960s and often held families of ten or so. Most were later built up to six or more levels, but even today, three-tier bunk beds are not uncommon, and in the summer months the street becomes an extended living room.

Since the beach clean-up, Barceloneta has enjoyed a much higher profile, and current redevelopment includes university housing and Enric Miralles's towering Gas Natural headquarters, which is covered in mirrored

glass. In the heart of the neighbourhood is the new market designed by Josep Mias; it features a wavy sea-green roof fitted with 180 solar panels and incorporates recycled materials from the original 1884 structure. The area has also been the beneficiary of a staggering amount of sculpture, particularly around the Port Vell. Lothar Baumgarten's *Rosa dels Vents* (Wind Rose) has the names of Catalan sea winds embedded in the pavement, and, at the other end of Passeig Joan de Borbó is Juan Muñoz's disturbing sculpture of five caged figures known as *Una habitació on sempre plou* (A Room Where it Always Rains). Behind it is the city's popular municipal swimming pool (*see p274*) newly marked by the soaring figures of Alfredo Lanz's *Homenatge a la Natació* (Homage to Swimming) to mark the 2003 World Swimming Championships held in Barcelona. Monuments within the quarter include the 18th-century church of Sant Miquel del Port, with a muscular sculpture of the Archangel Michael on the façade and the Font de Carmen Amaya at the sea end of C/Sant Carles, a fountain dedicated to the famous gypsy flamenco dancer who was born in 1913 in the squalid beach settlement of Somorrostro, although the slum no longer exists.

Nearby, the Port still preserves a small fishing area with the clock tower that gives its name to the wharf – Moll del Rellotge ('Clock Wharf'). Further down, the road leads to the Nova Bocana development, which should be finished by 2010. The complex will combine leisure and cultural facilities with offices and industry and will be dominated by Ricardo Bofill's Hotel Vela, a sail-shaped luxury hotel. If you head left at the end of Passeig Joan de Borbó, you'll reach Barceloneta beach and Rebecca Horn's tower of rusty cubes, *Estel Ferit* (Wounded Star), which pays homage to the much-missed beach shacks. The Passeig Maritim esplanade runs north from here, and is a popular hangout for in-line skaters, locals walking off their Sunday paella and outpatients from the enviably positioned Hospital del Mar. At its far end are Frank Gehry's shimmering copper *Fish*, the new U-shaped biomedical research park fronted by the pleasant wooden-decked Plaça Charles Darwin and the twin skyscrapers of the Hotel Arts (*see p65*) and the Torre Mapfre, which form an imposing gateway to the Port Olimpic.

Beaches

Now crowded with sunbathers, it's hard to believe that Barcelona's beaches were once a filthy Hell's Bathroom of slimy rocks, sewage, heavy industry and warehouses. Barceloneta was the only sandy part, but any usable parts of the narrow grey beach were clogged with private swimming baths and beach shacks (*xiringuitos*) that served seafood on trestle tables set up on the sand. Once the 1992 Olympics opened Barcelona's eyes to the commercial potential of its shoreline, the beaches were swiftly cleared and filled with tons of golden sand, imported palm trees and landscaped promenades.

However, the beaches have become a victim of their own popularity, and keeping them clean is something of a Sisyphean task for the city council. Dubbed the Bay of Pigs by the papers, the most central area was so dirty that in 2005 the nightly patrols collected over 4,000 cubic metres of rubbish, which included more

than 1.5 million cigarette butts. The massive clean-up campaign includes doubling the number of beachfront toilets, adding new bins, and endless posters and loudspeaker announcements reminding people to pick up their rubbish.

The beach furthest south is Platja de Sant Sebastià, right in front of the swimming pools, popular with nudists and anyone willing to swap an uninspiring background of industrial rubble for a bit more space. Next is Platja de Sant Miquel, which gets insanely crowded in the summer months; it's a slightly grubby version of Ibiza, with plenty of thongs and piercings on display, and *xiringuitos* pumping out house music. Platja de Barceloneta provides a sandy porch for restaurants and nightclubs; the covered walkway is home to tables where old men play dominoes, and it also houses the new beach centre – its small beach library lends out books, magazines and papers (some in English) in July and August. After the Port Olimpic and just down from the Ciutadella-Vila Olimpica metro station, Platja de Nova Icària is much broader, with plenty of space for volleyball and beach tennis, while Platja de Bogatell boasts the hippest *xiringuito* with torches and loungers out at night from May to October. Further north, Platja de Mar Bella is all about sport, with the sailing and water-sports club Base Nàutica and a popular half-pipe for skateboarders and BMXers behind. The more remote beaches of Nova Mar Bella and the new Llevant have the rather unexotic backdrops of high-rise residential blocks and are generally fairly quiet.

Vila Olímpica

The land lying further up the coast was once an area of thriving industry, but by the 1980s it had fallen into disuse and presented the perfect blank slate for a team of 30 prize-winning

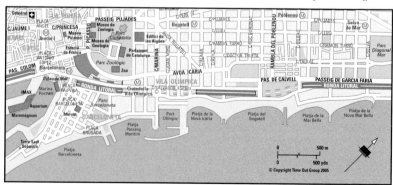

La Real thing

Hundreds of years of consolidation and gradual expansion followed, as the strength of the Byzantines was gradually whittled away until, a millennium after it had been founded, Constantinople fell in the year 1453 to the forces of the expanding Ottoman Empire and its great sultan, Mehmet II, dubbed 'the Conqueror'. Internal struggles temporarily brought a halt to the Ottoman onslaught, but with the accession of Suleiman I (1520-66) the attack on Europe resumed. Hungary was conquered and Vienna besieged in 1529. If freak rain storms had not caused Suleiman to abandon his artillery, it's almost certain that Vienna would have been taken, leaving the advance into Germany clear.

The Museu Marítim's most important exhibit is a full-scale replica of *La Real*, the flagship from which 24-year-old Don Juan of Austria commanded the fleet of the Holy League as it confronted the hitherto invincible Ottoman navy. Although few are aware of it today, the battle of Lepanto in 1571 was one of the most important in history. But why was this last battle between rowing galleys so crucial? After all, there was never any real doubt that the West would triumph over its enemies, was there?

Yes, there was. A neutral observer in the 16th century would have concluded that it was only a matter of time before the armies of Islam conquered all of Europe. Since the Arabs had burst from the desert in the seventh century, they had carried all before them. The first surge had seen all the previously Christian lands of north Africa and much of the Middle East become Muslim, while the Persian Sasanian Empire had also fallen. By 750, Islam ruled all the countries in a broad band from Spain in the west to what is now Pakistan in the east. Only the Byzantine Empire, the Christian successor to Rome founded by Constantine, prevented the advance of Muslim armies into Europe.

So, by the 16th century, the Christian world had been reduced to a remnant of its former extent and Europeans gloomily forsaw a time when Islam would have conquered all. Even the Crusades, which we so often see today as some sort of imperialist adventure, were more like a desperate attempt to turn an inexorable tide.

In this light, it's no wonder that at the time the battle of Lepanto caused rejoicing all over Europe. Poets, painters and writers celebrated the victory, the Protestant Queen Elizabeth I decreed services of thanksgiving for the triumph of the Catholic Holy League and Pope Gregory XIII declared 7 October, the anniversary of the battle, the feast of Our Lady of the Rosary. For once, Europe was united. Miguel de Cervantes, who fought in the battle, losing the use of his left hand, called it 'the most noble and memorable event that past centuries have seen or future generations can ever hope to witness'.

architects to design the model neighbourhood of the Olympic Village for the games in 1992. Based on Cerdà's Eixample grid (*see p125*), it provided accommodation for 15,000 athletes, parks, a cinema, four beaches and a leisure marina.

The lack of cafés and shops, however, leaves it devoid of Mediterranean charm. Most social activity takes place in the Port Olímpic, home to sailboats, restaurants, a large casino and a waterfront strip of cheesy nightclubs. Wide empty boulevards lend themselves to large-scale sculpture, including a jagged pergola on Avda Icària by Enric Miralles and Carme Pinós, in memory of the ripped-up railway tracks, and Antoni Llena's abstract *David i Goliat* in the Parc de les Cascades.

Montjuïc

Room for views.

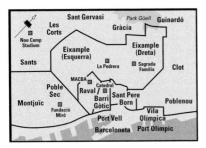

Maps p339 & p342

In a city with as few parks as Barcelona, the hills of Montjuïc offer a precious escape from the stresses of urban life, with pleasure gardens, spectacular views and all manner of outstanding museums and galleries. Here you'll find Santiago Calatrava's Olympic 'needle' and many other buildings from the 1992 games scattered over the landward side, while facing the sea are a lighthouse and an enormous cemetery. And skulking at the top of the hill, all but invisible from below, is the heavily fortified Castell de Montjuïc, a dark and brooding symbol of the centuries Catalonia spent under Castilian rule. Yet, despite all the reasons to visit, the difficulty of getting to Montjuïc means that its green spaces are greatly underused by local citizens; plans to convert it into the 'Central Park' of Barcelona involve opening up access from the neighbourhood of Poble Sec with broad boulevards and escalators leading up to Avinguda Miramar.

The mists of time obscure the etymology of Montjuïc, but one reasonably widely accepted educated guess is that 'juïc' comes from the old Catalan word meaning Jewish. It was here that the medieval Jewish community buried their dead; some of the excavated headstones are now to be found in the **Museu Militar**. Other headstones with Hebraic inscriptions can be seen plastered in to the walls of the 16th-century Palau de Lloctinent, just to the east of the cathedral; following the expulsion of all Jews from Spain by Ferdinand and Isabella in 1492, the cemetery was plundered and the stone reused. The sea-facing side of the mountain still houses a huge cemetery today, the **Cementiri del Sud-Oest**.

The 17th-century fortress, the Castell de Montjuïc, was rebuilt in its current form after Philip V's troops broke the siege of Barcelona in 1714. From its vantage point overlooking the city, the central government was able to impose its will on the unruly populace until the death of Franco. From here, in 1842, the city was bombed to repress an uprising against the government's policies. And in this fortress many Republicans were executed after the Civil War, including Generalitat President Lluís Companys, who was killed in 1940, victim no.2,761 of Franco's firing squads in Catalonia. However, the new Socialist government ceded formal ownership of the castle to the city of Barcelona in 2004, and approved a law that allows for the pardon of Civil War victims.

The 1929 Exhibition was the first attempt to turn the hill into a leisure area. Then, in the 1940s, thousands of immigrant workers from the rest of Spain settled on the hill. Some squatted in precarious shacks, while others rented brick and plaster sheds laid out along improvised streets that covered the hillside, then virtually treeless. These *barraques* thrived until the last few stragglers moved out in the 1970s, although the area still attracts intermittent waves of illegal tent and hut dwellers. Energetic visitors can follow the same steep routes these residents once took home, straight up C/Nou de la Rambla or C/Margarit in Poble Sec; the stairway at the top leaves you just a short distance from the **Fundació Joan Miró** and the Olympic stadium area.

The long axis from Plaça d'Espanya is still the most popular access to the park, with the climb now eased by a sequence of open-air escalators. In the centre of Plaça d'Espanya itself is a monument designed by Josep Maria Jujol (who created the wrought-iron balconies on La Pedrera), with representations of the rivers Ebre, Tagus and Guadalquivir. Where Paral·lel meets Plaça d'Espanya is Las Arenas, the old neighourhood bullring. The last bull met its fate here in the 1970s and until 2003 the bullring lay derelict. The ubiquitous Lord Rogers is currently overseeing the mammoth transformation project, to be completed who knows when, which will turn the ring into a circular leisure complex while restoring the existing neo-Mudéjar façade. The vision encompasses a 'piazza in the sky', a giant

Sightseeing

roof terrace that will allow for alfresco events and offer panoramic views over Barcelona.

On the other side of the square, two Venetian-style towers announce the beginning of the Fira, the trade-show area, with pavilions from 1929 and newer buildings used for conventions and congresses. To the left is the Palau d'Esports, recently converted into the **Barcelona Teatre Musical** (*see p266*) hosting large-scale musical theatre. Further up, the rebuilt **Pavelló Mies van der Rohe**, a modernist classic, contrasts sharply with the neo-classical structures nearby. Across the street, Puig i Cadafalch's Modernista factory has been converted into the excellent **CaixaForum** cultural centre. Further up the hill is the bizarre **Poble Espanyol**, a model village also designed in 1929 especially to showcase Spanish crafts and architecture.

Presiding over it all is the bombastic Palau Nacional, originally built as a 'temporary exhibition' for the Expo, and now home to the **MNAC (Museu Nacional d'Art de Catalunya)**, housing Catalan art from the last millennium and recently reopened after a lengthy refurbishment. At night, the entire setting is illuminated by a water-and-light spectacular, the **Font Màgica**, still operating with its complex original mechanisms. Other nearby buildings erected for the 1929 Expo have been converted into the **Museu d'Arqueologia de Catalunya** and the Ciutat del Teatre (theatre city) complex. From the same period are the nearby Teatre Grec (Greek theatre), used for summer concerts during the Grec Festival, and the beautifully restored Jardins Laribal, designed by French landscape architect JCN Forestier. At the top of this garden is the Font del Gat information centre. The **Museu Etnològic**, a typical 1970s construction, sits just below it.

If walking isn't your thing, another way up the hill is via the funicular railway, integrated with the city's metro system, leaving from the Paral·lel station. A more circuitous way up is by the Transbordador Aeri cable car across the harbour to Miramar, a peaceful spot with unmatchable views across the city that has been somewhat taken over by the new five-star Gran Hotel Miramar, which opened in August 2006.

Montjuïc's Anella Olímpica (Olympic Ring) is a convergence of diverse constructions all laid out for the 1992 Olympic Games. The Estadi Olímpic (home to the city's 'second' football team, Espanyol, until they moved to Cornellà in 2006), although entirely new, was built within the façade of a 1929 stadium by a design team led by Federico Correa and Alfonso Milà. The horse sculptures are copies of the originals by Pau Gargallo. Next to it is the most original and attractive of the Olympic facilities, Arata Isozaki's Palau Sant Jordi indoor arena, its undulating façade evoking Gaudi, and its high-tech interior featuring a transparent roof. Only 15 years after the Olympics, these two buildings are already falling into disrepair and underwent a ten-million euro renovation in 2007. In the

The dancing waters of the **Font Màgica de Montjuïc**. *See p120*.

hard, white *plaça* in front rises Santiago Calatrava's remarkable, Brancusi-inspired communications tower.

Across the square is the city's best swimming pool, the Piscines Bernat Picornell (*see p271*), while further down is the INEFC physical education institute, by architect Ricardo Bofill. Walk across the road and you look over a cliff on to a rugby pitch and an equestrian area, where children can take pony rides. The cliff itself is a favourite for rock-climbers.

The many parks and gardens include the **Jardins Mossèn Costa i Llobera**, which abounds in tropical plants, but particularly cacti, just below Miramar, on the steep flank nearest the port. Not far above are the Jardins del Mirador, from where there is a spectacular view over the harbour. These gardens are also the starting point for a new path for pedestrians and cyclists, running precariously below the castle and leading to a magical outdoor café, La Caseta del Migdia (*see p187*). One of the newest parks is the nearby Jardins de Joan Brossa, featuring humorous, hands-on contraptions where children can manipulate water courses and practise creative adventure sports. Walk down towards the funicular station and you will reach the enchanting Jardins Cinto Verdaguer, fresh from a €1.5-million makeover, with ponds filled with lotus flowers and water lilies. All these gardens play an adjunct role to the creative biospheres of the **Jardí Botànic**, just above the Olympic stadium, exquisitely designed and finally maturing into an important scientific collection.

Bus Montjuïc Turístic

Torres Venecianas, Plaça d'Espanya (93 415 60 20). Metro Espanya. **Open** *Mid Sept-June* 10am-9.20pm Sat, Sun. *July-mid Sept* 10am-9.20pm daily. **Tickets** *Day pass* €3; €2 reductions. **No credit cards.** **Map** p339 B9.

A new, open-top tourist bus. There are actually two routes: the blue line starts and ends at Plaça Espanya, the red one at Portal de la Pau, near the Monument a Colom; they coincide at the Olympic stadium and the castle. Tickets are valid for both routes.

CaixaForum

Casaramona, Avda Marquès de Comillas 6-8 (93 476 86 00/www.fundacio.lacaixa.es). Metro Espanya. **Open** 10am-8pm Tue-Fri, Sun; 10am-10pm Sat. **Admission** free. **Credit** (shop only) AmEx, DC, MC, V. **Map** p339 B9.

One of the masterpieces of industrial Modernisme, this red-brick former yarns and textiles factory was designed by Puig i Cadafalch in 1911. However, it spent most of the last century in a sorry state, acting briefly as a police barracks and then falling into dereliction. Fundació La Caixa, the charitable arm of Catalonia's largest savings bank, bought it and set about rebuilding it. The original brick structure was

supported, while the ground below was excavated to house a strikingly modern entrance plaza by Arata Isozaki, a Sol LeWitt mural, a 350-seat auditorium, bookshop and library. In addition to the smaller permanent contemporary art collection, upstairs there are three impressive spaces for temporary exhibitions – often among the most interesting shows to be found in the city. Exhibitions planned for 2008 include British photographer Hannah Collins (Apr-Aug) and a display of Chinese contemporary art (June-Sept). The Sala Montcada, the avant-garde art outpost that was formerly in the Born, has returned to its parental home, but it is still free to get in to.

Cementiri del Sud-Oest

C/Mare de Déu de Port 54-58 (93 484 17 00). Bus 38. **Open** 8am-6pm daily. **Admission** free.

Designed by Leandro Albareda in 1880, this enormous necropolis, perched at the side of the motorway out of town, serves as a daily reminder to commuters of their own mortality. It has housed the city's dead since 1883, originally placing them in four sections: one for Catholics, one for Protestants, one for non-Christians and a fourth for aborted foetuses. It now stretches over the entire south-west corner of the mountain, with family tombs stacked five or six storeys high. Many, especially those belonging to the gypsy community, are a riot of colour and flowers. The Fossar de la Pedrera memorial park remembers those fallen from the International Brigades and the Catalan martyrs from the Civil War. There is also a Holocaust memorial and a mausoleum to the former president of the Generalitat ,Lluís Companys. The cemetery is much visited, in

Fundació Joan Miró. *See p121.*

Walk on Garden art

Duration: 90 mins

From the gardens of the **Teatre Grec**, take the gateway to the right of the amphitheatre. From here, the **Escales del Generalife** lead up to the **Fundació Miró** (*see p121*). Named after the water gardens of Granada's Alhambra palace, this is a series of trickling fountains, flanked by stone steps, olive trees and benches for quiet contemplation. Instead of taking the steps, turn right into the **Jardins Laribal**, designed – like the Escales – by French landscape architect Jean-Claude Nicolas Forestier at the start of the 20th century. Ahead lie the **Colla de l'Arròs rose gardens**, at their best in late spring. From here a long pergola leads up to the **Font del Gat** (Fountain of the Cat), a clearing on the slope with a small restaurant (*see p163*)

designed by Josep Puig i Cadafalch, and the rather modest fountain itself.

With your back to the restaurant follow the path east towards the Miró and you'll arrive at a clearing, in the middle of which is Josep Viladomat's bronze *Noia de la Trena* (Girl with a Plait). Straight ahead is the stone *Repòs*, also by Viladomat, a scaled-up version of a Manolo Hugué figure, undertaken when Hugué was too ill to finish the commission.

Turn right on to the Avda Miramar, where, opposite the Miró museum you'll find a flight of steps which lead up and around to the **Tres Pins nursery**, where the plants are grown for the city's municipal parks and gardens. From here the Avda Miramar runs seaward, past the **Plaça Dante Alighieri**, where a bronze statue of the poet was presented by the city's

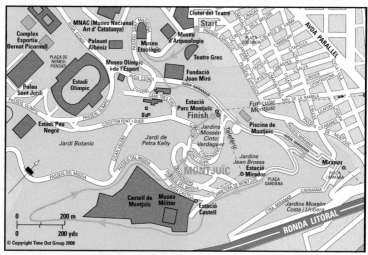

particular on All Saints' Day, when the roads are clogged solid with cars. In 2007, modernisation and expansion of the facilities started in order to provide more parking space, flower stalls, a new entrance and, eventually, a new home for the city collection of funeral carriages (*see p128*).

Font Màgica de Montjuïc

Plaça d'Espanya (93 316 10 00/www.bcn.cat/fonts).
Metro Espanya. **Shows** *Fountain* May-Sept 8-11.30pm Thur-Sun. *Music* every 30mins 9.30pm-midnight. Oct-Apr 7-9pm Fri, Sat; music every 30mins 7-9pm. **Map** p339 B9.

Still using its original art deco waterworks, the 'magic fountain' works its wonders with 3,600 pieces of tubing and more than 4,500 light bulbs. Summer evenings after nightfall see the multiple founts swell and dance to anything from soft rock to the *1812 Overture*, and, of course, Freddie Mercury and Montserrat Caballé's *Barcelona*, showing off its kaleidoscope of pastel colours, while searchlights play in a giant fan pattern over the palace dome. In July 2006, a new piece was inaugurated with the fountain choreographed to *El Moldava* by Czech composer Bedrich Smetana. *Photo p118.*

Italian residents to celebrate the 600th anniversary of the poet's death in 1921. In front of Dante, and in contrast to his stern salute, stands Josep Llimona's curvaceous and coquettish *Bellesa* (Beauty).

At the end of this road is the **Miramar area**, with its hotel (*see p61*), fronted by formal gardens, the station for the cable car over the port, and slightly south and below it, the **Costa i Llobera cactus gardens**. Backtracking slightly, a road leads behind the hotel up the hill towards the castle, passing the newly inaugurated **Joan Brossa gardens** en route. These were created on the site of the old fairground, and some of the stone statues from the time (such as *Charlie Chaplin*) are still in place. Just outside the gardens is the much-photographed *Sardana*, an uplifting representation of the Catalan national dance. Cross the road here to walk up via the fountains and ceramic mosaics of the recently spruced up **Mirador de l'Alcalde**. Beyond the Camí del Mar runs alongside the **castle** to the **Mirador del Migdia** (*see p187*), a wonderful outdoor café far from the madding crowds. (Note that during the winter months it only opens at weekends.)

Take the path around the landward side of the castle until you reach the moat on the right, then take a path down through the trees to the left. The road wiggles down to an underground entrance to the **Mossèn Cinto gardens**. These specialise in bulbous plants (daffodils, hyacinths and tulips) and various types of water lilies, with a series of terraced ponds running down the hillside to a small lake.

Exit from the lower side of the gardens and turn left to catch the funicular down the hill to Avda Paral·lel and the metro.

Fundació Joan Miró

Parc de Montjuïc (93 329 19 08/www.bcn.fjmiro.cat). Metro Paral·lel then Funicular de Montjuïc/61 bus. **Open** *July-Sept* 10am-8pm Tue, Wed, Fri, Sat; 10am-9.30pm Thur; 10am-2.30pm Sun. *Oct-June* 10am-7pm Tue, Wed, Fri, Sat; 10am-9.30pm Thur; 10am-2.30pm Sun. **Guided tours** 11.30pm Sat, Sun. **Admission** *All exhibitions* €7.50; €5 reductions. *Temporary exhibitions* €4; €3 reductions; free under-14s. **Credit** MC, V. **Map** p339 C11.
Josep Lluís Sert, who spent the years of the Franco dictatorship as dean of architecture at Harvard University, designed one of the greatest museum

buildings in the world on his return. Approachable, light and airy, these white walls and arches house a collection of more than 225 paintings, 150 sculptures and all of Miró's graphic work, plus some 5,000 drawings. The permanent collection, highlighting Miró's trademark use of primary colours and simplified organic forms symbolising stars, the moon, birds and women, occupies the second half of the space. On the way to the sculpture gallery is Alexander Calder's rebuilt Mercury Fountain, originally seen at the Spanish Republic's Pavilion at the 1937 Paris Fair. In other works, Miró is shown as a cubist (*Street in Pedralbes*, 1917), naïve (*Portrait of a Young Girl*, 1919) and surrealist (*Man and Woman in Front of a Pile of Excrement*, 1935). In the upper galleries, large, black-outlined paintings from Miró's final period precede a room of works with political themes.

Temporary shows have improved significantly, providing an often humorous contrast to Miro. February to May will see selections of Chinese contemporary art from the collection of Swiss diplomat Uli Sigg, and then from June to September the installations, incorporating natural elements, of Danish artist Olafur Eliason will feature. The Espai 13 in the basement features young contemporary artists. Outside is a pleasant sculpture garden with fine work by some contemporary Catalan artists. *Photo p119.*

Jardí Botànic

C/Doctor Font i Quer (93 426 49 35/www.jardi botanic.bcn.cat). Metro Espanya. **Open** *Apr-May, Sept* 10am-6pm Mon-Fri; 10am-8pm Sat, Sun. *June-Aug* 10am-8pm daily. *Oct-Mar* 10am-5pm Mon-Fri; 10am-8pm Sat, Sun. **Admission** €3; €1.50 reductions; free under-16s. Free last Sun of mth. **No credit cards**. **Map** p339 B11/12.
After the original 1930s botanical garden was disturbed by the construction for the Olympics, the only solution was to build an entirely new replacement. This opened in 1999, housing plants from seven global regions with a climate similar to that of the Western Mediterranean. Everything about the futuristic design, from the angular concrete pathways to the raw sheet steel banking (and even the design of the bins), is the complete antithesis of the more naturalistic gardens of England. It is meticulously kept, with all plants being tagged in Latin, Catalan, Spanish and English along with their date of planting, and has the added advantage of wonderful views across the city. There is a small space housing occasional temporary exhibitions and free audio guides to lead visitors through the gardens. Note that at the Natural History Museum (*see p99*) you can buy a combined entrance ticket for the museum and botanical garden.

Jardins Mossèn Costa i Llobera

Ctra de Miramar 1. Metro Drassanes or Paral·lel. **Open** 10am-sunset daily. **Admission** free. **Map** p339 D12.
The port side of Montjuïc is protected from the cold north wind, creating a microclimate two degrees centigrade warmer than the rest of the city, which

is perfect for 800 species of the world's cactus. It is said to be the most complete collection in Europe. Along with the botanic curiosities, there is a vast Josep Viladomat bronze of a young girl making lace.

MNAC (Museu Nacional d'Art de Catalunya)

Palau Nacional, Parc de Montjuïc (93 622 03 76/ www.mnac.cat). Metro Espanya. **Open** 10am-7pm Tue-Sat; 10am-2.30pm Sun. **Admission** (valid 2 days) *Permanent exhibitions* €8.50; €6 reductions. *Temporary exhibitions* €3-€5. *Combined ticket with Poble Espanyol* €12. Free over-65s, under-15s and 1st Sun of mth. **Credit** MC, V. **Map** p339 B10.

'One museum, a thousand years of art' is the slogan of the National Museum of Catalan Art, and the collection provides a dizzying overview of Catalan art from the 12th to the 20th centuries. Newly renovated, the museum now has a whole extra floor to absorb the holdings of the section of the Thyssen-Bornemisza collection that was previously kept in the convent in Pedralbes, along with the mainly Modernista holdings from the former Museum of Modern Art in Ciutadella park, a fine photography section, coins and the bequest of Francesc Cambó, founder of the autonomist Lliga Regionalista, a regionalist conservative party.

The highlight of the museum, however, is still the Romanesque collection. As art historians realised that scores of solitary tenth-century churches in the Pyrenees were falling into ruin – and with them were going extraordinary Romanesque mural paintings that had served to instruct villagers in the basics of the faith – the laborious task was begun of removing the murals from church apses. The display here features 21 mural sections in loose chronological order. A highlight is the tremendous *Crist de Taüll*, from the 12th-century church of Sant Climent de Taull. Even 'graffiti' scratchings (probably by monks) of animals, crosses and labyrinths have been preserved.

The Gothic collection is also excellent and starts with some late 13th-century frescoes that were discovered in 1961 and 1997, when two palaces in the city were being renovated. There are carvings and paintings from local churches, including works of the indisputable Catalan masters of the Golden Age, Bernat Martorell and Jaume Huguet. The highlight of the Thyssen collection is Fra Angelico's *Madonna of Humility* (c1430s), while the Cambó bequest contains some wonderful Old Masters – works by Titian, Rubens and El Greco among them. Also unmissable is the Modernista collection, which includes Ramon Casas' mural of himself and Pere Romeu on a tandem which decorated Els Quatre Gats (*see p149*). The rich collection of decorative arts includes original furniture from Modernista houses such as the Casa Amatller and Gaudí's Casa Batlló.

Temporary shows in 2008 include one curated by Tate Modern (mid May-Sept) featuring work by Man Ray and Marcel Duchamp among others, and (May-Jan 2009) Catalan sculptor Juli González .

Art ancient and modern at **MNAC (Museu Nacional d'Art de Catalunya).**

Museu d'Arqueologia de Catalunya

Passeig de Santa Madrona 39-41 (93 423 21 49/56 01/www.mac.cat). Metro Poble Sec. **Open** 9.30am-7pm Tue-Sat; 10am-2.30pm Sun. **Admission** €3; €2.10 reductions; free under-16s. **Credit** (shop only) MC, V. **Map** p339 C10.

The time frame for this archaeology collection starts with the Palaeolithic period, and there are relics of Greek, Punic, Roman and Visigothic colonisers, up to the early Middle Ages. A massive Roman sarcophagus is carved with scenes of the rape of Persephone, and an immense statue of Aesculapius, the god of medicine, towers over one room. A few galleries are dedicated to the Mallorcan Talayotic cave culture, and there is a very good display on the Iberians, the pre-Hellenic, pre-Roman inhabitants of south-eastern Spain. An Iberian skull with a nail driven through it effectively demonstrates a typical method of execution from that time. The display ends with the marvellous, jewel-studded headpiece of a Visigoth king. One of the best-loved pieces, inevitably, is an alarmingly erect Priapus, found during building work in Sants in 1848 and kept under wraps 'for moral reasons' until 1986.

Museu Etnològic

Passeig de Santa Madrona s/n (93 424 68 07/ www.museuetnologic.bcn.cat). Metro Poble Sec. **Open** Late June-late Sept noon-8pm Tue-Sat; 11am-3pm Sun. *Late Sept-late June* 10am-7pm Tue, Thur; 10am-2pm Wed, Fri-Sun. **Admission** €3; €1.50 reductions; free under-16s, over-65s. Free 1st Sun of mth. **No credit cards**. Map p339 B10.

Recently spruced up and expanded, the ethnology museum houses a vast collection of items, from Australian Aboriginal boomerangs to rugs and jewellery from Afghanistan, although by far the most comprehensive collections are from Catalonia. Of the displays upstairs, most outstanding are the Moroccan, Japanese and Philippine exhibits, though there are also some interesting pre-Columbian finds. Of the several attempts to arrange the pieces in thematically more interesting ways, 'Taboo' transpires to be a rather limp look at nudity in different cultures. However 'Sacred', a run through the world of religious rituals, is more successful.

Museu Militar

Castell de Montjuïc, Ctra de Montjuïc 66 (93 329 86 13/www.museomilitarmontjuic.es). Metro Paral·lel then funicular & cable car. **Open** Apr-Oct 9.30am-8pm Tue-Sun. *Nov-Mar* 9.30am-5pm Tue-Fri; 9.30am-8pm Sat, Sun. **Admission** €3; €1.50 reductions; free under-7s. **No credit cards**. Map p339 C12.

Appropriately housed in one wing of the old hilltop fortress, the Military Museum is a grim slice of local history. The fortress was used to bombard rather than protect Barcelona in past conflicts, and as a prison and place of execution, the castle has strong repressive associations. The exhibits here include armour, swords, lances, muskets (beautiful Moroccan *moukhala*), rifles and pistols. Other highlights include 23,000 lead soldiers representing a

Spanish division of the 1920s. Oddly, a display of Jewish tombstones from the mountain's desecrated medieval cemetery is the only direct reminder of death within its thick walls. The Spanish government finally ceded the castle to the city of Barcelona in May 2007 and there are plans to turn part of the building into a centre for peace studies.

Museu Olímpic i de l'Esport

Avda Estadi 60 (93 292 53 79). Bus 50, 55, 61. **Open** Apr-Sept 10am-6pm Mon, Wed-Sun. *Oct-Mar* 10am-1pm, 4-6pm Mon, Wed-Sun. **Admission** €8; €6 reductions; free under-5s. **Credit** AmEx, MC, V. **Map** p339 B11.

Opened in 2007 in a new building across from the stadium, the Olympic and Sports Museum gives an overview of the Games (and indeed all games) from Ancient Greece onwards. As well as photos and videos of great sporting moments and heroes, there are objects such as Ronaldinho's boots or Mika Häkkinen's Mercedes, along with a collection of opening ceremony costumes and Olympic torches. Perhaps more entertaining are the interactive displays, such as one that compares your effort at the long jump with that of the pros.

Pavelló Mies van der Rohe

Avda Marquès de Comillas (93 423 40 16/www. miesbcn.com). Metro Espanya. **Open** 10am-8pm daily. **Admission** €3.50; €2 reductions; free under-18s. **Credit** (shop only) MC, V. **Map** p339 B9.

Mies van der Rohe built the Pavelló Alemany (German Pavilion) for the 1929 Universal Exhibition not as a gallery, but as a simple reception space, sparsely furnished by his trademark 'Barcelona Chair'. The pavilion was a founding monument of modern rationalist architecture, with its flowing floor plan and a revolutionary use of materials. Though the original pavilion was demolished after the exhibition, a fine replica was built on the same site in 1986, the simplicity of its design setting off the warm tones of the marble and expressive Georg Kolbe sculpture in the pond.

Poble Espanyol

Avda Marquès de Comillas (93 325 78 66/www. poble-espanyol.com). Metro Espanya. **Open** Village & restaurants 9am-8pm Mon; 9am-2am Tue-Thur; 9am-4am Fri; 9am-5am Sat; 9am-midnight Sun. *Shops* Dec-May 10am-6pm daily. June-Aug 10am-8pm daily. Sept-Nov 10am-7pm daily. **Admission** €7.50; €4-€5.50 reductions; €15 family ticket; free under-7s. *Combined ticket with MNAC* €12. **Credit** AmEx, MC, V. **Map** p339 A9/B9.

Built for the 1929 Universal Exhibition, this mock Spanish Village is a minimally cheesy architectural theme park with reproductions of traditional buildings from every region in Spain. The cylindrical towers at the entrance are copied from the walled city of Ávila and lead on to a typical Castilian main square from which visitors can explore a tiny white-washed street from Arcos de la Frontera in Andalucia, then on to the 16th-century House of Chains from Toledo, and so on. There are numerous

Sightseeing

bars and restaurants, a flamenco *tablao* and more than 60 shops selling Spanish crafts although prices are not especially cheap. Outside, street performers recreate bits of Catalan and Spanish folklore; there are children's shows and 'The Barcelona Experience', an audio-visual presentation (available in English). The Poble is aimed at tourists, but it is attempting to raise its cultural profile by hosting music festivals such as B-estival (*see p222*) and opening a gallery of Iberian arts and crafts.

Telefèric de Montjuïc
Estació Funicular, Avda Miramar (93 441 48 20/ www.tmb.net). Metro Paral·lel then funicular. **Open** *June-Sept* 10.30am-8.15pm daily. *Sept-Oct* 10.30am-7.15pm daily. *Oct-June* 10am-6pm daily. **Admission** €9 one way; €12.50 return; free under-7s. **No credit cards. Map** p339 C11/D11.
The rebuilt cable-car system, with brand new, eight-person cable-cars that have disabled access, has reopened after two years of work. The prices have also been brought up to date, which may put many off, despite the fantastic views over the city.

Poble Sec & Paral·lel

Poble Sec, the name of the neighbourhood between Montjuïc and the Avda Paral·lel, actually means 'dry village', which is explained by the fact that it was 1894 before the thousands of poor workers who lived on the flanks of the hill celebrated the installation of

Poble Espanyol. *See p123*.

the area's very first water fountain (which is still standing today in C/Margarit).

Continuing on the entomological theme, the name Avda Paral·lel derives from the fact that it coincides exactly with 41° 44' latitude north, one of Ildefons Cerdà's more eccentric conceits. The avenue was the prime centre of Barcelona nightlife in the first half of the 20th century, and was full of theatres, nightclubs and music halls. A statue on the corner with C/Nou de la Rambla commemorates Raquel Meller, a legendary star of the street who went on to equal celebrity around the world. She now stands outside Barcelona's notorious live-porn venue, the Bagdad. Apart from this, most of the area's cabarets have long since disappeared, although there are still some theatres and cinemas along the Paral·lel (*see p266* **Windmill of the grind**).

These days, Poble Sec is a friendly, working-class area of quiet, relaxed streets and leafy squares. On the stretch of the Paral·lel opposite the city walls, three tall chimneys stand amid modern office blocks. They are all that remains of the Anglo-Canadian-owned power station known locally as La Canadença ('The Canadian'). This was the centre of the city's largest general strike, in 1919. Beside the chimneys an open space has been created and dubbed the Parc de les Tres Xemeneies (Park of the Three Chimneys).

Towards the Paral·lel are some distinguished Modernista buildings, which local legend maintains were built for *artistas* from the nude cabarets by their rich sugar daddies. At C/Tapioles 12 is a beautiful, narrow wooden Modernista door with particularly lovely writhing ironwork, while at C/Elkano 4 is La Casa de les Rajoles, which is known for its peculiar mosaic façade.

Refugi 307
C/Nou de la Rambla 169 (93 256 21 22). Metro Paral·lel. **Open** (guided tour & by appointment only) 11am, noon (Catalan), 1pm (Spanish) Sat, Sun. **Call to book** 10am-2pm, 4-6pm Mon-Thur; 10am-2pm Fri. **Admission** €3; free under-7s. **Meeting place** Biblioteca Francesc Boix, C/Blai 34. **No credit cards. Map** p339 D11.
C/Nou de la Rambla 169 (93 256 21 22/www. museuhistoria.bcn.es). Metro Paral·lel. **Open** 11am-2pm Sat, Sun. **Admission** €3; free under-7s. **No credit cards. Map** p339 D11.
About 1,500 Barcelona civilians were killed during the air bombings of the Civil War, a fact that the government long silenced. As Poble Sec particularly suffered the effects of bombing, a large air-raid shelter was built partially into the mountain at the top of C/Nou de la Rambla; this is one of some 1,200 in the entire city. Now converted into a museum, it is worth a visit. The tour takes about 90mins.

The Eixample

Elegant boutiques and exemplary urban planning.

Maps pp340-341

You would be hard put to find a more striking contrast to the narrow streets and serpentine alleys of the Old City than the geometrical regularity and broad boulevards of the Eixample. It should come as no surprise that Barcelona's 'enlargement' was built in the late 19th century, when belief in progress was at its height. Today, when belief seems to reside more in the therapeutic powers of shopping than the inevitable march of progress, the Eixample is home to some of Barcelona's most elegant boutiques and richest residents, as well as many unique buildings. So far as navigation is concerned, the grid system is bisected by the bisecting avenue of Passeig de Gràcia, which makes for a useful reference point when exploring the district. Incorporating some of the city's classiest boutiques, it's the showpiece of the **Quadrat D'Or** (Golden District) – a square mile between C/Muntaner and C/Roger de Flor that contains 150 protected buildings, many of them Modernista gems.

The Eixample was Europe's first expansive work of urban planning, necessitated by the chronic overcrowding of old Barcelona which, by the 1850s, had become rife with cholera and crime, hemmed in by its much-hated city walls. It was eventually decided the walls must come down, whereupon the Ajuntament held a competition to build an ambitious urban zone in the open land outside the city's ramparts. The competition was won by municipal architect Antoni Rovira i Trias, whose popular fan-shaped design can be seen at the foot of the statue of him in the Gràcia plaça that bears his name. The Madrid government, however, vetoed the plan, instead choosing the work of social idealist Ildefons Cerdà, a military engineer.

Cerdà's plan, reflecting the rationalist mindset of the era, was for a grid of uniform blocks to stretch from Montjuïc to the Besòs river, criss-crossed by two diagonal highways (Avda Diagonal and Avda de la Meridiana) meeting at Plaça de les Glòries, which was to become the hub of the modernised city. The ideas were utopian: each block was to be built on only two sides and be no more than two or three storeys high; the remainder of the space was to contain gardens, their leafy extremes joining at the crossroads and forming a quarter of a bigger park. Of course, when it came to the practical business of filling the grid (which never became as extensive as planned), many of the engineer's plans were ignored by developers. A concrete orchard of gardenless, fortress-like, six or seven-storey blocks grew up instead.

Fortunately, the period of construction coincided with Barcelona's golden age of architecture: the city's bourgeoisie employed Gaudí, Puig i Cadafalch, Domènech i Montaner and the like to build them ever more daring townhouses in an orgy of avant-garde one-upmanship. The result is extraordinary but can be tricky to negotiate on foot; the lack of open spaces and similarity of many streets can leave you somewhat confused. The city council, meanwhile, is attempting to make the area more liveable: in 1985 the ProEixample was set up to reclaim some of the courtyards proposed in Cerdà's plans so that everybody living in the area should be able to find an open space within 200 metres (650 feet) of their home. Two of the better examples are the palm-fringed mini-beach around the Torre de les Aigües water tower (C/Llúria 56; *see p231*) and the patio at Passatge Permanyer (C/Pau Claris 120).

The overland railway that ran down C/Balmes was the dividing line of the neighbourhood. Either side of this, the fashionable **Dreta** ('Right') contains the most distinguished Modernista architecture, the main museums and the shopping avenues. The **Esquerra** ('Left') was built slightly later; it contains some less well-known Modernista sights.

The Dreta

Trees, ceramic benches and idle ramblers make the **Passeig de Gràcia** appear like a calmer Champs-Elysées; this is one of the most pleasant walks in the city. From Plaça Catalunya, you can stroll all the way up the grand street, which, at the point it meets Diagonal, joins straight on to Gran de Gràcia which leads you straight through the heart of Gràcia. The Eixample's central artery is notable for its magnificent wrought-iron lamp-posts by Pere Falqués and for its pavement, hexagonal slabs decorated with intertwining nautilus shells and starfish. First designed for the patio of Gaudí's **Casa Batlló**, they were repeated in his aquatic-looking apartment block **La Pedrera** before covering the whole boulevard.

The Passeig de Gràcia has always been the Eixample's most desirable address, and it's where you'll find Modernisme's most flamboyant townhouses. For a primer, head to the block known as **Manzana de Discòrdia**, which has buildings designed by the era's three great architects. Its name is a pun on *manzana*, which in Spanish means both 'block' and 'apple', and alludes to the fatal choice of Paris when judging which of a group of divine beauties would win the golden Apple of Discord.

If the volume of camera-toting admirers is anything to go by, the fairest of these Modernista lovelies is undoubtedly Gaudí's Casa Batlló, permanently illuminated by flashbulbs. The runners-up are Domènech i Montaner's **Casa Lleó Morera** (*photo p128*), a decadently melting wedding cake of a building (partially defaced during the architecturally delinquent Franco era) on the corner of C/Consell de Cent at no.35, and Puig i Cadafalch's **Casa Amatller** (no.41; *photos p129*). Built for a chocolate baron,

the latter has a stepped Flemish pediment covered in shiny ceramics and looking good enough to eat, along with a gallery of medieval grotesques sculpted by Eusebi Arnau.

Other buildings on the Passeig de Gràcia hit parade also impress. There's the newly opened gallery of the **Fundació Suñol**, while the Casa Casas (no.96) was once home to Ramon Casas, one of the city's greatest painters, and now houses design emporium Vinçon. The first floor of the building has a Modernista interior; there's also a patio overlooking La Pedrera's rear façade. In addition, Enric Sagnier's neo-Gothic Cases Pons i Pascual (nos.2-4) is worth a look, while the Casa Vidua Marfà (no.66) has one of the most breathtakingly sumptuous entrance halls in the Eixample.

The other great building of the Modernisme movement is the towering mass of the **Família**. Whether you love it or hate it (George Orwell called it 'one of the most hideous buildings in the world'), it has become the city's emblem and sine qua non of Barcelona tourist itineraries. A less famous masterpiece in the shape of Domènech i Montaner's **Hospital de la Santa Creu i Sant Pau** bookends the northerly extreme of the Avda Gaudí. A few blocks south, there's more welcome space in the **Parc de l'Estació del Nord** and, on C/Marina, one of Barcelona's weirdest museums, the macabre **Museu de Carrosses Fúnebres**.

The streets above the Diagonal boast some striking Modernista buildings, such as Puig i Cadafalch's 1901 Palau Macaya at Passeig de Sant Joan 108. Other buildings of interest

La Pedrera (Casa Milà).
See p130.

include the tiled Mercat de la Concepció on C/Aragó, designed by Rovira i Trias, and the fairy-tale castle-esque Casa de les Punxes designed yet again by the prolific Joan Puig i Cadafalch. Moving down C/Roger de Llúria, you pass the Casa Thomas and the Palau Montaner, both designed by Lluís Domenech i Montaner, and on reaching C/Casp, you arrive at one of Gaudí's lesser-known works, the Casa Calvet. Over to the right is the egg-topped Plaça de Braus Monumental, but the city's last active bullring is now mainly frequented by tour buses from the Costa Brava; out of season, it hosts tatty travelling circuses. Not far from the bullring, at C/Lepant 150, are the ultra-modern premises of L'Auditori de Barcelona, where all major classical concerts are held (*see p262*). Back towards the bullring and just off the main drag is what is considered to be Modernisme's first ever building, designed by Domènech i Montaner, now housing the **Fundació Antoni Tàpies**. The area is rich in museums: over the other side is the **Museu Egipci de Barcelona**, next door to the varied collection in the **Fundació Francisco Godia**.

Casa Àsia

Avda Diagonal 373 (93 238 73 37/www.casaasia. org). Metro Diagonal. **Open** 10am-8pm Mon-Sat; 10am-2pm Sun. **Admission** free. **Map** p340 G6.
This much-needed Asian contribution to Barcelona's cultural scene is located in another of architect Puig i Cadafalch's creations, the Palau Baró de Quadras. The Casa Àsia cultural centre acts as both an exhibition space and ambassador for all things in Asia and the Asian Pacific. Recent exhibits include modern Chinese architecture and a homage to the relationship between pioneer video artist Nam June Paik (who died in 2006) and his country of birth, South Korea. It also features an oriental café on the ground floor and an excellent multimedia library on the fourth floor that offers visitors the opportunity to hire CDs, DVDs and books on presentation of their passport or ID card. In mid September, the centre runs Festival Asia (www.festivalasia.es), bringing Asian theatre, music, dance and food to Barcelona.

Casa Batlló

Passeig de Gràcia 43 (93 216 03 06/www.casa batllo.cat). Metro Passeig de Gràcia. **Open** 9am-8pm daily. **Admission** €16.50; €13.20 reductions; free under-7s. **Credit** V. **Map** p340 G8.
For many the Casa Batlló, sitting in the same block as masterworks by his two closest rivals, Domènech i Montaner and Puig i Cadafalch, is the most telling example of Gaudí's pre-eminence over his Modernista contemporaries. Opinions differ on what the building's remarkable façade represents, particularly its polychrome shimmering walls, its sinister skeletal balconies and its humpbacked scaly roof. Some say it's the spirit of carnival, others a Costa Brava cove. However, the most popular theory, which takes into

account the architect's deeply patriotic feelings, is that it depicts Sant Jordi and the dragon: the idea being that the cross on top is the knight's lance, the roof is the back of the beast, and the balconies below are the skulls and bones of its hapless victims.
The building was constructed for textile tycoon Josep Batlló between 1902 and 1906, and the chance to explore the interior (at a cost) offers the best opportunity of understanding how Gaudí, sometimes considered the lord of the bombastic and overblown, was really the master of tiny details, from the ingenious ventilation in the doors to the amazing natural light reflecting off the azure walls of the inner courtyard and the way the brass window handles are curved so as to fit precisely the shape of a hand. An apartment within is open to the public and access has been granted to the attic and roof terrace: the whitewashed arched rooms of the top floor, originally used for washing and hanging clothes, are among the master's most atmospheric spaces.

Fundació Antoni Tàpies

C/Aragó 255 (93 487 03 15/www.fundacio tapies.org). Metro Passeig de Gràcia. **Open** 10am-8pm Tue-Sun. **Admission** €6; €4 reductions; free under-16s. **Credit** (over €6) MC, V. **Map** p340 G8.
Antoni Tàpies, Barcelona's most celebrated living artist, set up the Tàpies Foundation in this, the former Montaner i Simon publishing house, in 1984, dedicating it to the study and appreciation of contemporary art. It is now a cultural centre and museum dedicated to the work and life of the man himself, with exhibitions, symposiums, lectures and films. Tàpies promptly crowned the building with a glorious tangle of aluminium piping and ragged metal netting (*Núvol i Cadira*, or Cloud and Chair), which

Plaça Catalunya.

Casa Lleó Morera.
See p126.

Fundació Suñol

*Passeig de Gràcia 98 (93 496 10 32/www.
fundaciosunol.org). Metro Diagonal.* **Open** 4-8pm
Mon-Wed, Fri, Sat. **Admission** €4; €2 reductions.
No credit cards. **Map** p340 G7.

Opened in May 2007, the foundation's two floors
house the contemporary art collection of businessman
Josep Suñol. There are 100 pieces, including painting,
sculpture and photography, on show at a time, shuf-
fled every six months (Jan and July) from an archive
of 1,200 artworks amassed over a 35-year period. The
collection includes historic artists of the avant-garde,
predominantly Catalan and Spanish: Picasso, Miró,
Gargallo, with international input from Giacometti,
Man Ray and Andy Warhol. With superfluities
removed, including labels, and chronology abandoned, works are arranged in careful, coherent
compositions, by style, colour or even mood, in
serene interlinking rooms of varying sizes. Helpful
English-speaking staff and a pamphlet aid visitors
and an additional information booklet costs €2.
Zero Nivell offers a large exhibition space to younger
avant-garde artists, with shorter-term poetry cycles,
installations and multimedia projects on the agenda.

Hospital de la Santa Creu i Sant Pau

*C/Sant Antoni Maria Claret 167 (93 291 90 00/
www.santpau.cat). Metro Hospital de Sant Pau.*
Map p341 L5/L6.

White-coated doctors mingle with recovering patients
and camera-wielding tourists in the green and pleasant grounds of Domènech i Montaner's 'garden city'
of a hospital, a collection of pavilions abundantly
adorned with the medieval flourishes that charac-
terise the architect's style. The hospital, now a
UNESCO World Heritage Site, comprises 18 pavilions connected by a tunnel system spreading over
nine blocks in the north-east corner of the Eixample.
It is set at a 45º angle from the rest of Ildefons
Cerdà's grid system, so that it catches more sun:
Domènech i Montaner built the hospital very much
with its patients in mind, convinced that aesthetic
harmony and pleasant surroundings were good for
the health. Unfortunately, the old buildings don't
suit the exigencies of modern medicine and patients
have been moved to the Nou Sant Pau (a recently
inaugurated white monstrosity on the north side of
the hospital grounds), leaving the old complex to be
used mainly for educational and research purposes.

The public enjoy free access to the grounds, and
guided tours (€5; €2.50 reductions) are held daily
between 10.15am and 1.15pm. Call 93 256 25 04 or
consult www.rutadelmodernisme.com to check
which languages are offered at which times.

Museu de Carrosses Fúnebres

C/Sancho de Avila 2 (93 484 17 10). Metro Marina.
Open 10am-1pm, 4-6pm Mon-Fri; 10am-1pm Sat,
Sun (wknds call to check). **Admission** free.
Map p343 K10.

Finding this, surely the most obscure and macabre
museum in Barcelona, hasn't got any easier. You'll
need to ask at the reception desk of the Ajuntament's

---

was a typically contentious act by an artist whose
work, a selection of which is on permanent display on
the top floor of the gallery, has caused controversy
since he burst on the scene in the 1960s. 'Give the
organic its rights,' he stated, and thus devoted his
time to making the seemingly insignificant significant, using materials such as mud, string, rags and
cardboard to build his rarely pretty but always striking works. The building remains one of the earliest
examples of Modernisme to combine exposed brick
and iron. Temporary exhibitions tend to be political
and, for the non-activist, rather dull. If you visit before
Easter 2008, check it's reopened after works.

Fundació Francisco Godia

*C/València 284 pral (93 272 31 80/www.
fundacionfgodia.org). Metro Passeig de Gràcia.*
Open 10am-8pm Mon, Wed-Sun. Closed Aug.
Admission €4.50; €2.10 reductions; free under-5s.
Credit (shop only) MC, V. **Map** p340 G7.

Godia's first love was motor racing: he was a Formula
1 driver for Maserati in the 1950s. His second love,
though, was art, which explains how this private
museum has come to house an interesting selection
of medieval religious art, historic Spanish ceramics
and modern painting. Exhibits date from the 12th century and are largely medieval sculptures and paintings. Highlights include Alejo de Vahía's medieval
Pietà and a Baroque masterpiece by Lucio Giordano,
along with some outstanding Romanesque sculptures
and 19th-century oil paintings by Joaquín Sorolla and
Ramon Casas. The modern collection has works by
Miró, Julio González, Tàpies and Manolo Hugué.

Casa Amatller. *See p126.*

funeral service and, eventually, a security guard will take you down to a perfectly silent and splendidly shuddersome basement housing the world's biggest collection of funeral carriages and hearses dating from the 18th century through to the 1950s. There are ornate Baroque carriages and more functional Berlins and Landaus, and a wonderful '50s silver Buick. The white carriages were designed for children and virgins; there's a windowless black-velour mourning carriage for the forlorn mistress. The vehicles are manned by ghoulish dummies dressed in period gear whose eyes follow you around the room, making you glad of that security guard. The museum is supposed to be moving to the cemetery on Montjuïc some day, although progress is, naturally, funereal.

Museu Egipci de Barcelona

C/València 284 (93 488 01 88/www.fundclos.com). Metro Passeig de Gràcia. **Open** 10am-8pm Mon-Sat; 10am-2pm Sun. **Admission** €7; €5 reductions; free under-5s. **Credit** Visa V. **Map** p340 G7.

Two floors of this museum showcase a well-chosen collection spanning 3,000 years of Nile-drenched culture. Exhibits include religious statuary, such as the massive baboon heads used to decorate temples, everyday copper mirrors or alabaster headrests, and oddly moving infant sarcophagi. Outstanding pieces include some painstakingly matched fragments from the Sixth Dynasty Tomb of Iny, a bronze statuette of the goddess Isis breastfeeding her son Horus, and mummified cats, baby crocodiles and falcons. Another highlight is a 5,000-year-old bed, which still looks comfortable enough to sleep in.

On Friday and Saturday nights, there are dramatic reconstructions of popular themes, such as the mummification ritual or the life of Cleopatra, for which reservations are essential. The museum is owned by renowned Egyptologist Jordi Clos, and the entrance fee is waived for guests staying at the Hotel Claris, which is also owned by Clos. If you go on Fridays at 5pm, there are free guided tours of the museum by English-speaking guides.

Museu del Perfum

Passeig de Gràcia 39 (93 216 01 21/www. museodelperfume.com). Metro Passeig de Gràcia. **Open** 10.30am-7.30 Mon-Fri; 10.30am-1.30 Sat. **Admission** €5; €3 reductions. **Map** p340 G8.

In the back room of the Regia perfumery sits this collection of nearly 5,000 scent bottles, cosmetic flasks and related objects. The collection is divided into two parts. One shows all manner of unguent vases and essence jars in chronological order, from a tube of black eye make-up from pre-dynastic Egypt to Edwardian atomisers and a prized double-flask pouch that belonged to Marie Antoinette. The second section exhibits perfumery brands such as Guerlain and Dior; some are in rare bottles, among them a garish Dalí creation for Schiaparelli and a set of rather disturbing golliwog flasks by Vigny Paris. The museum's most recent addition includes a collection of 19th-century perfume powder bottles and boxes.

Parc de l'Estació del Nord

C/Nàpols (no phone). Metro Arc de Triomf. **Open** 10am-sunset daily. **Admission** free. **Map** p343 J10/K10.

Otherwise known as Parc Sol i Ombra (meaning 'Sun and Shadow'), this slightly shabby space is perked up by the three pieces of art in glazed blue ceramic by New York sculptor Beverley Pepper. Along with a pair of incongruous white stone entrance walls, *Espiral Arbrat* (Tree Spiral) is a spiral bench set under the cool shade of lime-flower trees and *Cel Caigut* (Fallen Sky) is a 7m-high (23ft) ridge rising from the grass, while the tiles recall Gaudí's *trencadís* smashed-tile technique.

La Pedrera (Casa Milà)

Passeig de Gràcia 92-C/Provença 261-265 (93 484 59 00/www.caixacatalunya.cat/obrasocial). Metro Diagonal. **Open** 9am-8pm daily. **Admission** €8; €4.50 reductions; free under-12s. Guided tours (in English) 4pm Mon-Fri. **Credit** MC, V. **Map** p340 G7.
The last secular building designed by Antoni Gaudí, the Casa Milà (popularly known as La Pedrera, 'the stone quarry') has no straight lines and is a stupendous and daring feat of architecture, the culmination of the architect's experimental attempts to recreate natural forms with bricks and mortar (not to mention ceramics and even smashed-up cava bottles). Now a UNESCO World Heritage Site, it looks like it

might have been washed up on the shore, its marine feel complemented by Jujol's tangled balconies, doors of twisted kelp ribbon, sea-foamy ceilings and interior patios as blue as a mermaid's cave. When it was completed in 1912, it was so far ahead of its time that the woman who financed it as her dream home, Roser Segimon, became the laughing stock of the city – hence the ugly 'stone quarry' tag. Its rippling façade, bereft of straight lines, led local painter Santiago Rusiñol to quip that a snake would be a better pet than a dog for the inhabitants of the building. But La Pedrera has become one of Barcelona's best-loved buildings, and is adored by architects for its extraordinary structure: it is supported entirely by pillars, without a single master wall, allowing the vast asymmetrical windows of the façade to invite in great swathes of natural light.

There are three exhibition spaces. The first-floor art gallery hosts free shows of eminent artists, while upstairs is dedicated to a finer appreciation of Gaudí: you can visit a reconstructed Modernista flat on the fourth floor, with a sumptuous bedroom suite by Gaspar Homar, while the attic, framed by parabolic arches worthy of a Gothic cathedral, holds a museum offering an insightful overview of Gaudí's career.

Walk on Modernisme

Duration: 1 hour 30 minutes.
The tour begins with the splendid **Casa Comalat** by Valeri i Pupurull, which has the unusual distinction of two façades. The front (Avda Diagonal 442) has 12 voluptuously curvy stone balconies complete with ornate wrought-iron railings, while the more radical back façade (C/Còrsega 316) is a colourful harlequin effect with curiously bulging green-shuttered balconies. Almost opposite on Avda Diagonal is Puig i Cadafalch's sombre **Palau Baró de Quadras**, now home to the **Casa Àsia** exhibition space (*see p127*), and his **Casa Terrades** (nos.416-20), known colloquially as La Casa de les Punxes ('House of Spikes') for its spiky turrets and gables. Look out for the individual entrances and staircases built for each of the family's three daughters.

Turn down C/Girona and right on C/Mallorca to see Barenys i Gambús's fantasy **Casa Dolors Xiró** at no.302, followed by two Domènech i Montaner masterpieces: the **Casa Josep Thomas** (no.291) and the **Palau Ramón de Montaner** (no.278), which now houses offices. Double back a few steps and turn downhill on to C/Roger de Llúria. On the corner at no.80 is Fossas i Martinez's spike-topped **Casa Villanueva** and, just opposite at no.82, striking columns of stained-glass

windows decorate Granell i Manresa's **Casa Jaume Fern**. Just a few steps further down C/Roger de Llúria at no.85, the **Queviures Murrià** grocery retains original decoration by painter Ramon Casas and, on the right at no.74, is the lovely stained glass and floral decoration of the **Farmàcia Argelaguet**, one of many Modernista pharmacies in the area.

Retrace your steps up to the corner again, and turn right on to C/València. Continue for three blocks, and at no.339 is a stunning corner building by Gallissà i Soqué: the **Casa Manuel Llopis i Bofill**. The façade is a blend of red brick and white sgraffito by Josep Maria Jujol, while the neo-Mudéjar turrets, ceramics and keyhole shapes take their inspiration from the Alhambra in Granada.

Backtrack a block and turn left on C/Girona. At no.86 is the **Casa Isabel Pomar**, Rubió i Bellver's eccentric sliver of a building that squeezes in a neo-Gothic pinnacle, lively red brickwork and a staggered gallery window on the first floor. This contrasts with the spacious feel of Viñolas i Llosas's **Casa Jacinta Ruiz** (no.54). Glass galleries are a characteristic feature of Modernista houses, but here the jutting windows form the pivot for the design and give a three-dimensional effect. Further down, turn right on Gran Via, to another

Informative titbit-filled guided tours in English are run daily at 4pm. Best of all is the chance to stroll on the roof of the building amid its *trencadís*-covered ventilation shafts: their heads are shaped like the helmets of medieval knights, which led the poet Pere Gimferrer to dub the spot 'the garden of warriors'. *Photo p126*.

Sagrada Família

C/Mallorca 401 (93 207 30 31/www.sagradafamilia. org). Metro Sagrada Família. **Open** *Mar-Sept* 9am-8pm daily. *Oct-Feb* 9am-6pm daily. **Admission** €8; €5 reductions; €3 8-10 years; free under-8s. *Lift to spires* €2. **Credit** (shop only) MC, V. **Map** p341 K7.

The Temple Expiatori de la Sagrada Família manages to be both Europe's most fascinating building site and Barcelona's most emblematic creation. At times breathtaking, at times grotesque, it deserves the hubbub of superlatives that float around it, though not all are positive. George Orwell berated the 1930s anarchists for 'showing bad taste by not blowing it up'. They did, however, manage to set fire to Gaudí's intricate plans and models for the building, which was his final project before his death. Ongoing work is a matter of some conjecture and controversy, with the finishing date expected to be somewhere within the region of 25-30 years. It was hoped the masterpiece would be completed in 2026 to coincide with the 100th anniversary of Gaudí's death, although this now seems unlikely. This is, however, somewhat of an improvement on the prognosis in the 1900s, when construction was expected to last several hundred years; advanced computer technology is now being used to shape each intricately designed block of stone offsite to speed up the process. Nevertheless, the church's first mass has been put back a year and is now scheduled for Sant Josep's day (19 March) 2008, 126 years after its foundation stone was laid.

Gaudí, who is said to have once joked 'My client is not in a hurry', is buried beneath the nave; he dedicated more than 40 years to the project, the last 14 exclusively. Many consider the crypt, the apse and the Nativity façade, which were completed in his lifetime, as the most beautiful elements of the church. The last of these, facing C/Marina, looks at first glance as though some careless giant has poured candlewax over a Gothic cathedral, but closer inspection shows every protuberance to be an intricate sculpture of flora, fauna or human figure, combining to form an astonishingly moving stone tapestry

extravagant Modernista pharmacy, **Farmàcia Vilardell** (no.650), and Salvat i Espasa's elegant **Casa Ramon Oller** (no.658).

From there, turn left down C/Pau Claris and left again on to C/Casp. At no.22, **Casa Llorenç Camprubí**, Ruiz i Casamitjana's intricate stonework is a delight, but the real treasure lies a little further along at no.48. Gaudí's **Casa Calvet** may seem conventional, but closer study reveals characteristic touches: the columns framing the door and gallery allude to the bobbins used in the owner's textile factory, the wrought iron depicts a mass of funghi surrounded by stone flowers. The corbel underneath the gallery interweaves the Catalan coat of arms with Calvet's initial 'C'.

Turn right down C/Girona on to C/Ausiàs Marc, one of the most notable streets of the Quadrat d'Or. At nos.37-39 are the **Cases Tomàs Roger** by prominent Modernista architect Enric Sagnier, combining graceful arches with beautifully restored sgraffito. At no.31 is the **Farmàcia Nordbeck**, with a dark wood and stained-glass exterior. The last stop before reaching Plaça Urquinaona is the **Casa Manuel Felip** (no.20), designed by a little-known architect, Fernández i Janot, with sumptuous stonework and slender galleries connecting the first two floors.

depicting scenes from Christ's life. The other completed façade, the Passion, which faces C/Sardenya, is more austere, with vast diagonal columns in the shape of bones and haunting sculptures by Josep Maria Subirachs. Japanese sculptor Etsuro Sotoo has chosen to adhere more faithfully to Gaudí's intentions, and has fashioned six more modest musicians at the rear of the temple, as well as the exuberantly coloured bowls of fruit to the left of the Nativity façade.

An estimated five million tourists visit the Sagrada Familia each year, more than two-and-a-half million of them paying the entrance fee. (A combination of ticket revenues and charitable donations funds the continued construction of the project.) A ticket allows you to wander through the interior of the church, a marvellous forest of columns laid out in the style of the great Gothic cathedrals, with a multi-aisled central nave crossed by a transept. The central columns are fashioned of porphyry, perhaps the only natural element capable of supporting the church's projected great dome; destined to rise 170m (558ft), this will make the Sagrada Familia once again the highest building in the city. A range of tours are available.

An admission ticket also gives visitors access to the museum in the basement, offering insight into the history of the construction, original models for sculptural work and the chance to watch sculptors working at plaster-cast models through a large window. The highlight of any trip is a vertiginous hike up one of the towers (you can also take a lift), which affords unprecedented views through archers' windows.

The Esquerra

The left side of the Eixample was always a lot less fashionable than the right, and eventually it was to become the setting for the sort of city services the bourgeoisie didn't want ruining the upmarket tone of their new neighbourhood. A huge slaughterhouse was built at the eastern edge of the area (and was only knocked down in 1979, when it was replaced by the **Parc Joan Miró**). Also here is the busy Hospital Clínic, an ugly, functional building that covers two blocks between C/Corsega and C/Provença; on C/Entença, a little further out, was the grim, star-shaped La Model prison. It has been relocated out of town and replaced by subsidised houses and offices. The huge Escola Industrial on C/Comte d'Urgell, formerly a Can Batlló textile factory, was redesigned in 1909 as a centre to teach workers the methods used in the textile industry. Another building worth seeing is the central Universitat de Barcelona building on Plaça Universitat, completed in 1872. It is an elegant construction with a pleasant cloister-like garden. If you want to visit a market frequented by locals rather than tourists, try the Ninot, by the hospital. The Esquerra also contains a number of Modernista jewels, such as the Casa Boada (C/Enric Granados 106) and the Casa Golferichs (Gran Via 191), built in 1901 by Joan Rubio i Bellver, one of Gaudí's main collaborators. Beyond the hospital, the Esquerra leads to Plaça Francesc Macià, centre of the business district and a gateway to the Zona Alta.

Parc Joan Miró (Parc de l'Escorxador)

C/Tarragona (no phone). Metro Espanya or Tarragona. **Open** 10am-sunset daily. **Map** p339 C8.
The demolition of the old slaughterhouse provided much-needed parkland, although there's little greenery here. The rows of stubby palms and grim cement lakes are dominated by a library and Miró's towering phallic sculpture *Dona i Ocell* (Woman and Bird).

Sagrada Família. *See p131.*

Gràcia & Other Districts

From anarchist hotbed to bohemian heartland.

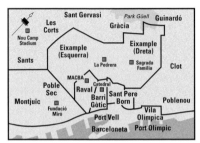

Maps pp340-341

So far as the inhabitants of Gràcia were concerned it was 'thanks, but no thanks' to incorporation in Barcelona. But the inexorable expansion that began when the city walls were demolished led to the devouring of the fields that once separated Gràcia from its neighbour. By 1897, Barcelona had pretty much swallowed up the fiercely independent conurbation. Gràcia's nominal independence was rendered pretty much irrelevant and amid howls of protest from its populace, the town was annexed. Since then, dissent has been a recurring feature in Gràcia's history: streets boast names such as Llibertat, Revolució and Fraternitat, and for the 64 years preceding the Civil War, there was a satirical political magazine called *La Campana de Gràcia*, named after the famous bell in Plaça Rius i Taulet.

The political activity came from the effects of rapid industrial expansion. This was a mere village in 1821, centred around the 17th-century convent of Santa Maria de Gràcia, with just 2,608 inhabitants. By the time of annexation, however, the population had risen to 61,935, making it the ninth largest town in Spain and a hotbed of Catalanism, republicanism and anarchism. Today, few vestiges of radicalism remain: sure, the *okupa* squatter movement inhabits a relatively high number of buildings in the area, but the middle-class population has been waging a campaign to dislodge them with increasing success.

Nowadays, the *barri* is a favourite hangout of the city's bohemians. There are numerous workshops and studios here and the many small, unpretentious bars are often frequented by artists, designers and students. However, Gràcia really comes into its own for a few days

in mid August, when its famous *festa major* grips the entire city (*see p222*). Residents spend months in advance preparing startlingly original home-made street decorations, and all of Barcelona converges on the tiny *barri* to party. Open-air meals are laid on for the residents of Gràcia, bands are dotted on every street, films are screened in *plaças* and bars, while old-timers sing along to *habaneros* (shanties) and resident squatters pogo to punk bands. Of Gràcia's many squares, Plaça de la Virreina is perhaps the most relaxing spot, silvered by the chairs and tables of bar terraces, and overlooked by Sant Joan church. Plaça del Sol is busier: home to half a dozen bars and restaurants, it's the main focus of the drinking crowd. Other favourites include Plaça Rius i Taulet, dominated by a 33-metre (108-foot) bell tower; the leafy Plaça Rovira (with a bronze statue of the neighbourhood's pensive planner, Antoni Rovira i Trias, sitting on a bench, his rejected plan for the Eixample at his feet); the rather rougher Plaça del Diamant, which was the setting for the Mercè Rodoreda novel *The Time of the Doves*; and Plaça John Lennon, where the singer is remembered with a huge model of the 'Give Peace a Chance' single. Photography buffs should also note the **Fundació Foto Colectània**. And, just off C/de Sants is C/Sant Medir, the starting point for the *barri*'s Festa de Sant Medir (*see p218*), held in mid March every year, where local representatives canter around in horse-drawn carriages throwing caramel sweets to children.

Much of Gràcia was built in the heyday of Modernisme, something evident in the splendid main drag, C/Gran de Gràcia. Many of the buildings are rich in nature-inspired curves and fancy façades, but the finest example is Lluís Domènech i Montaner's Casa Fuster at no.2, recently reopened as a luxury hotel (*see p73*). Gaudí's disciple Francesc Berenguer was responsible for much of the civic architecture, most notably the Mercat de la Llibertat (Barcelona's oldest covered market and still proudly adorned with Gràcia's old coat of arms) and the old Casa de la Vila (Town Hall) in Plaça Rius i Taulet.

However, the district's most overwhelming Modernista gem is one of Gaudí's earliest and most fascinating works, the **Casa Vicens** (*see p41*) of 1883-88, hidden away in C/Carolines.

Sightseeing

ate residence and thus
but the castellated red
rful tiled exterior with
influences should not be
the spiky wrought-iron
. And one of Gaudí's last
works, ... dinary **Park Güell**, is a walk
away, across the busy Travessera de Dalt and
up the hill. It's well worth the effort (there are
even escalators at certain points): not only for
the architecture, but also for the magnificent
view of Barcelona and the sea.

Fundació Foto Colectània

C/Julián Romea 6, D2 (93 217 16 26/www.
colectania.es). FGC Gràcia. **Open** 11am-2pm,
5-8.30pm Mon-Sat. **Admission** free. **Map** p340 F5.
This private foundation is dedicated to the promotion of the photography of major Spanish and
Portuguese photographers from the 1950s to the
present day. It also has an extensive library of
Spanish and Portuguese photography books,
including out-of-print ones.

Park Güell

C/Olot (Casa-Museu Gaudí 93 219 38 11). Metro
Lesseps/bus 24, 25. **Open** *Park* 10am-sunset daily.
Museum Apr-Sept 10am-7.45pm daily. Oct-Mar
10am-5.45pm daily. **Admission** *Park* free. *Museum*
€4; €3 reductions; free under-9s. **Credit** (shop only)
MC, V. **Map** p341 H2/H3/J2/J3.
Gaudí's brief for this spectacular project was to
emulate the English garden cities so admired by his
patron Eusebi Güell (hence the spelling of 'park'):

to lay out a self-contained suburb for the wealthy,
but also to design the public areas. The original
plan was for the plots to be sold off and the prop-
erties themselves subsequently designed by other
architects. The idea never took off – perhaps
because it was too far from the city, perhaps because
it was too radical – and the Güell family donated
the park to the city in 1922.

It is a real fairy-tale place; the fantastical exuber-
ance of Gaudí's imagination is breathtaking. The
visitor was previously welcomed by two life-sized
mechanical gazelles – a typically bizarre religious
reference by Gaudí to medieval Hebrew love poetry
– although these were unfortunately destroyed in
the Civil War. The two gatehouses that do still
remain were based on designs the architect made
earlier for the opera Hansel and Gretel, one of them
featuring a red and white mushroom for a roof.
From here, walk up a splendid staircase flanked
by multicoloured battlements, past the iconic mosaic
lizard sculpture, to what would have been the main
marketplace. Here, 100 palm-shaped pillars hold up
a roof, reminiscent of the hypostyle hall at Luxor.
On top of this structure is the esplanade, a circular
concourse surrounded by undulating benches in the
form of a sea-serpent decorated with shattered tiles
– a technique called *trencadís*, which was actually
perfected by Gaudí's overshadowed but talented
assistant Josep Maria Jujol. Like all of Gaudí's
works, these seats are by no means a case of design
over function; they are as comfortable as park
benches come, and no wonder – it's thought that
Gaudí used the mould of a woman's buttocks to
achieve the curvature of the bench surface.

Parc Güell.

The park itself, now a UNESCO World Heritage Site, is magical, with twisted stone columns supporting curving colonnades or merging with the natural structure of the hillside. The park's peak is marked by a large cross and offers an amazing panorama of Barcelona and the sea beyond. Gaudí lived for a time in one of the two houses built on the site (which was, in fact, designed by his student Berenguer). It has since become the Casa-Museu Gaudí; guided tours, some of which are in English, are available. The best way to get to the park is on the 24 bus; if you go via Lesseps metro, be prepared for a steep uphill walk.

Sants

For many arriving by bus or train, Estació de Sants is their first uninspiring sight of Barcelona. Most take one look at the forbidding Plaça dels Països Catalans, which looks like it was designed with skateboard tricks in mind, and get the hell out of the area. Over the next few years, however, the station is set for a long-overdue facelift as the new high-speed Barcelona-France train terminal is built (due to be finished in 2008). Still, there's no avoiding the fact that Sants (meaning 'Saints') is not exactly the most picturesque part of town – and be warned, the station is particularly popular among the city's bag-snatchers – but for those with time to spare, it's worth a few hours' investigation for historic, if not aesthetic, reasons. Mid August is one of the better times

to visit as, immediately following the Festa Major de Gràcia, Sants launches its own, albeit lower-key, version, and the *barri* sheds its drab industrial coat in favour of street parties, decorations and music.

Sants was originally built to service those who arrived after the town gates had shut at 9pm, with inns and blacksmiths there to cater for latecomers. In the 19th century, though, it became the industrial motor of the city. Giant textile factories such as the Vapor Vell (which is now a library), L'Espanya Industrial (now the **Parc de l'Espanya Industrial**) and **Can Batlló** (still a workplace) helped create the bourgeois wealth that the likes of Eusebi Güell spent on the Modernista dream homes that still grace the more salubrious areas of the city. The inequality did not go unnoticed. The *barri* has been a hotbed of industrial action: the first general strike in Catalonia broke out here in 1856, only to be violently put down by the infamous General Zapatero (known as the 'Tiger of Catalonia'). The left-wing nationalist ERC party, which now shares power in the Generalitat, was founded here in 1931, at C/Cros 9.

Most routes of interest start and end at the hub of the *barri*, Plaça de Sants, halfway up C/Sants high street, where Jorge Castillo's *Ciclista* statue is also to be found. Also worth checking out are the showy Modernista buildings at nos.12, 130, 145 and 151, all designed by local architect Modest Feu.

Sightseeing

Opera fans may also be interested in visiting one of Sant's oldest streets, the tiny commercial thoroughfare of C/Galileu, where tenor José Carreras was born at no.1 in 1946.

Returning back to Plaça de Sants and taking C/Olzinelles, you'll find the quaint Plaça Bonet i Mixi and the Parroquia de Santa Maria del Sants church, from which it is believed the *barri* got its name. This is the focal point for locals around Easter, when Semana Santa (Holy Week) grips Spain. Following C/Sants in the direction of Montjuïc, the road name suddenly changes to C/Creu Coberta, an old Roman road once known as the Cami d'Espanya, 'the road to Spain'. Following C/Creu Coberta further, you'll find the large, lively and colourful Mercat d'Hostafrancs, where there's also a stop for the tourist bus. Further along still is C/Sant Roc, where you will find the Modernista-inspired Església de l'Angel Custodi.

Parc de l'Espanya Industrial

Passeig de Antoni (no phone). Metro Sants-Estació. **Open** 10am-sunset daily. **Map** p339 B7.
In the 1970s, the owners of the old textile factory announced their intention to use the land to build blocks of apartments. The neighbourhood's residents, though, put their collective foot down and insisted on a park, which was eventually built in 1985. The result is a puzzling space, designed by Basque Luis Peña Ganchegui, with ten watchtowers overlooking a boating lake with a statue of Neptune in the middle, flanked by a stretch of mud used mainly by locals walking their dogs. By the entrance kids can climb over Andrés Nagel's Drac, a massive and sinister black dragon sculpture.

Les Corts

Row after row of apartment blocks now obscure any trace of the rustic origins of Les Corts (literally, 'cowsheds' or 'pigsties'), as the village itself was swallowed up by Barcelona in the late 19th century. But search and you will find Plaça de la Concòrdia, a quiet square dominated by a 40-metre (131-foot) bell tower. This is an anachronistic oasis housing the civic centre Can Deu, formerly a farmhouse and now home to a great bar that hosts jazz acts every other Thursday. The area is much better known, though, for what happens every other weekend, when tens of thousands pour in to watch FC Barcelona, whose **Nou Camp** takes up much of the west of the *barri*. The club recently hired Lord Foster to remodel the stadium, encasing it in a multi-coloured mosaic shell of glass and polycarbonate panels. The project is set to cost €250m and construction will begin in 2009. Visitors should note that at night the area is the haunt of transvestite prostitutes and their kerb-crawling clients.

Nou Camp – FC Barcelona

Avda Aristides Maillol, access 9, Les Corts (93 496 36 00/08/www.fcbarcelona.com). Metro Collblanc or Palau Reial. **Open** Apr-Oct 10am-8pm Mon-Sat, 10am-2.30pm Sun; *Nov-Mar* 10am-6.30pm Mon-Sat; 10am-2pm Sun. **Admission** €7; €5.60 reductions; free under-5s. Guided tour €11; €8.60 reductions. **Credit** (shop only) MC, V. **Map** p338 A3/4.
The Nou Camp, where FC Barcelona has played since 1957, is one of football's great stadiums, a vast cauldron of a ground that holds 98,000 spectators. That's a lot of noise when the team is doing well, and an awful lot of silence when it isn't. If you can't get there on match day (and you can usually pick up tickets if you try) but love the team, it's worth visiting the club museum. The excellent guided tour of the stadium takes you through the players' tunnel to the dugouts and then, via the away team's changing room, on to the President's box, where there is a replica of the European Cup, which the team won at Wembley in 1992. The club museum commemorates those glory years, making much of the days when the likes of Kubala, Cruyff, Maradona, Koeman and Lineker trod the hallowed turf, with pictures, video clips and souvenirs spanning the century that has passed since the Swiss business executive Johan Gamper first founded the club. *See p273* **More than a club**.

Tibidabo & Collserola

During the devil's temptation of Christ, he took Jesus to the top of a mountain and offered him all before him, with the words '*tibi dabo*' (Latin for 'To thee I will give'). This gave rise to the name of the dominant peak of the Collserola massif, with its sweeping views of the whole of the Barcelona conurbation stretching out to the sea: quite a tempting offer, given the present-day price of the city's real estate. The neo-Gothic **Sagrat Cor** church crowning the peak has become one of the city's most recognisable landmarks; it's clearly visible for miles around. At weekends, thousands of people head to the top of the hill in order to whoop and scream at the **funfair** (*see p227*). Nowadays the only one in Barcelona, it's been running since 1921 and has changed little since: the rides are creaky and old-fashioned, but very quaint. The marionette show is also a survivor from the early days, but a more recent addition is the first freefall ride in Spain, where visitors are dropped 38 metres (125 feet) in 2.8 seconds. Within the funfair is also the Museu d'Autòmats, a fine collection of fairground coin-operated machines from the early 1900s.

Getting up to the top on the clanking old **Tramvia Blau** (Blue Tram) and then the **funicular railway** is part of the fun, between the two is Plaça Doctor Andreu, a great place for an alfresco drink. For the best view of the city, either take a lift up Lord

Foster's communications tower, the **Torre de Collserola**, or up to the *mirador* at the feet of Christ atop the Sagrat Cor.

The vast **Parc de Collserola** is more a series of forested hills than a park; its shady paths through holm oaks and pines open out to spectacular views. It's most easily reached by FGC train on the Terrassa-Sabadell line from Plaça Catalunya or Passeig de Gràcia, getting off at Baixador de Vallvidrera station. A ten-minute walk from the station up into the woods (there's an information board just outside the station) will take you to the Vil·la Joana, an old *masia* covered in bougainvillea and containing the **Museu Verdaguer** (93 204 78 05, open 10am-2pm Sat, Sun, admission €5, free 1st Sat of mth) dedicated to 19th-century Catalan poet Jacint Verdaguer, who used this as his summer home. Just beyond the Vil·la Joana is the park's information centre (93 280 35 52,

Funicular de Tibidabo

open 10am-4pm daily), which has basic maps for free and more detailed maps for sale. Most of the information is in Catalan, but staff are helpful. There's also a snack bar.

Funicular de Tibidabo

Plaça Doctor Andreu to Plaça Tibidabo (93 211 79 42). FGC Avda Tibidabo then Tramvia Blau. **Open** As funfair (*see p227*), but starting 30mins earlier. **Tickets** *Single* €2; €1.50 reductions. *Return* €3; €2 reductions. **No credit cards.**
This art deco vehicle offers occasional glimpses of the city below as it winds through the pine forests up to the summit. The service has been running since 1901, but only according to a complicated timetable. If it's not running, take the FGC line from Plaça de Catalunya to Peu del Funicular, get the funicular up to Vallvidrera Superior, and then catch the 111 bus to Tibidabo (a process not half as complicated as it sounds). Alternatively, it's nearly an hour's (mostly pleasant) hike up from Plaça Doctor Andreu for those who are feeling energetic.

Torre de Collserola

Ctra de Vallvidrera al Tibidabo (93 211 79 42/ www.torredecollserola.com). FGC Peu Funicular then funicular. **Open** *Apr-June, Sept* 11am-2.30pm, 3.30-7pm Wed-Fri; 11am-7pm Sat, Sun. *July, Aug* 11am-2.30pm, 3.30-8pm Mon-Fri; 11am-8pm Sat, Sun. *Oct-Mar* 11am-2.30pm, 3.30-6pm Mon-Fri; 11am-6pm Sat, Sun. **Admission** €5; €4 reductions; free under-4s. **Credit** AmEx, MC, V.
Just five minutes' walk from the Sagrat Cor is its main rival and Barcelona's most visible landmark, Lord Foster's communications tower, built in 1992 to transmit images of the Olympics around the world. Visible from just about everywhere in the city and always flashing at night, the tower is loved and hated in equal measure. Those who don't suffer from vertigo attest to the wonderful views of Barcelona and the Mediterranean from the top.

Zona Alta

Zona Alta (the 'upper zone', or 'uptown') is the name given collectively to a series of smart neighbourhoods including Sant Gervasi, Sarrià, Pedralbes and Putxet that stretch out across the lower reaches of the Collserola hills. The handful of tourist sights found here include the Palau Reial, with its gardens and museums, the **Museu de Ceràmica** and **Museu de les Arts Decoratives**, the **CosmoCaixa** science museum and the remarkable **Pedralbes Monastery**, which is still well worth a visit despite the fact that its selection of religious paintings from the Thyssen-Bornemisza collection has been moved to the revamped Museu Nacional d'Art de Catalunya (MNAC; *see p122*). The centre of Sarrià and the streets of old Pedralbes around the monastery retain a flavour of the sleepy country towns these once were.

For many downtown residents, the Zona Alta is a favourite place to relax in the parks and gardens that wind into the hills. At the end of Avda Diagonal, next to the functional Zona Universitària (university district), is the Jardins de Cervantes, with its 11,000 rose bushes, the striking *Rombes Bessons* (Twin Rhombuses) sculpture by Andreu Alfaro and, during the week, legions of picnicking students, continuing in the scholastic traditions of the founder of Catalan literature, Ramon Llull. From the park, a turn back along the Diagonal towards Plaça Maria Cristina and Plaça Francesc Macià will take you to Barcelona's main business and shopping district. Here is the small Turó Parc, a semi-formal garden good for writing postcards amid inspirational plaques of poetry. The Jardins de la Tamarita, at the foot of Avda Tibidabo, is a pleasant dog-free oasis with a playground, while further up at the top of the tramline is the little-known Parc de la Font de Racó, full of shady pine and eucalyptus trees. A fair walk to the north-east, an old quarry has been converted into a swimming pool, the **Parc de la Creueta del Coll**.

Gaudí fans are rewarded by a trip up to the Pavellons de la Finca Güell at Avda Pedralbes 15; its extraordinary and rather frightening wrought-iron gate features a dragon into whose gaping mouth the foolhardy can fit their heads. Once inside the gardens, via the main gate on

Avda Diagonal, look out for a delightful fountain designed by the master himself. Across near Putxet is Gaudí's relatively sober Col·legi de les Teresianes (C/Ganduxer 85-105), while up towards Tibidabo, just off Plaça Bonanova, rises his remarkable Gothic-influenced Torre Figueres or Bellesguard.

CosmoCaixa

C/Teodor Roviralta 47-51 (93 212 60 50/ www.fundacio.lacaixa.es). Bus 60/FGC Avda Tibidabo then Tramvia Blau (see p140). **Open** 10am-8pm Tue-Sun. **Admission** €3; €2 reductions; free under-3s. *Planetarium* €2; €1.50 reductions; free under-3s. **Credit** AmEx, DC, MC, V.

The long-awaited revamp of the Fundació La Caixa's science museum and planetarium, to create the biggest in Europe, has been only partially successful. First off, its size is somewhat misleading: apart from a couple of new (and, admittedly, important) spaces – the Flooded Forest, a reproduction of a corner of Amazonia complete with flora and fauna, and the Geological Wall – the collection has not been proportionally expanded to fit the new building. A glass-enclosed spiral ramp runs down an impressive six floors, but actually represents quite a long walk to reach the main collection five floors down.

It is here that temporary exhibitions are housed too. From here, it's on to the Matter Room, which covers 'inert', 'living', 'intelligent' and then 'civilised' matter: in other words, natural history. However, for all the fanfare made by the museum about taking

CosmoCaixa.

exhibits out of glass cases and making scientific theories accessible, many of the displays still look very dated. Written explanations often tend towards the impenetrable, containing phrases such as 'time is macroscopically irreversible', and making complex those concepts that previously seemed simple.

On the plus side, the installations for children are excellent: the Bubble Planetarium pleases kids aged three to eight, and the wonderful Clik (ages three to six) and Flash (seven to nine) introduce children to science through games. Toca Toca! ('Touch Touch') educates children on which animals and plants are safe and which to avoid. One of the real highlights, for both kids and adults, is the hugely entertaining sound telescope outside on the Plaça de la Ciència.

The museum recently opened the Planeta Tierra section in collaboration with the European Space Agency, which looks at environmental preservation projects funded by the La Caixa Foundation and features lots of interesting interactive videos.

Monestir de Pedralbes

Baixada del Monestir 9 (93 256 21 22). FGC Reina Elisenda. **Open** 10am-5pm Tue-Sat, 10am-3pm Sun **Admission** €5; €3.50 reductions; free under-12s. Free 1st Sun of mth. **Credit** (shop only) AmEx, DC, MC, V.
In 1326, the widowed Queen Elisenda of Montcada used her inheritance to buy this land and build a convent for the Poor Clare order of nuns, which she soon joined. The result is a jewel of Gothic architecture with an understated single-nave church with fine stained-glass windows and a beautiful three-storey

14th-century cloister. The place was out of bounds to the general public until 1983, when the nuns, a closed order, opened it up as a museum in the mornings (when they escape to a nearby annexe).

The site offers a fascinating insight into life in a medieval convent, taking you through its kitchens, pharmacy and refectory, with its huge vaulted ceiling. To one side is the tiny chapel of Sant Miquel, with murals dating to 1343 by Ferrer Bassa, a Catalan painter and student of Giotto. In the former dormitory next to the cloister is a selection of illuminated books, furniture and items reflecting the artistic and religious life of the community. *Photos p140.*

Museu de Ceràmica & Museu de les Arts Decoratives

Palau Reial de Pedralbes, Avda Diagonal 686 (93 280 16 21/www.museuceramica.bcn.cat/ www.museuartsdecoratives.bcn.cat). Metro Palau Reial. **Open** 10am-6pm Tue-Sat; 10am-3pm Sun. **Admission** *Combined admission with Museu Tèxtil* €5; €3 reductions; free under-16s. Free 1st Sun of mth. **No credit cards. Map** p338 A2.
These two collections – accessible, along with the Textile Museum (*see p101*), on the same ticket – are housed in the august Palau Reial; originally designed for the family of Eusebi Güell, Gaudí's patron, it was later used as a royal palace but was reclaimed for the public when the Spanish Republic was declared in 1931. The Museum of Decorative Arts is informative and fun, and looks at the styles informing the design of artefacts in Europe since the Middle Ages, from Romanesque to art deco and beyond. A second section covers post-war Catalan design of objects as diverse as urinals and man-sized inflatable pens.

The Ceramics Museum is equally fascinating, showing how Moorish ceramic techniques from the 13th century were developed after the Reconquista with the addition of colours (especially blue and yellow) in centres such as Manises (in Valencia) and Barcelona. Two 18th-century murals are of sociological interest: one, *La Xocolatada*, shows the bourgeoisie at a garden party, while the other, by the same artist, depicts the working classes at a bullfight in the Plaza Mayor in Madrid. Upstairs is a section showing 20th-century ceramics, including a room dedicated to Miró and Picasso. The two museums, along with the Textile Museum and several smaller collections, are to be merged in the future in a Museu de Disseny (Design Museum) as part of the cultural overhaul of the Plaça de les Glòries.

Parc de la Creueta del Coll

C/Mare de Déu del Coll (no phone). Metro Penitents. **Open** 10am-sunset daily. **Admission** free.
Created from a quarry in 1987 by Josep Matorell and David Mackay, the team that went on to design the Vila Olímpica, this park boasts a sizeable swimming pool complete with a 'desert island' and a sculpture by Eduardo Chillida: a 50-ton lump of curly granite suspended on cables, called *In Praise of Water*. Three people were injured by it in 1998 when the cables snapped: make sure you view from a safe distance.

Sightseeing

The tranquil 14th-century cloister of **Monestir de Pedralbes**. *See p139*.

Tramvia Blau

Avda Tibidabo (Plaça Kennedy) to Plaça Doctor Andreu (93 318 70 74/www.tramvia.org/ tramviablau). FGC Avda Tibidabo. **Open** *Mid June-mid Sept* 10am-8pm daily. *Mid Sept-mid June* 10am-6pm Sat. Frequency 20mins. **Tickets** €2.20 single; €3.30 return. **No credit cards.**

Barcelonins and tourists have been clanking 1,225m (4,000ft) up Avda Tibidabo in the 'blue trams' since 1902. In the winter months, when the tram only operates on weekends, a rather more prosaic bus takes you up (or you can walk it in 15 minutes).

Poblenou & beyond

Poblenou has been many things in its time: a farming community, a fishing port, the site of heavy industry factories and a trendy post-industrial suburb. Now it's also a burgeoning technology and business district, snappily tagged 22@. Many of the factories around here closed down in the 1960s; these days, buildings not already been torn down or converted into office blocks are used as schools, civic centres, workshops, or, increasingly, coveted lofts.

The main drag, the pedestrianised Rambla de Poblenou, dating from 1886, is a much better place for a relaxing stroll than its busy central counterpart, and gives this still-villagey area a heart. Meanwhile, a bone's throw away, the city's oldest and most atmospheric cemetery, the Cementiri de l'Est, shows that most *barcelonins* spend their death as they did their life: cooped up in large high-rise blocks. Some were able to afford roomier tombs, many of which were built at the height of the

romantic-Gothic craze at the turn of the 19th century. A leaflet or larger guide (€15) sold at the entrance suggests a route around 30 of the more interesting monuments.

Nearby, Plaça de les Glòries finally seems ready to fulfil its destiny. The creator of the Eixample, Ildefons Cerdà, hoped that the square would become the new centre of the city, believing his grid-pattern blocks would spread much further north than they did and shift the emphasis of the city from west to east. Instead, it became little more than a glorified roundabout on the way out of town. Nowadays, it's best-known for its huge commercial shopping complex and the bustling market **Mercat Els Encants** (open Mon, Wed, Fri, Sat from 8.30am), which has everything from kitchen sinks to dodgy DVDs. From here, a wide and relatively quiet stretch of Diagonal is filled with joggers, cyclists and in-line skaters as it leads towards the sea.

Now, with the hugely phallic **Torre Agbar** to landmark the area from afar, the *plaça* has also become the gateway to Diagonal Mar and the new commercial and leisure area on the shoreline, known as the Fòrum, after the event in 2004 for which it was created. The tower, designed by French architect Jean Nouvel and owned by the Catalan water board, has been a bold and controversial project. A concrete skyscraper with a domed head and a glass façade, it's not unlike London's famed Gherkin. Nouvel says it's been designed to reflect the Catalan mentality: the concrete represents stability and severity; the glass, openness and transparency. At 144 metres (472 feet),

Saint alive Ramon Llull

All right, he's not strictly speaking a saint, only a blessed, but Ramon Llull (1232-1316) deserves a place in any list of Catalan holy men. However, the Fool of Love was for the first 30 years of his life fool to an altogether more earthly sort of love. Llull was attached to the household of the future Jaume II of Mallorca and he eventually became its seneschal. But marriage and two children did nothing to cool his pursuit of the court's women, for whom he composed many songs in the romantic troubadour style of the period.

'The more apt I found myself to sin, more I allowed my nature to obey the dictates of my body,' he wrote later. Not even the shock of one of his amours yielding to his advances, only to reveal breasts ravaged by cancer, could stop his philandering. But then, in the summer of 1263, while Ramon was busy writing another song in honour of a new love, he looked up from his work to see 'our Lord Jesus Christ hanging upon the Cross'. Llull, his poetic flow seriously interrupted, escaped to his bed, no doubt assuming that a good night's sleep would clear his mind. But when he next returned to songwriting, the figure returned and a terrified Llull again retired to bed. However, Ramon was no dilettante libertine and three times more he returned to his love song, only to be faced with the same figure. Llull decided that these must be authentic visions rather than mental phantoms and he set to working out what they meant. In the end, he decided to abandon the world and devote himself to Christ's service. This he was to do by trying to convert the unbelievers (in Ramon's world, this meant chiefly Muslims), by writing a book, 'the best in the world, against the errors of unbelievers', and setting up colleges to teach Arabic to missionaries.

Llull then sold his possessions, though keeping some back to support his wife and children, distributed the proceeds to the poor and spent the next nine years in study. It was only then, approaching his 40th year, that Ramon began the literary and missionary work for which he would become famous, known in later centuries as the *Doctor Illuminatus*, the 'Illuminated Doctor', from the series of mystical visions he had on Mount Randa in Majorca. The sheer scale of his labours almost defies belief. Llull was the author of 265 works in Catalan, Arabic and Latin; the writer of the seminal Catalan novel, *Blanquerna*; a missionary in almost constant travel between Europe and north Africa; a teacher at the University of Paris when it was the foremost institution of learning in Christendom; a suitor at papal and imperial courts; and the originator of the Ars Magna, a systematisation of, well, everything with respect to God's attributes. This was the book, 'the best in the world', that Llull believed showed the truth and which he illustrated through diagrams, tables and, literally, millions of words.

This man continued working throughout his long life. At 75, still travelling, he was on a mission to north Africa, where he was 'beaten with sticks and with fists, and forcibly dragged along by his beard, which was very long, until he was locked in the latrine of the thieves' jail'. The details of his death are subject to dispute – some say he died at the hands of a Muslim mob in Tunis, others that he succumbed to disease when sailing back – but whatever the truth few men can ever have packed so much into the second half of a life.

it's Barcelona's third highest building (behind the two Olympic towers) and contains no fewer than 4,400 multiform windows. Remarkably, it has no air-conditioning: the windows let the breeze do the job. Nouvel claims Gaudí as the inspiration for the multicoloured skin – it has 4,000 LED lights that change colour at night – of a building that has already polarised public opinion and come to dominate the district.

One breath of fresh air in the rather stagnant area north of here is the **Parc del Clot**. Just beyond it is the Plaça de Valentí Almirall, with the old town hall of Sant Martí and a 17th-century building that used to be the Hospital de Sant Joan de Malta somewhat at odds with the buildings that have mushroomed around them. Further north, up C/Sagrera, the entrance to a former giant truck factory now leads to the charming **Parc de la Pegaso**. The area also has a fine piece of recent architecture, the supremely elegant Pont de Calatrava bridge. Designed by Santiago Calatrava, it links to Poblenou via C/Bac de Roda.

Diagonal Mar

Many detractors of the **Fòrum**, which was the six-month cultural symposium that was held in 2004, felt that its real purpose was to regenerate this post-industrial wasteland. Certainly, a large element of its legacy are the enormous conference halls and hotels that it is hoped will eventually draw many wealthy business clients into the city, together with a scarcely believable increase in real-estate values. More recently, the Fòrum has benefited the city's youth, with its wide-open spaces providing an excellent venue for two of the Barcelona's biggest music festivals, Primavera Sound (*see p221*) and Summercase (*see p222*).

If you're approaching from the city, the first sign of this resurgent *barri* is **Parc de Diagonal Mar** (*see p42* **Not-so-green spaces**), containing an angular lake decorated with scores of curling aluminium tubes and vast Gaudian flowerpots. Designed by the late Enric Miralles (he of Scottish Parliament fame), the park may not be to most *barcelonins'* taste, but the local seagull population has found it to be an excellent roosting spot. Just over the road from here is the Diagonal Mar shopping centre, a still woefully undervisited three-storey mall of high-street chains, cinemas and the grand Hotel Princesa, a triangular skyscraper designed by architect, designer, artist and local hero Óscar Tusquets.

The **Edifici Fòrum**, a striking blue triangular construction by architects Herzog and de Meuron (responsible for London's Tate Modern), is the centrepiece of the €3-billion redevelopment. The remainder of the money was spent on the solar panels, marina, new beach and the Illa Pangea, an island 60 metres (197 feet) from the shore, reachable only by swimming. It's all a far cry from the local residential neighbourhood, Sant Adrià de Besòs, a poor district of tower blocks that includes the notorious La Mina neighbourhood, a hotbed of drug-related crime. It's hoped that the new development will help regenerate the area, best known for its Feria de Abril celebrations in April (*see p219*), the Andalucian community's version of the more famous annual celebrations in Seville. There's also a fine *festa major* in Badalona, just up the coast, in May, in which a large effigy of a devil is burned on the beach in a shower of fireworks.

Horta & around

Horta, which is to the far west of the blue metro line, is a picturesque little village that remains aloof from the city that swallowed it up in 1904. Originally a collection of farms (its name means

Pont de Calatrava.

'market garden'), the *barri* is still peppered with old farmhouses, such as Can Mariner on C/Horta, dating back to 1050, and the medieval Can Cortada at the end of C/Campoamor, which is now a huge restaurant located in beautiful grounds. An abundant water supply also made Horta the place where much of the city's laundry was done: a whole community of *bugaderes* (washerwomen) lived and worked in lovely C/Aiguafreda, where you can still see their wells and open-air stone washtubs.

To the south, joined to Gràcia by Avda Mare de Déu de Montserrat, the steep-sided neighbourhood of Guinardó, with its steps and escalators, consists mainly of two big parks. Parc del Guinardó, a huge space designed in 1917 (making it Barcelona's third oldest park) full of eucalyptus and cypress trees, is a relaxing place to escape. The smaller Parc de les Aigües shelters the neo-Arabic Casa de les Altures from 1890, Barcelona's most eccentrically beautiful council building.

The Vall d'Hebron is a leafy area located just above Horta in the Collserola foothills. Here, formerly private estates have been put to public use; among them are the chateau-like Palauet de les Heures, now a university building. The area was one of the city's four major venues for the Olympics and is rich in sporting facilities, including public football pitches, tennis courts, and cycling and archery facilities at the Velòdrom. It's also the home to one of Barcelona's major concert venues. Around these environs there are several striking examples of street sculpture, including Claes Oldenburg's Matches and Joan Brossa's Visual Poem (in the shape of the letter 'A'). The area also conceals the rationalist **Pavelló de la República** and the zany **Parc del Laberint**, dating back to 1791 and surrounded by a modern park. More modern still is the Ciutat Sanitària, Catalonia's largest hospital; a good proportion of *barcelonins* first saw the light of day here.

Parc del Laberint

C/Germans Desvalls, Passeig Vall d'Hebron (no phone). Metro Mundet. **Open** 10am-sunset daily. **Admission** €2; €1.20 reductions Mon, Tue, Thur-Sat; free under-6s, over-65s. Free Wed, Sun.
In 1791, the Desvalls family, owners of this marvel-lously leafy estate, hired Italian architect Domenico Begutti to design scenic gardens set around a cypress maze, with a romantic stream and a water-fall. The mansion may be gone (replaced with a 19th-century Arabic-influenced building), but the gardens are remarkably intact, shaded in the summer by oaks, laurels and an ancient sequoia. Best of all, the maze, an ingenious puzzle that intrigues those brave enough to try it, is also still in use. Nearby stone tables provide a handy picnic site. On paying days, last entry is one hour before sunset.

Pavelló de la República

Avda Cardenal Vidal y Barraquer (93 428 54 57). Metro Montbau. **Open** 9am-8pm Mon-Fri. **Admission** free.
This functionalist building houses a university library specialising in materials from the Civil War and the clandestine republican movement that oper-ated during Franco's dictatorship. It was built in 1992 as a facsimile of the emblematic rationalist pavilion of the Spanish Republic designed by Josep Lluís Sert for the Paris Exhibition in 1937 and later to hold Picasso's *Guernica*. It makes an interesting juxtapo-sition to Oldenburg's pop art Matches over the road.

The outer limits

L'Hospitalet de Llobregat lies beyond Sants, completely integrated within the city's transport system but nevertheless a distinct municipality, one with its own sense of separateness. The area also boasts a rich cultural life, with good productions at the Teatre Joventut (C/Joventut 10, 93 448 12 10) and excellent art exhibitions at the **Tecla Sala Centre Cultural**.

Sant Andreu is another vast residential district in the north-east of the city, and was once a major industrial zone. Apart from the Gaudí-designed floor mosaic in the Sant Pacià church on C/Monges, there's little reason to venture here, unless you have an historical interest in Josep Lluís Sert's rationalist Casa Bloc, which were originally workers' residences from the brief republican era.

The name of Nou Barris, across the Avda Meridiana, translates as 'nine neighbourhoods', but the area is actually a collection of 11 former hamlets. The council has compensated for the area's poor housing (many tower blocks were built in the area in the 1950s and have fallen into disrepair) with the construction of public facilities such as the Can Dragó, a sports centre incorporating the biggest swimming pool in the city, and Parc Central. The district is centred on the roundabout at Plaça Llucmajor, which also holds Josep Viladomat's bold *La República*, a female nude holding aloft a sprig of laurel as a symbol of freedom. The renovation of the nearby Seu de Nou Barris town hall has brightened up an area that badly needed it, although it's not quite a tourist draw yet.

Tecla Sala Centre Cultural

Avda Josep Tarradellas 44, Hospitalet de Llobregat (93 338 57 71/www.l-h.es/ccteclasala). Metro La Torrassa. **Open** 11am-2pm, 5-8pm Tue-Sat; 11am-2pm Sun. **Admission** free.
Tecla Sala is an old textile factory now housing a number of cultural concerns, including a vast library and this excellent gallery, which exhibits a varied mixture of national and international artists.

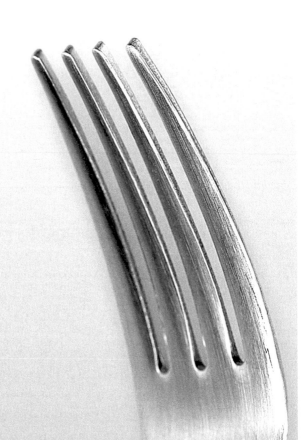

taxidermista...cafè restaurant
Plaça Reial 8   08002 Barcelona   tel. 93 412 45 36
www.taxidermistarestaurant.com   info@taxidermistarestaurant.com

Eat, Drink, Shop

Mundial Bar. *See p156.*

Restaurants

Move over Paris.

Gastronomic tremors have been shaking the culinary world for the last couple of decades and their epicentre has been south of the Pyrenees. First, it was the Basques who emerged from their linguistic fastnesses to steal stars and column inches from the French. Now, it's the turn of the Catalans. And once again the standard bearer is a chef, this time Ferran Adrià and his legendary restaurant **El Bulli** (*see p174*) on the Costa Brava.

While Adrià's kitchens have spawned many notable alumni, such as Carles Abellan at **Comerç 24** (*see p151*) and Jordi Ruiz at **Neri Restaurante** (*see p147*), the trickledown effect of his global success (in April 2006 and again in 2007, El Bulli was voted 'Best Restaurant in the World' by over 500 international critics) has also had a huge impact on the gastronomy of the region. Not only is cookery the new rock 'n' roll among young Spaniards, but suddenly food tourists from the States, Japan and Australia are showing up with the express intention of splashing some cash in restaurants.

This has led to an increase in overall quality, with some new and excellent dining options, among them **Cinc Sentits** (*see p164*), **Lasarte** (*see p167*) and **Oleum** (*see p163*). Other welcome new additions, albeit of a less rarefied nature, include the wonderfully homely **Tapioles 53** (*see p163*), excellent Asian food at **Wushu** (*see p155*) or just a really good pizza at **Ravalo** (*see p159*). Generally, though, local resistance to spices and the difficulty of

sourcing key ingredients make it hard to find good Indian, Chinese or Italian food. Middle Eastern and Japanese restaurants have been rather more successful, along with a growing number of Latin American places. Most ethnic variety is found in Gràcia.

WHAT HAPPENS WHEN
Lunch starts around 2pm and goes on until roughly 3.30pm or 4pm; dinner is served from about 9pm until 11.30pm or midnight. Some restaurants open earlier in the evening, but arriving before 9.30pm or 10pm generally means you'll be dining alone or in the company of foreign tourists. Reserving a table is generally a good idea at weekends, and also on Monday lunchtimes, when few restaurants are open. Many also close for lengthy holidays, including about a week over Easter, two or three weeks in August or early September, and often the first week in January. We have listed closures of more than a week where possible.

PRICES AND PAYMENT
Eating out in Barcelona is not as cheap as it used to be, but low mark-ups on wines keep the cost relatively reasonable for northern Europeans and Americans. All but the most upmarket restaurants are required by law to serve an economical fixed-price *menú del dia* (*menú* is not to be confused with the menu, which is *la carta*) at lunchtime; this usually consists of a starter, main course, dessert, bread and something to drink. The idea is to provide cheaper meals for the workers, but while it can be a real bargain, it is not by any means a taster menu or a showcase for the chef's greatest hits; rather, they're a healthier version of a snatched lunchtime sandwich.

Laws governing the issue of prices are routinely flouted, but, legally, menus must declare if the seven per cent IVA (VAT) is included in prices or not (it rarely is), and also if there is a cover charge (generally expressed as a charge for bread). Catalans, and the Spanish in general, tend to tip very little, but tourists let their conscience decide.

The best Restaurants

For bragging about back home
El Bulli (*see p174*).

For celebrity spottting
Noti (*see p169*).

For distressed wallets
Can Culleretes (*see p147*).

For new Catalan cooking
Cinc Sentits (*see p164*).

For seafood
La Paradeta (*see p156*).

> ❶ Purple numbers given in this chapter correspond to the location of the restaurants on the street maps. See pp338-345.

Where the cool cats eat. **Els Quatre Gats**. *See p149.*

Barri Gòtic

Catalan

Cafè de l'Acadèmia

C/Lledó 1 (93 319 82 53). Metro Jaume I. **Open** 9am-noon, 1.30-4.30pm, 8.45pm-11.30pm Mon-Fri. Closed 3wks Aug. **Main courses** €13. **Set lunch** €9.25-€12.95. **Credit** AmEx, DC, MC, V. **Map** p345 D6 ❶

Enjoy a power breakfast among the suits from the nearby town hall, bask in the sunshine over lunch at one of the tables outside on the evocative little Plaça Sant Just, or take a date for an alfresco candle-lit dinner. The regular menu of creative Catalan classics offers superb value and has had no need to change direction over the years, so you can expect to find home-made pasta (try shrimp and garlic), guinea fowl with a tiny tarte tatin and lots of duck.

Can Culleretes

C/Quintana 5 (93 317 30 22). Metro Liceu. **Open** 1.30-4pm, 9-11pm Tue-Sat; 1.30-4pm Sun. Closed July. **Main courses** €9. **Set lunch** €12-€15. **Credit** MC, V. **Map** p345 B5 ❷

The rambling dining rooms at the 'house of tea-spoons' have been packing 'em in since 1786 and show no signs of slowing. The secret to this restaurant's longevity is a straightforward one: honest, hearty cooking and decent wine served at the low-est possible prices. Under huge oil paintings and a thousand signed black-and-white photos, diners munch sticky boar stew, tender pork with prunes and dates, goose with apples, partridge *escabeche* and superbly fresh seafood.

Mercè Vins

C/Amargós 1 (93 302 60 56). Metro Urquinaona. **Open** 8am-5pm Mon-Fri. **Set lunch** €9.30 Mon-Fri. **Credit** V. **Map** p344 D3 ❸

In the morning, this cosy restaurant, with its green beams, buttercup walls and fresh flowers, functions as a breakfast bar, before moving on to serve a set lunch, while on Friday nights it dishes up *pica-pica* plates of ham and cheese, with generous rounds of bread rubbed with tomato. The standard of cooking on the lunch deals can vary a bit, but occasionally a pumpkin soup or inventive salad might appear, along with sausages with garlicky sautéed potatoes. Dessert regulars are flat, sweet coca bread with a glass of muscatel, chocolate flan or figgy pudding.

Neri Restaurante

C/Sant Sever 5 (93 304 06 55/www.hotelneri.com). Metro Jaume I. **Open** 1.30-3.30pm, 8.30-11pm daily. **Main courses** €28. **Credit** AmEx, DC, MC, V. **Map** p345 C5 ❹

These days, any Barcelona restaurant worth its *fleur de sel* has an alumnus of enfant terrible Ferran Adrià heading up its kitchens, and the Neri is no exception. Jordi Ruiz has eschewed the wilder excesses of

CULLERA de BOIX

RESTAURANT

Paellas and Catalan Cuisine

Rda. Sant Pere, 24 BCN · Phone 93 268 79 82
info@culleradeboix.com · www.culleradeboix.com

molecular gastronomy, however, and cooks with a quiet assurance in tune with the sombre Gothic arches, crushed velvet and earthy tones of his dining room, creating a perfect, tiny lamb Wellington to start; cannelloni formed with artichoke petals and stuffed with wild mushrooms, or a fillet of hake on creamed parsnip with apricots and haricot beans.

Pitarra

C/Avinyó 56 (93 301 16 47/www.restaurant pitarra.cat). Metro Liceu. **Open** 1-4pm, 8.30-11pm Mon-Sat. Closed Aug. **Main courses** €15. **Set lunch** €11 Mon-Sat. **Credit** MC, V. **Map** p345 C7 ➎
Once home to the Catalan playwright Frederic 'Pitarra' Soler and his watchmaking uncle, this smart, bright, traditional restaurant is still a shrine to the art of horology, as well as a virtual museum of poems, photographs and drawings presented to the author by the Catalan great and good. The classic dishes include partridge casserole, pheasant in a creamy cava sauce and langoustines with wild mushrooms; the desserts are not quite so accomplished.

Els Quatre Gats

C/Montsió 3 (93 302 41 40/www.4gats.com). Metro Catalunya. **Open** 1pm-1am daily. **Main courses** €19. **Set lunch** €12.80 Mon-Fri; €22.50 Sat. **Credit** AmEx, DC, MC, V. **Map** p344 C3 ➏
This Modernista classic, designed by Puig i Cadafalch and once frequented by Picasso and other luminaries of the period, nowadays caters substantially to tourists. The consequences include higher prices, so-so food and, worst of all, house musicians. It's still dazzling in its design, however, so to avoid the worst excesses, come at lunchtime for a reasonably priced and respectably varied *menú* and spare yourself in the process. *Photo p147.*

Chilean

Xeroga

C/Parc 1 (93 412 62 75). Metro Drassanes. **Open** 1-4pm, 8pm-midnight Tue-Sun. **Main courses** €10. **Set lunch** €8.75. **Credit** MC, V. **Map** p345 B8 ➐
Under the same ownership as El Paraguayo (*see p150*) next door, Xeroga is the Chilean arm, slightly cheaper and slightly shabbier, but sharing the same good-natured South American vibe, its walls hung with bright oil paintings, a gold-stitched sombrero and a cracked and burnished guitar. On offer are various *empanadas* (*pino* is the classic – meat, olives, egg and raisin), *ceviche, mariscal* (shellfish and hake in a fish broth) and *bife a lo pobre* – a trucker's breakfast of thin steak, two fried eggs and a stack of chips.

Japanese

Shunka

C/Sagristans 5 (93 412 49 91). Metro Jaume I. **Open** 1.30-3.30pm, 8.30-11.30pm Tue-Fri; 2-4pm, 8.30-11.30pm Sat, Sun. Closed Aug & ten days at Christmas. **Main courses** €18 Tue-Fri. **Credit** AmEx, DC, MC, V. **Map** p344 D4 ➑

Increasingly compromised by its own success, Shunka is still one of the better Japanese restaurants in town, and a favourite haunt of superchef Ferran Adrià. Reserve a table for the sumo-sized set lunch of rich miso soup, a leafy salad topped with salmon and punchy vinegar and teriyaki dressing, followed by vegetable and shrimp tempura and six pieces of maki and extremely good nigiri-zushi. The best seats are in front where you can watch the performing chefs hard at work.

Tokyo

C/Comtal 20 (93 317 61 80). Metro Catalunya. **Open** 1.30-4pm, 8-11pm Mon-Sat. Closed Aug. **Main courses** €15. **Set lunch** €13.91 Mon-Thur. **Credit** MC, V. **Map** p344 D3 ➒
We suggest that you resist the temptation to forgo the *menú*, for this is in fact the best way to eat here. A zingy little salad is followed by a mountain of prawn and vegetable tempura and a platter of maki rolls, nigiri and a bowl of miso soup. It's a simple, cosy space that's been cleverly divided with slatted wooden partitions, with a reassuring Japanese presence. If you decide to go with the à la carte menu, the speciality is *edomae* (hand-rolled nigiri-zushi), but the meat and veg sukiyaki, which is cooked at your table, is also good. Check out Javier Mariscal's grateful signed drawing of Cobi (the Olympic mascot) dressed as a Japanese chef.

Mediterranean

El Gran Café

C/Avinyó 9 (93 318 79 86). Metro Liceu. **Open** 1-4.30pm, 7.30pm-midnight daily. **Main courses** €15. **Set lunch** €12.85 Mon-Fri. **Credit** AmEx, DC, MC, V. **Map** p345 C6 ➓
The fluted columns, bronze cavorting nymphs, suspended globe lamps and wood panelling all go towards successfully replicating a classic Parisian vibe. But that would count for nothing if the food didn't match up. Thankfully, those cornerstones of brasserie cuisine – onion soup, duck magret, tarte tatin and even crêpes suzette – are all present and correct. The imaginative Catalan dishes spliced into the menu also work, but what is less convincing is the waiters' need to sport headphones and other assorted gadgetry, and a distinctly non-Gallic attitude towards the hastily assembled set lunch.

El Salón

C/Hostal d'en Sol 6-8 (93 315 21 59). Metro Jaume I. **Open** 8.30-11.30pm Mon-Sat. **Main courses** €13. **Credit** MC, V. **Map** p345 D7 ⓫
Under new ownership, El Salón remains as welcoming as before and has retained its faintly bohemian style. Also welcome is the fact that prices have come down a notch, and the dishes have become a little simpler – creamed carrot soup, lamb brochettes, tuna with ginger and brown rice, botifarra and beans, and ice-cream made with Galician Arzoa-Ulloa cheese to finish – but this remains one of the more charming places to eat in the Barri Gòtic.

Taxidermista.

Taxidermista

Plaça Reial 8 (93 412 45 36). Metro Liceu. **Open** 1.30-4pm, 8.30pm-12.30am Tue-Sun. Closed 3wks Jan. **Main courses** €15. **Set lunch** €10 Tue-Fri. **Credit** AmEx, DC, MC, V. **Map** p345 B6 ⓬

When this was a taxidermist's, Dali famously ordered 200,000 ants, a tiger, a lion and even a rhinoceros – the latter was wheeled into the Plaça Reial so that the artist could be photographed sitting on top of the beast. Those who leave here stuffed nowadays are generally tourists, though, and this really is a surprise, this hasn't affected standards, which remain reasonably high. À la carte offerings include foie gras with quince jelly; langoustine ravioli with seafood sauce; steak tartare; and some slightly misjudged fusion elements, such as wok-fried spaghetti with vegetables. The lunch *menú* is excellent, with two- or three-course deals.

Pan-Asian

Matsuri

Plaça Regomir 1 (93 268 15 35). Metro Jaume I. **Open** 1.30-3.30pm, 8.30-11.30pm Mon-Fri; 8.30pm-midnight Sat. **Main courses** €12. **Set lunch** €9.95-€10.95. **Credit** MC, V. **Map** p345 C6 ⓭

Matsuri is more convincing than most of the city's Asian restaurants, with a perfectly executed look – trickling fountain, dark shades of terracotta and amber, wooden carvings and wall-hung candles – saved from cliché by the thoroughly occidental lounge soundtrack. Reasonably priced tom yam soup, sushi, pad Thai and other South-east Asian favourites top the list, while the less predictable choices include a zingy mango and prawn salad dressed with lime and chilli, and a rich, earthy red curry with chicken and aubergine.

Paraguayan

El Paraguayo

C/Parc 1 (93 302 14 41). Metro Drassanes. **Open** 1-4pm, 8pm-midnight Tue-Sun. **Main courses** €17. **Credit** AmEx, DC, MC, V. **Map** p345 B8 ⓮

As with most South American restaurants, the best plan of attack at El Paraguayo is to order a fat juicy steak, a bottle of the good cheap house Rioja and a bowl of piping hot yucca chips. The rest is all just so much menu filler. As to which steak, a helpful chart walks you through the various cuts, most of them unfamiliar to European butchers, but a *bife de chorizo* should satisfy the ravenous. The place itself is cosy and wood-panelled, brightened with oil paintings of buxom madams and their dapper admirers.

Peruvian

Peimong

C/Templers 6-10 (93 318 28 73). Metro Jaume I. **Open** 1-4pm, 8-11.30pm Tue-Sat; 1-4pm Sun. Closed mid Aug-Sept. **Main courses** €8.50. **Credit** DC, MC, V. **Map** p345 C6 ⓯

With its tapestries of Macchu Pichu and plastic flowers, Peimong wins no prizes for design, but it makes up for its rather unforgiving and overlit interior with some tasty little South American dishes. Start with

Mesón Jesús.

a pisco sour and a dish of big fat yucca chips, or maybe some stuffed corn tamales, and then move on to *ceviche*, *pato en aji* (a hunk of duck with a spicy sauce and rice) or the satisfying *lomo saltado* – pork fried with onions, tomatoes and coriander.

Spanish

Mesón Jesús

C/Cecs de la Boqueria 4 (93 317 46 98). Metro Jaume I or Liceu. **Open** 1-4pm, 8-11pm Mon-Fri. Closed Aug-early Sept. **Main courses** €14. **Set lunch** €15 Mon-Fri. **Set dinner** €16 Mon-Fri. **Credit** MC, V. **Map** p345 B5 🔞
The feel of Mesón Jesús is authentically Castilian, with gingham tablecloths, oak barrels, cartwheels and pitchforks hung around the walls, while the waitresses are incessantly cheerful with a largely non-Spanish-speaking clientele, and especially obliging when it comes to dealing with children. The menu is limited and never changes, but the dishes are reliably good and inexpensive to boot – try the sautéed green beans with ham to start, then the superb grilled prawns or a tasty fish stew.

Les Quinze Nits

Plaça Reial 6 (93 317 30 75). Metro Liceu. **Open** 1-3.45pm, 8.30-11.30pm daily. **Main courses** €7.50. **Set lunch** €8.20 Mon-Fri. **Credit** AmEx, MC, V. **Map** p345 B6 🔞
Top of many tourists' dining agenda, with a queue stretching halfway across the Plaça Reial, the Quinze Nits (and its many other incarnations across town) manages all this with distinctly so-so food.

The secret? Combining fast-food speed and prices with striking spaces, smart table linen and soft lighting. Diners get to feel special, eat local dishes and come away with nary a dent in their wallets. Order simply – soups, salads, grilled fish – and a reasonable meal can still be had. The queues tend to be shorter at the other branches.
Other locations La Dolça Herminia, C/Magdalenes 27 (93 317 06 76); La Fonda, C/Escudellers 10 (93 301 75 15), and throughout the city.

Born & Sant Pere

Catalan

Comerç 24

C/Comerç 24 (93 319 21 02/www.comerc24.com). Metro Arc de Triomf. **Open** 1.30-3.30pm, 8.30pm-11pm Tue-Sat. **Main courses** (tapas) €12. **Credit** MC, V. **Map** p344 F4 🔞
One of the acknowledged masters of Catalan new wave cuisine, Carles Abellan was, unsurprisingly, a disciple of Ferran Adrià in the kitchens of El Bulli (*see p174*). But nowadays he ploughs his own, very successful furrow in this urbane and sexy restaurant. A selection of tiny playful dishes (described as 'tapas') changes seasonally but might include a 'Kinder egg' (lined with truffle); tuna sashimi and seaweed on a wafer-thin pizza crust; a fun take on the bikini (a cheese and ham toastie); or a densely flavoured fish suquet. Order a selection in the shape of the *menú* festival to understand Catalonia's food revolution a little better.

Eat, Drink, Shop

Cuban

Habana Vieja
C/Banys Vells 2 (93 268 25 04). Metro Jaume I.
Open 1.30-3.30pm, 8.30-11.30pm Mon-Sat. **Main courses** €13. **Credit** AmEx, DC, MC, V.
Map p345 E6 ⑲
A tiny, laid-back Cuban restaurant, with plenty of *son* and rumba to get the evening going. The sharp taste of limes in the *mojitos* and *caipirinhas* complements the love-it-or-hate-it parade of Havana cuisine, which involves lots of meat, stodge and frying pans. Rice and beans accompany tender *ropa vieja* (shredded chilli beef), or there is fried yucca with *mojo cubano* (garlic sauce) and banana or *malanga* (a taro-like root vegetable) fritters with fresh guava for dessert. The prices seem high, but portions are big.

Global

Cuines Santa Caterina
Mercat Santa Caterina, Avda Francesc Cambó (93 268 99 18). Metro Jaume I. **Open** 1-4pm, 8-11.30pm daily. **Main courses** €11. **Credit** AmEx, DC, MC, V. **Map** p344 E4 ⑳
It's not as dazzling as it was when it opened in 2005, with higher prices and a slightly more lax attitude to quality control, but CSC still has its charms. The menu holds a little of everything you fancy, from langoustine tempura to a baked spud with cheese and *sobrassada* sausage, with an excellent chocolate tart or red-fruit millefeuille to finish. The rice, flour, crates of veg and so on arrayed along the vast windows, coupled with the well-made olive wood furniture, give everything a pleasant Mediterranean feel.

Hofmann
C/Argenteria 74-78 (93 319 58 89/www.hofmann-bcn.com). Metro Jaume I. **Open** 1.30-3pm, 9-11.15pm Mon-Fri. Closed Aug. **Main courses** €25. **Set lunch** €37. **Credit** AmEx, DC, MC, V. **Map** p345 E6 ㉑
Said to be the best cookery school in the world after the Cordon Bleu, Hofmann puts its pupils to good use in its top-class restaurant. A succession of small dining rooms holds a bright atrium, and another decorated in deep reds, orange and green – adorned with plants and dramatic flower arrangements. The affordable lunch *menú* might start with a truffle salad, followed by bream in bacon or carré of lamb with mustard sauce, but, as with the à la carte menu, the puddings are really the high point here. Artful constructions such as a jam jar and lid made of sugar and filled with red fruit, or a tarte tatin in a spun-sugar 'cage', are as delicious as they are clever.

Re-Pla
C/Montcada 2 (93 268 30 03). Metro Jaume I. **Open** 1.30-4pm, 8.30pm-midnight daily. **Main courses** €18. **Credit** DC, MC, V. **Map** p345 E5 ㉒
A casually hip but nonetheless welcoming restaurant serving Asian-Mediterranean fusion. The varied menu might include anything from a sushi platter to ostrich with green asparagus, honey and

grilled mango slices. Veggie options are clearly marked, and desserts are rich and creative. For once, the lighting is wonderfully romantic and the sleek artwork easy on the eye, though some may feel uncomfortable with the sort of waiters who pull up a chair while recounting the day's specials.
Other locations Pla, C/Bellafila 5, Barri Gòtic (93 412 65 52).

Indian

Kama
C/Rec 69 (93 268 10 29). Metro Barceloneta. **Open** 1-4pm, 7.30pm-3am Tue-Sun. **Main courses** €12. **Credit** MC, V. **Map** p345 F7 ㉓
The default spiciness setting for Kama's mostly Indian food is mild (in deference to the Catalan palate), but if owner Ketan hears a British accent, he'll ask if you'd like the heat turned up a little. Once you've factored in rice and naan, the prices can seem a little steep for a Ruby, but you're paying for the Barcelona Treatment: moody lighting; a hot-pink neon bar area; banquette seating; a covetable Kama Sutra frieze and ethno-chill-out on the sound system. Happy-hour cocktails are available 6-8pm.

French

La Cua Curta
C/Carassa s/n (93 310 00 15). Metro Jaume I. **Open** 8.30pm-midnight Tue-Sun. **Main courses** €10. **Credit** MC, V. **Map** p345 E6 ㉔
Having tired of mullets and swingers' bars, the retro-obsessed of Barcelona have turned their attention to the quietly thriving fondue restaurants. Yes, it's hip to dip once again, but *Abigail's Party* this is not: quaintly Gallic, with its etched mirrors and lacy embroidered lampshades, La Cua Curta is a refined affair, where only the menus glued to record sleeves evoke anything but the 1920s. Start with a generous salad before tackling one of the dozen variations on the emmenthal and gruyère theme, and stay off the water if you intend to digest the cheese.

Malaysian

Bunga Raya
C/Assaonadors 7 (93 319 31 69). Metro Jaume I. **Open** 8pm-midnight Tue-Sun. **Main courses** €7. **No credit cards. Map** p345 E5 ㉕
The 'Hibiscus Flower' beautifully (and almost certainly unwittingly) evokes a genuine Malaysian restaurant, with its slightly musty and forgotten air, its faded tourist-board posters and its dusty bamboo panelling. It has a faithful local following for the excellent-value taster menu (€12.95), consisting of a pile of coconut rice accompanied by beef rendang, fried peanuts with coconut shavings, spicy pineapple, marinated beansprout salad, chicken and beef satay, and a bowl of chicken curry. Other dishes worth trying include the curried anchovies and a thoroughly tasty tom yam soup.

Menu glossary

rosat/blanc	rosado/blanco	white wine
bon profit	Aproveche	Enjoy your meal
sóc	soy	I'm a...
vegetarià/ana	vegetariano/a	vegetarian
diabètic/a	diabético/a	diabetic

Cooking terms

a la brasa	a la brasa	char-grilled
a la graella/ planxa	a la plancha	grilled on a hot metal plate
a la romana	a la romana	fried in batter
al forn	al horno	baked
al vapor	al vapor	steamed
fregit	frito	fried
rostit	asado	roast
ben fet	bien hecho	well done
a punt	medio hecho	medium
poc fet	poco hecho	rare

Carn i aviram/Carne y aves/ Meat & poultry

ànec	pato	duck
bou	buey	beef
cabrit	cabrito	kid
colomí	pichón	pigeon
conill	conejo	rabbit
embotits	embotidos	cold cuts
fetge	higado	liver
gall dindi	pavo	turkey
garrí	cochinillo	suckling pig
guatla	codorniz	quail
llebre	liebre	hare
llengua	lengua	tongue
llom	lomo	loin (usually pork)
oca	oca	goose
ous	huevos	eggs
perdiu	perdiz	partridge
pernil (serrà)	jamón serrano	dry-cured ham
pernil dolç	jamón york	cooked ham
peus de porc	manos de cerdo	pigs' trotters

Essential terminology

Catalan	Spanish	
una cullera	una cuchara	a spoon
una forquilla	un tenedor	a fork
un ganivet	un cuchillo	a knife
una ampolla de	una botella de	a bottle of
una altra	otra	another (one)
més	más	more
pa	pan	bread
oli d'oliva	aceite de oliva	olive oil
sal i pebre	sal y pimienta	salt and pepper
amanida	ensalada	salad
truita	tortilla	omelette
(note: **truita** can also mean 'trout')		
la nota	la cuenta	the bill
un cendrer	un cenicero	an ashtray
vi negre/	vino tinto/	red/rosé/

Mexican

Itztli

C/Mirallers 7 (93 319 68 75/www.itztli.es). Metro Barceloneta or Jaume I. **Open** noon-11pm Tue-Sun. **Main courses** €3.50. **No credit cards**. **Map** p345 E6 ㉖

One thing the Ajuntament rarely mentions in its tourist literature is the massively long queues for entry to the Picasso Museum. Fortify yourself during the long wait with a takeaway chicken burrito from this nearby Mexican snack bar. Keenly priced around the €3.50 mark, burritos also come with beef, chili con carne or veg, as do tacos. Also on offer are quesadillas, wraps, nachos and salads, and there's a good range of Mexican beers, tinned goods and fiery chilli sauces for sale. **Other locations** C/Sant Miquel 60, Barceloneta.

Eat, Drink, Shop

pintada	gallina de Guinea	guinea fowl
pollastre	pollo	chicken
porc	cerdo	pork
porc senglar	jabalí	wild boar
vedella	ternera	veal
xai/be	cordero	lamb

Peix i marisc/Pescado y mariscos/Fish & seafood

anxoves	anchoas	anchovies
bacallà	bacalao	salt cod
besuc	besugo	sea bream
caballa	verat	mackerel
calamarsos	calamares	squid
cloïsses	almejas	clams
cranc	cangrejo	crab
escamarlans	cigalas	crayfish
escopinyes	berberechos	cockles
espardenyes	espardeñas	sea cucumbers
gambes	gambas	prawns
llagosta	langosta	spiny lobster
llagostins	langostinos	langoustines
llamàntol	bogavante	lobster
llenguado	lenguado	sole
llobarro	lubina	sea bass
lluç	merluza	hake
moll	salmonete	red mullet
musclos	mejillones	mussels
navalles	navajas	razor clams
percebes	percebes	barnacles
pop	pulpo	octopus
rap	rape	monkfish
rèmol	rodaballo	turbot
salmó	salmón	salmon
sardines	sardinas	sardines
sípia	sepia	squid
tallarines	tallarinas	wedge clams
tonyina	atún	tuna
truita	trucha	trout

(note: **truita** can also mean 'omelette')

Verdures/Legumbres/Vegetables

albergínia	berenjena	aubergine
all	ajo	garlic
alvocat	aguacate	avocado
bolets	setas	wild mushrooms
carbassos	calabacines	courgette
carxofes	alcahofas	artichokes
ceba	cebolla	onion
cigrons	garbanzos	chickpeas
col	col	cabbage
enciam	lechuga	lettuce
endivies	endivias	chicory
espinacs	espinacas	spinach
mongetes blanques	judías blancas	haricot beans
mongetes verdes	judías verdes	French beans
pastanagues	zanahorias	carrot
patates	patatas	potatoes
pebrots	pimientos	peppers
pèsols	guisantes	peas
porros	puerros	leek
tomàquets	tomates	tomatoes
xampinyons	champiñones	mushrooms

Postres/Postres/Desserts

flam	flan	crème caramel
formatge	queso	cheese
gelat	helado	ice-cream
música	música	dried fruit and nuts, served with muscatel
pastís	pastel	cake
tarta	tarta	tart

Fruïta/Fruta/Fruit

figues	higos	figs
gerds	frambuesas	raspberries
maduixes	fresas	strawberries
pera	pera	pear
pinya	piña	pineapple
plàtan	plátano	banana
poma	manzana	apple
préssec	melocotón	peach
prunes	ciruelas	plums

Pan-Asian

Wushu

C/Colomines 2, off Plaça Santa Caterina (93 310 73 13/www.wushu-restaurant.com). Metro Jaume I.
Open 1-4.30pm, 7-11pm Tue-Sat. **Main courses** €13.50. **Credit** MC, V. **Map** p345 E5 ㉗

A year after Wushu's opening, its six tables have become so sought-after that securing one for lunch has become something of a lottery (the hunt is on for bigger premises to handle the large number of people who want to eat here, so check the website or call ahead for any updates as to alternative locations). The reason for its great popularity is easy to understand: superb Asian wok cooking (pad Thai, lo mein and the only laksa to be found in Barcelona) courtesy of Australian chef Bradley Ainsworth; friendly, charming service and generous portions.

Pizzeria

Pizza Paco
*C/Allada-Vermell 11 (mobile 670 338 992). Metro
Arc de Triomf.* **Open** 1pm-midnight Mon-Thur,
Sun; 1pm-2am Fri, Sat . **Main courses** €7.
Credit MC, V. **Map** p345 F5 ㉘
Spawned from the improbably successful hole-in-
the-wall bar opposite, Casa Paco, this one aims to
provide the ballast. In fact, it functions better as a
bar than a pizza restaurant (though the pizzas are
really pretty good), and you'll struggle to get your
order heard over the general hubbub (and the
Strokes). One to incorporate into a night on the tiles,
rather than an evening's outing in itself.

Seafood

Cal Pep
*Plaça de les Olles 8 (93 310 79 61/www.calpep.com).
Metro Barceloneta.* **Open** 8-11.45pm Mon; 1.30-4pm,
8-11.45pm Tue-Sat. Closed Aug. **Main courses** €15.
Credit AmEx, DC, MC, V. **Map** p345 E7 ㉙
As much tapas bar as restaurant, Cal Pep is always
packed: get here early for the coveted seats at the
front. There is a cosy dining room at the back, but
it's a shame to miss the show. The affable Pep will
take the order steering the neophytes towards the
trifàsico – a mélange of fried whitebait, squid rings
and shrimp. Other favourites are the exquisite little
tallarines (wedge clams), and botifarra sausage with
beans. Then, squeeze in four shot glasses of foam –
coconut with rum, coffee, crema catalana and lemon.

Mundial Bar
*Plaça Sant Agustí Vell 1 (93 319 90 56). Metro Arc
de Triomf or Jaume I.* **Open** 1-4pm, 9pm-midnight
Tue-Sat; noon-3.30pm Sun. Closed Aug. **Main
courses** €17. **Credit** MC, V. **Map** p344 F4 ㉚
Since 1925, this venerable family establishment has
been dishing up no-frills platters of seafood, cheeses
and the odd slice of cured meat. Colourful tiles and
a marble trough of a bar add charm to the rather
basic decor, but it's not as cheap as it looks. People
come for the steaming piles of fresh razor clams,
shrimp, oysters, fiddler crabs and the like, but
there's also plenty of tinned produce, so check the
bar displays to see exactly which is which.

La Paradeta
*C/Comercial 7 (93 268 19 39). Metro Arc de Triomf
or Jaume I.* **Open** 8-11.30pm Tue-Fri; 1-4pm, 8pm-
midnight Sat; 1-4pm Sun. **Main courses** €10.
No credit cards. Map p345 F6 ㉛
Superb seafood which is served refectory-style.
Choose from glistening mounds of clams, mussels,
squid, spider crabs and whatever else the boats have
brought in, let them know how you'd like it cooked
(grilled, steamed or *a la marinera*), pick a sauce
(Marie Rose, spicy local romesco, *all i oli* or onion),
buy a drink and wait for your number to be called.
A great – and cheap – experience for anyone not too
grand to clear their own plate.

Raval

Catalan

Drassanes
*Museu Marítim, Avda Drassanes (93 317 52 56).
Metro Drassanes.* **Open** 1-4pm Mon-Sat; 1-4pm,
9pm-midnight Thur-Sat. **Main courses** €15.
Set lunch €10.75 Mon-Fri. **Credit** DC, MC, V.
Map p345 A8 ㉜
Drassanes is dwarfed by the towering 14th-century
Gothic arches of the former shipyard, now housing
the Maritime Museum. The restaurant fills up at
lunchtime with office workers who come here for in
particular for the generally good-value set menu.
The quality of the food varies, but at its best, it is
unbeatable, with Catalan classics such as botifarra
sausage with wild mushrooms appearing alongside
grilled fish and pasta. Going à la carte, the dishes
traverse the globe, from wok-fried prawns and vegetables on yakisoba noodles, to duck magret with
sour apple sauce or Thai curry. *Photo p159.*

Elisabets

C/Elisabets 2-4 (93 317 58 26). Metro Catalunya.
Open 7am-11pm Mon-Sat. Closed 3wks Aug. **Set
lunch** €9 Mon-Fri. **Set dinner** €12 Fri. **No credit
cards**. **Map** p344 B3 ㉝
Also open in the mornings for breakfast, and late
night for drinking at the bar, Elisabets maintains a
sociable local feel, despite the recent gentrification
of its street. Dinner, served only on Fridays, is actually a selection of tapas, and otherwise only the set
lunch or myriad *bocadillos* are served. The lunch deal
is terrific value, however, with osso buco, vegetable
and chickpea stew, baked cod with garlic and parsley, and roast pork knuckle all making regular
appearances on the menu.

Filipino

Fil Manila

*C/Ramelleres 3 (93 318 64 87). Metro Catalunya
or Liceu.* **Open** 11am-midnight daily. **Main courses**
€8. **Credit** AmEx, DC, MC, V. **Map** p344 B3 ㉞

Mundial Bar.

Unpretentious and undervisited, Fil Manila may
have the longest menu in Barcelona. Malay, Chinese
and Spanish influences all contribute to the classic
flavours of sour fish soup, *pancit* (noodles), chicken
and pork adobo, fried *lumpia* (crispy vegetable or
meat rolls) or a halo-halo dessert of fruits, crushed
ice and milk. The bamboo-lined decor doesn't try too
hard to be exotic, and the faithful patronage of local
Filipinos augurs well for the food's authenticity.

Global

Dos Trece

C/Carme 40 (93 301 73 06). Metro Liceu. **Open**
1.30-4pm, 9pm-midnight Tue-Sun. **Main courses**
€12. **Set lunch** €9.50 Tue-Fri. **Credit** AmEx, DC,
MC, V. **Map** p344 A4 ㉟
Another to fall victim to the council's crackdown on
late-night music, Dos Trece had to ditch its DJs and
jam sessions, and instead has turned its cosy basement space into another dining room – this one with
cushions and candles for post-prandial lounging.
Apart from a little fusion confusion (ceviche with
nachos, and all manner of things with yucca chips)
the food's not half bad for the price, and includes one
of the few decent burgers to be had in Barcelona.

El Pati

C/Montalegre 7 (93 318 65 04). Metro Catalunya.
Open 9am-9pm Mon-Fri. Closed Aug. **Set lunch**
€10.50. **Credit** MC, V. **Map** p344 A2 ㊱
The charm of this café comes from its situation in
the Pati Manning, an arcaded 18th-century patio
decorated with colourful tiling and sgraffiti. The
lunch deal is a good option, where €10.50 gets you
spinach ravioli with courgette sauce, followed by
layers of pork and aubergine slices in a balsamic
vinegar reduction, or roast chicken with fat wedge
chips, a drink and a dessert. Outside lunch hours,
croissants, sandwiches and so on are served.

Zarabanda

*C/Ferlandina 55 (mobile 653 169 539). Metro Sant
Antoni.* **Open** 8pm-2am daily. Closed 2wks Aug; Sun
in July, Aug. **Main courses** €7. **No credit cards**.
Map p342 E9 ㊲
Probably the only place in town to have a shared bowl
of nachos as a signature dish, Zarabanda attracts a
fair few students looking for somewhere more comfortable than a bar but cheaper than a restaurant. Its
cosy vibe is nudged along with low lighting, creative
paintwork and the much sought-after space on the
one, battered, sofa; the food is decent and good value,
particularly the salads and crêpes. Occasional jazz,
flamenco and even electro take over the tiny stage.

Mediterranean

Biblioteca

*C/Junta de Comerç 28 (93 412 62 21/www.biblio
tecarestaurant.com). Metro Liceu.* **Open** 8-11.30pm
Mon-Sat. Closed 2wks Aug. **Main courses** €13.
Credit AmEx, MC, V. **Map** p345 A5 ㊳

Eat, Drink, Shop

A tranquil, elegant space with beige minimalist decor, Biblioteca is all about food. Food and books about food, that is. From Bocuse to Bourdain, they are all for sale, and their various influences collide in the menu. Increasingly, though, it draws from the Catalan culinary canon, with a good *esqueixada* (salt cod salad) or a reasonable onion *coca* (flat, crispy bread) with anchovies to start, followed by gamier mains that might include venison pie or pigs' trotters stuffed with prunes on a bed of spinach.

Pla dels Àngels

C/Ferlandina 23 (93 329 40 47). Metro Universitat. **Open** 1.30-4pm, 9-11.30pm Mon-Thur, Sun; 1.30-4pm, 9pm-midnight Fri, Sat. **Main courses** €6.50. **Set lunch** €6.40 Mon-Fri. **Credit** DC, MC, V. **Map** p342 F9 ③

Beautifully designed in keeping with its position opposite the MACBA, Pla dels Àngels is a riot of colour and chimera, something that also translates to its menu (which you'll find glued to a wine bottle, no less). The range of salads on offer might include mango, yoghurt and mint oil, or radicchio, serrano ham and roast peppers, followed by a short list of pasta and gnocchi and a couple of meat dishes. 'Delirium tremens' is a rich chocolate fantasy that might induce tremors of delight. The cheap-as-chips set lunch includes two courses and a glass of wine.

Silenus

C/Àngels 8 (93 302 26 80). Metro Liceu. **Open** 1.30-4pm, 8.30-11.30pm Mon-Thur; 1.30-4pm, 8.30pm-midnight Fri, Sat. **Main courses** €16.50. **Set lunch** €13 Mon-Sat. **Credit** AmEx, DC, MC, V. **Map** p344 A3 ④

Run by arty types for arty types, Silenus works hard to maintain its air of scuffed elegance, with artfully chipped and stained walls on which the ghost of a clock is projected and the faded leaves of a book float in a ghostly manner up on high. The food, too, is artistically presented, and never more so than with the lunchtime tasting menu. This allows a tiny portion of everything on the menu, from French onion soup to a flavoursome haricot-bean stew and entrecôte with mashed potatoes.

Pizzeria

Ravalo

Plaça Emili Vendrell 1 (93 442 01 00). Metro Sant Antoni. **Open** 6pm-1.30am Tue-Sun. **Main courses** €9. **Credit** MC, V. **Map** p342 E10 ④

Perfect for fans of the thin and the crispy, Ravalo's table-dwarfing pizzas take some beating, thanks to flour (and a chef) imported from Naples. All the pizzas, like the Sienna, come with the cornerstone toppings you'd expect in any pizzeria – in this case mozzarella di bufala, speck, cherry tomatoes and rocket – but the less familiar offerings include the Pizza Soufflé, which comes filled with ham, mushrooms and an eggy mousse (better than it sounds, really). The restaurant's terrace overlooking a quiet square is open year-round.

La Verònica

C/Rambla de Raval 2-4 (93 329 33 03). Metro Liceu. **Open** *Sept-July* noon-2am Tue-Sun. *Aug* 7pm-1am Tue-Sun. **Main courses** €10. **Credit** MC, V. **Map** 342 E10 ④

La Verònica's pizzas are properly crisp, thin and healthy, and come with such toppings as smoked salmon, or apple, gorgonzola and mozzarella. Salads include the Nabocondensor, a colourful tumble of parsnip, cucumber and apple, and there is a short but reliable wine list.

Spanish

Las Fernández

C/Carretas 11 (93 443 20 43). Metro Paral·lel. **Open** 9pm-2am Tue-Sun. **Main courses** €7.50. **Credit** DC, MC, V. **Map** p342 E10 ④

An inviting entrance, pillar-box red, is a beacon of cheer on one of Barcelona's less salubrious streets. Inside, the three Fernández sisters have created a bright and unpretentious bar/restaurant that specialises in wine and food from their native León. Alongside *cecina* (dried venison), gammon and sausages from the region are lighter, Mediterranean dishes and generous salads; smoked salmon with mustard and dill; pasta filled with wild mushrooms; and sardines with a citrus escabeche.

Shipshape at **Drassanes**. *See p156.*

Eat, Drink, Shop

Bestial.

Vegetarian

Juicy Jones

C/Hospital 74 (93 443 90 82). Metro Liceu. **Open**
noon-11pm daily. **Main courses** €6. **Set lunch**
€8.50 daily. **No credit cards. Map** p342 F10 **44**

A new branch of this colourful, vegan restaurant,
with an inventive list of juices, salads and baguettes.
While its heart is in the right place, it's mostly aimed
at backpackers and staffed, it would seem, by clue-
less language-exchange students; this is not somewhere you can expect a speedy lunch. Bring a book.
Other locations C/Cardenas 7 (93 302 43 20).

Organic

C/Junta de Comerç 11 (93 301 09 02). Metro Liceu.
Open 12.30pm-midnight daily. **Main courses** €9.
Set lunch €10 Mon-Fri. **Set dinner** €18 daily. **Set
lunch** €13 Sat; €14 Sun. **Credit** AmEx, DC, MC, V.
Map p345 A5 **45**

The last word in refectory chic, Organic is better
designed and lighter in spirit (its motto: 'Don't panic,
it's organic!') than the vast majority of the city's vegetarian restaurants. The friendly staff will usher you
inside and give you a rundown on meal options.
Beware the extras, which hitch up the prices.

Sésamo

*C/Sant Antoni Abat 52 (93 441 64 11). Metro Sant
Antoni.* **Open** 1-3.30pm Mon; 1-3.30pm, 8.30-11.30pm
Wed-Sat; 8.30-11.30pm Sun. **Main courses** €11.
Set lunch €9 Mon-Fri; €10 Sat. **Credit** MC, V.
Map p342 E10 **46**

Another veggie restaurant not taking itself too seriously (yoga adverts, but thankfully no wailing
whale song), Sésamo offers an interesting and creative bunch of dishes served in a cosy, buzzing back
room. Salad with risotto and a drink is a bargain at
just €6.50, or you could try cucumber rolls stuffed
with smoked tofu and mashed pine nuts; crunchy
polenta with baked pumpkin, gorgonzola and radicchio; or spicy curry served in popadom baskets with
dahl and wild rice. There is also a selection of
Japanese tapas on offer.

Barceloneta & the Ports

Global

Somorrostro

*C/Sant Carles 11 (93 225 00 10/www.restaurante
somorrostro.com). Metro Barceloneta or Ciutadella
Vila Olímpica.* **Open** 7-11.30pm Mon, Thur-Sun.
Main courses €12.50. **Credit** DC, MC, V.
Map p343 H13 **47**

Named after the shanty town of Andalucian immigrants that once stood nearby on the beach,
Somorrostro is a refreshingly non-traditional, non-
fishy restaurant for these usually unchanging, at
least as far as food is concerned, parts. Its bare-
bricked walls and red-and-black decor attract a
young, buzzy crowd, attended to by permanently
confused waiters. The food ranges from cucumber,
tomato and yoghurt soup with home-made bread, to
an unexpectedly successful tandoori duck magret.

Italian

Bestial

C/Ramón Trias Fargas 2-4 (93 224 04 07). Metro Barceloneta. **Open** 1-4pm, 8-11.30pm Mon-Fri daily. **Main courses** €16.50. **Set lunch** €18.20 Mon-Fri. **Credit** AmEx, DC, MC, V. **Map** p343 K13 ⓭
Its tiered wooden decking and ancient olive trees making it the most elegant restaurant on this stretch of beach, Bestial is a peerless spot for alfresco seaside dining. The interior design manages to match the splendour of the exterior, with black-clad waiters sashaying along sleek runways holding their trays high. At weekends, coloured lights play over the tables as a DJ takes to the decks. The food is modern Italian: dainty mini-pizzas, rocket salads with parma ham and a lightly poached egg, tuna with black olive risotto and all the puddings you'd expect to find – panna cotta, tiramisu and limoncello sorbet.

Mediterranean

Agua

Passeig Marítim 30 (93 225 12 72/www.aguadel tragaluz.com). Metro Barceloneta/bus 45, 57, 59, 157. **Open** 1-3.45pm, 8-11.30pm Mon-Thur, Sun; 1-4.30pm, 8pm-12.30am Fri, Sat. **Main courses** €15. **Credit** AmEx, DC, MC, V. **Map** p343 J13 ⓭
One of the freshest, most relaxed places to eat in the city, with a large terrace smack on the beach and an animated sunny interior. The menu rarely changes, but regulars never tire of the competently executed monkfish tail with *sofregit*, the risotto with partridge, and fresh pasta with juicy little prawns. Scrummy puddings include marron glacé mousse and sour apple sorbet. The wine mark-up is quite high for such reasonably priced food; a couple of notable exceptions are white Creu de Lavit or red Añares.

Seafood

Can Majó

C/Almirall Aixada 23 (93 221 54 55). Metro Barceloneta. **Open** 1-4pm, 8-11.30pm Tue-Sat; 1-4pm Sun. **Main courses** €21. **Credit** AmEx, MC, V. **Map** p343 H13 ⓭
Famous for its fresh-from-the-nets selection of oysters, scallops, Galician clams, whelks and just about any other mollusc you care to mention. While the menu reads much as you'd expect for a Barceloneta seafood restaurant, with plates of shellfish or (exemplary) fish soup to start, followed by rich paellas and exquisitely tasty fideuà, the quality is a cut above the norm. Sit inside the dapper green and yellow dining room, or within the periwinkle blue picket fence, overlooking the sea.

Can Ramonet

C/Maquinista 17 (93 319 30 64). Metro Barceloneta. **Open** noon-midnight daily. Closed 2wks Jan. **Main courses** €20. **Credit** AmEx, DC, MC, V. **Map** p343 H12 ⓭

A classic among Barceloneta's seafood restaurants, this quaint, rose-coloured space with two quiet terraces is mostly overlooked by tourists, being set away from the tourist runs deep in the heart of the neighbourhood. Consequently, it suffers none of the drop in standards of some of those paella joints on nearby Passeig Joan de Borbó. Spectacular displays of fresh seafood show what's on offer that day, but it's also worth sampling the velvety fish soup and the generous paellas.
Other locations C/Carbonell 5 (93 268 33 13).

Can Solé

C/Sant Carles 4 (93 221 50 12). Metro Barceloneta. **Open** 1.30-4pm, 8-11pm Tue-Thur; 1.30-4pm, 8.30-11pm Fri, Sat; 1.30-4pm Sun. Closed 2wks Aug. **Main courses** €20. **Credit** AmEx, DC, MC, V. **Map** p342 H13 ⓭
One of Barceloneta's most traditional seafood restaurants, where for over a century portly, jovial waiters have been charming moneyed regulars. Over the years, many of these have added to the framed photos, sketches and paintings that line the sky-blue walls. What continues to lure them is the freshest shellfish (share a plate of chipirones in onion and garlic, Cantabrian anchovies or red shrimp to start) and fillets of wild turbot, lobster stews and sticky paellas. Beware the steeply priced extras (coffee, cover).

Set Portes

Passeig Isabel II 14 (93 319 30 33/www.7portes. com). Metro Barceloneta. **Open** 1pm-1am daily. **Main courses** €18. **Credit** AmEx, DC, MC, V. **Map** p345 E7 ⓭
The eponymous seven doors open on to as many dining salons, all kitted out in elegant 19th-century decor. Long-aproned waiters bring regional dishes, served in enormous portions, including a stewy fish *zarzuela* with half a lobster, a different paella daily (shellfish, for example, or rabbit and snails), and a wide array of fresh seafood or heavier dishes such as herbed black-bean stew with pork sausage, and *orujo* sorbet to finish. Reservations are available only for certain tables (two to three days in advance is recommended); without one, get there early or expect a long wait outside.

El Suquet de l'Almirall

Passeig Joan de Borbó 65 (93 221 62 33). Metro Barceloneta. **Open** 1-4pm, 8.30-11pm Tue-Sat; 1-4pm Sun. Closed 2wks Aug. **Main courses** €20. **Credit** MC, V. **Map** p342 G13 ⓭
One of the famous beachfront *chiringuitos* that was moved and refurbished in time for the 1992 Olympics, El Suquet remains a friendly family-run concern despite the smart decor and mid-scale business lunchers. The fishy favourites range from xató salad to arròs negre and include a variety of set menus, such as the 'blind' selection of tapas, a gargantuan taster menu and, most popular, the *pica-pica*, which includes roast red peppers with anchovies, a bowl of steamed cockles and clams, and a heap of *fideuà* with lobster.

Eat, Drink, Shop

Montjuïc & Poble Sec

Catalan

La Font del Gat
Passeig Santa Madrona 28 (93 289 04 04).
Funicular Parc Montjuïc/bus 55. **Open** 1-4pm Tue-
Sun. Closed 3 wks Aug. **Main courses** €17. **Set**
lunch €11.20. **Credit** MC, V. **Map** p339 B11 ⑤
A welcome watering hole perched high on Montjuïc
between the Miró and ethnological museums. This
small and informal-looking restaurant, has a surprisingly sophisticated menu: ravioli with truffles and
wild mushrooms, for example, or foie gras with
Modena caramel. However, most come for the set
lunch: start with scrambled egg with Catalan sausage
and peppers or a salad, follow it with baked cod or
chicken with pine nuts and basil, and finish with fruit
or a simple dessert. Tables outside have a surcharge.

Oleum
Palau Nacional (93 289 06 79). Metro Espanya.
Open 1-4pm Tue-Sun. **Main courses** €22. **Credit**
AmEx, DC, MC, V. **Map** p339 B10 ⑤
That the MNAC's restaurant is to be considered a
serious contender in Barcelona's dining scene is indicated by the two Antoni Tàpies canvases flanking
– and almost outdoing – the striking view across the
city. Dishes run the gamut from scallops on squid-
ink noodles with lime foam to suckling pig with an
onion tarte tatin, or St Peter's fish poached in a fen-
nel broth. Despite one or two teething troubles (dis-
tracted service and a couple of deliquescent foams),
your average museum caff this is not. *Photo p165.*

Global

La Soleá
Plaça del Sortidor 14 (93 441 01 24). Metro Poble
Sec. **Open** noon-midnight Tue-Sat; noon-4.30pm Sun.
Main courses €9. **Set lunch** €6.50. **No credit**
cards. Map p339 D11 ⑤
From the name to the sprawling terrace and the
cheerful waiters to the orange-and-yellow decor,
everything about La Soleá radiates sunshine. There's
barely a continent that isn't on the menu, which holds
houmous, tabouleh and goat's-cheese salad alongside
juicy burgers served with roquefort or mushrooms,
smoky tandoori chicken, Mexican tacos, vegetable
samosas and slabs of Argentine beef. For all its international appeal, however, the location in a quiet
Poble Sec square makes this a firmly local restaurant, buzzing with children, dogs and the greeting
cries of neighbours, with prices to match.

Italian

La Bella Napoli
C/Margarit 12 (93 442 50 56). Metro Paral·lel.
Open 8.30pm-midnight Tue; 1.30-4pm, 8.30pm-
midnight Wed-Sun. **Main courses** €12. **Credit**
DC, MC, V. **Map** p339 D10 ⑤

La Bella Napoli's once-legendary queues (which
would snake out of the door) are thankfully a thing
of the past thanks to a major renovation and the
addition of a new and spacious bare-bricked dining
room. Welcoming Neapolitan waiters, in nifty red T-
shirts to match the red gingham tablecloths, can talk
you through the long, long list of antipasti and pasta
dishes, while you can't go wrong with the crispy
baked pizzas, such as the Sofia Loren, with provolone, basil, bresaola, cherry tomatoes, rocket and
parmesan. Beer is Moretti, the wine list all-Italian.

Xemei
Passeig de la Exposició 85 (93 553 5140). Metro
Poble Sec. **Open** 1.30-3.30pm, 9.30pm-midnight Mon,
Wed-Sun. **Main courses** €14. **Credit** MC, V.
Map p339 C10 ⑤
Heartwarming Venetian country cooking, from
home-made pasta to peppered ribbons of liver and
onions with fried polenta. The *cicchetti* is a great way
to start: a plate of antipasti involving fresh
anchovies, figs with pecorino and *sarda in saor* (sardines marinated in vinegar and onions), while peach
crostata makes for an indulgent finish. When the
weather allows, book a pavement table; the dining
room can get a little cramped and noisy.

Mediterranean

Tapioles 53
C/Tapioles 53 (93 329 22 38/www.tapioles53.com).
Metro Paral·lel or Poble Sec. **Open** 9-11pm Tue-Sat.
Set menu €34-€54. **Credit** MC, V. **Map** p339 D11 ⑥
Eating at Tapioles 53 would be a little like eating at
a friend's house; if, that is, you had any friends who
could cook this well with as canny an eye for seductive lighting. Tucked down a residential Poble Sec
street, behind a doorbell and slatted blinds, it's the
brainchild of Australian chef Sarah Stothart, who
wanted to create a cosy atmosphere with accomplished but unpretentious food – fabulous home-
made bread with wild mushroom soup; boeuf
bourguignon; fresh pasta with baby broad beans
and artichokes; rose-water rice pudding with pome-
granate, or ginger and mascarpone cheesecake. The
freshest produce is bought daily, and Sarah cooks
according to demand, so it helps to book ahead.

Eixample

Catalan

Alkimia
C/Indústria 79 (93 207 61 15). Metro Joanic or
Sagrada Família. **Open** 1.30-3.30pm, 8.30-11pm
Mon-Fri. Closed 2wks Aug. **Main courses** €29.50.
Credit DC, MC, V. **Map** p341 J6 ⑥
It came as no surprise to Alkimia's regulars when it
was awarded a Michelin star (as a consequence of
which, reservations are now all but essential). A
great way to explore is to sample the gourmet menu,
which offers four good savoury courses, including

complex dishes that play with Spanish classics – for instance, liquid pa amb tomàquet with fuet sausage, wild rice with crayfish, strips of tuna on a bed of foamed mustard – and a couple of desserts. An excellent wine cellar adds to the experience.

Casa Calvet

C/Casp 48 (93 412 40 12). Metro Urquinaona.
Open 1-3.30pm, 8.30-11pm Mon-Sat. Closed 2wks Aug. **Main courses** €28.50. **Credit** AmEx, DC, MC, V. **Map** p344 E1 ⓷²

The loafer's guide to sightseeing would surely have Casa Calvet at the top of the list: a place where you can sample stellar cuisine and appreciate the master of Modernisme at the same time. One of Gaudí's more understated buildings from the outside, Casa Calvet has an interior full of glorious detail in the carpentry, stained glass and tiles. The food is up to par, with surprising combinations almost always hitting the mark: squab with puréed pumpkin, risotto of duck confit and truffle with yoghurt ice-cream, and smoked foie gras with mango sauce. The puddings are supremely good, particularly the pine-nut tart with foamed crema catalana, and the cheeseboard contains some unexpected finds. *Photo p167.*

Cinc Sentits

C/Aribau 58 (93 323 94 90/www.cincsentits.com). Metro Passeig de Gràcia or Universitat. **Open** 1.30-3.30pm Mon; 1.30-3.30pm, 8.30-11.15pm Tue-Sat. Closed 2wks Aug. **Main courses** €22.50. **Credit** AmEx, MC, V. **Map** p340 F7 ⓷³

Run by Catalan-Canadian siblings, the 'Five Senses' is the most reasonably priced of Barcelona's top-end restaurants, and should be on everyone's dining agenda. Talented chef Jordi Artal shows respect for the classics (melt-in-the-mouth suckling pig with apple compôte, or Catalan flat coca bread with foie gras and crispy leeks), while adding a personal touch in dishes such as lamb cutlets with a crust of porcini dust. To finish, save room for the artisanal Catalan cheese pairings or the 'five textures of lemon'. Reservations are generally essential at night; visit for lunch if you're after a more peaceful experience. *See p172* **Artal soul**. *Photo p171.*

Gaig

Hotel Cram, C/Aragó 214 (93 429 10 17/www. restaurantgaig.com). Metro Passeig de Gràcia. **Open** 9-11pm Mon; 1.30-3.30pm, 9-11pm Tue-Sat. Closed 3wks Aug, 1wk Easter. **Main courses** €35. **Credit** AmEx, DC, MC, V. **Map** p340 F8 ⓷⁴

Sadly displaced from its long-term (for over 130 years, in fact) home in Horta after structural problems made it unsafe, Gaig has lost none of its shine in the move to a new location. The eponymous chef Carles Gaig's cooking never fails to thrill the visitor. From the crayfish tempura amuse-gueule, served with a dip of creamed leek salted with a piece of pancetta, through to a shot glass holding layers of tangy lemon syrup, crema catalana mousse, caramel ice-cream and topped with burned sugar (to be eaten by plunging the spoon all the way down), every dish

is as surprising and perfectly composed as the last. The one drawback resulting from the new hotel location, however, is the increase in prices.

Manairó

C/Diputació 424 (93 231 00 57/www.manairo.com). Metro Monumental. **Open** 1.30-4pm, 8.30-11pm Tue-Sat. **Main courses** €21. **Credit** AmEx, MC, V. **Map** p340 F8 ⓷⁵

If you've ever been curious to try some of the more extreme experiences in postmodern haute cuisine (we're talking tripe and brains rather than the latest flights of fancy from the Blumenthal school), Manairó is the place to start. Its divine tasting menu takes in small portions of Catalan specialities such as *cap i pota* (a stew of calves' head and feet) and langoustine with botifarra sausage and cod tripe, and renders them so delicately that the most squeamish diner will be seduced. Other star turns include a 'false' anchovy – actually a long strip of marinated tuna dotted prettily with pearls of red vermouth. Using some nifty design to make the most of a small and awkwardly shaped dining room, Manairó makes customers instantly at ease. *Photo p172.*

Moo

C/Rosselló 265 (93 445 40 00/www.hotelomm.es). Metro Diagonal. **Open** 1.30-3.45pm, 8.30-10.45pm Mon-Sat. **Main courses** (half portions) €18.50. **Credit** AmEx, DC, MC, V. **Map** p340 G6 ⓷⁶

As desirable as the rooms at the Hotel Omm, the tables in its fine restaurant, Moo. Superbly inventive cooking is overseen by renowned Catalan chef Joan Roca – from El Celler de Can Roca (*see p289*) in Girona – and designed as half portions, the better to experience the full range, from sea bass with lemongrass to exquisite suckling pig with a sharp Granny Smith purée. Particular wines (from a list of 500) are suggested to go with every course, and many dishes are even built around them: finish, for example, with 'Sauternes', the wine's bouquet perfectly rendered in mango ice-cream, saffron custard and grapefruit jelly. To top it off, service is exemplary.

Saüc

Ptge Lluís Pellicer 12 (93 321 01 89). Metro Hospital-Clínic. **Open** 1.30-3.30pm, 8.30-10.30pm Tue-Sat. Closed 3wks Aug. **Main courses** €29.50. **Credit** AmEx, MC, V. **Map** p340 E6 ⓷⁷

Despite its considerable reputation locally, it came as a pleasant surprise when the unassuming little Saüc ('elderberry') received a Michelin star recently. It's now essential to book, particularly for lunch. Dishes range from accomplished Catalan comfort food in the shape of spicy Mallorcan sobrassada sausage with potatoes and poached egg to more sophisticated fare such as cod with apple aïoli, spinach and cherry tomatoes.

Toc

C/Girona 59 (93 488 11 48/www.tocbcn.com). Metro Girona. **Open** 1.30-3.30pm, 8.30-10.45pm Mon-Fri; 8.30-11.30pm Sat. **Main courses** €18.50. **Set lunch** €31.90. **Credit** AmEx, MC, V. **Map** p343 H8 ⓷⁸

Oleum. *See p163.*

Eat, Drink, Shop

Minimalist to the point of clinical, Toc nonetheless offers a menu that is all heart and colour. Old Catalan favourites such as *esqueixada* (salt cod salad) and *cap i pota* (calves' head stew) are revived with pzazz alongside squab and truffled pâté or chilled beetroot gazpacho. Look out for the green-tea fruitcake with pears in red wine to finish, and a well-thought-out wine list with some excellent local bottles.

Windsor

C/Còrsega 286 (93 415 84 83 www.restaurantwind sor.com). Metro Diagonal. **Open** 1-4pm, 8.30-11pm Mon-Fri; 8.30-11pm Sat. Closed Aug. **Main courses** €25. **Credit** AmEx, DC, MC, V. **Map** p340 F6 ⑱

Let down slightly by a smart but drab dining room, Windsor nevertheless serves some of the most creative and uplifting food around. Most dishes riff on the cornerstones of Catalan cuisine – pigs' trotters stuffed with cap i pota and so on – while others have a lighter, Mediterranean feel: turbot with orange risotto and citrus powder, or salt cod with stewed tomatoes and olives.

French

Ty-Bihan

Ptge Lluis Pellicer 13 (93 410 90 02). Metro Hospital Clínic. **Open** 1.30-3.30pm Mon; 1.30-3.30pm, 8.30-11.30pm Tue-Fri; 8.30-11.30pm Sat. Closed Aug. **Main courses** €7.80. **Set lunch** €11 Mon-Fri. **Credit** V. **Map** p340 E6 ⑳

Functioning both as a crêperie and a cultural centre for Bretons, Ty-Bihan has chosen a smart, spacious look over wheat sheaves and pitchforks. A long list of sweet and savoury *galettes* (crêpes that are made with buckwheat flour) is followed up with scrumptious little blinis – try them smothered with strawberry jam and cream – and crêpes suzettes served in a pool of flaming Grand Marnier. The Petite menu will take care of *les enfants*, while a bowl or two of Breton cider takes care of the grown-ups.

Mediterranean

Lasarte

Hotel Condes de Barcelona, C/Mallorca 259 (93 445 32 42/www.restaurantlasarte.com). Metro Passeig de Gràcia. **Open** 1.30-3.30pm, 8.30-11pm Mon-Fri. Closed Aug. **Main courses** €35.50. **Credit** AmEx, DC, MC, V. **Map** p340 G7 ㉑

Triple-Michelin-starred San Sebastián chef Martin Berasategui has now established a culinary outpost in Barcelona, overseeing a menu that incorporates many of his signature dishes. One of the most spectacular of these is the layered terrine of foie gras, smoked eel and caramelised apple, while among the other dishes of note you'll find a succulent pigeon breast with a foie gras prepared from its own liver, or roast sea bass with hot citrus vinaigrette and creamed 'marrowbone' of cauliflower. Puddings range from superbly refreshing – apple 'ravioli' in a mint and lime jus with coconut ice-cream and rum

Eat with your eyes too at **Casa Calvet**. *See p164.*

Eat, Drink, Shop

Catalan dishes

Many dishes apparently from other cuisines – risotto, *canelons*, ravioli – are entrenched in the Catalan culinary tradition. Two names borrowed from the French are *foie* (as opposed to *fetge/higado* or foie gras), which has come to mean hare, duck or goose liver prepared with liqueur, salt and sugar; and *coulant* – rather like a small soufflé, but melting in the centre.

a la llauna literally 'in the tin' – baked on a metal tray with garlic, tomato, paprika and wine

all i oli garlic crushed with olive oil to form a mayonnaise-like texture, similar to aïoli

amanida catalana/*ensalada catalana* mixed salad with a selection of cold meats

arròs negre/*arroz negro* 'black rice', seafood rice cooked in squid ink

botifarra/*butifarra* Catalan sausage. Variants include *botifarra negre* (blood sausage) and *blanca* (mixed with egg)

botifarra amb mongetes/*butifarra con judías* sausage with haricot beans

calçots a variety of large spring onion, available only from December to spring, and eaten char-grilled, with *romesco* sauce

carn d'olla traditional Christmas dish of various meats stewed with *escudella*, then served separately

conill amb cargols/*conejo con caracoles* rabbit with snails

crema catalana custard dessert with burned sugar topping, similar to crème brûlée

escalivada/*escalibada* grilled and peeled peppers, onions and aubergine

escudella winter stew of meat and vegetables

espinacs a la catalana/*espinacas a la catalana* spinach fried in olive oil with garlic, raisins and pine nuts

esqueixada summer salad of marinated salt cod with onions, olives and tomato

fideuà/*fideuá* paella made with vermicelli instead of rice

mar i muntanya a traditional Catalan combination of meat and seafood, such as lobster and chicken in the same dish

mel i mató curd cheese with honey

pa amb tomàquet/*pan con tomate* bread prepared with tomato, oil and salt

picada a mix of nuts, garlic, parsley, bread, chicken liver and little chilli peppers, which is often used to enrich and thicken dishes

romesco a spicy sauce from the coast south of Barcelona, made with crushed almonds and hazelnuts, tomatoes, oil and a special type of red pepper (*nyora*)

samfaina a mix of onion, garlic, aubergine and red and green peppers (like ratatouille)

sarsuela/*zarzuela* fish and seafood stew

sípia amb mandonguilles/*sepia con albóndigas* cuttlefish with meatballs

suquet de peix/*suquet de pescado* fish and potato soup

torrades/*tostadas* toasted *pa amb tomàquet*

xató salad containing tuna, anchovies and cod, with a *romesco*-type sauce

granita – to the almost impossibly indulgent: a rich bread and butter pudding with coffee ice-cream and plum compôte. Afterwards we suggest a long sleep.

Noti

C/Roger de Llúria 35 (93 342 66 73/www.noti-universal.com). Metro Passeig de Gràcia or Urquinaona. **Open** 1.30-4pm, 8.30pm-midnight Mon-Fri; 8.30pm-midnight Sat. **Main courses** €25. **Set lunch** €20 Mon-Fri. **Credit** AmEx, DC, MC, V. **Map** p342 G8 ⓧ

Housed in the award-winning former offices of *El Noticiero* newspaper (hence the name), Noti pulls in a glamorous selection of the great and the good for its globetrotting range of dishes. Centrally positioned tables surrounded by reflective glass and gold panelling make celebrity-spotting unavoidable, but other reasons for coming here include steak tartare, squid stuffed with pigs' trotters and a good selection of French cheeses.

Tragaluz

Ptge de la Concepció 5 (93 487 01 96/www.grupo tragaluz.com). Metro Diagonal. **Open** 1.30-4pm, 8.30pm-midnight daily. **Main courses** €17. **Set lunch** €24.60 Mon-Fri. **Credit** AmEx, DC, MC, V. **Map** p340 G7 ⓧ

The stylish flagship for this extraordinarily successful restaurant group (which includes Agua and Bestial, for both *see p161*) has weathered the city's culinary revolution well and is still covering new ground in Mediterranean creativity. Prices have risen a bit recently, and the wine mark up is hard to swallow, but there's no faulting tuna tataki with a cardamom wafer and a dollop of ratatouille-like pisto; monkfish tail in a sweet tomato sofrito with black olive oil; or juicy braised oxtail with cabbage. Finish your meal with cherry consommé or a thin tart of white-and-dark chocolate.

La Verema

C/Comte d'Urgell 88 (93 451 68 91). Metro Urgell. **Open** 1.30-4pm Mon; 1.30-4pm, 8.30-11pm Tue, Wed; 1.30-4pm, 8.30pm-midnight Fri, Sat. **Main courses** €10.50. **Set lunch** €10.70. **Credit** AmEx, MC, V. **Map** p342 E8 ⓧ

An unexpected little neighbourhood find, La Verema doesn't look much from the outside, but takes its food very seriously. Sit up at the bar to enjoy three oysters and a glass of cava (€7) or nibble on some tapas while tasting some of its superb wines, or step down into a small dining room for a great-value *menú del día*. From the night-time à la carte menu, don't miss the artichoke hearts filled variously with wild mushrooms and quail's egg, goat's cheese and anchovy or Iranian caviar.

Vietnamese

Hanoi II

Avda Sarrià 37 (93 444 10 99). Metro Hospital Clínic. **Open** 12.30-4pm, 8.30pm-midnight Mon-Sat; 8.30pm-midnight Sun. **Main courses** €12. **Credit** AmEx, MC, V. **Map** p340 D5 ⓧ

Opened in 2006, this little sister of the frenetic original Hanoi on C/Enric Granados is a muted version, with low lighting, teak chairs and prints of Miró paintings. It's also considerably easier to get a table. The Vietnamese menu is the same, however, with duck or prawn nem rolls, chicken *musi* (chopped with water chestnuts and pine nuts, and rolled in lettuce leaves) and beef *chempy* (with orange peel and vegetables, fried with honey).

Gràcia

Catalan

Octubre

C/Julián Romea 18 (93 218 25 18). Metro Diagonal/ FGC Gràcia. **Open** 1.30-3.30pm, 9-11pm Mon-Fri; 9-11pm Sat. Closed Aug. **Main courses** €10. **Credit** V, MC. **Map** p340 F5 ⓧ

Time stands still in this quiet little spot, with its quaint old-fashioned decor, swathes of lace and brown table linen. Time often stands still, in fact, between placing an order and receiving any food, but this is all part of Octubre's sleepy charm. Also contributing to its appeal is a roll-call of reasonably priced, mainly Catalan dishes. Beef in mustard sauce is excellent, and the wild mushroom risotto, while not outstanding, is fine for the reasonable price. The puddings also vary a fair bit, but Octubre is more about atmosphere than anything else.

Iraqi

Mesopotamia

C/Verdi 65 (93 237 15 63). Metro Fontana. **Open** 8.30pm-midnight Tue-Sat. Closed 2 weeks Dec. **Main courses** €12.75. **Set dinner** €28. **No credit cards.** **Map** p341 H4 ⓧ

The policy at Barcelona's only Iraqi restaurant is to have everything on the menu at the same price, so that the cost won't hold anybody back from ordering what they want. The menu is based on Arab 'staff of life' foods, such as yoghurt and rice. Best value is the enormous taster menu, which includes great Lebanese wines, a variety of dips for your riqaq bread, bulgur wheat with aromatic roast meats and vegetables, sticky baklava and Arabic teas. Also good are the potato croquettes stuffed with minced meat, almonds and dried fruit.

Japanese

Shojiro

C/Ros de Olano 11 (93 415 65 48). Metro Fontana. **Open** 1.30-3.30pm Mon; 1.30-3.30pm, 9-11.30pm Tue-Sat. Closed 3wks Aug. **Set lunch** €14.15 (all incl). **Set dinner** €46 (only food). **Credit** MC, V. **Map** p340 G5 ⓧ

A curious but surprisingly successful mix of Catalan and Japanese applies to the decor as much as the food, with original mosaic flooring and dark-green paintwork setting off a clean feng-shuied look. There

Eat, Drink, Shop

modern-indian-culinary-experience

Reservations - English Spoken
t   93 502 49 52   -   f   93 500 69 14

info@bembi-barcelona.com
www.bembi-barcelona.com

In Bembì, authentic Indian recipes are passionately prepared and presented in a modern stylish way. Experience Bembi in exotic surroundings.

Open	Mon to Sat	
Lunch	Mon to Sat	13:15 - 15:45
Dinner	Mon to Thurs	20:30 - 23:30
	Fri and Sat	20:30 - 23:45
	Closed Sunday	

Consell de Cent 377, 08009 Barcelona
Metro: Girona Yellow Line 4 & Passeig de Gracia Green Line 3

are only set meals on offer (water, wine, coffee and tax are all included in lunch), starting with an amuse-bouche, then offering sushi with strips of nori, sticky rice and salad, or courgette soup with pancetta as a starter, then salmon teriyaki or spring-chicken confit with a potato dauphinois as mains. Puddings might include a wonderfully refreshing own-made apple ice-cream.

Korean

San Kil

C/Legalitat 22 (93 284 41 79). Metro Fontana or Joanic. **Open** 1-4pm, 8.30pm-midnight Mon-Sat. Closed 2wks Aug. **Main courses** €11. **Credit** MC, V. **Map** p341 J4 ❼
If you've never eaten Korean food before, it pays to gen up a bit before you head to this bright and spartan restaurant. *Panch'an* is the ideal starter for the beginner in this cuisine: four little dishes containing vegetable appetisers, one of which will be tangy *kimch'i* (fermented cabbage with chilli). Then try mouth-watering *pulgogi* – beef served sizzling at the table and eaten rolled into lettuce leaves – and maybe *pibimbap* – rice with vegetables (and occasionally meat) topped with a fried egg. Just as you're finishing up with a shot of soju rice wine, the Korean telly sparks up, and it's time to move on.

Mexican

Cantina Machito

C/Torrijos 47 (93 217 34 14). Metro Fontana or Joanic. **Open** 1-4pm, 7pm-1.30am daily. **Main courses** €10 **Credit** MC, V. **Map** p341 H5 ❽
Every day is Day of the Dead – in a good sense – in this cheerily decked out little Mexican joint, with its tissue paper bunting and chaotic hubbub. The miniscule writing on the menu and low lighting make for some guesswork when placing your order, but the choices are standard enough – quesadillas, tacos, ceviche and enchiladas – with a couple of surprises thrown in for good measure, such as the tasting platter of insects. Service can be slow and the kitchen is heavy-handed with the sauces, but the portions are huge and prices reasonable.

Nepalese

Himali

C/Milà i Fontanals 68 (93 285 15 68). Metro Joanic. **Open** noon-4pm, 8pm-midnight Tue-Sun. **Main courses** €9. **Set lunch** €8.25. **Credit** AmEx, MC, V. **Map** p341 H6 ❺
Cocking a snook at the many mediocre Indian restaurants around town, Barcelona's first Nepalese eaterie has become a real hit with the locals. Faced with an alien and impenetrable menu, you might be tempted by the set meals but they are not always the best option: be sure to press the waiters for recommendations or try *mugliaco kukhura* (barbecued butter chicken in creamy tomato sauce) or *khasi*

Cinc Sentits. *See p164.*

masala tarkari (baked spicy lamb). Meat cooked in the tandoori oven (*txulo*) is also worth a try, and there are plenty of vegetarian options.

Pizzeria

La Tarantella

C/Fraternitat 37 (93 284 98 57). Metro Fontana. **Open** 8.30pm-midnight Tue; 1.30-3.30pm, 8.30-11.30pm Wed-Sun. **Main courses** €10.50. **Set lunch** €9.20. **Credit** MC, V. **Map** p340 H6 ❻
To get to the restaurant you need to make your way through the unpromising, brightly lit tunnel of a bar to a cosy, low-ceilinged backroom warmed with yellow paintwork, beams and oil paintings. Here you can dine on decent budget Italian grub – salads, fresh pasta and a long list of pizzas. Toppings are generous, rather too much so at times, and the house pizza, for example, comes slathered in mozzarella, ham, mushrooms and onion, while the Extremeño is a mountain of mozzarella, chorizo and egg.

Seafood

Botafumeiro

C/Gran de Gràcia 81 (93 218 42 30). Metro Fontana. **Open** 1pm-1am daily. **Main courses** €25. **Credit** AmEx, DC, MC, V. **Map** p340 G5 ❻
Love it or hate it (and the size, the racket and the overwhelmingly arriviste diners mean no one leaves here undecided), there's no denying Botafumeiro's

success, and its dozens of tables are rarely empty for long. The speciality here is seafood in every shape and form, which is served with military precision by the fleet of nautically clad waiters. The turbot with clams is excellent and, at the other end of the scale, cod with chickpeas is not half bad either. The non-fish-eaters have a reasonable choice of Galician numbers to choose from, including a rich *caldo gallego* (a delicious cabbage and pork broth) and *lacón con grelos* (boiled gammon with turnip tops).

Spanish

Envalira
Plaça del Sol 13 (93 218 58 13). Metro Fontana. **Open** 1.30-4pm, 9pm-midnight Tue-Sat; 1.30-5pm Sun. Closed Aug. **Main courses** €12. **Credit** MC, V. **Map** p340 G5
Old-school Spain lives on as penguin-suited waiters solemnly hand out brown PVC menus at plastic teak-effect tables under painfully austere lighting. But it's all worth it for the food: as traditionally brown as the drab decor, it runs the full gamut of hefty Iberian classics. Start your meal with fish soups or lentils and go on to paellas, roast meats and seafood stews, followed by serious, own-made crema catalana or tarta de Santiago. Arrive early for the leather banquettes at the front.

Extreme cuisine at **Manairo**. *See p164.*

Other districts

Catalan

Can Travi Nou
C/Jorge Manrique, Horta (93 428 03 01). Metro Horta or Montbau. **Open** 1.30-4pm, 8.30-11pm Mon-Sat; 1.30-4pm Sun. **Main courses** €16.50. **Credit** AmEx, DC, MC, V.
An ancient rambling farmhouse clad in bougainvillea and perched high above the city, Can Travi Nou offers wonderfully rustic dining rooms with roaring log fires in winter, while in summer the action moves out to a covered terrace in a bosky, candlelit garden. The food is hearty, traditional Catalan cuisine though it's a little expensive for what it is, and suffers from the sheer volume being churned out of the kitchen. Puddings are better and served with a *porrón* (a glass jug with a drinking spout) of muscatel. But Can Travi Nou is really all about location.

La Parra
C/Joanot Martorell 3, Sants (93 332 51 34). Metro Hostafrancs. **Open** 8.30am-12.30pm Tue-Fri; 2-4.30pm, 8.30pm-12.30am Sat; 2-4.30pm Sun. Closed Aug. **Main courses** €14.50. **Credit** MC, V. **Map** p339 B7
A charming converted 19th-century coaching inn with a shady vine-covered terrace. The open wood grill sizzles with various parts of goat, pig, rabbit and cow, as well as a few more off-piste items such as deer and even foal. Huge, oozing steaks are slapped on to wooden boards and accompanied by baked potatoes, calçots, grilled vegetables and *all i oli*, with jugs of local wines from the giant barrels.

Japanese/Spanish

Icho
C/Deu i Mata 69-95, Les Corts (93 444 33 70/ www.ichobcnjapones.com). Metro Maria Cristina. **Open** 1.30-3.30pm, 9-11.30pm Tue-Sat. Closed 2 wks Aug. **Main courses** €20. **Credit** AmEx, MC, V. **Map** p338 C5
In a coolly designed space under the NH Constanza, Icho (in Japanese it means gingko tree – of which three graceful examples sit outside) fuses Japanese with Spanish cooking. This really shouldn't work, but in fact it does, beautifully – perhaps because you can offset the digestive demands of tender suckling pig and pumpkin pureé with a platter of sushi, or balance a starter of foie and eel with tuna tartare and creamed tofu with wasabi. The portions aren't large, so order several and share them around.

Mediterranean

Hisop
Passatge Marimon 9, Sant Gervasi (93 241 32 33/ www.hisop.com). Metro Hospital Clinic or Diagonal. **Open** 1.30-3.30pm, 9-11pm Mon-Fri; 9-11pm Sat. **Main courses** €23. **Credit** MC, V. **Map** p340 E5

Artal soul

The idea is to bring certain dishes (like a smoky Japanese-style broth that is poured over sushi-grade tuna belly) to the table under a glass cloche so that the diner can properly smell it.

Inspirations?
More than any individual, I would say our dishes are inspired by the produce itself, and the changing tastes of the seasons. Apricots are really good right now, so we thought we'd use them to balance veal cheeks, along with a camomile gelée. I get depressed when I see peaches in the market in January. A properly ripened peach should trickle down the chin, that's the fun. Don't be eating them out of season.

What's different?
We like to muck around with people's expectations. Our amuse-bouche is a shot containing maple syrup, cava sabayon and a pinch of Maldon sea salt. It shouldn't work, but it wakes up the palate for what is to come.

Molecular gastronomy. Discuss.
It makes for an interesting experience, but it's not the kind of soul-satisfying food

Born in Toronto to a Catalan mother and Canadian father, **Jordi Artal** threw away a successful career in Silicon Valley to move to the land of his European forefathers and indulge his real passion – for cooking. Together with his sister, sommelier Amèlia Artal, he set up **Cinc Sentits** (*see p164*); one of the hottest restaurants of the moment.

What's cooking?
Hmm, langoustine tails with *botifarra* sausage and shellfish consommé is a great new dish, or the Iberian pork belly with apple risotto and rosemary is an old favourite revisited.

What's next?
We're introducing some great types of lesser-known, local fish – so many are overlooked because the public demand is for sea bass, monkfish and so on. We're also looking at in-house smoking with herbs and woodchips.

you want to eat often. Also, not everyone can be Ferran Adrià, Heston Blumenthal or Grant Achatz – what people don't realise is that these guys all have a solid base in classic cooking. Ferran, for example, spent years studying and creating French haute cuisine before taking over at El Bulli.

And where do you eat for fun?
When I can I'll grab a plate of *pulpo* (octopus) at Bar Celta (*see p177*) in the Barri Gòtic and then the flaming chorizo over the road at El Corral (C/Mercè 17). The best tapas, though, are probably those at Quimet i Quimet (*see p187*) in Poble Sec. Uptown, the *patatas bravas* at Bar Tomás (C/Major de Sarrià 49) are legendary. For dinner I might go to Alkimia (*see p163*) or Gaig (*see p164*), but really the choice is endless in Barcelona these days.

Eat, Drink, Shop

Run by two young, enthusiastic and talented chefs, Hisop aims to bring serious dining to the non-expense-account masses by keeping its prices on the low side and its service approachable. The €52 tasting menu is a popular choice among diners with dishes that vary according to the season, but often includes their rich 'monkfish royale' (served with its liver, a cocoa-based sauce and tiny pearls of saffron) and a pistachio soufflé with Kaffir lime ice-cream and rocket 'soup'.

La Venta

Plaça Doctor Andreu (93 212 64 55). FGC Avda Tibidabo, then Tramvia Blau. **Open** 1.30-3.15pm, 9-11.15pm Mon-Sat. **Main courses** €15. **Credit** AmEx, DC, MC, V.
La Venta's Moorish-influenced interior is pleasant but it definitely plays second fiddle to the terrace during every season: shaded by day and uncovered by night in summer, sealed and warmed with a wood-burning stove in winter. But what about the food? Complex starters include lentil and spider crab salad; sea urchins au gratin (a must); and langoustine ravioli, filled with leek and foie mousse. Simpler, but high-quality mains run from rack of lamb to delicate monkfish in filo pastry with pesto.

Seafood

Els Pescadors

Plaça Prim 1, Poblenou (93 225 20 18/www.els pescadors.com). Metro Poblenou. **Open** 1-3.45pm, 8.30pm-midnight daily. **Main courses** €25. **Credit** AmEx, DC, MC, V.

In a forgotten, almost rustic square of Poblenou lies this first-rate fish restaurant, with tables under the canopy formed by two huge and ancient *ombú* trees. Suspend your disbelief with the crunchy sardine skeletons that arrive as an aperitif (trust us, they're delicious), and move on to tasty fried chipirones, followed by cod and pepper paella or creamy rice with prawns and smoked cheese. Creative desserts include the likes of strawberry gelatine 'spaghetti' in a citric soup. The waiters are exceptional.

Out of town

El Bulli

Cala Montjoi (972 15 04 57/www.elbulli.com). By train to Figueres, then bus to Roses, then taxi. **Open** *Apr-June* 8-10pm Wed-Sat; 1-2.30pm, 8-10pm Sun. *July-Sept* 7.30-10pm daily. Closed Oct-Mar. **Set dinner** €198. **Credit** AmEx, DC, MC, V.
Darling of the Sunday papers, El Bulli is possibly the most talked-about restaurant in the world today; thus it merits a mention here, despite its location up on the Costa Brava. There is only a *degustación*, and diners must arrive by 8.30pm if they are to finish the 30 or so courses by midnight. Dinner is an extraordinary experience, occasionally exalted and frequently frustrating: diners are cossetted guinea pigs, their reactions scanned by the maître d' and the great Ferran Adrià himself. Raw quail's yolk in caramelised gold leaf; sautéed rabbit brains with a truffled cigar of veal marrowbone; edible clingfilm peppered with trout's eggs – every dish is as much food for the mind as the stomach.

Hisop. *See p172.*

Cafés, Tapas & Bars

Café society, tapas talk and the Barna bar boom.

Anyone observing the proliferation of bars in Barcelona – many open all day and most of the night – could easily conclude that the Catalans are heavy drinkers. They would be wrong. The bars, which run the gamut from fiercely lit, zinc-countered old men's social clubs to ersatz Maghrebi lounges with sofas and hookahs, exist to facilitate conversation and social interaction, not drunkeness and fighting. Mind you, that means that alcohol is a constant accompaniment throughout the day starting, perhaps, with a thoughtful shot of *anis* with a morning coffee and ending with *la penúltima*, the final drink of the night with friends (*última* is never uttered, and to do so would be bad luck), with all manner of snifters in between.

BEER BEFORE WINE

If you ask for a *caña*, you'll be given a small draught beer; a *jarra* is closer to a pint. Ask for a *cerveza*, meanwhile, and you'll be given a bottle. Damm beer is ubiquitous in Catalonia, with Estrella, a strong lager, the most popular variety. Damm also produces an even stronger lager (Voll Damm) and a dark one (Bock Damm). Shandy (*clara*) is popular, untainted by the stigma it has in the UK.

Among wines, Rioja is well known, but there are many excellent wines from other regions in the north of Spain, such as the Penedès in Catalonia, Navarra or El Duero. Most wine drunk here is red (*negre/tinto*), but Galicia produces good whites too, including a slightly sparkling and very refreshing wine called *vino turbio*. Of course, Catalonia has its many cavas, running from *semi-sec* (which is 'half-dry', but actually pretty sweet) to *brut nature* (very dry).

ETIQUETTE

Except in busy bars, or when sitting outside, you won't usually be required to pay until you leave. If you have trouble attracting a waiter's attention, a loud but polite '*oiga*' or, in Catalan, '*escolti*' is acceptable. On the vexed question of throwing detritus on the floor (cigarette ends, paper napkins, olive pits and so on), it's safest to keep an eye on what the locals are doing and act accordingly.

❶ Pink numbers given in this chapter correspond to the location of each café, tapas or bar on the maps. *See pp338-346.*

Barri Gòtic

Cafés

Arc Café

C/Carabassa 19 (93 302 52 04). Metro Drassanes or Jaume I. **Open** noon-1.30am Mon-Thur, Sun; noon-2am Fri, Sat. **Credit** AmEx, DC, MC, V. **Map** p345 C7 ❶

A sunny and convivial café popular with expats. The winning strategy is in predicting exactly what the foreigners might be missing, from a Thai curry (properly spicy) on Thursdays to a slice of cheesecake in the afternoons. Sadly, though, the eggs 'n' bacon brunches are a thing of the past and the café now opens only at noon.

Café de l'Opera

La Rambla 74 (93 317 75 85). Metro Liceu. **Open** 8am-2.30am Mon-Thur, Sun; 8.30am-3am Fri, Sat. **No credit cards. Map** p345 B5 ❷

The last oasis of old-style class on the increasingly commercial La Rambla, Café de l'Opera has bags of fin-de-siècle charm and attentive bow-tied waiters to dish out coffee, *ensaimadas* (Mallorcan spiralled pastries, dusted with sugar, which go quickly and are best caught in the morning) and a small selection of tapas. Its situation means that nowadays it sees a largely tourist clientele, but few venture upstairs, which is where peace is to be found. *Photo p176.*

Čaj Chai

C/Sant Domènec del Call 12 (mobile 610 334 712). Metro Jaume I. **Open** 3-10pm daily. **No credit cards. Map** p345 C5 ❸

The best Cafés

For architecture buffs
Els Quatre Gats (*see p176*).

For tapas
Inopia (*see p188*).

For tea
Čaj Chai (*see above*).

For thespians
L'Antic Teatre (*see p180*).

For views
La Caseta del Migdia (*see p187*).

One for serious drinkers of the brown stuff, Čaj Chai is based on a Prague tearoom. Here, serenity reigns and First Flush Darjeeling is approached with reverence. A range of leaves comes with tasting notes describing, not only the origins, but suggestions for maximum enjoyment, and in summer iced teas are accompanied by a dollop of sorbet. Baklava and home-made cakes are on hand to aid contemplation further. The place is non-smoking.

La Clandestina
Baixada Viladecols 2 (93 319 05 33). Metro Jaume I. **Open** 10am-10pm Mon-Thur; 10am-midnight Fri; 11am-midnight Sat; 11am-10pm Sun. Closed 2wks Aug. **No credit cards. Map** p345 D6 ❹
Turn in at the sign of the hanging kettle for a mellow, New Age teahouse serving breakfasts, home-made cakes and a huge range of interesting teas – including *masala chai*, lotus flower, or cherry and redcurrant – along with an array of fresh fruit juices and *lassis* for those wanting a cold refreshment.

La Granja
C/Banys Nous 4 (93 302 69 75). Metro Liceu. **Open** *June-Sept* 9.30am-2pm, 5-9pm Mon-Sat. *Oct-May* 9.30am-2pm, 5-9pm Mon-Sat; 5-10pm Sun. **No credit cards. Map** p345 C5 ❺
There are a number of these old *granjes* (milk bars, often specialising in hot chocolate) around town, but this is one of the loveliest, with handsome antique fittings and its very own section of Roman wall at the back. You can stand your spoon in the chocolate, which won't be to all tastes. However, the spicy version with chilli or the mocha espresso will set you up for a hard day's shopping. It's non-smoking too.

Milk
C/Gignas 21 (93 268 09 22/www.milkbarcelona.com). Metro Jaume I. **Open** 6.30pm-3am Mon-Sat; noon-3am Sun. **Credit** AmEx, DC, MC, V. **Map** p345 D7 ❻
Milk's candlelit, low-key Baroque look, charming service and cheap prices make it ideal for that first date, set to a laid-back soundtrack ranging from Al Green to Hotel Costes. Cocktails are a speciality, as is good solid home-made bistro grub from Caesar salad to fish and chips. A good Sunday brunch includes fruit smoothies, fry-ups and pancakes.

Els Quatre Gats
C/Montsió 3 bis (93 302 41 40/www.4gats.com). Metro Catalunya. **Open** 8am-2am daily. **Credit** AmEx, DC, MC, V. **Map** p344 C3 ❼
Housed in a gorgeous building designed in 1897 by Puig i Cadafalch, Els Quatre Gats was once the popular hangout of the city's finest artists, including Pablo Picasso, who held his first exhibition here, and Modernistes Santiago Rusiñol and Ramon Casas, who painted pictures for the place. The food served in the adjoining restaurant could be better, but the setting certainly couldn't. *Photo p180.*

Schilling
C/Ferran 23 (93 317 67 87). Metro Liceu. **Open** *Sept-July* 10am-3am Mon-Sat; noon-2.30am Sun. *Aug* 5pm-3am daily. **Credit** (over €10) AmEx, DC, MC, V. **Map** p345 B5 ❽
Schilling's airy, smart interior and position smack in the centre of the Old City make it a meeting place par excellence (not to mention the city's prime spot for budding travel writers to scribble in their journals), but the aloofness of the staff can be tiring. *Photo p181.*

Café de l'Opera. *See p175.*

Tapas

Bar Celta

C/Mercè 16 (93 315 00 06). Metro Drassanes.
Open noon-midnight Tue-Sun. **Credit** AmEx,
MC, V. **Map** p345 C7 **9**
No-frills, noisy, brightly lit and not recommended
for anyone feeling a bit rough, Bar Celta is nonetheless one of the more authentic experiences to be had
in the Gòtic. A Galician tapas bar, it specialises in
food from the region, such as *lacón con grelos* (boiled
gammon with turnip tops) and good seafood – try
the steamed *navajas* (razor clams) or the *pulpo*
(octopus) – and crisp Albariño wine served in the
traditional white ceramic bowls.

Bar Pinotxo

La Boqueria 466-467, La Rambla 89 (93 317 17 31).
Metro Liceu. **Open** 6am-4.30pm Mon-Sat. Closed
3wks Aug. **No credit cards. Map** p344 B4 **10**
Just inside the entrance, on your right-hand side, of
the Boqueria, is this essential market bar, run by
Juanito, one of the city's best-loved figures. The
place is popular with ravenous night owls on their
way home and lunchtime foodies in the know.
Tapas are available, along with excellent daily
specials such as tuna casserole or scrambled eggs
with clams. Recommended.

Cervecería Taller de Tapas

C/Comtal 28 (93 481 62 33/www.tallerdetapas.com).
Metro Urquinaona. **Open** 8.30am-midnight Mon-
Thur; 8.30am-1am Fri, Sat; noon-midnight Sun.
Credit AmEx, DC. MC. V. **Map** p344 D3 **11**.

A new venture from the people behind Taller de
Tapas (*see p179*), and still serving tapas, but this
time with an emphasis on beers from around the
world. The list provides a refreshing alternative to
Estrella, with Argentinian Quilmes, Brazilian
Brahma (this one, admittedly, via Luton), Bass Pale
Ale, Leffe and Hoegaarden, among others.

Onofre

C/Magdalenes 19 (93 317 69 37/www.onofre.net).
Metro Urquinaona. **Open** 10am-4.30pm, 8pm-
12.30am Mon-Fri; 1pm-4.30pm, 8pm-1am Sat. Closed
2wks Aug. **Credit** DC, MC, V. **Map** p344 D3 **12**
A reasonably priced wine bar and tapas restaurant,
specialising in cured meats, hams and artisanal
cheeses from around the country (while the wines,
unusually for a Spanish tapas bar, come from all
over the globe). Dishes include a superb goat's
cheese salad with anchovies and a rather tasty cod
carpaccio. The bar's diminutive size and stone floors
mean it can get noisy when full.

El Portalón

C/Banys Nous 20 (93 302 11 87). Metro Liceu.
Open 9am-midnight Mon-Sat. Closed Aug.
Credit MC, V. **Map** p345 C5 **13**
A rare pocket of authenticity in the increasingly
touristy Barri Gòtic, this traditional tapas bar is
located in what were once medieval stables, and it
doesn't seem to worry too much about inheriting
the ancient dust. The tapas list is extensive, but the
torrades are good too: toasted bread topped with red
peppers and anchovy, cheese, ham or whatever
takes your fancy. These are washed down with
house wine from terracotta jugs.

Eat, Drink, Shop

La Granja.

Taller de Tapas

Plaça Sant Josep Oriol 9 (93 301 80 20/www.taller detapas.com). Metro Liceu. **Open** noon-midnight Mon-Thur, Sun; noon-1am Fri, Sat. **Credit** AmEx, DC, MC, V. **Map** p345 B5 **14**

The more successful the two branches of this tourist-oriented tapas bar become, the more frequently quality control is inclined to dip. At its best, though, it's an easy, multilingual environment, with plentiful outdoor seating at both of its branches, in which to try tapas from razor clams to locally picked wild mushrooms. At busy periods, however, the service can be hurried and unhelpful, with dishes prepared in haste and orders confused, so it pays to avoid the lunchtime and evening rush hours.

Other locations C/Argenteria 51, Born (93 268 85 59).

La Vinateria del Call

C/Sant Domènec del Call 9 (93 302 60 92). Metro Jaume I or Liceu. **Open** 8.30pm-1am Mon-Sat; 8.30pm-midnight Sun. **Credit** AmEx, DC, MC, V. **Map** p345 C5 **15**

La Vinateria's narrow entrance, furnished with dark wood and dusty bottles, has something of the Dickensian tavern about it, but once inside there's a varied music selection, from flamenco to rai, and lively multilingual staff. The wine list and range of hams and cheeses are outstanding; try the *cecina de ciervo* – wafer-thin slices of cured venison – and finish with home-made fig ice-cream.

Bars

Bar Bodega Teo

C/Ataulf 18 (93 315 11 59). Metro Drassanes or Jaume I. **Open** 9am-4pm, 5pm-2am Mon-Thur; 9am-4pm, 5pm-3am Fri, Sat. Closed Aug. **Credit** AmEx, MC, V. **Map** p345 C7 **16**

The split personality of BBT means that mornings see it filling with ancient locals, who've been coming to this old *bodega* since 1951 to fill their jugs and bottles with wine from huge oak barrels. Night times are a different proposition altogether, with young foreigners and *barcelonins* sipping Moscow Mules amid the changing decor – fairy lights, futuristic insect lamps, a backlit panel of an expensive mandarin duck have all featured – and an extravagant floral display on the bar. *Photo p182.*

Ginger

C/Palma de Sant Just 1 (93 310 53 09). Metro Jaume I. **Open** 7pm-2.30am Tue-Thur; 7pm-3am Fri, Sat. Closed 2wks Aug. **Credit** MC, V. **Map** p345 D6 **17**

Ginger manages to be all things to all punters: swish cocktail bar; purveyor of fine tapas and excellent wines, and, above all, a superbly relaxed place to chat and listen to music. The foreigner quotient has risen in recent years but it would be short-sighted to dismiss this little gem of Barcelona nightlife for that.

Kiosko de la Cazalla

C/Arc del Teatre (93 301 50 56). Metro Drassanes. **Open** 10am-2am Tue, Wed, Sun; 10am-3am Thur-Sat. **No credit cards. Map** p345 A7 **18**

Recently reopened, this emblematic hole-in-the-wall bar set in to the arch at the entrance of C/Arc del Teatre was for most of the last century a favourite of bullfighters and flamenco dancers, prostitutes and sailors. Little has changed since it first raised its hatch in 1912, and the tipple of choice is still the *cazalla*, an aniseedy firewater to warm the cockles.

Born & Sant Pere

Cafés

La Báscula

C/Flassaders 30 (93 319 98 66). Metro Jaume I. **Open** 7pm-11.30pm Wed-Fri, 1pm-11.30pm Sat. **No credit cards. Map** p345 E6 **19**

Still under threat from demolition (check before going and, if it's still there, sign the petition near the till), this former chocolate factory is a real find, with good vegetarian food and a large dining room situated out back. An impressive list of drinks runs from chai to Glühwein, taking in cocktails, milkshakes, smoothies and iced tea, and the pasta and cakes are as good as you'll find anywhere. Non-smoking.

Bocamel

C/Comerç 8 (93 268 72 44/www.bocamel.com). Metro Arc de Triomf. **Open** *Sept-July* 8.30am-8.30pm Mon-Fri; 8.30am-3pm, 5-8.30pm Sat; 8.30am-3pm Sun. *Aug* 8.30am-3pm, 5-9pm Mon-Sat; 8.30am-3pm Sun. Closed 2wks Aug. **Credit** MC, V. **Map** p345 F4 **20**

It's the mouthwatering, home-made chocolate bon-bons, Sachertorte, petits fours and brownies that bring most customers through the door, but Bocamel is also worth knowing about for its breakfast pastries and a short but sweet lunch menu. Needless to say, it's a good idea to hold out for pudding.

Bubó

C/Caputxes 10, Plaça Santa Maria (93 268 72 24/ www.bubo.ws). Metro Jaume I. **Open** 4-10pm Mon; 11am-10pm Tue, Wed, Sun; 11am-11pm Thur; 10am-1am Fri, Sat; 10am-10pm Sun. **Credit** AmEx, MC, V. **Map** p345 E7 **21**

Be a hit at any dinner party with a box of Bubó's exquisitely sculpted petits fours or make afternoon tea fashionable with a tray of its colourful fruit sablés, brandy snaps or dreamily rich Sachertorte. Or just sit in a window seat and gorge yourself silly.

Tèxtil Cafè

C/Montcada 12 (93 268 25 98). Metro Jaume I. **Open** *Nov-Feb* 10am-8pm Tue, Wed; 10am-midnight Thur, Sun; 10am-1am Fri, Sat. *Mar-Oct* 10am-midnight Tue-Thur, Sun; 10am-2am Fri, Sat. **Credit** MC, V. **Map** p345 E6 **22**

Perfectly placed for museum-goers, and with a graceful 14th-century courtyard, Tèxtil Cafè is an elegant place to enjoy a coffee in the shade, or under gas heaters in winter, with decent breakfast and lunch menus to boot. March to October, for music lovers, there's a DJ on Wednesday evenings and on Sundays live jazz (€5 supplement, with a drink included).

Eat, Drink, Shop

Els Quatre Gats. *See p176.*

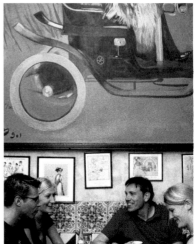

Rococó

C/Gombau 5-7 (93 269 16 58). Metro Jaume I.
Open 9am-midnight Mon-Thur; 9am-1am Fri, Sat.
Credit MC, V. **Map** p344 E4
On the ground floor of a nondescript apartment
block, Rococó manages to live up to its name thanks
to an array of red velvet seating, along with flock
wallpaper and gilt-edged paintings. The Vietnamese
rolls and chocolate brownies are fun, but the real
stars are the *bocadillos* on home-made ciabatta.

Tapas

El Bitxo

*C/Verdaguer i Callis 9 (93 268 17 08). Metro
Urquinaona.* **Open** 1-4pm, 7pm-midnight Mon-
Thur, Sun; 1-4pm, 7pm-1am Fri, Sat. **No credit
cards. Map** p344 D3
This area is not blessed with decent watering holes;
a surprising fact, given the presence of the Palau de
la Música and its concert-going crowds. Now the balance is being redressed with this small, lively tapas
bar specialising in excellent cheese and charcuterie
from the small Catalan village of Oix. Kick off the
evening with a Power Vermut (made up of red vermouth, Picon, gin and Angostura bitters) and end it
with a bottle of fine wine.

Euskal Etxea

*Placeta Montcada 1-3 (93 310 21 85). Metro Jaume
I.* **Open** *Bar* 7pm-midnight Mon; noon-4pm, 7pm-
midnight Tue-Sat. *Restaurant* 8.30-11.30pm Mon;
1.30-4pm, 8.30-11.30pm Tue-Sat. Closed 1wk Dec-Jan.
Credit AmEx, MC, V. **Map** p345 E6

A Basque cultural centre and *pintxo* bar. Help yourself to dainty *jamón serrano* croissants, chicken
tempura with saffron mayonnaise, melted *provolone*
with mango and crispy ham, or a mini-brochette of
pork, but hang on to the toothpicks spearing each
one: they'll be counted and charged for at the end.

Mosquito

*C/Carders 46 (93 268 75 69/www.mosquitotapas.
com). Metro Arc de Triomf or Jaume I.* **Open** 1pm-
1am Tue-Thur, Sun; 1pm-2am Fri, Sat. **Credit** MC,
V. **Map** p345 F5
Don't be put off. The announced 'exotic tapas' are
not another lame attempt to sex up fried calamares
by way of tower presentation and yucca chips, but
tiny versions of good to excellent dishes from the
Indian subcontinent and elsewhere in Asia. Food
ranges from chicken tikka to Thai omelettes and
masala dosas and daisy-fresh sashimi.

Bars

L'Antic Teatre

*C/Verdaguer i Callis 12 (93 315 23 54/www.lantic
teatre.com). Metro Urquinaona.* **Open** noon-11pm
daily. **No credit cards. Map** p344 E4
A slightly madcap theatre run by a slightly madcap crew has, as its most fabulous feature (unless
you count a bloke who uses his own blood to make
black pudding on stage), a hidden garden dotted
with tables cloaked in fruity vinyl and reverberat-
ing to the sound of young-enough-to-know-better
hippies. These days you must be a member (€3) to
drink. *Photo p186.*

Casa Paco

C/Allada Vermell 10 (no phone). Metro Arc de Triomf or Jaume I. **Open** *Apr-Sept* 9am-2am Mon-Thur, Sun; 9am-3am Fri, Sat; *Oct-Mar* 6pm-2am Tue-Thur, Sun; 6pm-3am Fri, Sat. **No credit cards.** **Map** p345 F5 ❷⑧

It may sound like an old man's bar and it may look like an old man's bar, but this scruffy, yet amiable, hole-in-the-wall has been the underground hit of recent years, thanks largely to occasional visits from Barcelona's DJ-in-chief, Christian Vogel. Other contributing and crucial factors include a sprawling terrace and probably the biggest vodka and tonics in the known world.

Espai Barroc

C/Montcada 20 (93 310 06 73). Metro Jaume I. **Open** 8pm-2am Tue-Sat; 6-10pm Sun. **Admission** €7 incl 1 drink Mon-Wed, Fri-Sun; €20 incl 1 drink Thur. **Credit** MC, V. **Map** p345 E6 ❷⑨

A sombre-hued riot of Baroque excess, with hundreds of flickering candles lighting up oil paintings, tapestries, sculptures, flowers and bowls of fruit, to the accompaniment of Handel, Brahms and live opera on Thursdays. The location is also great: deep within the 17th-century Palau Dalmases, with tables outside in the summer. Expensive and undeniably elitist, but utterly unique.

Gimlet

C/Rec 24 (93 310 10 27). Metro Barceloneta or Jaume I. **Open** 10pm-3am daily. **No credit cards.** **Map** p345 F6 ❸⓿

This subdued little wood-panelled cocktail bar has an Edward Hopper feel on quiet nights. The long mahogany counter has been burnished by the same well-clad elbows and patrolled by the same laconic barman for many years, and Gimlet is considered something of a classic, though the measures can be a little too ladylike for modern tastes.

Mudanzas

C/Vidrieria 15 (93 319 11 37/www.mudanzas. barceluca.com). Metro Barceloneta or Jaume I. **Open** *Sept-July* 10am-2.30am Mon-Thur, Sun; 10am-3am Fri, Sat. *Aug* 5.30pm-2.30am Mon-Thur, Sun; 5.30pm-3am Fri, Sat. **Credit** MC, V. **Map** p345 E6 ❸①

Eternally popular with all ages and nationalities, Mudanzas has a beguiling, old-fashioned look, with marble-topped tables, a black-and-white tiled floor and a jumble of well-thumbed newspapers. Be warned: it gets very smoky in the winter months, though some relief is to be had at the upstairs tables.

Va de Vi

C/Banys Vells 16 (93 319 29 00). Metro Jaume I. **Open** 6pm-1am Mon-Wed, Sun; 6pm-2am Thur; 6pm-3am Fri, Sat. **Credit** MC, V. **Map** p345 E6 ❸②

Opened a few years ago by a former sommelier, artist and sculptor, this Gothic-style wine bar looks like it's been around forever. There are more than 1,000 wines on the list, many available in a *cata* (small tasting measure) – at a price. The usual Spanish selections are accompanied by wines from around the world.

La Vinya del Senyor

Plaça Santa Maria 5 (93 310 33 79). Metro Barceloneta or Jaume I. **Open** noon-1am Mon-Thur; noon-2am Fri, Sat; noon-midnight Sun. **Credit** AmEx, DC, MC, V. **Map** p345 E7 ❸③

Another classic wine bar, this one has an unmatchable position right in front of Santa Maria del Mar. With high-quality tapas and so many excellent wines on its list (the selection changes every two weeks), it is, however, a crime to do as most tourists do and take up its terrace tables just for the view.

El Xampanyet

C/Montcada 22 (93 319 70 03). Metro Jaume I. **Open** noon-4pm, 7-11.30pm Tue-Sat; noon-4pm Sun. Closed Aug. **Credit** MC, V. **Map** p345 E6 ❸④

Schilling. *See p176.*

Eat, Drink, Shop

Bar Bodega Teo. *See p179.*

The eponymous poor man's champagne is actually a fruity and drinkable sparkling white, served in old-fashioned saucer glasses accompanied by the house tapa, a little plateful of delicious fresh anchovies from Cantàbria. Run by the same family since the 1930s, El Xampanyet is lined with coloured tiles, barrels and antique curios, and with a handful of marble tables.

Raval

Cafés

Baraka
C/Valldonzella 25 (93 304 10 61). Metro Universitat. Open 11am-10.30pm Mon-Fri. Closed Aug. Credit AmEx, MC, V. Map p342 F9 ⑤
At the back of a beautiful old building converted into a health-food shop is this cosy little bar, where everything from the wine and beer to the milk used in the fair-trade coffee, is organic and cheap – not a common combination. Should anything ail you, the amiable staff will make up an appropriate medicinal tea from the shop's stock of more than 100 herbs.

Bar Fidel
C/Ferlandina 24 (93 317 71 04). Metro Sant Antoni. Open 8pm-2am Mon-Thur, Sun; 8pm-2.30am Fri, Sat. No credit cards. Map p342 E9 ⑥
There are no Mojitos or cigars and no sign of the bearded one, but Bar Fidel is popular, particularly among students, for its legendary bocadillos (filled baguettes). The basic ingredients – though there are 100 permutations – are cured Canary Islands ham, chicken and pork. There are veggie options too.

Bar Kasparo
Plaça Vicenç Martorell 4 (93 302 20 72). Metro Catalunya. Open May-Aug 9am-midnight daily. Sept-Apr 9am-10pm daily. Closed Dec-mid Jan. No credit cards. Map p344 B2 ⑤
The favourite bar of Barcelona's beleaguered parents, Australian-run Bar Kasparo has outdoor seating (only) overlooking a playground on a quiet, traffic-free square. As well as sandwiches and tapas, there is a daily-changing choice of dishes from around the globe, soups and salads. The kitchen is open all day.

Bar Mendizábal
C/Junta de Comerç 2 (no phone). Metro Liceu. Open June-Oct 10am-1am daily. Nov-May 10am-midnight daily. No credit cards. Map p344 A4 ⑧
An emblematic Raval bar, its multicoloured tiles a feature in thousands of holiday snaps, Mendizábal has been around for decades but is really little more than a pavement stall. On offer are myriad fruit juices, bocadillos and, in winter, soup, served to tables across the road in the tiny square opposite.

Buenas Migas
Plaça Bonsuccés 6 (93 318 37 08). Metro Liceu. Open June-Sept 10am-midnight Mon-Thur, Sun; 10am-1am Fri, Sat. Oct-May 10am-11pm Mon-Thur, Sun; 10am-midnight Fri, Sat. Credit MC, V. Map p344 B3 ⑨

'Good Crumbs' (from a phrase meaning 'to get on with someone'), is a ferociously wholesome kind of place, all gingham and pine and chewy spinach tart. The speciality is tasty focaccia with various toppings, along with the usual high-fibre, low-fun cakes you expect to find in a vegetarian café. This branch has several tables outside.
Other locations Baixada de Santa Clara 2, off Plaça del Rei, Barri Gòtic (93 319 13 80); Passeig de Gràcia 120, Eixample (93 238 55 49).

Granja M Viader
C/Xuclà 4-6 (93 318 34 86). Metro Liceu. Open 5-8.45pm Mon; 9am-1.45pm, 5-8.45pm Tue-Sat. Closed 3wks Aug. Credit AmEx, MC, V. Map p344 B3 ⑩
The chocolate milk drink Cacaolat was invented in this old granja in 1931, and it is still on offer, along with strawberry and banana milkshakes, orxata (tiger nut milk) and hot chocolate. It's an evocative, charming place with century-old fittings and enamel adverts, but the waiters refuse to be hurried.

Iposa
C/Floristes de la Rambla 14 (93 318 60 86). Metro Liceu. Open Sept-July 1pm-2.30am Mon-Sat. Aug 7pm-2.30am Mon-Sat. Closed 2wks Dec-Jan. Credit MC, V. Map p344 A4 ⑪
At lunch and dinner, Iposa functions almost exclusively as a restaurant, serving a handful of simple and low-priced dishes. The rest of the time it makes for a cosy, vaguely bohemian bar with chilled-out music, decent art exhibited on its walls and coveted tables outside on a quiet, traffic-free square.

El Jardí
C/Hospital 56 (93 329 15 50). Metro Liceu. Open 10am-11pm Mon-Sat. Credit MC, V. Map p344 A4 ⑫
A small terrace café in the dusty tree-lined grounds of the Antic Hospital (see p107), El Jardí provides a tranquil spot just off La Rambla. Breakfast pastries and all the usual tapas are present and correct, along with pasta dishes, quiches and salads.

Madame Jasmine
Rambla del Raval 22 (no phone). Metro Liceu. Open 10am-2.30am Tue-Fri, Sun; 10am-3am Fri, Sat. No credit cards. Map p342 E10 ⑬
Kitted out like a somewhat bizarre and crumbling theatre set, Madame Jasmine sports geckos painted silver, oriental lamps and feather boas amid its beams and retro 1970s tiling. Its generous salads and heaped bocadillos are named after historical Raval characters and local street names.

Tapas

Mam i Teca
C/Lluna 4 (93 441 33 35). Metro Sant Antoni. Open 1-4pm; 8.45pm-midnight Mon, Wed-Fri, Sun; 8.45pm-midnight Sat. Closed 2wks Aug. Credit AmEx, MC, V. Map p342 E10 ⑭
A bright little tapas restaurant with only three tables, so it pays to reserve. All the usual tapas, from anchovies to cured meats, are rigorously sourced,

and complemented by superb daily specials such as organic *botifarra*, pork confit and asparagus with shrimp. The bar (which is also open afternoons) is worth mentioning for a superior vodka and tonic.

Els Tres Tombs
Ronda Sant Antoni 2 (93 443 41 11). Metro Sant Antoni. **Open** 6am-2am daily. **No credit cards.** **Map** p342 E10 ⓯

Not, perhaps, the most inspired tapas bar in town, with its overcooked *patatas bravas*, sweaty Manchego and vile loos, but Els Tres Tombs is still a long-time favourite for its pavement terrace and proximity to the Sunday morning book market. The *tres tombs* in question are nothing more ghoulish than the 'three turns' of the area performed by a procession of men on horseback during the Festa dels Tres Tombs in January.

Bars

23 Robador
C/Robador 23 (no phone). Metro Liceu. **Open** 8pm-2am Tue-Sun; 8pm-3am Fri, Sat. **No credit cards.** **Map** p345 A5 ⓰

Inside this stone-walled and smoke-filled lounge, Raval denizens dig the jazz jam on Wednesdays, the flamenco on Sundays and, in between times, a DJ who plays a genre-defying range of music that might include Joy Division and DJ Shadow on the same night. A manga-style mural painted on the back wall by one of Barna's many graffiti artists adds to the underground appeal. You'll need to ring the bell by the door to get in.

Bar Lobo
C/Pintor Fortuny 3 (93 481 53 46). Metro Catalunya. **Open** noon-midnight Mon-Wed, Sun; noon-2am Thur-Sat. **Credit** MC, V. **Map** p344 B3 ⓱

Bar Lobo is a stark, monochrome space, with punky artwork from celebrated graffiti artists. The watchword is moody (not least among the waiting staff) but the bar comes alive with DJs and studied lounging on the mezzanine at night, and by day its terrace is a peaceful, sunny space for coffee or a light lunch.

Boadas
C/Tallers 1 (93 318 95 92). Metro Catalunya. **Open** *Sept-June* noon-2am Mon-Thur; noon-3am Fri, Sat. *July, Aug* noon-3pm, 6pm-2am Mon-Thur; noon-3pm, 6pm-3am Fri, Sat. **No credit cards.** **Map** p344 B3 ⓲

Set up in 1933 by Miguel Boadas, born to Catalan parents in Havana (where he became the first barman at the legendary La Floridita), this classic cocktail bar has changed little since Hemingway used to come here. In a move to deter the hordes of rubbernecking tourists, they have instituted a dress code. Courteous staff.

Cafè de les Delícies
Rambla del Raval 47 (93 441 57 14). Metro Liceu. **Open** 6pm-2am Mon, Tue, Thur, Sun; 6pm-3am Fri, Sat. Closed 3wks Aug. **No credit cards.** **Map** p342 E10 ⓳

David Soul! Boney M! Olivia Newton-John! The functioning 1970s jukebox is reason enough to visit this cosy little bar, even without the excellent G&Ts, the chess, the variety of teas, the terrace and the shelves of books for browsing. A coveted alcove with a sofa, low armchairs and magazines is opened at busy times, or there is a quiet dining room at the back.

London Bar
C/Nou de la Rambla 34 (93 318 52 61). Metro Liceu. **Open** 7.30am-3pm Mon; 7.30am-3.30am daily. **Credit** AmEx, MC, V. **Map** p345 A6 ⓾

The only thing familiar to Londoners will be the punters; otherwise, the Modernista woodwork and smoky, yellowing charm is 100% Barcelona. Problems with the Ajuntament meant the end of live music, but the owners promise the jazz, blues and rock will return.

Marsella
C/Sant Pau 65 (93 442 72 63). Metro Liceu. **Open** 10pm-2.30am Mon-Thur; 10pm-3am Fri, Sat. **No credit cards.** **Map** p342 E/F11 ⓼

Marsella was opened in 1820 by a native of Marseilles, who may just have changed the course of Barcelona's artistic endeavour by introducing absinthe, still a mainstay of the bar's delights. Untapped 100-year-old bottles of the stuff sit in glass cabinets alongside old mirrors and William Morris curtains, probably covered in the same dust kicked up by Picasso and Gaudí.

The Quiet Man
C/Marqués de Barberà 11 (93 412 12 19). Metro Liceu. **Open** 6pm-3am daily. **No credit cards.** **Map** p345 A6 ⓼

One of the original and best of the city's many Oirish pubs, the Quiet Man's a peaceful place with wooden floors and stalls that eschews the beautiful game for occasional poetry readings and pool tournaments on its two back-room tables. There is Guinness (properly pulled) and Murphy's, and you're just as likely to find Catalans here as you are to see homesick expats and holidaymakers.

Barceloneta & the Ports

Cafés

La Miranda del Museu
Museu d'Història de Catalunya, Plaça Pau Vila 3 (93 225 50 07). Metro Barceloneta. **Open** 10am-7pm Tue; 10am-8pm Wed; 10am-7pm, 9-11pm Thur-Sat; 10am-5pm Sun. **Credit** MC, V. **Map** p345 E8 ⓺

Don't go spreading this about, but there's a secret rooftop café with terrific views, cheap and reasonable set lunches (along with coffee and pastries at breakfast time) and a vast terrace, sitting right at the edge of the marina, perched high above the humdrum tourist traps. Walk into the Catalan History Museum and take the lift to the top floor. You don't need to buy a ticket to the museum to have a cup of coffee at the café. *Photo p188.*

Eat, Drink, Shop

L'Antic Teatre. *See p180.*

La Piadina

C/Meer 48 (mobile 660 806 172). Metro Barceloneta. **Open** 1-10pm Tue-Sun. **No credit cards. Map** p343 H13 ⬤

A *piadina* is a warmed Italian wrap, made using something akin to a large pitta. The fillings here come in 30 different permutations on the standard tomato, mozzarella, ham, rocket and mushroom theme. La Piadina is a comfortable little place with newspapers and makeshift sofas, and it really exists to provide superior takeaway snacks to beach-goers. To find it, turn inland at Rebecca Horn's tower of rusting cubes on the beach.

Tapas

Bar Colombo

C/Escar 4 (93 225 02 00). Metro Barceloneta. **Open** noon-3am daily. Closed 2wks Jan-Feb. **No credit cards. Map** p342 G13 ⬤

Deck-shod yachties and moneyed locals stroll by all day, oblivious to this unassuming little bar and its sunny terrace overlooking the port. In fact, nobody seems to notice it; odd, given its fantastic location and generous portions of *patatas bravas*. The only drawback is the nerve-jangling techno that occasionally fetches up on the stereo.

Can Paixano

C/Reina Cristina 7 (93 310 08 39/www.canpaixano. com). Metro Barceloneta. **Open** 9am-10.30pm Mon-Sat. Closed 3wks Aug-Sept. **No credit cards. Map** p345 E8 ⬤

It can be impossible to talk, get your order heard or move your elbows, and yet the 'Champagne Bar', as it's invariably known, has a global following. Its narrow, smoky confines are always mobbed with Catalans and adventurous tourists making the most of the dirt-cheap house cava and sausage *bocadillos* (you can't buy a bottle without buying a couple as ballast). A must.

La Cova Fumada

C/Baluard 56 (93 221 40 61). Metro Barceloneta. **Open** 9am-3pm Mon-Wed; 9am-3pm, 6-8.15pm Thur, Fri; 9am-1pm Sat. Closed Aug. **No credit cards. Map** p343 H13 ⬤

This cramped little *bodega* is said to be the birthplace of the *potato bomba*, served with a chilli sauce. Here, when they say spicy, they mean it. Especially tasty are the chickpeas with *morcilla* (black pudding), roast artichokes and marinated sardines. Its huge following of lunching workers means it can be hard to get a table after 1pm.

El Vaso de Oro

C/Balboa 6 (93 319 30 98). Metro Barceloneta. **Open** 9am-midnight daily. Closed Sept. **No credit cards. Map** p343 H12 ⬤

The enormous popularity of this long, narrow cruise-ship style bar tells you everything you need to know about the tapas, but it also means that he who hesitates is lost when it comes to ordering. Elbow yourself out a space and demand, loudly, *chorizitos, patatas bravas, solomillo* (cubed steak) or *atún* (tuna, which here comes spicy).

Bars

The loud, tacky bars lining the Port Olímpic draw a mixture of drunken stag parties staring at the go-go girls and curious locals staring at the drunken stag parties.

Luz de Gas – Port Vell
Opposite the Palau de Mar, Moll del Dipòsit (93 484 23 26). Metro Barceloneta or Jaume I. **Open** Apr-Oct noon-3am daily. Closed mid Nov-mid Mar. **Credit** AmEx, DC, MC, V. **Map** p345 E8 ❺❾
It's cheesy, but this boat/bar also has its romantic moments. By day, bask in the sun with a beer on the upper deck, or rest in the shade below. With night-fall, candles are brought out, wine is uncorked and, if you can blot out the Lionel Richie, it's everything a holiday bar should be.

Montjuïc & Poble Sec

Cafés

Bar Seco
Passeig Montjuïc 74 (93 329 63 74). Metro Paral·lel. **Open** 9am-1am Tue-Thur; 9am-2.30am Fri, Sat. **No credit cards**. **Map** p339 D11 ❻⓪
The 'Dry Bar' is anything but, and its ethically friendly choices range from local beers and organic wines to fair-trade Brazilian *cachaça*. Opened in late 2006 and despite a quiet location, it has already gathered quite a following for the quality of its Italian-Spanish vegetarian dishes and tapas, its fresh milkshakes and a heavenly home-made chocolate and almond cake.

Tapas

Quimet i Quimet
C/Poeta Cabanyes 25 (93 442 31 42). Metro Paral·lel. **Open** noon-4pm, 7-10.30pm Mon-Fri; noon-4pm Sat. Closed Aug. **Credit** MC, V. **Map** p339 D11 ❻①
Packed to the rafters with dusty bottles of wine, this classic but minuscule bar makes up for in tapas what it lacks in space. The specialities are preserved clams, cockles, mussels and so on, which are not to all tastes, but the *montaditos*, sculpted tapas served on bread, are spectacular. Try salmon sashimi with cream cheese, honey and soy, or cod, *passata* and black olive pâté. The bar is now no-smoking.

Bars

La Caseta del Migdia
Mirador del Migdia, Passeig del Migdia s/n (mobile 617 956 572). Bus 55 or bus Parc de Montjuïc/funicular de Montjuïc then 10min walk. Follow signs to Mirador de Montjuïc. **Open** June-Sept 8pm-2.30am Thur, Fri; 11am-2.30am Sat; 11am-1am Sun. *Oct-May* 10am-6pm Sat, Sun. **No credit cards**. **Map** p339 A12 ❻②
Follow the Camí del Mar footpath around Montjuïc castle to find one of the few vantage points from which to watch the sun set. Completely alfresco, high up in a clearing among the pines, this is a magical space, scattered with deckchairs, hammocks and candlelit tables. DJs spinning funk, rare groove and lounge alternate surreally with a faltering string quartet; food is pizza and other munchies.

Eixample

Cafés

Bauma
C/Roger de Llúria 124 (93 459 05 66). Metro Diagonal. **Open** 8am-midnight Mon-Fri, Sun. Closed 3wks Aug. **Credit** AmEx, DC, MC, V. **Map** p340 G6 ❻③
Bauma is an old-style café-bar that's good for lazy Sunday mornings, with its battered leather seats and ceiling fans, although staff can be surly. Along with well-priced, substantial dishes such as baked cod and wild boar stew, there's an impressive list of tapas and sandwiches.

Café Berlin
C/Muntaner 240-242 (93 200 65 42). Metro Diagonal. **Open** *Sept-July* 10am-2am Mon-Wed; 10am-3am Thur-Sat. *Aug* 5.30pm-2am Mon-Wed; 5.30pm-3am Thur-Sat. **Credit** V. **Map** p340 E5 ❻④
Downstairs in the basement, the low sofas fill up with amorous couples, while upstairs everything is sleek and light, with brushed steel, dark leather and a Klimtesque mural. A rack of newspapers and plentiful sunlight make Berlin popular for coffee or

The strong stuff

Spanish coffee is very strong and generally excellent. The three basic types are *cafè sol/café solo* (in Catalan, also known simply as 'café'), a small strong black coffee; *tallat/cortado*, the same but with a little milk; and *cafè amb llet/café con leche*, the same but with more milk. Cappuccino has yet to catch on; whipped cream as a substitute for foam is not unheard of. Then there's café americano (a tall black coffee diluted with more water) and spiked coffee: a *carajillo*, which is a short, black coffee with a liberal dash of brandy. If you want another type of liqueur, you have to specify, such as *carajillo de ron* (rum) or *carajillo de whisky*. A *trifásico* is a *carajillo* with a layer of milk. Decaffeinated coffee (*descafeinado*) is widely available, but specify for it *de máquina* (from the machine) unless you want Nescafé. Decaff is popular and is also very good.

Tea, on the other hand, is pretty poor. If you can't live without it, ask for cold milk on the side ('*leche fría aparte*') or run the risk of getting a glass of hot milk and a teabag. Basic herbal teas, such as chamomile (*manzanilla*), limeflower (*tila*) and mint (*menta*), are common.

La Miranda del Museu. *See p185.*

snacks all day; as well as tapas, there are also pasta dishes, *bocadillos* and cheesecake, but be aware of the 20% surcharge for pavement tables.

Dolso

C/València 227 (93 487 59 64). Metro Passeig de Gràcia. **Open** 9am-10.30pm Mon; 9am-11.30pm Tue-Thur; 9am-1am Fri; 11am-1am Sat. **Credit** AmEx, DC, MC, V. **Map** p340 F7 **⑥⑤**
Heaven on earth for sweet tooths: even the retro-Baroque wallpaper is chocolate-coloured at this 'pudding café'. Desserts run from refreshingly light (a 'gin and tonic' rendered in clear jelly, lemon sorbet, candied peel and juniper berries) to wickedly indulgent (chocolate fondant with sherry reduction and passion fruit sorbet). A short range of sandwiches and topped ciabatta keeps the spoilsports happy.

La Paninoteca Cremoni

C/Rosselló 112 (93 451 03 79). Metro Hospital Clínic. **Open** 9.30am-5pm, 7.30pm-midnight Mon-Fri; 1.30-5pm, 8.30pm-midnight Sat. Closed 3wks Aug. **Credit** AmEx, DC, MC, V. **Map** p340 E7 **⑥⑥**
Named after the 19th-century inventor of the famous Italian sandwich, this is a sunny spot, with a white-painted rustic look enlivened by a huge photograph of Siena. Neither the owners nor the ingredients can make much claim to Italian provenance, but nonetheless *panini* such as the siciliano – olive bread, mozzarella, aubergine, tomato and basil – make a wonderful change from endless *bocadillos de jamón.*

Tapas

Bar Mut

C/Pau Claris 192 (93 217 43 38). Metro Diagonal. **Open** 8.30am-midnight Mon-Fri; 10.30am-midnight Sat; noon-5pm, 8.30pm-midnight Sun. **Credit** AmEx, DC, MC, V. **Map** p340 G6 **⑥⑦**

There's more than a *soupçon* of the *16ème arrondissement* in this smart, traditional bar; well-heeled Catalans, BCBG to the core, chatter loudly and dine on excellent, well-sourced tapas – foie gras, wild sea bass and *espardenyes* (sea cucumbers). The wine selection is similarly upmarket, and the bottles are displayed so seductively behind plate glass that you may find yourself drinking and spending rather more than you bargained for.

La Bodegueta

Rambla de Catalunya 100 (93 215 48 94). Metro Diagonal. **Open** 8am-2am Mon-Sat; 6.30pm-1am Sun. Closed 2wks Aug. **No credit cards. Map** p340 G7 **⑥⑧**
Resisting the rise of the surrounding district, this former wine *bodega* is unreconstructed, dusty and welcoming, supplying students, businessmen and everyone in between with reasonably priced wine, vermouth on tap and prime-quality tapas amid the delicate patterns of century-old tiling. In summer, there are tables outside on the almost pedestrianised Rambla de Catalunya.

Cerveseria Catalana

C/Mallorca 236 (93 216 03 68). Metro Passeig de Gràcia. **Open** 8am-1.30am Mon-Fri; 9am-1.30am Sat, Sun. **Credit** AmEx, DC, MC, V. **Map** p340 F7 **⑥⑨**
The 'Catalan Beerhouse' lives up to its name with a winning selection of brews from around the world, but the real reason to come is the tapas. A vast array is yours for the pointing; only hot *montaditos*, such as bacon, cheese and dates, have to be ordered from the kitchen. Arrive early for a seat at the bar, and even earlier to sit at one of the pavement tables.

Inopia

C/Tamarit 104 (93 424 52 31). Metro Poble Sec. **Open** 7pm-midnight Mon-Fri; 1-3.30pm, 7pm-midnight Sat. Closed Aug. **Credit** MC, V. **Map** p339 D9 **⑦⓪**

Being brother (and pastry chef) to infamous chef Ferran Adrià has been both a curse and a blessing for Albert Adrià. On the one hand, his traditional tapas bar has been rammed since it opened; on the other, its glaringly bright old-school look and approach has disappointed those expecting El Bulli-style culinary fireworks. If classic tapas – *patatas bravas*, Russian salad, croquettes and tripe – are to your liking, however, Inopia does them better than anywhere.

TapaÇ24

C/Diputació 269 (93 488 09 77/www.carlesabellan. com). Metro Passeig de Gràcia. **Open** 8am-midnight Mon-Sat. **Credit** AmEx, DC, MC, V. **Map** p342 G8 ⓱
A new venture from Carles Abellan of Comerç 24 fame (*see p151*), this is ostensibly an old-school tapas bar, but among the lentils with *chorizo* or ham croquettes you'll find playful snacks more familiar to his fans. The McFoie Burger is an exercise in fast-food heaven, as is the Bikini – a small version of his signature take on the ham and cheese toastie, this one with truffle.

Bars

Dry Martini

C/Aribau 162-166 (93 217 50 72). FGC Provença. **Open** *Sept-July* 1pm-2.30am Mon-Thur; 1pm-3am Fri; 6.30pm-3am Sat; 6pm-2.30am Sun. *Aug* 6.30pm-2.30am Mon-Thur, Sun; 6.30pm-3am Fri, Sat. **Credit** AmEx, DC, MC, V. **Map** p340 F6 ⓰
This is a shrine to the eponymous cocktail, honoured in Martini-related artwork and served in a hundred forms. All the trappings of a traditional cocktail bar are here – bow-tied staff, leather banquettes, drinking antiques and wooden cabinets displaying a century's worth of bottles – but the stuffiness is absent: music owes more to trip hop than middle-aged crowd-pleasers, and the barmen welcome all comers.

Xix Bar

C/Rocafort 19 (93 423 43 14/www.xixbar.com). Metro Poble Sec. **Open** 9am-4.30pm, 6.30pm-1.30am Mon-Thur; 9am-4.30pm, 6.30pm-3am Fri, Sat. **No credit cards. Map** p339 C/D9 ⓳
Xix (pronounced 'chicks', and a play on the address, among other things) is a new, unconventional cocktail bar in the candlelit surroundings of an old tiled *granja* (milk bar). It's dead cosy but a little bit scruffy, which makes the list of 20 brands of gin all the more unexpected. Simple pasta dishes, salads and *bocadillos* are served during the day.

Gràcia

Cafés

Flash Flash

C/Granada del Penedès 25 (93 237 09 90). FGC Gràcia. **Open** 1.30pm-1.30am daily. **Credit** AmEx, DC, MC, V. **Map** p340 F5 ⓴
Opened back in 1970, this bar was a design sensation in its day, with its white leatherette banquettes and walls imprinted with silhouettes of a life-size frolicking, Twiggy-like model. They describe it as a *tortilleria*, with 60 or so tortilla variations available, alongside a list of child-friendly dishes and adult-friendly cocktails. Non-smoking.

Salambó

C/Torrijos 51 (93 218 69 66). Metro Fontana or Joanic. **Open** noon-1am Mon-Thur, Sun; noon-3am Fri, Sat. **Credit** MC, V. **Map** p341 H5 ⓵
The time-honoured meeting place for Verdi cinema-goers, Salambó is a large and ever-so-slightly staid split-level café that serves coffee, teas and filled ciabatta to the *barri*'s more conservative element. At night, those who are planning to eat are given preference when it comes to bagging a table.

Eat, Drink, Shop

Flash Flash.

Tapas

Bodega Manolo

C/Torrent de les Flors 101 (93 284 43 77).
Metro Joanic. **Open** 10am-6pm Tue, Wed; 10am-
6.30 9pm-1am Thur, Fri; 12.30-6.30pm, 8.30pm-1am
Sat; noon-3pm Sun. Closed Aug. **No credit cards.**
Map p341 H4 ⑩
Another old family *bodega* with a faded, peeling
charm (though under renovation at the time of writing), barrels on the wall and rows of dusty bottles,
Manolo specialises not only in wine, but in classy
food: try the foie gras with port and apple. At the
other end of the scale, and also with its place, comes
the 'Destroyer': egg, bacon, sausage and chips.

Sureny

Plaça de la Revolució 17 (93 213 75 56). Metro
Fontana or Joanic. **Open** 8.30pm-midnight Tue-
Thur; 8.30pm-1am Fri, Sat; 1-3.30pm, 8pm-midnight
Sun. Closed last wk Oct, 2nd wk Apr.
Credit MC, V. **Map** p341 H5 ⑰
A well-kept gastronomic secret (until now), Sureny
boasts superb gourmet tapas and waiters who know
what they are talking about. In addition to the usual
run-of-the-mill tortilla 'n' calamares fare, look out for
tuna marinated in ginger and soy sauce, partridge
and venison when in season, and a sublime duck foie
gras with redcurrant sauce.

Bars

Bar Elèctric

Travessera de Gràcia 233 (no phone). Metro Joanic.
Open 7pm-2am Tue-Thur, Sun; 7pm-3am Fri, Sat.
Closed last wk July, 1st wk Aug. **No credit cards.**
Map p341 H5 ⑱
Elèctric was the first bar in Gràcia to be connected to
the mains (as local legend has it), yet this once bastion
of modernity seems not to have changed since. An
innocuous entry opens into a sprawling bohemian
den that has an agenda as colourful as its clientele:
theatre, puppetry and storytelling on weekdays,
Brazilian jazz and cabaret at weekends.

Bo!

Plaça Rius i Taulet 11 (93 368 35 29). Metro
Fontana. **Open** 10am-1am Mon-Thur; 10am-
2.30am Fri-Sun. **Credit** MC, V. **Map** p340 G5 ⑲
Decent tapas, creative sandwiches and generous
portions, plus plenty of terrace tables, make this a
favourite spot in one of Gràcia's most emblematic,
lively squares. If Bo!'s black chairs are all taken,
you'll do nearly as well on one of neighbouring bar
Amelie's white ones. The terrace closes at 12.30am.

Casa Quimet

Rambla de Prat 9 (93 217 53 27). Metro Fontana.
Open 6.30pm-2am Tue-Sun. Closed Aug. **No credit**
cards. Map p340 G5 ⑳
Yellowing jazz posters cover every inch of wall-
space, dozens of ancient guitars hang from the
ceiling and a succession of ticking clocks compete

to be heard over the voice of Billie Holiday at Casa
Quimet. This other-worldly 'Guitar Bar' (as the place
is invariably known to locals) occasionally springs
to life with an impromptu jam session but, most of
the time, it's a perfect study in melancholy.

Noise i Art

C/Topazi 26 (93 217 50 01). Metro Fontana.
Open 6pm-2.30am Tue-Thur, Sun; 7pm-3am Fri,
Sat. Closed 2wks end Aug, 1st wk Sept. **No credit**
cards. Map p340 H4 ㉛
Although some of the furniture looks like it might
have come from IKEA, Noise i Art's interior is a
colourful and playful pop art melange. The food is a
cut above the normal grub served in bars around
Gràcia and the spirit measures are generous – two
G&Ts being enough to ensure wobbling home. A convivial atmosphere is livened up by Madonna videos
playing at one end of the bar; there are occasional
flamenco sessions. One of the best bars in the area.

Puku Café

C/Guilleries 10 (93 368 25 73). Metro Fontana.
Open 7pm-1.30am Mon-Wed; 7pm-2pm Thur; 7pm-
3am Fri, Sat. Closed 1st 2wks Aug. **Credit** AmEx,
DC, MC, V. **Map** p340 H5 ㉜
Puku Café has two different vibes going on. During
the week it's a colourful meeting place, where the
casually hip hang out over a bottle of wine and maybe
some cactus and lime ice-cream. At weekends, however, there's a transformation: the amber walls and
deep orange columns prop up a younger, scruffier
crowd, nodding along to some of the city's best DJs
spinning a varied playlist based around electropop.

Samsara

C/Terol 6 (93 285 36 88). Metro Fontana or Joanic.
Open *June-Sept* 8.30pm-2am Mon-Thur; 8.30pm-3am
Fri, Sat. *Oct-May* 1.30-4pm, 8.30pm-2am Mon-Thur;
1.30-4pm, 8.30pm-3am Fri; 8.30pm-3am Sat. **Credit**
MC, V. **Map** p341 H5 ㉝
A combination of Moroccan-themed decor and intelligent cooking, Samsara has built up quite a following among Gràcia foodies. Its tapas are diminutive
but don't want for flavour or imagination: try monkfish ceviche with mango, or watermelon gazpacho
with basil oil. Photos line the walls, and a DJ plays
lounge and the smoothest of house later in the week.

Tibidabo

Bars

Merbeyé

Plaça Doctor Andreu, Tibidabo (93 417 92 79).
FGC Avda Tibidabo then Tramvia Blau/bus 60.
Open 11am-2.30am Tue-Thur; noon-3.30am Fri,
Sat; noon-2am Sun. **Credit** MC, V.
A cocktail bar that comes straight from central casting: moodily lit, plush with red velvet and hung with
prints of jazz maestros. In summer, there's a peaceful, stylish terrace. The clientele runs from shabby
gentility to flashy Barça players and their WAGs.

Shops & Services

Unique boutiques and global home-grown chains.

Maremàgnum. *See p193.*

Catalonia's mercantile tradition and the quality of its local products – from silverware to olive oil – have meant Barcelona has always been good for shopping. Many stores still have their original 150-year-old façades, or have been in the same hands for four generations, offering a great contrast to today's homogeneous high streets. Of course, much of Barcelona is now given over to Zaras and Mangos, but you can still find the store that roasts its own nuts in a century-old oven, and the workshop that has made carnival costumes since the 1900s.

Most shops don't open until 10am and then close for lunch from 2pm to around 5pm. Many small shops also close on Saturday afternoons and all day Monday. Large shops and chains, however, soldier through until 8pm, an hour later on Saturdays. The regulations governing Sunday and holiday opening hours are complex. Generally speaking, however, restaurants, bakeries, flower stalls, convenience stores and shops in tourist zones can open seven days a week, and nearly all stores open on the four Sundays before Christmas.

The rate of sales tax (IVA) depends on the type of product: it's currently seven per cent on food and 16 per cent on most other items.

In any of the 700 or so shops that display a Tax-Free Shopping sticker on their door, non-EU residents can request a Tax-Free Cheque on purchases of more than €90.15. Before leaving the EU, these must be stamped at customs (at Barcelona airport, this is located in Terminal A by the Arrivals gate) and can immediately be reclaimed in cash at La Caixa bank.

The best Shops

For everything
El Corte Inglés (*see p193*).

For books
Hibernian Books (*see p196*).

For ham
Jamonísimo (*see p208*).

For gifts
Art Escudellers (*see p208*).

For hats
Sombreria Obach (*see p210*).

Where to shop

BARRI GOTIC

The Saturday-afternoon hordes head to the big-name chain stores that line **Avda Portal de l'Àngel** and **C/Portaferrissa**, but there are plenty of less mainstream retail options. It's possible to lose hours while browsing antiques on **C/Banys Nous**, where tiny shops specialise in furniture, posters or textiles. The streets around **Plaça Sant Jaume** house some lovely, old-fashioned stores selling hats, candles, stationery or magic tricks. For something more contemporary, try the independent boutiques on **C/Avinyó**, which offer affordable, streetwise fashion and household items with a twist.

BORN & SANT PERE

The streets leading off the **Passeig del Born** are a rabbit's warren of stylish little boutiques offering quality, rather than quantity. Hip music, intimidating sales assistants and heartbreaking prices are part of the shopping experience, but so are gorgeous clothing, shoes and accessories from a clique of fast-rising local and international designers. Nearby **C/Argenteria** was named after its denizen silversmiths, and a handful of shops there follow the tradition, selling affordable, if mainstream, trinkets.

RAVAL

Raval's shopping, concentrated on the streets between the Boqueria market and Plaça dels Angels, has a youthful bent: head to **C/Riera Baixa** and **C/Tallers** for second-hand clothing and streetwear, and **C/Bonsuccès** for specialist record shops. **C/Doctor Dou** and **C/Elisabets** feature some trendy boutiques and shoe shops; the latter also has a couple of design stores. **C/Pelayo**, along Raval's top edge, has an impressive number of shoe stores.

BARCELONETA & THE PORTS

Barcelona's seafront shopping is concentrated in the shopping centre of **Maremàgnum** (*see right*), which houses a large, if sterile, confection of high-street fashion that are at least open late.

MONTJUIC

The area's museum and gallery shops tend to offer rather more than the usual guidebooks, posters and Gaudí-related bric-a-brac, which make for ideal gifts and souvenirs.

THE EIXAMPLE

Passeig de Gracia is home to enough high fashion and statement jewellery to satisfy even a footballer's wife. Chanel, Dior, Cartier and friends are present and correct, as are Spanish luxury brands Tous, Loewe and, on adjacent Consell de Cent, Catalan fashion hero Antoni Miró. A stone's throw away, the tree-lined **Rambla de Catalunya** is a pleasant place for browsing high-street fashion.

GRACIA & OTHER DISTRICTS

Independent shops rule in bohemian Gràcia: head to the bottom end of **C/Verdi** or the streets around **Plaça Rius i Taulet** for quirky little boutiques selling clothing, accessories and gifts. Local design collective Ruta Gràcia (www.rutagracia.com) lists dozens of independent retailers on its website.

Returning goods, even when they are faulty, can be difficult. However, all shops are required to provide a complaints book (ask for an *hoja de reclamación*). The mere act of asking for it sometimes does the trick, but, if not, take your receipt and copy of the complaint form to the consumer information office, OMIC (Ronda Sant Pau 43-45, Raval, 93 402 78 41, www.omic.bcn. cat, open 9am-5pm Mon-Thur, 9am-2pm Fri).

Note that if you're paying by credit card, you usually have to show photographic ID, such as a passport or driving licence. Bargain-hunters should note that sales (*rebaixes/rebajas*) begin after the retail orgy of Christmas and Epiphany, running from 6 January to mid February, and again during July and August.

General

Department stores

El Corte Inglés
Plaça Catalunya 14, Eixample (93 306 38 00/www. elcorteingles.es). Metro Catalunya. **Open** 10am-10pm Mon-Sat. **Credit** AmEx, DC, MC, V. **Map** p344 C2.
El Corte Inglés flagship store (shaped like a cruise liner) is a dominant landmark in Plaça Catalunya. It flies in the face of Barcelona's retail traditions – goods are relatively easy to return, and the staff are generally helpful when you want assistance, and unobtrusive when you don't. Visitors are catered for with store directories in other languages and a translation service. The Plaça Catalunya branch is the place for toiletries and cosmetics, clothes and accessories and homewares. It also houses a well-stocked but pricey supermarket and gourmet food store, plus services ranging from key cutting to currency exchange. The Avda Portal de l'Àngel branch stocks music, books, electronic equipment, stationery and sports gear from trainers to training bikes.
Other locations Avda Portal de l'Àngel 19-21, Plaça Catalunya (93 306 38 00); Avda Diagonal 471-473, Eixample (93 493 48 00); Avda Diagonal 617, Eixample (93 366 71 00); L'Illa (sports clothing only), Avda Diagonal 545, Eixample (93 363 80 90).

FNAC
El Triangle, Plaça Catalunya 4, Eixample (93 344 18 00/www.fnac.es). Metro Catalunya. **Open** 10am-10pm Mon-Sat. *Newsstand* 10am-10pm daily. **Credit** AmEx, MC, V. **Map** p344 B2.
At FNAC you'll find a sweeping book selection in several languages, and at low prices. On the other floors of this French multimedia megastore there are CDs, DVDs, hi-fis, TVs, computers, mobile phones, film processing and so on. The downside of the FNAC shopping experience is the mainly young, surly and poorly informed staff.
Other locations Diagonal Mar, Avda Diagonal 3, Poblenou (93 502 99 00); L'Illa, Avda Diagonal 545-557, Eixample (93 444 59 00).

Malls

Barcelona Glòries
Avda Diagonal 208, Eixample (93 486 04 04/ www.lesglories.com). Metro Glòries. **Open** *Shops* 10am-10pm Mon-Sat. **Credit** varies. **Map** p343 L8.
Since opening in 1995, this mall, office and leisure centre has become the focus of local life. There's a seven-screen cinema (films are mostly dubbed into Spanish) and more than 220 shops, including a Carrefour supermarket, an H&M, a Mango and a Disney Store, facing on to a large, café-filled square decorated with jets of coloured water. Family-friendly attractions include a free pram-lending service, play areas and entertainment such as bouncy castles and trampolines. As a leisure zone, Glòries stays open until 1am.

Diagonal Mar
Avda Diagonal 3, Poblenou (93 567 76 37/ www.diagonalmar.com). Metro El Maresme-Forum. **Open** *Shops* 10am-10pm Mon-Sat. *Food court & entertainment* 10am-midnight Mon-Thur; 10am-2am Fri, Sat; 11am-midnight Sun. **Credit** varies.
This three-level mall at the end of Avda Diagonal east of the city centre has an airy marine theme and a sea-facing roof terrace filled with cafés and restaurants of the fast-food variety. As business is a little slow (except at the giant Alcampo supermarket), it's a good queue-free option. Other anchors include El Corte Inglés, Zara, Mango and FNAC.

L'Illa
Avda Diagonal 545-557, Eixample (93 444 00 00/ www.lilla.com). Metro Maria Cristina. **Open** 10am-9.30pm Mon-Sat. *Supermarket* 9.30am-9.30pm Mon-Sat. **Credit** varies. **Map** p338 C4.
This monolithic mall's design is based on the idea of a skyscraper lying on its side, stretching 334m (1,100ft) along Avda Diagonal. It features all the usual fashion favourites but has a good range of Catalan brands such as Camper, Custo and Antonio Miró. It has been gaining a good reputation for its food offerings, with specialist gourmet food stalls and interesting eateries such as sushi and oyster bars.

Maremàgnum
Moll d'Espanya, Port Vell (93 225 81 00/www. maremagnum.es). Metro Drassanes. **Open** 10am-10pm daily. **Credit** varies. **Map** p342 F12/13.
When Viaplana and Piñon's black-mirrored shopping centre opened in 1995, it was *the* place to hang out. After years of declining popularity, it has been spruced up, ditched most of the bars and discos and taken a step upmarket with shops such as Xocoa (for great chocolate), Calvin Klein and Parisian accessories from boudoirish Lollipops. High-street staples are all present (Mango, H&M, Women's Secret), and the ground floor focuses on the family market, with sweets, children's clothes and a Barça shop. There's also a Starbuck's and a handful of tapas restaurants. *Photo p191.*

Eat, Drink, Shop

Diagonal Mar®
centre comercial

Fashion & Accessories-Culture-Electronics-Restaurants-Cinemas & Leisure

3, Diagonal Avenue Public Transport: Ⓜ El Maresme / Fòrum Metro Station, Bus: 7 and 41
For additional information: **902 530 300** or visit **www.diagonalmarcentre.es**

Markets

For details of the 40 permanent neighbourhood food markets in Barcelona, check www.bcn.cat/mercatsmunicipals. **Mercat Santa Caterina** (Avda Francesc Cambó, 93 319 57 40, www.mercatsantacaterina.net), in a remarkable Gaudiesque building designed by the late Enric Miralles, is especially worthy of note.

Other markets to look out for include the **stamp and coin market** on Plaça Reial (9am-2.30pm Sun) and the **Fira de Santa Llúcia** on Plaça Nova (*see p225*). Of the city's various **artisan food fairs**, the most central is usually held on picturesque Plaça del Pi on the first and third Friday, Saturday and Sunday of every month, as well as during local fiestas. *See also below, p206, p211 and p213.*

Specialist

Books & magazines

Museum shops are often the best bet for books on art, photography, film, architecture and design. A glut of shops specialising in comics, film and other visual art forms can be found in the Arc de Triomf area. In other areas, **Kowasa** (C/Mallorca 235, Eixample, 93 215 80 58, www.kowasa.com) runs excellent exhibitions in addition to its extensive stock of books about photography. For books on Catalonia, head to the **Palau Robert** shop (*see p323*).

English language

BCN Books

C/Roger de Llúria 118, Eixample (93 457 76 92/www.bcnbooks.com). Metro Passeig de Gràcia. **Open** *July, Aug* 10am-8pm Mon-Fri. *Sept-June* 10am-8pm Mon-Fri; 10am-2pm Sat. **Credit** MC, V. **Map** p340 G/H7.

This well-stocked English-language bookstore has a wide range of learning and teaching materials for all ages. There's also a decent selection of contemporary and classic fiction, a good kids' section, some travel guides and plenty of dictionaries. **Other locations** C/Rosselló 24, Eixample (93 476 33 43); C/Amigó 81, Eixample (93 200 79 53).

Casa del Llibre

C/Passeig de Gràcia 62, Eixample (93 272 34 80/www.casadellibro.com). Metro Passeig de Gràcia. **Open** 9.30am-9.30pm Mon-Sat. **Credit** AmEx, DC, MC, V. **Map** p340 G7.

Part of a well-established Spanish chain, this bookstore offers a diverse assortment of titles that includes some English-language fiction. Glossy, Barcelona-themed coffee-table tomes with good gift potential sit by the front right-hand entrance.

Hibernian Books

C/Montseny 17, Gràcia (93 217 47 96/www.hibernian-books.com). Metro Fontana. **Open** 4-8.30pm Mon; 10.30am-8.30pm Tue-Sat. **No credit cards**. **Map** p340 G5.

Hibernian Books feels like a proper British second-hand bookshop, with its air of pleasantly dusty intellectualism. There are books here for all tastes – from beautifully bound early editions to classic Penguin paperbacks, biographies, cookbooks, poetry and plays – in all more than 30,000 titles.

Specialist

Altaïr

Gran Via de les Corts Catalanes 616, Eixample (93 342 71 71/www.altair.es). Metro Universitat. **Open** 10am-2pm, 4.30-8.30pm Mon-Fri; 10am-3pm, 4-8.30pm Sat. **Credit** AmEx, DC, MC, V. **Map** p342 F8.

Every aspect of travel is covered in this, the largest travel bookshop in Europe. You can pick up guides to free eating in Barcelona, academic tomes on geolinguistics, handbooks on successful outdoor sex, and CDs of tribal music. Of course, all the less arcane publications are here too: maps for hikers, travel guidebooks, multilingual dictionaries, travel diaries and equipment such as mosquito nets.

Book & Coin Market

Mercat de Sant Antoni, C/Comte d'Urgell 1, Eixample (93 423 42 87). Metro Sant Antoni. **Open** 8am-2pm (approx) Sun. **No credit cards**. **Map** p342 D/E9.

Trestle tables around the outside of the Mercat Sant Antoni's metal structure are packed with every manner of reading material from arcane old tomes to well-pawed bodice-rippers and yellowing comics. There are also stacks of coins and more contemporary wares such as music, software and posters. Arrive early to beat the crowds.

Children

Fashion

One floor of the Plaça Catalunya branch of **El Corte Inglés** is devoted to children, while **Galeries Maldà** (C/Portaferrissa 22, no phone, Barri Gòtic) is a small shopping centre with plenty of kids' shops. Larger branches of **Zara** (*see p200*) have decent clothes sections. Kiddy's Class, which has branches all over town, sells exclusively Zara's children's clothing.

Chicco

Ronda Sant Pere 5, Eixample (93 301 49 76/www.chicco.es). Metro Catalunya. **Open** 10am-8.30pm Mon-Fri; 10am-9pm Sat. **Credit** AmEx, DC, MC, V. **Map** p344 D2.

The market leader in Spain, this colourful store has every conceivable baby-care item, from dummies and high chairs to bottle-warmers and travel cots.

Altaïr: Europe's largest travel bookshop has a global reach.

Its clothes and shoes are practical and well designed, and made to fit children up to eight years old.
Other locations Diagonal Mar, Avda Diagonal 3, Poblenou (93 356 03 74).

Monkey Biz
C/Casanova 211, Eixample (93 272 27 08/www.mon-key-biz.com). Bus 14, 67, 68. **Open** 10.30am-8.30pm Mon-Sat. **Credit** AmEx, MC, V. **Map** p340 D5.
The Monkey Biz monkeys have been busy collecting the coolest clothes and accessories from around the world: cute cotton Mikihouse togs from Japan and Naturino shoes from Italy are just two examples. The shop also has handmade and recycled toys and furniture, and stages workshops and activities.

Prénatal
Gran Via de les Corts Catalanes 611, Eixample (93 302 05 25/www.prenatal.es). Metro Passeig de Gràcia. **Open** 10am-8.30pm Mon-Sat. **Credit** AmEx, DC, MC, V. **Map** p342 G8.
This ubiquitous but pricey chain has slightly frumpy maternity wear, clothes for under-eights, buggies, car seats, cots, feeding bottles and toys.
Other locations Diagonal Mar, Avda Diagonal 3, Poblenou (93 356 04 03); throughout the city.

Toys

Drap
C/Pi 14, Barri Gòtic (93 318 14 87/www.ample24.com/drap). Metro Liceu. **Open** 9.30am-1.30pm, 4.30-8.30pm Mon-Fri; 10am-1.30pm, 5-8.30pm Sat. **Credit** MC, V. **Map** p344 C4.
Painstakingly crafted dolls' mansions that are perfect in every detail down to the doorbells and tiny padded hangers for the hand-carved wardrobes. *Photos p198.*

El Ingenio
C/Rauric 6, Barri Gòtic (93 317 71 38/www.el-ingenio.com). Metro Liceu. **Open** 10am-1.30pm, 4.15-8pm Mon-Fri; 11am-2pm, 5-8.30pm Sat. **Credit** (for purchases over €6) MC, V. **Map** p345 B5.
At once enchanting and disturbing, El Ingenio's handcrafted toys, tricks and costumes are reminders of a pre-digital world where people made their own entertainment. Its cabinets are full of practical jokes and curious toys; its fascinating workshop produces the oversized heads and garish costumes used in Barcelona's traditional festivities.

Joguines Monforte
Plaça Sant Josep Oriol 3, Barri Gòtic (93 318 22 85). Metro Liceu. **Open** 9.30am-1.30pm, 4-8pm Mon-Fri; 10am-2pm, 4.30-8.30pm Sat. **Credit** MC, V. **Map** p345 B5.
Make sure you try the Spanish version of snakes and ladders (*el juego de la oca*, or the 'goose game') and ludo (*parchís*) at this old-school toy shop, which is dedicated to traditional board games. Other items for quiet pursuits sold here include chess boards, jigsaw puzzles, wooden solitaire sets, croquet sets and kites.

Electronics & photography

If Casanova Foto doesn't have what you need, try **ARPI** (La Rambla 38-40, Barri Gòtic, 93 301 74 04), which has a wide range but poor service.

Casanova Foto
C/Pelai 18, Raval (93 302 73 63/www.casanova foto.com). Metro Universitat. **Open** 10am-2pm, 4.30-8.30pm Mon-Fri; 10am-2pm, 5-8.30pm Sat. **Credit** MC, V. **Map** p344 B1.

Drap has little people (and their homes) for your little people. *See p197.*

One for the pros and enthusiastic amateurs (they'll take two days to process your snaps). It's not the most user-friendly of establishments, either, but if you know what you want and what you're talking about, you should be able to find it among the extensive stock of new and second-hand digital and film equipment: camera bodies, lenses, tripods, darkroom gear, bags and more. There's also a slow but thorough repair lab.
Other locations Casanova Professional, C/Tallers 68, Raval (93 301 61 12); Casanova Col·lecció, C/Pelai 9, Raval (93 317 28 69).

Fotoprix

C/Pelai 6, Raval (93 318 20 36/www.fotoprix.es). Metro Universitat. **Open** 9.30am-8.30pm Mon-Fri; 10am-8.30pm Sat. **Credit** MC, V. **Map** p344 A1.
All 45 branches of Fotoprix offer one-hour APS and standard film development and copies from negatives. Other services are also on offer, such as passport photos, slide processing, printing from CDs and memory cards, and converting Super 8 film to video or DVD.
Other locations C/Ferran 33, Barri Gòtic (93 317 02 13); and throughout the city.

Fashion

Designer

Antonio Miró

C/Consell de Cent 349, Eixample (93 487 06 70/ www.antoniomiro.es). Metro Passeig de Gràcia. **Open** 10.30am-8.30pm Mon-Sat. **Credit** AmEx, DC, MC, V. **Map** p340 G8.
Catalan designer Miró caused a bit of a stir when he displayed his 2007 collection on eight Senegalese illegal immigrants. Quite what that has to do with Miró's sober, almost uniform-like clothes for men and women in muted tones is unclear. His diffusion line, Miró jeans, is a bit more relaxed and playful.
Other locations C/Vidrieria 5, Born (93 268 82 03).

Giménez y Zuazo

C/Elisabets 20, Raval (93 412 33 81/www.boba.es). Metro Catalunya. **Open** 10.30am-3pm, 5-8.30pm Mon-Sat. **Credit** AmEx, DC, MC, V. **Map** p344 A3.
This effortlessly cool designer duo has always been quirky. Previously, they've let themselves go when it comes to colour and print, although they have

been quite restrained with the silhouette of their women's clothing line. However, lately, they seem to have thrown the A-line shape rule book out of the window and have started playing with layers. **Other locations** C/Rec 42, Born (93 310 67 43).

Lydia Delgado

C/Minerva 21, Gràcia (93 415 99 98/www.lydia delgado.es). Metro Diagonal. **Open** *Sept-July* 10am-2pm, 4.30-8.30pm Mon-Sat. *Aug* 10.30am-2pm, 8.30pm Mon-Fri; 10.30am-2pm Sat. **Credit** AmEx, DC, MC, V. **Map** p340 G6.

Lydia Delgado's womenswear and accessories pull off purposeful femininity without descending into frothiness. Expect luxuriant brocades and satins, appliqué motifs, diaphanous layers, flowing cuts and tailored wools and tweeds.

Purificación García

Passeig de Gràcia 21, Eixample (93 487 72 92/ www.purificaciongarcia.es). Metro Passeig de Gràcia. **Open** 10am-8.30pm Mon-Sat. **Credit** AmEx, DC, MC, V. **Map** p342 G8.

Spanish-Uruguayan designer Purificación's sleek, sophisticated creations have appeared in many film and theatre productions. García creates clothes for those who want to make a subtle statement in the office or at the dinner party.
Other locations L'Illa, Avda Diagonal 545-557, Eixample (93 444 02 53).

Discount

One of Barcelona's hotspots for bargain clothes shopping is C/Girona. The two blocks between C/Ausiàs Marc and Gran Via de les Corts Catalanes are lined with numerous remainder stores and factory outlets of fluctuating quality. **Mango Outlet**, crammed with last season's unsold stock, far outshines the competition: the C/Girona branch (no.37, 93 412 29 35) is larger and more frantic, while the uptown branch (C/Pau Casals 12, 93 209 07 73) offers a more select choice of clothing.

If you're a dedicated designer bargain-hunter, make the 30-minute pilgrimage just outside the city to **La Roca Village** (93 842 39 39, www.larocavillage.com), where more than 50 discount outlets will tempt you with designer apparel from popular brands such as Antonio Miró, Versace, Diesel and Camper.

Contritem

C/Riera Sant Miquel 30, Gràcia (93 218 71 40). Metro Diagonal. **Open** 11am-2pm, 5-9pm Mon-Fri; 11am-2pm Sat. Closed 2wks Aug. **Credit** AmEx, DC, MC, V. **Map** p340 G6.

Discount designerwear for men and women in an airy store on the fringes of the uptown shopping district. An impressive array of international designers is represented: on a good day you could walk off with *gangues* (bargains) from the likes of Cacharel, Comme des Garçons, Moschino or Versace.

Stockland

C/Comtal 22, Barri Gòtic (93 318 03 31). Metro Urquinaona. **Open** 10am-8.30pm Mon-Sat. **Credit** AmEx, DC, MC, V. **Map** p344 D3.

A far cry from the elbow-deep frenzy of many remainder stores, this elegant boutique specialises in end-of-line clothing for women designed by respected Spanish names such as Josep Font, Jesús del Pozo and Purificación García at discount prices. Smart styles predominate; eveningwear is upstairs.

General

Adolfo Domínguez

C/Ribera 16, Born (93 319 21 59/www.adolfo dominguez.com). Metro Barceloneta. **Open** 11am-9pm Mon-Sat. **Credit** AmEx, DC, MC, V. **Map** p345 F7.

Men's tailoring remains Domínguez's forte, with his elegantly cut suits and shirts. The women's line reciprocates with tame, immaculately refined outfits, also squarely aimed at the 30- to 45-year-old market. The more casual U de Adolfo Domínguez line courts younger traditionalists, but doesn't quite attain the effortless panache of its grown-up precursor. This undervisited two-storey flagship store is supplemented by several others around the city.
Other locations Avda Diagonal 490, Gràcia (93 416 17 16); Passeig de Gràcia 32, Eixample (93 487 41 70); Passeig de Gràcia 89, Eixample (93 215 13 39); and throughout the city.

Cortefiel

Avda Portal de l'Àngel 38, Barri Gòtic (93 301 07 00/www.cortefiel.com). Metro Catalunya. **Open** 10am-8.30pm Mon-Sat. **Credit** AmEx, DC, MC, V. **Map** p344 C3.

A popular chain that casts a wider net than Mango or Zara, its fine tailored jackets and elegant, mature renditions of current trends appealing to a variety of women, from conservative students to fashion-conscious fiftysomethings. If you like a bit of glitz in your wardrobe, take a peek at the swankier Pedro del Hierro collection downstairs. Both labels have less prominent, but successful, menswear lines.
Other locations L'Illa, Avda Diagonal 545-557, Eixample (93 405 35 44); and throughout the city.

Custo Barcelona

Plaça de les Olles 7, Born (93 268 78 93/www.custo-barcelona.com). Metro Jaume I. **Open** 10am-10pm Mon-Sat. **Credit** AmEx, DC, MC, V. **Map** p345 E7.

The Catalan Dalmau brothers had to make it in LA before bringing their garish cut-and-paste style T-shirts back home, but now the Custo look is synonymous with Barcelona style, and has spawned a thousand imitations. Custo's signature prints can now be found on everything from coats to jeans to swimwear for both men and women, but a T-shirt is still the most highly prized (and highly priced) souvenir for any visiting fashionista.
Other locations C/Ferran 36, Barri Gòtic (93 342 66 98). L'Illa, Avda Diagonal 545-557, Eixample (93 322 26 62). La Rambla 109; Barri Gòtic (93 481 39 30).

Eat, Drink, Shop

Free

C/Ramelleres 5, Raval (93 301 61 15). Metro Catalunya. **Open** *Sept-June* 10am-2pm, 4.30-8.30pm Mon-Sat. *July, Aug* 10am-8.30pm Mon-Sat. **Credit** V. **Map** p344 B3.

A skate emporium that has grown exponentially to cater for Barcelona's expanding population of enthusiasts. For boys, there's casual wear from Stüssy, Carhartt, Fresh Jive et al; girls get plenty of Compobella and Loreak Mendian. The requisite chunky or retro footwear comes courtesy of Vans, Vision and Etnies.
Other locations C/Viladomat 319, Eixample (93 321 72 90); C/Rec 16, Born (93 295 50 36).

La Gauche Divine

Passatge de la Pau 7-10, Barri Gòtic (93 301 61 25/ www.lagauchedivine.com). Metro Drassanes. **Open** 5-8.30pm Mon; 11am-2.30pm, 5-8.30pm Tue-Sat. Closed 1wk Aug. **Credit** AmEx, DC, MC, V. **Map** p345 B7.

Tucked away among the sidestreets running off C/Ample, La Gauche Divine enlivens the clothes shopping experience with art exhibitions, video projections and DJ sets. It has a laid-back friendly vibe that belies the serious quality of its collections: this includes elegant tailoring from Ailanto, and complex, ambitiously constructed pieces from the young and talented Txell Miras.

Jean-Pierre Bua

Avda Diagonal 469, Eixample (93 439 71 00/www. jeanpierrebua.com). Bus 6, 7, 15, 33, 34, 67, 68. **Open** 10am-2pm, 4.30-8.30pm Mon-Sat. **Credit** AmEx, DC, MC, V. **Map** p340 E5.

The clothes are the highest of high-end fashion, the assistants are model-beautiful, and the shop itself has the air of a runway at a Paris catwalk show. No inferiority complexes are allowed: if you have the money, figure and label knowledge (and only if), come to worship at the altar of Miu Miu, Dries van Noten, Alexander McQueen and many more.

Mango

Passeig de Gràcia 65, Eixample (93 215 75 30/ www.mango.es). Metro Passeig de Gràcia. **Open** 10am-9pm Mon-Sat. **Credit** AmEx, DC, MC, V. **Map** p340 G7.

A small step up from Zara in quality and price, Mango's womenswear is less chameleon-like but still victim to the catwalks. Strong points include funky winter coats, tailored trouser suits and skirts, knitwear and stretchy tops. Unsold items end up at the Mango Outlet (*see p199*), which is packed with frenzied girls on a mission.
Other locations Passeig de Gràcia 8-10, Eixample (93 412 15 99); Avda Portal de l'Àngel, Barri Gòtic (93 317 69 85); and throughout the city.

On Land

C/Princesa 25, Born (93 310 02 11/www.on-land. com). Metro Jaume I. **Open** *Sept-July* 5-8.30pm Mon; 11am-3pm, 5-8.30pm Tue-Fri; 11am-8.30pm Sat. *Aug* 11am-3pm, 5-8.30pm Tue-Sat. Closed 1wk Aug. **Credit** AmEx, DC, MC, V. **Map** p345 C3.

On Land's two shops show a refreshing lack of pretension, with simple decor and a hint of playfulness echoed in the fashions they stock: local boy Josep Font's girly frocks are made for fun rather than flouncing, Petit Bateau's cute T-shirts are perfect for playing sailor girl, and Divinas Palabras' cartoony T-shirts put a smile on your face.
Other locations C/València 273, Eixample (93 215 56 25).

Suite

C/Verdi 3-5, Gràcia (93 210 02 47/www. martargustems.com). Metro Fontana. **Open** *Mar-July* 5-9pm Mon; 11am-2pm, 5-9pm Tue-Sat. *Aug* 5-9pm Mon-Thur; 11am-2pm, 5-9pm Fri, Sat. *Sept-Feb* 5-8.30pm Mon; 10.30am-2pm, 5-8.30pm Tue-Sat. Closed 2wks end Aug, 1wk Sept and 1st wknd Feb. **Credit** AmEx, V. **Map** p341 H5.

The designers showcased in this Gràcia boutique tend towards the sober rather than the showy in their pieces. But it doesn't mean school marms only need apply. P-Pi's bags combine prim tweed with pretty ribbons in avant-garde shapes and La Casita de Wendy's fairy-tale inspired designs are a favourite with Björk.

Tribu

C/Avinyó 12, Barri Gòtic (93 318 65 10). Metro Jaume I or Liceu. **Open** 11am-2.30pm, 4.30-8.30pm Mon-Fri; 11am-8.30pm Sat. **Credit** MC, V. **Map** p345 C6.

One of the countless clued-up fashion platforms in Barcelona for both international and home-grown casual labels such as Jocomomola, Nolita, Diesel and Freesoul. Be sure to seek out the designer trainers at the back of the shop.

Zara

Avda Portal de l'Àngel 32-34, Barri Gòtic (93 301 08 98/www.zara.com). Metro Catalunya. **Open** 10am-9pm Mon-Sat. **Credit** AmEx, DC, MC, V. **Map** p344 C3.

Zara's recipe for success has won over the world, but items are cheaper on its home turf. Well-executed, affordable copies of catwalk fashions appear on the rails in a fashion heartbeat; while the women's section is the front-runner, the men's and children's sections cover good ground. The Zara Home department has also been a success. The price you pay (for the price you pay) becomes apparent in the despair-inducing queues at peak times.
Other locations C/Pelai 58, Eixample (93 301 09 78); Passeig de Gràcia 16, Eixample (93 318 76 75); and throughout the city.

Used & vintage

The narrow C/Riera Baixa in the Raval is where most of Barcelona's second-hand clothes retailers cluster, making it a great place to hunt for bargains and unique items. **Holala! Ibiza** at no.11 (93 441 99 94) has affordable thrift-store staples, while at no.7, **Smart And Clean**'s 1960s and '70s second-hand gear is largely made up of mod essentials, with a decent range of leather jackets and vintage trainers on hand as well (93 441 87 64, www.smartandclean.com).

Lailo

C/Riera Baixa 20, Raval (93 441 37 49). Metro Liceu or Sant Antoni. **Open** 11am-2pm, 5-8pm Mon-Sat. Closed 1wk end Aug. **Credit** AmEx, DC, MC, V. **Map** p342 E10.

Lailo stands out from the second-hand crowd by the quality of its stock. It even has a 'museum' of old costumes from the Liceu theatre, some dating back to the 18th century. If you want something for a one-off occasion, you can hire everything from the tuxedos to the coming-out gowns.

Le Swing

C/Riera Baixa 13, Raval (93 324 84 02). Metro Liceu or Sant Antoni. **Open** 10.30am-2.30pm, 4.30-8.30pm Mon-Sat. **Credit** AmEx, DC, MC, V. **Map** p342 E10.

Today's second-hand is known as vintage, and thrift is not on the agenda. Fervent worshippers of Pierre Cardin, YSL, Dior, Kenzo and other fashion deities scour all corners of the sartorial stratosphere and deliver their booty back to this little powder puff of a boutique. The odd Zara number and other mere mortal brands creep in as well.

Produit National Brut

C/Avinyó 29, Barri Gòtic (93 268 27 55). Metro Jaume I or Liceu. **Open** 11am-9pm Mon-Sat. **Credit** MC, V. **Map** p345 C7.

Wear your *barri* on your chest with PNB's sweat tops emblazoned with the names of Barcelona's hipster neighbourhoods, such as Barrio Chino. This store also stocks a good supply of second-hand fashions: the usual range of ironic US high-school ties, 1960s-styled shirts, smock dresses, denim, corduroy and leather. If that doesn't tempt you, perhaps a kitsch knick-knack or piece of grafittiesque artwork will.

Fashion accessories & services

Cleaning & repairs

Any shop marked '*rapid*' or '*rápido*' does shoe repairs and key cutting; **El Corte Inglés** (*see p193*) has both in the basement.

La Hermosa

C/Formatgeria 3, Born (93 319 97 26). Metro Jaume I. **Open** 10am-9pm Mon-Sat. **No credit cards**. **Map** p345 E6.

A washing and dry-cleaning facility. Opt for self-service washing and drying (€5 for a standard load) or go for the drop-off service (€12 for 8kg, €179 for 14kg). Dry-cleaning takes two to three days.

LavaXpres

C/Ferlandina 34, Raval (no phone). Metro Sant Antoni or Universitat. **Open** 8am-11pm daily. **No credit cards**. **Map** p342 E9.

This completely self-service, American-owned launderette is open 365 days a year. There are machines big enough to wash a rucksack-full of dirty clothes and still have room. Smaller 9kg loads cost €3.50.

Tintorería Ferran

C/Ferran 11, Barri Gòtic (93 301 87 30). Metro Liceu. **Open** 9am-2pm, 4.30-8pm Mon-Fri. **Credit** V. **Map** p345 B5.

A competent, reasonably priced dry-cleaners. Services include cleaning of large items like duvets and rugs, mending (which can be pricey), service washes and delivery. Look out for offers.

Jewellery

The Born's C/Argentería takes its name from the numerous silversmiths who established themselves there in the 15th century. Even

La Gauche Divine.

A unique place

Maremagnum

A mall with a view

Seen one mall, seen them all? Not at Maremagnum you haven't. Take a walk down La Rambla and pass the statue of Columbus, pointing your way to a new world of fashion, shopping and culture. Cross the sea (though you can do this by bridge instead of a rather leaky boat) and enter the world of Maremagnum.

Here you'll find a whirl of constant activity to amaze and entice the visitor, from every variety of retail therapy to an eclectic collection of eateries. This is a place where the commercial and the cultural entwine in a series of stunning developments.

So, with the best of fashion, music festivals and events from the frivolous to the serious, Maremagnum is the place to visit. And remember, it's the only place in the city centre that is open all year round, from 10am to 10pm daily, including holidays.

Shopping!

At Maremagnum you will find all the best outlets for fashion and also plenty of places to buy that little something to take home in memory of your time in Barcelona. There's no need to labour around the city centre, sweating in the sun, when you can do all your shopping in air-conditioned comfort here, with the added bonus of beautiful views of the port and sea.

When and Where

TIMETABLE: Open from Monday to Sunday, from 10am - 10pm, holidays included.
ADDRESS: Maremagnum Building
Moll d'Espanya, 5
08039 Barcelona

HOW TO GET THERE: By underground: L3 Drassanes or L4 Barceloneta.
By bus: 14 - 17 - 19 - 36 - 39 - 40 - 57 - 59 - 64 - 157 (daytime bus) / NO - N9 - N12 - N15 (night bus). **Tourist bus:** Southern Route. **By car:** Exit 22 de Ronda Litoral. **On foot:** Crossing Rambla del Mar.

www.maremagnum.es

There are more than 30 outlets featuring the best brands in the city, including H&M, Desigual, Oysho, Mango, QuikSilver, Jack&Jones, Pull&Bear, Springfield and many others besides. Take your time, enjoy the city, stroll around unencumbered with bags and then come to Maremagnum safe in the knowledge that it's waiting for you, seven days a week, every day of the year.

Take a break!

Should all the shopping get too much for you, or you simply want a chance to unwind from the hustle and bustle of the city, then why not take a ramble on our light and airy terraces, enjoying the views of the ships in the harbour and the ever-changing glitter of light on water, before settling down for a coffee at one of the many cafés and restaurants in Maremagnum. You can even catch a movie at our cinema or simply watch the world sail by.

What would you like to eat?

Dining well by the sea is no longer difficult. At Maremagnum we have a great variety of places to eat, ranging from simple cafés where you can sip a slow coffee to the most fashionable restaurants serving the latest in Catalan cuisine. Whatever your fancy, you won't get hungry at Maremagnum.

today, this street and the surrounding area are home to a number of shops selling silver jewellery, such as **joid'art** (Plaça Santa Maria 7, 93 310 10 87, www.platamundi.com), part of a successful chain that has pretty, affordable pieces in its shops throughout Barcelona. Nearby, boutiques such as **Ad Láter** (C/Ases 1, 93 310 66 00) exhibit pieces by innovative local jewellery designers.

Upmarket jewellers naturally gravitate towards the glamorous shopping districts, such as Passeig de Gràcia and Avda Diagonal.

Alea Majoral Galería de Joyas

C/Argenteria 66, Born (93 310 13 73/www. majoral.com). Metro Jaume I. **Open** *Sept-July* 10.30am-8.30pm Mon-Fri; 11am-8.30pm Sat. *Aug* 11am-8.30pm Mon-Sat. Closed 1wk Aug. **Credit** AmEx, DC, MC, V. **Map** p345 E6.

This elegant jewellery gallery dedicates its street-front space to Enric Majoral's structural silver and gold pieces. A small room tucked in the back plays host to a changing exhibition of works by various up-and-coming artists. In fact, many of the creations are more artworks than accessories.
Other locations Majoral, C/Consell de Cent 308, Eixample (93 467 72 09); Majoral Pedralbes Centre, Avda Diagonal 609, Zona Alta (93 363 12 91).

Bagués

Passeig de Gràcia 41, Eixample (93 216 01 73/ www.bagues.com). Metro Passeig de Gràcia. **Open** *Sept-July* 10am-8.30pm Mon-Fri; 10am-1.30pm, 5-8.30pm Sat. *Aug* 10am-1.30pm, 4.30-8.30pm Mon-Fri; 10am-1.30pm Sat. **Credit** AmEx, DC, MC, V. **Map** p340 G8.

Housed in a jewel of a building – the Modernista palace Casa Amatller (*see p126*) – Bagués is, perhaps, Barcelona's most prestigious and historic jeweller. The original master jeweller of the house, Lluis Masriera, created revolutionary pieces using a 'translucid enamel' technique at the beginning of the 20th century. His signature motifs, the art nouveau favourites of flowers, insects and birds, are reflected in today's designs.
Other locations Rambla de les Flors 105, Raval (93 481 70 50).

Hipotesi

C/Provença 237, Eixample (93 215 02 98). Metro Diagonal. **Open** *Sept-July* 10am-1.30pm, 5-8.30pm Mon, Sat; 10am-8.30pm Tue-Fri. *Aug* 10.30am-2pm, 5-8.30pm Mon-Fri. **Credit** AmEx, DC, MC, V. **Map** p340 F7.

The friendly owner of Hipotesi loves jewellery and seems as happy for fellow fans to browse in this gallery/shop and ask about the artists whose work she sells as he is for them to buy. Both local artisans, such as Ramon Puig Cuyàs, head of Barcelona's Massana jewellery school, and international jewellers, like Briton Kathryn Marchbank, are represented. Styles vary considerably, and materials can range from the finest spun gold to plastic, felt or ribbon.

Hipotesi.

Lingerie & underwear

Rambla de Catalunya is a mecca for underwear shoppers: boutiques brimming with lingerie, such as **La Perla** (no.88, 93 467 71 49), sit beside traditional retailers, among them **La Perla Gris** on the crossing with C/Rosselló (no.220, 93 215 29 91). And then there's the inexpensive swimwear and underwear at high-street chains such as **Oysho** (no.77, 93 488 36 01, www.oysho.com), from the same stable as Zara. **Vanity Fair** (no.11, 93 317 65 45) strikes a happy medium with reasonably priced Spanish labels as well as its own range. **El Corte Inglés** (*see p193*) has men's and women's underwear for all ages.

Janina

Rambla de Catalunya 94, Eixample (93 215 04 84). Metro Diagonal/FGC Provença. **Open** *Sept-July* 10am-8.30pm Mon-Sat. *Aug* 10am-2pm, 5-8.30pm Mon-Sat. **Credit** AmEx, MC, V. **Map** p340 G7.
Good-quality women's underwear and nightwear by Calvin Klein, Christian Dior, La Perla and others. Some larger sizes are stocked; alternatively, bras can be sent to a seamstress to be altered overnight.
Other locations Avda Pau Casals 8, Eixample (93 202 06 93).

Le Boudoir

C/Canuda 21, Barri Gòtic (93 302 52 81/www. leboudoir.net). Metro Catalunya. **Open** *Sept-July* 10am-8.30pm Mon-Fri; 10.30am-9pm Sat. *Aug* 11am-9pm Mon-Sat. **Credit** AmEx, DC, MC, V. **Map** p344 C3.
Sensuality abounds in Barcelona's classy answer to Agent Provocateur. Sexy lingerie comes with designer labels (and prices), the swimwear is not intended for shrinking violets, and fluffy kitten-heeled mules are not made with practicality in mind.
Other locations Pedralbes Centre, Avda Diagonal 609, Pedralbes (93 321 05 39).

Women's Secret

C/Portaferrissa 7-9, Barri Gòtic (93 318 92 42/www. womensecret.com). Metro Liceu. **Open** 10am-9pm Mon-Sat. **Credit** AmEx, DC, MC, V. **Map** p344 B4.
What's the secret? Women would rather wear underwear that's cute, colourful and comfortable than some fussy, itchy pieces of black nylon string. There are some sexy pieces here, but mostly it's versatile strap bras, cool cotton Japanesey wraparound PJs and a funky line of under/outerwear in cartoonish stylings: skimpy shorts, miniskirts and vest tops.
Other locations Avda Portal de l'Àngel, Barri Gòtic (93 318 70 55); and throughout the city.

Luggage

Capricho de Muñeca

C/Brosoli 1, Born (93 319 58 91/www.capricho demuneca.com). Metro Jaume I. **Open** 5-9.30pm Mon-Sat. **Credit** MC, V. **Map** p345 E6.

Soft leather handbags in cherry reds, chocolate browns and parma violet made by hand just upstairs by designer Lisa Lempp. Sizes range from the cute and petit to the luxuriously large. Belts and wallets complement the handbags.

Casa Antich SCP

C/Consolat del Mar 27-31, Born (93 310 43 91/ www.casaantich.com). Metro Jaume I. **Open** 9am-8.30pm Mon-Fri; 9.30am-8.30pm Sat. **Credit** AmEx, DC, MC, V. **Map** p345 D7.
Under the arches at the back end of the Born you'll find a luggage wares shop that in levels of service and size of stock recalls the golden age of travel. Here you can still purchase trunks for a steam across the Atlantic and ladies' vanity cases that would be perfect for a sojourn on the Orient Express. But you'll also find computer cases and shoulder bags from the likes of Mandarina Duck and Kipling.

Loewe

Passeig de Gràcia 35, Eixample (93 216 04 00/ www.loewe.com). Metro Passeig de Gràcia. **Open** 10am-8.30pm Mon-Sat. **Credit** AmEx, DC, MC, V. **Map** p342 G8.
The price tags are bigger than the handbags at this couturier, where the Daddy Warbucks prices go well into the thousands. With a decadent setting on two floors of Domènech i Montaner's Casa Morera, the store's products, from crocodile-skin demi bags to men's sheepskin coats, are of superb quality.
Other locations Avda Diagonal 570, Eixample (93 200 09 20); Hotel Arts, C/Marina 19-21, Barceloneta (93 225 99 27).

Scarves & textiles

Textiles were once one of Barcelona's main industries. It's a legacy visible in many of the street names of the Born, where you'll find the highest concentration of textile shops and workshops in the city.

Almacenes del Pilar

C/Boqueria 43, Barri Gòtic (93 317 79 84/www. almacenesdelpilar.com). Metro Liceu. **Open** 9.30am-2pm, 4-8pm Mon-Sat. Closed 2wks Aug. **Credit** AmEx, MC, DC, V. **Map** p345 B5.
An array of fabrics and accessories for traditional Spanish costumes is on display in this colourful, shambolic interior dating back to 1886. Making your way through bolts of material, you'll find bolts of the richly hued brocades used for Valencian *fallera* outfits and other rudiments of folkloric dress from various parts of the country. Lace *mantillas,* and the high combs over which they are worn, are stocked, along with fringed, hand-embroidered pure silk *mantones de manila* (shawls) and colourful wooden fans.

Alonso

C/Santa Ana 27, Barri Gòtic (93 317 60 85/www. tiendacenter.com). Metro Liceu. **Open** 10am-8pm Mon-Sat. Closed 1wk Aug. **Credit** AmEx, DC, MC, V. **Map** p344 C3.

Elegant Catalan ladies have come here for those important finishing touches for their outfit for more than 100 years. Behind the Modernista façade lie soft gloves in leather and lace, intricate fans, both traditional and modern, and scarves in mohair or silk.

Shoes

In summer, people of all ages wear *abarcas*, sloppy, peep-toe leather shoes from Menorca, or the traditional Catalan *espardenyes,* espadrilles of hemp and canvas. Footwear outlets line the main shopping strips, such as Avda Portal de l'Àngel or C/Pelai; chains include **Casas**, **Mar Bessas**, **Royalty**, **Querol**, **Tascón** and **Vogue**, which have huge but similar collections.

Camper

C/Pelai 13-37, Eixample (93 302 41 24/www. camper.com). Metro Catalunya. **Open** 10am-10pm Mon-Sat. **Credit** AmEx, DC, MC, V. **Map** p344 B2.
Mallorca-based eco shoe company Camper has sexed up its ladies' line recently. Each year it seems to flirt

Le Boudoir.

more with high heels (albeit rubbery wedgy ones) and girly straps. Of course, it still has its classic round-toed and clod-heeled classics, and the guys still have their iconic bowling shoes, but it's worth another look if you've previously dismissed this lot.
Other locations Passeig de Gràcia 30, Eixample (93 481 61 75); Plaça del Àngels 6, Raval (93 342 41 41); and throughout the city.

Czar

Passeig del Born 20, Born (93 310 72 22). Metro Jaume I. **Open** 5-9.30pm Mon; noon-2pm, 5-9.30pm Tue-Sat. **Credit** MC, V. **Map** p345 E6.
The hippest trainers are presented here like valuable pieces in a museum. You should be able to find an Adidas Originals or Vision Streetwear pair to suit even the most demanding of street feet. The collection is mainly aimed at men, but girls have a small and sassy range at the back.

La Manual Alpargatera

C/Avinyó 7, Barri Gòtic (93 301 01 72/www.la manual.net). Metro Liceu. **Open** Sept-Jun 9.30am-1.30pm, 4.30-8pm Mon-Fri; 10am-1.30pm, 4.30-8pm Sat. *July, Aug* 9.30am-1.30pm, 5-8.30pm. **Credit** AmEx, DC, MC, V. **Map** p345 C6.
The catwalk-blessed revival of the espadrille may not have convinced everyone, but a stop at handmade espadrille emporium La Manual Alpargatera, open since 1910, is a must for any Barcelona visitor. The store has shod such luminaries as Pope John Paul II and Jack Nicholson during its years of service.

Muxart

C/Rosselló 230, Eixample (93 488 10 64/www. muxart.com). Metro Diagonal. **Open** 10am-2pm, 4.30-8.30pm Mon-Fri; 10am-2pm, 5-8.30pm Sat. **Credit** AmEx, DC, MC, V. **Map** p340 G6/7.
Muxart sells shoes around which to build an outfit. Materials are refined, styles are sharp, avant-garde and blatantly not intended to hide under a pair of baggy beige slacks. Lines for men and women are complemented by equally creative and attractive bags and accessories.
Other locations Rambla de Catalunya 47, Eixample (93 467 74 23).

U-Casas

C/Espaseria 4, Born (93 310 00 46/www.casas club.com). Metro Jaume I. **Open** 10.30am-9pm Mon-Thur; 10.30am-9.30pm Fri, Sat. **Credit** MC, V. **Map** p345 E7.
The pared-down, post-industrial decor so beloved of this neighbourhood provides the perfect back-drop for bright and quirky shoes. Strange heels and toes are out in force this season, and after trying on all those snub-nosed winklepickers and rubber wedgies from the likes of Helmut Lang, Fly, Fornarina and Irregular Choice, you can rest your weary pins on the giant, shoe-shaped chaise longue.
Other locations C/Tallers 2, Raval (93 318 3405); L'Illa, Avda Diagonal 345-557, Eixample (93 419 14 85); Barcelona Glòries, Avda Diagonal 208, Eixample (93 486 0145).

Eat, Drink, Shop

Jamonísimo: this little piggy went to market – and boy did he taste good. *See p208.*

Food & drink

Drinks

Craft shop **Art Escudellers** (*see p208*) has a good selection of wines in its cellar.

Lavinia

Avda Diagonal 605, Eixample (93 363 44 45/www. lavinia.es). Metro Maria Cristina. **Open** 10am-9pm Mon-Sat. **Credit** AmEx, DC, MC, V. **Map** p340 D5.
This ultra-slick store houses the largest selection of wines in Europe. Knowledgeable, polyglot staff happily talk customers through the thousands of horizontally displayed Spanish and international wines, including exceptional vintages and special editions at good prices. They'll also help you put together cases to send home and let you try before you buy.

Torres

C/Nou de la Rambla 25, Barri Gòtic (93 317 32 34/ www.vinosencasa.com). Metro Drassanes or Liceu. **Open** 9am-2pm, 4-9pm Mon-Sat. **Credit** MC, V. **Map** p345 A6.
After moving from its old and dusty grocery store across the road, Torres' shiny new shop is a bit out of place in the run-down end of the Raval. Now it stocks a good range of Spanish wines (with a particularly good cava section) and interesting international beers and spirits, including black Mallorcan absinthe. Handily, the shop's competitive prices weren't also revamped during the move.

Vila Viniteca

C/Agullers 7, Born (93 268 32 27/www.vila viniteca.es). Metro Jaume I. **Open** *Sept-June* 8.30am-8.30pm Mon-Sat. *July, Aug* 8.30am-8.30pm Mon-Fri; 8.30am-2pm Sat. **Credit** DC, MC, V. **Map** p345 D7.
Newly renovated and expanded, this family-run business has built up a stock of more than 6,000 wines and spirits since 1932. With everything from a 1953 Damoiseau rum, which costs as much as €500,

through to €6 bottles of table wine, the selection here is mostly Spanish and Catalan, but it also takes in international favourites. The new food shop next door at no.9 stocks fine cheeses, cured meats and oils. The perfect stop for upmarket foodie gifts.
Other locations Vinacoteca, València 595, Eixample (93 232 58 35).

General

The supermarket in the basement of **El Corte Inglés** (*see p193*) in Plaça Catalunya has a gourmet section of local and foreign specialities.

Carrefour Express

La Rambla 113, Barri Gòtic (93 302 48 24). Metro Catalunya. **Open** 10am-10pm Mon-Sat. **Credit** MC, V. **Map** p344 B3.
The opening hours, a chemist and an unbeatable location make up for its slight shabbiness, confusing layout and agonisingly slow checkout queues.

Colmado Quilez

Rambla Catalunya 63, Eixample (93 215 23 56). Metro Passeig de Gràcia. **Open** *Jan-mid Oct* 9am-2pm, 4.30-8.30pm Mon-Fri; 9am-2pm Sat. *Mid Oct-Dec* 9am-2pm, 4.30-8.30pm Mon-Sat. **Credit** MC, V. **Map** p340 F/8.
Colmados – old-school grocery stores – are relics of the old way of shopping before the invasion of the supermarkets. This is one of the few surviving examples in the Modernista Eixample, with floor-to-ceiling shelves stacked full of gourmet treats, such as local preserved fungi in cute mushroom-shaped bottles (Delicias del Bosque), and the store's own-label caviar, cava, saffron and anchovies.

Markets

La Boqueria

La Rambla 89, Raval (93 318 25 84/www. boqueria.info). Metro Liceu. **Open** 8am-8.30pm Mon-Sat. **Map** p344 A/B4.

Riding the current wave of fascination with all things gastronomic in Barcelona, the city's most famous food market is now a must-stop for any visitor. Prices are inflated by the gaggle of tourists at the market's front and outer limits: penetrate to the centre and rear for better deals. If you visit in the morning, you'll see the best produce, including the smallholders' fruit and vegetable stalls in the little square attached to the C/Carme side of the market. If you do come to ogle, remember that this is where locals come to shop, so don't touch what you don't want to buy, ask before taking photos and watch out for vicious old ladies with ankle-destroying shopping trolleys.

Specialist

La Botifarreria de Santa Maria

C/Santa Maria 4, Born (93 319 97 84). Metro Barceloneta or Jaume I. **Open** 8.30am-2.30pm, 5-8.30pm Mon-Fri; 8.30am-3pm Sat. Closed Aug. **Credit** MC, V. **Map** p345 E7.
Coarse farmhouse pâtés, hand-cut smoked salmon, fine melting chèvre cheeses and free-range chickens are not why this shop is always so crowded. The main draw is the sausage that gives the Botifarreria its name. This traditional Catalan pork sausage is almost worshipped here, and curious versions (squid, chocolate) are made up fresh each day.

Caelum

C/Palla 8, Barri Gòtic (93 302 69 93). Metro Liceu. **Open** 5-8.30pm Mon; 10.30am-8.30pm Tue-Thur; 10.30am-midnight Fri, Sat; 11.30am-9pm Sun. Closed 2wks Aug. **Credit** AmEx, DC, MC, V. **Map** p344 C4.
Spain's monks and nuns have a naughty sideline in trad sweets including candied saints' bones, sugared egg yolks and drinkable goodies such as eucalyptus and orange liqueur, all beautifully packaged. If you'd like to sample before committing to a whole box of holy honey cake, there's a taster café downstairs on the site of the medieval Jewish thermal baths.

Cafés El Magnífico/Sans & Sans

C/Argenteria 64/59, Born (93 310 33 61/www. cafeselmagnifico.com). Metro Jaume I. **Open** 10am-2pm, 4-8pm Mon-Fri; 10am-2pm Sat. Closed 3wks Aug. **Credit** AmEx, MC, V. **Map** p345 E6.
For the finest coffees roasted on the premises and the widest range of teas in elegant lacquer boxes, visit this pair of shops that stand opposite each other on C/Argenteria. As well as the various infusions, you can also purchase all the paraphernalia necessary to enjoy them at their best. **Other locations** Avda Diagonal 520, Eixample (93 414 56 23).

Casa Gispert

C/Sombrerers 23, Born (93 319 75 35/www.casa gispert.com). Metro Jaume I. **Open** *Jan-Sept* 9.30am-2pm, 4-7.30pm Tue-Fri; 10am-2pm, 5-8pm Sat. *Oct-Dec* 9.30am-2pm, 4-7.30pm Mon-Fri; 10am-2pm, 5-8pm Sat. **Credit** MC, V. **Map** p345 E6.

Casa Gispert radiates a warmth that has something to do with more than just its original wood-fired nut and coffee roaster. Like a stage-set version of an olde schoole shoppe, its wooden cabinets and shelves groan with the finest and most fragrant nuts, herbs, spices, preserves, sauces, oils, seasonings and, most importantly, huge hand-made chocolate truffles. The pre-packed kits for making local specialities such as *panellets* (Hallowe'en bonbons) make great gifts.

Delishop

C/Mallorca 241, Eixample (93 215 15 46/www. delishop.es). Metro Diagonal. **Open** *Sept-July* 10.30am-9pm Mon-Sat. *Aug* noon-9pm Mon-Sat. **Credit** MC, V. **Map** p340 F7.
Opened in November 2006 by a pair of well-travelled foodies, Delishop brings together several hundred products from around the world. Most are selected for taste, while some add colour with wonderful packaging. Plenty of recipes are laid on if you're unsure what to do with hoisin sauce or vine leaves.

Enric Rovira Shop

Avda Josep Tarradellas 113, Les Corts (93 419 25 47/www.enricrovira.com). Metro Entença. **Open** 10am-2.30pm, 5-8pm Tue-Fri; 10am-2pm Sat. Closed Aug. **Credit** MC, V. **Map** p338 D6.
Perhaps the best place in Barcelona for designer chocolates, this is where substance actually keeps up with style. Locally born Rovira's Gaudí-esque chocolate tile is an iconic gift for any choc lover, and his pink peppercorn truffles make great after-dinner conversation pieces.

Escribà

Gran Via de les Corts Catalanes 546, Eixample (93 454 75 35/www.escriba.es). Metro Urgell. **Open** *Sept-July* 8am-3pm, 5-9pm Mon-Fri; 8am-9pm Sat, Sun. *Aug* 9am-3pm daily. **Credit** DC, MC, V. **Map** p342 E8.
Antoni Escribà, the 'Mozart of Chocolate', died in 2004, but his legacy lives on. His team produces jawdropping creations for Easter, from a hulking chocolate Grand Canyon to a life-size model of Michelangelo's *David*. The smaller miracles include cherry liqueur encased in red chocolate lips. The Rambla branch is particularly worth visiting as it's situated in a pretty Modernista building. **Other locations** La Rambla 83, Raval (93 301 60 27).

Formatgeria La Seu

C/Dagueria 16, Barri Gòtic (93 412 65 48/ www.formatgerialaseu.com). Metro Jaume I. **Open** 10am-2pm, 5-8pm Tue-Fri; 10am-3pm, 5-8pm Sat. Closed Aug. **No credit cards. Map** p345 D6.
Spain has long neglected its cheese heritage, which perhaps explains why this is the only shop in the whole country to specialise in Spanish-only farmhouse cheeses. Scottish owner Katherine hand-picks her wares, such as the fruity blue Valdeón and the melting, bittersweet Torta de la Serena. Her *tast* of three cheeses and a glass of wine for just a few euros is a great way to explore what's on offer.

Get a new look at **Arlequí Mascares**.

Jamonísimo

C/Provença 85, Eixample (93 439 0847/www.
jamonisimo.com). Metro Hospital Clínic. **Open**
Sept-July 5-9pm Mon; 9.30am-2.30pm, 5-9pm Tue-Fri;
9.30am-2.30pm, 5.30-9pm Sat. *Aug* 9.30am-2.30pm,
5-9pm Mon-Fri; 9.30am-2.30pm Sat. **Credit** AmEx,
DC, MC, V. **Map** p340 D7.
If you really want to know what all the fuss with
regard to *jamón ibérico* is about, you have to come
to Jamonísimo and try its plate of 'the three textures'
of *jamón*. It will spoil you for ham sandwiches at the
local bar, but it's worth it. *Photo p206.*

Papabubble

C/Ample 28, Barri Gòtic (93 268 86 25/www.
papabubble.com). Metro Barceloneta or Drassanes.
Open 10am-2pm, 4-8.30pm Tue-Fri; 10am-8.30pm
Sat; 11am-7.30pm Sun. Closed Aug. **Credit** AmEx,
MC, V. **Map** p345 C7.
You can watch the Australian owners create their
kaleidoscope-coloured humbugs before your eyes in
flavours both usual (orange, mint) and unusual
(lavender, passion fruit).

Planelles Donat

Avda Portal de l'Àngel 7, Barri Gòtic (93 317 29
26). Metro Catalunya. **Open** *Apr-mid Oct, Nov,*
Dec 10am-10pm Mon-Sat. **Credit** V. **Map** p344 C4.
Turrón is Catalunya's traditional sweet treat eaten
at Christmas. It comes in two types: the nougat-
like *turrón de Alicante* and the grainy marzipan-ish
turrón de Jijona. You can try both, along with dusty
'*polvorones*' (marzipan-like sweets similar to *turrón*),
ice-cream and refreshing *horchata* (tiger nut milk)
here and at its nearby ice-cream parlour (Avda
Portal de l'Àngel 25).

Gifts & souvenirs

The city's museums have some good gift shops.
The Espai Gaudí at **La Pedrera** (*see p130*)
is the mother of all Gaudiana purveyors, while
the **MACBA** (*see p107*) and **CaixaForum**
(*see p117*) shops are excellent sources of games,
gifts, designer gizmos and kooky postcards.
The **Fundació Joan Miró** (*see p118*) has
plenty of boldly designed espresso cups,
coasters and so on, while the **Museu Tèxtil**
(*see p101*) has a good supply of creative
scarves, ties, shirts, bags and quirky jewellery.

Arlequí Mascares

C/Princesa 7, Born (93 268 27 52/www.
arlequimask.com). Metro Jaume I. **Open** 10.30am-
8.30pm Mon-Sat; 10.30am-4.30pm Sun. **Credit** MC,
V. **Map** p345 D5.
The walls here are dripping with masks, crafted
from papier mâché and leather. Whether gilt-laden
or in feathered commedia dell'arte style, simple
Greek tragicomedy styles or traditional Japanese
or Catalan varieties, they make striking fancy dress
or decorative staples. Other trinkets and toys include
finger puppets, mirrors and ornamental boxes.
Other locations Plaça Sant Josep Oriol 8, Barri
Gòtic (93 317 24 29); C/Caballeros 10, Poble Espanyol
(93 426 21 69).

Art Escudellers

C/Escudellers 23-25, Barri Gòtic (93 412 68 01/
www.escudellers-art.com). Metro Drassanes.
Open 11am-11pm daily. **Credit** AmEx, DC,
MC, V. **Map** p345 C6.
Art Escudellers sells an extravaganza of stunning
clay and glassware that's mostly handmade by
Spanish artists and labelled by region. Decorative
and practical items include sturdy kitchenware, traditional *azulejos* (tiles) and Gaudi-themed coffee cups.
Downstairs is a wine cellar and diminutive café,
while the nearby branch (at no.12) specialises in some
unusual glassware: a kitsch-fest of lurid Swarovski
crystal bonsais, to be precise. *Photos p210.*

Cereria Mas

C/Carme 3, Raval (93 317 04 38/www.cereriamas.
com). **Open** 10am-2pm, 4.30-8pm Mon-Thur; 10am-
2pm, 4.30-8.30pm Fri; 10.30am-2pm, 5-8.30pm Sat.
Closed last 2wks Aug. **Credit** MC, V. **Map** p344 B4.
The Mas candle-makers have been making award-
winning bundles of wax for more than a hundred
years. The shop specialises in extremely realistic
representations of fruit and other objects, as well
as the usual range of tapered dinner-table candles,
votive candles, scented floating candles and a variety of candles for every occasion, from birthdays
to Christmas to Hallowe'en.

Flora Albaicín

C/Canuda 3, Barri Gòtic (93 302 10 35). Metro
Catalunya. **Open** 10.30am-1pm, 5-8pm Mon-Sat.
Credit AmEx, MC, V. **Map** p344 B3.

If you're even mildly tempted by all of those frilly flamenco dresses hanging forlornly in the tourist traps lining La Rambla, make a beeline for this haven of ruffles and polka dots. The tiny boutique is bursting to the seams with brightly coloured flamenco frocks, shoes, head combs, bangles, shawls and everything else you'd need.

Herboristeria del Rei

C/Vidre 1, Barri Gòtic (93 318 05 12). Metro Liceu. **Open** 10am-2pm, 5-8pm Tue-Sat. Closed 1-2wks Aug. **Credit** MC, V. **Map** p345 B6.
Designed by a theatre set designer in the 1860s, this atmospheric shop's intricate wooden shelving hides myriad herbs and infusions, ointments and unguents for health and beauty. Its more up-to-date stock includes vegetarian foods, organic olive oils and organic mueslis.

El Rei de la Màgia

C/Princesa 11, Born (93 319 39 20/www.elreidela magia.com). Metro Jaume I. **Open** *Sept-July* 10am-2pm, 5-8pm Mon-Fri; 11am-2pm Sat. *Aug* 11am-2pm, 5-8pm Mon-Fri. **Credit** MC, V. **Map** p345 E5.
Although the 'King of Magic' is a serious set-up that prepares stage-ready illusions for pros, it also welcomes the amateur magician, curious fan and even prank-obsessed schoolboy, who may levitate with joy on seeing its sublime range of fake turds, itching powder and the like.

Greed is green

In Barcelona being resourceful is all the rage: it's perfectly normal to see grown men nip about town on little girls' bikes, and no accessory is really fashionable unless you found it in the bin. With numerous recycling points in the city and the common, if officially discouraged, practice of leaving unwanted household furniture on the street for passers-by, recycling is already ingrained into the local culture. Only now it's being turned into art.

The association Drap-Art centres on the shop/exhibition space **La Carboneria** (C/Groch 1, Barri Gòtic, 93 268 48 89). Run by Tanja Grass, it offers a kaleidoscope of curiosities for sale, fashioned of recycled materials. Bel y Bel (www.belybel.com) rescue rusting SEATs

and Vespas, resurrecting them as swivel chairs and retro lamps. Artisan fare includes Zenzele or Fantastik's intricate animal sculpture made of tins or twisted-wire. In the summertime, the space hosts a fashion show offering T-shirts or less wearable Tetra Brik bras and bottle dresses. Accessories abound: chunky jewellery incorporates seeds, beads, buttons or sweetie wrappers (Edith Lasierra). Similar items are sold in second-hand shops such as **Amateur** (C/Reira Baixa 16, Raval) or in spontaneous street markets organised by Pulgas Mix (www.pulgasmix.com).

Following the example of Swiss pioneers Freitag, Catalan designer Francesc Liebana was the first in Barcelona to attach seatbelts to truck tarpaulin to create colourful Kolombo bags (www.kolombo.com); find them in urban clothing stores like **Hackney** (Travessera de Gràcia 164, 93 217 84 75). Eco-design crew Demano (93 300 48 07, www.demano.net) work with obsolete PVC banners advertising cultural events, turning them into bags, hats and wellies, which can be bought to design on their website or in stores such as **Anna Povo** (Vidrieria 11, Barri Gòtic). Similarly, Girona-based duo **Vaho** (C/Cotoners 8, 93 268 05 30, www.vaho.ws) offer a cheerful Boldo bag range made of balcony covers.

For sophisticated, durable furniture, **Homâ** (C/Rec 20, Born, 93 315 27 55) is an atmospheric grotto selling sculpture, lamps, twisted bed-frames and ingenious useable bicycles made of recycled iron.

Local musical group Cabosanroque (www.cabosanroque.com; *pictured*), under the technical expertise of Roger Aixut, wrangle industrial materials, domestic appliances and discarded toys into extraordinary instruments. Check the website for upcoming concerts.

Sombreria Obach

C/Call 2, Barri Gòtic (93 318 40 94). Metro Jaume I or Liceu. **Open** *Oct-July* 9.30am-1.30pm, 4-8pm Mon-Fri; 10am-2pm, 4.30-8.30pm Sat. *Aug, Sept* 9.30am-1.30pm, 4-8pm Mon-Fri; 10am-2pm Sat. **Credit** MC, V. **Map** p345 C5.

Sombreria Obach's old-fashioned display windows are worth seeing for themselves: Kangol's mohair berets share space with fedoras, while stetsons nod to trilbies and matador's caps (like Mickey Mouse ears) face off with traditional red Catalan beanies.

Xilografies

C/Freneria 1, Barri Gòtic (93 315 07 58). Metro Jaume I. **Open** *Jan-July, Sept, Oct* 10am-2pm Mon-Sat. *Nov, Dec* 10am-2pm, 4.30-7.30pm Mon-Sat. Closed Aug. **No credit cards**. **Map** p345 D5.

Using painstakingly detailed 18th-century carved boxwood blocks that have been passed down in her family for generations (some of which you will see displayed in a glass cabinet in this tiny shop), Maria creates *ex libris* stickers for books, bookmarks, notepaper, address books and prints. She also sells prints of 18th-century maps, pens, birthday cards and reproduction pocket sundials.

Flowers

The 18 flower stalls dotting the Rambla de les Flors originated from the old custom of Boqueria market traders giving a free flower to their customers. There are also stands at the **Mercat de la Concepció** (C/Aragó 311, Eixample, 93 457 53 29, www.laconcepcio.com), on the corner of C/València and C/Bruc (map p341 H7), some of which are open all night. Many local florists offer the Interflora delivery service.

Flors Navarro

C/València 320, Eixample (93 457 40 99/www.flores navarro.com). Metro Verdaguer. **Open** 24hrs daily. **Credit** AmEx, MC, V. **Map** p340 H7.

At Flors Navarro, fresh-cut blooms, pretty house plants and stunning bouquets are available to buy 24 hours a day. A dozen red roses can be delivered anywhere in the city, day or night, for €30.

Health & beauty

Hairdressers

Llongueras

Passeig de Gràcia 78, Eixample (93 215 41 75/ www.llongueras.com). Metro Passeig de Gràcia. **Open** *Sept-July* 9am-7pm Mon-Sat. *Aug* 9am-6pm Mon-Fri; 9am-2pm Sat. **Credit** AmEx, DC, MC, V. **Map** p340 G7.

A safe bet for all ages, this pricey Catalan chain of hairdressers has well-trained stylists, who take the time to give a proper consultation, wash and massage. The cuts themselves are up to the minute but generally as natural as possible.
Other locations throughout the city.

Art Escudellers. *See p208.*

Eat, Drink, Shop

Rock & Roll

C/Palma de Sant Just 12, Barri Gòtic (93 268 74 75). Metro Jaume I. **Open** 10.30am-8pm Tue-Fri; 10am-4pm Sat. Closed 2wks Aug. **Credit** AmEx, MC, V. **Map** p345 C6.

Blinding white decor and bleeping electronica usually indicate tyrannical stylists, but the friendly and experienced Laura and Christian, don't insist on the latest fashion foibles: if you want a tiny trim, that's what you'll get. A basic cut and blow-dry is €35 for women and €23 for men.

La Tijereta

C/Vidrieria 13, Born (93 319 70 01). Metro Barceloneta or Jaume I. **Open** *Sept-July* 3-7pm Mon; 10am-7pm Tue-Fri; 9am-2pm Sat. *Aug* 10am-7pm Mon-Fri. **Credit** MC, V. **Map** p345 E7.

As long as you don't mind passers-by gawking at you through the goldfish-bowl windows, tiny La Tijereta is cheaper than the rest of the Born crop of hi-design hairdressers with no discernible drop in quality. A wash, cut and blow-dry is around €23 for women and €14 for men.

Opticians

Grand Optical

El Triangle, Plaça Catalunya 4, Eixample (93 304 16 40/www.grandoptical.com). Metro Catalunya. **Open** 10am-10pm Mon-Sat. **Credit** AmEx, DC, MC, V. **Map** p344 B2.

There are some English-speaking staff at this handy optical superstore in the centre of town. Efficient service means that you should be able to have your prescription sunglasses or standard specs ready in as little as an hour. Products have a year's guarantee, which is redeemable in any Grand Optical outlet worldwide.

Pharmacies

See p312.

Shops

The ground floor of **El Corte Inglés** (*see p193*) also has a good range of toiletries.

Regia

Passeig de Gràcia 39, Eixample (93 216 01 21/ www.regia.es). Metro Passeig de Gràcia. **Open** 10am-8.30pm Mon-Sat. **Credit** AmEx, DC, MC, V. **Map** p340 G8.

Regia was founded in 1928, and all half-dozen of its Barcelona branches have a good selection of upmarket perfumes and cosmetics on sale, as well as its own house line of skin and hair products. What makes this particular outlet special is the outstanding perfume museum (*see p129*) hidden at the back of the shop, past the offices.
Other locations Bulevard Rosa, Passeig de Gràcia 55, Eixample (93 215 73 48); C/Muntaner 242, Sant Gervasi (93 200 63 48); and throughout the city.

Sephora

El Triangle, C/Pelai 13-37, Eixample (93 306 39 00/ www.sephora.es). Metro Catalunya. **Open** 10am-10pm Mon-Sat. **Credit** AmEx, DC, MC, V. **Map** p344 B2.

Sephora is your best bet for unfettered playing around with scents and make-up. Make-up and toiletries include most of the usual mid- to high-end brands, plus there are handy beauty tools, such as eye-brow tweezers and pencil sharpeners.
Other locations La Maquinista, C/Potosi s/n, Sant Andreu (93 360 87 21); Diagonal Mar, Avda Diagonal 3, Poblenou (93 356 23 19).

Spas & salons

Instituto Francis

Ronda de Sant Pere 18, Eixample (93 317 78 08). Metro Catalunya. **Open** 9.30am-8pm Mon-Fri; 9am-4pm Sat. **Credit** DC, MC, V. **Map** p344 D2.

Europe's largest beauty centre has seven floors and more than 50 staff all dedicated to making you beautiful – inside and out. As well as offering all the usual facials, massages, anti-cellulite treatments and manicures, the institute specialises in depilation, homeopathic therapies and non-surgical procedures such as teeth whitening and micropigmentation.

Masajes a 1000

C/Mallorca 233, Eixample (93 215 85 85/ www.masajesa1000.com). Metro Diagonal/ FGC Provença. **Open** 8am-midnight daily. **Credit** MC, V. **Map** p340 F7.

An efficient and economic beauty centre in the Eixample, operating via a voucher system. You can try a half-hour massage and siesta in an ergonomic chair, or a luxurious 90-minute 'four-hand' massage. There are also pedicures, manicures, hair and skin care and tanning, with no need to book ahead.
Other locations Travessera de les Corts 178, Les Corts (93 490 92 90); C/Numancia 76, Les Corts (93 410 87 82).

House & home

Antiques

A long-standing antiques market is held outside the cathedral every Thursday (*see p196*), and dealers set up stands at **Port Vell** at weekends. **C/Palla** is the main focus for antiques in the Barri Gòtic; however, they're of variable quality. Dazzlingly expensive antiques can be found on **C/Consell de Cent** in the Eixample, and the more affordable around **C/Dos de Maig**, near Els Encants flea market (*see p213*).

Antiques Market

Plaça Nova, Barri Gòtic (93 302 70 45). Metro Jaume I. **Open** 10am-9pm Thur. Closed Aug. **No credit cards.** **Map** p344 C4.

With its location in front of the cathedral, this market charges prices that are targeted at tourists, so be prepared to haggle. The market dates from the

Middle Ages, but antiques generally consist of small items such as sepia postcards, *manila* shawls, pocket watches, typewriters, lace, cameras and jewellery among bibelots and bric-a-brac. In the first week of August and for all of December, the market is held at Avda Portal de l'Àngel.

L'Arca de l'Àvia

C/Banys Nous 20, Barri Gòtic (93 302 15 98/ www.larcadelavia.com). Metro Liceu. **Open** 10am-2pm, 5-8pm Mon-Fri; 11am-2pm Sat. **Credit** AmEx, DC, MC, V. **Map** p345 C5.

The 'Grandmother's Ark' is a treasure trove of delicate lacy things from the era when a lady wouldn't think of leaving the house without a collection of fine-edged hankies to drop in a suitor's path. The silk *camisetas de suerte* make a fine gift for any newborn, or treat yourself to a fringed shawl, exquisite fan or some flouncy white underthings.

Bulevard dels Antiquaris

Passeig de Gràcia 55, Eixample (93 215 44 99/ www.bulevarddelsantiquaris.com). Metro Passeig de Gràcia. **Open** Oct-June 10.30am-1.30pm, 4.30-8.30pm Mon-Sat. *July-Sept* 10am-1.30pm, 4.30-8.30pm Mon-Fri. **Credit** AmEx, MC, V. **Map** p340 G7.

One of the most convenient and safest places to shop for antiques in Barcelona (experts inspect every object for authenticity). Miró and Tapies fans can buy limited-edition prints of works by these local artists at March (no.42). Check out the style of ethnic art that influenced the likes of Miró at Raquel Montagut (no.11), where you can pick up a Nigerian funeral urn if that's just what your hallway is missing. Collectors will love the antique playthings at Tric Trac (no.43) and Govary's (no.54).

Els Encants

C/Dos de Maig 177-187, Plaça de la Glòries, Eixample (93 246 30 30). Metro Glòries. **Open** 9am-6pm Mon, Wed, Fri, Sat. *Auctions* 7.30-9am Mon, Wed, Fri. **No credit cards. Map** p343 L8.

It's increasingly hard to find a bargain at Barcelona's old fleamarket. Still, it's a diverting way to pass the time strolling around this suntrap: the buyers and sellers are as varied and curious as the bric-a-brac, big pants, Barça memorabilia, cheap electrical gadgets, religious relics and ancient Spanish school books that make up the majority of the stalls' booty. If you want to buy furniture at a decent price come to the auctions at 7am with the commercial buyers or at noon, when unsold stuff drops in price. Don't forget to check out the cavernous warehouses on the market's outskirts, where you may find a bargain – even if you have to dig your way through a pile of junk to find it. Avoid Saturdays, when prices shoot up (except in the early morning) and the crowds move in, and be on your guard for pickpockets and short-changing.

Novecento

Passeig de Gracia 75, Eixample (93 215 1183). Metro Passeig de Gràcia. **Open** 10am-2pm, 4-8.30pm Mon-Fri; 10am-2pm, 5-8pm Sat. Closed 3wks Aug. **Credit** AmEx, V. **Map** p340 G7.

Antiques Market. *See p211.*

If you had a very rich great-grandma, this might be what her jewellery box would look like: tumbling strings of raw amber, fiery precious stones set into crosses, delicate cameos on gossamer ribbons. It's not all diamond chokers, however. Some pretty costume pieces can be picked up for a pittance.

General

Gotham

C/Cervantes 7, Barri Gòtic (93 412 46 47/www. gotham-bcn.com). Metro Jaume I. **Open** Sept-June 11am-2pm, 5-8pm Mon-Fri; 11am-2pm Sat. *July, Aug* 11am-2pm, 5-8pm Mon-Fri. Closed 2wks end Aug. **Credit** V. **Map** p345 C6.

Fab 1950s ashtrays in avocado green, bubble TV sets, teak sideboards, coat stands that look like molecular models… Take a trip down nostalgia lane with Gotham's classic retro furniture. Be warned, however, that the prices will have you wishing you'd never given that lampshade to the local jumble sale.

Recdi8

C/Espaseria 7, Born (93 268 02 57/www.recdi8.com). Metro Jaume I. **Open** 11.30am-2.30pm, 5-8.30pm Mon-Thur; 11.30-2pm, 5-9pm Fri, Sat. Closed 2wks Aug. **Credit** AmEx, DC, MC, V. **Map** p345 E7.

At first glance this may seem like yet another shop selling student knick-knacks – plastic flower garlands, jokey welcome mats and the like. But, while Recdi8 does score high on the quirkometer, it also has a fairly healthy showing in taste tests. All the products are made by top design houses using quality materials and have some serious design thought behind them – even the cutesy cuckoo clocks.

Vinçon

Passeig de Gràcia 96, Eixample (93 215 60 50/www. vincon.com). Metro Diagonal. **Open** 10am-8.30pm Mon-Sat. **Credit** AmEx, DC, MC, V. **Map** p340 D4.

Eat, Drink, Shop

This is one of the vital organs that keeps Barcelona's reputation as a city of cutting-edge design alive. The building itself is a monument to the history of local design: the upstairs furniture showroom is surrounded by Modernista glory (and you get a peak at Gaudí's La Pedrera); downstairs in the kitchen, bathroom, garden and other departments, everything is black, minimalist and hip. Although not cheap, almost everything you buy here is, or will be, a design classic, whether it's a Bonet armchair or the so-called 'perfect' corkscrew.

Other locations TinçÇon, C/Rosselló 246, Eixample (93 215 60 50).

Music & entertainment

C/Tallers, C/Bonsuccès and C/Riera Baixa in the Raval are dotted with music shops catering to all tastes and formats, with plenty of sheet music and instruments. Mainstream music selections are found in the huge Avda Portal de l'Àngel branch of **El Corte Inglés** (*see p193*) and, more cheaply, at **FNAC** (*see p193*), which also has world music and acres of classical.

Casa Beethoven
La Rambla 97, Raval (93 301 48 26/www.casa beethoven.com). Metro Liceu. **Open** 9am-2pm, 4-8pm Mon-Fri; 9am-1.30pm, 5-8pm Sat. Closed 3wks Aug. **Credit** MC, V. **Map** p344 B4.
The sheet music and songbooks on sale in this old shop cover the gamut from Wagner to the White Stripes, with a concentration on opera. Books cover music history and theory, while CDs are particularly strong on both modern and classical Spanish music.

CD Drome
C/Valldonzella 3, Raval (93 317 46 46/www. cddrome.com). Metro Catalunya or Universitat. **Open** Sept-July 10.30am-8.30pm Mon-Fri; 10.30am-2pm, 4.30-8.30pm Sat. Aug 10.30am-8.30pm Mon-Fri. **Credit** DC, MC, V. **Map** p344 A2.
Budding DJs come to CD Drome just to absorb the hipness in the air. Genres are precisely delineated into groups such as minimal beats and hands-up vinyl. Once you've decided what your particular flavour is, you can listen to your selections on the professional-looking decks. It's also good for picking up flyers, listings magazines and for buying tickets.

Discos Castelló
C/Tallers 3, 7, 9 & 79, Raval (93 302 59 46/ www.discoscastello.es). Metro Catalunya. **Open** 10am-8.30pm Mon-Sat. **Credit** AmEx, DC, MC, V. **Map** p344 B2.
Discos Castelló is a homegrown cluster of small shops, each with a different speciality in music: no.3 is devoted to classical; the largest, no.7, covers pretty much everything; no.9 does hip hop, rock and alternative pop plus T-shirts and accessories; and no.79 is best for jazz and '70s pop. The branch at no.79 is good for ethnic music and electronica.
Other locations throughout the city.

Gong
C/Consell de Cent 343, Eixample (93 215 34 31/ www.gongdiscos.com). Metro Passeig de Gràcia. **Open** 10am-9pm Mon-Sat. **Credit** AmEx, MC, V. **Map** p340 G8.
An unglamorous but serious record shop chain with a wide range of stock. The poor can flick through the always extensive bargain rack. Gong is a good source of concert tickets and information.
Other locations Barcelona Glòries, Avda Diagonal 208, Eixample (93 486 00 28).

New Phono
C/Ample 35-37, Barri Gòtic (93 315 13 61/ www.newphono.com). Metro Jaume I. **Open** 10am-2pm, 4.30-8pm Mon-Fri; 10am-2pm Sat. Closed 2wks Aug. **Credit** AmEx, DC, MC, V. **Map** p345 C7.
Budding Segovias will splurge on a fine Ramirez classical guitar; others will just want a dirt-cheap Admira to strum on the beach. New Phono's cluster of display rooms holds a range of wind, string and percussion instruments and accessories, while keyboards and recording equipment reside over the road (nos.39-40). Check the noticeboard for musical contacts.

Sports & fitness

The tourist shops on La Rambla stock a huge range of football strips.

La Botiga del Barça
Maremàgnum, Moll d'Espanya, Port Vell (93 225 80 45). Metro Drassanes. **Open** 10am-10pm daily. **Credit** AmEx, DC, MC, V. **Map** p342 F12/13.
Everything for the well-dressed Barça fan, from the standard blue and burgundy strips to scarves, hats, crested ties, aftershave and even underpants, plus calendars, shirts printed with your name, shield-embossed ashtrays, beach towels and so on.

Vinçon. *See p213.*

Other locations C/Jaume I, Barri Gotic (93 269 15 32); Museu del FC Barcelona, Nou Camp (93 409 02 71); Ronda Universitat 24, Barri Gòtic (93 318 64 77).

Decathlon

C/Canuda 20, Barri Gòtic (93 342 61 61/www. decathlon.es). Metro Catalunya. **Open** 9.30am-9.30pm Mon-Sat. **Credit** AmEx, DC, MC, V. **Map** p344 C3.

This multi-storey French chain is a handy sports-gear department store. Services include bike repair and hire, and team kit stamping.

Other locations L'Illa, Avda Diagonal 545-557, Eixample (93 444 01 65); Gran Via 2, Gran Via de les Corts Catalanes 75-97, Hospitalet de Llobregat (93 259 15 92).

Tickets

FNAC (*see p193*) has a very efficient ticket desk situated on its ground floor: it sells tickets to theme parks and sights, but it's especially good for contemporary music concerts and events. Concert tickets for smaller venues are often sold in record shops and at the venues themselves; check street posters for further details. For Barça tickets, *see p270 and below.*

Servi-Caixa – La Caixa

902 332 211/www.servicaixa.com. **Credit** AmEx, DC, MC, V.

Use the special Servi-Caixa ATMs (you'll find them in most larger branches of La Caixa), dial 902 332 211 or check the website above to purchase tickets for cinemas, concerts, plays, museums, amusement parks and Barça games. You'll need to show the card with which you made the payment when you collect the tickets; but be sure to check the pick-up deadline so that you don't risk being too late.

Tel-entrada – Caixa Catalunya

902 101 212/www.telentrada.com. **Credit** MC, V.

Through the Tel-entrada agency you can purchase tickets for theatre performances, cinemas (including shows at the IMAX), concerts, museums and sights over the phone, online from the website above, or even over the counter at any branch of the Caixa Catalunya savings bank. Tickets can be collected from either Caixa Catalunya ATMs or the tourist office at Plaça Catalunya (*see p323*).

Travellers' needs

FNAC (*see p193*) and El Corte Inglés (*see p193*) also have travel agencies. Alternatively, one very worthwhile Spanish travel website can be found at www.rumbo.es.

Halcón Viajes

C/Aribau 34, Eixample (93 454 59 95/902 300 600/www.halconviajes.com). Metro Universitat. **Open** 9.30am-1.30pm, 4.30-8pm Mon-Fri; 10am-1pm Sat. **Credit** AmEx, DC, MC, V. **Map** p340 F8.

This mammoth chain has exclusive deals with Air Europa and Globalia, among others, and can offer highly competitive rates in most areas. Service tends to be quite brisk but efficient.

Other locations throughout the city.

Viajes Zeppelin

C/Villarroel 49, Eixample (93 412 00 13/www. viajeszeppelin.com). Metro Urgell. **Open** 9am-8pm Mon-Fri; 10am-1pm Sat. **Credit** AmEx, DC, MC, V. **Map** p342 E9.

The friendly staff at this agency speak some English and it offers all the usual travel services. Viajes also provides international student identity cards (ISIC) and youth discount cards for those aged under 25. Check online for special offers.

Eat, Drink, Shop

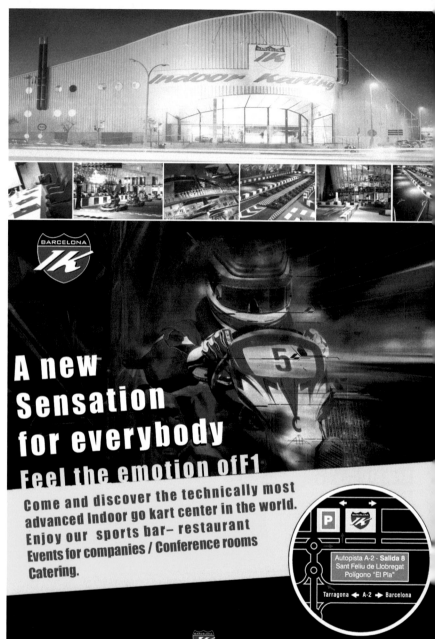

Arts & Entertainment

Fundació Joan Miró. *See p120.*

Festivals & Events

Barcelona's abuzz.

Does Barcelona need any more festivals? All right, the city has to do something with the hordes of young cyber sculptors, DJs and graffiti artists that come here, but it's a moot question whether there's any need for yet another multimedia arts/music festival.

But it's not all spray cans and knob-twiddling: Barcelona's great strength has always been its traditional street festivals. The most fertile time of year is undoubtedly September, when the **Festes de la Mercè**, Barcelona's main city celebrations, inspire entertainment ranging from wine-tasting fairs to street art competitions and free music concerts. The Mercè and the other 30 or so neighbourhood festes share many traditional ingredients; among them are the *correfoc* and the *sardana*, dwarves, *castellers* (human castles) and *gegants* (five-metre/16-foot-high papier-mâché/fibreglass giants dressed as princesses, fishermen, swarthy sultans and even topless chorus girls; *photo p224*). The *correfoc* ('fire run') is a frenzy of pyromania, when groups of horned devils dance through the streets, brandishing tridents that spout fireworks, and generally flouting just about every safety rule in the book. The more daring onlookers, protected by cotton caps and long sleeves, try to stop the devils and touch the fire-breathing dragons being dragged along in their wake.

The orderly antidote to this pandemonium is the *sardana*, Catalonia's folk dance. Watching the dancers executing their fussy little hops and steps in a large circle, it's hard to believe that *sardanes* were once banned as a vestige of pagan witchcraft. The music is similarly restrained, a reedy noise played by an 11-piece *cobla* band. The *sardana* is much harder than it looks, and the joy lies in taking part rather than watching. To try your luck, check out the *sardanes populars* held in front of the cathedral (noon-2pm Sun, 6.30-8.30pm Sat from March to November) or www.fed.sardanista.com for monthly programmes around the city.

INFORMATION

Organisers are prone to change dates. For more information, try tourist offices, the city's information line on 010, or the cultural agenda section at www.bcn.es. Newspapers also carry details, especially in their Friday or Saturday supplements. Events listed below that include public holidays (when many shops will be closed for the day) are marked *.

Spring

Festes de Sant Medir de Gràcia

Information www.santmedir.org. Gràcia to Sant Cugat & back, usually via Plaça Lesseps, Avda República Argentina & Ctra de l'Arrabassada. Starting point Metro Fontana. **Date** 3 Mar. **Map** p340 G4/5 & p341 H4/5.
Since 1830, decorated horses and carts have gathered bright and early around the Plaça Trilla to ride up to the hermitage of Sant Medir in the Collserola hills. Mass is celebrated, *sardanes* are danced and barbecued *botifarres* are eaten with beans. At mid-morning and again in the evening, neighbourhood societies drive horse-drawn carts around the main streets of Gràcia and shower the crowd with more than 100 tons of blessed boiled sweets.

Nous Sons – Músiques Contemporànies

L'Auditori (see p262) & CCCB (see p107). Metro Catalunya or Marina. **Date** Mar-Apr. **Map** p343 K9 & p344 A4.
See p265 Performing Arts.

Festival Guitarra

Various venues (93 481 70 40/www.theproject.es). **Date** Mar-June.
This prestigious guitar festival is a classic on the Barcelona music scene and has the ability to attract world-class players, from Jackson Browne to John Williams. Styles span everything from flamenco to Latin sounds, classical guitar and gypsy jazz.

Setmana Santa* (Holy Week)

Date 17-23 Mar 2008.
The main Easter event in Barcelona is the blessing of the palms on *diumenge de rams* (Palm Sunday). Crowds surge into the cathedral clutching bleached palm fronds bought from the stalls along Rambla de Catalunya and outside the Sagrada Família. On Good Friday, a series of small processions and blessings takes place in front of the cathedral; a procession sets out from the church of Sant Agustí on C/Hospital at around 5pm and arrives at the cathedral a couple of hours later. On Easter Sunday, godparents dole out the *mones*: originally, marzipan cakes decorated with boiled eggs, but these days more likely to be a chocolate cartoon character.

Sant Jordi

La Rambla & all over Barcelona. **Date** 23 Apr.
On the feast day of Sant Jordi (St George), the patron saint of Catalonia, nearly every building bears the red and gold Catalan flag, while bakeries sell Sant

Jordi bread streaked with red *sobrassada* pâté. Red roses decorate the Palau de la Generalitat and the city's many statues and paintings of George in all his dragon-slaying glory. It's said that as the drops of the dragon's blood fell, they turned into red flowers; for more than five centuries, this has been the Catalan version of St Valentine's Day.

Men traditionally give women a rose tied to an ear of wheat, and women reciprocate with a book, many now give both. This is also the 'Day of the Book', *see p20* **Saint alive**. The day accounts for an amazing ten per cent of Catalonia's annual book sales; street stalls and bookshops give good discounts.

Festival de Música Antiga

L'Auditori (see p262). **Concerts** €5-€20. **Date** 30 Apr-21 May. **Map** p343 K9.
Go for Baroque at the Festival of Early Music, which features performers from around the world. The accompanying El Fringe festival is held over three days around the Barri Gòtic and offers young performers an opportunity to perform alongside more established musicians.

Feria de Abril de Catalunya

Fòrum area (information Federación de Entidades Culturales Andaluces en Cataluña www.fecac.com). Metro El Maresme-Fòrum. **Date** end Apr/May.
The move to its new site at the seaside Fòrum area means a greatly improved venue for this enormous and joyously tacky event, but a sad goodbye to the entrances on horseback. The city's Andalucian population parties furiously and, unlike elitist Seville's equivalent, the Barcelona version is a free-for-all, with more than 60 open *casetas* (decorated marquees) offering manzanilla sherry, free flamenco shows, throbbing speakers and heaving dancefloors.

Dia del Treball* (May Day)

Various venues. **Date** 1 May.
A day of demonstrations led by trade unionists representing various left-wing organisations. The main routes cover Plaça da la Universitat, Via Laietana, Passeig de Gràcia, Passeig Sant Joan and Plaça Sant Jaume, as well as the Sants neighbourhood.

Barcelona Poesia & Festival Internacional de Poesia

All over Barcelona (information Institut de Cultura 93 316 10 00/www.bcn.es/barcelonapoesia). **Date** early May.
This poetry festival started in 1393 as the courtly Jocs Florals (Floral Games), which were named after the prizes: a silver violet for third prize; a golden rose as second; and, naturally, a real flower for the winner. The games died out in the 15th century but were resuscitated in 1859 as a vehicle for the promotion of the Catalan language. Prizes went to the most suitably florid paeans to the motherland; these days, however, Spanish is also permitted, as are Basque and Galician; many foreign languages can be heard at the International Poetry Festival.

The best in flamenco, and more, at the **Festival de Flamenco.** *See p220.*

Arts & Entertainment

Sant Ponç

C/Hospital. Metro Liceu. **Date** 11 May.
Map p344 A4.
In honour of the patron saint of beekeepers and herbalists, C/Hospital becomes a charming outdoor market for the day, full of fresh herbs, natural infusions, home-produced honey and candied fruit, most of it straight off the farmer's cart.

Festa Major de Nou Barris

All over Nou Barris (www.bcn.es). Metro Poblenou.
Date mid May.
Nou Barris has a very lively *festa major*, which is particularly strong on music, attracting top-notch local acts such as Ojos de Brujo. The music also incorporates the Nou Barris flamenco festival, with stars such as Farruquito or Chocolate attracting huge crowds. But the event is not solely limited to music: other festivities include a medieval market and all the usual ingredients of street theatre, fireworks, parades and *castellers*.

Festival de Flamenco

*Information (93 443 43 46/www.tallerdemusics.com).
Metro Catalunya.* **Date** May. **Map** p344 A2.
Although there are plenty of traditional performers for the fan of flamenco, hard-line flamenco purists should be warned that this festival also includes DJs fusing the Andalucian music with anything from electronica to jazz and rock. *Photos p219.*

B-estival. *See p222.*

Dia Internacional dels Museus

All over Barcelona. **Date** 18 May.
Free entrance to all city-owned museums.

L'Ou Com Balla

*Ateneu Barcelonès, C/Canuda 6; Casa de l'Ardiaca,
C/Santa Llúcia 1; Cathedral cloisters; Museu Frederic
Marès; all in Barri Gòtic (information Institut de
Cultura 93 301 77 75/www.bcn.es/icub).*
Date 23-25 May 2008.
L'Ou Com Balla (the 'dancing egg') is a local Corpus
Christi tradition dating from 1637: a hollowed-out
eggshell is set in spinning and bobbing apparent
perpetuum mobile on the spout of a fountain that is
garlanded for the occasion with flowers and cherry
blossom. The Sunday Corpus Christi procession
itself leaves from the cathedral in the early evening,
while on the Saturday there's free entrance to the
Ajuntament, the Palau Centelles behind it and the
Museu d'Història de la Ciutat, along with *sardanes*
at 7pm outside the cathedral.

Primavera Sound

Fòrum (information www.primaverasound.com).
Tickets *3 days* €85. **Date** 29-31 May.
Fast stealing Sónar's thunder, this three-day, six-
stage music festival is one of the best in Spain. Credit
for its success is due to its range of genres. There
are rafts of electronica acts, DJs and local bands, plus
a record fair and the Soundtrack Film Festival.

Summer

Festa dels Cors de la Barceloneta

Barceloneta. **Date** early June. **Map** p343 H12/13.
In a tradition dating back 150 years, some 24 choirs
of workers and regulars from Barceloneta's restaurants and bars sing traditional *caramelles* and march
in carnival parades around the district. The singers
wear costumes garlanded with objects that are typical of their profession – nets and oars for a fisherman, cereal boxes and sausage for a grocer – and
carry long, decorated hatchets, oars or pitchforks
bearing their choir's symbol. The more sober parade
is on Saturday morning; at midday, the choirs take
off for an overnight jolly on the coast, returning
rather the worse for wear on Monday afternoon for
song, dance, drink and fireworks.

Sónar

Information www.sonar.es. **Tickets** approx
€28-€140. **Date** mid June.
The three-day International Festival of Advanced
Music and Multimedia Art (or Sónar it is more snappily known) is still a must for anyone into electronic music, contemporary urban art and media
technologies. The event is divided into two parts:
SónarDay comprises multimedia art, record fairs,
conferences, exhibitions and sound labs around the
CCCB, while DJs play. Later, SónarNight means a
scramble for the desperately overcrowded shuttle
bus from the bottom of La Rambla out to the vast
hangars of the site in Hospitalet (tip: share a cab

between four – it'll cost you the same – and get there
by midnight to avoid the queues), where concerts
and DJs are spread out over SónarClub, SónarPark
and SónarPub. Advance tickets are available online
or from the Palau de la Virreina.

Sant Joan*

All over Barcelona. **Date** night of 23 June.
The beach is the place to be for an orgy of all-night
pyromania on the eve of Sant Joan (St John the
Baptist). Being summer solstice, it's traditional to
stay up till dawn, munching *coca de Sant Joan* – flat,
crispy bread topped with candied fruit – and drinking endless bottles of cava while partying by the
light of huge bonfires. The biggest fireworks displays are at Montjuïc, Tibidabo and L'Estació del
Nord. Don't miss Barceloneta's Nit del Foc (Night of
Fire), where devils incite the crowds to dance around
the bonfires before everyone drunkenly heads down
to the beach to watch the sunrise. Special metro and
FGC trains run all night.

Festa de la Música

*All over Barcelona (information Institut de
Cultura 93 316 10 00/www.bcn.es/icub or
www.festadelamusica.info).* **Date** late June.
Started in France in 1982 and now celebrated in
more than 100 countries, the three-day Festival of
Music sees amateur musicians from 100 countries
take to the streets. All events are free, and you're as
likely to see a child slapping a bongo as a first-rate
blues band, symphonic orchestra or choir.

Gran Trobada d'Havaneres

*Passeig Joan de Borbó, Barceloneta (information
Institut de Cultura 93 316 10 00/www.bcn.es/icub).*
Date last Sat in June. **Map** p345 E7/8.
The barnacled legacy of Catalonia's old trade links
with Cuba, *havaneres* are melancholy 19th-century
sea shanties accompanied by accordions and guitars. The main event is at the port town of Calella de
Palafrugells, but the Barcelona satellite is no less
fun. Performances by groups dressed in stripy
shirts, with salty sea-dog names such as Peix Fregit
(fried fish) and Xarxa (fishing net), are followed by
cremat (flaming spiced rum) and fireworks.

Dies de Dansa

*Information Associació Marató de l'Espectacle
(93 268 18 68/www.marato.com).* **Date** June/July.
This three-day Festival of Dance is free, with shows
on the terraces of the CCCB (*see p107*), MACBA (*see
p107*), CaixaForum (*see p119*) and Fundació Miró
(*see p121*), including popular events such as the
Spanish-Portuguese breakdancing championships.

Festival del Grec

*Information Institut de Cultura (93 316 10 00/
www.bcn.es/grec).* **Date** June-Aug.
An integral part of summer in the city, El Grec
began in 1976 as a series of plays in the eponymous
Greek-style amphitheatre on Montjuïc and three
decades on has grown into a two-month spree of
dance, music and theatre all over the city.

De Cajón!

Various venues (www.theproject.es). **Date** June-July.
This high-quality new mini festival has snagged
some of Barcelona's top venues to showcase spectacular flamenco talents such as *cantaor* Antonio
Vargas 'Potito', flamenco pianist Diego Amador and
the world-famous guitarist Paco de Lucía.

Clàssics als Parcs

*Information Parcs i Jardins (93 413 24 00/
www.bcn.es/parcsijardins).* **Date** July.
What nicer way can there be to spend a balmy summer evening than listening to classical music in one
of Barcelona's most beautiful parks? Throughout
July, young musicians perform a varied concert programme, alfresco and for free. On Thursdays, concerts are held at the secluded Jardins de la Tamarita
and the pretty Turó Park, on Fridays at the futuristic Diagonal Mar and the Jardins de Ca n'Altimira,
and on Saturdays at the Parc de la Ciutadella.

B-estival

*Poble Espanyol, Avda Marquès de Comillas s/n
(www.b-estival.com). Metro Espanya.* **Date** July.
Defining itself as Barcelona's 'festival of rhythms',
B-estival was born in 2006, and the impressive programming covers blues, soul, R&B, Brazilian music
with flamenco and rai to fill in the gaps. *Photo p220.*

Summercase

*Parc del Fòrum (www.summercase.com). Metro El
Maresme-Fòrum.* **Date** two days mid July.
Summercase, a two-day festival, is the sunny partner to Wintercase (*see p224*), with a healthy line-up
of indie rock and some big-name dance acts.

Mas i Mas Festival

*Information (93 319 17 89/www.masimas.com).
Various venues.* **Date** late July-early Sept.
This impeccably tasteful music festival stretches
over the summer months and has gone from concentrating on Latin sounds to providing a little bit of
everything. Concerts take place at various venues,
including the Palau de la Música (*see p263*).

Festa de Sant Roc

*Information (010/www.bcn.es). Various venues
around Plaça Nova, Barri Gòtic. Metro Jaume I.*
Date 12-16 Aug. **Map** p344 C4.
The Festa de Sant Roc, celebrated every year since
1589, is the Barri Gòtic's street party. It's hard to
beat for lovers of Catalan traditions: there are
parades with the giants and fat heads, *sardana* dancing and 19th-century street games. The festivities,
which centre around the Plaça Nova in front of the
cathedral, conclude with a *correfoc* and fireworks.

Festa Major de Gràcia

*All over Gràcia (information 93 459 30 80/
www.festamajordegracia.org). Metro Fontana.*
Date 3rd wk in Aug. **Map** p340 G4/5 & p341 H4/5.
Gràcia's extravagant *festa major* is most distinctive
for its street competition, where residents transform

some 25 streets into pirate ships, rainforests and even
a giant strawberry gateau. The festival opens with
giants and castles in Plaça Rius i Taulet, and climax-
es with a *correfoc* and a *castell de focs* (castle of fireworks). In between, 600 activities, from concerts to
sardanes and kids' bouncy castles, are centred
around Plaça Rius i Taulet, Plaça de la Revolució,
Plaça del Sol and Plaça de la Virreina.

Festa Major de Sants

*All over Sants (information Federació Festa Major
de Sants 93 490 62 14/www.festamajordesants.org).
Metro Plaça de Sants or Sants Estació.*
Date last wk in Aug.
One of the lesser-known *festes majors*, Sants has a
traditional flavour, with floral offerings to images
of St Bartholomew at the local church and the mar-
ket. Major events, such as the *correfoc* on the night
of the 24th, are held in the Parc de l'Espanya
Industrial; others are held at Plaça del Centre,
C/SantAntoni, Plaça de la Farga and Plaça Joan
Peiro, behind Sants station.

Autumn

Diada Nacional de Catalunya*

All over Barcelona. **Date** 11 Sept.
Catalan National Day commemorates Barcelona's
capitulation to the Bourbon army in the 1714 War
of the Spanish Succession, a bitter defeat that led to
the repression of many Catalan institutions. It's lost
some of its vigour but is still a day for national
re-affirmation, with the Catalan flag flying on buses
and balconies. There are several marches throughout the city, the centre being the statue of Rafael
Casanova (who directed the resistance) on the Ronda
Sant Pere. Many make a pilgrimage to the
monastery at Montserrat, the spiritual heart of the
region and an important guardian of Catalan language and culture during the dictatorship.

Festes de la Mercè*

*All over Barcelona (information tourist offices or
www.bcn.es).* **Date** Sept.
What was once a small religious parade in honour of
the patron saint of the city, Our Lady of Mercy, has
gradually swollen to a week-long party with all
things bright and Catalan hitched to its wagon. The
event opens with *castellers* in the Plaça de la Mercè
followed by more than 400 events including *gegants*,
capgrosses (little scampering dwarves with large
fibreglass heads), *sardanes* and the biggest and bold-
est *correfoc* of them all on the Saturday night. The
highlights of this immense event include dazzling
fireworks displays along the city beaches, a seafront
air show and the solidarity festival, now returned to
its original location on the Passeig de Gràcia. Free
concerts fill the squares, while sporting events
include a swim across the port and a regatta. Add to
that exhibitions, children's activities, street entertainers and free entrance to many museums on 24
September, and it's a full week. *See p223* **Saint alive.**

Saint alive Our Lady of Mercè

You'd have thought that being mother to God would take up all of your time, but you'd be wrong. In fact, as with her Son, not even death has been able to put a stop to the activities of the young woman from Nazareth, and on 1 August 1218 Mary appeared in a vision to a young Frenchman named Peter Nolasco, instructing him on how to continue his work of freeing captives. During the seven-and-a-half centuries of conflict between Christian and Muslim Spain, a common feature was the taking of captives for ransom. Now this was all very well if you were a member of the nobility and had someone to pay for your release, but many people from poor families were also captured in the general trawling for profit and plunder that took place during a *gaza* (a religiously sanctioned raid). To be captured during a *gaza* was by definition to become a slave, a state which could be escaped only by conversion to Islam (which many prisoners did) or paying a lot of money. It was this work of buying the poor out of slavery that Peter Nolasco embarked upon, helped by his mercantile background. In fact, Nolasco switched from buying goods to buying people, but all his efforts seemed only to swell the number of captives.

It was at this point that Mary advised him to form an order dedicated to the redemption of captives. The next day, Nolasco sought an audience with the king, Jaume I, who agreed to help in the foundation of the Order of the Virgin Mary of Mercy of the Redemption of Captives (or Mercedarians as they are called). The order set up a fund to buy back captives but, if all else failed, each member took vows to hand himself over in place of a prisoner. The order brought 11,615 slaves out of captivity between 1218 and 1301.

As if that wasn't enough, Our Lady of Mercy delivered the city of Barcelona from a plague of locusts in 1637. A grateful city adopted her as patron and celebrated her feast on 24 September, or at least it did until Franco clamped down on all things Catalan. But sometimes things suppressed simply wait for an opportunity to burst forth, and that's precisely what happened with the Festes de la Mercè. What had been a simple religious feast turned into today's week-long celebration of Catalan identity, yet it all remains inextricably bound up with a long-dead Jewish girl. But then, what else would one expect of her?

Barcelona Acció Musical (BAM)

Various venues (information 93 427 42 49/ www.bam.es). **Date** during the Festes de la Mercè, Sept.

BAM stages free concerts, mostly of jazz and singer-songwriters, on Plaça del Rei, while more famous names perform outside the cathedral, with dance oriented acts at the Fòrum and rumba at Portal de la Pau, near the Maritime Museum. The prime mover of what has become known as So Barcelona (Barcelona Sound), BAM largely promotes left-field *mestissa* (vaguely, ethnic fusion) in its mission to provide 'music without frontiers'.

Mostra de Vins i Caves de Catalunya

Moll d'Espanya, Port Vell (93 552 48 00). Metro Drassanes. **Date** during Festes de la Mercè, Sept. **Map** p342 F12.

This outdoor wine and cava fair has been running since 1980 and now showcases more than 400 labels from around 50 Catalan *bodegas*. Big names include Torres, Freixenet, Codorníu, Pinord and Mont Marçal; also on show are fine cheeses and charcuterie. Ten wine or cava tastings with a free glass cost €6; four food tastings cost €5.

Festa Major de la Barceloneta

All over Barceloneta (information 93 221 72 44/www.cascantic.net). Metro Barceloneta. **Date** last wk Sept. **Map** p343 H12/13.

This tight-knit maritime community throws itself into the local *festes* with incredible gusto. The fun kicks off with fireworks on the beach, a 24-hour football tournament, *falcons* (acrobatic groups), *sardana* dancing and a free tasting of traditional crispy coca bread washed down with muscatel, and ends with more of the same ten days later. In between, expect parades, music, fire-breathing dragons, open-air cinema and bouncy castles. Look out, too, for a character called General Bum Bum, who parades with a wooden cannon but stops periodically to fire sweets into crowds of scrabbling children.

Festival de Músiques del Món
L'Auditori (see p262). Metro Marina. **Tickets** €10; €8 reductions. **Date** Oct. **Map** p343 K9.
A World Music Festival featuring around 20 concerts, along with related exhibitions, films and workshops. Concerts might include anything from Mongolian throat-singing to Turkish whirling dervishes alongside home-grown talent such as flamenco singer Miguel Poveda, a regular at this event.

Festival de Tardor Ribermúsica
Various venues, Born (information www.ribermusica.org). Metro Barceloneta or Jaume I. **Date** 17-21 Oct. **Map** p345 E6/7.
A lively autumn music festival that boasts more than 100 free performances around the Born, and fills the squares, bars, galleries, shops, churches and clubs with concerts of all stripes.

Artfutura
Mercat de les Flors, C/Lleida 59, Poble Sec (www.artfutura.org). Metro Espanya or Poble Sec. **Date** last weekend in Oct. **Map** p339 C10.

A pioneer festival in the field of cyber-art, Artfutura is a great place to check out the latest progeny of the union between mind and machine.

La Castanyada*
All over Barcelona. **Date** 31 Oct-1 Nov.
All Saints' Day and the evening before are known as the Castanyada after the traditional treats of *castanyes* (roast chestnuts) along with *moniatos* (roast sweet potatoes) and *panellets* (small almond balls that are covered in pine nuts). The imported tradition of Hallowe'en has grown in popularity of late, and there are now several celebrations around town. *Tots Sants* (All Saints') is also known as the *Dia dels Difunts* (Day of the Dead); the snacks switch to white, bone-shaped *ossos de sant* cakes. Thousands visit local cemeteries over the weekend to sprinkle the graves with holy water, leave flowers and hold vigils.

Wintercase Barcelona
Sala Razzmatazz 1, C/Almogàvers 122, Poblenou. Information www.wintercase.com). Metro Marina. **Tickets** from €18. **Date** late Nov. **Map** p343 L10.
This music festival showcases some of the finest indie bands over four nights. The Barcelona leg takes place in Razzmatazz (*see p259*), with past players including the likes of Ian Brown, Mercury Rev and Teenage Fanclub.

Gegants. *See p218.*

Arts & Entertainment

Festival Internacional de Jazz de Barcelona

(Information The Project 93 481 70 40/www.the-project.net). **Date** late Nov/early Dec.
See p257 **Jazz it up**.

Winter

Fira de Santa Llúcia

Pla de la Seu & Avda de la Catedral (93 402 70 00/ www.bcn.es/nadal). Metro Jaume I. **Dates** 2-23 Dec. **Map** p344-345 D4/5.

Dating from 1786, this traditional Christmas fair has expanded to more than 300 stalls selling all manner of handcrafted Christmas decorations and gifts, along with mistletoe, poinsettias and Christmas trees. The most popular figure on sale for nativity scenes is the curious Catalan figure of the *caganer* (shitter), a small figure crouching over a steaming turd with his trousers around his ankles. Kids line up for a go on the giant *caga tió*, a huge, smiley-faced 'shit log' that poops out pressies upon being beaten viciously by a stick; smaller versions are on sale in the stalls. There's also a nativity scene contest, musical parades and exhibitions, including the popular life-size nativity scene in Plaça Sant Jaume.

Resfest

Various venues, mainly El Mercat de les Flors (www.resfest.com). **Date** Dec.
Coolhunters unite. This travelling event celebrates the convergence of innovative film, music, art, design, fashion and technology.

Nadal* & Sant Esteve* (Christmas Day & Boxing Day)

Dates 25 & 26 Dec.

The Catalan equivalent of the Christmas midnight mass is the *missa del gall* (cockerel's mass), held at dawn. Later, the whole family enjoys a traditional Christmas feast of *escudella i carn d'olla* (a meaty stew), seafood and roast truffled turkey, finishing off with great ingots of *turrón*. The *caga tió* (see above Fira de Santa Llúcia) gives small gifts but the real booty doesn't arrive until the night of 5 January.

Cap d'Any (New Year's Eve)*

Date 31 Dec & 1 Jan.

During the day, look out for L'Home dels Nassos, the man who has as many noses as days of the year – it being the last day, the sly old fox has only one – who parades and throws sweets to the children. At night, bars and discos charge hiked-up prices, but free public celebrations are held around the city, mainly on La Rambla and Plaça Catalunya. At midnight, everyone stops swilling cava and starts stuffing 12 grapes into their mouths, one for every chime of the bell. Wear red underwear for good luck.

Cavalcada dels Reis

Kings usually arrive at Parc Ciutadella then parade along C/Marquès de l'Argentera up Via Laietana to Plaça Catalunya & continue to Montjuïc. The detailed
route changes each year *(information Centre d'Informació de la Virreina 010/www.bcn.es/nadal).* **Date** 5 Jan, 5-9pm. **Map** p343 J11; p345 D6, p344 C2 & p341 B9.

Melchior, Gaspar and Balthasar arrive aboard the Santa Eulàlia boat at the bottom of La Rambla before beginning a grand parade around town with a retinue of acrobats, circus clowns and pages. The televised route is published in the newspapers, but the biggest crowds are on C/Marquès de l'Argentera. Later that night, children leave their shoes out on the balcony stuffed with hay for the kings' camels; in the morning, they're either full of presents or edible coal (lumps of coloured sugar) depending on their behaviour.

Festa dels Tres Tombs

Sant Antoni. Metro Sant Antoni. **Date** 17 Jan. **Map** p342 E10.

St Anthony's day also marks the *festa major* of the district; all the usual ingredients of music and gegants here include a monstrous, symbolic fire-breathing pig. The devil is meant to have tempted the saint by taking the form of a pig; indeed, Sant Antoni is often depicted with a porker by his side. However, he is in fact the patron saint of all domestic animals and on his feast day it's still the custom to bring animals to the church of St Anthony to be blessed. Afterwards, horsemen ride three circuits (*tres tombs*) in a formal procession from Ronda Sant Antoni, through Plaça Catalunya, down La Rambla and along C/Nou de la Rambla.

Santa Eulàlia

All over Barcelona. **Date** wk of 12 Feb.

The city's blowout winter festival is in honour of Santa Eulàlia (Laia), Barcelona's co-patron saint and a special favourite of children, *see p88* **Saint alive**. Her feast day on 12 February kicks off with a ceremony in Plaça Sant Jaume, followed by music, *sardanes* and parades, with masses and children's choral concerts held in the churches and cathedral. In the evening, the female giants gather in Plaça Sant Josep Oriol, then go to throw flowers on the Baixada de Santa Eulàlia before a final boogie in the Plaça Sant Jaume. The Ajuntament and the cathedral crypt (where she's buried) are free and open to the public, as are more than 30 museums. The festival closes on Sunday evening with *correfocs* (for adults and children) centred around the cathedral.

Carnestoltes (Carnival)

All over Barcelona. **Date** Shrove Tuesday/ Ash Wednesday (5 Feb & 6 Feb 2008).

The city drops everything for a last hurrah of overeating, overdrinking and underdressing prior to Lent. The celebrations begin on Dijous Gras (Mardi Gras) with the appearance of potbellied King Carnestoltes – the masked personification of the carnival spirit – followed by the grand weekend parade, masked balls, *fartaneres* (neighbourhood feasts, typically with lots of pork), food fights and a giant *boti-farrada* (sausage barbecue) on La Rambla, with most of the kids and market traders in fancy dress.

Arts & Entertainment

Children

Rambla on.

CosmoCaixa.

Barcelona, like most Mediterranean cities, has little specifically for children but makes up for it with beaches, mountains and an atmospheric Old City. It helps that *barcelonins* find it very natural to touch and coo over other people's children; don't be surprised if an old lady comes over to pull up your child's droopy socks. However, the nuts and bolts of childcare, such as nappy-changing rooms and special breastfeeding areas, are not widely provided. There are mother-and-baby facilities in El Corte Inglés (third floor) department store, the airport, the large shopping malls and Poble Espanyol, but be warned that most nappy changes occur in the car or the pram; breastfeeding is totally accepted in public as long as you are discreet.

So far as keeping children amused is concerned, parents will be helped by the city's compact centre. A well-planned itinerary can easily include plenty of traffic-free squares, play parks and outdoor terraces for frequent refreshment stops. The obvious first stop (and there will be plenty of stops) is La Rambla (*see p95*). Once the children tire of the entertainers, artists and general life on display, they can be entertained with visits to the **Zoo de Barcelona** and the Font Màgica de Montjuïc (*see p120*) or trips on the cable car (*see p124*). Even the local museums are feeling the pull of small, sticky hands on the purse strings and

provide a growing choice of extra children's activities, from making chocolate figurines at the **Museu de la Xocolata** to blowing giant paint bubbles at **CosmoCaixa**.

Public transport is only free for children under four, and only metro stations on line 2 and some on line 4 have lifts. Officially, pushchairs are supposed to be folded up on the metro, but in practice most people just grapple gamely with the obstacle course and the guards don't interfere. All buses are low enough to wheel prams straight on.

Entertainment

Attractions

In the summer, it's hard to drag the children away from the city's beaches (*see p114*). These have plenty of lifeguards, play areas, showers and ice-cream kiosks and an increasing number of public toilets. Go early and bear in mind that the beaches on the far side of the Port Olimpic tend to be cleaner and less crowded than Barceloneta. Those further out of town towards the south, such as Castelldefels or Sitges, have shallower waters and fine, pale sands.

The pedestrianised streets and squares of the Barri Gòtic and the Born are especially child-friendly areas, as is Poble Espanyol (*see p123*).

From a child's-eye view, La Rambla, with its Boqueria market, entertainers and caricature artists, can easily fill an afternoon. At the bottom end, the Maremàgnum (*see p193*) centre attracts families with ice-creams, a summer carousel and sea views. Many museums run children's activities for the Estiu als Museus summer programme from June to September, but there's also a spectrum of year-round children's options. The CaixaForum (*see p119*) runs 'Playing with Art', for children aged three and above, every Saturday and Sunday (11am-2pm, 4-8pm). MACBA (*see p107*) has various free Sunday morning workshops for children up to 14. See also www.toc-toc.cat for a round-up of events, though you'll need some Catalan to work your way through it.

A must-see for junior footie fiends is the Museu del FC Barcelona (*see p136*), where the tour includes a walk from the dressing rooms through the tunnel, a few steps on the pitch and a spell on the bench.

L'Aquàrium

Moll d'Espanya, Port Vell (93 221 74 74/www. aquariumbcn.com). Metro Barceloneta or Drassanes. **Open** *Oct-May* 9.30am-9pm Mon-Fri; 9.30am-9.30pm Sat, Sun. *June, Sept* 9.30am-9.30pm daily. *July, Aug* 9.30am-11pm daily. **Admission** €16; €11-€12.50 reductions; free under-4s. **Credit** AmEx, DC, MC, V. **Map** p342 G13.

Barcelona's modest aquarium houses an important collection of Mediterranean marine life with more than 450 species on display. The information panels are child-friendly and in English. Miniaquària is devoted to the smaller animals such as sea cucumbers, anemones and the ever-popular seahorses, all displayed at tot's-eye level, but the main draw here is the Oceanari, a giant shark-infested tank traversed via a glass tunnel on a wooden conveyor belt. The upstairs section is devoted to children: for pre-schoolers, Explora! has 50 knobs-and-whistles style activities, such as turning a crank to see how ducks' feet move underwater or climbing inside a deep-sea diver's suit. Older children should head to Planet Aqua – a quite extraordinary, split-level circular space with Humboldt penguins and a walk through model of a sperm whale.

CosmoCaixa

C/Teodor Roviralta 47-51 (93 212 60 50/www.cosmo caixa.com). Bus 17, 22, 58/FGC Avda Tibidabo then Tramvia Blau (see p140). **Open** 10am-8pm Tue-Sun. **Admission** €3; €1.50 reductions; free under-3s. *Planetarium* €2; €1.50 reductions; free under-3s. **Credit** AmEx, DC, MC, V.

Permanent exhibitions at the new science museum include the interactive Material Room, explaining everything from hormones to fire; the 90-ton geological wall of Iberian rocks; and the Flooded Forest, the world's first living, breathing bit of Amazonian rainforest inside a museum. Outside, the enormous

Archimedes Gardens hold a number of games illustrating his principles and a scale model T-rex. Other attractions include the Bubble Planetarium (a digital 3D simulation of the universe); the Toca Toca! space where supervisors guide the exploration of natural phenomena such as tarantula and snakes, and the candy-bright Javier Mariscal-designed spaces of Clik (for three- to six-year-olds) and Flash (for seven- to nine-year-olds), where children learn how to make electricity and how a kaleidoscope works.

Museu de Cera

Ptge de la Banca 7, Barri Gòtic (93 317 26 49/ www.museocerabcn.com). Metro Drassanes. **Open** *Mid July-mid Sept* 10am-10pm daily. *Mid Sept-mid July* 10am-1.30pm, 4-7.30pm Mon-Fri; 11am-2pm, 4.30-8.30pm Sat, Sun. **Admission** €7.50; €4.50 reductions; free under-5s. **No credit cards**. **Map** p345 B7.

The Museu de Cera offers more of a giggle than an essential educational visit. This is a wax museum that belongs to the so-bad-it's-good school of entertainment. Expect the savvy PlayStation generation to be underwhelmed by clumsy renderings of Gaudí and Princess Di jumbled in with Frankenstein and ET. Recover with a cool drink at the museum's interesting enchanted-forest-cum-café.

Museu de la Màgia

C/Oli 6, Born (93 319 73 93/www.elreydelamagia. com). Metro Jaume I. **Open** *Show* 6pm Sat; noon Sun. Closed July-Sept. **Admission** €7. **No credit cards**. **Map** p345 B3.

This collector's gallery of 19th- and 20th-century tricks and posters from the magic shop El Rei de la Màgia will enchant any budding magicians. To see some live sleight of hand, book for the shows; places are limited. They're not in English, but they are fairly accessible regardless. *Photo p230.*

Museu de la Xocolata

C/Comerç 36, Born (93 268 78 78/www.museudela xocolata.cat). Metro Arc de Triomf or Jaume I. **Open** 10am-7pm Mon, Wed-Sat; 10am-3pm Sun. **Admission** €3.90; €3.30 reductions; free under-7s. **Credit** MC, V. **Map** p345 F7.

This delicious collection of chocolate sculptures includes characters from *Finding Nemo*, *Chicken Run*, *Ben-Hur* and so on, along with painstaking reproductions of Gaudí's buildings. Audio-visual shows and touch-screen computers help children make their way through what would otherwise be the rather dry history of the cocoa bean. Reserve in advance for weekend chocolate figurine-making courses and lessons in cooking desserts. *Photo p231.*

Tibidabo Funfair

Plaça del Tibidabo, Tibidabo (93 211 79 42/www. tibidabo.es). FGC Avda Tibidabo. **Open** *Nov-mid Dec, mid Jan-Feb* noon-6pm Sat, Sun. *Mar, Apr* noon-7pm Sat, Sun. *May, June* noon-8pm Sat, Sun. *July* noon-8pm Wed-Fri; noon-11pm Sat; noon-10pm Sun. *Aug* noon-10pm Mon-Thur; noon-11pm Fri-Sun. *1st 2wks Sept* noon-8pm Wed-Fri; noon-9pm Sat, Sun.

Arts & Entertainment

L'Home del Sac (the 'bag man') is a sinister old man who tosses children out alone in to his sack. Back in his castle, he boils the children down for oil.

Caçamentides ('liar hunter') is as tall as the cathedral and with fingers as sharp as claws, which he uses to snatch up children who tell lies.

La Pesanta is a huge black dog with human hands made of steel. She jumps on to the chest of those who sleep on their backs, suffocating them.

Night terrors

Forget the tooth fairy and the bogeyman, Barcelona's under-the-bed fauna is of an entirely more grisly variety. From child-abducting bag men to manic hairdressers, Catalan folklore is full of decidedly non-PC *espantanens* ('child-frighteners'), designed to make kids behave and – as a side effect – turn them into gibbering emotional wrecks. Illustration by **Dave McKean**.

Cardapeçols is obsessed with well-combed hair. She visits little girls with long, tangled locks and combs until she's pulled all the hair out, and the offender is left bleeding and bald.

2nd 2wks Sept noon-9pm Sat, Sun. *Oct* noon-7pm Sat, Sun. Closed mid Dec-mid Jan. **Admission** *individual rides* €11-€14. *Unlimited rides* €24; €19 reductions; €7-€14 children under 1.2m (3ft11in); free children under 90cm (2ft11in). **Credit** MC, V.

It may date from 1889 but this mountain-top fairground is investing millions in getting itself bang up to date. After years of falling profits, the fair has boomed in popularity again with a terrifying new free-fall ride called the Pendulum and a new hot-air balloon style ride for smaller children. The raft of other attractions includes a house of horrors and bumper cars to the emblematic Avió, the world's first popular flight simulator when it was built in 1928. Don't miss the antique mechanical puppets and contraptions at the Museu d'Autòmats or the hourly puppet shows at the Marionetàrium (from 1pm). At the weekends, there are circus parades at the end of the day and, in the summer, *correfocs* (fire runs) and street theatre.

Zoo de Barcelona

Parc de la Ciutadella, Born (93 225 67 80/www. zoobarcelona.com). Metro Barceloneta or Ciutadella-Vila Olímpica. **Open** *Mar, Oct* 10am-6pm daily. *Apr-Sept* 10am-7pm daily. *Nov-Feb* 10am-5pm daily. **Admission** €14.95; €9 3-12s. **Credit** MC, V. **Map** p343 J11/12.

The live dolphin shows (hourly at weekends) are the big draw now that Snowflake the albino gorilla has gone to the great swinging tyre in the sky. Other favourites include the hippos, sea lions, elephants and wide-open monkey houses, although there's

Museu de la Màgia. *See p227.*

barely enough room to move in some of the enclosures. Child-friendly features include a farmyard zoo, pony rides and plenty of restaurants, picnic areas and a brand-new adventure playground. If all that walking is too much, there's a zoo 'train', or you can rent electric cars from the C/Wellington entrance. Bear in mind that on hot days many of the animals are sleeping and out of sight.

Festivals

The **Festes de Santa Eulàlia** in February are specially geared towards children, with hands-on activities and even a mini *correfoc*. **La Mercè** and the local *festes majors* of each neighbourhood also have plenty of parades and music; the decorated streets of **Festa Mejor de Gràcia** are especially popular with younger children, and there's a raft of bouncy castles, circus performers and story telling in many of the district's squares. Older children will enjoy the late-night pyromania of the **Sant Joan** festival and music festivals such as **Primavera Sound**, while younger ones will go for the carnival parades of **Carnestoltes** or gathering sweeties from the streets at the **Festes de Sant Medir de Gràcia**. Christmas traditions are also particularly child-centred, with racks of pooping *caganers* (*see p225*) and pooping logs at the **Santa Llúcia** market. The **Three Kings**' procession on 5 January is also a guaranteed hit. For all, *see pp218-225*.

Music, film & theatre

At weekends from September to May, the Auditori (*see p262*) runs a cycle of 55-minute family concerts centred around various themes, such as metal instruments, and with audience participation. The Teatre Principal (La Rambla 27, 93 301 47 50, www.grupbalana.com) often puts on Spanish-language theatre shows based on familiar children's television programmes such as the *Tweenies*, and in the summer months the **Parc del Fòrum** lays on theatre, circus and music acts, some of them free. English-language children's theatre is rare, with the exception of the Christmas pantomime; check *Metropolitan* magazine for details. To catch a **film** in English, the best bet is the huge Yelmo Icària Cineplex (*see p234*) for mainstream blockbusters, while the FilmoTeca de la Generalitat (*see p234*) shows original-language children's films on Sundays at 5pm. On a rainy or cold day, a good but pricey standby can be the IMAX Port Vell (*see p236*), although the films here are only shown in Spanish and Catalan, and tend to be the usual rather dreary nature or sport documentaries. For all, *see pp233-236* and *pp262-269*.

Parks & playgrounds

The **Parc del Fòrum** is working hard to establish itself as an all-day family destination and has a specially designed new area entirely devoted to children that includes plenty of free activities. The Parc de la Ciutadella (*see p102*) has shady gardens, a giant mammoth sculpture, play parks, picnic areas, rowing boats and a zoo, which make for a packed day out. At the Ludoteca, in the Ciutadella's main play park (by the lake), young children can make free use of the many toys.

Gaudí's quirky Park Güell (*see p134*) makes up for its lack of grass with bright gingerbread houses and winding coloured benches. High above the city, the Parc de la Creueta del Coll (*see p139*) has a large playground, ping-pong tables, a picnic area and great views, and the large artificial lake is filled up in the summertime for use as an outdoor public swimming pool. The delightful Parc del Laberint (*see p143*) has hidden benches and elfin tables, picnic areas and a deceptively difficult maze, while the Jardins de la Tamarita (*see p138*) form a tranquil dog-free enclave of swings and slides hidden away next to the stop for the Tramvia Blau. The largest of them all is the Parc de Collserola (*see p137*), perfect for young nature lovers. The beachfront esplanades are ideal places for bicycle riding.

Jardíns de la Torre de les Aigües

C/Roger de Llúria 56 interior (93 291 62 60/637 40 28 66). Metro Girona. **Admission** €1.30; free under-1s. **Open** *End June-July* 10am-8pm Mon-Sat; 10am-3pm Sun. *Aug* 10am-8pm Mon-Fri; 10am-3pm Sat, Sun. **No credit cards. Map** p340 G8.

In the summer, this leafy inner patio becomes the 'beach of the Eixample', an oasis for under-sevens. There's a knee-high wading pool, plenty of sand with buckets and spades provided, trees for shade and the eponymous water tower in the centre along with outdoor showers, changing tents and toilets.

Parc del Castell de l'Oreneta

Camí de Can Caralleu & Ptge Blada, Zona Alta (93 413 24 80/010/www.bcn.cat/parcsijardins). By car Ronda de Dalt exit 9/bus 22, 34, 64, 66, 75. **Open** *May-Aug* 10am-9pm daily. *Apr, Sept, Oct* 10am-8pm daily. *Mar* 10am-7pm daily. *Nov-Feb* 10am-6pm daily.

The castle (*castell*) may be long gone, but the old grounds remain a wonderful place to roam through forest glades and flowery meadows. There are two signposted walks with great views, plus picnic areas, supervised pony rides for three- to 12-year-olds on Saturdays and Sundays (Sept-July 10.30am-2pm, €5), ping-pong tables and adventure playgrounds. On Sundays, hop aboard the miniature train.

Parc del Fòrum

Rambla Prim, Sant Martí (93 356 10 50/www.bcn. cat/parcdelforum). Metro El Maresme Fòrum. **Open** *Zona de Banys* May-Oct 11am-7pm daily. *Àrea Lúdica Infantil i Familiar* June-Oct 11.30am-2pm, 5.30-8.30pm Sat, Sun. **Admission** free.

Museu de la Xocolata. *See p227.*

The Àrea Lúdica Infantil i Familiar offers free children's activities, including bouncy castles, arts and crafts workshops and performances, an area for playing traditional games, and music concerts. Paying activities in the same enormous area include two skating rinks, a miniature train, go karts, PlayStation, minigolf and the like. To top off what can only be called nipper nirvana, the vast Zona de Banys swimming area is just next door, with free pools and plenty of extra paying activities such as kayaking, canoeing and snorkelling.

Out of town

As well as the water parks mentioned below, Catalonia has four others: Aqua Brava (in Roses), Aquadiver (Platja d'Aro), Water World (Lloret de Mar) along the Costa Brava and Marineland (Palafolls). For the endlessly popular Port Aventura theme park (*see p285*).

Catalunya en Miniatura

Can Balasch de Baix, Torrelles de Llobregat (93 689 09 60/www.catalunyaenminiatura.com). By car A2 south to Sant Vicens dels Horts then left to Torrelles de Llobregat (5km/3 miles)/by bus 62 Soler i Sauret (info 93 632 51 33) from Travessera de les Corts. **Open** *July, Aug* 10am-8pm daily. *Sept-June* 10am-6pm Tue-Sun. **Admission** €9.50; €6.50 4-12s; free under-4s. **Credit** MC, V.
Imagine Gulliver as you stroll around tiny renderings of 170 of Catalonia's most emblematic buildings and sights. Highlights include a miniature Montserrat, Girona cathedral and everything Gaudí ever laid a finger on. An appropriately munchkin-sized train circles part of the complex, and clowns perform at 1pm on Sundays in the amphitheatre.

Illa de Fantasia

Finca Mas Brassó, Vilassar de Dalt (93 751 45 53/ www.illafantasia.com). By car NII north to Premiàde Mar then left (24km/15 miles). **Open** *Mid June-1st wk Sept* 10am-7pm daily. **Admission** €16; €12 3-10s; free under-3s. **Credit** AmEx, DC, MC, V.
A bit like Port Aventura on a budget, this water park has foam slides, kamikaze-style rides and rubber-dinghy chutes, along with pools, a restaurant, super-market and a range of activities. There's also a picnic/barbecue area in a pine grove.

Eating & drinking

It's rare to find a children's menu in Barcelona, but many restaurants will provide smaller portions on request. That said, there's little need to do so when children and tapas were so clearly made for each other. Basque *pintxo* bars such as Euskal Etxea (*see p180*) are an even better option, as children can simply serve themselves from the food that is laid out, waiting for hungry young mouths, on the bar. An important point to remember for families with early eating children is that most

restaurants in Barcelona don't serve lunch before 1.30pm or dinner before 9pm, so play it like the locals and encourage a siesta followed by tea at 5pm so the children can hold out for a late dinner. However, if the children need a snack, there are plenty of options available: Bar Mendizábal (*see p183*) and Juicy Jones (*see p160*) are good for fresh juices and healthy sandwiches, and there's all-day pizza at Al Passatore (Pla del Palau 8, Born, 93 319 78 51). For relaxing in the sun (near a playground), you could try the outdoor terraces at Bar Kasparo (*see p183*), Iposa (*see p183*), Casa Paco (*see p181*) or Filferro (C/Sant Carles 29, Barceloneta, 93 221 98 36). There's also lots of safe open space around the beachfront terraces.
Museum cafés are often child-friendly and you don't always have to buy a ticket for the museum itself to enjoy them. La Miranda del Museu (*see p185*), at the Catalan history museum, has fantastic views and plenty of terrace space on which to play, while the Bosc de les Fades, next to the wax museum, is gussied up like a fairy grotto.

Babysitting & childcare

Canguro Gigante

Passeig de Sant Gervasi 16-20, Sant Gervasi (93 211 69 61). FGC Avda Tibidabo. **Open** 9am-9pm Mon-Fri. Closed Aug. **Rates** from €6/hr. **No credit cards**.
A day care centre for children aged from one to ten. Meals are available. Some English is spoken.

Cinc Serveis

C/Pelai 50, 3º 1ª, Eixample (93 412 56 76/24hr mobile 639 361 111/609 803 080/www.5serveis. com). Metro Catalunya. **Open** 9.30am-1.30pm, 4.30-8.30pm Mon-Fri. Closed 2wks Aug. **No credit cards. Map** p344 B2.
The basic rate after 8pm is €11 per hour, plus the cost of the sitter's taxi home. Long-term rates are cheaper and vary according to the age of the child.

Happy Parc

C/Pau Claris 97, Eixample (93 317 86 60/www. happyparc.com). Metro Passeig de Gràcia. **Open** 5-9pm Mon-Fri; 11am-9pm Sat, Sun. Closed last 2wks Aug. **Rates** €4.50/hr; €1.50 each subsequent 15mins. **No credit cards. Map** p342 G8.
Ball pools, twister slides and more at this giant indoor fun park and drop-in day care centre for children up to 11 years old (maximum height 1.45m/4ft 7in).

Tender Loving Canguros

Information Mobile 647 605 989/www.tlcanguros. com. **Open** 9am-9pm Mon-Sat. **No credit cards**.
English residents Lucie Bloor, Julie Stephenson and Julia Fossi provide short- and long-term nannies and babysitters for Barcelona and surrounds. All babysitters and nannies speak fluent English. Prices start at €7 an hour; the agency fee is €15 per session.

Film

Reel life.

Casablanca-Gràcia. *See p234.*

Yes, Spain has a healthy local film industry and national stars, but in 2007 Hollywood, in the bespectacled form of Woody Allen and the spectacular form of Scarlett Johansson, came to town, and everything else pretty much stopped. Allen spent July filming his love letter to the city, which also stars Penélope Cruz and Javier Bardem, and even dropped into the local jazz clubs to blow his horn. No doubt his feelings towards the city grew even warmer after receiving the Ajuntament's generous subsidy.

But of course, the iconic figure of Spanish cinema, both at home and abroad, continues to be Pedro Almodóvar, whose place in the pantheon of Spanish cinema is assured, sitting at the right hand of Luis Buñuel, whence he shall judge the quick and the dull. Almodóvar shows no signs of slowing down, the histrionics of his early style having been replaced by a more mature, slightly less melodramatic approach to human drama. His films invariably shoot to the top of the charts. In fact they are so popular, he seems to have claimed the Spanish Oscar nomination for Best Foreign Film as his by right, causing the Spanish Film Academy a major headache when other, more deserving but less idiosyncratic, films come along.

As a key member of the next generation of filmmakers, Fernando León de Aranoa (*Barrio, Princesas*) has built up an impressive body of work as a social realist in the vein of Ken Loach, though with greater doses of well-observed naturalist comedy. Equally distinctive

are the ethereal dreamscapes of Julio Medem, including *Cows, Lovers of the Arctic Circle, Sex and Lucia* and *Chaotic Ana*.

But perhaps the two best-known filmmakers of this generation, at least internationally, are Alejandro Amenábar (*The Others, The Sea Inside*) and Isabel Coixet (*My Life Without Me, The Secret Life of Words, Elegy*), who cleverly produce Hollywood-friendly films, generally in English, starring Hollywood-friendly actors.

Given the complete acceptance of Americana at Spanish cinemas, this has increased their audience internationally, while doing nothing to harm it domestically. Even irreverent, genre-hopping wildchild Álex de la Iglesia (*The Day of the Beast, Ferpect Crime*) is returning to the language of Shakespeare and Joel Silver for his next film, *Oxford Murders*, also due out in 2008. Meanwhile, his regular collaborator Santiago Seguro continues to break all records as writer, director and star of the detective comedy franchise *Torrente*, currently on two sequels and counting, which is as Spanish as Manchego, and no less cheesy.

SEEING FILMS
Where once Barcelona boasted a fine array of cinemas screening subtitled foreign films, there has been a gradual 'consolidation'. In other words, all the small, charming venues have been forced to close down by the sterile multi-screens, leading to a corresponding reduction in choice. Hollywood blockbusters predominate,

with Asian and European independents fighting it out for the remaining screen space. Release dates vary widely: blockbusters are usually released more or less simultaneously worldwide, while smaller productions can sometimes take up to three years to arrive at cinemas, long after they are available on DVD.

Newspapers carry full details of all cinema screenings, as does the weekly *Guía del Ocio* and its online version at www.guiadelocio.com/barcelona/cine/. Subtitled films are marked VO or VOSE (for '*versió original subtitulado en espanyol*'). Some of the larger cinemas open at 11am, though most have their first screenings around 4pm. Evening showings start between 7.30pm and 8.30pm; later screenings begin between 10.15pm and 10.45pm. Weekend evenings can be very crowded, especially for recent releases, so turn up early. On Fridays and Saturdays, many cinemas have a late-night session starting around 1am. All cinemas have a cheap night: usually Monday, occasionally Wednesday. You can buy tickets for a number of cinemas online at www.entradas.com or via Servi-Caixa (*see p215*).

Original-language cinemas

Casablanca-Kaplan
Passeig de Gràcia 115, Eixample (93 218 43 45). Metro Diagonal. **Tickets** *Mon* €4.50. *Tue-Sun* €6. **No credit cards. Map** p340 G6.
This centrally located cinema is the smallest in Barcelona, with two screens offering independent Spanish and European films.
Other locations Casablanca-Gràcia, C/Girona 173-175, Eixample (93 459 03 26). *Photo p233.*

Méliès Cinemes
C/Villarroel 102, Eixample (93 451 00 51/www. cinesmelies.net). Metro Urgell. **Tickets** *Mon* €2.70. *Tue-Sun* €4. **No credit cards. Map** p340 E8.
A small, two-screen cinema that is the nearest the city comes to arthouse, with an idiosyncratic roster of accessible classics alongside more recent films that aren't quite commercial enough for general release. This is the place to bone up on your Billy Wilder, Antonioni, Hitchcock and others, with up to eight films per week and a ten-films-for-€20 offer.

Renoir-Floridablanca
C/Floridablanca 135, Eixample (93 228 93 93/www. cinesrenoir.com). Metro Sant Antoni. **Tickets** *Mon* €4.80. *Tue-Thur* €6.20. *Fri-Sun* €6.50. *Late show Fri, Sat* €4.80. **Credit** MC, V. **Map** p342 E9.
The closest first-run original-version cinema to the centre of town, this four-screen branch of the Renoir chain screens up to eight independent, offbeat American, British and Spanish films per day, though note that programming tends towards the worthy.
Other locations Renoir-Les Corts, C/Eugeni d'Ors 12, Les Corts (93 490 43 05).

Verdi
C/Verdi 32, Gràcia (93 238 79 90/www.cines-verdi.com). Metro Fontana. **Tickets** *1st screening daily* €4.50. *Mon* €4.50. *Tue-Fri* €6. *Sat, Sun* €6. **Credit** MC, V. **Map** p341 H5.
The five-screen Verdi and its four-screen annexe Verdi Park on the next street have transformed this corner of Gràcia, bringing with them vibrant bars and cheap eats for the crowds that flock to their diverse programme of independent, mainly European and Asian cinema. At peak times, chaos reigns; arrive early and make sure you don't mistake the line to enter for the ticket queue, which can stretch as far as Madrid on rainy Sundays. *Photo p236.*
Other locations Verdi Park, C/Torrijos 49, Gràcia (93 238 79 90).

Yelmo Icària Cineplex
C/Salvador Espriu 61, Vila Olímpica (information 93 221 75 85/tickets 902 22 09 22/www.yelmo cineplex.es). Metro Ciutadella-Vila Olímpica. **Tickets** *Mon* €5.30. *Tue-Sun* €6.80; €5.30 before 3pm & reductions. **Credit** AmEx, MC, V. **Map** p343 K12.
The Icària has all the atmosphere of the empty shopping mall that surrounds it, but what it lacks in charm, it makes up for in choice, with 15 screens offering a very commercial roster of films, particularly Hollywood blockbusters, but also mainstream English and Spanish releases. Weekends are seat-specific, so queues tend to be slow-moving; it's worth booking your seat on the internet before you go.

Specialist cinemas

Some bars serve films with the drinks. Planeta Rai (C/Carders 12, principal, 93 268 13 21, Born, www.pangea.org/rai, closed Aug) runs mainly classic movies twice a week on Tuesdays and Thursdays (€2).

Cine Maldà
Cine Maldà, C/Pi 5, Barri Gòtic (93 481 37 04/www.cinemalda.com). Metro Catalunya or Liceu. **Tickets** *Mon* €5. *Tue-Sun* €6. **No credit cards. Map** p344 C4.
After extensive remodelling, the well-loved Cine Maldà, perched in a small shopping precinct off plaça del Pi, has been resurrected as the city's first cinema boasting a regular Bollywood cycle. It also shows an array of independent films, in four daily screenings. On Tuesday nights, Maldà plays host to Cine Ambigú, showing accessible but alternative arthouse films from around Europe. See www.retinas.org for details.

FilmoTeca de la Generalitat de Catalunya
Cinema Aquitania, Avda Sarrià 31-33, Eixample (93 410 75 90/http://cultura.gencat.net/filmo). Metro Hospital Clínic. **Shows** 3 screenings daily. Closed Aug. **Tickets** €2.70; €2 reductions; €18 for 10 films. **Credit** (block tickets only) AmEx, MC, V. **Map** p340 D5.

City in lights

With its intense light, sea and mountain views, and architectural backdrops spanning millennia, director Pedro Almodóvar was right to call Barcelona 'a splendid natural film set'. Indeed, the Old City has become so clogged with cameramen and dolly tracks that the Ajuntament now only allows two shoots a month in certain areas.

Woody Allen's latest project, reportedly titled *Midnight in Barcelona*, was shot in July 2007 and the director intends it to be 'a love letter from me to Barcelona'. The feeling was reciprocated when Pompeu Fabra University awarded Allen an honorary doctorate for his services to the city. The film, starring Penélope Cruz, Javier Bardem and Allen's new muse, Scarlett Johansson, who plays an American tourist on holiday, is based on a series of bilingual romantic entanglements. Locations included Barceloneta, Gaudí's La Pedrera and the Picasso Museum.

Tom Tykwer's *Perfume* (2006) converted the old town into 18th-century Paris by covering shop fronts in a mixture of latex batter and mashed potato. Plaça Sant Felip Neri and the Parc del Laberint d'Horta staged two of the murder scenes, while Poble Espanyol was packed, Spencer Tunick-style, with 750 naked extras for the orgy scene, which was directed by Jürgen Müller of outré local theatre troupe, La Fura dels Baus.

Manuel Huerga's acclaimed *Salvador* (2006) used 1970s-style locations in its telling of the grim story of Salvador Puig Antich, the last anarchist to be executed by garrotte under Franco.

Calista Flockhart starred in Jaume Balagueró's supernatural gore flop *Fragile* (2005). Far more interesting to the local paparazzi was her boyfriend, Harrison Ford, pretending to drop her in a bin.

Keeping costs down, Barcelona's industrial suburbs stood in for an anonymous West Coast American backdrop in Brad Anderson's *The Machinist* (2004), starring a famously emaciated Christian Bale.

Starring Marcia Gay Harden and Judy Davis, Susan Seidelman's *Gaudí Afternoon* (2001) got the Barcelona tourist board all excited but turned out to be a straight-to-DVD yawn-fest.

Almodóvar's Oscar-winning *All About My Mother* (1998) starred Penélope Cruz and featured Plaça Duc de Medinaceli, the red light district around Camp Nou, the Hospital del Mar, and the Montjuïc cemetery.

The city grabbed the title role in Whit Stillman's semi-autobiographical comedy of manners *Barcelona* (1994), which starred a still unknown Mira Sorvino and chronicled Stillman's experiences in Spain in the 1990s.

Michelangelo Antonioni's thriller *The Passenger* (1975) featured La Rambla, the port, the shade house in Parc Ciutadella and a scene between Maria Schneider and Jack Nicholson in the Palau Güell where Gaudí's modernist interiors almost stole the show.

Woody Allen on a night off in Barcelona.

Arts & Entertainment

Funded by the Catalan government, the Filmoteca is a little dry for some tastes, offering comprehensive seasons of cinema's more recondite auteurs, alongside better-known classics, plus screenings each spring of all films nominated in the Goya Awards. Overlapping cycles last two or three weeks, with each film screened at least twice at different times. Books of 20 and 100 tickets bring down the price per film to a negligible amount. The 'Filmo' also runs an excellent library of film-related books, videos and magazines at Portal Santa Madrona 6-8 (93 316 27 80), just off La Rambla.

IMAX Port Vell

Moll d'Espanya, Port Vell (93 225 11 11/www.imax portvell.com). Metro Barceloneta or Drassanes. **Tickets** €7-€10. **Credit** MC, V. **Map** p342 G12.
A squat white hulk in the middle of the marina, the IMAX has yet to persuade many that it's anything more than a gimmick. Its predictable programming, recognisable from similar enterprises the world over, covers fish, birds, ghosts and adventure sports, possibly in 3D. (If it's fish in 3D you want, the Aquarium is next door; *see p227.*)

Rush to beat the queue at **Verdi**. *See p234.*

Festivals

Barcelona is home to an increasing number of film festivals. Though none is as big or brash as Sitges' (*see below*), they all show interesting work unlikely to feature elsewhere. New events pop up every year, but regular festivals include the following: Asian (April/May), Women's (June), Animation (June), Jewish (July), Gay and Lesbian (July and October), Open Air Shorts (September), Documentaries (February and October), Human Rights (October), African (November) and Alternative Film (November). OVNI, a well-established alternative video festival, takes place every 18 months, in early spring and late autumn; the next is scheduled for autumn 2008.

Festival Internacional de Cinema de Catalunya, Sitges

93 894 99 90/www.cinemasitges.com.
Advance tickets available from Tel-entrada (902 101 212/www.telentrada.com). **Date** Oct.
Despite suffering occasional identity crises, the Sitges Film Festival, which celebrated its 40th anniversary in 2007, is widely recognised as the leading European festival for gore, horror, sci-fi and fantasy, offering dozens of screenings, as well as a host of conferences, retrospectives, premieres and appearances from the leading figures in the rarefied world of genre filmmaking. The festival would like to be taken more seriously by the mainstream, and has experimented with different times of year, although now it's back to its traditional slot in early October. During the festival, a special late-night train service returns to Barcelona after the final screening of the evening.

Open-air cinema

OK, it's not quite a drive-in, but Sala Montjuïc (www.salamontjuic.com, €4) has transformed the grassy moat of the castle on Montjuïc into Barcelona's main outdoor cinema, making it a wonderful way to spend a balmy evening. Bring a picnic, a rug and a bottle of wine, turn up early for the jazz band, then lie back and watch the film. A blend of classics and recent independent cinema is shown every Monday, Wednesday and Friday throughout the season, from July to early August.

A special free bus service runs from Metro Espanya before and after the film (8.30pm to 9.30pm going up, returning after the 10pm screening), though as screenings regularly attract hundreds, you're faced with a scrum, a wait or a rather long (though pleasant) walk.

Every August, the CCCB (*see p107*) takes over with Gandules (or 'Slackers'), offering free screenings of experimental/arthouse cinema on Tuesdays, Wednesdays and Thursdays at 10pm, complete with bar. Space is limited, though, and the courtyard tends to get fairly full.

Other outdoor film cycles tend to come and go, depending on short-lived initiatives and the granting of official licences; check the *Guía del Ocio* or www.bcn.cat for the latest information.

Galleries

Art and soul.

The rivalry between Madrid and Barcelona is not confined to the football pitch or the political arena: art, too, is the locus of competition. Until recently Barcelona was content to let its rival reap the cold, hard cash from the big art brought in by shows like Arco and PhotoEspaña, but with ever more international artists coming into the city it's only a matter of time until Barcelona makes a grab for the glory, and the gold.

In the near term, though, public sponsorship for festivals remains scarce, so the arts scene has tried to insert itself into other large-scale performance events. So you'll find experimental art with audiovisual work by groups such as graphic designers No-domain at music festival Sónar (*see p221*) and, if you look past the writhing bodies that normally feature in La Fura dels Baus (*see p268*) shows, you'll see spectacular stage sets by German-born local Roland Olbeter, while film festivals like September's Mecal (www.mecalbcn.org) incorporate an art film section. This does mean that a particular type of visual art tends to get promoted: the more technological wizardry, the better. Commercial galleries offer 'traditional' art exhibitions in painting, sculpture and photography featuring big names only, while multimedia shows can play a wild card, seeking input from young locals. Still, it provides an opportunity for graduates of design schools such as IED (www.ied.it) and Mecad (www.mecad.org), and residents of arts production centre **Hangar**, to strut their stuff. Commercial galleries such as **ProjecteSD**, **NIU** and **Àngels Barcelona** are particularly supportive.

Many purely visual arts events still find it difficult to survive. But an exception is the international video art festival Loop (www.loop-barcelona.com), with its emphasis on aesthetics rather than experimentalism. Well worth a look.

Galleries tend to reflect their neighbourhoods, with the trendy Raval boasting chic and cheek: Ester Partegàs and Jaume Pitarch exhibit in the area. Barri Gòtic and Gràcia are hubs for the city's international artists, many of whom dwell and/or work in the areas; their work is varied in quality but sometimes surprising. Innovative youngsters Frederic Amat, Alicia Framis and Tere Recarens are ones to watch in the Eixample.

The public institutions have become increasingly adventurous in their exhibition policies. Centre d'Art Santa Mònica (*see p96*)

Galeria Loft. *See p238*.

does a great job of promoting young artists and the MACBA (*see p107*) has overcome its identity crisis to offer original, interesting-to-excellent multidisciplinary shows. The CCCB (*see p107*) has a mixed bag of goodies, with digital art and film particularly well represented.

On the festival front, the high-tech, high-profile OFFF (www.offf.ws), in May, is one for the technologically savvy. Interferència in July grapples with the relationship between art and the public space (www.marato.com).

Gallery listings appear in *Guía del Ocio* and *Time Out Barcelona*. The information office at Palau de la Virreina (La Rambla 99, Barri Gòtic, 93 316 10 00, www.bcn.cat/cultura) has a plethora of publicity materials, as does FAD (Plaça dels Àngels 5-6, Raval, 93 443 75 20, www.fadweb.org), opposite the MACBA.

Commercial galleries

Barri Gòtic

For those looking for slightly older art a walk down C/Palla, which winds from the cathedral's Plaça Nova to Plaça Sant Josep Oriol, might

Arts & Entertainment

Galeria Trama.

well prove profitable. Watch for the various outlets of local dealer **Artur Ramón** (C/Palla 10, 23 & 25, 93 302 59 70, www.arturamon.com), including some lovely lithographs by Picasso, Mariano Fortuny and Joan Serrà at no.23.

Galeria Loft

C/Ample 5 (93 301 11 12/www.espace-ample.com). Metro Drassanes or Jaume I. **Open** 11am-2pm, 5-8.30pm Tue-Sat. Closed 3wks Aug. **Credit** AmEx, MC, V. **Map** p345 B7.

Specialising in Chinese avant-garde art, Loft is wonderfully decked out in chic-kitsch decor, with a patio out back. Frenchman Bertrand Cheuvreux also owns Dart gallery downstairs, which shows European art, and Off*Ample, a small space for installations on nearby Passatge de la Pau 10. Loft focuses on photography in 2008, with Rong Rong, Zeng Zicheng and the Gao Brothers all showing. Frenchman Mauro Corda takes Dart in the springtime. *Photo p237.*

Galeria Trama

C/Petritxol 8 (93 317 48 77/www.galeriatrama.com). Metro Liceu. **Open** 10.30am-2pm, 4-8pm Tue-Sat. Closed Aug. **Credit** AmEx, MC, V. **Map** p344 B4.

Opposite lavish Parès, the unassuming Trama gallery quietly shows brilliant contemporary photography. Established American duo Aziz + Cucher, and Anna Miquel are coming up in spring 2008. Scottish artist Jo Milne features and Garikoitz Cuevas take us into the summer.

Sala Parés

C/Petritxol 5 (93 318 70 20/www.salapares.com). Metro Liceu. **Open** *July-Sept* 4-8pm Mon; 10.30am-2pm, 4.30-8.30pm Tue-Sat. *Oct-June* 4-8pm Mon. 10.30am-2pm, 4.30-8.30pm Tue-Sat; 11.30am-2pm Sun. Closed 3wks Aug. **Credit** AmEx, MC, V. **Map** p344 B4.

Sombre Sala Parés (c1840) has long dealt in figurative and historical painting, dealing out art to the local bourgeoisie. It was here that Picasso had his first solo show in 1905 and it remains almost time-less in its tranquillity. Miquel Vilà, Jaume Roure and Perico Pastor feature in 2008. In September, Sala Parès hosts the Young Painters Prize. *Photo p240.*

Raval

Art/design bookshop **Ras** (C/Doctor Dou 10, 93 412 71 99, www.actar.es) is good for a quiet browse. Be sure to pop into the gallery space at the back while you're there.

Àngels Barcelona

C/Àngels 16 (93 412 54 54/www.galeriadels angels.com). Metro Catalunya. **Open** noon-2pm, 5-8.30pm Tue-Sat. Closed Aug. **No credit cards.** **Map** p344 A3.
Sparky Àngels resonates to the personality of its energetic owner, local entrepreneur Emilio Álvarez, who is the driving force behind the Loop festival (*see p237*). Locals Jaume Pitarch (sculpture and installations) and Mayte Vieta (photography) feature alongside young internationals. Angels has a new space nearby in C/Pintor Fortuny 27, while on the next street restaurant Carmelitas shows silent low-fi video art at dinnertime (C/Doctor Dou 1, 93 412 46 84, www.carmelitasgallery.com).

Galeria NoguerasBlanchard

C/Xuclà 7 (93 342 57 21/www.noguerasblanchard. com). Metro Liceu. **Open** Sept-June 10.30am-2pm, 4-8pm Tue-Sat. July 10.30am-2pm, 4-8pm Tue-Fri. Closed Aug. **No credit cards.** **Map** p342 B3.
Tucked behind a terrace café, NoguerasBlanchard occupies a sociable little spot on the winding C/Xuclà and offers smart, fun and hands-on exhibitions from locals, such as Ester Partegàs and Taiwanese artist Michael Lin. Look for the characterful cats sketched on the wall outside.

Born

Galeria Maeght

C/Montcada 25 (93 310 42 45/www.maeght.com). Metro Jaume I. **Open** 10am-2pm, 4-7pm Tue-Fri; 10am-3pm Sat. Closed 3wks Aug. **Credit** AmEx, DC, MC, V. **Map** p345 E6.
The sistership of the prestigious Paris-based gallery, Galeria Maeght occupies what was once a Renaissance palace, with a lovely courtyard and winding stone steps. It's a tad shabby inside, but its taupe paintwork and worn carpets seem somehow appropriate for the sombre Spanish greats such as Antoni Tàpies, Eduardo Arroyo and Pablo Palazuelo, among others.

Eixample

Relatively few galleries have survived the soaring prices of the Eixample. Those that have cluster on C/Consell de Cent, between Rambla de Catalunya and Balmes. The exceptions are **Galeria Toni Tàpies** (C/Consell de Cent 282,

93 487 64 02, www.tonitapies.com), owned by the son of the prestigious painter, and the two branches of **Galeria Joan Prats** (Rambla Catalunya 54, 93 216 02 84 and C/Balmes 54, 93 488 13 98, www.galeriajoan prats.com). Nearby **Galeria ADN** (C/Enric Granados 49, 93 451 00 64, www.adngaleria. com) is one to watch, favouring less-established but well-selected contemporaries.

Galeria Carles Taché

C/Consell de Cent 290 (93 487 88 36/www.carles tache.com). Metro Passeig de Gràcia. **Open** Sept-May 10am-2pm, 4-8.30pm Tue-Sat. June, July 10am-2pm, 4-8.30pm Tue-Fri. Closed Aug. **No credit cards.** **Map** p342 F8.
Quality meets reputation at Carles Taché. Here you'll find Sean Scully's abstracts, the wriggly personable rocks of Tony Cragg, the juicy scrawlings of Frederic Amat and the fiendishly clever pop of Carlos Pazos. Don't forget your wallet.

Galeria Estrany de la Mota

Ptge Mercader 18 (93 215 70 51/www.estranyde lamota.com). FGC Provença. **Open** Sept-June 10.30am-1.30pm, 4.30-8.30pm Tue-Sat. July 10.30am-1.30pm, 4.30-8.30pm Mon-Fri. Closed Aug. **No credit cards.** **Map** p340 F7.
This cavernous basement is one of the most interesting art spaces in the city: outstanding contemporary exhibitions, particularly in photography, combine established and lesser known artists from local art production house, Hangar.

Galeria Senda

C/Consell de Cent 337 (93 487 67 59/www. galeriasenda.com). Metro Passeig de Gràcia. **Open** 10.30am-2pm, 4-8pm Tue-Sat. Closed Aug. **Credit** V. **Map** p342 F8.
Senda occupies the best spot on the street and makes good use of it, with ample space for large-scale photographic exhibitions, abstract art and sculpture shows. The gallery has opened a smaller space just opposite, Espai 2nou2 (C/Consell de Cent 292, 93 487 57 11), that showcases local work.

Kowasa Gallery

C/Mallorca 235 (93 487 35 88/www.kowasa.com). Metro Passeig de Gràcia. **Open** 11am-2pm, 5-8.30pm Mon-Sat. Closed Aug. **Credit** AmEx, DC, MC, V. **Map** p340 F7.
A must for photography buffs. Kowasa Gallery, located above a well-stocked bookshop, exhibits Spanish and international classical, modern and contemporary photography covering a wide variety of genres. Agustí Centelles, Joan Colom and Eugeni Forcano set the standards for contemporary Catalan photographers such as Toni Catany.

ProjecteSD

Ptge Mercader 8 (93 488 13 60/www.projecte sd.com). FGC Provença. **Open** Sept-June 11am-8.30pm Tue-Sat. July 11.30am-8.30pm Tue-Fri. Closed Aug. **No credit cards.** **Map** p340 F7.

Silvia Dauder's penchant for new photography and film is sculpted into subtle, provocative and highly original shows at the ProjecteSD space. Limited-edition artists' texts, detailed explanations in English and Silvia's own bilingual talents complement the exhibitions. Look out for Patricia Dauder, Pieter Vermeersch and Raimond Chaves.

Gràcia & Other Districts

In comfy **La Camara Lucida** (Gran de Gracia 9, 93 368 30 72, www.lacamaralucida.com), photography fans on a budget can browse bargain prints from an extensive selection of photographers, from Nobuyoshi Araki to Mariano Zuzunaga.

Galeria Alejandro Sales

C/Julián Romea 16, Gràcia (93 415 20 54/www. alejandrosales.com). FGC Gràcia. **Open** *Oct-June* 11am-2pm, 5-8.30pm Tue-Sat. *July, Sept* 11am-2pm, 5-8.30pm Tue-Fri. Closed Aug. **No credit cards**. **Map** p340 F5.
Alejandro Sales's contemplative, sophisticated exhibitions are given the space and tranquillity they deserve. High-profile painters José Cobo, Mark Cohen and Pep Duran are regulars. While you're there, pop into the Fundació Foto Colectània (*see p134*) on the same street.

Galeria H20

C/Verdi 152, Gràcia (93 415 18 01/www.h2o.es). Metro Lesseps. **Open** 4-8pm Tue-Fri; 11am-1pm Sat. Closed Aug. **Credit** V. **Map** p341 H4.
Local architect Joaquim Ruiz Millet and writer Ana Planella founded this gorgeous Gràcia gallery in 1989. Diverse design and photography shows, book publications and spontaneous musical performances fuel the liveliest inaugurations in town.

NIU

C/Almogàvers 208, Poblenou (93 356 88 11/www. niubcn.com). Metro Glòries or Llacuna/bus 40, 42. **Open** 4-10pm Mon-Sat. Closed 2wks Aug. **Credit** MC, V. **Map** p343 off L10.

NIU, in Poblenou, is a buzzing centre for media and audio-visual art, incorporating a small exhibition space, live music, conferences, workshops and information on a kaleidoscopic array of musical and art events. Check the website for a comprehensive list.

The fringe

Much of Barcelona's visual arts fringe wallows in the amateur or the tried and tested. Some gallery spaces moonlight as bars, which is often just as well. Downtown **Miscelänea** (C/Guardia 10, Raval, 93 317 93 98, www.miscelanea.info) or uptown **Saladestar** (C/Martinez de la Rosa 40, www.saladestar.com, 93 218 39 20) incorporate exhibition spaces and cinema. Funky night spot **Maumau** (*see p255*) offers decent audio-visual fare. Many artists take part in Barri Gòtic's **Tallers Oberts** (93 443 75 20, www.tallersoberts.org), opening their studios to the public for two weekends in late May. The event is administered by FAD, who also run the database Terminal B (www.terminalb. org), aimed at visual artists, designers and filmmakers in the city. Barcelona Creativa (www.barcelonacreativa.info) does a similar job, offering an electronic classified ads page with the aim of promoting creative projects.

Centres such as Poblenou's **Centre Civic Can Felipa** (C/Pallars 277, 93 266 44 41) and **Hangar** (Passatge del Marqués de Santa Isabel 40, Poblenou, 93 308 40 41, www.hangar.org) have a limited number of studios snapped up by artists who can prove their worth.

La Xina A.R.T.

C/Doctor Dou 4, Raval (93 301 67 03/www.laxina art.org). Metro Catalunya. **Open** 5.30-8.30pm Mon-Fri; 11am-2pm, 5.30-8.30pm Sat. Closed Aug. **No credit cards**. **Map** p344 A3.
An artists' collective runs this unassuming space near the MACBA, which features exhibitions from the likes of Benxamin Álvarez and Tito Inchaurralde.

Sala Parés. *See p238.*

Gay & Lesbian

Queen of the Spanish scene.

Átame.

Enthusiastic *barcelonins* have been acclaiming their city as Europe's new gay capital for a while now but, and let's be honest here, cities like Berlin and London aren't yet ready to relinquish their crowns. For Barcelona to accede to the throne the clubbing scene in particular could do with more variety and less hair gel. But considering that homosexuality was illegal in Spain until 1978, it's no wonder that the locals have got a little overexcited: since legalisation we've seen gay marriage, gay adoption, even gay hotels. Queer Catalonia has never had it so good.

The gay scene, or *el ambiente* as it's known in Spanish, is roughly centred around an area in the Eixample bordered by the streets Diputació, Villarroel, Aragó and Balmes, delightfully/dizzily nicknamed the Gaixample. But there are also shops and bars dotted throughout the Old City, or if it's alfresco entertainment you're after, head up to the leafy shadows of Montjuïc, behind Plaça d'Espanya.

It is worth noting that, as most of the city's nightlife is pretty mixed, there's a lot of fun to be had off the official scene; a keen ear to the ground and the occasional flyer will often deliver an embarrassment of riches when it comes to partying in Barcelona. The summer's

fiestas at shacks on gay-friendly Marbella beach are a particularly fine example of minimum advertising, maximum raving.

For more information, pick up free copies of *Shanguide*, *Nois* and *Gay Barcelona* in bars and gay shops around town. Alternatively, for online info check out www.mensual.com, www.naciongay.com, www.barcelonagay.com and www.guiagay.com.

Bars

Gaixample

Bars and clubs open and close with bewildering rapidity in Barcelona, so it's worth checking that that favourite haunt from a previous trip is still in business before heading out.

Átame

C/Consell de Cent 257 (93 454 92 73). Metro Universitat. **Open** 6.30pm-2.30am Mon-Thur, Sun; 6.30pm-3am Fri, Sat. **Credit** MC, V. **Map** p342 E8.
Endless diva nonsense on the TV screens keeps the largely older local crowd grinning along. On Tuesdays, Thursdays and Sundays, there's a drag show, which varies from run-of-the-mill sing-song to hilarious (Hispanic) bitch-fest. On Tuesdays there's free tapas and a happy hour until 10pm.

Col·lectiu Gai de Barcelona

*Ptge Valeri Serra 23 (93 453 41 25/www.
colectiugai.org). Metro Universitat or Urgell.* **Open**
7-9.30pm Mon-Thur; 7-9.30pm, 11pm-3am Fri;
11pm-3am Sat. **No credit cards**. **Map** p342 E8.
The headquarters of this local gay association is
home to an easygoing, quiet and unpretentious bar,
with cheap drinks and few tourists. It occupies a
long, narrow space, where strangers have little
choice but to talk to each other.

Dietrich

*C/Consell de Cent 255 (93 451 77 07). Metro
Universitat.* **Open** 10.30pm-2.30am Mon-Thur,
Sun; 10.30pm-3am Fri, Sat. **Admission** (incl drink)
€6 Fri, Sat in July & Aug. **Credit** AmEx, MC, V.
Map p342 E8.
Dietrich is a classic club, although now somewhat
careworn, that generally attracts a mixed and lively
crowd. Drag shows and acrobats perform on the
dancefloor, and the friendly international bar crew
all speak English.

Punto BCN

*C/Muntaner 63-65 (93 453 61 23/www.arena
disco.com). Metro Universitat.* **Open** 6pm-2.30am
Mon-Thur, Sun; 6pm-3am Fri, Sat. **No credit cards**.
Map p342 E8.
A large, bright and airy (read: rather cold) place
popular with all sorts that's been around for many
years in the Gaixample. Snag a table on the mezzanine and get gawping at the variety of fine-looking
chaps that pre-party here before heading elsewhere. Free passes to the Arena clubs (*see p243*)
are available behind the bar.

Sweet

C/Casanova 75 (no phone). Metro Universitat. **Open**
10.30pm-2.30am Wed, Thur; 10.30pm-3am Fri, Sat;
8pm-2.30am Sun. **No credit cards**. **Map** p345 E8.
A slick affair, that, like many of the city's bars, makes
you feel like you're in a hip vodka ad. A young gay
crowd (most people are in their 20s) and their female
friends dress up for the occasion. Toni, the owner, is
always good for advice on where to go next.

Z:eltas Club

*C/Casanova 75 (93 451 84 69/www.zeltas.net).
Metro Universitat.* **Open** 10.30pm-3am daily.
Credit MC, V. **Map** p342 E8.
Z:eltas is one of the more stylish of the Gaixample's
bars. Although open every day, it only really comes
into its own later on in the week, when the trendy
young *guapos* show their appreciation for the DJ's
tunes (mainly funky house) by squashing together
on the mini dancefloor. *Photo p246*.

The rest of the city

Schilling (*see p176*), La Concha (*see p252*) and
Zelig (C/Carme 116, no phone), though not gay
per se, are worth a look.

La Bata de Boatiné

C/Robadors 23, Raval (no phone). Metro Liceu.
Open 11.30pm-3am Wed-Sat; 11.30pm-2.30am Sun.
No credit cards. **Map** p345 A5.
The most alternative gay bar in Barcelona, this squat-
like former brothel is popular with all shapes and
forms. It's not a huge place, but cheap drinks and the
lack of attitude mean it can be packed at weekends.

Camping it up in the centre of Barcelona's gay nightlife, the **Gaixample**. *See p241*.

Burdel 74

C/Carme 74, Raval (mobile 678 464 515). Metro Liceu. **Open** 8pm-3am Tue-Sun. **No credit cards.** **Map** p342 E10.
A bit of a Raval staple, Burdel's louche, intimate interior has more than a touch of Almodóvar's high-camp chic about it. Deep reds and hallowed divas on the walls make it ideal for taking a date, or swing by for the bingo on Sunday nights.

New Chaps

Avda Diagonal 365, Eixample (93 215 53 65/ www.newchaps.com). Metro Diagonal or Verdaguer. **Open** 9pm-3am Mon-Sat; 7pm-3am Sun. **No credit cards.** **Map** p338 G6.
The more mature clientele which frequents this sex bar avoids studying the rather bizarre collection of objects hung around the place and instead heads for the busy darkroom downstairs. If you are tempted, make sure you check in your valuables first.

La Penúltima

Riera Alta 40 (mobile 675 246 262). Metro Sant Antoni, Raval. **Open** 7pm-3am Tue-Sun. **No credit cards.** **Map** p342 E9.
Away from the tight T-shirts and high prices of the Gaixample is this relaxed and friendly bar, which is mixed rather than exclusively gay. Converted from a former *bodega*, it retains the large barrels in the entrance and has plenty of tables at the back. Look out for the collection Barbie dolls. A good place to start the evening.

Clubs

Gaixample

Arena

Classic & Madre *C/Diputació 233 (93 487 83 42). Metro Universitat.* **Open** 12.30-5am Tue-Sat; 7.30pm-5am Sun. **Admission** (incl 1 drink) €7 Fri; €12 Sat. **No credit cards.** **Map** p338 F8. **VIP & Dandy** *Gran Via de les Corts Catalanes 593 (93 487 83 42/www.arenadisco.com). Metro Universitat.* **Open** 1-6am Fri, Sat. **Admission** (incl 1 drink) €5 Fri; €10 Sat. **No credit cards.** **Map** p342 F8.
Ten years on, and the four Arena clubs are still packed to the rafters every week with a huge variety of punters. The USP is that you pay once, get your hand stamped and can then switch between all four clubs as well as lesbian club Aire (*see p245*). Madre is the biggest and most full-on, with thumping house and a darkroom; there are shows and strippers at the beginning of the week but Wednesday's semi-riotous foam party is where it's really at. VIP doesn't take itself too seriously and is popular with everyone from mixed gangs of Erasmus students to parties of thirtysomethings down from Sabadell, all getting busy to Snoop Dogg and vintage Mariah. Classic is similarly mixed, if even cheesier, playing only '80s and '90s chart hits and, finally, Dandy bangs away with somewhat unimaginative house.

Bear Factory

Ptge Domingo 3 (no phone/www.bearfactory barcelona.com). Metro Passeig de Gràcia. **Open** 11pm-3am Wed, Thur, Sun; 11pm-5am Fri, Sat. **Admission** €6 Fri; (incl 1 drink) €6 Sat. **No credit cards.** **Map** p338 G7.
This spacious and well-designed bar has become very popular – and not just with bears. There is, however, bearaphernalia everywhere and, on closer examination, even the bar has hair! The good-sized dancefloor is open for hard house on Fridays and Saturdays, while the small darkroom never closes.

Martins

Passeig de Gràcia 130 (93 218 71 67/www.martins-disco.com). Metro Diagonal. **Open** midnight-5am Wed-Sun. **Admission** (incl 1 drink) €12. **Credit** MC, V. **Map** p338 G6.
Catching up with Metro, with three bars, porno lounge and decent dancefloor, it can be packed at the weekends (especially Saturdays).

Metro

C/Sepúlveda 185 (93 323 52 27/metrodisco.bcn). Metro Universitat. **Open** 1-5am Mon; midnight-5am Tue-Sun. **Admission** (incl 1 drink) €14. **Credit** MC, V. **Map** p342 C5.
Fully refurbished and with a redesigned bar, Metro's dingier corners now have a better shine. With stiffer competition around, it's to be seen if this will be enough to sustain it as the pre-eminent gay club in town. Latin beats predominate on the smaller dancefloor, with house on the main one to keep the boys entertained (that is, when they're not entertaining each other).

Admire the view down below at **Punto BCN**.

Comic hero

Transsexual/transvestite, part prostitute, part detective, Anarcoma haunts La Rambla and its environs – her exaggerated breasts and cock bulging out of tight-fitting clothes. Her debut was on the front cover of the first edition of *El Víbora*, published in 1979, the ground-breaking, subversive comic published in Barcelona. She is the masterpiece of Nazario Vera Luque, probably the most famous comic artist in Spain and considered the father of modern Spanish comics.

Nazario was born in 1944 in Seville and later went on to teach at primary school for more than ten years. A lover of film, literature and poetry, he identified with the American hippy and beatnik movements. Taking inspiration from the new generation of comic artists such as Robert Crumb and Gilbert Shelton, he drew short stories with contemporary themes such as gay life and women's liberation. By 1971, he realised that life in repressed Seville would never provide what he needed, so abandoning his career he moved to Barcelona.

He never looked back, and during the revolutionary and subversive atmosphere of Barcelona in the early '70s he came into contact with a wide range of like-minded people including the artists Ocaña and Javier Mariscal and a young Pedro Almodóvar. He formed a famous friendship with Ocaña, even ending up in prison together following one of Ocaña's happenings on La Rambla. With Mariscal and other activists he co-founded El Rrollo Enmascarado, an underground collective that published the semi-clandestine magazine, *El Rrollo*.

Nazario's openly gay characters and subversive storylines meant that most of his work was unpublishable during the dictatorship and it was not until the late 1970s that he was able to work freely. *El Víbora* was launched in 1979, going on to huge success. By the mid '80s – the golden era of Spanish comics – it was selling upwards of 40,000 copies per issue with Nazario as its star.

However, outside Spain Nazario is probably more famous for his 23-years-long copyright battle with RCA records. In 1976, he drew the front cover for an edition of the Spanish magazine *Rock Comix* that was dedicated to Lou Reed. Reed apparently liked the drawing enough to want it for the front cover of his album *Take No Prisoners*, which was released in 1978. However, Nazario was never asked for his permission and his signature was removed from the work. For Nazario the issue was never the money: he simply wanted recognition for his work, and there ensued a 20-year legal battle complicated by the fact that the album was released in Spain with a different cover. But in 2001 the case was resolved in the US courts and he received damages of £16,000.

Although Nazario retired from comics over ten years ago, he continues to paint, draw and write and his work has gradually come to be recognised for its artistic merit and groundbreaking themes. A major retrospective took place in the Palau de la Virreina in 2002 and in 2004 he published *La Barcelona de los Años 70 Vista por Nazario y sus Amigos* (*Barcelona in the '70s by Nazario and his Friends*), which used drawings, articles and memorabilia of the period to reconstruct the Barcelona he knew and loved.

The rest of the city

La Luna
Avda Diagonal 323, Eixample (no phone). Metro Verdaguer. **Open** 5am-8.30am Mon; 5am-8.30am, 11pm-3am Thur, Fri; 5am-10.30am, 11pm-3am Sat, Sun. **Admission** (incl 1 drink) €20. Free before 3am. **No credit cards. Map** p341 J7.
As the Spanish saying goes, 'never the last drink, always the penultimate', and so it is for La Luna, the only genuine 'after hours' in the centre of Barcelona. While a friendly kind of place, the faces of those still clinging on by their fingertips or other body parts speak for themselves.

Salvation
Ronda Sant Pere 19-21, Eixample (93 318 06 86/ www.matineegroup.com). Metro Urquinaona. **Open** midnight-5am Thur-Sat. **Admission** (incl 1 drink) €15. **No credit cards. Map** p342 E2.
It's been said of Salvation – one of the city's more enduringly popular gay clubs – that 'everyone you see naked on Gaydar… you can see them in here with their clothes on'. One room is full of said tanned, buff torsos lurching around to house; in the other sprightly young things bounce about to pop.

Lesbian bars & nightclubs

Sadly, Barcelona's lesbian scene doesn't seem to have much consistency, with bars struggling to survive amid constant changes of ownership. On the other hand, there are several thriving groups that organise regular parties, including Nextown Ladys (www.nextownladys.com) and Silk (www.silkbcn.com). Check online for details. You'll also find lesbians in some spots favoured by gay men, such as Arena (*see p243*) or La Bata de Boatiné (*see p242*). Other events are organised by a variety of groups: Casal Lambda (C/Verdaguer i Callis 10, Barri Gòtic, 93 319 55 50, www.lambdaweb.org) is a reliable source of information, as is Complices (*see p246*). Admission to the bars listed below is free unless otherwise stated.

Aire
C/València 236, Eixample (93 454 63 94/www. arenadisco.com). Metro Passeig de Gràcia. **Open** 11pm-3am Thur-Sat. **Admission** (incl 1 drink) €5 Fri; €6 Sat. **No credit cards. Map** p338 F7.
The girly outpost of the Arena group is the city's largest lesbian club and as such sees a decent variety of girls (and their male friends, by invitation) head down to shoot pool and dance to pop, house and 1980s classics. On the first Sunday of the month, there's a women-only strip show.

La Femme
C/Plató 13, Sant Gervasi (no phone). Metro Lesseps/FGC Muntaner. **Open** midnight-3am Fri, Sat. **No credit cards. Map** p338 E3.

Hip dance music, comfortable seating, red and green neon lighting and pretty people on both sides of the bar. Lots of trendy young things and fortysomethings. This is not a place for boys.

Kiut
C/Consell de Cent 280 (no phone). Metro Passeig de Gracia. **Open** midnight-5.30am Thur-Sat. **Admission** Free women; €10 men. **Credit** (Bar only) AmEx, MC, V. **Map** p342 F8.
Kiut, pronounced 'cute', is the latest addition to the fragile lesbian scene, brought to you by the owner of Z:eltas (*see p242*). There's lots of shiny black marble and mirrors for preening. The resident DJs play happy house to liven up the smallish dancefloor, while the smokers take refuge in the back bar.

Prados
Maria Cubi 4 (mobile 605 099 942), Gràcia. Metro Fontana/FGC Gracia. **Open** 11.30pm-5.30am Fri, Sat. **No credit cards. Map** p338 F5.
It may have a new name (it was called Via before) but Prados remains one of the longest-running lesbian haunts in Barcelona. A friendly atmosphere and small dancefloor means that it fills up after the others close their doors.

Restaurants

In addition to those listed here, plenty of mixed restaurants in Barcelona have thriving gay followings. Among the most popular are the Barri Gòtic's La Verònica (Rambla de Raval 2-4, 93 329 33 03) and Venus Delicatessen (C/Avinyó 25, 93 301 15 85) and the Eixample's Café Miranda (C/Casanova 30, 93 453 52 49).

Castro
C/Casanova 85, Eixample (93 323 67 84/www. castrorestaurant.com). Metro Universitat. **Open** 1-4pm, 9pm-midnight Mon-Fri; 9pm-midnight Sat. **Main courses** €12. **Set lunch** €8.80 Mon-Fri. **Credit** MC, V. **Map** p342 C5.
Still ahead of the crowd as far as gay restaurants go, Castro continues to provide imaginative dishes such as duck breast with wild strawberries or deer in balsamic vinegar, all served up by the cutest of staff.

Cubaneo
C/Casanova 70, Eixample (93 454 83 94). Metro Universitat. **Open** *Oct-June* 1-4pm, 8.30pm-1am Mon-Sat. *July-Sept* 8.30pm-1am Tue-Sun. **Main courses** €10. **Set lunch** €8. **Credit** MC, V. **Map** p342 E8.
Cuban soul food, invigorating Mojitos and handsome muscled waiters, not to mention an unholy mix of Cuban personalities and gay icons on the walls. The set meals start with salads, followed by a choice of mains, and include a bottle of wine or cava.

Iurantia
C/Casanova 42, Eixample (93 454 78 87/www. iurantia.com). Metro Universitat. **Open** 1.30-4pm, 9pm-midnight Mon-Fri; 9pm-midnight Sat. **Main courses** €12. **Credit** MC, V. **Map** p342 E8.

Though not a gay eaterie per se, Iurantia's Gaixample location assures it's frequented by a stylish crowd keen on the slick red paint job, downbeat tunes and the menu, which varies from imaginative fusion – octopus carpaccio – to popular and fairly priced pasta and pizzas. Leave room for the home-made bitter chocolate truffles with a touch of mint.

Shops & services

General shops

Antinous Libreria Café
C/Josep Anselm Clavé 6, Barri Gòtic (93 301 90 70/ www.antinouslibros.com). Metro Drassanes. **Open** 10.30am-2pm, 5-8.30pm Mon-Fri; noon-2pm, 5-8.30pm Sat. **Credit** AmEx, DC, MC, V. **Map** p345 B7.
A large bright bookshop with an appealing café at the back. Ideal for checking out your purchases, from DVDs to postcards, poetry to magazines, art to comics all with a queer twist; they also have a great selection of nude photobooks. Its website lists the top ten best-selling items so you know what's popular; it also features online reviews.

Complices
C/Cervantes 2, Barri Gòtic (93 412 72 83/www. libreriacomplices.com). Metro Jaume I. **Open** 10.30am-8pm Mon-Fri; noon-8pm Sat. **Credit** AmEx, MC, V. **Map** p345 C6.
Barna's oldest gay bookshop is run by a helpful lesbian duo who stock a variety of literature and films – from highbrow paperback classics (some in English) and *Queer as Folk* box sets to porn mags and DVDs.

D'Arness
C/Casanova 63, Eixample (www.d-arness.com). Metro Universitat. **Open** 5-9pm Mon-Fri. **Credit** MC, V. **Map** p342 E8.
This small specialist leather shop has all the gear you could need. The fully kitted-out room at the back is available for hire by the hour.

Ovlas
Via Laietana 33, Barri Gòtic (93 268 76 91). Metro Jaume I. **Open** 10.15am-8.30pm Mon-Fri; 10.15am-9pm Sat. **Credit** AmEx, MC, V. **Map** p345 D4.
A large space that keeps Barcelona's boys in lurid briefs, singlets and revealing garments – making it a perfect one-stop shop for a weekend in Sitges.

Hairdressers

Fashion Chaning
C/Diputació 159, Eixample (93 454 24 10). Metro Urgell. **Open** 4-8pm Mon; 11am-8.30pm Tue-Sat. **Credit** V. **Map** p342 E8.
A gay hairdressing salon for boys and girls, where men can ask for manicures, pedicures and facials without getting odd looks. You can get your eyebrows, eyelashes and even your body hair dyed.

Saunas

At both the establishments listed below, you will find enough showers, steam rooms and dry saunas to justify the name, along with bars and colourful porn lounges. On arrival, you will be supplied with locker key, towel and flip-flops.

Share a laugh with the stylish set at **Z:eltas Club**. *See p242.*

Corinto
C/Pelai 62, Eixample (93 318 64 22). Metro Catalunya. **Open** noon-5am Mon-Thur; 24hrs Fri-Sun. **Admission** €14. **Credit** MC, V. **Map** p342 B2.
Nothing really changes at the Corinto, smack in the centre, on perhaps the busiest corner in town, and it still remains the most popular place for tourists to go get busy, aided by some fine vistas of Plaça Catalunya and La Rambla.

Sauna Casanova
C/Casanova 57, Eixample (93 323 78 60). Metro Urgell. **Open** 24hrs daily. **Admission** €14 Mon, Wed, Fri-Sun; €11 Tue, Thur. **Credit** MC, V. **Map** p342 E8.
Recently refurbished, Casanova is the city's most popular sauna, attracting plenty of well-muscled eye candy for the visitor. It's at its busiest on Tuesday and Thursday evenings, every night after the clubs close and all day Sunday.

Sex shops
The following gay-oriented sex shops have viewing cabins for videos.

Nostromo
C/Diputació 208, Eixample (93 451 33 23). Metro Universitat. **Open** 11am-11pm Mon-Fri; 3-11pm Sat, Sun. **No credit cards. Map** p342 E8.

Zeus
C/Riera Alta 20, Raval (93 442 97 95). Metro Sant Antoni. **Open** 10am-9pm Mon-Sat. **Credit** MC, V. **Map** p342 E10.

Sitges
Just a short (30min) train ride down the coast is Sitges, the internationally renowned gay capital of Spain. For nine months of the year, this pretty little town is the bolt-hole for city-weary *barcelonins*, but in the summer months the streets heave with muscled flesh and the party atmosphere goes on and on. There is a small (and packed) gay beach in the centre of town, but for the more adventurous, the nudist beach, which has a small, but pricey *xiringuito*, is about another hour's walk (plenty of water and comfortable shoes advisable).

Accommodation
Be aware that finding somewhere in August is a nightmare and book at least three months in advance for anything decent. This goes in particular for **El Xalet** (C/Illa de Cuba 35, 93 894 55 79, www.elxalet.com, rates €80-€128 incl breakfast) and its sister **Hotel Noucentista** (C/Illa de Cuba 21, 93 894 85 53, rates €80-€128 incl breakfast, closed Nov-Feb), both of which occupy Modernista palaces and are furnished with period furniture. Almost next door is

Hotel Liberty (C/Illa de Cuba 45, 93 811 08 72, www.libertyhotelsitges.com, rates €76-€130 incl breakfast), with spacious rooms, a lush garden and, if you feel like splashing out, a luxury penthouse with two terraces overlooking the town. The owners also have 41 apartments for rent – see www.staysitges.com. The romantics' choice, naturally, is the **Hotel Romàntic**, a beautifully restored 19th-century house with a secluded palm-filled garden (C/Sant Isidre 33, 93 894 83 75, www.hotel romantic.com, rates €90-€114 incl breakfast, closed Nov-Mar). In a quieter residential area is the friendly French-run **Hotel Los Globos** (Avda Nuestra Señora de Montserrat s/n, 93 894 93 74, www.hotellosglobos.com, rates €60-€95 incl breakfast), in need of slight redecoration but with a balcony or private garden for each room. Peter and Rico at **RAS** (mobile 607 14 94 51, www.raservice.com) may be able to help you out if you're stuck.

Bars & nightclubs
For a night out in Sitges, first squeeze your way through the sweating herd at the beginning of C/Primer de Maig, aka Sin Street, and take a seat at one of the numerous pavement cafés to watch the world go by. Later, head round the corner to **Privilege** (C/Bonaire 24, no phone) with its friendly atmosphere and small but packed dancefloor, passing **Mari Pili** (C/Joan Tarrida Ferratges 14, mobile 653 771 071), the local lesbian hangout on the way. Two minutes from there is the much larger but rammed **Mediteraneo** (C/Sant Bonaventura 6, no phone) frequented by a slightly older but equally lively crowd; beware of the rather intimate toilets. If you feel the urge to keep going, there is the eternal **Organic** (C/Bonaire 15, no phone) or **Trailer** (C/Angel Vidal 36, 93 894 04 01) in the centre of town. On Tuesdays from June to September head for the gay beach party at **L'Atlantida** (Platja les Coves, no phone), a short taxi ride from the centre.

Restaurants
Finding good food in Sitges can be a problem, but if you're looking for a particularly gay experience and are not too bothered about the food try **Parrots Restaurant** (C/Joan Tarrida Ferratges 18, 93 811 12 19, mains €16, closed Nov-Dec). Also worth a mention is **Monroe's** (C/Sant Pau 36, 93 894 16 12, mains €14), dedicated to Marilyn and serving a range of international cuisine. If it's charm you're after try **Flamboyant** (C/Pau Barrabeitg s/n 16, 93 894 58 11, mains €16, closed Oct-May). The food is fairly average, but served in a magical leafy courtyard.

Arts & Entertainment

Music & Nightlife

From superclubs to salsatecas, this city knows how to party.

Will it be back? **La Paloma**. *See p254.*

Sure, Barcelona has a reputation as a party city. There's a reason all those stag and hen parties head here, and it's not just because of cheap flights. Yet, 24-hour, seven-days-a-week party heaven is actually more a facet of Ibiza than Barcelona. So why do they keep coming here? Well, there's an energy and creativity in the local nightlife that you won't find anywhere else. This is reflected primarily in the mix of people in bars, a willingness to experiment with sound and art, and a proud resolve to continue the city's fine devotion to excellence in interior bar design.

But, and it's a big but, the present government's acquiescence over growing, and quite often irrational, neighbourhood protests about noise pollution has transformed, and will continue to transform, the nightlife landscape. Two areas have fallen victim already – the Born and Gràcia. Both have been issued with indefinite bans on new bar licences. It was certainly a sign of what was to come when,

in 2005, **La Terrrazza**, the city's best-loved club, closed after noise complaints. And while La Terrrazza managed to reopen, many other venues have gone to the big party in the sky.

Clampdowns on premises aside, Barcelona has it all – from superclubs hosting famed international celebrity DJs to tiny little clubs specialising in the latest electro, drum 'n' bass and techno. There are lounge clubs and gilded ballrooms, salsatecas and Brazilian samba bars, seductive tango emporiums and alternative club nights offering anything from northern soul to Bollywood bhangra and crooning drag queens. There's even a bar with beds (**CDLC**), so why would you ever go home?

Going out in Barcelona happens late, but that's mainly Thursday until Saturday. Barcelona on a Monday evening is a dead city. Tuesday and Wednesday things pick up slightly. People rarely meet for a drink much before 11pm – if they do, it's a pre-dinner thing. Bars are officially supposed to close at 1.30am or so, depending on their licence, but in practice many close at 2am or 3am and it's not until they kick people out that the clubs (cutesily still known as *discotecas*) really get going. If you're still raring to go at 6am, there's a good chance you'll find an after-party party for even more hedonism. 'Afters', some better known than others, can usually be found by asking around clubbing regulars. Traditionally, you had to head uptown to hit the posh clubs, but the Port Olímpic is putting on some serious competition with places like **Club Catwalk** and CDLC luring the *pijos* (well-groomed uptowners) downtown. There are also nightly beach parties running up and down the coast from Bogatell to Mataró through the summer. Meanwhile, you'll find smaller venues pulsating with life in the Barri Gòtic, particularly around the Plaza Reial and C/Escudellers. Across La Rambla, in the Raval, you can skulk in the grittier, grungier places, though in the last year or so many have fallen prey to the Ajuntament's drive to wipe out late-night noise. If hippie chic, joints and chillums are your thing, Gràcia is good for hanging with the artsy crowd, though in truth it's a far better place for drinking than it is for dancing.

In the end, if it's beautiful people you want to see and you don't mind the try-hard pretension and steep prices, then the clubs are worth a go. But the unpretentious local bar has always been

Barcelona's real strength, and it offers a more genuine experience than standing in a queue with a couple of hundred desperate wannabes.

LIVE MUSIC

The term 'live music' has been threatening to become a bit of a misnomer in Barcelona over the last few years. The closure of grown-up venues La Boîte and Jazzroom and the threatened closure of **Harlem Jazz Club** were seen by some as a worrying symptom of the music scene's sickly state, particularly as these venues were run by long-time champions of live music in Barcelona. But perhaps the rumours of the death of music in the city are exaggerated. There is still plenty of variety, with a healthy dose of genres and bands from northern Europe and America – good news for visitors, who often get to see their favourite bands in venues half the size they'd normally play at home. But rocketing ticket prices (perhaps to support seemingly ever-growing guest lists – blaggers, take note!) mean you pay for such privilege.

For a city that's hardly booming with smaller live-music venues, over the past five or so years Barcelona has, incredibly, managed to garner somewhat of a reputation for a burgeoning local music movement that is claiming considerable international recognition. *Mestizaje* (basically meaning 'mix') performers generally draw from a blend of influences including rock, flamenco, rai, hip hop and various South American, Asian and African styles. The top *mestizaje* draws at the moment are Manu Chao, Ojos de Brujo and the Raval's 08001.

As well as the venues listed below, you can catch the occasional visits of pop-rock superstars in one of Montjuïc's sports stadiums, one of which has become the Barcelona Teatre Musical (C/Joaquim Blume s/n, 93 423 15 41), and Vall d'Hebron, or even way out in Badalona's Palau Olímpic. The other main music venues for seeing international names (as well as hotly tipped unknowns and local musicians) are the multifaceted industrial space **Razzmatazz** and the old dance halls **La Paloma** and **Sala Apolo**, the former hosting both cutting-edge live and electronic music, the latter specialising in feel-happy DJs and special theme nights. In July, there are concerts on the roof of **La Pedrera**. Not exactly cutting edge (tickets come with cava so you can sip wine and stare out over the city to the accompaniment of soft jazz) but the location is unique.

The mall-like **Bikini**, which has recently revived the quality of its programming with an impressively varied roster of recent acts including Radio 4, Terry Callier, Marianne Faithfull and Everlast, is the grand old survivor of the Barcelona scene.

INFORMATION AND TICKETS

For concert information, buy the weekly listings guide *Guía del Ocio*, the new *Time Out Barcelona* or the Friday papers, which usually include listings supplements. Look in bars and music shops for free magazines such as *Go*, *AB*, *Mondo Sonoro* (all mostly independent pop/rock/electronica) and *Batonga!* (which covers world music). *Punto H* and *Suite* are good for keeping up to date on the club scene.

Try web listings sites www.lecool.com, ww.atiza.com,www.salirenbarcelona.com, www.barcelonarocks.com, and www.clubbing spain.com. For festivals, try www.festivales. com and www.whatsonwhen.com. You can also get information and tickets from Tel-entrada and Servi-Caixa, and FNAC. Specialist record shops, such as those on C/Tallers in the Raval, are good for info and club flyers.

Barri Gòtic

Barcelona Pipa Club

Plaça Reial 3, pral (93 302 47 32/www.bpipa club.com). Metro Liceu. **Open** 11pm-3am daily. **Admission** free. **No credit cards**. **Map** p345 B6. Once up some stairs and through a door, the chaos of the Plaça Reial below couldn't seem further away. That's not to say it's quiet – it's usually rammed with bright young things – but that the heavy curtains, wooden cabinets and ornate chandeliers conjure up a relaxed and relaxing atmosphere. You have to ring the bell next to the pipe to get in.

Fonfone

C/Escudellers 24 (93 317 14 24/www.fonfone.com). Metro Drassanes or Liceu. **Open** 11pm-2.30am Mon-Thur, Sun; 11pm-3am Fri, Sat. **Admission** free. **Credit** MC, V. **Map** p345 B6.

Clubs

If you only visit one club
La Terrrazza (*see p256*). There's reason for its reputation.

For music
Harlem Jazz Club (*see p251*). Not just jazz, but all worth listening to.

For those with money
CDLC (*see p255*). Is that Ronaldinho?

For trashy delights
Baja Beach (*see p254*). Plastic fantastic.

Out of the ordinary
La Paloma (*see p254*). Part dancehall, part club, completely extraordinary.

Arts & Entertainment

THE SHORTLIST
WHAT'S NEW | WHAT'S ON | WHAT'S BEST

 Amsterdam

 Barcelona

 Berlin

 Dubai

 Dubrovnik

 Edinburgh **NEW IN 2008**

 Florence

 Las Vegas

 London

 Malta

 Manchester

 Marrakech

 New York

 Nice & Cannes **NEW IN 2008**

 Paris

 Prague

 Rome

 San Francisco **NEW IN 2008**

 Sydney **NEW IN 2008**

 Tokyo

 Venice

- **POCKET–SIZE GUIDES**
- **WRITTEN BY LOCAL EXPERTS**
- **KEY VENUES PINPOINTED ON MAPS**

Available at all major bookshops at only
£6.99 and from timeout.com/shop

 Time Out SHORTLIST

A refreshingly spacious bar on a seedy backstreet, Fonfone stands out by virtue of its green-and-orange glowing decor. It pulls a mixed crowd of locals and lost tourists of a studenty bent. Pop, electronica, house and breakbeats attempt to distract the punters from their conversation.

Harlem Jazz Club

C/Comtessa de Sobradiel 8 (93 310 07 55). Metro Jaume I. **Open** 8pm-4am Tue-Thur, Sun; 8pm-5am Fri, Sat. **Gigs** 10.30pm, midnight Tue-Thur, Sun; 11.30pm, 1am Fri, Sat. Closed 2wks Aug. **Admission** free Mon-Thur; (incl 1 drink) €7 Fri-Sun. **No credit cards. Map** p345 C6.

For a time, the gig looked over for this Barcelona institution. To cut a long story short, it's managed to come back bigger and stronger than ever, remodelled and, as a nod to the times, with a DJ booth. But live music is still what it does best, and it's for this reason that it's a regular hangout for not-so-cashed up musicians, serious music buffs and students. A lot of history's gone down at Harlem – some of the city's most promising talent and the occasional special international artist have played here. Jazz, klezmer and flamenco fusion all get a run in a venue that holds no musical prejudices.

Jamboree/Los Tarantos

Plaça Reial 17 (93 319 17 89 /www.masimas.com). Metro Liceu. **Open** 8pm-11am daily. **Gigs** 8.30pm, 9.30pm, 10.30pm daily. **Admission** €6. **Credit** V. **Map** p345 B6.

Every night Jamboree hosts jazz, Latin or blues gigs by mainly Spanish groups; when they're over the beatbox comes out. On Mondays, particularly, the outrageously popular What the Fuck (WTF) jazz jam session is crammed with a young local crowd waiting for the funk/hip-hop night that follows. Upstairs, sister venue Los Tarantos stages flamenco performances, then joins forces with Jamboree as a smooth-grooves chill-out space.

La Macarena

C/Nou de Sant Francesc 5 (no phone/www. macarenaclub.com). Metro Drassanes. **Open** 11.30pm-4.30am Mon-Thur, Sun; 11.30pm-5.30am Fri, Sat. **Admission** free before 1.30am; €5 afterwards. **No credit cards. Map** p345 B7.

This is not a centre for embarrassing synchronised arm movements and dance steps performed to cheesy pop tunes, but a completely soundproofed cosy little dance space/bar with a kicking sound system that will pound away electro, minimal and house beats until just before the sun rises. Guest house DJs Brett Johnson and Vincenzo have shared the decks with local talent, usually a day before or after a bigger gig elsewhere.

New York

C/Escudellers 5 (93 318 87 30). Metro Drassanes or Liceu. **Open** midnight-5am Thur-Sat. **Admission** (incl 1 drink) €5 with flyer and before 2am; €10 without flyer & after 2am. **No credit cards. Map** p345 B6.

After a facelift and a change of management, this ancient former brothel-turned-rock-club is now indulging Spain's obsession for Depeche Mode and other newly trendy '80s sounds, alongside the typical floppy-haired party fare from the likes of Franz Ferdinand, the Strokes et al. A long hallway bar leads on to the main dancefloor, where fairground figures leer from the stage and wallflowers gaze from the mezzanine. In its previous incarnation, such well-known figures as Gilles Peterson, King Britt and Norman Jay all played here.

Sidecar Factory Club

Plaça Reial 7 (93 302 15 86/www.sidecar factoryclub.com). Metro Liceu. **Open** 6pm-4.30am Tue-Thur, Sun; 6pm-5am Fri, Sat. **Admission** (incl 1 drink) €4-€6 before 2am Tue-Thur, Sun; €5-€7 before 2am Fri, Sat. **Gigs** €5-€15. **No credit cards. Map** p345 B6.

Sidecar still has all the ballsy attitude of the spit 'n' sawdust rock club that it once was and, while the gigs and weekend's rock-pop extravaganza continue to pack in the local indie kids and Interrailers, the programming has diversified considerably to include DJs playing breakbeat on Wednesdays and Brazilian tunes on Tuesdays.

Born & Sant Pere

Club Mix

C/Comerç 21 (93 319 46 96/www.clubmixbcn.com). Metro Jaume I. **Open** 8pm-3am daily. **Admission** free. **Credit** MC, V. **Map** p345 F5.

Mix is an urbane and classy DJ bar serving cocktails and 'international tapas' to a grown-up, dressed-up crowd. As well as occasional live acts (most regularly, jazz on Wednesdays), DJs spin rare groove, neo soul and the like from a deeply cool booth set high up in a copper-panelled wall.

Diobar

C/Marquès de l'Argentera 27 (93 221 19 39). Metro Barceloneta. **Open** 11pm-3am Thur-Sat. **Admission** free. **Credit** MC, V. **Map** p345 F7.

The latest underground hit has popped up in one of the most unlikely places imaginable – the basement of a Greek restaurant. Forget Zorba and plate smasking, from Thursday through Saturday nights, this cosy, stone-walled space transforms into a temple of funk and soul as the sofas and dancefloor host lounging urbanites and DJ Fred Spider hits the decks.

Dr Astin

C/Abaixadors 9 (mobile 676 220 736). Metro Jaume I. **Open** 11pm-2.30am Mon-Thur; 11pm-3am Fri, Sat. **Admission** free. **No credit cards. Map** p345 D6.

Minute and slightly grungy, the good Dr Astin has been hammering out house and techno beats for years. The Born's hipsters come here to get in to their groove before heading on out to the bigger venues. Since it's free and completely soundproofed, it makes for a good place to start the night.

Arts & Entertainment

Don't say we didn't warn you. **Baja Beach**. *See p254.*

Raval

Aurora

C/Aurora 7 (93 442 30 44/mobile 680 518 250).
Metro Paral·lel. **Open** 8pm-2.30am Mon-Thur;
9.30pm-3am Fri, Sat. **Admission** free. **No credit
cards. Map** p342 E10.

Aurora used to be an unkempt ramshackle place, but
it was given a makeover a few years ago and now
has a considerably smarter look. It's today inhabited by arty types who remain here well into the small
hours, and its mini dancefloor appeals to students
and Raval locals, who cram on to it for weekends of
varied DJ sounds. During the week, the cocktails and
the conversation forthcoming from the party-hun-
gry bar staff will keep you sustained at the bar till
the clock strikes 'close'.

Bar Pastis

C/Santa Mònica 4 (93 318 79 80). Metro Drassanes.
Open 7.30pm-2am Tue-Thur, Sun; 7.30pm-3am Fri,
Sat. **Admission** free. **Credit** AmEx, MC, V.
Map p345 A7.

This quintessentially Gallic bar once served *pastis*
to the visiting sailors and the various undesirable
denizens of the Barrio Chino underworld. It has since
moved on but, thankfully, not much: it still has a
louche Marseilles feel, floor-to-ceiling indecipherable
oil paintings (painted by the original owner when he
was drunk, apparently), Edith Piaf gracing the

stereo, and latter day troubadours on Tuesdays,
Wednesdays and Sundays. It's kind of touristy these
days, but if your Spanish is up for it there are enough
regular locals here who can tell you what the Raval
was really like pre-Olympic Games.

Big Bang

C/Botella 7 (93 443 28 13/www.bigbangbcn.net).
Metro Liceu or Sant Antoni. **Open** *Bar* 9.30pm-
2.30am Wed, Thur, Sun; 10.15pm-3am Fri, Sat. **Gigs**
around 10.30pm-1am Fri, Sat. *Jam sessions* 11pm-
1am Wed, Thur, Sun. **Admission** *Bar & jam
sessions* free. *Gigs* prices vary. **No credit cards.**
Map p342 E10.

Brothers Jesús, Robert and Ran of heavy rock group
DE KALLE run Big Bang, one of the few ungentri-
fied bars in the Raval and one of the few hosting free
rock jam sessions. On top of the gigs, throw in film
nights on Thursdays, a cruddy table football
machine and straight-down-the-line bar staff, and it's
no surprise that it attracts all sorts – crusty types,
ageing rockers, boyz from the 'hood and some slightly confused-looking backpackers. Bang on the shutters if you're wandering the streets after everything
else has closed to try your luck at getting a drink.

La Concha

C/Guàrdia 14 (93 302 41 18). Metro Drassanes.
Open 5pm-2.30am Mon-Thur, Sun; 5pm-3am Fri,
Sat. **Admission** free. **No credit cards.**
Map p345 A6.

Still in fashion. **Club Catwalk**. *See p255.*

The often imitated, never bettered, original drag queen cabaret La Concha closed down at the end of 2006, but resurfaced in a newly botoxed version of its former self: the meringue ceiling studded with sea shells and fishing net alas is a thing of the past.

Fellini
C/La Rambla 27 (93 272 49 80/www.clubfellini.com). Metro Liceu. **Open** midnight-5am Mon-Sat. **Admission** Mon-Thur free before 1.30am, €6 before 3am, €9 afterwards. Fri, Sat €9-€12. **No credit cards. Map** p345 A6.

Due to its location on the Rambla, Fellini, with its themed club spaces, has had to work pretty hard to earn kudos but, with its manic flyering and some good programming, it's managed to establish itself as the most talked-about new club in town. The monthly polysexual Puticlub parties are quite mixed and lots of fun, and the last Thursday of the month is the semi-legendary Mond Club, with everyone from the Glimmers to Freelance Hellraiser playing dancey rock and rocky dance for a muso crowd.

Guru
C/Nou de la Rambla 22 (93 318 08 40/www. gurubarcelona.com). Metro Liceu. **Open** 8pm-3am daily. **Admission** free. **No credit cards. Map** p345 A6.

Guru has its eyes set on becoming the latest addition to the Raval bar scene's sleekification, but, palm trees and mood lighting aside, you can't help think-

ing that, with its white padded walls, it looks rather like a rest room for the suicidal. As a newcomer in tourist central, it hasn't yet achieved the exclusive status it's aiming for and, as such, Cosmo-sipping, black-clad Parisians are still having to deal with gangs of tipsy Scousers hopping about madly to live salsa. For the moment.

Jazz Sí Club
C/Requesens 2 (93 329 00 20/www.tallerdemusics. com). Metro Sant Antoni. **Open** 5pm-2.30am Mon-Thur, Sun; 5pm-3am Fri, Sat. **Admission** free. **No credit cards. Map** p342 E10.

This tiny music-school auditorium-cum-bar is a space where students, teachers and music lovers can meet, perform and listen: heaven or hell depending on your preference. Each night is dedicated to a different musical genre: trad jazz on Mondays, pop/rock/blues jams on Tuesdays, jazz jams on Wednesdays, Cuban music on Thursdays, flamenco on Fridays, rock on Saturdays and Sundays. A place for people who are serious about their music.

Moog
C/Arc del Teatre 3 (93 301 72 82/www. masimas.com). Metro Drassanes. **Open** midnight-5am daily. **Admission** €9. **Credit** DC, MC, V. **Map** p345 A7.

Moog's an odd club; almost like partying on an aeroplane: it's long, narrow and enclosed, with full-blast air-conditioning and service with a smile, although thankfully not quite as cramped as economy class. Some fine techno and house keep everything ticking along just right; Angel Molina, Laurent Garnier and Jeff Mills, among countless others, have all played here, with Wednesday nights being especially popular. Upstairs there's a tiny concession to those not feeling the bleeps – an even smaller dancefloor that plays R&B and 1970s tunes into the night.

La Paloma

C/Tigre 27 (93 301 68 97/www.lapaloma-bcn.com). Metro Universitat. **Open** 6-9.30pm, 11.30pm-5am Thur; 6-9.30pm, 11.30pm-2am; 2.30-5am Fri, Sat; 5.45-9.45pm Sun. **Admission** (incl 1 drink) €3-€8. **Credit** (bar only) MC, V. **Map** p342 E9.

Although La Paloma is currently closed as it fights with the Ajuntament and its neighbours about noise pollution, the management promises, and we certainly hope, that it will reopen sometime soon. Since it's Barcelona's most extraordinary club, we have retained its listing in the hope that you'll eventually be able to see what we're excited about. Arrive early and you'll see older *barcelonins*, in full evening wear elegantly circling the dancefloor. Take a seat in one of the plush balconies to admire the chandeliers and belle époque fittings. Once the foxtrot and tango have finished, DJs mix funk and Latin on Thursdays, with everything from electro to acid at the weekend. But telephone first before going; we don't know how this battle will end. *Photo p248.*

Zentraus

Rambla del Raval 41 (93 443 80 78/www. zentraus.com). Metro Liceu. **Open** noon-5pm Mon; noon-2.30am Tue-Thur; noon-3am Fri, Sat. Closed mid Aug-mid Sept. **Admission** free. **No credit cards**. **Map** p342 E10.

Stepping into this minimalist black, grey and red setting, you could forget that you're smack in the middle of the Raval and not in some uptown dig. The uplit bar, black-clad bartenders and completely soundproofed dancefloor make this a prime hotspot for beat-seekers in the area, bringing in a diverse and unpredictable crowd. The harder side of techno, electro, drum 'n' bass, breakbeats and minimal house normally take control of the dancefloor.

Barceloneta & the Ports

Around the right-angled quayside of the Port Olímpic, you'll find dance bars interspersed with seafood restaurants, fast-food outlets, ice-cream parlours, coffee shops and mock-Irish pubs; with video screens, glittery lights and go-go girls and boys in abundance, it makes little difference which one you choose.

Baja Beach

Passeig Marítim 34 (93 225 91 00/www.baja beach.es). Metro Ciutadella-Vila Olímpica. **Open** *June-Oct* 11am-midnight Mon-Wed, Sun; 11am-6am

Le Kasbah.

Thur-Sat. *Nov-May* 11am-6am Thur-Sat; 11am-midnight Sun. **Admission** (incl 1 drink) Wed €10, €12 Thur, Sun; €14 Fri; €18 Sat. **Credit** AmEx, MC, V. **Map** p343 J13.
Baja Beach, the epitome of the Port Olímpic's brashness, is like one endless wedding disco, student night and Planet Hollywood extravaganza rolled into one but, providing you've got money to spend, there's loads of fun to be had. Nearly nude barstaff play on espaneesh holiday-romance fantasies, blowing whistles and serving up body-shots to everyone from fresh-faced school leavers (turning green) to businesstrippers (turning 50). This is not a place for the shy and retiring. Meanwhile, the DJ commands from his speedboat overlooking the dancefloor, giving the masses what they want: cheeeese. *Photo p252.*

CDLC
Passeig Marítim 32 (93 224 0470/www.cdlc barcelona.com). Metro Ciutadella-Vila Olímpica. **Open** 10pm-2.30am Mon-Wed; noon-3am Thur-Sun. **Admission** free. **Credit** AmEx, MC, V. **Map** p343 J13.
Carpe Diem Lounge Club remains at the forefront of Barcelona's splash-the-cash, see-and-be-seen celeb circuit – the white beds flanking the dancefloor, guarded by a clipboarded hostess, are perfect for showing everyone who's the daddy. Or, for those not celebrating six-figure record deals, funky house and a busy terrace provide an opportunity for mere mortals (and models) to mingle and discuss, first, who's going to finance their next drink and, secondly, how to get chatting to whichever member of the Barça team that has just walked in.

Club Catwalk
C/Ramon Trias Fargas s/n (93 221 61 61/www. clubcatwalk.net). Metro Ciutadella-Vila Olímpica. **Open** midnight-5.30am Wed-Sun. **Admission** €15-€18. **Credit** DC, MC, V. **Map** p343 J13.
Maybe it's the name or maybe it's the location (slap bang under the celeb-tastic Hotel Arts), but most of the Catwalk queue seems to think they're headed straight for the VIP room – that's crisp white collars and gold for the boys and short, short skirts for the girls. Inside it's suitably snazzy; upstairs there's R&B and hip hop, but the main house room is where most of the action is, with regular appearances from the likes of Erick Morillo and Roger Sánchez keeping the club's prestige firmly intact. *Photo p253.*

Le Kasbah
Plaça Pau Vilà (Palau del Mar) (93 238 07 22/ www.ottozutz.com). Metro Barceloneta. **Open** 11pm-3am daily. **Admission** free. **Credit** AmEx, MC, V. **Map** p345 E8.
A white awning over terrace tables heralds the entrance to this louche bar behind the Palau de Mar. Inside, a North African harem look seduces a young and up-for-it mix of tourists and students on to its plush cushions for a cocktail or two before heading on out to other venues. But as the night progresses, so does the music, from chill-out early in the night to full-on boogie after midnight.

Mondo
Edifici IMAX, Moll d'Espanya (93 221 39 11/ www.mondobcn.com). Metro Barceloneta or Drassanes. **Open** 11.30pm-3am Wed-Sat. **Credit** MC, V. **Map** p342 G12.
Arrive by yacht or Jaguar – anything less might not get you past the door. Upscale dining alongside amazing views of the port precede late-night caviar and champagne house parties with DJs from Hed Kandi and Hotel Costes. Multiple intimate VIP rooms provide privacy, pleasure and prestige.

Shôko
Passeig Marítim 36 (93 225 92 03/www.shoko.biz). Metro Ciutadella-Vila Olímpica. **Open** 11.30pm-3am daily. **Admission** free. **Credit** AmEx, MC, V. **Map** p343 J13.
Another restaurant-club in the Port Olímpic. The tried and tested formula continues to go down a treat with a CDLC-like crowd and meanwhile, outside on the terrace, civilised sets of chino-clad tourists recline on the comfy beds sipping cocktails.

Suite Royale
Passeig Joan de Borbó 54 (93 268 00 12). Metro Barceloneta. **Open** 10pm-3am daily. **Admission** free. **Credit** MC, V. **Map** p345 E8.
Barcelona night owls suffered last year when hotspot Café Royale closed, but the same crew have revamped the club in a new portside hotel. Jazz-funk DJ Fred Guzzo still has his swing, while the softly lit, retro bachelor pad decor has been successfully reproduced in a cosy subterranean setting.

Montjuïc & Poble Sec

Barcelona Rouge
C/Poeta Cabanyes 21 (93 442 49 85). Metro Paral·lel. **Open** 11pm-4am Tue-Sat. **Admission** free. **No credit cards**. **Map** p342 D11.
A hidey hole of a place tucke away in one of Barcelona's more unsung *barris*. It's small enough to get packed even though it's little known, hard to get into and hard on the wallet once you're inside. Should you decide to make the trip, there's ambient music, good cocktails and battered sofas draped with foreign and local thirtysomethings – those with a bit of money and a bit of class who want to avoid the more obvious nightspots. Occasionally, there's a performance or two. Ring the buzzer to get in.

Maumau
C/Fontrodona 33 (93 441 80 15/www. maumaunderground.com). Metro Paral·lel. **Open** 11pm-2.30am Thur; 11pm-3am Fri, Sat; 7pm-midnight Sun. **Admission** (membership) €5. **No credit cards**. **Map** p342 D11.
Recently renovated to include, among other things, a wheelchair ramp (unusual) and better lavatories (very welcome), Maumau is our long-time favourite among the Poble Sec haunts. Behind the anonymous grey door (ring the bell in order to get in), first timers to this likeable little chill-out club pay €5 to become

Arts & Entertainment

members. In practice, though, it rarely charges out-of-towners. Inside, a large warehouse space is humanised with colourful projections, IKEA-style sofas and scatter cushions, and a friendly, laid-back crowd. DJ Wakanda schools us in the finer points of deep house, jazz, funk or whatever other musical development has currently taken his fancy.

Sala Apolo

C/Nou de la Rambla 113 (93 441 40 01/www.sala-apolo.com). Metro Paral·lel. **Open** midnight-5am Wed, Thur; midnight-7am Fri, Sat; 10.30pm-3am Sun. **Admission** varies. **No credit cards**. **Map** p342 E11.
Sala Apolo, one of Barcelona's most popular clubs, is a 1940s dancehall, with all that implies for atmosphere (good) and acoustics (bad). A smaller space downstairs features intimate relaxed gigs from up-and-coming talent, while upstairs on Wednesdays and Thursdays is a more upbeat affair, with an international crowd of music buffs, from hipster geeks to hip-hop gals, trekking across the Raval for funk and Latin grooves from the likes of Kid Koala and Gotan Project. There are still epic queues for the weekend's bleeping techno extravaganza, Nitsa.

La Terrrazza

Poble Espanyol, Avda Marquès de Comillas s/n (93 272 49 80/www.laterrrazza.com). Metro Espanya. **Open** May-mid October midnight-6am Thur-Sat. **Admission** (incl 1 drink) €18 without flyer, €15 with flyer. **Credit** MC, V. **Map** p339 A9/B9.
Despite being Barcelona's most famous club, La Terrrazza closed in 2005 after noise complaints from local residents. Thankfully, it reopened in May 2006 and reclaimed its crown as the city's top club in the manner of one born to rule. Driven by resident DJ Sergio Patricio, the club packs them in on its huge outdoor space that moves to a tech house beat. Compilation albums, international guest DJs and partner club Fellini in La Rambla (*see p253*) make it one energetic enterprise. If you get to go to only one nightclub in Barcelona, or Spain for that matter, make it this one. A long cold drink on a balmy night checking out the eye candy prancing, preening and boogieing is pretty hard to beat.

Tinta Roja

C/Creu dels Molers 17 (93 443 32 43/www.tintaroja. net). Metro Poble Sec. **Open** *Bar* 8pm-2am Wed, Thur; 8pm-3am Fri, Sat; 7pm-1am Sun. *Shows* 10pm-midnight Wed-Sat. Closed 2wks Aug. **Admission** *Bar* free. *Shows* (incl 1 drink) €8-€10. **No credit cards**. **Map** p339 D10.
Word has it that this smooth and mysterious club was once a dairy farm. Push through the depths of the bar to be transported to a Buenos Aires bordello/theatre/circus/cabaret by plush red velvet sofas, smoochy niches and ancient ticket booth. It's an atmospheric place to go for a late-ish drink, and a distinctly different entertainment experience from Friday to Sunday when there are performances of tango, jazz and flamenco in a small theatre at the back. Tango classes are also offered.

The Eixample

Antilla BCN Latin Club

C/Aragó 141 (93 451 45 64/www.antillasalsa.com). Metro Urgell. **Open** 11pm-3.30am Mon-Wed, Sun; 11pm-4.30am Fri, Sat. **Gigs** around 1am. **Admission** (incl 1 drink) €10. **No credit cards**. **Map** p340 E8.
The Antilla prides itself on being a 'Caribbean cultural centre', hosting exhibitions and publishing its magazine Antilla News. But, its true calling lies in being the self-claimed best salsateca in town, offering dance classes (including acrobatic salsa and Afro-Cuban styles) and a solid programme of live music, which covers all Latin flavours from son to merengue and Latin jazz.

Astoria

C/Paris 193 (93 200 98 25/www.grupocostaeste.com/ astoria). Metro Diagonal. **Open** 11.30pm-2.30am Tue-Thur, Sun; 11.30pm-3.30am Fri, Sat. Closed Aug. **Admission** free. **Credit** AmEx, MC, V. **Map** p340 F6.
From the same people who brought you Bucaro and the Sutton Club, Astoria offers a break from the norm. For a start, the club is housed in a converted 1950s cinema, which means the projections are big and actually watchable. There are three bars, so you're spared endless queues; there's plenty of comfortable seating along with a small dancefloor; and if you're very wonderful, you may get to sit on a heart-shaped cushion in the tiny VIP area. With all this going for it, it has inevitably become the domain of Barcelona's moneyed classes.

Bucaro

C/Aribau 195 (93 209 65 62/www.grupocostaeste. com/bucaro). FGC Provença. **Open** 11.30pm-4.30am Mon-Thur; 11pm-5.50am Fri, Sat. **Admission** free before 1am (incl. one drink) €10 after. **Credit** AmEx, MC, V. **Map** p340 F5.
Looking a tad jaded, Bucaro's worn leather sofas and grubby pouffes still manage to pull a crowd of glamour pusses. With the giant skylight looming above the dancefloor like a portal to another world, and a mezzanine from where you can stalk your prey, this is a place that knows class when it sees it. Drinks are a couple of euros more expensive if you're sitting at a table. A list of dress code dos and don'ts and a friendly but firm bouncer to enforce them, greet you at the entrance.

Buda Restaurante

C/Pau Claris 92 (93 318 42 52/www.budarestaurante. com). Metro Catalunya. **Open** 9pm-3am daily. **Admission** free. **Credit** MC, V. **Map** p344 D1.
The centre of Barcelona is strangely devoid of glamorous nightspots, or at least it was until Buda came along. The place has lots of throne-style furniture and gilded wallpaper, topped off with a colossal chandelier. The laid-back nature of the staff (dancing on the bar seems completely acceptable) and upbeat house music make it excellent for drinks and an ogle.

Jazz it up

As a musical metropolis, Barcelona is something of a mixed bag. Aside from excellent opera, classical music is not well catered for and, aside from a handful of concerts, the fare on offer is generally of a mainstream, bums-on-seats type. On the other hand, despite not being 'Spain', it is a great city to hear that most Spanish of music, flamenco, especially at the festivals of Nou Barris and Ciutat Vella, and during the excellent annual Festival de la Guitarra. In the course of a year, most of the big flamenco stars of the day will pass through the city, and there is a thriving local scene.

The stand-out music festival, however, is the annual **Barcelona International Jazz Festival**, which over the years has established itself as one of the most important jazz festivals to be found anywhere in the world, putting together slates of big names while not stinting on giving a platform to homegrown talent (boosted by the fact that a number of American jazz musicians have made the city their home).

The festival runs from October to December and is spread over a number of venues, principally l'Auditori, the Palau de la Música Catalunya and Luz de Gas, in ascending order of intimacy. L'Auditori is a typical modern concert hall, which is to say it

has great acoustics but rather less atmosphere than Mars. Fine, therefore, for the stand-out show of the 2006 festival, the pianist Brad Mehldau's solo concert, but a bit on the cold side for the recent Wayne Shorter and Herbie Hancock gigs.

Any music lover should go to a concert of whatever kind in the Palau de la Música just for the experience of hearing music in this extraordinary venue. Claimed as the first steel-framed building in the world, this fabulous hall, the work of Modernista architect Domènech i Montaner, was not designed with acoustics in mind, although it was commissioned by a choir, and the abundance of glass is a sound mixer's nightmare. However, much has been done to soften the sound in recent years. Luz de Gas has great atmosphere and good sound but, as it is less central, doesn't host the headline gigs.

Whatever the venues, it's the bill that gives the Barcelona festival its credibility. While other festivals try to 'soften' the line-up with acts that aren't strictly jazz, in Barcelona they only occasionally resort to a Norah Jones or a Madeleine Peyroux to boost the press previews, and are not afraid to put on relatively inaccessible acts such as Abbey Lincoln or Joe Lovano. For information and acts see www.theproject.cat.

La Pedrera de Nit.

City Hall

Rambla Catalunya 2-4 (93 317 21 77/www.grupo-ottozutz.com). Metro Catalunya. **Open** midnight-6am Tue-Sun. **Admission** (incl 1 drink) €12. **Credit** (door only) MC, V. **Map** p344 C1.

City Hall ain't that big, but it is surprisingly popular with Barcelona's night watch. The music is mixed, from deep house to electro rock, and there's an older post-(pre-?) work crowd joining the young, tanned and skinny to show the dancefloors some love. Outside, the terrace is a veritable (and in summer, literal) melting pot of tourists and locals, who rub shoulders under the watchful (and definitely anti-pot-smoking) eye of the bouncer.

Danzarama

Gran Via de les Corts Catalanes 604 (93 301 97 43/reservations 93 342 5070/www.gruposalsitas.com). Metro Universitat. **Open** 7am-3am Mon-Sat. **Admission** free. **Credit** AmEx, DC, MC, V. **Map** p342 F8.

Make your way past the flash restaurant upstairs – we're talking white sofas swinging from the ceiling – and down on to the brick-walled, loud dancefloor. With no entry charge and lots of tables, Danzarama has become a popular pre-party venue with a free shuttle bus and thumping tunes making up for the club-priced drinks.

Distrito Diagonal

Avda Diagonal 442 (mobile 607 113 602/www.distritodiagonal.com). Metro Diagonal. **Open** midnight-6am Fri, Sat. **Admission** free before 3am, (incl 1 drink) €15 after. **No credit cards**. **Map** p340 G6.

Distrito Diagonal attracts a slightly older crowd with an easygoing atmosphere. The venue's bathed in red light, there are sounds from nu jazz to deep house and plenty of chairs to sink into. It's become a sought-after place for small promoters and one-off parties, which means the music can veer anywhere from Bollywood to hip hop.

Luz de Gas

C/Muntaner 246 (93 209 77 11/www.luzdegas.com). FGC Muntaner. **Open** *Club* 11.30pm-5am daily. **Gigs** 12.30am daily. **Admission** (incl 1 drink) €18. **Credit** AmEx, DC, MC, V. **Map** p340 E5.

This lovingly converted old music hall, garnished with chandeliers and classical friezes, is a real stayer. In between the visits from international 'names' like Monica Green, you'll find nightly residencies: blues on Mondays, Dixieland jazz on Tuesdays, and disco on Wednesdays.

La Pedrera de Nit

C/Provença 261-265 (93 484 59 00/www.caixacatalunya.es/obrasocial). Metro Diagonal. **Open** *July* 9-11.30pm Fri, Sat. Closed Aug-June. **Admission** (incl 1 drink) €12. **Credit** MC, V. **Map** 340 G7.

In summer, the swerving, rolling roof terrace of Gaudí's visionary La Pedrera is open on Friday and Saturday evenings for drinks, live music and fine views of the city. It's definitely a stand, sip and look

contemplative sort of evening. Concerts are at 10pm and book as far in advance as possible, as the shows only take place in July and tickets sell fast.

Raum

Gran Via 593 (mobile 600 422 318/www.raum.es). Metro Universitat. **Open** midnight-5am Thur. **Admission** €10. **No credit cards**. **Map** p340 F8.

Raum's cold industrial decor lends itself well to this weekly electronic night, where the tunes run the gamut from minimal to hard techno to the occasional chunk of deep electro-house. The Thursday slot ensures that the crowd – a chatty bunch of expats and locals – come for the tunes rather than to pose among the steel pillars and lunar-style projections.

Santa Locura

C/Consell de Cent 294 (93 200 14 66). Metro Passeig de Gràcia. **Open** midnight-5.30am Thur-Sat. **Admission** €10 one drink, €15 two drinks. **Credit** V. **Map** p342 F8.

Perhaps Barcelona's most extraordinary (if that's the right word) clubbing experience, Santa Locura has three floors filled with weird and wonderful nocturnal pleasures: get married at the bar; watch a Chippendale-style show; plead guilty at the confessional box; and hit the dancefloor to the music of Kylie and Sophie Ellis-Bextor. *Photo p261.*

Space Barcelona

C/Tarragona 141-147 (93 426 84 44/www.spacebarcelona.com). Metro Tarragona. **Open** midnight-6am Fri, Sat; 9pm-3am Sun. **Admission** (incl 1 drink) €15 without flyer; €12 with flyer. **No credit cards**. **Map** p339 C7.

Like its superclub rival Pacha, Space tries desperately to cash in on Barcelona's Balearic party aspirations and with equally limited success. A young crowd of fashionistas and diehard clubbers descends en masse to strike poses under the deep lights and pounding bass, or to lean against one of the four bars. Occasional appearances from the likes of Carl Cox keep the brand's reputation safe.

Poblenou

Razzmatazz

C/Almogàvers 122 (93 320 82 00/www.salarazzmatazz.com). Metro Bogatell or Marina. **Open** 1-5am Fri, Sat. **Admission** varies. **Credit** V. **Map** p343 L10.

Skinny jeans, battered Converse and a heavy dose of party-rock dominate this warehouse superclub, and while some of the punters are a bit young and the toilets a bit vile, line-ups are on the ball, diverse and international. As it's essentially five clubs in one, if you're tired of 2 ManyDjs or Miss Kittin in the main Razz Room, you can head upstairs to check out Queens of Noize, Four Tet or Tiga playing the Loft. It's also one of the best venues for live music, with acts from Arctic Monkeys to Queens of the Stone Age to, no word of a lie, Bananarama, producing awesome crowd-surfing mayhem.

Arts & Entertainment

Gràcia

El Dorado

Plaça del Sol 4 (93 237 36 96/mobile 607 548 273).
Metro Fontana. **Open** *May-Sept* 7pm-2.30am Mon-
Thur; 7pm-3am Fri, Sat. *Oct-Apr* 10pm-2.30am Tue-
Thur; 10pm-3am Fri, Sat. **Admission** free. **Credit**
MC, V. **Map** p340 G5.

El Dorado is the nightclub equivalent of your disco
night at the local pub in some English village. A
place for the locals, it's as unpretentious as they
come – a cosy (sometimes too cosy) bar/dancefloor
that doesn't charge a fortune for drinks and
unashamedly plays the hits, from local heroes
Estopa through to Michael Jackson.

Gusto

*C/Francisco Giner 24 (no phone) com). Metro
Diagonal.* **Open** 10pm-2.30am Tue-Thur; 10pm-
3am Fri, Sat. **Admission** free. **No credit cards**.
Map p340 G6.

Gusto gets full to bursting on weekend nights, seemingly due to one rather bizarre feature – past the normal but attractive red-painted front bar, where a DJ
plays chilled electronica, a quirky back room lures
a young crowd with a floor covered in sand.
Actually, the fact that it's Gràcia's funkiest space by
a long shot might be another reason.

KGB

*C/Alegre de Dalt 55 (93 210 59 06/www.salakgb.
net). Metro Joanic.* **Open** 1-6am Thur, Fri, Sat.
Admission free before 3am with flyer; (incl
1 drink) €12 after 3am or without flyer. **Gigs**
varies. **No credit cards**. **Map** p341 J4.

KGB is a cavern-like space that was, in its heyday,
the rock 'n' roll disco barn capital of the city and the
'after' where Sidecar heads would bolt to at 6am on
the weekend. It still remains loud, whether featuring concerts or DJ sessions. The concerts tend
towards rock and hip hop, the DJ sets feature reg-
gae, hip hop, techno electro house and house.
Thursdays have rumba music to get you dancing.

Otto Zutz

*C/Lincoln 15 (93 238 07 22/www.grupo-ottozutz.
com). FGC Gràcia.* **Open** midnight-5am Tue, Wed;
midnight-5.30am Thur-Sat. **Admission** (incl 1 drink)
€15. **Credit** AmEx, DC, MC, V. **Map** p340 F4.

Run by the same people as City Hall, Otto Zutz has
a similar feel to its more central sister club, but would
do well to be a little less pretentious and a little more
concerned with the music. Three floors of an old textile factory feature R&B, hip hop and some electro,
but the main focus is on same old not-so-funky house.
Not that the uptown boys and girls, who arrive by
the Audi-load, seem to care. The monthly Poker Flat
parties are the exception to the rule.

Universal

*C/Marià Cubí 182 bis-184 (93 201 35 96/www.
grupocostaeste.com). FGC Muntaner.* **Open** 11pm-
3.30am Mon-Thur; 11pm-5am Fri, Sat. **Admission**
free. **Credit** AmEx, MC, V. **Map** p340 E5.

One of a very few clubs in the city that caters to an
older, well-dressed crowd, Universal doesn't charge
admission, but the drink prices are steep as a result.
Renovations by the designer of the Salsitas chain
have brought slide projections in the upstairs chill-
out area, along with a sharper look downstairs. Later,
the music moves from downtempo to soft house,
which works the crowd up to a gentle shimmy.

Vinilo

*C/Matilde 2 (mobile 626 464 759/http://vinilus.
blogspot.com). Metro Fontana.* **Open** 8pm-2.30am
Mon-Thur, Sun; 7pm-3am Fri, Sat. **Admission** free.
No credit cards. **Map** p340 G5.

A venue for grown-ups like this was long overdue in
Gràcia, indeed in Barcelona. Local musician Jordi
opened this cosy red-velveted bar/café almost a year
ago and he's having rip-roaring success. Doubling
up as a casual eating place that serves up damn fine
savoury and sweet crêpes, Vinilo gets a mention in
this section simply because of its immaculate music
selection – Sparklehorse, Rufus Wainwright, Antony
and the Johnsons, Coco Rosie and the Sleepy Jackson
all get good runs here, so too do the Beatles and Pink
Floyd. No chill-out in sight and it's a good bet that
most of his clients come in for that reason. A place
that comes into its own during the colder months.

Other areas

Bikini

*C/Déu i Mata 105, Les Corts (93 322 08 00/www.
bikinibcn.com). Metro Les Corts or Maria Cristina.*
Open *Club* midnight-5am Wed-Sat; 8.30pm-5am Sun.
Admission (incl 1 drink) €15. **Credit** MC, V.
Map p338 C5.

A legendary Barcelona venue, Bikini is hard to find
in the soulless streets behind the L'Illa shopping centre, but it's worth seeking out for top-flight gigs by
serious musicians of any stripe, from Femi Kuti to
the Thievery Corporation, Marianne Faithfull and
Amp Fiddler. After the gigs, stay for club nights
with house, funk and hip hop on the turntables. On
Sunday, watch Barça football matches on the big
screen from 8.30pm, then party on to the latest dance
sounds from 10.30pm.

Danzatoria

*Avda Tibidabo 61, Tibidabo (93 211 62 61/
www.danzatoria-barcelona.com). FGC Avda Tibidabo
then 10min walk.* **Open** *Club* 11pm-2.30pm Tue,
Wed; 11.30pm-3am Thur-Sat. *Restaurant* 9-11.30pm
Tue-Sat. **Admission** free. **Credit** AmEx, DC, MC, V.
The uptown location attracts an upscale crowd to
this spectacular converted manor house on a hill
overlooking Barcelona. If you want to hang with the
hipsters then climb the stairs: the hipness factor goes
up as you ascend the club's glamour-glutted storeys.
Preened flesh is shaken on hothouse dancefloors, or
laid across sofas hanging from the ceiling in the
chill-out lounges. We've had reports of snotty staff,
and the champagne is expensive, but the gardens
are beautiful, as are the people.

Arts & Entertainment

Santa Locura. See p259.

Elephant

Passeig dels Til·lers 1, Pedralbes (93 334 02 58/
www.elephantbcn.com). Metro Palau Reial. **Open**
11.30pm-4am Wed, 11.30pm-5am Thu Fri, Sat.
Admission free Wed, €12 Thu, Fri, Sat. **Credit**
MC, V. **Map** 338 A2.
If you have a Porsche and a model girlfriend, this is
where you meet your peers. Housed in a converted
mansion, Elephant is as elegant and hi-design as its
customers. The big attraction is the outdoor bar and
terrace dancefloor – though the low-key, low-volume
(due to the neighbours' complaints) house music
doesn't inspire much hands-in-the-air action.

Espacio Movistar

C/Martí i Franquesa, Parc de Bederrida, Zona
Universitària (www.espacio.movistar.es/tickets 902
150 025/www.ticktackticket.com). Metro Palau Reial.
Open times vary. **Admission** prices vary. **Credit**
AmEx, DC, MC, V.
Up in the vicinity of Nou Camp, the main attraction
of this mammoth two-tier white tent, owned by
telecommunications giant Telefónica, is a 1,000sq m
(10,800sq ft) concert space that plays host to national and international money-spinning acts such as
Alejandro Sanz, Arctic Monkeys and Scissor Sisters,
plus music festivals and sporadic cinema and audio-
visual events. There's also an exhibition space, a
restaurant, a cybercafé and a chill-out zone, where
you can almost escape the feeling of being digested
by a giant publicity machine.

Mirablau

Plaça Doctor Andreu 1, Tibidabo (93 418 58 79).
FGC Avda Tibidabo then Tramvia Blau. **Open**
11am-4am Mon-Thur; 11am-5.30am Fri-Sun.
Admission free. **Credit** V.
It doesn't get any more uptown than this, geographically and socially. Located at the top of Tibidabo,
this small bar is packed with the high rollers of
Barcelona, from local footballers living on the hill to
international businessmen on the company card. Its
main attraction is the breathtaking view.

Pacha

Avda Doctor Marañon 17, Zona Universitària (93
334 32 33/www.clubpachabcn.com). Metro Zona
Universitària. **Open** *June-Sept* midnight-6am daily.
Oct-May midnight-6am Thu-Sun. **Admission** (incl 1
drink) €15. **Credit** MC, V.
When Pacha was set to open in Barcelona a few
years back, the queues of potential barstaff were so
long that they made the evening news. Such is the
power of the global clubbing giant that armies of
tourists, out-of-towners and locals, many deluded
about their party-animal status, continue rolling up
for fair sound quality, a so-so venue and heaps of
attitude. Regular sets from David Guetta, Paul
Oakenfold and Jeff Mills etc are more worthwhile.

Sala Salamandra

Avda Carrilet 301, L'Hospitalet (93 337 06 02/www.
salamandra.cat). Metro A Carrilet. **Open** midnight-
5am Fri, Sat. **Admission** *Gigs* Prices vary. *Club* €8
after 2am. **No credit cards.**
It's often lamented that some of Barcelona's best
home-grown acts are hard to see in Barcelona outside of festivals. But that's not strictly true. If you're
happy to travel 30 minutes on the metro's red line to
L'Hospitalet, you'll find a 500-person venue, which
doubles as a nightclub, that regularly hosts the
cream of local artists, such as Macaco, Muchachito
Bombo Infierno, Kinky Beat, as well as Spanish acts
like Amparanoia. Local and visiting DJs take over
afterwards. It also promotes emerging Catalan musicians, so you may well discover the next big thing
too. Drawing a mainly local crowd, the atmosphere's
unprentious and the drinks fairly cheap.

Arts & Entertainment

Performing Arts

Barcelonaaahhh!

Classical Music & Opera

Barcelona's rich musical heritage was, until quite recently, easier to appreciate on CD than live. But with the addition of **L'Auditori** and the appearance of a number of smaller venues, including the **Auditori Winterthur**, this has changed. Barcelona's two most venerable institutions are also experiencing something of a renaissance: the **Liceu** has begun to take more risks with its programming policy and the extraordinary **Palau de la Música Catalana** is undergoing a facelift to mark its centenary; major renovations in 2004 also added a modern subterranean auditorium. These venue changes have been supplemented by a subtle switch in repertoire. The canon still reigns, of course. But, as a younger generation of cultural programmers takes charge, newer work has also found an audience. You no longer have to be dead to get your music heard.

The main musical season runs September to June. During this time the city orchestra, the **OBC**, plays weekly at the Auditori, while the Liceu hosts a different opera every three or four weeks. Both the Auditori and the Palau de la Música hold several concert cycles of various genres, either programmed by the venues or by independent promoters (Ibercamera and Euroconcert are the most important). Several festivals are also staged, the foremost of which are the Festival de Música Antiga (see *p219*) and the Nous Sons festival of contemporary music (see *p218*).

In summer, the focus moves. Various museums, among them the Fundació Miró (see *p121*), the CaixaForum (see *p119*) and La Pedrera (see *p130*), hold small outdoor concerts, and there are weekly events in several of the city's parks. More serious musical activity, though, follows its audience and heads up the coast, to festivals in the towns of Vilabertrán, Perelada, Cadaqués and Torroella de Montgri.

INFORMATION AND TICKETS

The monthly *Informatiu Musical*, published by Amics de la Música (93 268 01 22, www.amics musica.org), lists concerts in all genres. Pick up a copy at tourist offices and record shops.

Weekly entertainment guide *Guía del Ocio* has a music section as does the new weekly *Time Out Barcelona*; both *El País* and *La Vanguardia* list forthcoming concerts. For children's events, see www.toc-toc.cat, although note that the site is in Catalan. The council website, www.bcn.cat, also has details of many forthcoming events. Tickets for most major venues can be bought by phone or online from venues, or from Tel-entrada or Servi-Caixa (see *p215*).

Venues

In addition to the venues below, several churches also hold concerts. The most spectacular is Santa Maria del Mar (see *p103*) in the Born, whose tall, ghostly interior exemplifies the Gothic intertwining of music, light and spirituality. It's a wonderful place to hear a performance. Concerts include everything from Renaissance music to gospel. There's a monthly free organ concert at the cathedral, usually (but not always) held on the second Wednesday of the month (see www. euroconcert.org for programme). Other churches with regular programmes include Santa Maria del Pi, Sant Felip Neri, Santa Anna and the monastery in Pedralbes.

L'Auditori

C/Lepant 150, Eixample (93 247 93 00/www. auditori.org). Metro Marina. **Open** *Information* 8am-10pm daily. **Box office** noon-9pm Mon-Sat; 1hr before performance Sun. Closed Aug. **Tickets** vary. **Credit** MC, V. **Map** p343 K9.
Serious music lovers in Barcelona prefer to see concerts at Rafael Moneo's sleek L'Auditori: what it lacks in architectural warmth, it more than makes up for in acoustics and facilities. The 2,400-seat hall has provided the city with a world-class music venue and a home to its orchestra, the OBC, now under the baton of conductor Eiji Oue (although it frequently performs with guest conductors). There's also a 600-seat space that tends to get the jazz and flamenco gigs as well as chamber music, and one with 400 seats which shows experimental work as well as children's programming. The 2008 programme features the pathetic and the fantastic: Tchaikovsky's *Symphony No.6 Pathetique* (late March) and Berlioz's *Symphony Fantastique* (in May). Guest conductors include Leonard Slatkin and the young (and rather dashing) Tugan Sokhiev. A late-night bus service connects the Auditori with Plaça Catalunya after evening performances.

(margin) **Arts & Entertainment**

A suitably grand venue for grand opera. **Gran Teatre del Liceu**.

Auditori Winterthur

L'Illa, Avda Diagonal 547, Les Corts (93 290 11 02/ www.winterthur.es). Metro Maria Cristina. **Open** *Information* 8.30am-1.30pm, 3-5.30pm Mon-Fri. Closed Aug. **Tickets** vary. **Credit** varies. **Map** p338 C4.

A charming, intimate venue in the unlikely setting of L'Illa, a monolithic shopping centre. Though it hosts few concerts, they're generally of a high quality; the Schubert cycle and series of song recitals, both annual events, are well worth catching.

Gran Teatre del Liceu

La Rambla 51-59, Barri Gòtic (93 485 99 13/tickets 902 53 33 53/www.liceubarcelona.com). Metro Liceu. **Open** *Information* 11am-2pm, 3-8pm Mon-Fri. **Box office** 2-8pm Mon-Fri; 1hr before performance Sat, Sun. Closed 2wks Aug. **Tickets** vary. **Credit** AmEx, MC, V. **Map** p345 A/B5.

The impressive speed with which the Liceu was resurrected after a fire, as well as the meticulous recreation of the original 1847 design, is indicative of the central importance the city's opera house has in the cultural life of Barcelona. Compared with the restrained façade, the 2,292-seat auditorium is an elegant, classical affair of red plush, gold leaf and ornate carvings, but with mod cons that include seat-back subtitles in various languages that complement the Catalan surtitles above the stage. Under the stewardship of artistic director Joan Matabosch and musical director Sebastian Weigle, the Liceu has consolidated its programming policy, which mixes in-house productions (with occasional forays into the cutting-edge with productions directed by the likes of Calixto Bieito and the Fura dels Baus) with

co-productions with leading opera houses in Europe, as well as major international dance companies. The large basement bar hosts pre-performance talks, recitals, children's shows and other musical events; the Espai Liceu is a 50-seat auditorium with a regular programme of screenings of past operas.

Palau de la Música Catalana

C/Sant Francesc de Paula 2, Sant Pere (93 295 72 00/www.palaumusica.org). Metro Urquinaona. **Box office** 10am-9pm Mon-Sat; 1hr before performance Sun. Closed Aug for concerts. **Tickets** vary. **Credit** MC, V. **Map** p344 D/E3.

This extraordinary visual explosion of Modernista architectural flights of fancy is on the UNESCO list of World Heritage sites. Built in 1908 by Lluís Domènech i Montaner, it is certainly one of the most spectacular music venues anywhere in the world and much work has been done to improve its acoustics. A recent extension, adding a terrace, a restaurant and a subterranean hall, has been controversial: concertgoers approve, but architecture critics have been less sure. The Palau has seen some of the best international performers over the years, including the likes of Leonard Bernstein and Daniel Barenboim. This year sees the centenary of the Palau, which will be celebrated with a season of orchestral music called Palau 100. *See also p101. Photo p264.*

Orchestras & ensembles

La Capella Reial de Catalunya, Le Concert des Nations & Hespèrion XXI

Information 93 580 60 69/www.alia-vox.com.

Arts & Entertainment

Palau de la Música Catalana. *See p263.*

The popularity of Catalonia's rich heritage in early music is due in large part to the indefatigable Jordi Savall, the driving force behind these three inter-linked groups which, between them, play around 300 concerts a year worldwide. La Capella Reial specialises in Catalan and Spanish Renaissance and Baroque music; Le Concert des Nations is a period-instrument ensemble playing orchestral and symphonic work from 1600 to 1850; and Hespèrion XXI plays pre-1800 European music.

Orfeó Català

Information 93 295 72 00/www.palaumusica.org.
The Orfeó Català, which began life as one of 150 choral groups that sprang up as part of the patriotic and social movements at the end of the 19th century, was banned by Franco as a focus of Catalan nationalism. While it's no longer as pre-eminent as it once was, the group still stages around 25 performances a year, giving a cappella concerts, as well as providing a choir for the Orquestra Simfònica and other Catalan orchestras. The largely amateur group also includes a small professional nucleus, the Cor de Cambra del Palau de la Música, which gives 50 performances a year.

Orquestra Simfònica de Barcelona Nacional de Catalunya (OBC)

Information 93 247 93 00/www.obc.cat.
Representing both Barcelona and Catalonia, the awkwardly named Orquestra Simfònica de Barcelona is the busiest orchestra in the city, performing at the Auditori almost every weekend of the season. Under the right baton, the Simfònica can excel, though it's difficult to know who wields it, with so many different conductors performing in a single season. The orchestra provides a fairly standard gallop through the symphonic repertoire, though the director Eiji Oue and principal guest conductor Ernest Martinez Izquierdo have brought in a more adventurous programme. The orchestra is also committed to new Catalan composers, commissioning two works a year.

Orquestra Simfònica i Cor del Gran Teatre del Liceu

Information 93 485 99 13/www.liceubarcelona.com.
Upcoming operatic productions for the 2008 season include Richard Wagner's *Tannhäuser* in March and April, Benjamin Britten's *Death in Venice* in May, both co-produced with major international opera companies, and radical stage director Calixto Bieito's vision of a drug-crazed *Don Giovanni* in July. There's also a programme of concerts and recitals, and half a dozen mini operas for children; in 2008 these include Engelbert Humpeldinck's *Hansel i Gretel*, and *The Superbarber of Seville*.

Orquestra Simfònica del Vallès

Information 93 727 03 00/www.osvalles.com.
This run-of-the-mill provincial orchestra, based in the nearby town of Sabadell, performs regularly in Barcelona, often at the Palau de la Música, where it plays a dozen symphonic concerts each season.

Contemporary music

AvuiMúsica

Associació Catalana de Compositors, Passeig Colom 6, space 4, Barri Gòtic (93 268 37 19/ www.accompositors.com). Metro Jaume I. **Open** *Information* 9.30am-1.30pm Mon-Fri. Closed 3wks Aug. **Tickets** €10; €5 reductions. **No credit cards. Map** p345 D7.

A season of small-scale contemporary concerts run by the Association of Catalan Composers at various venues around the city. Members of the association are well represented, and around half the works each year have not been played in public before.

Barcelona 216

Information 93 487 87 81.
A small ensemble with a strong commitment to contemporary music of all types, including written compositions and more experimental works. The dancers regularly feature in the Nous Sons programme at L'Auditori in March.

CAT

Travessia de Sant Antoni 6-8, Gràcia (93 218 44 85/ www.tradicionarius.com). Metro Fontana. **Open** Gigs about 10pm Thur, Fri. Closed Aug. **Tickets** €8-€10. **No credit cards. Map** p340 G5.
The Centre Artesà Tradicionàrius promotes traditional Catalan music and culture and hosts a number of festivals, including a showcase of folk music and dance staged between January and April. The centre's concerts and workshops also cover indigenous music from Spain as well as other countries.

Diapasón

Information 60 508 10 60/telungc@hotmail.com.
Diapasón comprises a septet specialising in Erik Satie and more playful works of contemporary classical music. The group is led by composer/performer Domènec González de la Rubia.

Festival d'Òpera de Butxaca i Noves Creacions

Information 93 301 84 85/mobile 659 454 879/ www.fobnc.org. **Date** Oct-Nov.
A successful series of innovative and entertaining small-scale chamber operas performed in various venues, including the former anatomy theatre of the Royal Academy of Medicine.

Fundació Joan Miró

See p121. **Open** Mid June-July. **Box office** 1hr before performance Thur. **Tickets** €10; €40 for 6 concerts. **Credit** MC, V. **Map** p339 C11.
When the rest of the city gets too hot, head up to the Fundació Miró for its annual Nits de Música series of jazz, improv and other performance-based music. It's not the greatest venue in the city, but the electric performances soon dispel any discomfort. Some concerts take place on the roof terrace.

Gràcia Territori Sonor

Information 93 237 37 37/www.gracia-territori.com.
The main focus of this dynamic collective is the month-long LEM festival in autumn: held in various venues in Gràcia, it's a rambling series of musical happenings, much of them experimental, improvised and electronic, and most of them free. The concerts themselves are supplemented by various dance performances, sound installations and even poetry readings. The larger-scale events are held at MACBA, La Pedrera and CaixaForum.

Nous Sons – Músiques Contemporànies

Information 93 247 93 00/www.auditori.org.
Date 9 Feb-15 Mar 2008.
Previously known as the festival of contemporary music, New Sounds is a burst of new music that continues to evolve yearly, and features national and international ensembles. The 12 or so concerts range from symphonic and chamber music to experimental, improvisation and free jazz; the festival is also increasingly multi-media in its focus, incorporating cinema and plastic arts into performances.

Trio Kandinsky

Information 93 301 98 97/www.triokandinsky.com.
Formed in 1999, the Trio Kandinsky has an excellent reputation, performing contemporary repertoire as well as the classical canon.

Theatre & Dance

Catalan theatre is known for physical spectacle and there's one simple reason: during the Franco years the Catalan language was banned. Theatre companies responded by doing away with the text. However, the big names such as **La Fura dels Baus**, **Els Comediants** and **Tricicle** are beginning to look a little old, although all are in receipt of what appear to be subsidies for life from the Generalitat. Since the Generalitat subsidises Catalan theatre, you'll find international works tend to be translated into the local language, although there are some touring shows in Spanish. Two fine festivals are the Festival d'Opera de Butxaca (*see left*) and the Grec Festival (*see p221*).

Although Barcelona has many thriving contemporary dance companies, there are few major dance venues, and most companies spend a large amount of their time touring. Performers such as Pina Bausch and the Compañía Nacional de Danza (directed by the revered Nacho Duato) have played to sell-out crowds in the **Teatre Nacional** and the Liceu (*see p263*), and the **Teatre Lliure** hosts quite a lot of new work. However, it's generally difficult for companies to find big audiences.

Companies such as **Sol Picó** and **Mar Gómez** usually run a new show every year, as do influential troupes such as **Metros**, **Mudances** and **Gelabert-Azzopardi**.

SEASONS AND FESTIVALS

The Grec Festival (*see p221*) brings in major international acts, although of late there has been more emphasis on local acts. It is held at venues all over the city but the open-air Grec amphitheatre is magical on a summer night. New companies have a chance to launch their work at the Mostra de Teatre (93 436 32 62,

Arts & Entertainment

Teatre Nacional de Catalunya (TNC).

www.mostradeteatredebarcelona.com) in October and November, when they're assigned two nights apiece and judged by a panel of directors. The Marató de l'Espectacle at the Mercat de les Flors is a showcase for new talent on nights of non-stop five-minute performances. Dies de Dansa (*see p221*), run by the same cultural association, offers three days of national and international dance in public sites such as the Port, the CCCB or the MACBA.

TICKETS AND TIMES

Main shows start around 9-10.30pm, although many theatres have earlier (and cheaper) shows at 6-7pm on Saturdays. On Sundays, there are morning matinées aimed at family audiences; most theatres are dark on Mondays. Advance bookings are best made through Servi-Caixa or Tel-entrada (*see p215*). The best places to find information are *Guía del Ocio, Time Out Barcelona* and the *cartelera* (listings) pages of the newspapers. Online, check www.teatral.net and www.teatrebcn.com; for dance, try www.dancespain.com. You can also visit Canal Cultura in the pull-down menu on www.bcn.cat.

Major venues

Large-scale commercial productions are shown in the vast **Teatre Condal** (Avda Paral·lel 91, Poble Sec, 93 442 31 32); the **Borràs** (Plaça

Urquinaona 9, Eixample, 93 412 15 82), and the **Tívoli** (C/Casp 10-12, Eixample, 93 412 20 63), which hosts giant productions such as *Bollywood: The Show* (a musical late Feb-March 2008). For more information on these two venues, see www.grupbalana.com. The same group is returning the **Coliseum** (Gran Via de les Corts Catalanes, 595, 902 424 243) to its original role as a theatre. The **Monumental** bullring (*see p270*) and the **Barcelona Teatre Musical** (C/Guàrdia Urbana s/n, Montjuïc, 93 423 64 63) are used for mega-shows, with the latter due to play host to *Mamma Mia!* the Abba musical.

Mercat de les Flors

Plaça Margarida Xirgú, C/Lleida 59, Poble Sec (93 426 18 75/www.mercatflors.org). Metro Poble Sec. **Box office** 1hr before show. Advance tickets also available from Palau de la Virreina. **Tickets** vary. **No credit cards. Map** p339 C10.
The former flower market has been converted into a theatre city (Ciutat de Teatre) housing three performance spaces, making the Mercat one of the most innovative venues in town. Performances here experiment with unusual formats and mix new technologies, pop culture and performing arts, as well as staging more conventional theatre and providing a venue for jazz. Shows planned for 2008 include a piece inspired by Patagonia, radical Belgian group Les Ballets C de la B and Ferrán Carvajal's choreography of Bach's *Goldberg Variations*.

Teatre Lliure

Plaça Margarida Xirgú, Montjuïc (93 289 27 70/ www.teatrelliure.com). Metro Poble Sec. **Box office** 11am-3pm, 4.30-8pm Mon-Fri; 2hrs before show Sat, Sun. **Tickets** €12-€16 Tue, Wed; €16-€22 Thur-Sun; reductions 25% discount. **Credit** MC, V. **Map** p339 C10.
The Lliure is one of the most prestigious venues for serious theatre, and under director Álex Rigola it has taken an adventurous turn, although to somewhat mixed reviews. Are *Hamlet* without text and *Richard III* in a mafia setting groundbreaking productions or exercises in attention-seeking? The critics are divided. March 2008 will see interesting Belgian group Needcompany showcasing *The Lobster Shop* (in English and French). Bigger shows are surtitled in English on Thursdays and Saturdays.

Teatre Nacional de Catalunya (TNC)

Plaça de les Arts 1, Eixample (93 306 57 00/www. tnc.cat). Metro Glòries. **Box office** 3-9pm Tue-Sun. **Tickets** €15-€25; €10-€15 reductions. **Credit** AmEx, DC, MC, V. **Map** p343 K9.
The Generalitat-funded theatre designed by Ricardo Bofill boasts three superb performance spaces. Its main stage promotes large-scale Catalan and Spanish classical theatre, while more contemporary European theatre and works by new writers are normally staged in the more experimental Sala Tallers. March 2008 will see Brecht's *Caucasian Chalk Circle*,

with a live soundtrack by Cabo San Roque (*see p208* **Greed is green**) and *King Lear* in Spanish is on in May. The Projecte Tdansa is set up to give young dancers their first professional experience.

Teatre Poliorama

La Rambla 115, Barri Gòtic (93 317 75 99/ www.teatrepoliorama.com). Metro Catalunya. **Box office** 5-8pm Tue; 5-8.30pm Wed-Sat; 5-7pm Sun. **Open** till 9.30pm Wed-Sat for same day purchase. Closed 2wks Aug. **Tickets** varies. **Credit** MC, V. **Map** p344 B3.

Run by private producers 3xtr3s, this once adventurous theatre now stages mainly mainstream comedies and musicals, plus the odd piece of serious theatre. It also stages shows for children.

Teatre Romea

C/Hospital 51, Raval (information 93 301 55 04/ tickets 902 10 12 12/www.teatreromea.com). Metro Liceu. **Box office** 5-8pm Tue-Sat. Performances 9pm Tue-Fri; 6.30pm, 10pm Sat; 6.30pm Sun. **Tickets** €16-€24. **Credit** (phone bookings only) AmEx, DC, MC, V. **Map** p344 A4.

Windmill of the grind

Louche, lewd and loud, fin-de-siècle Barcelona was known as 'the Paris of the South', and its sleazily throbbing groin was the Paral.lel district. Packed with bordellos, music halls, casinos, theatres and cafés, it became the centre of city nightlife when outdoor electric lighting, installed for the 1881 exhibtion, lit up the Avda Paral.lel, transforming it from just another workers' district to the Montmartre of Barcelona, replete with pouting red lips, highkicking legs and absinthe-fuelled nights.

Of the many music halls, the most notorious was **El Molino**. It started life in 1899 as a cabaret café called La Pajarera Catalana, but in 1913 was rebuilt as a Parisian-style music hall fronted by a revolving windmill. It was rechristened Le Petit Moulin Rouge, but with the arrival of the Franco dictatorship in 1939, its name was switched to the Spanish El Molino (quietly dropping the rouge, now the colour of the political left).

The post-war decline in the popularity of music hall forced the closure of even the much-loved El Molino in the 1990s. Its derelict state was symbolic of the general shabbiness of the Paral·lel, lined with abandoned theatres and once decadent cafés converted into cheap kebab joints.

Renovation started in March 2007 and such is the old theatre's hold on its fans that it opened one last time to the public before construction began – an event attended by the mayor, 70 ex-artistes and nearly 5,000 members of the public. The progress of the project is tracked on www.molinolandia.com and the neon red sails are due to turn again in early 2009. This project is the figurehead for the Ajuntament's plan to recover the spirit of the area, spruce up the Paral·lel and create a Barcelona Broadway; next up for renovation is the neighbouring, 100-year-old Teatre Arnau, which is to be converted into a cultural centre for performance arts.

Only the paintwork is old at **L'Antic Teatre**.

Calixto Bieito, the artistic director of Teatre Romea, looks to contemporary European theatre for inspiration, although most works are in Catalan. Shows for 2008 include Aeschylus' *The Persians*, Ibsen's *Ghosts* and Marlowe's *Doctor Faustus*.

Alternative theatres

Smaller venues struggle for funding and audiences, however, theatres such as the **Nou Tantarantana** (C/Flors 22, Raval, 93 441 70 22, www.tantarantana.com), the **Espai Escènic Joan Brossa** (C/Allada-Vermell 13, Born, 93 310 13 64, www.espaibrossa.com), **L'Antic Teatre** (C/Verdaguer i Callis 12, Barri Gòtic, 93 315 23 54, www.lanticteatre.com) and the **Versus Teatre** (C/Castillejos 179, Eixample, 93 232 31 84, www.versusteatre.com) and **Sala Muntaner** (C/Muntaner 4, Eixample, 93 451 57 52, www.salamuntaner.com) often produce interesting work. The **Teatre de la Riereta** (C/Reina Amalia 3, Raval, 93 442 98 44, www.lariereta.es) hosts a few English works as does **Café-Teatre Llantiol** (C/Riereta 7, Raval, 93 329 90 09, www.llantiol.com) which also hosts monthly Guiggling Guiri comedy nights on Saturdays (www.gigglingguiri.com).

Sala Beckett

C/Alegre de Dalt 55 bis, Gràcia (93 284 53 12/ www.salabeckett.com). Metro Joanic. **Box office** from 8pm Wed-Sat; from 5pm Sun. Closed Aug. **Tickets** €6-€16; €4-€12 reductions. **No credit cards. Map** p341 J4.

This small venue was founded by the Samuel Beckett-inspired Teatro Fronterizo group, run by playwright José Sanchis Sinisterra. He's no longer based at the theatre, but his influence prevails. The theatre is also among the venues for the annual Opera de Butxaca (pocket opera) festival, *see p265*.

Theatre companies

As well as those reviewed below, companies to check include the satirical, camp Chanclettes, and the Compañia Nacional Clásica for versions of the Spanish masters. For English-language theatre, look out for the Jocular company and Black Custard Theatre.

Els Comediants

www.comediants.com.
Now a national institution, Els Comediants has its roots in commedia dell'arte and street performance; its mix of mime, circus, music, storytelling and fireworks is as likely to appear on the street to celebrate a national holiday as at any major theatre festival.

Compañia Mar Gómez

www.danzamargomez.com.
Compañia Mar Gómez provides a wonderful mix of contemporary dance and theatre with a wicked sense of humour and good music.

La Cubana

www.lacubana.es.
Both satirical and spectacular, La Cubana's shows have a cartoonish quality, using multimedia effects, camp music and audience participation.

La Fura dels Baus

www.lafura.com.
Barcelona's bad boy company has been going for years, touring the world with polemical and stimulating shows such as the infamous *XXX*, a porn cabaret inspired by the Marquis de Sade. In April, the company will perform Pushkin's *Aleksandr Godunov* at Teatre Nacional de Catalunya.

Els Joglars

www.elsjoglars.com.
Darkly satirical, Els Joglars has been at the forefront of political theatre for 30-odd years. Albert Boadella, the company's founder and leader, was imprisoned under the Franco regime for his political stance.

Tricicle

93 317 4747/www.tricicle.com.
Local boys Carles Sans, Paco Mir and Joan Gràcia founded this mime trio 25 years ago. The goofy, clean-cut humour appeals to the Spanish taste for slapstick; they're not above the odd Benny Hill moment of cross-dressing or chase sequences.

Dance companies

In addition to those listed below, groups worth seeing include the collective **La Caldera** (www.lacaldera.info), newer group **Búbulus** (www.bubulus.net) and Toni Mira's company **Nats Nus** (www.natsnus.com). Its highly successful offshoot Nats Nens produces contemporary dance shows for children.

Compañia Metros

www.metrosdansa.com.
Led by local choreographer Ramón Oller, Metros are presently working on a dance version of *The Little Prince*, aimed at younger audiences.

Erre que erre

www.errequerredanza.net.
This company of younger dancers gives fresh, original performances, with well-measured doses of excellent theatre. A new piece inspired by writers Harold Pinter and Haruki Murakami is due in June.

Gelabert-Azzopardi

www.gelabertazzopardi.com.
The duo of Barcelona's Cesc Gelabert and Londoner Lydia Azzopardi is at its peak and displays an extraordinary emotional range. Their activities for 2008 include a new (as-yet untitled) production for London-based company Union Dance in June and July.

Mal Pelo

www.malpelo.com.
Mal Pelo has a Catalan sensibility, creating expressive, earthy and somewhat surreal choreographies.

Marta Carrasco

www.martacarrasco.com.
Carrasco has choreographed many plays and musicals, and is one of Catalonia's finest dancers.

Mudances

www.margarit-mudances.com.
Director Àngels Margarit has been growing in stature as a choreographer for the past decade, producing highly structured work with creative use of video. Mudances often holds children's shows.

Raravis-Andrés Corchero-Rosa Muñoz

http://raravisdanza.com.
This is the dancers' dance company, but its experimental and intimate style can make it a little difficult for the uninitiated.

Sol Picó

www.solpico.com.
Through perserverance, charisma, hard work and lots of energy, Sol Picó and her company are probably the best known outside Catalonia.

Flamenco

Bar-restaurant **TiriTiTran** (C/Buenos Aires 28, Gràcia, 93 410 86 77, www.tirititran.com) is a favourite with flamenco aficionados; impromptu performances often happen at weekends, with concerts every Wednesday. The Friday night flamenco shows at the restaurant **Nervion** (C/Princesa 2, Born, 93 315 21 03, closed end Aug, 1st wk Sept) seem to be aimed at tourists, but it is a lot cheaper than the established *tablaos*: if you don't eat, entry is €12, which includes a drink. **Flamenco Barcelona** (C/Marquès de Barberà 6, Raval, 93 443 66 80, www.flamencobarcelona.com) is a shop specialising in flamenco paraphernalia and music, with exhibitions and occasional concerts. It also offers flamenco guitar, singing and dance courses.

El Tablao de Carmen

Poble Espanyol, Avda Marquès de Comillas, Montjuïc (93 325 68 95/www.tablaodecarmen.com). Metro Espanya. **Open** 7pm-midnight Tue-Sun. **Shows** 7.45pm, 10pm Tue-Sun. Closed 2wks Jan. **Admission** show & 1 drink €34; show & dinner €64. **Credit** AmEx, DC, MC, V. **Map** p339 A/B9.
This rather sanitised version of the flamenco *tablao* sits in faux-Andalucian surroundings in the Poble Espanyol. You'll find both stars and new young talent, displaying the various styles of flamenco singing, dancing and music. You must reserve in advance (up to a week ahead in summer), which will allow you to enter the Poble Espanyol free after 7pm.

Los Tarantos

Plaça Reial 17, Barri Gòtic (93 319 17 89/www. masimas.com/tarantos). Metro Liceu. **Open** *Flamenco show* 8.30pm, 9.30pm, 10.30pm daily. **Admission** €6. **Credit** MC, V. **Map** p342 B6.
This flamenco *tablao* has presented many top stars over the years, as well as offering some *rumba catalana*. It now caters mainly to the tourist trade.

Sport & Fitness

To Barça and beyond.

Catalans love their sport, and it is a passion that transcends social class, age and background. Of course, football reigns supreme, and every *barri* in town has its own local team and most (nearly always male) *barcelonins* like a run-out at weekends, either in six-a-side matches at the numerous indoor gyms around town, or on the dusty wastelands that pass for football pitches in this grass-challenged city.

The ultimate symbol of the Catalan love of sport, however, is FC Barcelona. The fetishistic love of the *azulgrana* (the burgundy and red shirt), and pride in the Nou Camp, Europe's biggest football stadium, make membership of the club de rigueur for any self-respecting football fan (unless they are one of those stick-in-the-muds who prefer to support Espanyol).

Spectator sports

Tickets can often be purchased by credit card with Servi-Caixa or Tel-entrada (*see p216*). Check www.agendabcn.com or newspapers such as *El Mundo Deportivo* for event details.

Basketball

Baloncesta or, simply, 'basket', is easily Spain's second most popular sport, and the country hosts Europe's most competitive league, the ACB. The season runs September to early June; league matches are on weekend evenings, with European matches played midweek.

AXA FC Barcelona

Palau Blaugrana, Avda Aristides Maillol, Les Corts (93 496 36 00/www.fcbarcelona.com). Metro Collblanc or Palau Reial. **Ticket office** *Sept-June* 9am-1.30pm, 3.30-6pm Mon-Thur; 9am-2.30pm Fri. *Aug* 8.30am-2.30pm Mon-Fri; also 2hrs before a game. Advance tickets available from day before match; if match is Sun, tickets available from Fri. **Tickets** €7-€35. **No credit cards**.

Barcelona are an ambitious side and, after a disappointing 2005/06 , the team bounced back with an impressive 2006/07 season, beating Real Madrid to win the Copa del Rey and coming second in the championship. Although Roko Ukic has left and local star Juan Carlos Navarro was lured to NBA, players like Marion Kasun and Jaka Lakovic, and new signings Pepe Sánchez and Ersan Illyasova ensure that Barcelona have arguably the strongest squad in Europe. Barça are also rumoured to be on the lookout for an NBA star to complete the line-up for this year.

Bullfighting

Plaza de Toros Monumental

Gran Via de les Corts Catalanes 749, Eixample (93 245 58 04/93 215 95 70). Metro Monumental. **Open** *Bullfights* Apr-Sept 6.30-7pm Sun. *Museum* Apr-Sept 11am-2pm, 4-8pm Mon-Sat; 10.30am-1pm Sun. **Admission** *Bullfights* €20-€97. Advance tickets available from Servi-Caixa. *Museum* €5; €4 reductions. **No credit cards**. **Map** p343 K8.

In April 2004, the council voted the city to be *anti-taurino* (anti-bullfighting), though this was largely a symbolic gesture: 100 bulls are still killed every year at the city's one remaining bullring. *Corridas* take place on Sundays in summer, largely in front of tourists and immigrant Andalusians.

Football

Barcelona boasts two Primera (top flight) teams, FC Barcelona and the somewhat less well-known RCD Espanyol. Every weekend from mid August to May, one or the other will be playing, usually on Saturday or Sunday evening; check the press for details, and keep checking as kick-off times can change. Europa (based in Gràcia) and Júpiter (in Poblenou) are worthwhile semi-pro teams.

FC Barcelona

Nou Camp, Avda Aristides Maillol, Les Corts (93 496 36 00/www.fcbarcelona.com). Metro Collblanc or Palau Reial. **Ticket office** *Sept-June* 9am-1.30pm, 3.30-6pm Mon-Thur; 9am-2.30pm Fri. *Aug* 8.30am-2.30pm Mon-Fri; from 11am match days. Tickets available from 2wks before each match. **Tickets** €19-€125. Advance tickets for league games available from Servi-Caixa. **Credit** AmEx, DC, MC, V. **Map** p338 A4.

See p273 **More than a club**.

RCD Espanyol

Estadi Olímpic de Montjuïc, Passeig Olímpic 17-19, Montjuïc (93 292 77 00/www.rcdespanyol.com). Metro Espanya then free bus or Paral·lel then Funicular de Montjuïc. **Ticket office** *Sept-June* (matchdays only). Opening times vary so check website first. **Tickets** €25-€55. **Credit** V. **Map** p339 A/B11.

Espanyol had a good season in 2006/07 with the highlight being a place in the UEFA Cup final, although the team lost 3-1 on penalties to Seville, the match having been tied 2-2 after extra time. This season, manager Ernesto Valverde is hoping to prove that Espanyol deserve its place in the Primera Liga. To do so, he will be putting his faith

Remember to ride on the right. Cyclists on Passeig Marítim Port Olímpic.

in a talented crop of young Catalan players (Espanyol have always been regarded as a good *cantera* – 'mine' – of footballing talent), alongside their two veterans: 'the little Buddha' Ivan de la Peña and their faithful top scorer and captain, Raúl Tamudo. The club is scheduled to move to a new, 42,000-capacity, ground in Cornellà in 2008.

Special events

La Cursa del Corte Inglés
93 270 17 30/www.elcorteingles.com. **Date** May.
Barcelona's biggest fun run in May is sponsored by the city's favourite department store.

Motorsports
Circuit de Catalunya, Ctra de Parets del Vallès a Granollers, Montmeló (93 571 97 00/www. circuitcat.com). By car C17 north to Parets del Vallès exit (20km/13 miles). **Times & tickets** vary by competition; available from Servi-Caixa.
Credit MC, V.
Until 1975, Barcelona's Formula One track used to be a death-defying race through the roads of Montjuïc. Now, the city boasts one of the world's best racing circuits at Montmeló. Since Spaniard Fernando Alonso won the World Championship in 2006/07 tickets have become harder to come by. Book well in advance if you want to see the race.

Tennis
Reial Club de Tennis Barcelona-1899, C/Bosch i Gimpera 5, Les Corts (93 203 78 52/www.rctb 1899.es). FGC Reina Elisenda/bus 63, 78. **Ticket office** During competitions 8.30am-1.30pm, 3.30-6.30pm Mon-Fri; 9am-1pm Sat. **Tickets** €20-€64; available from Servi-Caixa. **Credit** AmEx, MC, V.
Map p338 B2.
The annual Open Seat Comte de Godó tournament in Pedralbes, is considered one of the ATP circuit's most important clay-court tournaments. All the top players usually attend, including Rafael Nadal, who has already won the competition twice. The 2008 tournament takes place at the end of April.

Active sports & fitness

The 237 municipally run facilities include an excellent network of *poliesportius* (sports centres). Visitors should note that one-day entry tickets are usually available for these. But should the great outdoors prove an irresistible lure you can always just head to the beach: there's a free outdoor gym and ping-pong table at Barceloneta, and the sea is warm enough for swimming in between May and October. All beaches have wheelchair ramps, and most of the city's pools are also fully equipped for disabled people. See Servei d'Informació Esportiva below for details.

Servei d'Informació Esportiva
Avda de l'Estadi 30-40, Montjuïc (93 402 30 00). Metro Espanya then escalators or Paral·lel then Funicular de Montjuïc/bus 50. **Open** Oct-June 8am-2pm, 3.45-6pm Mon-Thur; 8am-2.30pm Fri. *July-Sept* 8am-2.30pm Mon-Fri. **Map** p339 B10/11.
The Ajuntament's sports' information service is based at the Piscina Bernat Picornell. Call for information (although note that not all the staff speak English). Alternatively, you can consult the Ajuntament's very thorough listings on the Esports section of its website: www.bcn.cat.

Bowling

Bowling Pedralbes
Avda Dr Marañón 11, Les Corts (93 333 03 52/ www.bowlingpedralbes.com). Metro Collblanc or Zona Universitaria. **Open** 10am-2am Mon-Thur; 10am-4am Fri, Sat; 10am-midnight Sun. *Aug* open only from 5pm daily. **Rates** €2.50-€4.75/person.
Credit MC, V.
There are 14 lanes to try for that perfect 300, in an alley that hosts international tournaments. Early afternoons are quiet; otherwise, sit at the bar and wait to be paged. Shoe hire is available (€1), as are pool, snooker and *futbolín* (table football).

Cycling

Tourist offices have maps detailing cycle routes. These make cycling just about viable as a mode of transport, though major roads in the Eixample can get a bit hairy. The seafront is a good bet for leisure cycling; otherwise, try the spectacular Carretera de les Aigües, a flat gravel road that skirts along the side of Collserola mountain. To avoid a killer climb, take your bike on the FGC to Peu del Funicular station, then take the Funicular de Vallvidrera to the midway stop. For serious mountain biking, check http://amicsbici.pangea.org, which also has information on when you can take your bike on public transport. A really good lock is a must; bicycle theft is big business, with thieves stealing even bells.

Probike

C/Villarroel 184, Eixample (93 419 78 89/www. probike.es). Metro Hospital Clínic. **Open** 10am-8.30pm Mon-Sat. **Credit** AmEx, MC, V. Closed 1wk Aug. **Map** p340 E6.
The Probike club organises regular excursions, from day trips to a summertime cross-Pyrenees run. Its centre, which has a broad range of equipment and excellent service, plus maps and information on all manner of routes, is a magnet for mountain bikers.

Football

Barcelona International Football League

www.bifl.info/nicksimonsbcn@yahoo.co.uk.
Matches, of Sunday League standard, are generally played at weekends from September to June among teams of expats and locals. New players are welcome.

Golf

Catalonia is currently *a la moda* as a golfing-holiday destination. Thus visitors hoping to swing a club or two should book in advance; courses can be full at weekends.

Club de Golf Sant Cugat

C/Villa, Sant Cugat del Vallès (93 674 39 58/ www.golfsantcugat.com). By train FGC from Plaça Catalunya to Sant Cugat/by car Túnel de Vallvidrera (C16) to Valldoreix. **Open** 8am-8pm Mon; 7.30am-8.30pm Tue-Fri; 7am-9pm Sat, Sun. **Rates** *Non-members* €65 Mon-Thur; €150 Fri-Sun. **Club hire** €40. **Credit** MC, V.
Designed by Harry S Colt back in 1917 and built by British railway workers, the oldest golf course in Catalonia is a tight, varied 18-hole set-up, making the most of natural obstacles, that's challenging enough to host the Ladies' World Matchplay Tour. There's a restaurant and swimming pool on site. You may be asked to pay a membership fee depending on the time of year: call ahead.

Gyms & fitness centres

Sports centres run by the city council are cheaper and generally more user-friendly than most private clubs. Phone the council's sport information service, Servei d'Informació Esportiva (*see p271*), for more details on prices and locations.

Centres de Fitness DiR

C/Casp 34, Eixample (902 10 19 79/93 301 62 09/ www.dir.es). Metro Urquinaona. **Open** 7am-10.45pm Mon-Fri; 9am-3pm Sat, Sun. **Rates** vary. **Credit** MC, V. **Map** p344 D1.
This plush, well-organised private chain has ten fitness centres. Additional installations vary from a huge outdoor pool (at DiR Diagonal) to a squash centre (DiR Campus).
Other locations DiR Campus, Avda Dr Marañón 17, Les Corts (93 448 41 41); DiR Diagonal, C/Ganduxer 25-27, Eixample (93 202 22 02); and throughout the city.

Europolis

Travessera de les Corts 252-254, Les Corts (93 363 29 92/www.europolis.es). Metro Les Corts. **Open** 7am-11pm Mon-Fri; 8am-8pm Sat; 9am-3pm Sun. **Rates** *Non-members* €10.40/day. *Membership* approx €46/mth, plus €81 joining fee. **Credit** MC, V. **Map** p338 B5.
Europolis centres, as large and well equipped as any private gym in town, are municipally owned but run by the British chain Holmes Place. They provide exercise machines, as well as pools, classes, trainers and weight-lifting gear.
Other locations C/Sardenya 549-553, Gràcia (93 210 07 66).

Ice skating

FC Barcelona Pista de Gel

Nou Camp, entrance 7 or 9, Avda Joan XXIII, Les Corts (93 496 36 30/www.fcbarcelona.com). Metro Collblanc or Maria Cristina. **Open** 10am-2pm, 4-6pm Mon-Thur; 10am-2pm, 4-8pm Fri; 10.30am-1.30pm, 5-8pm Sat, Sun. Closed Aug. **Rates** (incl skates) €10.50. **No credit cards. Map** p338 A4.
This functional rink is situated right next to the Nou Camp complex which makes it a perfect place for the non-football fans in the family to spend 90 minutes or more. Gloves are obligatory, and on sale at €2 a pair. The rink is also used for ice-hockey matches.

Skating Roger de Flor

C/Roger de Flor 168, Eixample (93 245 28 00/ www.skatingclub.cat). Metro Tetuan. **Open** *July-mid Sept* 10.30am-1.30pm, 5-9pm Mon-Fri, Sun; 10.30am-2pm, 4.30-10pm Sat. *Mid Sept-June* 10.30am-1.30pm, 5-9pm daily. **Rates** (incl skates) €13. **Credit** MC, V. **Map** p341 J8.
A family-orientated ice rink off Avda Diagonal in the Eixample. Gloves are compulsory and are on sale for €3. Any non-skaters in a group can get in for €1 and then have use of the café.

Arts & Entertainment

More than a club

left within 24 hours – for Real. Gaspart desperately threw money at mediocrity. Average players idly earned fortunes. Barça flopped, even skirted relegation. Real signed Figo, then Ronaldo, then Zidane, then Beckham.

As Cruyff griped in one of the three sports dailies of his adopted city, his young lawyer Joan Laporta was heading an independent supporters' group, Elefant Blau, to challenge the moribund club leadership. With Cruyff whispering advice, Laporta won the 2003 election by a landslide.

Sewn into the collar of every bright Barça replica shirt is the motto: *Més de un club* ('More than a club'). On the front of each, the prime advertising space used by clubs of Barça's stature to earn billions from gambling concerns and car companies, is the acronym Unicef. Announced in September 2006, the Unicef deal not only means global recognition for the international children's charity but an annual £1 million put into its coffers by FC Barcelona. Let bwin sponsor the eternal enemy Real Madrid and Toyota nearest rivals Valencia – FCB sported their iconic stripes brand-free for 107 years before a publicity stunt like this one. 'More than a club', indeed.

Current incumbent Joan Laporta presides over Barça's most successful spell since the Dream Team of Johan Cruyff in the early 1990s. Europe's most exciting football club are again at full tilt thanks to a revival secretly masterminded by the mercurial Dutchman. Cruyff arrived here in 1974. Barcelona, flagship club for Catalonia in the still ongoing Franco era, hadn't won the Spanish title since 1960. In 1974, Cruyff's Barça went to Real and won 5-0. The subsequent title was almost an afterthought.

Later as coach, Cruyff won Barça the ultimate triumph: the elusive European Cup of 1992. His Dream Team, the last word in thrilling football, were Spanish champions four years running.

An ego clash with club president, Basque construction mogul José Luis Nuñez, saw Cruyff leave. Nuñez was replaced by his deputy Joan Gaspart. Star player Luis Figo

He threw out boardroom fuddy-duddies and spoiled players, slashed budgets and brought in young directors. Another Cruyff whisper saw him appoint relatively untried Dutchman Frank Rijkaard as manager. Laporta's right-hand man, Sandro Rosell, a former Nike executive in Brazil, had enough clout to sign Ronaldinho, the world's best player.

The momentum and newly found money attracted Europe's most exciting players while Rijkaard, as Cruyff had done before him, kept a core of gritty Catalans such as Xavi and Puyol. Barça complemented back-to-back league titles in 2005 and 2006 with a first Champions League win since 1992. Although Barcelona was beaten in the closing minutes of the 2006/07 campaign, the season will be best remembered for a Maradonaesque wonder goal by new hero Lionel Messi. The arrival of Thierry Henry in the summer of 2007 will keep Barça close to the chequered flag in the world's most exciting league and most lucrative international club competition – and sales of replica shirts at a healthy level.

Getting tickets, though, can be something of a lottery. Around 4,000 tickets usually go on sale on the day of the match: phone to find out when, and join the queue an hour or so beforehand at the intersection of Travessera de les Corts and Avenida Arístides Maillol. 'Rented out' seats go on sale from these offices and can also be bought through Servi-Caixa. If there are none left, buy a *reventa* ticket from touts at the gates. The 'B' team plays in the mini-stadium over the road.

In-line skating

The APB (Asociacion de Patinadores de Barcelona, www.patinar-bcn.com) organises skating convoys: beginners meet at the Fòrum at 10.15pm on Fridays. Pro skaters hook up at Plaça Catalunya at 10.30pm on Thursday and follow an 'unofficial' route. See www.sat.org. es/bcnskates for details. RODATS (635 629 948, www.rodats.com/tours) organises skating convoys and classes at four levels of difficulty (€10 per 1.5 hour class, and monthly courses for €30 or €55, depending on how many classes you do, €8 for equipment) on Monday on the beach front at platja Mar Bella, on Friday at the Fòrum (both days 7.30pm) and on Wednesday (10pm) in Parc Clot.

Going it alone, you're not officially allowed on roads or cycle paths, and the speed limit is 10 kilometres/hour. The pedestrian broadways of Rambla de Catalunya, Avda Diagonal and Passeig Marítim are popular haunts.

Jogging & running

The seafront is a good location. If you can handle the climb, or use other transport for the ascent, there are scenic runs on Montjuïc, especially around the castle and Olympic stadium, the Park Güell/Carmel hills and Collserola.

Sailing

Base Nàutica de la Mar Bella

Avda Litoral, between Platja Bogatell & Platja de Mar Bella (93 221 04 32/www.basenautica.org). Metro Poblenou. **Open** *Apr-Aug* 10am-8pm daily. *Sept-Oct* 10am-7pm daily. *Nov-Dec* 10am-6pm daily. *Jan-Mar* 10am-5.30pm daily. **Rates** *Windsurfing* €171/10hr course; €20/hr equipment hire. *Catamaran* €200/16hr course; €26-€60/hr equipment hire. *Kayak* €115/10hr course; €15-€25/hr equipment hire. **Credit** MC, V.

Situated next to Barcelona's official nudist beach, the Base Nàutica hires out catamarans and windsurf gear to those with experience. There's a proficiency test when you first get on the water (€20 fee if you fail); unofficial registered 'friends', who will join your catamaran team for a fee, are usually available for beginners. You can hire a kayak without a test. There are also different options available for intensive or longer-term sailing proficiency courses.

Skiing

If you sicken of the urban bustle, within three hours you can be in the Pyrenees. The best bet for a skiing day trip is the resort of La Molina (972 89 20 31, www.lamolina.cat). A RENFE train from Plaça Catalunya at 7.05am or 9.22am (€7.50 single, €15 return) takes you to the train station (get off at La Molina) and a bus takes you up to the resort. A day's ski pass (known as the *forfait*) will set you back around €36.50, or you can buy combined return train ticket and *forfait* for around €43. Trains return at 4.55pm and 7.15pm (check the timetable in the station or www.renfe.es). There are runs to suit all. More information is available at the La Molina office in El Triangle (C/Pelai, 93 205 15 15).

Swimming

The city has dozens of municipal pools, many of them open air. It also has more than three miles of beach, patrolled by lifeguards in summer. For a list of pools, contact the Servei d'Informació Esportiva (*see p271*). Flip-flops and swimming caps are generally obligatory.

Club de Natació Atlètic Barceloneta

Plaça del Mar, Barceloneta (93 221 00 10/www. cnab.org). Metro Barceloneta then bus 17, 39, 64. **Open** *Oct-Apr* 6.30am-11pm Mon-Fri; 7am-11pm Sat; 8am-5pm Sun. *May-Sept* 6.30am-11pm Mon-Fri; 7am-11pm Sat; 8am-8pm Sun. **Admission** *Non-members* €9.80/day. **Membership** €33/mth, plus €67 joining fee. **Credit** AmEx, DC, MC, V. **Map** p342 G13.

This historic beachside centre, which celebrated its centenary in 2007, has an indoor pool and two outdoor pools (one heated), as well as sauna (which costs extra) and gym facilities. There's a *frontón* (Spanish ball sports court) if you fancy a go at the world's fastest sport: *jai alai*, a fierce Basque game somewhere between squash and handball.

Poliesportiu Marítim

Passeig Marítim 33-35 (93 224 04 40/www. claror.org). Metro Ciutadella-Vila Olímpica. **Open** *Sept-July* 7am-midnight Mon-Fri; 8am-9pm Sat; 8am-4pm Sun. *Aug* 7am-10pm Mon-Fri; 8am-9pm Sat; 8am-9pm Sun. **Admission** *Non-members* €14 Mon-Fri; €16.50 Sat, Sun; 5-visit pass €57; 10-visit pass €101. **Credit** AmEx, DC, MC, V. **Map** p343 K12.

This spa centre specialises in thalassotherapy, a popular hydrotherapy treatment using seawater. There are seven saltwater pools of differing temperatures, including a vast whirlpool with waterfalls to massage your shoulders and an icy plunge-pool. There's also a sauna, a steam room and a really fab slab of hot marble that you lie on after exerting yourself in the, er, jacuzzi. Other services include a bigger freshwater pool, a gym, bike hire and classes.

Tennis

Club Tennis Pompeia

C/Foixarda, Montjuïc (93 325 13 48). Bus 13, 50. **Open** 8am-10pm daily. **Rates** *Non-members* €13/hr; €4.60 floodlights. €146/pass for July-Sept. **No credit cards.**

There are good rates for non-members at this pleasant club above the Poble Espanyol. There are seven clay courts and racket hire is free.

Trips Out of Town

Features

Girona. *See p288.*

Getting Started

Discover Catalonia.

Catalonia boasts one of the most diverse landscapes in Spain: sea, mountains, islands, virtual deserts and wetlands. It's an outdoors person's paradise, but that's not to say there isn't plenty to entertain culture vultures. There's Ferran Adrià's celebrated El Bulli restaurant (*see p171*), little boutique wineries, honeypot villages, art and architecturally rich medieval cities, weird and wonderful festivals and daredevil sporting events.

For information on roads and public transport, see the Generalitat's www.mobilitat.org. The Palau Robert tourist centre (*see p323*) is a hub of useful information about the region.

Catalonia has a network of *casa de pagès* – country houses or old farmhouses – where you can rent a room or a whole house. For details, see the Generalitat's widely available guide *Residències – Casa de pagès*. For holiday cottages, try the Rural Tourism Association, online at www.ecoturismocatalunyarural.com.

On foot

Catalonia's hills and low mountain ranges make it hugely popular for walking. In many places this is made easier by GR (*gran recorregut*) long-distance footpaths, indicated with red-and-white signs. Good places for walking within easy reach of the city include the **Parc de Collserola** (*see p136*), **Montserrat** (*see p280*) and **La Garrotxa** (*see p301*). Another excellent Generalitat website, **www.gencat.net** (click on 'Catalonia', and then 'Touring routes in Catalonia'), has particularly good information on walks. For detailed walking maps, try **Altaïr** (*see p191*) or **Llibreria Quera** (C/Petritxol 2, 93 318 07 43).

By bus

Transport around the region is reliable and reasonably priced. It's a good way to get to main hubs, though a rental car is better for exploring more out-of-the-way areas. The **Estació d'Autobusos Barcelona-Nord** (C/Ali Bei 80, map p343 J9) is the principal bus station for coach services around Catalonia. General information and timetables for all the different private companies are on 902 26 06 06, www.barcelonanord.com. The Costa Brava is better served by buses than trains.

By road

Be warned that over the last few years Spain's roads have undergone a gradual process of renaming, and many locally bought maps are still out of date. Road signs generally post both the new and the old name, but signage often doesn't make itself clear until you're right on top of your junction. Plan your route in advance.

Roads beginning C1 run north–south; C2 run east–west; C3 run parallel to the coast. Driving in or out of Barcelona, you will come across either the **Ronda de Dalt**, running along the edge of Tibidabo, or the **Ronda Litoral** along the coast, meeting north and south of the city. They intersect with several motorways (*autopistes*): the C31 (heading up the coast from Mataró); the C33/A7 (to Girona and France) and the C58 (Sabadell, Manresa), which both run into Avda Meridiana; the A2 (Lleida, Madrid), a continuation of Avda Diagonal that connects with the A7 south (Tarragona, Valencia); and the C32 to Sitges, reached from the Gran Via.

All are toll roads, which in Catalonia tend to be quite expensive; where possible, we've given toll-free alternatives. Avoid the automatic ticket dispensers if on a motorbike: you'll pay less in the 'Manual' lanes. The **Túnel de Vallvidrera**, the continuation of Via Augusta that leads out of Barcelona under Collserola to Sant Cugat and Terrassa, also has a high toll, as does the **Túnel de Cadí**, running through the mountains just south of Puigcerdà. For more information on tolls, call 902 20 03 20 or see www.autopistas.com.

By train

All **RENFE** (902 24 02 02, www.renfe.es) trains stop at **Sants** station, and some at **Passeig de Gràcia** (Girona, Figueres, the south coast), **Estació de França** (the south coast) or **Plaça Catalunya** (Montseny, Vic, Puigcerdà). RENFE's local and suburban trains (*rodalies/cercanías*) are integrated into the metro and bus fares system (*see p305*). Tickets for these are sold at separate windows. Catalan Government Railways (**FGC**) serves destinations from **Plaça d'Espanya** (including Montserrat) and **Plaça Catalunya** (Tibidabo, Collserola, Sant Cugat and Terrassa). FGC information is available on 93 205 15 15 and at www.fgc.net.

Around Barcelona

Take a spiritual retreat to the mountains or hit a high-spirited beach resort.

South along the coast

A short train ride from Barcelona can take you to the beach or mountains. About 30 minutes south is the broad strand at **Castelldefels**, popular with sun worshippers and water sports fanatics. It's also become something of a mecca for kite-surfers, and although the sport is banned in the summer months, it is fun to watch the multicoloured kites perform when the sea gets too cold for swimming. **Escola Náutica Garbí** (mobile 609 752 175, www.escolagarbi.com) can teach you how. The town also has a large recreational port, where kayaks and catamarans can be hired from the **Catamaran Center** (Port Ginesta, local 324, 93 665 22 11, www.catamaran-center.com).

For bathing of a more relaxed nature, stay on the train past Castelldefels, and get off at the tiny port of **Garraf**, with its small curved beach backed by green-and-white striped bathing huts. Miraculously, it is still relatively undiscovered, and the steep-sided mountains that surround it mean that development is not a worry. It's worth taking a stroll to the **Celler de Garraf** at the northern tip of the bay, a magical Modernista creation built by Gaudí for the Güell family in 1895, and now housing a restaurant. Behind the village stretches the **Parc del Garraf** nature reserve, with hiking and biking trails (marked out on maps available from the tourist office in Sitges). The more adventurous can also go spelunking here in its intricate network of caves and grottoes. Contact the **Oficina i Centre d'Informació del Parc del Garraf** (93 597 18 19, www.diba.es).

The pretty, whitewashed streets of **Sitges** burst with party-goers in the summertime, while providing a relaxing getaway in the winter. Sitges was 'discovered' by Modernista artist Santiago Rusiñol in the 1890s: this legendary figure threw massive parties for the great and the good of Barcelona's cultural heyday, among them a teenage Pablo Picasso.

It has remained a magnet for artists, writers and assorted leisure-lovers, and since the 1960s it has become Spain's principal gay resort, served by a hotchpotch of gay bars and discos

Sitges.

(*see p247*). The madre of all Sitges's parties, in the week leading up to Shrove Tuesday, is the camp-as-they-come carnival, a riot of floats, fancy dress and men in high heels.

In the 19th century, Sitges was a fashionable retirement spot for the merchants, known as '*los americanos*', who had made their fortunes in the Caribbean. More than 100 of their palaces are dotted around the centre of town: in the tourist office you can pick up an excellent booklet that highlights the most important. Alternatively, **Agis Sitges** (C/Lope de Vega 9, 2°-2ª, mobile 619 793 199, €9) offers guided tours of these houses the first three Sundays of the month, plus a Modernista route on the first Sunday.

Sitges's highest building, topping a rocky promontory overlooking the sea, is the pretty 17th-century church of **Sant Bartomeu i Santa Tecla**, offering wonderful views of the sea. Behind the church is the **Museu Cau Ferrat** (C/Fonollar, 93 894 03 64, www.diba.es/museus/sitges.asp, closed Mon). Rusiñol set up his home here: the building houses his collection of paintings (including works by El Greco, Picasso and Ramon Casas, as well as his own) and wrought-iron sculptures. Over the road is the **Palau Maricel** (C/Fonollar, 93 811 33 11, guided tours €10, 8pm Tue & 10pm Thur, book beforehand, closed Oct-June), an old hospital that's been converted into a Modernista palace and is now used as a concert hall in summer. The building contains medieval and Baroque paintings and sensuous marble sculptures.

Also worth visiting is the **Museu Romàntic** in the Casa Llopis (C/Sant Gaudenci 1, 93 894 29 69, closed Mon), which portrays the lifestyle of the aristocratic 19th-century family that once lived there. The original furnishings and decorations haven't been changed; you can wander from room to room among grandfather clocks, music boxes and antique dolls. Those who prefer messing about in boats are served well at the Port Esportiu Aiguadolç. The **Centro Náutico Aiguadolç-Vela** (93 811 31 05, www.advela.net, closed Mon & Dec-Feb) rents sailing boats and organises sailing excursions; a private hour-long session costs €40. The **Yahoo Motor Centre** rents jet skis with guides (93 811 30 61, €40 for 15min ride).

Beyond, **Vilanova i la Geltrú** is a working fishing port. From it you can walk along the cliffs all the way back to Sitges (about two hours).

Where to eat

For a long, lazy lunch looking out to sea, commandeer a table at one of the terraces at **La Cúpula** (93 632 00 15, mains €15) in Garraf. Booking is essential and note that if you specify the *xiringuito*, it's a little bit cheaper.

In Sitges, a fisherman's lunch of steamed mussels, clams and razor clams, and *arròs negre* doesn't come better than from friendly **El Tambucho** (Port Alegre 49, Platja Sant Sebastià, 93 894 79 12, mains €18). A little more upmarket, **Restaurant Maricel** (Passeig de la Ribera 6, 93 894 20 54, www.maricel.es, mains €22) gives local produce an elegant twist along the lines of foie with curried plums and mango, and red mullet with anchovy parmentier. For classics, such as rabbit with snails and *xató* (a local salad of salt cod, tuna and escarole lettuce), head to **La Masia** (Passeig de Vilanova 164, 93 894 10 76, mains €14). The restaurant in hotel **El Xalet** (C/Illa de Cuba 35, 93 811 00 70, www.elxalet.com, mains €18) is on the pricey side but worth it for the Modernista decor in the dining room. Be sure to leave time for a cava cocktail on the terrace at the delightful **Hotel Romàntic** (C/Sant Isidre 33, 93 894 83 72, 93 894 83 75, www.hotelromantic.com, closed Nov-Mar).

It's possible to get superb fish and seafood in Vilanova and generally it's less pricey than in Sitges. Those in the know go to **La Fitorra** (C/Isaac Peral 8, 93 815 11 25, www.hotelcesar.net, set menu €18.50) where, despite a rather uninspiring façade, the accomplished cooking offers superbly fresh fish from the local market, as does **Peixerot** (Passeig Marítim 56, 93 815 06 25, closed Sun dinner, mains €25).

Tourist information

Oficina de Turisme de Castelldefels

C/Pintor Serrasanta 4 (93 635 27 27/www.turismo castelldefels.com). **Open** *June-Sept* 10am-2pm; 4-8pm daily. *Oct-May* 9am-1pm, 3-5pm Mon-Fri.

Oficina de Turisme de Sitges

C/Sinia Morera 1 (93 894 42 51/www.sitgestur.com). **Open** *June-Sept* 9am-8pm Mon-Sat. *Oct-May* 9am-2pm, 4-6.30pm Mon-Sat.

Getting there

By bus

Mon-Bus (93 893 70 60) runs a frequent service from 7.20am to 10.20pm to Sitges, and an hourly night service between 12.10am and 3.10am to Ronda Universitat 33 in Barcelona.

By car

C32 toll road to Castelldefels, Garraf and Sitges (41km/25 miles), or C31 via a slow, winding drive around the Garraf mountains.

By train

Frequent trains leave from Passeig de Gràcia for Platja de Castelldefels (20min journey) and Sitges (30mins); not all stop at Castelldefels and Garraf.

Montserrat. *See p281*.

Saint alive La Moreneta

On 25 March 1522, a soldier hung his sword in front of a small statue of Mary. He crossed himself and looked up at the dark features of a crowned woman and the child seated upon her knee, hand raised in benediction. Then he turned and limped away, his leg still weak from the cannonball that had wrecked it. The man was Ignatius of Loyola and he would go on to found the Jesuits. The statue was the Black Virgin of Montserrat, and she would go on to greet pilgrims by the million.

Black Madonnas – pictures or statues of Mary that depict her with dark skin – are widespread in the Catholic world and often come with a reputation for working miracles. Theories as to why Mary is thus represented vary from the spurious (they're depictions of Isis and Horus) to the practical (centuries of candle smoke have stained them), but for whatever reason they always seem to evoke popular devotion. La Moreneta, or 'Little Dark One', as the Virgin of Montserrat is usually called, is no exception. Pious enthusiasts date the statue to St Luke in the first century, sceptics to the 12th. Whichever is true – and there exists evidence for the statue having been hidden from the Moors and then rediscovered in the ninth century – what is certain is how quickly the statue became an object of pilgrimage from the 12th century onwards. This was no doubt helped by the identification of the mountain as the site of the Holy Grail in Wolfram von Eschenbach's medieval romance *Parsifal*. But what really swung it was the miracles. And it certainly didn't hurt that King Alfonso X ascribed healings to Our Lady of Montserrat in his canticles. The shrine was to remaine popular over the centuries: even today two million people visit the Little Dark One each year.

North along the coast

The beaches of the **Maresme fringe** – the coast immediately north of Barcelona – are all far better options than any of the city beaches, with trains leaving every 30 minutes from Plaça Catalunya. If you walk back towards Barcelona from **Montgat Nord**, you'll come across a clutch of white fishermen's cottages with blue shutters on the beach and a good *xiringuito* that gets rammed at the weekends for its paella and mussels. Go a little further afield, and the beaches at **Caldes d'Estrac** (popularly known as **Caldetes**), **Sant Pol de Mar** and **Calella**, are better still, although the railway separating land from littoral can dampen the atmosphere. Caldetes (45 minutes away) was the playground of the Barcelona bourgeoisie around the turn of the 20th century, and a string of ostentatious Modernista mansions lines the seafront. Pretty Sant Pol is a few kilometres further. Calella is more touristy, but its lush Parc Dalmau is worth a visit and there are several interesting Gothic buildings. Thanks to massively improved cycle paths, it's now possible to cycle all the way from Barcelona to Blanes along the seafront.

Where to eat

In Caldes d'Estrac, the **Fonda Manau Can Raimón** (C/Sant Josep 11, 93 791 04 59, closed Tue & dinner Sun-Thur Oct-May, mains €14) is a small pensión with great food, while **Hispania** (Ctra Real 54, Arenys de Mar-Caldetes, 93 791 03 06, mains €35) is revered for the staunchly traditional dishes turned out by the hands of sisters Francisca and Dolores Rexach, who've been pleasing upmarket Catalan punters since 1952. In Sant Pol, **La Casa** (C/Riera 13, 93 760 23 73, closed Mon, mains €12) serves simple food in a pretty dining room, while **Carme Ruscalleda** at Sant Pau (C/Nou 10, 93 760 06 62, www.ruscalleda.com, closed all Mon, Thur lunch & Sun dinner, 3wks May & all Nov, mains €40) now boasts three Michelin stars.

Getting there

By car

NII to El Masnou (10km/6 miles), Caldes d'Estrac (36km/22 miles), Sant Pol (48km/30 miles) and Calella (52km/32 miles).

By train

RENFE trains leave every 30mins from Sants or Plaça Catalunya for El Masnou, Caldes d'Estrac, Sant Pol and Calella. Journey approx 1hr.

Montserrat & Colònia Güell

It's unsurprising that **Montserrat** ('jagged mountain'; *photos p279*), the vast bulbous-peaked sandstone mass that dominates the landscape to the west of Barcelona, is seen as the spiritual heart of Catalonia: its other-worldly appearance lends it a mystical aura that has for centuries made it a centre of worship and veneration. In the Middle Ages, the mountain was an important pilgrimage destination; the Benedictine monastery that sits near the top became the jewel in the crown of a politically independent fiefdom. Surrounded by a number of tiny chapels and hermitages, the monastery is still venerated by locals, who wait in line in the 16th-century basilica to say a prayer while kissing the orb held by **La Moreneta** (the 'Black Virgin', *see left* **Saint alive**). The **basilica** (7.30am-8.30pm daily) is at its most crowded around 1pm, when the monastery's

celebrated boys' choir sings mass, so you might want to plan your visit around this. The monastery's **museum** is stocked with fine art, including paintings by Picasso, Dalí, El Greco, Monet and Caravaggio, as well as a collection of liturgical gold and silverware, archaeological finds and gifts for the Virgin.

If all this piety isn't to your taste, it's still worth the trip up the mountain (there's a road, a cable car and a rack railway if you don't fancy the walk). The tourist office gives details of a number of fine walks to the various caves, among them **Santa Cova**, where the statue was discovered, a 20-minute hike from the monastery or take the funicular. The most accessible hermitage is **Sant Joan**, also 20 minutes or a funicular ride away. But the most rewarding trek is the longest, to the peak of **Sant Jeroni**, at 1,235 metres (4,053 feet), which offers 360-degree views from a vertigo-inducing platform. Montserrat is something of a tourist trap and gets unbearably crowded in the summer. Its characterless, overpriced restaurants are also best avoided. But it is nonetheless a worthwhile excursion, if only to appreciate the fine views.

Closer to Barcelona, on the western outskirts of Santa Coloma de Cervelló, is the **Colònia Güell** (93 630 58 07), which was commissioned by the textile baron Eusebi Güell, designed by Antoni Gaudí and, like so many of the great architect's projects, never actually completed. The utopian idea was to build a garden city for the textile workers around the factory where they worked. Gaudí did, however, manage to complete the crypt of the church, which, with its ribbed ceiling and twisted pillars, is an extraordinary achievement. It's sometimes closed for private events so call ahead.

Tourist information

Oficina de Turisme de Montserrat

Plaça de la Creu, Montserrat (93 877 77 77/www.montserratvisita.com). **Open** *June-Sept* 9am-8pm daily. *Oct-May* 9am-6pm daily.

Getting there

By bus

Montserrat A Julià-Via (93 490 40 00) bus leaves at 9.15am from Sants bus station and returns at 5pm (6pm July-Sept) daily; journey time is approx 80mins.

By train

Montserrat FGC trains from Plaça d'Espanya hourly from 8.36am to Montserrat-Aeri (1hr) for the cable car (every 15mins); or to Monistrol de Montserrat for the rack train (every hour) to the monastery. Last cable car and rack train 6pm. **Colònia Güell** FGC trains from Plaça d'Espanya.

Tarragona &
the Costa Daurada

Drink in some history.

Tarragona

Tárraco, as Tarragona was known back then, was the first Roman city to be built outside Italy and dates back to the year 218 BC. It outranked Barcelona both economically and strategically for centuries. Nowadays, though, Tarragona can feel rather staid; but what it lacks in pzazz, it more than makes up for in ancient architecture. Start with the Roman walls that once ringed the city. The path along them is known as the **Passeig Arqueològic** (Avda Catalunya, 977 24 57 96) and has its entrance at **Portal del Roser**, one of three remaining towers, two of which are medieval. Inside the walls, the superb Roman remains include the ancient **Pretori**, or 'praetorium' (977 22 17 36), used as both palace and government office and reputed to have been the birthplace of Pontius Pilate. From here, walk to the ruins of the **Circ Romans** (977 23 01 71), the first-century Roman circus where chariot races were held. The **Museu Nacional Arqueològic**, home to an important collection of Roman artefacts and mosaics, is nearby.

To see all of the **Catedral de Santa Maria** (*photos p285*), not to mention some wonderful religious art and archaeological finds, you'll need a ticket for the **Museu Diocesà** (Pla de la Seu, 977 23 86 85, closed Mon). The majestic cathedral was built on the site of a Roman temple to Jupiter, and is Catalonia's largest. The cloister, built in the 12th and 13th centuries, is glorious; the carvings alone are worth the trip.

Leading from the Old Town towards the sea, the **Passeig de las Palmeres** runs to the **Balcó del Mediterrani** overlooking the Roman **amphitheatre** (Parc del Miracle, 977 24 25 79). The same street also leads to the bustling, pedestrianised **Rambla Nova**, from where you can follow C/Canyelles to the **Fòrum** (C/Lleida, 977 24 25 01) to the remains of the juridical basilica and Roman houses. A couple of miles north of the city (but an unpleasant walk along a busy main road; take bus no.5 from the top of the Rambla Nova) is the spectacular **Pont del Diable** (Devil's Bridge), a Roman aqueduct built in the first century AD.

Entry to the Passeig Arqueològic, the circus and praetorium, the amphitheatre and the Fòrum costs €2.40 (€1.20 reductions, free under-16s); entry is free to holders of **Port Aventura** tickets (*see p285*). An all-in ticket for the city's five main museums is €9 (€4.50 reductions). All are closed on Mondays.

There's a decent **antiques market** on Sunday mornings next to the cathedral.

Museu Nacional Arqueològic de Tarragona
Plaça del Rei 5 (977 23 62 09/www.mnat.es). **Open** *June-Sept* 9.30am-8.30pm Tue-Sat; 10am-2pm Sun. *Oct-May* 9.30am-1.30pm, 3.30-7pm Tue-Sat; 10am-2pm Sun. **Admission** (incl entrance to Museu i Necròpolis Paleocristians) €2.40; €1.20 reductions; free under-18s, over-65s. **No credit cards**.

Where to eat

In the old city **Les Coques** (C/Sant Llorenc 15, 977 22 83 00, closed Sun, mains €16) serves traditional roast kid and cod dishes. The neighbourhood of El Serrallo is the place to head for fish and seafood. Try the paella at **Cal Martí** (C/Sant Pere 12, 977 21 23 84, closed Mon & dinner Sun, Tue, Wed, and Sept, mains €22.50) or the super-fresh fish at **La Puda** (Moll Pescadors 25, 977 21 15 11, closed dinner Sun and Oct-May, mains €25). Alternatively, head out of the centre to the west to **Sol-Ric** (Via Augusta 227, 977 23 20 32, closed Mon & dinner Sun, and Jan, mains €15).

Those on a budget can fall back on **Bufet el Tiberi** (C/Marti d'Ardenya 5, 977 23 54 03, www.eltiberi.com, closed Mon & dinner Sun, buffet €10.40-€11.85), while below the cathedral is **La Cuca Fera** (Plaça Santiago Rusiñol 5, 977 24 20 07, closed Tue, set lunch €13.90), which has great fish *suquet* (stew).

Where to stay

In town the smartest hotel is the towering **Imperial Tarraco** (Passeig de les Palmeres, 977 23 30 40, www.husa.es, €123-€289). The **Lauria** (Rambla Nova 20, 977 23 67 12, www.hlauria.es, €64-€75) has a swimming pool and

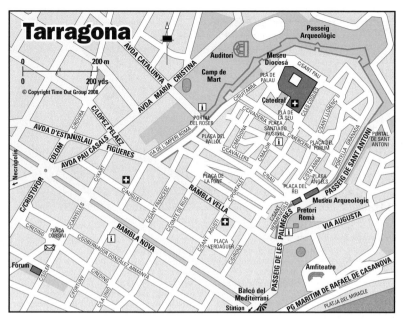

offers large discounts for weekends out of season. Some other mid-range hotels include the **Astari** (Via Augusta 95, 977 23 69 00, €68-€90), which also has a swimming pool, and the central **Hotel Urbis** (C/Reding 20 bis, 977 24 01 16, www.urbis.com, €59.50-€113). **Alexandra Aparthotel** (Rambla Nova 71, 977 24 87 01, www.ah-alexandra.com, €70-€80) is a good option if you want a little more independence. You'll find cheaper stays on the Plaça de la Font at the **Pensión Forum** (no.37, 977 23 17 18, closed Dec, €40-€43) and **Pensión La Noria** (no.53, 977 23 87 17, €34-€44); there's little to choose between them in either price or amenities.

Tourist information

Tarragona

C/Fortuny 4 (977 23 34 15/www.tarragona turisme.es). **Open** 9am-2pm, 4-6.30pm Mon-Fri; 9am-2pm Sat.

Getting there

By bus

Alsa (902 42 22 42, www.alsa.es) runs 12 buses daily from Barcelona Nord station.

By train

RENFE from Sants or Passeig de Gràcia. Trains depart hourly (journey time 1hr 6mins).

The Wine Country

Just south-west of Barcelona you'll find prime wine terrain, where the majority of Catalan wines are produced. Various of the region's many *denominaciones de origen* are found here, but the main suppliers are found in the **Penedès**, with vineyards dating back to Roman times. **Vilafranca** is the winemaking capital of this region, and a handsome medieval town in its own right, presided over by the elegant 14th-century **Basílica de Santa Maria**. The town's wine museum, the **Museu del Vi** (Plaça Jaume I 1-3, 93 890 05 82, www. vinseum.cat, closed Mon), has old wooden presses and wine jugs, some dating to the fourth century. The Saturday morning market here is the region's best, and a great place to stock up on local produce.

The two main wineries in the area are both owned by the Torres family. **Torres** (Finca El Maset, Pacs del Penedès, 93 817 74 87, www. torres.es) itself, is Penedès' largest winemaker and runs tours at its cellars outside town. More interesting for serious wine-lovers is **Jean León** (Pago Jean León, 93 899 55 12, www.jean leon.com, admission €5), a pioneering brand credited with introducing cabernet sauvignon and chardonnay to Spain. Nearby **Albet i Noya** (Can Vendrell de la Codina, Sant Pau

Trips Out of Town

Tarragona: a scenic town to look at, and to look away from. *See p282.*

d'Ordal, 93 899 48 12, www.albetinoya.com, tours €5.50) was Spain's first organic winery and now leads the way in restoring traditional, pre-phylloxera varietals to the area.

North of here is **Sant Sadurní d'Anoia**, the capital of the Penedès cava industry. It's not a pretty town, but it's easier to visit by public transport than the more remote wine producers. More than 90 per cent of Spain's cava is made here. **Codorníu** (Avda Codorniu, 93 818 32 32, www.grupocodorniu.com, admission €2, booking necessary), one of the largest producers, offers a wonderful tour of its Modernista headquarters, designed by Puig i Cadafalch. A train takes visitors through parts of the 26 kilometres (16 miles) of underground cellars, finishing, of course, with a tasting. **Freixenet** (C/Joan Sala 2, 93 891 70 96, www.freixenet.es, admission €5, booking necessary) another mega wine producer, is opposite Sant Sadurní station and offers free tours and tastings.

The **Priorat** area is renowned for its full-bodied (and full-priced) red wines. Monks were producing wine here as long ago as the 11th century, but the area had been all but abandoned as a centre of viticulture when young winemaker **Alvaro Palacios** set up a tiny vineyard here in the late 1980s. He battled steep hills and a sceptical wine industry, but within a few years he won global acclaim, and the region is now one of Spain's most popular among wine buyers. *Bodegas* to look out for in and around the town of Gratallops include **Clos l'Obac** (Costers del Siurana, C/Manyetes, s/n, 977 83 92 76, admission €15), **Mas Igneus** (Ctra Falset a La Vilella Baixa km 11.1, 977 26 22 59, www.masigneus.com, admission €7) and **Clos Mogador** (Camí Manyetes, 977 83 91 71). The Priorat wineries are less accessible to

casual visitors and it pays to call ahead to let them know you're coming if you want to visit.

The small **Alella** district, east of Barcelona, is best known for light, dry whites, but more important is **Terra Alta**: near the Priorat in Tarragona, with Gandesa as its capital, this area is renowned for its heavy reds. **Montsant**, a newly created DO, is also growing in popularity. Montsant's **Celler Capçanes** makes one of the world's top kosher wines and is also visitor-friendly.

Where to stay & eat

To try excellent local wines in Vilafranca, head to the **Inzolia** wine bar and store (C/Palma 21, 93 818 19 38, www.inzolia.com). **El Purgatori** (Plaça Campanar 5, 93 892 12 63, dinner only, mains €9) serves *pa amb tomàquet* (bread with tomato) with charcuterie and cheese. **Cal Ton** (C/Casal 8, 93 890 37 41, closed Mon & dinner Sun, Tue, mains €20) offers Catalan dishes like salt-cod tripe salad, and *mató* (fresh cheese) mousse with tomato jam. In Sant Sadurni, **Cal Blay** (C/Josep Rovira, 11, 93 891 00 22, www.calblay.com, mains €13.50) is also of the new wave and serves a good fixed lunch.

The three-star **Hotel Pere III** (Plaça del Penedès 2, 93 890 31 00, www.hotelpedro tercero.com, €61), in the centre of Vilafranca is good if you're travelling here by train as there are several wineries within walking distance; ask at the museum. In Torrelavit is **Masia Can Cardús** (93 899 50 18, www.masiasdelpenedes. com, €45), a farm and vineyard with rooms to rent. In the Priorat, the dreamy **Mas Ardèvol** (Ctra Falset a Porrera km 5.3, 630 324 578, www.masardevol.net, €91-€139, dinner €28) has cheerful decor and gardens of fruit trees and flowers. For updated regional cooking, try **El Cairat** (C/Nou 3, 977 83 04 81, closed Mon, mains €14.50) in Falset.

Tourist information

Falset
C/Sant Marcel 2 (977 83 10 23/www.priorat.org). **Open** 10am-2pm, 4-7pm Mon-Fri; 10am-2pm Sat; 11am-2pm Sun.

Sant Sadurní d'Anoia
C/Hospital 26 (93 891 31 88). **Open** *Sept-July* 10am-2pm, 4.30-6.30pm Mon-Fri; 10am-2pm Sat, Sun. *Aug* 10am-2pm Tue-Sun.

Vilafranca del Penedès
C/Cort 14 (93 818 12 54). **Open** 4-7pm Mon; 9am-1pm, 4-7pm Tue-Sat.

Getting there

By bus
Alella Sagales Barcelona Bus (902 13 00 14, www.sagales.es) from Plaça Urquinaona.
Alt Penedès Hispano Igualadina (93 804 44 51) provides 15 buses daily from Sants.
Falset & Gandesa Hispano Igualadina (93 804 44 51). There are two buses daily from Sants.

By train
Alt Penedès RENFE from Sants or Plaça Catalunya; trains hourly 6am-10pm (journey time 45mins), then taxi for Torres, Jean León and Codorníu.
Falset & Gandesa RENFE from Sants or Passeig de Gràcia to Marcà-Falset. Six trains daily (2hrs). For Gandesa go to Mora d'Ebre (20mins) and catch a bus.

Costa Daurada

Known as the Costa Daurada, or 'Gold Coast', the area beyond Sitges and Vilanova boasts long strands of sand, backed by alluvial plains. Development has been rife, however, and most of it is lined by concrete apartment blocks. Before you hit Tarragona, the seaside town of **Calafell** is popular with yachties, and its Iberian citadel is worth a mooch.

Further along the coast, the town of **Altafulla** hugs the sea with an esplanade of low-rise houses. Altafulla Pueblo, meanwhile, is a jumble of cobbled streets with a medieval feel; it's a ten-minute walk inland. Further south along the coast, towards the unlovely resort of **Salou**, is the **Port Aventura** theme park.

Universal Mediterránea Port Aventura
977 77 90 90/www.portaventura.es. By car A2, then A7 or N340 (108km/67 miles)/by train from Passeig de Gràcia (1hr 15mins). **Open** *Mid Mar-mid June, mid Sept-Oct* 10am-7pm daily. *Mid June-mid Sept* 10am-midnight daily. *Nov, Dec* 10am-6pm Fri; 10am-7pm Sat, Sun. **Admission** *Port Aventura* €39; €31 reductions. Night ticket (7pm-midnight) €25; €20.50 reductions. Free under-4s. *Costa Caribe* (mid June-mid Sept) €20; €16.50 reductions. *3-day combined ticket* €68; €54 reductions. **Credit** AmEx, DC, MC, V.
Port Aventura theme park is the main attraction of this beach resort, but there are also two hotels and the tropically landscaped Costa Caribe water park. Port Aventura has some 90 rides spread across five internationally themed areas (Mexico, the Far West, China, Polynesia and the Mediterranean), while

Catedral de Santa Maria.
See p282.

Popeye and the Pink Panther roam the time-space continuum and hug your kids. The truly stomach-curdling Dragon Khan rollercoaster is one of the highlights; for the little ones, there's the usual slew of carousels and spinning teacups. There are also 100 daily live shows and a spectacular lakeside Fiesta Aventura with lights, music and fireworks.

Where to stay & eat

Located in Calafell, the **Hotel Ra** is a sleek spa and thalassotherapy centre (Avda Sanatori 1, 977 69 42 00, www.hotelra.com, €265-€417). For great breakfasts and artisan pastries by the sea try **Calafell 66** (San Juan de Dios 83, 977 69 29 18). For a blowout, head to **Giorgio** (C/Àngel Guimerà 4, 977 69 11 59, closed Mon-Thur) and sample the dishes of eccentric chef-painter Giorgio Serafini.

Altafulla has the elegant **Hotel Gran Claustre** (C/Cup 2, 977 65 15 57, www.gran claustre.com, €150-€203), housed in an old convent with a central patio and swimming pool. The **Hotel San Martín** (C/Mar 7, 977 65 03 07, www.hotelsanmartin.com, €56.70-€87.74) is basic, but has a pool. The **Faristol** (C/Sant Marti 5, 977 65 00 77, closed lunch June-Sept, closed Mon-Thur Oct-May, €60-€70, mains €11), in the Old Town, is a hotel, bar and particularly good restaurant in an 18th-century house. For seafood tapas on the seafront, try **El Braser** (C/Botigues de Mar 15, 977 65 11 62, closed Wed, mains €11) and for cheap eats, **La Chunga** (C/Mar 13, 977 65 22 81, mains €8).

Tourist information

Altafulla
Plaça dels Vents (977 65 07 52/www.altafulla.org). **Open** *June-Sept* 11am-1pm, 5-9pm daily.

Getting there

By bus
Autobuses Plana (977 21 44 75) runs one bus each day to Altafulla from Passeig Sant Joan. Hispano Igualadina (93 804 44 51) runs one bus a day (Mon-Fri) to El Vendrell from Sants.

By train
RENFE from Sants or Passeig de Gràcia to Altafulla (1hr 15mins). Trains run hourly, approx 6am-9.20pm.

The Cistercian Route

The three architectural gems of the area inland from Tarragona are the Cistercian monasteries in **Poblet**, **Santes Creus** and **Vallbona de les Monges**. A signposted path, the GR175, runs between them; the trail, more than 100 kilometres (62 miles) long, is known as **La**

Ruta del Cister (the Cistercian Route). There are plenty of places to stay en route, though, and all three monasteries are easily accessible by car from **Montblanc**, 112 kilometres (70 miles) west of Barcelona and a beautiful town in its own right. In the Middle Ages, it was one of Catalonia's most powerful centres, with an important Jewish community. Its past is today reflected in its narrow medieval streets, magnificent 13th-century town walls, its churches, the **Palau Reial** and the **Palau del Castlà** (Chamberlain's Palace).

Poblet, to the west, was founded in 1151 as a royal residence and monastery. The remarkable complex includes a 14th-century **Gothic royal palace**, the 15th-century chapel of **Sant Jordi** and the main **church**, which houses the tombs of most of the count-kings of Barcelona. **Santes Creus**, founded in 1158, grew into a small village when families moved into the old monks' residences in the 1800s. Fortified walls shelter the **Palau de l'Abat** (Abbot's Palace), a monumental fountain, a 12th-century church and a superb Gothic cloister and chapterhouse.

Santa Maria de Vallbona, the third of these Cistercian houses, was, unlike the others, a convent of nuns. It has a fine part-Romanesque cloister but is less grand than the other two. Like them, it still houses a religious community.

Monestir de Poblet
977 87 02 54/www.abadia-poblet.org. **Open** *Mar-Sept* 10am-12.45pm, 3-6pm daily. *Oct-Feb* 10am-12.30pm, 3-5.30pm daily. **Admission** €5; €3 reductions. **No credit cards.**

Monestir de Santa Maria de Vallbona
973 33 02 66/www.vallbona.com. **Open** *Mar-Oct* 10.30am-1.30pm, 4.30-6.30pm Mon-Sat; noon-1.30pm, 4.30-6.30pm Sun. *Nov-Feb* 10.30am-1.30pm, 4.30-5.30pm Mon-Sat; noon-1.30pm, 4.30-5.30pm Sun. **Admission** €3; €2 reductions. **No credit cards.**

Monestir de Santes Creus
977 63 83 29. **Open** *Mid Mar-mid Sept* 10am-1pm, 3-6.30pm Tue-Sun. *Mid Sept-mid Jan* 10am-1.30pm, 3-5pm Tue-Sun. *Mid Jan-mid Mar* 10am-1.30pm, 3-5.30pm Tue-Sun. **Admission** €3.60; €2.40 reductions. Free Tue. **No credit cards.**

Where to stay & eat

In Montblanc, you'll need to book in advance in order to secure a room at the popular **Fonda dels Àngels** (Plaça dels Àngels 1, 977 86 01 73, closed Sun and 3wks Sept, €41, set menu €15 & €20), which also has a great restaurant. The **Fonda Colom** is a friendly old restaurant located behind the Plaça Major (C/Civaderia 5, 977 86 01 53, closed dinner Sun & Mon, 2 wks Sept & 2 wks Dec, mains €13.50).

In L'Espluga de Francolí, en route to Poblet, the **Hostal del Senglar** (Plaça Montserrat Canals 1, 977 87 01 21, ww.hostaldelsenglar.com, €64-€72) is a great-value country hotel with lovely gardens, a swimming pool and an atmospheric, if slightly pricey, restaurant (mains €12). In Santes Creus the **Hotel La Plana del Molí** (Avda Plana del Molí 21, 977 63 83 09, €48) is set in extensive gardens. Try the delicious partridge broth or wild-boar stew at its restaurant (mains €10). The **Hostal Grau** (C/Pere El Gran 3, 977 63 83 11, www.pension grau.com, closed mid Oct-June, €36, restaurant closed Mon and mid Dec-mid Jan, mains €13) is a reasonable option, with good Catalan food, as is the **Restaurant Catalunya** (C/Arbreda 2, 977 63 84 32, closed Wed, mains €14).

Tourist information

Montblanc
Antiga Església de Sant Francesc (977 86 17 33/ www.montblancmedieval.org). **Open** 10am-1.30pm, 3-6.30pm Mon-Sat; 10am-2pm Sun.

Getting there

By bus
Hispano Igualadina (93 804 44 51) runs a service to Montblanc from Sants station leaving at 3.30pm Mon-Fri. There are more buses running from Valls and Tarragona.

By train
RENFE trains leave from Sants or Passeig de Gràcia to Montblanc. There are five trains a day. The journey takes about 2hrs.

Tortosa & the Ebre Delta

An hour further down the coast from Tarragona is **Tortosa**, a little-visited town with a rich history evident in the fabric of its buildings. A magnificent Gothic cathedral, built on the site of a Roman temple, is surrounded by medieval alleyways, and traces of the town's Jewish and Arab quarters can still be seen (and are clearly signposted). Interesting Modernista buildings around the town include the colourful, Mudéjar-inspired pavilions of the former slaughterhouse (Escorxador), on the banks of the Ebre river.

East of here is the astonishing **Parc Natural del Delta de l'Ebre**, an ecologically remarkable protected area. The towns of the delta are themselves nothing special, but the immense, flat, green expanses of wetlands, channels, dunes and still-productive rice fields are eerily beautiful. It's this variety of habitat, so attractive to birds, that makes the area such a popular birdwatching destination, since birders can hope to tick off nearly half the 600

bird species that are found in Europe at this one site. The flocks of flamingos make a spectacular sight as they shuffle around filter feeding, and the wetlands are full of herons, great crested grebes, spoonbills and marsh harriers.

The town of **Deltebre** is the base for most park services; from here, it's easy to embark on day trips to the bird sanctuaries, especially the remote headland of **Punta de la Banya**. The delta's flatness makes it an ideal place for walking or cycling; for bicycle hire, check at the tourist office in Deltebre. Small boats offer trips along the river from the north bank about eight kilometres (five miles) east of Deltebre.

Where to stay & eat
Tortosa has a wonderful parador, **Castell de la Suda** (977 44 44 50, €123-€201), built on the site of a Moorish fortress with panoramic views of the countryside. See www.paradors.es for occasional offers. On the eastern edge of the Ebre delta is a wide, sweeping beach, Platja dels Eucaliptus, where you'll find the **Camping Eucaliptus** (977 47 90 46, www.camping eucaliptus.com, closed mid Oct-mid Mar, €4.05-€5.15/person; €5.93-€6.42/tent; €3.64-€4.45/car). The **Hotel Rull** in Deltebre is friendly and organises occasional 'safaris' (Avda Esportiva 155, 977 48 77 28, www. hotelrull.com, €68-€95, mains €18). You can also stay and eat at the ecologically friendly **Delta Hotel** (Avda del Canal, Camí de la Illeta, 977 48 00 46, www.deltahotel.net, €74-€95). Local specialities include dishes made with delta rice, duck, frogs' legs and the curious *chapadillo* (sun-dried eels): try them all at **Galatxo** (Desembocadura Riu Ebre, 977 26 75 03, mains €15), at the mouth of the river.

Tourist information

Delta de l'Ebre
C/Doctor Marti Buera 22, Deltebre (977 48 96 79/ www.parcsdecatalunya.net). **Open** *Oct-Apr* 10am-2pm, 3-6pm Mon-Sat; 10am-2pm Sun. *May-Sept* 10am-2pm, 3-7pm Mon-Sat; 10am-2pm Sun.

Tortosa
Plaça Carrilet 1 (977 44 96 48/www.turismetortosa. com). **Open** *Oct-Mar* 10am-1.30pm, 3.30-6.30pm Tue-Sat; 10.30am-1.30pm Sun. *Apr-Sept* 10am-1.30pm, 4.30-7.30pm Tue-Sat; 10.30am-1.30pm Sun.

Getting there

By train & bus
RENFE from Sants or Passeig de Gràcia every 2hrs to Tortosa (journey time 2hrs) or L'Aldea (journey time 2hrs 30mins), then three buses daily (run by HIFE; 977 44 03 00) to Deltebre.

Girona & the Costa Brava

Handsome towns and heavenly coves on Spain's wild coast.

Girona

Smart, peaceful and solidly middle class, Girona is a city far more staunchly Catalan than its cosmopolitan cousin Barcelona, and increasingly it is becoming almost as much a destination thanks to Ryanair's monopoly on the airport. Time spent in Girona rewards with a carefully restored Jewish quarter dominating the handsome medieval heart, an imposing cathedral and a handful of interesting museums. These include the one-off **Museu del Cinema** (C/Sequia 1, 972 41 27 77, www.museudelcinema.org, closed Mon) – a fascinating collection of early animation techniques right through to the present day.

The **River Onyar**, which is lined by buildings in red and ochre, divides the Old City from the new, and connects one to the other by the impressive Eiffel-designed bridge, the **Pont de les Peixateries**. A walk up the lively riverside **Rambla de la Llibertat** takes you towards the city's core and major landmark, the magnificent **cathedral**. Its 1680 Baroque façade conceals a graceful Romanesque cloister and understated Gothic interior, which happens to boast the widest nave in Christendom. In the cathedral museum is the stunning 12th-century **Tapestry of Creation** and the **Beatus**, an illuminated tenth-century set of manuscripts.

Before its expulsion in 1492, the city's sizeable Jewish population had its own district, the **Call**, whose labyrinthine streets running off and around the C/Força are among the most beautifully preserved in Europe. The story of this community is told in the Jewish museum in the **Centre Bonastruc ça Porta** (C/Força 8, 972 21 67 61, www.ajuntament.gi/call/cat/index.php), built on the site of a 15th-century synagogue. Nearby is the **Museu d'Història de la Ciutat** (C/Força 27, 972 22 22 29, www.ajuntament.gi/museu_ciutat, closed Mon), set in an 18th-century monastery. Look out for the alcoves with ventilated seating on the ground floor: this is where the deceased monks were placed to dry out for two years, before their mummified corpses were put on display.

Heading north from here, the **Mudéjar Banys Àrabs** (C/Ferran el Catòlic, 972 19 07 97) is actually a Christian creation, a 12th-century bathhouse blending Romanesque and Moorish architecture. The nearby monastery of **Sant Pere de Galligants** is a fine example of Romanesque architecture, its beautiful 12th-century cloister rich with intricate carvings. The monastery also houses the **Museu Arqueològic** (Plaça Santa Llúcia 1, 972 20 26 32, www.mac.es, closed Mon), which shows day-to-day objects from the Paleolithic to the Visigothic periods. Continuing from here, the **Passeig Arqueològic** runs along what's left of the old city walls, intact until 1892.

Of particular appeal to visitors of a more active disposition, the **carrilet** (an old steam-rail route dating back to 1892) has been reincarnated as a cycle path running from Girona to Sant Feliu de Guixols. It starts at the Plaça dels Països Catalans and continues along a lovely route of ancient Iberian villages, iron bridges and long-dry river beds. It takes about three hours going at a gentle pace.

Where to stay & eat

The **AC Palau de Bellavista** (C/Pujada Polvorins 1, 872 080 670, www.ac-hotels.com, €91-€149) is the business option in the New Town. It has a terrace with wonderful views of the city and the gourmet restaurant **Numun**, headed by the Roca brothers. The **Hotel Ciutat de Girona** (C/Nord 2, 972 48 30 38, www.hotel-ciutatdegirona.com, €130.54-€150.87) is similar, and is enhanced by the odd designer touch.

In the Old Town, the **Hotel Històric** (C/Bellmirall 6, 972 22 35 83, www.hotel historic.com, €122) is a shade cheaper. The owners also rent fully equipped apartments for two or three people (€96) in the adjacent building. **Pensión Bellmirall** (C/Bellmirall 3, 972 20 40 09, closed Jan & Feb, €65-€75) is in an attractive 14th-century building with a shady breakfast courtyard. The **Hotel Peninsular** (C/Nou 3 & Avda Sant Francesc 6, 972 20 38 00, www.novarhotels.com, €66-€75) is good value.

A warren of medieval streets lies behind **Girona**'s colourful riverfront façades.

The best restaurant in town, and one of the best in Spain, is the **Celler de Can Roca** (C/Taialà 40, 972 22 21 57, www.cellercanroca. com, closed Mon & Sun, mains €30). Located in a quiet suburb just north of the city, it's an essential trip for food-lovers, though you will need to book ahead. If the coffers won't quite stretch to this, the affordable tasting menu at **Massana** (C/Bonastruc de Porta 10, 972 21 38 20, closed Sun & dinner Tue, tasting menu €59.65) offers yet more creativity. Over the river from the Old Town, you'll find Girona's oldest and possibly best-value restaurant, **Casa Marieta** (Plaça de la Independència 5-6, 972 20 10 16, www.casamarieta.com, closed

Mon, mains €12), while the old Modernista flour factory houses **La Farinera** (Ptge Farinera Teixidor 4, 972 22 02 20, menu €9), which has good tapas. Nearby, halfway up a medieval flight of steps, is a Francophile's delight, **Le Bistrot** (Pujada Sant Domènec 4, 972 21 88 03, mains €6), with a cheap (and good) set lunch in a pretty setting.

Tourist information

Girona
Rambla de la Llibertat 1 (972 22 65 75/ www.ajuntament.gi). **Open** 8am-8pm Mon-Fri; 8am-2pm, 4-8pm Sat; 9am-2pm Sun.

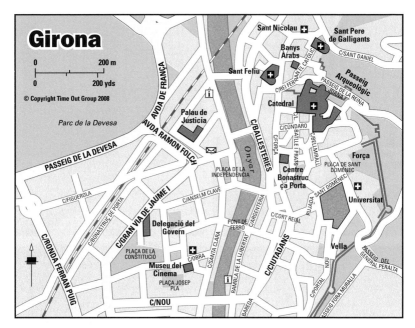

Getting there

By bus

Sagales Barcelona Bus (902 26 06 06, www.sagales.
com) runs approximately five buses daily from
Estació del Nord.

By train

RENFE from Sants or Passeig de Gràcia (1hr
15mins). Trains leave hourly from 6am-9.15pm.

From Girona to the coast

The C66 takes you from Girona to the coast
through the Baix (Lower) Empordà, coined the
'Golden Triangle' by locals, and the 'Tuscany of
Spain' by foreigners. Both amount to much the
same thing: a postcard-perfect patchwork of corn
fields, oak copses and sunflowers, and a wealthy,
part-time population. The region's strategic
importance in medieval times is demonstrated
by a legacy of castles and walled, honey-coloured
towns and villages. The road splits in dignified
La Bisbal, where you can buy no end of
ceramic goods. Nearby **Verges** is most famous
for its grotesque 'dance of death' procession on
Maundy Thursday. Up the road is the 12th-
century **Castell de Púbol**, bought by Salvador
Dalí to house (and eventually bury) his wife-
muse Gala in her later years. Relations were
strained by then: Dalí had to book appointments
to see her, and the tomb that he prepared for
himself next to hers lies empty (he changed
his mind), guarded by a stuffed giraffe.

A few miles east lies the walled, moated town
of **Peratallada**. Dominated by an 11th-century
castle, it's famous for its indigo-painted arcades
and fine restaurants. Nearby **Ullastret** takes
you further back in time, with extensive ruins
from a third-century BC Iberian settlement,
explained in the small **Museu d'Arqueològic**
(Puig de Sant Andreu, 972 17 90 58, www.mac.es,
closed Mon). The medieval town of **Pals**, with
its imposing **Torre de les Hores**, has great
views of the coast, as does **Begur**, a 14th-
century town built around its castle. The latter,
a steep three-kilometre (two-mile) walk from the
sea, acts as a gateway to the Costa Brava.

Castell de Púbol

*Information Teatre-Museu Dalí (972 48 86 55/
www.salvador-dali.org).* **Open** *15 Mar-14 June,
16 Sept-1 Nov* 10.30am-5.15pm Tue-Sun. *15 June-
15 Sept* 10.30am-7.15pm daily. *2 Nov-31 Dec*
10.30am-4.15pm. Closed 1 Jan-14 Mar. **Admission**
€6; €4 reductions. **No credit cards**.

Where to stay & eat

In Peratallada, the **Hostal Miralluna** (Plaça de
l'Oli 2, 972 63 43 04, www.hostalmiralluna.com,
€160-€192) is a tranquil 14th-century place to

stay, and filled with antiques. **El Cau del Papibou** (C/Major 10, 972 63 40 18, www. hotelelcau.net, €107-€133) is a pleasant, eight-room hotel with all the latest technology. The charming **Ca l'Aliu** (C/Roca 6, 972 63 40 61, www.calaliu.com, €57-€64) is probably the best value accommodation in town. In Ullastret the **Hotel Restaurant El Fort** (C/Presó 2, 972 75 77 73, www.hotelelfort.com, €107-€160) has four comfortable studio apartments, and offers a range of packages. In Pals, the **Hotel Mas Salvi** (C/Carmany 13, 972 63 64 78, www. massalvi.com, closed mid Jan-mid Feb, €269-€327) is a sprawling, converted farmhouse in the middle of pristine countryside. It has immense rooms, landscaped gardens, indoor and outdoor pools, tennis courts and an avant-garde restaurant. At the other end of the scale is the **Barris** (C/Enginyer Algarra 51, 972 63 67 02, €45). If you're staying in Begur, try the **Hotel Rosa** (C/Pi i Ralló 19, 972 62 30 15, www. hotel-rosa.com, closed Nov-Feb, €70-€115).

Locals travel from far and wide to eat in Peratallada's restaurants; try the famous *galtes de porc a l'empordanesa* (pigs' cheeks with artichoke and carrots) at the **Restaurant Bonay** (Plaça de les Voltes 13, 972 63 40 34, www.bonay.com, closed Jan & Dec, mains €14). Also making a name for itself in the centre of town is **La Païssa d'en Cardina** (C/Jaume II 10, 972 63 47 08, mains €15, closed dinner Tue & all day Wed), which has superb Empordan and Italian fare, with a wood-fired pizza oven and dishes such as home-made ravioli stuffed with anis-flavoured carrots. The €10 set lunch is fantastic. In Begur, **Els Patis de Begur** (C/Pi i Rallo 9, 972 62 37 41, mains €14) specialises in paellas; in Pals, **Restaurant Sa Punta** (Urbanizació Sa Punta, 972 66 73 76, mains €25) serves excellent Mediterranean dishes by a pool. In Ullastret, try **Restaurant Ibèric** (C/Valls 11, 972 75 71 08, mains €18) for truly great regional fare such as snails, *suquet* and wild-boar stew, with home-grown vegetables. Another superb-value little eaterie is **Sa Torre Volver a Llamar** (Plaça de la Mota 6, Palau-sator, 972 63 41 18, closed Wed, mains €12) serving exceptional grilled meats. It is also famed for its *arrós a la cassola* (a dark stew made with Pals rice, baked in terracotta and beefed out with *botifarra*, calamares and pork). Make like a local and take it to the beach.

Tourist information

Begur
Avda 11 de Setembre 5 (972 62 45 20/www. begur.es). **Open** *June-Sept* 9am-2pm, 4-9pm Mon-Fri; 10am-2pm, 4-9pm Sat, Sun. *Oct-May* 9am-2pm, Mon-Fri; 10am-2pm Sat, Sun.

Pals
Plaça Major 7 (972 63 73 80/www.pals.es). **Open** *mid June-Oct* 10am-2pm, 5-8pm Tue, Wed, Sat, Sun. 10am-8pm Mon, Thur, Fri. *Oct-mid June* 10am-5pm Mon-Sat; 10am-2pm Sun.

Getting there

By bus
Sarfa (902 30 20 25, www.sarfa.com) runs nine daily buses from Estació del Nord to Palafrugell (some continue to Begur), and regular buses to La Bisbal, which stop at Púbol.

Costa Brava

In its heyday, before the arrival of the bulldozers, high-rises and masses of pink-fleshed tourists, the Costa Brava (meaning 'wild' or 'rugged' coast) was the most exclusive resort area in Spain, attracting legions of film stars, artists and writers. Today, despite the concrete resorts that have swamped towns like **Calella**, **Blanes** and **Lloret de Mar**, it's still possible to find pockets of prettiness along the coast thanks to the soaring cliffs and rocky, sea-buffeted coves that prevent overdevelopment. A train will get you as far as Blanes, beyond which the road spins into a series of cliff-hugging hairpin bends that mark the start of the Costa Brava proper, with **Tossa del Mar** as its gateway. While the new town has been constructed with little thought, Tossa still has one of the loveliest medieval quarters in Spain, crowning a hill jutting into the sea. It used to be a favourite haunt of Ava Gardner – a bronze statue of her marks the entry to the Old Town – harking back to the days when it looked like Tossa might be the new Capri. **Cala Bona** and **Cala Pola** are both lovely and relatively isolated beaches a short walk from here.

The tortuous 20-kilometre (12-mile) drive through coastal pine forests from here to **Sant Feliu de Guíxols** offers brief, but unforgettable, views of the sea. Sant Feliu itself has some fine Modernista buildings along the dignified Passeig Marítim, and the town museum has a fine collection of local ceramics. **Sant Pol** beach is three kilometres (two miles) north of the crowded town sands, and offers more towel room. Just north of Sant Pol the GR92 path, or 'Camino de Ronda', starts out from below the Hostal de la Gavina in S'Agaró and continues on along many secluded coves and rocky outlets for swimming. The sandy bay of **Sa Conca** – considered to be one of the most beautiful beaches on the Costa Brava – has a couple of good *xiringuitos* for a sardine lunch. Continue on at a leisurely pace all the way to Torre Valentina, from where you can catch a

Costa Brava. *See p291.*

bus back. The only tedious stretch is the one that traverses **Platja d'Aro**. This and **Palamós** are worth avoiding generally; the latter has never recovered from an attack by the infamous pirate Barba Roja (Redbeard) in 1543. Instead, continue to **Palafrugell**, which has a great Sunday market and offers access to a number of picturesque villages built into the rocky coves. The **Fundació Vila Casas** (Plaça Can Mario 7, 972 30 62 46, www.fundaciovila casas.com, closed Tue) houses a surprisingly good collection of works by local artists and sculptures, and gives an idea of the kind of creativity the environment inspires. **Calella de Palafrugell**, not to be confused with its ugly near-namesake down the coast, is a quiet, charming town, even during its annual Cantada d'Havaneres song festival in July. A scenic 20-minute walk away, **Llafranc** offers a long curved beach where you can swim between fishing boats at anchor in the bay. The cliff-top botanical gardens at **Cap Roig** (972 61 45 82) host a wonderful music and arts festival every July and August, attracting names such as Bob Dylan and Roberta Flack.

Tamariu, known for its good seafood, is the perfect base for waterskiing and fishing. Giro Nàutic (www.gironautic.com) is a useful portal for all things aquatic in the area. Next up is **Aiguablava**, with its modern parador and white sandy beach, and **Fornells** – both are accessible from **Begur**, as is the small **Aiguafreda**, a cove that's sheltered by pines. Nearby **Sa Riera**, the northernmost cove, shelters two beaches: **La Platja del Raco**, where bathing costumes must be worn, and **Illa Roja**, where they mustn't.

Beyond the Ter estuary and the Montgri hills, which divide the Baix and Alt Empordà, is **L'Estartit**. This small resort town caters for tourists interested in exploring the **Illes Medes**, a group of rocky limestone outcrops. The biggest housed a British prison in the 19th century, but Les Illes are now home only to a unique ecosystem, an underwater paradise where divers can contemplate colourful coral and hundreds of different species of sea life. For a view of the islands, it's worth the climb up to the 12th-century **Castell de Montgrí**.

Where to eat

In Tossa, **Santa Marta** (C/Francesc Aromir 2, 972 34 04 72, mains €18) has a pretty terrace in the Old Town and specialises in Catalan cuisine. **Da Nino** (C/Pola 9, 972 34 11 26, mains €8) is a friendly pizzeria in the centre. In Sant Feliu de Guíxols, try the **Nàutic** (Port Esportiu, 972 32 06 63, closed Mon, set lunch €14.70, set dinner €36) in the Club Nàutic sailing club, for great

views and superb seafood. In Mont-ras, just outside Palafrugell, **La Cuina de Can Pipes** (Barri Canyelles s/n, Mont-ras, 972 30 66 77, www.canpipes.com, closed Mon, Tue, mains €34.50) is one of the finest restaurants in the area, with tables on a large lawn. Calella has the excellent **Tragamar** (Platja de Canadell s/n, 972 61 43 36, www.grupotragaluz.com, mains €14.50), a branch of the restaurant Tragaluz in Barcelona. In Tamariu, there's good seafood at the **Royal** on the beachfront (Passeig de Mar 9, 972 62 00 41, closed Dec-Feb, mains €17); while in Aiguablava, the **Hotel Aiguablava** (Platja de Fornells, 972 62 20 58, www.aiguablava.com, closed Nov-Feb, mains €24.50, set lunch/dinner €39) has an excellent beachfront restaurant.

Where to stay

In Tossa, the **Hotel Diana** (Plaça España 6, 972 34 18 86, www.diana-hotel.com, €72-€149) is situated in a Modernista building with a beautifully preserved marble staircase and tiled floors. Bargain rooms are to be had at **Fonda Lluna** (C/Roqueta 20, 972 34 03 65, www.fondalluna.com, €38-€42). In Sant Feliu de Guíxols, try the small, friendly **Hotel Plaça** (Plaça Mercat 22, 972 32 51 55, www. hotelplaza.org, €75-€113), close to the beach. North of Sant Feliu, in **S'Agaró**, is the nearest luxury option, the **Hostal de la Gavina** (Plaça de la Rosaleda, 972 32 11 00, www. lagavina.com, closed Nov-Easter, €203-€446), a five-star in the European grand-hotel tradition. Near the Platja d'Aro, **Mas Torrellas** (Ctra de Santa Cristina a Platja d'Aro km2, 972 83 75 26, €64-€90) is removed from the madness somewhat. It is an 18th-century farmhouse with bags of charm and a pretty garden pool. Llafranc has the **Hotel Llafranch** (Passeig de Cipsela 16, 972 30 02 08, www.hllafranch.com, €97-€143), which is run by two brothers, and was a favourite haunt of Salvador Dalí and various of his cronies back in the 1960s. Alternatively, the friendly **Hotel Casamar** (C/Nero 3-11, 972 30 01 04, closed Jan-mid Mar, €55-€130) is a good budget option.

Tamariu is home to the relaxed **Hotel Tamariu** (Passeig de Mar 2, 972 62 00 31, www.tamariu.com, closed Nov-Mar, €87-€122), while in Aiguablava, choose from the pleasant parador, **Platja d'Aiguablava** (972 62 21 62, www.parador.es, €140-€171) or the stately, family-run **Hotel Aiguablava** (*see above* **Where to eat**, €144.50-€234). In Begur, try **AiguaClara** (972 62 29 05, www.aiguaclara. com, €95-€145), a colonial-style palace dating back to 1876. Light, airy rooms, original tiles and colourful paintwork give it a chilled-out, funky edge. There's live jazz in the restaurant on Friday evenings. Nearby, in Sa Tuna, the **Hostal Sa Tuna** (Platja Sa Tuna, 972 62 21 98, www.hostalsatuna.com, closed mid Oct-mid Mar, €107-€134) has five rooms and enjoys a perfect position by the sea. L'Estartit is home to the **Santa Clara** (Passeig Marítim 18, 972 75 17 67, €43-€58).

Tourist information

L'Estartit

Passeig Marítim (972 75 19 10/www.torroella.org). **Open** *June, Sept* 9.30am-2pm, 4-8pm daily. *July, Aug* 9.30am-2pm, 4-9pm daily. *Oct-May* 9am-1pm, 3-6pm daily.

Palafrugell

C/Carrilet 2 (972 30 02 28/www.palafrugell.net). **Open** *May-June, Sept* 10am-1pm, 5-8pm Mon-Sat; 10am-1pm Sun. *July, Aug* 9am-9pm Mon-Sat; 10am-1pm Sun. *Oct-Apr* 10am-1pm, 4-7pm Mon-Sat; 10am-1pm Sun.

Sant Feliu de Guíxols

Plaça del Mercat 28 (972 82 00 51/www.guixols.net). **Open** *Mid June-mid Sept* 10am-2pm, 4-8pm daily. *Mid Sept-mid June* 10am-1pm, 4-7pm Mon-Sat; 10am-2pm Sun.

Getting there

By bus

Sarfa (902 30 20 25, www.sarfa.com) runs 13 buses daily to Sant Feliu from Estació del Nord (journey time 1hr 20mins), and nine to Palafrugell (2hrs); some continue to Begur. Change in Palafrugell or Torroella for L'Estartit.

North to France

The port town of **L'Escala** is well known for its anchovies, best enjoyed from one of its seafront terraces. A mere 15-minute walk away, in **Empúries**, you'll find the remains of an ancient city that dates back to 600 BC, when it was founded by the Phoenicians, before being recolonised by the Greeks and finally the Romans. Today, ruins from all three periods – including a stunning mosaic of Medusa, as well as the layout of the original Greek harbour – are clearly visible.

On the other side of the huge Golf de Roses is the overcrowded tourist resort of **Roses**, which has little to recommend it apart from a 16th-century citadel and the nearby legendary restaurant **El Bulli** (*see p174*) in Cala Montjoi. From Roses, the road coils over the hills that form the **Cap de Creus** nature reserve, before dropping spectacularly down to **Cadaqués**. The town's relative isolation has made it the chosen destination for the discerning: Picasso

painted much of his early cubist work here, but it was Salvador Dalí who really put the place on the map. The artist spent his childhood summers here, brought his surrealist circle to see it, and ended up building his home in **Port Lligat**, a short walk away. Cadaqués later became the preferred resort among the Catalan cultural elite. It has kept its charm primarily thanks to a ban on the high-rise buildings that have blighted much of the rest of coastal Spain. Dalí's house, with its collections of zany furniture, peculiar fittings and stuffed animals, is now a museum that offers extraordinary insight into the eccentric genius's strange lifestyle. Note that you should book well in advance of your visit, as only eight people are allowed in at a time.

On the north side of the cape, you'll find **Port de la Selva**, which looks towards France. Less touristy than Cadaqués, it's also within hiking distance of the remarkable **Sant Pere de Rodes** fortified abbey (972 38 75 59, closed Mon, admission €3.60; €2.40 reductions, free Tue), the area's most accomplished example of Romanesque architecture. A further climb takes you up to the imposing **Castell de Sant Salvador**, an imposing tenth-century castle that seems to grow out of the rock, with unparalleled views out over the Pyrenees to France, and back into Catalonia.

The capital of the Alt Empordà region is **Figueres**, where Dalí was born and is buried in his own museum in the city's old theatre, the **Teatre-Museu Dalí**. The artist donated many of his works to the museum and also redesigned the place, putting thousands of yellow loaves on the external walls and huge eggs on its towers. The highlight inside is the three-dimensional room-sized Mae West face, a collection of furniture arranged to look like the star when viewed from a certain angle, with a plump red sofa for her famous pout. All of this somewhat overshadows the city's other two (rather good) museums: the **Museu de l'Empordà** (Rambla 2, 972 50 23 05, www. museuemporda.org, closed Mon, admission €2, reductions €1), which gives an overview of the history of the area, and the **Museu del Joguet** (C/Sant Pere 1, 972 50 45 85, closed Mon, admission €5, reductions €4), full of 19th- and early 20th-century toys, some of which belonged to Dalí and Miró.

Between Figueres and the sea sits the **Parc Natural dels Aiguamolls de l'Empordà**, which is a haven for rare species of birds that flock to the marshy lowlands at the mouth of the Fluvia river in spring and autumn. As well as flamingos, bee-eaters and moustached warblers, this nature reserve is home to turtles, salamanders and otters.

Casa-Museu de Port Lligat

972 25 10 15/www.dali-estate.org. **Open** *Mid Mar-mid June, mid Sept-Dec* 10.30am-5.10pm Tue-Sun. *Mid June-mid Sept* 9.30am-8.10pm daily. Closed Jan-mid Mar. **Admission** €10; €8 reductions. Advisable to book ahead.

Teatre-Museu Dalí

Plaça Gala-Salvador Dalí 5, Figueres (972 67 75 00/ www.dali-estate.org). **Open** *July-Sept* 9am-7.15pm daily. *Oct-June* 10.30am-5.15pm Tue-Sun. **Admission** €10; €7 reductions.

Where to stay & eat

Next to the ruins in Empúries, the **Hostal Empúries** (Platja Portitxol, 972 77 02 07, www.hostalempuries.com, €102-€155, set menu €31) offers sparse but clean rooms in a fantastic setting in front of the rocky beach. It also does good Mediterranean food all year round. Fifteen minutes' walk away, in the pretty village of Sant Martí d'Empúries, is the comfortable **Riomar** (Platja del Riuet, 972 77 03 62, www.riomarhotel.com, closed late Oct-Easter, €75-€124). Over the bay, a twisting seven-kilometre (four-and-a-half-mile) drive from Roses, is the extraordinary and world-famous **El Bulli** (*see p174*).

Perched on a cliff-top between Roses and Cadaqués, the **Hotel Cala Jóncols** (Ctra Vella de Roses a Cadaqués, 972 25 39 70, www.calajoncols.com, closed Dec-Mar, €56-€77 full board) is completely isolated and basic; a blissful hideaway for those who can do without luxuries, it makes for a great romantic weekend, especially out of season.

Cadaqués has few hotels, and most are closed in winter, so always call first. The **Hotel Rocamar** (C/Virgen del Carment s/n, 972 25 81 50, www.rocamar.com, €76-€180) is the finest hotel in Cadaqués and set away from the rest of the town, looking back over the bay. Alternatively, **Playa Sol** (Platja Pianc 3, 972 25 81 00, www.playasol.com, closed Jan & Dec, €105-€180) puts you in the thick of things and also has lovely sea views. Over the hill in Port Lligat, the two-star **Hotel Port Lligat** (972 25 81 62, €67-€125) is right next door to the Dalí museum and has a boutiquey feel to it, while the **Hotel Calina** (Avda Salvador Dali, 33, 972 25 88 51, www.hotelcalina.com, incl breakfast €64-€133) is more modern, more comfortable and has a decent-sized swimming pool overlooking the beach. Restaurants, too, have a habit of closing in winter, so it pays to call ahead. **Restaurant Can Rafa** (C/Passeig Maritim 7, 972 15 94 01, www.restaurant canrafa.com, closed Wed and Dec, mains €22) specialises in local lobster, while the pretty **Es Balconet** (C/Sant Antoni 2, 972 25 88 14, closed Tue and Jan, Feb, Nov, mains €15), up a winding street back from the bay, is good for paella. **Casa Anita** (C/Miguel Rosen, 972 25 84 71, www.casa-anita.com, closed Mon and Nov, mains €18) is a popular, friendly and family-owned place with excellent fresh seafood and long queues. Dalí used to eat here. At Cap de Creus, the **Restaurant Cap de Creus** (972 19 90 05, www.cbrava.com/restcapc.es.htm, mains €16.50) serves an eclectic range of dishes from seafood to curry, all in a stunning setting on a headland jutting out to sea. Rooms are also available here (€85).

In Figueres, the **Hotel Duran** (C/Lasauca 5, 972 50 12 50, www.hotelduran.com, €86-€118, set menu €16.05) was an old haunt of Dali and exudes comfortable, battered elegance. The restaurant serves fine game and seafood. For clean and simple rooms, head for **La Barretina** (C/Lasauca 13, 972 67 34 25, www.hostallabarretina.com, closed Nov, €48). **President** (Ronda Firal 33, 972 50 17 00, set lunch €16.05) offers good, solid Catalan fare and excellent seafood. C/Jonquera is the main drag for cheap *menús del dia*, which you can sample at alfresco tables. A couple of kilometres west, **Mas Pau** (Ctra de Figueres a Besalú, Avinyonet de Puigventós, 972 54 61 54, www.maspau.com, closed Sun dinner, all day Mon and Tue lunch, mains €25) is an excellent and creative restaurant.

Tourist information

Cadaqués

C/Cotxe 2A (972 25 83 15/www.cadaques.org). **Open** *June-Sept* 9am-9pm Mon-Sat; 10.30am-1pm Sun. *Oct-May* 9am-1pm, 4-7pm Mon-Sat.

L'Escala

Plaça de les Escoles 1 (972 77 06 03/www. lescala.org). **Open** *Mid June-mid Sept* 9am-8.30pm daily. *Mid Sept-mid June* 9am-1pm, 4-7pm Mon-Fri; 10am-4pm Sat; 10am-1pm Sun.

Figueres

Plaça del Sol (972 50 31 55). **Open** *Mar-June, Oct* 9am-2pm, 4-7pm Mon-Fri; 9.30am-2pm, 3.30-6.30pm Sat. *July-Sept* 9am-8pm Mon-Sat; 10am-3pm Sun. *Feb* 9am-2pm Mon-Fri. Closed Nov-Jan.

Getting there

By bus

Sagales (902 26 06 06, www.sagales.com) runs several buses daily to Figueres from Estació del Nord (2hrs 30mins). Sarfa (902 30 20 25) runs two buses daily to Roses and Cadaqués (2hrs 15mins).

By train

RENFE from Sants or Passeig de Gràcia to Figueres (journey 2hrs). Trains leave every hour.

Vic to the Pyrenees

Head out on the high roads.

Vic & around

Vic reveals its magic gradually, offering a good deal more than one might expect on first impressions. The capital of the verdant Osona region has at its heart the impressive arcaded Plaça Major, home to a famous market that is nearly as old as the town itself (Tuesday and Saturday mornings). In one corner of the market square is the Modernista Casa Comella. Sgraffiti designed by Gaietà Buïgas depict the four seasons. Buïgas was also responsible for the Monument a Colom in Barcelona. Of Vic's many churches, the **Catedral de Sant Pere** contains Romanesque, Gothic and neo-classical elements, along with a set of dramatic 20th-century murals by Josep Lluis Sert, who is buried here. The **Temple Romà** was only discovered in 1882, when the 12th-century walls that surrounded it were knocked down. It's since been well restored, and now houses an art gallery that shows some of Sert's work. The **Museu Episcopal** (Plaça del Bisbe Oliva 3, 93 886 93 60, www.museuepiscopalvic.com, closed Mon, admission €4) is worth a visit for its magnificent 12th-century murals and a superb collection of Romanesque and Gothic art.

The beech forests, medieval villages, steep gorges and Romanesque hermitages make this area rewarding to explore by foot but it is also a centre of both parapenting and hot air ballooning (Osona Globus, 609 832 974, www. osonaglobus.com). Following the C153 road towards Olot, **Rupit** makes a remarkably beautiful stop. An ancient village built on the side of a medieval castle, it has a precarious hanging bridge across the Ter gorge. Later building has been done so sympathetically to the style that it's difficult to tell the old from the new. Almost as lovely, and not quite as touristy, is nearby **Tavertet**.

Where to stay & eat

In **Vic** itself, there's very little in the way of accommodation; its only *pensión* is **Hostal Osona** (C/Remei 3, 93 883 28 45, €28). It does, however, have some great restaurants. **Cardona 7** (C/Cardona 7, 93 886 38 15, tapas €6.50, closed Sun dinner and all day Mon) serves new-wave tapas such as pig's trotter salad and salt cod in rosemary. **La Taula**

(C/Sant Marius 8, 93 417 28 48, closed lunch Sat, all day Sun and Aug, mains €14.50) offers a range of excellent-value set menus.

If you have transport, the nicest places to stay are outside Vic. The **Hotel Torre Martí** (C/Ramon Llull 11, St. Julià de Vilatorta, 93 888 83 72, www.hoteltorremarti.com, €133-€171) is one of the loveliest in the area. Painted fire-red with blue galleries, it was built in 1945 by local architect Riera Clariana. It's now an enclave of music and art, fine wine and gastronomy. The **Parador de Vic** (Paraje el Bac de Sau, 93 812 23 23, www.parador.es, €167-€200) is modern and comfortable, and sits in a fabulous location overlooking the Ter gorge; take the C153 north of Vic and follow the signs (around 14km/10 miles). Just before Tavèrnoles, **Mas Banús** (93 812 20 91, www.elbanus.com) is a giant old farmhouse, with self-contained cottages (from €250 per weekend for four people). In Tavèrnoles is the **Fussimanya** (Ctra del Parador km 7, 93 812 21 88, closed dinner Mon, Tue, Wed & all day Thur, mains €12), a rambling old restaurant famous for its sausages; it's popular at the weekends. In Rupit, **Hostal Estrella** (Plaça Bisbe Font 1, 93 852 20 05, www.hostal estrella.com, €98, set lunch €18) is a *pensión* with a huge and popular restaurant.

Tourist information

Vic
C/Ciutat 4 (93 886 20 91/www.victurisme.cat).
Open 10am-2pm, 4-8pm Mon-Fri; 9.30am-2pm, 4-7pm Sat; 10am-1.30pm Sun.

Getting there

By bus
Empresa Sagalès (902 13 00 14) from the Fabra i Puig bus station (near the metro of the same name) to Vic. For Rupit, take a local bus from Vic.

By train
RENFE from Sants or Plaça Catalunya to Vic. Trains leave about every 90mins. Journey time is 1hr 20mins.

Berga to Puigcerdà

To the west, on the most popular approach to the Pyrenees from Barcelona, is **Berga**, famous for the frenzied festival of La Patum, held each May. Just north from there, the giant cliffs of

Besalú. *See p300.*

the **Serra del Cadí**, one of the ranges of the Pre-Pyrenees, or Pyrenees foothills, loom above the town. Berga has **Sant Ferran**, a medieval castle with a suitably storybook air, but the blight of endless holiday apartment blocks has taken its toll on the charm of its old centre.

Far prettier is the little town of **Bagà**, north of here on the C17. With its partially preserved medieval walls around an atmospheric old quarter, Bagà marks the beginning of the **Parc Natural del Cadí-Moixeró**, a mountain park containing wildlife and forest reserves, and some 20 or so ancient villages. All retain some medieval architecture, and many offer stunning views. Picasso stayed and painted in the village of **Gósol** in 1906. Rising above this are the twin peaks of **Pedraforça**, practically a pilgrimage for hiking enthusiasts and well worth the effort (allow a full day to get up there and back).

Above Bagà, the C16 road enters the Túnel del Cadí to emerge into the wide, fertile plateau of the **Cerdanya**. Described by writer Josep Pla as a 'huge casserole', the area has a clear geographical unity, but the French/Spanish border runs through its middle. **Puigcerdà**, the capital of the area (on the Spanish side), is a lively ski-resort town; while not particularly interesting in its own right, it does make a good base (and a memorable train journey from Barcelona) for exploring the area on foot: the tourist office has maps and itineraries. Head over the border a few miles from here and you'll stumble across the charming and quirky town of **Llívia**. When 33 villages were ceded to the French under the treaty of the Pyrenees in 1659, it was pointed out that Llívia was technically a town, and therefore exempt from inclusion. It remains Catalan to this day, despite being geographically part of France.

One of the more charming places to stay in the area is **Bellver de Cerdanya**, a lovely hilltop village with a lively market and Gothic church. There is an information centre and all over town noticeboards list hikes of varying degrees of difficulty.

Where to stay & eat

On the C26 outside Berga, the tiny village of Les Llosses has a couple of rustic *cases rurales* tucked away in the pine forests. **Domus de Maçanós** (mobile 645 403 337, www.elripolles. com/masmacanos, €108 half-board) is open year-round and has pretty stone arches, beams, log fires and fabulous views. In Bagà, the **Hotel Ca L'Amagat** (C/Clota 4, 93 824 41 60, www. hotelcalamagat.com, €53.50) has rooms with large balconies, and a restaurant serving dishes such as trout with almonds or veal with redcurrants (mains €15, closed Mon Oct-May).

Puigcerdà has no shortage of hotels in the town centre, including the small and charming **Avet Blau** (Plaça Santa Maria 14, 972 88 25 52, €80-€110) and the newly opened **Hospes Villa Paulita** (Avda Pons i Gash 15, 972 88 46 22, €130-€160), which is right by the lake. The **Hotel Rita-Belvedere** (C/Carmelites 6-8, 972 88 03 56, mobile 608 088 085, closed May to mid July, €42-€53) has a small garden and terrace. The **Hotel del Lago** (Avda Doctor Piguillem 7, 972 88 10 00, www.hotellago.com, €97), with its terracotta paintwork and green shutters, is not quite so pretty inside, but both the staff and the atmosphere are friendly, and there's a heated pool, a sauna and a jacuzzi. For modern French-Mediterranean food, try **La Col d'Hivern** (C/Baronia 7, 972 14 12 04, closed Mon-Wed, mains €17).

A little further, out in Bolvir, the sumptuous **Torre del Remei** (C/Cami Reial, 972 14 01 82, www.torredelremei.com, €251-€727) also has one of the best (and the most expensive) restaurants in the area (mains €25). In Bellver, the **Fonda Bianya** (C/Sant Roc 11, 973 51 04 75, €60-€80) is utterly charming, with its sweet cornflower-blue woodwork, a sunny bar and a lively feel. The rooms are simple but clean.

In Llívia the **Hostal Rusó** (Pujada de l'Església 2, 972 14 62 64, €70) is a small, fairly basic village house and one of the best deals for accommodation locally. For eats, check out **Can Ventura** (Plaça Major 1, Llívia, 972 89 61 78, mains €22) for regional cooking in an 18th-century stone house. The **Xalet de la Formatgeria** (Pla de Ro, Gorguja-Llívia, 972 14 62 79, mains €20) is an old dairy that now does good, hearty country fare.

Tourist information

Berga

C/Angels 7 (93 822 15 00/www.elbergueda.cat). **Open** 9am-1pm, 3-6pm Mon-Sat; 9am-2pm Sun.

Puigcerdà

C/Querol (972 88 05 42). **Open** 9am-1pm, 4-7pm Mon-Fri; 10am-1pm, 4.30-7pm Sat; 10am-1pm Sun.

Getting there

By bus

Alsina-Graëlls (93 265 68 66) runs five buses daily to Berga from the corner of C/Balmes and Ronda de Universitat 11-13; journey time is about 2hrs. The same company has daily buses to Puigcerdà from Estació del Nord; journey time is 3hrs.

By train

RENFE from Sants or Plaça Catalunya to Puigcerdà. A train leaves about every 2hrs, and the journey generally takes about 3hrs.

Ripoll to the Vall de Núria

Ripoll is best known for its extraordinary monastery, **Santa Maria de Ripoll**, founded in 879 by Wilfred the Hairy, one of the founding fathers of Catalonia, who is buried here. The church has a superb 12th-century stone portal, its carvings among the finest examples of Romanesque art in Catalonia. Wilfred also founded the monastery and town of **Sant Joan de les Abadesses**, ten kilometres (six miles) east up the C26, which is worth a visit for its Gothic bridge as well as the 12th-century monastery buildings. Neither town holds much charm outside its monastery.

Ribes de Freser, the next town on the C17 north of Ripoll, is an attractive base from which to travel to the pretty, if slightly gentrified, villages of **Campelles** and **Queralbs**. Ribes is also the starting point for the *cremallera*, or 'zipper train', a narrow-gauge cog railway that runs via Queralbs along the Freser river up to the sanctuary of **Núria**, affording incredible views. Many choose to walk back to Queralbs (around two hours), following the path through dramatic rock formations, crumbling scree, pine-wooded slopes and dramatic, crashing waterfalls.

Núria itself nestles by a lake on a plateau at over 2,000 metres (6,500 feet), and was the first ski resort on this side of the border. Home to the second most famous of Catalonia's patron virgins, a 12th-century wooden statue of the Madonna, Núria was a refuge and a place of pilgrimage long before then. The mostly 19th-century monastery that surrounds the shrine is nothing special, but its location is spectacular. You can bury your head in a pot to gain fertility or ring a bell to cure headaches, but most opt to hike, ski, row boats or ride horses. Pick up maps and information from the tourist office.

Besalú gets all medieval. *See p300.*

(Ctra de Sant Joan 68, 972 70 21 06, www.reccapolis.com, closed dinner Wed, mains €15.50) is intimate and romantic, offering unusual twists on regional specialities.

In Núria is the **Hotel Vall de Núria** (Estació de Muntanya Vall de Núria, 972 73 20 30, www.valldenuria.com, closed mid Oct-Nov, €111-€163 half-board), with a two-night minimum stay. This is your only option for a bite to eat up here.

Where to stay & eat

In Ribes de Freser, the family-run **Hotel Els Caçadors** (C/Balandrau 24-26, 972 72 77 22, closed Nov, €98-€104) is the first eco-hotel in the Pyrenees and has good food and comfortable rooms. If it's full, try **Hostal Porta de Núria** (C/Nostra Senyora de Gràcia 3, 972 72 71 37, closed May, €62-€51). In Queralbs, there's **Calamari Hostal l'Avet** (C/Major 17-19, 972 72 73 77, closed Mon-Thur Oct-May, €80 half-board). **La Perdiu Blanca** (C/Puigcerdà 5, 972 72 71 50, closed Wed, mains €9) in Ribes, is a village classic and good value. The one good place to eat in Queralbs is **De La Plaça** (Plaça de la Vila 2, 972 72 70 37, closed Tue, closed 2wks July-Oct, mains €8.50), especially for regional specialities. **Reccapolis**

Tourist information

Núria
Estació de Montanya del Vall de Núria (972 73 20 20/www.valldenuria.cat). Open Mid July-mid Sept 8.30am-5.45pm daily. Mid Sept-mid July 8.30am-5.45pm daily.

Ribes de Freser
Plaça del Ajuntament 3 (972 72 77 28). Open Sept-June 10am-2pm, 5-8pm Tue-Sat; 11am-1pm Sun. July, Aug 10am-2pm, 5-8pm Mon-Sat; 11am-1pm Sun.

Getting there

By bus
TEISA (93 215 35 66) runs one bus a day from the corner of C/Pau Claris and C/Consell de Cent to Ripoll, Sant Joan de les Abadesses and Camprodon.

By train

RENFE from Sants or Plaça Catalunya (journey time to Ripoll 2hrs). For Queralbs and Núria, change to the *cremallera* train in Ribes de Freser.

Besalú & Olot

The medieval fortified town of **Besalú** (*photos p297 and p299*) has to be one of the loveliest in Catalonia, its impressive 12th-century fortified bridge spanning the Fluvià river marking its entrance. Once home to a sizeable Jewish community, it boasts the only remaining Jewish baths (*mikveh*) in Spain. These extraordinary structures date back to the 13th century but were only discovered in the 1960s. Charmingly, if the doors are locked when you arrive, the tourist office will give you a key so that you can let yourself in. Also worth a visit are the Romanesque church of Sant Pere and the arcaded Plaça de la Llibertat.

West from here the N260 runs to **Olot**, past a spectacular view of **Castellfollit de la Roca**, a village perched on the edge of a precipitous crag. The town is prettier from below than it is once you get inside, but the old part still makes for an interesting stroll. **Olot** was destroyed in an earthquake in 1427, and so lost much of its oldest architecture, but it has some impressive 18th-century and Modernista buildings. In the last century, it was home to a school of landscape painters: the local **Museu de la Garrotxa** (C/Hospice 8, 972 27 91 30, closed Mon) has works by them, along with Ramon Casas, Santiago Rusiñol and other Modernista artists. The town is not especially interesting, however, and is mainly worth visiting due to its position amid the 30-odd inactive volcanoes and numerous lava flows of the volcanic region of **La Garrotxa**. Just south of town, on the road to Vic, is elegant **Casal dels Volcans** (Ctra Santa Coloma 43, 972 26 67 62, closed Mon), an information centre and museum where you can pick up maps detailing hikes.

Off the G1524 toward Banyoles you'll see a vast beech forest, the **Fageda d'en Jordà**, immortalised by Catalan poet Joan Maragall, and the pretty, if touristy, village **Santa Pau**, with an impressive castle and arcaded squares.

Where to stay & eat

In Besalú a 19th-century riverside inn, **Fonda Siqués** (Avda Lluis Companys 6-8, 972 59 01 10, €44.34-€73.36), offers clean if drab rooms and is located above a charming restaurant (set meal €9). For nicer, though still simple, rooms, try **Els Jardins de la Martana** (C/Pont 2, 972 59 00 09, www.lamartana.com, €90-€103). Restaurants in Besalú include the **Pont Vell**

(C/Pont Vell 24, 972 59 10 27, closed dinner Mon & Tue €16), which offers magnificent views of the bridge and an interesting menu including sweet and sour rabbit, pigs' trotters stuffed with wild mushrooms and foie gras, and a good vegetarian selection. The terrace of the **Cúria Reial** (Plaça de la Llibertat 8-9, 972 59 02 63, closed dinner Mon & all day Tue, Feb, mains €15) is very popular, with good traditional cooking. A couple of miles north of the town in Beuda, is a pretty *masia* (farmhouse) with a pool, **Mas Salvanera** (972 59 09 75, www.salvanera.com, €125). If you stop to explore Castellfollit de la Roca, **Can Bundacia** (Ctra de Castellfollit de la Roca a Oix, 972 29 44 81, closed Mon & Tue, mains €7) is good for regional fare in hearty portions.

In Olot, **La Perla** (Avda Santa Coloma 97, 972 26 23 26, www.laperlahotels.com, €68-€76) is a large hotel with a good restaurant, or **Pensión La Vila** (C/Sant Roc 1, 972 26 98 07, €48-€56) is modern and very central. **Can Guix** (C/Mulleres 3-5, 972 26 10 40, closed dinner Wed & all day Sun, mains €5) has great, cheap local dishes. **La Deu** (Ctra de la Deu s/n, 972 26 10 01, closed Thur, mains €12) specialises in '*cocina volcánica*', including beef stewed in onions and beer, and duck breast stuffed with foie gras. North of the town is the **Restaurant Les Cols** (Crta de la Canya, 972 26 92 09, closed Sun, Mon & dinner Tue, mains €23), which is famed as much for the design as the food. The structure is a work of architectural brilliance that seamlessly combines a modernist steel-and-glass dining room with an 18th-century farmhouse. South of Olot, in La Pinya, is **Mas Garganta** (972 27 12 89, www.masgarganta.com, closed Jan & Feb, €68), an 18th-century *masia* with magnificent views that has walking tours in conjunction with two *masies* nearby, so you can stay in one place and walk without bags to the next.

In Banyoles, try the red mullet with tomato confit at the **Restaurant Fonda La Paz**, which also has rooms (C/Ponent 18, 972 57 04 32, closed Mon, dinner Sun, Jan & 2wks Sept, €40, mains €13).

Tourist information

Olot
C/Hospici 8 (972 26 01 41/www.olot.cat). **Open** *Mid Sept-June* 9am-2pm, 5-7pm Mon-Sat; 11am-2pm Sun. *July-mid Sept* 10am-8pm Mon-Sat; 11am-2pm Sun.

Getting there

By bus
TEISA (93 215 35 66) to Besalú and Olot from the corner of C/Pau Claris and C/Consell de Cent.

Directory

Features

Directory

Getting Around

Barcelona's centre is compact and easily explored on foot. Bicycles are good for the Old City and port: there is a decent network of bike lanes across the city. The metro and bus systems are best for longer journeys. Cars can be a hindrance: there's little parking, and most of the city is subject to one-way systems. For transport outside Barcelona, see p276.

For transport outside Barcelona, see p276.

Arriving & leaving

By air

Aeroport de Barcelona

91 393 60 00/www.aena.es.
Barcelona's airport is at El Prat, south-west of the city. There are three main terminals (A, B or C), with a fourth due for completion in 2009. Tourist information desks and currency exchanges are in terminals A and B.

Aerobús

The airport bus (93 415 60 20) runs from each terminal to Plaça Catalunya, with stops at Plaça d'Espanya, C/Urgell and Plaça Universitat. Buses to the airport go from Plaça Catalunya (in front of El Corte Inglés), stopping at Sants station and Plaça d'Espanya. Buses run every 8-10mins, leaving the airport 6am-1am Mon-Fri and 6.30am-1am on weekends, returning from Plaça Catalunya 5.30am-12.15am Mon-Fri and 6am-12.15am at weekends. The trip takes 35-45mins; a single is €3.90, a return (valid one week) €6.70.

At night the N17 runs every hour, on the hour, between the airport (from 10pm) and Plaça Catalunya (from 11pm), with several stops on the way, including Plaça d'Espanya and Plaça Universitat. Last departures are at 5am. Journey time is 45mins; the cost is a single metro fare.

Airport trains

By train: the long overhead walkway between terminals A and B leads to the train station. The Cercanías train (C10) leaves the airport at 29mins and 59mins past the hour, 6.29am-10.59pm, with an extra train at 11.44pm daily, stopping at Barcelona Sants, Passeig de Gràcia and Estació França. Trains to the airport leave Barcelona Sants at 25mins and 55mins past the hour, 5.25am-10.55pm daily (13mins earlier from Estació França and 5mins earlier from Passeig de Gràcia). The journey takes 20-30mins and costs €2.60 one way (no return tickets). Be aware that tickets are valid only for 2hrs after purchase (information 902 24 02 02, www.renfe.es/cercanias; www.spanish-rail.co.uk, 020 7725 7063).

The T-10 metro pass (see p303) can also be used.

Taxis from the airport

The basic taxi fare to central Barcelona should be €15-€26, including a €3 airport supplement. Fares are about 15 per cent higher after 9pm and at weekends. There is a 90¢ supplement for each large piece of luggage placed in the car boot. All licensed cab drivers use the ranks outside the terminals.

Airlines

Terminals are shown in brackets. UK numbers are listed second.
Air Berlin (B) 93 478 7594/0870 738 8880/www.airberlin.com
Aer Lingus (A) 902 502 737/www.aerlingus.com
Air Europa (B) 91 540 16 82/www.air-europa.com
bmi (B) 902 100 737/0870 607 0555/www.flybmi.com
bmibaby (B) 902 100 737/0871 224 0224/www.bmibaby.com
British Airways (B) 902 111 333/0870 850 9850/www.ba.com
easyJet (A) 807 260 026/0871 244 2366/www.easyjet.com
Iberia (B or C) 902 400 500/0870 609 0500/www.iberia.com
Jet2 (A) 0871 226 1737/www.jet2.com
Monarch Airlines (A) 902 502 737/0870 0405 040/www.flymonarch.com
Ryanair (from Girona or Reus) 807 220 220/0871 246 0000/www.ryanair.com
Spanair (B) 971 916 047/902 131 415/www.spanair.com
Thomsonfly (B) 91 414 1481/0870 190 0737/www.thomsonfly.com
Vueling (B) 902 333 933/93 378 78 78/www.vueling.com

By bus

Most long-distance coaches (national and international) stop or terminate at Estació d'Autobusos Barcelona-Nord (C/Ali Bei 80, 902 26 06 06, www.barcelonanord.com, map p343 J9). The Estació d'Autobusos Barcelona-Sants at C/Viriat, between Sants rail station and Sants-Estació metro stop, is only a secondary stop for many coaches, though some international Eurolines services (information 93 490 40 00, www.eurolines.es) both begin and end their journeys at Sants.

By car

The easiest way to central Barcelona from almost all directions is the Ronda Litoral, the coastal half of the ring road. Take exit 21 (Paral·lel) if you're coming from the south, or exit 22 (Via Laietana) from the north. Motorways also feed into Avda Diagonal, Avda Meridiana and Gran Via, which all lead to the city centre. Tolls are charged on most of the main approach routes, payable in cash (the lane marked *'manual'*; motorbikes are charged half) or by credit card (*'automatic'*). For more on driving in Barcelona, see p305.

For more on driving in Barcelona, see p305.

By rail

Most long-distance services operated by the Spanish state railway company RENFE run from Barcelona-Sants station, easily reached by metro. A few services from the French border or south to Tarragona stop at the Estació de França in the Born, near the Barceloneta metro which is otherwise sparsely served. Many trains stop at Passeig de

Gràcia, which can be the handiest for the city centre and also has a metro stop.

The long-awaited RENFE high-speed service AVE (Alta Velocidad) will, allegedly, be up and running between Barcelona Sants station and Madrid, via Zaragoza and Lleida, by early 2008, although its launch has been beset by delays over the past few years. The AVE will travel at speeds of up to 330 km/hour (205 mph), whisking travellers to the Spanish capital in just over three hours, with some 20 trains daily.

RENFE

National 902 24 02 02/ international 902 24 34 02/ www.renfe.es. **Open** *National* 5am-10pm daily. *International* 7am-midnight daily. **Credit** AmEx, DC, MC, V.
Some English-speaking operators. RENFE tickets can be bought at train stations or travel agents, or reserved over the phone and delivered to an address or hotel for a small extra fee.

By sea

Balearic Islands ferries dock at the Moll de Barcelona quay, at the bottom of Avda Paral·lel; Trasmediterránea (902 45 46 45, 91 663 2850, www.trasmedi terranea.es) is the main operator.

Grimaldi Lines runs a ferry a day, except Sundays, between Barcelona and Civitavecchia (near Rome) from the Moll Sant Bertran (information and reservations 93 508 88 50, www.grimaldi-ferries.com); or to Genoa three times a week from the Moll de Ponent, a few hundred metres south (902 40 12 00).

Cruise ships use several berths around the harbour. The PortBus shuttle service (information 93 415 60 20) runs between them and the bottom of La Rambla when ships are in port.

Maps

For street, local train and metro maps, *see pp336-352*. Tourist offices provide a reasonable free street map, or a better-quality map for €1. Metro maps (ask for *una guía del metro*) are available free at all metro stations; bus maps can be obtained from the main

Oficines d'Informació Turística (*see p322*). There is an excellent interactive street map at www.bcn.cat/guia.

Public transport

Although it's run by different organisations, Barcelona's public transport is now highly integrated, with the same tickets valid for up to four changes of transport (within 75 minutes) on bus, tram, local train and metro lines. The metro is generally the quickest and easiest way of getting around the city. All metro lines operate from 5am to midnight Monday to Thursday, Sunday and public holidays; 5am to 2am Friday and non stop on Saturday. Buses run throughout the night and to areas not covered by the metro system. Local buses and the metro are run by the city transport authority (TMB). Two underground train lines connect with the metro, run by Catalan government railways, the FGC. One runs north from Plaça Catalunya; the other runs west from Plaça d'Espanya to Cornellà. Two tram lines are of limited use to visitors.

FGC information

Vestibule, Plaça Catalunya FGC station (93 205 15 15/www. fgc.net). **Open** 7am-9pm Mon-Fri. **Map** p344 C1.
Other locations FGC Provença (open 9am-7pm Mon-Fri, closed Aug); FGC Plaça d'Espanya (open 9am-2pm, 4-7pm Mon-Fri).

TMB information

Main vestibule, Metro Universitat, Eixample (93 318 70 74/www. tmb.net). **Open** 8am-8pm Mon-Fri. **Map** p344 A1.
Other locations vestibule, Metro Sants Estació and Sagrada Família (both open 7am-9pm Mon-Fri; Sants also open 9am-7pm Sat, 9am-2pm Sun); vestibule, Metro Diagonal (8am-8pm Mon-Fri).

Fares & tickets

Travel in the Barcelona urban area has a flat fare of €1.25 per journey, but multi-journey tickets or *targetes* are better value. The basic ten-trip *targeta* is the T-10 (*Te-Deu* in Catalan, *Te-Diez* in Spanish), which can be shared by

any number of people travelling simultaneously; the ticket is validated in the machines on the metro, train or bus once per person per journey.

Along with the other integrated *targetes* listed below, the T-10 offers access to all five of the city's main transport systems (local RENFE and FGC trains within the main metropolitan area, the metro, the tram and buses). To transfer, insert your card into a machine a second time; unless 75 minutes have elapsed since your last journey, no other unit will be deducted. Single tickets do not allow free transfers.

You can buy T-10s in newsagents and Servi-Caixa cashpoints, as well as on the metro and train systems (from machines or the ticket office), but not on buses. More expensive versions of all *targetes* take you to the outer zones of the metropolitan region, but the prices listed below will get you anywhere in central Barcelona, and to the key sights on the outskirts of the city itself.

Integrated targetes

T-10 Valid for ten trips; can be shared by two or more people. €6.90.
T-Familiar Gives 70 trips in any 30-day period; can be shared. €42.
T-50/30 Gives 50 trips in any 30-day period; but can only be used by one person. €28.60.
T-Dia A one-day travelcard. €5.25.
T-Mes Valid for any 30-day period. €44.35.
T-Trimestre Valid for three months. €122.
T-Jove Valid for three months; for under-21s only. €104.

Other *targetes*
2, 3, 4 & 5 Dies Two-, three-, four- and five-day travelcards on the metro, buses and FGC trains. Also sold at tourist offices. €9.60, €13.70, €17.50 and €20.80.
Barcelona Card A tourist discount scheme offering unlimited use of public transport for up to five days. *See p83.*

Buses

Many bus routes originate in or pass through Plaça Catalunya, Plaça Universitat and Plaça Urquinaona. However, they often run along parallel streets, due to the city's one-way system. Not all stops are labelled, and street signs are not always easy to locate.

Most routes run 6am-10.30pm daily except Sundays; some begin earlier and finish later. There's usually a bus every 10-15mins, but they're less frequent before 8am, after 9pm and on Saturdays. On Sundays, buses are less frequent still; a few do not run at all. Only single tickets can be bought from the driver; if you have a *targeta*, insert it into the machine behind the driver as you board.

Useful routes

The following services connect Plaça Catalunya with popular places:

22 via Gràcia to the Tramvia Blau up to Tibidabo and the Pedralbes monastery.
24 goes up Passeig de Gràcia and to Park Güell.
39 connects Gràcia, the town centre and the beach.
41, 59, 67 and **68** go to the Plaça Francesc Macià area, which is not served by the metro.
41 also goes to Ciutadella and the Vila Olímpica.
45 stops in Plaça Urquinaona and goes to the beach near Port Olímpic.

Three good cross-town routes:
7 runs the length of Avda Diagonal, from the Zona Universitària to Diagonal Mar and along Passeig de Gràcia and Gran Via to Glòries.
50 goes from north-east Barcelona past Sagrada Família, along Gran Via and then climbs Montjuïc from Plaça d'Espanya to Miramar.
64 goes from Barceloneta beach, past Colom, Avda Paral·lel, Plaça Universitat to Sarrià and Pedralbes.

Night buses

There are 16 urban night bus (*Nitbus*) routes (information 902 02 33 93, or TMB, *see p303*), most of which run from around 10.30-11.30pm to 4.30-6am nightly, with buses every 20-30mins, plus an hourly bus to the airport; *see p302*. Most pass through Plaça Catalunya. Fares and *targetes* are as for daytime buses. Plaça Catalunya is also the terminus for all-night bus services linking Barcelona with more distant parts of its metropolitan area.

Local trains

Regional trains to Sabadell, Terrassa and other towns beyond Tibidabo depart from FGC Plaça Catalunya, those for Montserrat from FGC Plaça d'Espanya.

All trains on the RENFE local network ('Rodalies/Cercanías') stop at Sants but can also be caught at either Plaça Catalunya and Arc de Triomf (for Vic and the Pyrenees, Manresa, the Penedès and Costa del Maresme) or Passeig de Gràcia (for the southern coastal line to Sitges and the Girona-Figueres line north).

Metro

The metro is the easiest way to get around Barcelona. There are six lines, each colour coded: L1 (red), L2 (purple), L3 (light green), L4 (yellow), L5 (blue), L11 (dark green). For information on tickets and running times, *see p303*; for a map *see pp350-351*.

Trams

Lines T1, T2 and T3 go from Plaça Francesc Macià, Zona Alta, to the outskirts of the city. T1 goes to Cornellà via Hospitalet and Esplugues de Llobregat; T2 goes the same way but contines further to Sant Joan Despi; and T3 runs to Sant Just Desvern. The fourth line runs from Ciutadella-Vila Olímpica (also a metro stop), via Glòries and the Fòrum, on to Sant Adrià (also a RENFE train station) and the fifth line follows the same route, splitting off at Glòries to go on to Badalona.

All trams are fully accessible for wheelchair-users and are part of the integrated TMB *targeta* system. You can buy integrated tickets and single tickets from the machines at tram stops.

Tram information

Trambaix (902 19 32 75/www. trambcn.com). **Open** 9am-2pm, 4-7pm Mon-Thur; 9am-2pm Fri.

Taxis

It's usually easy to find one of the 10,500 black-and-yellow taxis. There are ranks at railway and bus stations, in main squares and throughout the city, but taxis can also be hailed on the street when

they show a green light on the roof and a sign saying *lliure/libre* ('free') behind the windscreen. Information on taxi fares, ranks and regulations can be found at www.emt-amb.com/links/cat/cimtaxi.htm.

Fares

Current rates and supplements are shown inside cabs on a sticker on the rear side window (in English). The basic fare for a taxi hailed in the street is €1.75 (or €1.85 at nights, weekends and holidays), which is what the meter should register when you set off. The basic rates (78¢/km) apply 7am-9pm Mon-Fri; at other times, including public holidays, the rate is 20-30 per cent higher (€1/km).

There are supplements for luggage (90¢), for the airport (€3) and the port (€2), and for nights such as New Year's Eve (€3), as well as a waiting charge. Taxi drivers are not required to carry more than €20 in change; few accept credit cards. There is a €2 supplement from midnight to 6am on Friday, Saturday and Sunday. And if a public holiday falls on one of these days there is an additional €3 supplement.

Radio cabs

These companies take bookings 24 hours daily. Phone cabs start the meter when a call is answered but, by the time it picks you up, it should not display more than €3.09 during weekdays and €3.86 at night, at weekends or public holidays (supplements are added at the end of the journey).

Autotaxi Mercedes Barcelona 93 307 07 07.
Barnataxi 93 357 77 55.
Fono-Taxi 93 300 11 00.
Ràdio Taxi '033' 93 303 30 33.
Servi-Taxi 93 330 03 00.
Taxi Groc 93 322 22 22.
Taxi Miramar 93 433 10 20.

Receipts & complaints

To get a receipt, ask for *un rebut/un recibo*. It should include the fare, the taxi number, the driver's NIF (tax) number, the licence plate, the driver's signature and the date; if you have a complaint about a driver, insist on all these, and the more details (time, route) the better. Complaints must be filed in writing to the Institut Metropolità del Taxi (93 223 51 51 ext 2168, www.taxi barcelona.com).

Driving

For information (only in Catalan or Spanish) on driving in Catalonia, call the Servei Català de Trànsit (93 567 40 00); the local government's general information line (012), which has a more extended timetable and English speakers, or see www.gencat.net/ transit. Driving in the city can be intimidating and time-consuming. If you do drive, remember:

● Keep your driving licence, vehicle registration and insurance documents with you at all times.
● Do not leave anything of value, including car radios, in your car. Foreign plates can attract thieves.
● Be on your guard at motorway service areas, and take care to avoid thieves in the city who may try to make you stop, perhaps by indicating you have a flat tyre.

Breakdown services

If you're planning to take a car, join a motoring organisation such as the AA (www.theaa.co.uk) or the RAC (www.rac.co.uk) in the UK, which usually have reciprocal agreements.

RACE (Real Automóvil Club de España)

Information 91 593 33 33/902 40 45 45/24hr assistance 902 30 05 05/www.race.es.

Car & motorbike hire

Car hire is relatively pricey, but it's a competitive market, so shop around. Ideally, you want unlimited mileage, 16 per cent VAT (IVA) included and full insurance cover (*seguro todo riesgo*) rather than the third-party minimum (*seguro obligatorio*). You'll need a credit card as a guarantee. Most companies require you to have had a licence for at least a year; many also enforce a minimum age limit.

Europcar

Plaça dels Països Catalans, Sants (93 491 25 65/reservations 902 10 50 30/www.europcar.com).

Metro Sants Estació. **Open** 7am-11pm Mon-Fri; 8am-8pm Sat; 8am-10pm Sun. **Credit** AmEx, DC, MC, V. **Map** p339 B7.
Other locations Airport, terminals B & C (93 298 33 00); Gran Via de les Corts Catalanes 680, Eixample (93 302 05 43); C/Viladomat 214, Eixample (93 439 84 01).

Motissimo

C/Comandante Benítez 25, Sants (93 490 84 01/www.motissimo.es). Metro Badal. **Open** *Oct-June* 9am-1.30pm, 4-8pm Mon-Fri; 10am-1pm Sat. *July-Sept* 9am-1.30pm, 4-8pm Mon-Fri. **Credit** AmEx, DC, MC, V. **Map** p338 A5.

Pepecar

C/Rivadeneyra, underground car park (807 41 42 43/902 36 05 35/www.pepecar.com). Metro Catalunya. **Open** 8am-8pm daily. **Credit** AmEx, MC, V. **Map** p344 C2/C3.

Vanguard

C/Viladomat 297, Eixample (93 439 38 80/www.vanguard rent.com). Metro Hospital Clínic. **Open** 8am-1.30pm, 4-7.30pm Mon-Fri; 9am-1pm Sat, Sun. **Credit** AmEx, DC, MC, V. **Map** p338 D6.

Legal requirements

For full details of driving laws and regulations (in Spanish), see the Ministry of Interior's website (www.dgt.es).

Parking

Parking is fiendishly complicated and municipal police are quick to hand out tickets or tow away cars. In some parts of the Old City, access is limited to residents for much of the day. In some Old City streets, time-controlled bollards pop up, meaning your car may get stuck. Wherever you are, don't park in front of doors marked '*Gual Permanent*', indicating an entry with 24-hour right of access.

Pay & display areas

The Àrea Verda contains zones exclusively for residents' use (most of the Old City), and 'partial zones' (found in Gràcia, Barceloneta and the Eixample), where non-residents pay €2.75/hr with a 1hr or 2hr maximum stay, as indicated on the meter.

If you overstay by no more than an hour, you can cancel the fine by paying an extra €6; to do so, press *Anul·lar denùncia* on the machine, insert €6, then press Ticket. Some machines accept credit cards (AmEx, MC, V); none accepts notes or gives change. For information, check www.bcn.es/areaverda or call 010. There's a drop-in centre for queries on the ground floor of the Ajuntament building on Plaça Carles Pi i Sunyer 8-10, open 8.30am-5.30pm Mon-Fri.

Car parks

Car parks (*parkings*) are signalled by a white 'P' on a blue sign. Those run by SABA (Plaça Catalunya, Plaça Urquinaona, Rambla de Catalunya, Avda Catedral, airport and elsewhere; 93 230 56 00, www.saba.es) cost around €2.40/hr, while SMASSA car parks (Plaça Catalunya 23, C/Hospital 25-29, Avda Francesc Cambó 10, Passeig de Gràcia 60 and elsewhere; 93 409 20 21, www.bsmsa.es/mobilitat) cost €2-€2.45/hr. The €5.50 fare at the Metro-Park park-and-ride (Plaça de les Glòries, Eixample, 93 265 10 47, open 4.30am-12.30am Mon-Sat) includes a day's travel on the metro and buses.

Towed vehicles

If the police have towed your car, they should leave a triangular sticker on the pavement where it was. The sticker should let you know to which pound it's been taken. If not, call 901 513 151; staff generally don't speak English. Recovering your vehicle within 4hrs costs €141.90, with each extra hour costing €1.85, or €18.50/day. On top of this, you'll have to pay a fine to the police. You'll need your passport and documentation, or rental contract, to prove ownership.

Cycling

There's a network of bike lanes (*carrils bici*) along major avenues and alongside the seafront; local authorities are very keen to promote cycling. No more than two bikes are allowed to ride side by side. Be warned too that bike theft is rife: always carry a good lock. For information see www.bcn.cat/bicicleta.

Resources A-Z

Addresses

Most apartment addresses consist of a street name followed by a street number, floor level and flat number, in that order. So, to go to C/València 246, 2° 3ª, find no.246, go to the second floor and find the door marked 3 or 3ª. Ground-floor flats are usually called *baixos* or *bajos* (often abbreviated *bxs/bjos*); one floor up, the *entresol/ entresuelo* (*entl*), and the next is often the *principal* (*pral*). Confusingly, numbered floors start here: first, second, up to the *àtic/ático* at the top.

Age restrictions

The minimum legal age for drinking alcohol or smoking is 18. The age of consent is just 13. In Spain, you must be 18 to drive a car.

Attitude & etiquette

The Catalans are less guarded about personal space than people in the UK or US. The common greeting between members of the opposite sex and between two women, even if it is the first time that the two parties have met, is a kiss on both cheeks. Men usually greet each other by shaking hands. Don't be surprised if people bump into you on the street, or crowd or push past you on the bus or metro without saying sorry: it's not considered rude.

Business

Anyone wanting to set up shop in Barcelona needs to know the intricacies of local, Spanish and EU regulations. A visit to the Cambra de Comerç (*see p308*) is a must;

some consulates can refer you to professionals, and a *gestoria* (*see below*) will save you time and energy.

Admin services

The *gestoria* is a very Spanish institution. Its main function is to lighten the weight of local bureaucracy – which can be quite crushing – by dealing with it for you. A combination of bookkeeper, lawyer and business adviser, a good *gestor* can be helpful in handling all of the paperwork the state and the Generalitat generate and advising on various short cuts, although *gestoria* employees only rarely speak English.

Martin Howard Associates

C/Aribau 177, entl 1ª, Eixample (93 240 52 75/mobile 600 905 078/ www.mhasoc.com). **Open** *Sept-July* 9am-6pm Mon-Thur; 9am-2pm Fri. *Aug* 8am-3pm Mon-Fri.
Map p340 F5.
British accountant Alex Martin and his Spanish associate offer consultancy, accounting, tax services and advice on buying property for English-speaking expats in Spain.

Tutzo Assessors

C/Aribau 226, pral 2ª, Eixample (93 209 67 88/www.tutzo-assessors. com). Metro Diagonal/FGC Gràcia. **Open** *Sept-June* 8.30am-2pm, 4-7pm Mon-Fri; *July, Aug* 9am-2pm Mon-Fri. Closed 2wks Aug.
Map p340 F5.
Lawyers and economists as well as a *gestoria*. Some English speakers are available.

Conventions & conferences

Barcelona Convention Bureau

Rambla Catalunya 123, pral, Eixample (93 368 97 00/www. barcelonaturisme.com). Metro Diagonal. **Open** *Sept-mid June* 9am-2.30pm, 3.30-6.30pm Mon-Thur; 9am-3pm Fri. *Mid June-Aug* 8am-3pm Mon-Fri. **Map** p340 F6.
Specialist arm of the city tourist authority that assists organisations with conferences.

Fira de Barcelona

Avda Reina Maria Cristina, Montjuïc (93 233 20 00/www. firabcn.es). Metro Espanya. **Open** *Mid Sept-mid June* 9am-1.30pm, 3.30-5.30pm Mon-Fri. *Mid June-mid Sept* 9am-2pm Mon-Fri.
Map p339 B9.
The Barcelona Trade Fair is one of the largest exhibition complexes in Europe. In addition to the main area, it includes a huge site, Montjuïc-2, towards the airport, and administers the Palau de Congressos conference hall in the Plaça d'Espanya site, which can be let separately.

World Trade Center

Moll de Barcelona, Port Vell (93 508 88 88/www.wtcbarcelona. com). Metro Drassanes. **Open** *Sept-June* 9am-2pm, 4-7pm Mon-Thur; 9am-3pm Fri. *July, Aug* 9am-3pm Mon-Fri. **Map** p342 F13.
The WTC rents 130,000sqm (72,624 sq ft) of office space in a modern complex in the old port. Conferences can be arranged.

Courier services

Estació d'Autobusos Barcelona-Nord

C/Ali Bei 80, Eixample (93 232 43 29). Metro Arc de Triomf. **Open** 7am-9.30pm Mon-Fri; 7am-1.30pm Sat. **No credit cards. Map** p343 J9.
An inexpensive service available at the bus station for sending parcels on scheduled buses within Spain.

Missatgers Trèvol

C/Antonio Ricardos 14, La Sagrera (93 498 80 70/www.trevol.com). Metro Sagrera. **Open** *Sept-July* 8am-7.30pm Mon-Fri. *Aug* 8am-3pm Mon-Fri. **No credit cards.**
Courier firm serving central Barcelona. Check online for rates.

Seur

902 10 10 10/www.seur.es. **Open** 8am-8pm Mon-Fri; 9am-2pm Sat. **No credit cards.**
An efficient (though not always cheap) service for national and international deliveries. Call by 6pm for same-day pick-up.

UPS

902 88 88 20/www.ups.com. **Open** 8am-8pm Mon-Fri. **Credit** AmEx, MC, V.
Next-day delivery to both Spanish and international destinations. There are some English-speaking operators available.

Office & computer services

The area round Ronda Sant Antoni is the best place to go if you're looking for hardware for your PC. You can look in the shop windows or try Life Informática (C/Sepúlveda 173, Sant Antoni, 902 90 15 32, www.lifeinformatica.com) is good for parts; PC City (C/Casanova 2, Eixample, 902 10 03 02, www.pccity.es) is a reliable option for hardware.

Centro de Negocios

C/Pau Claris 97, 4º 1ª, Eixample (93 304 38 58/www.centro-negocios.com). Metro Passeig de Gràcia. **Open** *Sept-July* 8am-9pm Mon-Fri. *Aug* 9am-2pm Mon-Fri. **No credit cards. Map** p342 G8.
Desks in shared offices, mailboxes, meeting rooms, secretarial services and administrative services.

CTA Serveis

C/Consell de Cent 382, Eixample (93 244 03 50/www.cta.es). Metro Girona. **Open** 9am-2pm, 4-7pm Mon-Fri. Closed 3wks Aug. **Credit** MC, V. **Map** p343 H8.
Computer installation and repairs, including Macs.

Microrent

C/Rosselló 35, Eixample (93 363 32 50/www.microrent.es). Metro Entença. **Open** *Sept-June* 9am-6pm Mon-Fri. *July, Aug* 8am-3pm Mon-Fri. **No credit cards. Map** p339 C6.
Computer equipment for rent: PCs, Macs, laptops, printers, projectors and everything else.

Translators

For more translators, see www.act.es.

DUUAL

C/Ciutat 7, 2º 4ª, Barri Gòtic (93 302 29 85/www.duual.com). Metro Jaume I or Liceu. **Open** *Sept-June* 9am-2pm, 4-7pm Mon-Thur; 9am-2pm Fri. *July* 8.30am-3pm Mon-Fri. Closed 3wks Aug. **No credit cards. Map** p345 C6.

Traduit

C/Ribeira 6, 1º 2ª, Born (93 268 74 95/www.traduit.com). Metro Jaume I. **Open** 9am-2pm, 4-6.30pm Mon-Fri. **Credit** MC, V. **Map** p345 F7.

Useful organisations

Ajuntament de Barcelona

Plaça Sant Miquel 4-5, Barri Gòtic (93 402 70 00/www.bcn.es). Metro Jaume I. **Open** *Sept-June* 8.30am-5.30pm Mon-Fri. *July, Aug* 8.15am-2.15pm Mon-Fri. **Map** p345 C6.
The city council. The Ajuntament is an important stop for any businessman as the council does try hard to encourage investment inward investment in to Barcelona. Permits for new businesses are issued by the ten municipal districts.

Borsa de Valors de Barcelona

Passeig de Gràcia 19, Eixample (93 401 35 55/www.borsabcn.es). Metro Passeig de Gràcia. **Open** *Reception* 9am-5.30pm Mon-Fri. *Library* 9am-noon Mon-Fri. **Map** p344 C1.
The stock exchange.

Cambra de Comerç de Barcelona

Avda Diagonal 452-454, Eixample (902 448 448/www.cambrabcn.es). Metro Diagonal/FGC Provença. **Open** 9am-5pm Mon-Thur; 9am-2pm Fri. **Map** p340 G6.
The Chamber of Commerce.

Generalitat de Catalunya

Information 012/new businesses 902 20 15 20/www.gencat.net.
The Catalan government provides a range of consultancy services for businesses.

Consumer

Ask for a complaint form (*full de reclamació/hoja de reclamación*), which many businesses and all shops, bars and restaurants are required to keep. Leave one completed copy with the business. Take the other forms to the consumer office.

Oficina Municipal d'Informació al Consumidor

Ronda de Sant Pau 43-45, Barri Gòtic (93 402 78 41/www.omic.bcn.es). Metro Paral·lel or Sant Antoni. **Open** 9am-1pm Mon-Fri. **Map** p342 E10.
The official centre for consumer advice and complaints follow-up. You can file complaints in English through the website. Best get there early if you don't want to queue for hours.

Telèfon de Consulta del Consumidor

012. **Open** 9am-6pm Mon-Fri.
A telephone line run by the Generalitat that offers helpful consumer advice.

Customs

Custom declarations are not usually necessary if you arrive from another EU country and are carrying legal goods for personal use. The amounts given below are guidelines only: if you come close to the maximums in several of these categories, you may still have to explain your personal habits to an interested but sceptical customs officer.

Travel advice

For up-to-date information on travelling to a specific country – including the latest news on safety and security, health issues, local laws and customs – contact your home country government's department of foreign affairs. Most of them have websites that are packed with useful advice for would-be travellers.

Australia
www.smartraveller.gov.au
Canada
www.voyage.gc.ca
New Zealand
www.mft.govt.nz/travel

Republic of Ireland
http://foreignaffairs.gov.ie
UK
www.fco.gov.uk/travel
USA
www.state.gov/travel

● 800 cigarettes, 400 small cigars, 200 cigars or 1kg loose tobacco

● 10 litres of spirits (more than 22% alcohol), 90 litres of wine (less than 22% alcohol) or 110 litres of beer

Coming from a non-EU country or the Canary Islands, you can bring:

● 200 cigarettes, 100 small cigars, 50 regular cigars or 250g (8.82oz) of tobacco.

● 1 litre of spirits (more than 22% alcohol) or 2 litres of wine or beer (more than 22% alcohol).

● 50g (1.76oz) of perfume.

● 500g coffee; 100g tea.

Visitors can also carry up to €6,000 in cash without having to declare it. Non-EU residents can reclaim VAT (IVA) on some large purchases when they leave. For details, *see p191.*

Disabled

www.accessiblebarcelona.com, run by a British expat wheelchair-user living in Barcelona, is a useful resource.

Institut Municipal de Persones amb Disminució

Avda Diagonal 233, Eixample (93 413 27 75/www.bcn.cat/accessible). Metro Glòries or Monumental/bus 56, 62. **Open** 9am-2pm Mon-Fri. **Map** p343 K8. The official city organisation for the disabled has information on access to venues and transport, and can provide a map with wheelchair-friendly itineraries. It's best to call in advance to make an appointment, rather than just turning up. There are some English speakers available.

Access to sights

Although many sights claim to be accessible, you may still need assistance. Phoning ahead to check is always a good idea.

Newer museums such as the Museu Egipci de Barcelona (*see*

p129) have good accessibility (and, occasionally, adapted toilets), but others, such as the MACBA (*see p107*), despite appearances, are impractical for the disable. The process of converting older buildings is proceeding slowly.

Wheelchair-friendly museums & galleries

All of the below should be accessible to wheelchair users. CCCB; Espai Gaudí - La Pedrera; Fundació Joan Miró; Fundacio Antoni Tàpies; MNAC; Museu Barbier-Mueller d'Art Precolombi; Museu d'Arqueologia de Catalunya; Museu de les Arts Decoratives; Museu del Calçat; Museu de Cera de Barcelona; Museu del Temple Expiatori de la Sagrada Família; Museu d'Història de Catalunya; Museu d'Història de la Ciutat; Museu de la Ciència - CosmoCaixa; Museu de la Xocolata; Museu Frederic Marès; Museu Picasso; Museu Tèxtil i d'Indumentaria; Palau de la Música; Palau de la Virreina.

Transport

Access for disabled people to local transport is improving but still leaves quite a lot to be desired. For wheelchair-users, buses and taxis are usually the best bets. For transport information, call TMB (93 318 70 74) or 010. Transport maps, which can be picked up from transport information offices and some metro stations, indicate wheelchair access points and adapted bus routes. For a list of accessible metro stations and bus lines, check www.tmb.net and click on Transport for Everyone, or see the map on pages 350-352. However, even those stations with lifts can sometimes prove inaccessible, so wheelchair users might do best to avoid the metro altogether.

Buses

All the Aerobús airport buses, night buses and the open-topped tourist buses are fully accessible, though you may need assistance with the steep ramps. Adapted buses also alternate with standard buses on many daytime routes. Press the blue button with the wheelchair symbol to alert the driver before your stop.

Metro & FGC

Only L2 has lifts and ramps at all stations. On L1 and L3, some stations have lifts. There is usually a step on to the train, the size of which varies; some assistance may be required. The Montjuïc funicular railway is fully wheelchair-adapted. Accessible FGC stations include Provença, Muntaner and Avda Tibidabo. The FGC infrastructures at Catalunya and Espanya stations are accessible, but interchanges with metro lines are not.

RENFE trains

While Sants and Plaça Catalunya stations are wheelchair-accessible, the trains themselves are not. If you go to the Atenció al Viajero office ahead of time, help on the platform can be arranged.

Taxis

All taxi drivers are officially required to transport wheelchairs and guide dogs for no extra charge, but cars can be small, and the willingness of drivers to co-operate varies widely. Special minibus taxis adapted for wheelchairs can be ordered from the Taxi Amic service, as well as from some general taxi services such as Servi-Taxi (93 330 03 00). You need to book at least 24-48 hours ahead.

Taxi Amic

93 420 80 88/ www.taxi-amic-adaptat.com. **Open** 7am-11pm Mon-Fri; 9am-10pm Sat, Sun. Fares are the same as for regular cabs, but there is a minimum fare of €9.50 for Barcelona city (€10.50 at weekends), and more for the surrounding areas. Numbers are limited, so call well in advance (two days if possible) to request a specific time.

Trams

All the tram lines throughout Barcelona are fully accessible for wheelchair-users, with ramps that can access all platforms. Watch out for the symbol on each platform that indicates where the wheelchair-accessible doors will be situated.

Drugs

Many people smoke cannabis openly in Spain, but possession or consumption in public is illegal. In private, the law is contradictory: smoking is OK, but you can be nabbed for possession or distribution. Enforcement is often not the highest of police priorities, but you could theoretically receive a fine. Larger amounts entail a fine and, in extreme cases, prison. Smoking in bars is also prohibited; most proprietors are strict on this issue because it could cost them their licences. Having said that, it's not unheard of to catch a whiff of spliff on some terraces in summer. However, if you are caught in possession of any other drugs, you are looking at minimum at some hefty fines and possibly a long prison sentence.

Electricity

The standard current in Spain is 220V. Plugs are of the two-round-pin type. You'll need a plug adaptor to use British-bought electrical devices. If you have US (110V) equipment, you will need a current transformer as well as an adaptor.

Embassies & consulates

Australian Consulate
Plaça Gal.la Placídia 1, Gràcia (93 490 90 13/www.spain.embassy. gov.au). FGC Gràcia. **Open** 10am-noon Mon-Fri. Closed Aug. **Map** p340 F5.

British Consulate
Avda Diagonal 477, 13°, Eixample (93 366 62 00/www.ukinspain.com). Metro Hospital Clínic. **Open** Mid Sept-mid June 9.30am-2pm Mon-Fri. Mid June-mid Sept 8.30am-1.30pm Mon-Fri. **Map** p340 E5.

Canadian Consulate
C/Elisenda de Pinós 10, Zona Alta (93 204 27 00/www.canada-es.org). FGC Reina Elisenda. **Open** 10am-1pm Mon-Fri.

Irish Consulate
Gran Via Carles III 94, 10°, Zona Alta (93 491 50 21). Metro Maria Cristina. **Open** 10am-1pm Mon-Fri. **Map** p338 B4.

New Zealand Consulate
Travessera de Gràcia 64, 2°, Gràcia (93 209 03 99). Metro Diagonal. **Open** 9am-2pm, 4-7pm Mon-Fri. **Map** p340 F5.

South African Consulate
Parque Empresarial Mas Blau II, Alta Ribagorza, 6-8, El Prat de Llobregat (93 506 91 00/ laffont@indukern.es). **Open** 9.30am-noon Mon-Fri.

US Consulate
Passeig Reina Elisenda 23, Zona Alta (93 280 22 27/www. embusa.es). FGC Reina Elisenda. **Open** 9am-1pm Mon-Fri. **Map** p338 B1.

Emergencies

The following are available 24 hours a day.

Emergency services
112
Police, fire or ambulance.

Ambulance/ Ambulància
061.
For hospitals and other health services, see pp310-13.

Fire/Bombers/ Bomberos
080.

Policía Nacional
091.
First choice in a police emergency.

Guàrdia Urbana
092.
The city police; for traffic but also general law and order. For more information on police forces, see p317.

Mossos d'Esquadra
088.

Electricity/ Fecsa-Endesa
900 77 00 77.

Gas/Gas Natural
900 75 07 50.

Water/Aigües de Barcelona
900 70 07 20.

Gay & lesbian

Casal Lambda
C/Verdaguer i Callís 10, Barri Gòtic (93 319 55 50/www.lambdaweb.org). Metro Urquinaona. **Open** 5-9pm Mon-Fri. Closed Aug. **Map** p344 D4. Gay cultural organisation that is the focus for a wide range of activities and publishes the monthly magazine Lambda.

Coordinadora Gai-Lesbiana
C/Violant d'Hongria Reina d'Aragó 156, Sants (93 298 00 29/www. cogailes.org). Metro Plaça de Sants. **Open** 7-9pm Mon-Fri. Closed Aug. **Map** p339 A7.
This gay umbrella group works with the Ajuntament on concerns for the gay, bisexual and transsexual communities. Its Telèfon Rosa service (900 601 601, open 6-10pm daily) gives help or advice and is open all year round.

Front d'Alliberament Gai de Catalunya
C/Verdi 88, Gràcia (93 217 26 69/www.fagc.org). Metro Fontana. **Open** 7-9pm Mon-Thur. **Map** p341 H4.
A vocal group that produces the Debat Gai information bulletin.

Health

Visitors can obtain emergency care through the public health service, Servei Català de la Salut. EU nationals are entitled to free basic medical attention if they have the European Emergency Health Card, also known as the Health Insurance Card. This replaced the E111 form and is valid for one year. Contact the health service in your country of residence for details. If you don't have one but can get one sent or faxed within a few days, you will likely be exempt from charges.

Directory

On yer bike

Back in the 1960s, the White Bike experiment in Amsterdam left bikes lying around the city for citizens to use, abuse and (mostly) steal. Barcelona is far less idealistic about bike sharing: here, utopia comes with a digital tracking system and a register of users. Introduced in March 2007, the distinctive red 'smart' bikes have spread like a rash over the city and with over 50,000 users signing up in the first four months alone, the project has been a runaway success. If the project can keep up with the demand from local residents, there are plans to make it more accessible to tourists.

Following the trend for jabberwocky Euro-English, the city council christened its new bike lending service Bicing (pronounced bee-sing in Catalan, bee-thing in Spanish).

Bicing (www.bicing.com, 902 31 55 31) is part of the much publicised 'greening' of the city, a scheme designed to encourage residents to make short trips by bicycle and to reduce the number of cars on the street. The system also cuts out many of the hassles of owning a bike in Barcelona: lack of storage space in the cramped apartment buildings, limited parking, theft and vandalism. To avoid competing with the many bike hire shops in Barcelona, Bicing is intended to be part of the public transport system rather than a daily bike hire service and as such, the bikes are only free for 30-minute trips. The system is similar to other

lending systems in Scandinavia and is run by Clearchannel, which has just been awarded a 10-year contract in Barcelona.

By the end of 2007, there are to be over 3,000 bikes distributed over more than 100 parking stations. These points are located by metro and bus stations, shopping centres and major sights in the city centre. Users simply go online or to the office at Plaça Carles Pi i Sunyer 8, in the Barri Gòtic, and buy a personal, nontransferable card (€24 a year or €1 a week). This is swiped to release a bike from the parking rack, giving the cyclist 30 minutes to get to their destination and drop off the bike in an available parking slot. Should no space be available, an electronic screen indicates the nearest bike-park with a free bay. The first half hour is free, after which there is a surcharge of 30 cents per 30 minutes up to a maximum of two hours; there is no limit to the number of sessions in one day.

Hogging the bike for more than two hours brings more severe penalties; every further fraction of an hour costs €3 and if the bike is not returned within 24 hours, €150 is charged to your credit card. Those who keep the bike over three hours on more than three occasions have their contract terminated. The bikes are available from 5am to midnight Sunday to Thursday and 24 hours on Friday and Saturday, a timetable designed to coincide with the local metro service.

Citizens of certain other countries that have a special agreement with Spain, among them several Latin American states, can also have access to free care. For general details, check the website www.gencat.net/temes/eng/salut.htm, or call the Catalan government's 24-hour health information line on 902 11 14 44 or the Instituto Nacional de Seguridad Social on 900 16 65 65, 901 50 20 50, www.seg-social.es.

For non-emergencies, it's usually quicker to use private travel insurance rather than the state system. Similarly, non-EU nationals with private

medical insurance can also make use of state health services on a paying basis, but private clinics are simpler.

Accident & emergency

In an emergency, go to the casualty department (*Urgències*) of any of the main public hospitals in the city. All are open 24 hours daily. The most central are the Clínic, which also has a first-aid centre for less serious emergencies two blocks away (C/València 184, 93 227 93 00, open 9am-9pm Mon-Fri, 9am-1pm Sat) and Perecamps. Call 061 for an ambulance.

Centre d'Urgències Perecamps
Avda Drassanes 13-15, Raval (93 441 06 00). Metro Drassanes or Paral·lel. **Map** p342 E11.

Hospital Clínic
C/Villarroel 170, Eixample (93 227 54 00). Metro Hospital Clínic. **Map** p340 E6.

Hospital Dos de Maig
C/Dos de Maig 301, Eixample (93 507 27 00). Metro Hospital de Sant Pau or Cartagena. **Map** p341 L6.

Hospital del Mar
Passeig Marítim 25-29, Barceloneta (93 248 30 00). Metro Ciutadella-Vila Olímpica. **Map** p343 J12.

Directory

Hospital de Sant Pau

C/Sant Antoni Maria Claret 167, Eixample (93 291 90 00). Metro Hospital de Sant Pau. **Map** p341 L5.

Complementary medicine

Integral: Centre Mèdic i de Salut

C/Diputació 321, 1º 1ª, Eixample (93 467 74 20/www.integralcentre medic.com). Metro Girona. **Open** (by appointment only) 9am-9pm Mon-Fri. Closed Aug. **Map** p341 H8.
Acupuncture, homeopathy and other forms of complementary medicine are offered at this well-established clinic. A few practitioners speak English, including the osteopath.

Contraception & abortion

All pharmacies sell condoms (*condons/preservativos*) and other forms of contraception including pills (*la píndola/la píldora*), which can be bought without a prescription. You'll generally need a prescription to get the morning-after pill (*la píndola del dia seguent/la píldora del día siguiente*) but some CAP health centres (*see right*) will dispense it free themselves. Many bars and clubs have condom-vending machines.

While abortion is decriminalised (the law is ambiguous in not using the term 'legal'), during the first 11 weeks of pregnancy, terminations usually take place in private clinics. Under-18s must have parental consent. The only time when abortions might be carried out in public hospitals is when there is foetal abnormality, in which case it's legal up to 22 weeks.

Centre Jove d'Anticoncepció i Sexualitat

C/La Granja 19-21, Gràcia (93 415 10 00/www.centrejove.org). Metro Lessems. **Open** Sept-mid June noon-6.30pm Mon-Thur; 10am-2pm Fri. Mid June-July 10am-5pm Mon-Thur; 10am-2pm Fri. Aug 10am-2pm Mon-Fri. Closed 2wks Aug. **Map** p341 H4.

A family-planning centre aimed at young people (under 25s). It can provide information on the morning-after pill; free HIV tests are given to people under 30. There's a small fee for pregnancy tests.

Dentists

Most dentistry is not covered by the Spanish public health service (to which EU citizens have access). Check the classified ads in *Barcelona Metropolitan* (*see p315*) for English-speaking dentists.

Institut Odontològic Calàbria

Avda Madrid 141-145, Eixample (93 439 45 00/www.ioa.es). Metro Entença. **Open** 9am-1pm, 3-8pm Mon-Fri. **Credit** DC, MC, V. **Map** p339 C6.

These well-equipped clinics provide a complete range of dental services. Some staff speak English.
Other locations Institut Odontològic Sagrada Família, C/Sardenya 319, Eixample (93 457 04 53); Institut Odontològic, C/Diputació 238, Eixample (93 342 64 00).

Doctors

A **Centre d'Assistència Primària** (CAP) is a local health centre (aka *ambulatorio*), where you should be seen fairly quickly by a doctor, but you may need an appointment. There are around 40 in Barcelona; see www.bcn.cat for a full list of locations.

CAP Casc Antic

C/Rec Comtal 24, Sant Pere (93 310 14 21). Metro Arc de Triomf. **Open** 9am-8pm Mon-Fri; (emergencies only) 9am-5pm Sat. **Map** p344 F4.

CAP Doctor Lluís Sayé

C/Torres i Amat 8, Raval (93 301 27 05). Metro Universitat. **Open** 9am-8pm Mon-Fri; (emergencies only) 9am-5pm Sat. **Map** p344 A1.

CAP Drassanes

Avda Drassanes 17-21, Raval (93 329 39 12). Metro Drassanes. **Open** 8am-8pm Mon-Fri. **Map** p342 E11.

CAP Vila Olímpica

C/Joan Miró 17, Vila Olímpica (93 221 37 85). Metro Ciutadella-Vila Olímpica or Marina. **Open** 8am-8.30pm Mon-Fri. **Map** p343 K11.

Centre Mèdic Assistencial Catalonia

C/Provença 281, Eixample (93 215 37 93). Metro Diagonal. **Open** 8am-9pm Mon-Fri. **Map** p340 G7.

Dr Lynd is a British doctor. She can be seen at this surgery 3.50-7.10pm every Wednesday, but it is best to call beforehand.

Dr Mary McCarthy

C/Aribau 215, pral 1ª, Eixample (93 200 29 24/mobile 607 220 040). FGC Gràcia/bus 14, 58, 64. **Open** by appointment. **Credit** MC, V. **Map** p340 F5.

Dr McCarthy is an internal medicine specialist from the US. She will also treat general patients at American health-care rates.

Hospitals

See p311 Accident & emergency.

Opticians

See p211.

Pharmacies

Pharmacies (*farmàcies/ farmacias*) are signalled by large green-and-red neon crosses. Most are open 9am-1.30pm and 4.30-8pm weekdays, and 9am-1.30pm on Saturdays. About a dozen operate around the clock, while more have late opening hours; some of the most central are listed below. The full list of chemists that stay open late (usually until 10pm) and overnight on any given night is posted daily outside every pharmacy door and given in the day's newspapers. You can also call the 010 and 098 information lines. At night, duty pharmacies often appear to be closed, but knock on the shutters and you will be attended to.

The Spanish attitude to dispensing drugs is relaxed. You can legally obtain many things that are more tightly regulated in other countries, including contraceptive pills and some antibiotics, without a prescription. This state of affairs, coupled with the fact that they tend to be quite knowledgeable, means that pharmacists' advice is often sought in order to avoid an unnecessary trip to the doctor. Some have even been known to dispense drugs that do require prescriptions over the counter. Those with the EU Health Insurance Card will pay the same for prescriptions as residents: 40 per cent less than full price.

Farmàcia Alvarez

Passeig de Gràcia 26, Eixample (93 302 11 24). Metro Passeig de Gràcia. **Open** 8am-10.30pm Mon-Thur; 8am-midnight Fri; 9am-midnight Sat. **Credit** MC, V. **Map** p342 G8.

Farmàcia Cervera

C/Muntaner 254, Eixample (93 200 09 96). Metro Diagonal/FGC Gràcia. **Open** 24hrs daily. **Credit** AmEx, MC, V. **Map** p340 E5.

Farmàcia Clapés

La Rambla 98, Barri Gòtic (93 301 28 43). Metro Liceu. **Open** 24hrs daily. **Credit** AmEx, MC, V. **Map** p344 B4.

Farmàcia Vilar

Vestibule, Estació de Sants, Sants (93 490 92 07). Metro Sants Estació. **Open** 7am-10.30pm Mon-Fri; 8am-10.30pm Sat, Sun. **Credit** AmEx, MC, V. **Map** p339 B7.

STDs, HIV & AIDS

Spain's high death rate from AIDS might be falling somewhat, but the HIV virus continues its lethal spread through many groups, such as drug-users and, particularly, heterosexuals. Local chemists take part in a needle-exchange and condom distribution programme for intravenous drug-users. Anti-retroviral drugs for HIV treatment are covered by social security in Spain. Free, anonymous blood tests for HIV and other STDs are given at the Unidad de Infección de Transmisión Sexual (93 441 46 12, open by appointment 8.30am-1pm, 2.30-7pm Mon-Fri) at CAP Drassanes (*see p312*). HIV tests are also available at the

Coordinadora Gai-Lesbiana (*see p310*), at the Asociació Ciutadana Antisida de Catalunya (C/Junta de Comerç 23, Raval, 93 317 05 05, www.acasc.info, open 10am-2pm, 4-7pm Mon-Thur, 10am-2pm Fri) and at Projecte dels Noms (C/Comte Borrell 164 izq, 93 318 20 56, www.hispano sida.com, open by appointment 10am-2pm, 3-7pm Mon-Thur, 10am-2pm Fri).

Actua

C/Gomis 38, Zona Alta (93 418 50 00/www.actua.org.es). Metro Vallcarca/bus 22, 27, 28, 73. **Open** (by appointment only) 10am-2pm, 4-7pm Mon-Thur; 10am-2pm Fri. Support group for people with HIV. There are some English speakers available.

AIDS Information Line

Freephone 900 21 22 22. **Open** Mid Sept-May 8am-5.30pm Mon-Thur; 8am-3pm Fri. *June-mid Sept* 8am-3pm Mon-Fri.

Helplines

Alcoholics Anonymous

93 317 77 77/www.alcoholicos-anonimos.org. **Open** 10am-1pm, 5-8pm Mon-Fri.
Among the local AA groups, several have dedicated English-speaking sections. Call for details.

Narcotics Anonymous

902 11 41 47/www.na-esp.org. **Open** hours vary.
Check the website for details of twice-weekly meetings in English.

Telèfon de l'Esperança

93 414 48 48/www.telefono esperanza.com. **Open** 24hrs daily.
Apart from 24-hour counselling, the staff at this local helpline run by a private foundation can put you in contact with other specialist help groups, from psychiatric to legal. English is occasionally spoken by the staff, but is not always guaranteed.

ID

From the age of 14, Spaniards are legally obliged to carry their DNI (identity card). Foreigners are also meant to carry an ID card or passport, and are in theory subject to a fine – in practice, you're more likely to get a warning. If you

don't want to carry it around with you (wisely, given the prevalence of petty crime), it's a good idea to carry a photocopy or a driver's licence instead: technically, it's not legal, but usually acceptable. ID is needed to check into a hotel, hire a car, pay with a card in shops and exchange or pay with travellers' cheques.

Insurance

For health-care and EU nationals, *see p310*. Some non-EU countries have reciprocal health-care agreements with Spain, but for most travellers it's usually more convenient to have private travel insurance, which will also, of course, cover you in case of theft and flight problems.

Internet

Broadband (ADSL), now more affordable than ever, is fast taking over from basic dial-up. Ex-monopoly Telefónica (902 35 70 00, www.telefonica online.es) controls most of the infrastructure, but is obliged to rent its lines to other firms. Telefónica (Terra), Orange (902 012 240, www.orange.es), Ya (902 90 29 02, www.ya.com) and Auna (ONO) (902 50 00 60, www.auna.es) all offer high-speed Router or Wi-Fi connection with 24-hour access for a flat monthly rate. Many firms also offer discount 'package' deals for phone lines and high-speed internet (and, increasingly, cable TV). Initial connection times can vary. Be aware that rock-bottom price deals may slow down the process considerably, and/or be applicable for a short time.

Internet access

There are internet centres all over Barcelona. Some libraries (*see p314*) have internet points and wireless access for public use.

Bornet Internet Cafè

*C/Barra de Ferro 3, Born (93 268
15 07/www.bornet-bcn.com). Metro
Jaume I.* **Open** 10am-12pm Mon-Fri;
3-10pm Sat, Sun. **No credit cards.**
Map p345 E6.
There are ten terminals in this small
café and six more for laptops. One
hour is €2.60; but you're really
paying for the atmosphere.

easyEverything

*La Rambla 31, Barri Gòtic (93
301 75 07/www.easyeverything.
com). Metro Drassanes or Liceu.*
Open 8am-2am daily. **No credit
cards. Map** p345 A6.
There are 330 terminals here and
240 at Ronda Universitat 35 (open
8am-2am daily). Buy credit from the
machines; price then increases with
demand. Alternatively, buy passes
that allow unlimited access during a
set period (from 24 hours to 30 days).

Language

See pp324-325.

Left luggage

Look for signs to the *consigna*.
**Aeroport del Prat
Terminal B**.
Open 24hrs daily.
Rates €4/day.
**Estació d'Autobusos
Barcelona-Nord**
*C/Alí Bei 80, Eixample.
Metro Arc de Triomf.*
Open 24hrs daily. **Rates**
€3-€4.50/day. **Map** p343 E5.
**Train stations Sants-
Estació & Estació de
França**, Born.
Open 6am-11.45pm daily.
Rates €3-€4.50/day. **Map**
p339 A4 & p343 E6.
Some of the smaller railway
stations also have left-
luggage lockers.

Legal help

Consulates (*see p310*) help
tourists in emergencies, and
recommend lawyers.

Marti & Associats

*Avda Diagonal 584, pral 1ª,
Eixample (93 201 62 66/www.
martilawyers.com). Bus 6, 7, 15,
33, 34.* **Open** *Sept-July* 9am-8pm
Mon-Thur; 9am-7pm Fri. *Aug* 9am-
2pm, 4-7pm Mon-Thur, 9am-2pm Fri.
Map p340 E5.

Australian John Rocklin is one of
the lawyers at this Catalan firm that
also has native speakers of other
languages on staff. The firm can
help with work and obtaining
residency permits.

Libraries

There is a network of public
libraries around the city that
offers free internet access,
some English novels and
information on cultural
activities. Membership is free.
Opening times are generally
10am-2pm, 3.30-8.30pm
Monday-Saturday and 10am-
2pm Sunday. See www.bcn.
cat/icub/biblioteques/ or call
93 316 10 00 for details. Private
libraries (*see below*) are better
stocked but generally require
paid membership to use
their facilities.

Ateneu Barcelonès

*C/Canuda 6, Barri Gòtic (93 343
61 21/www.ateneubcn.org). Metro
Catalunya.* **Open** 9am-11pm daily.
Map p344 C3.
This venerable cultural and
philosophical society has the city's
best private library, plus a quite
wonderfully peaceful interior
garden patio and a quiet bar. It
also organises cultural events.
Membership is €21.44 a month.

Biblioteca de
Catalunya

*C/Hospital 56, Raval (93 270 23
00/www.bnc.cat). Metro Liceu.*
Open 9am-8pm Mon-Fri; 9am-
2pm Sat. **Map** p344 A4.
The Catalan national collection is
housed in the medieval Hospital de
la Santa Creu and has an excellent
stock reaching back through the
centuries. Readers' cards are
required, but free one-day research
visits are allowed for over-18s (take
your passport with you to prove
your identity). It also stages the
occasional theatre show.

British Council/
Institut Britànic

*C/Amigó 83, Zona Alta (93 241 97
11/www.britishcouncil.es). FGC
Muntaner.* **Open** *Oct-mid June*
9.30am-12.30pm, 3.30-9pm Mon-Fri;
10.30am-2pm Sat. *Mid June-July, Sept*
9.30am-12.30pm, 4-8.30pm Mon-Fri.
Aug 9.30-12.30pm Mon-Fri.
Map p340 E4.
The British Council has the UK
press, English books, satellite TV,
internet access and a multi-media

section oriented towards helping
students learn English. Membership
is obligatory for use of the library
and borrowing materials. The
charge is €62 a year.

Mediateca

*CaixaForum, Avda Marquès de
Comillas 6-8, Montjuïc (902 22 30
40/93 476 86 51/www.mediateca
online.net). Metro Espanya.* **Open**
Sept-July 10am-8pm Tue-Fri; 10am-
2pm, 4-10pm Sat. *Aug* 4-8pm Tue,
Thur-Sun; 4pm-midnight Wed.
Map p339 B9.
A high-tech art, music and media
library in the arts centre of Fundació
la Caixa. Most materials are open-
access, though use of the internet is
limited to Mediateca-related subjects.
You can borrow books, magazines,
CDs, etc. Membership is €6 (€3
reductions). The lending desk is
open 10am-7.30pm Tue-Fri and
10am-2pm Sat (closed Sat in Aug).

Lost property

If you lose something at the
airport, report it to the lost
property centre (Oficina
d'objectes perduts/Oficina
de objetos perdidos, Bloque
Técnico building, between
terminals B and C, 93 298
33 49). If you have mislaid
anything on a train, look for
the Atenció al Passatger/
Atención al Viajero desk or
Cap d'Estació office at the
nearest station to where your
property went astray. Call
ahead to the destination
station, or call station
information and ask for
objetos perdidos.

Municipal Lost
Property Office

*Oficina de Troballes, Plaça Carles
Pi i Sunyer 8-10, Barri Gòtic
(lost property enquiries 010).
Metro Catalunya or Jaume I.*
Open 9am-2pm Mon-Fri.
Map p344 C4.
All items found on city public
transport and taxis, or picked up
by the police in the street, should
eventually find their way to this
Ajuntament office, just off Avda
Portal de l'Àngel, hopefully within
a few days of being lost. Call 010
for information. Within 24 hours
of the loss, you can also try ringing
the city transport authority on 93
318 70 74, or, for taxis, the Institut
Metropolità del Taxi lost property
office on 93 400 50 26.

Media

Spanish and Catalan newspapers tend to favour serious political commentary. There are no sensationalist tabloids in Spain: for scandal, the *prensa rosa* ('pink press', or gossip magazines) is the place to look. Television channels, though, go straight for the mass market, with junk television (*telebasura*) prevalent. Catalan is the dominant language on both radio and TV, less so in print.

Daily newspapers

Free daily papers of reasonable quality, such as *20 Minutes* and *Metro*, are handed out in the city centre every morning. Articles in these papers jump between Spanish and Catalan for no apparent reason.

ABC

Heavyweight, right-wing reading (www.abc.es).

Avui

A conservative, nationalist Catalan-language newspaper (www.avui.cat).

El Mundo

A decent centrist option (www.elmundo.es).

El País

A serious, left-wing paper (www.elpais.es).

El Periódico

Of the local press, this is the most akin to the British tabloid in terms of format, with bright colours and bold headlines, but it has serious content. Catalan and Spanish editions (www.elperiodico.com).

La Vanguardia

The city's top-selling daily newspaper is conservative in tone, with a daily Barcelona supplement. Written in Spanish (www.lavanguardia.es).

English language

Foreign newspapers are available at most kiosks on La Rambla, Barri Gòtic, and Passeig de Gràcia, Eixiample and there is an international newsstand at FNAC (*see p193*).

Barcelona Connect

A small free magazine with tips for travellers to the city (www.barcelonaconnect.com).

Barcelona Metropolitan

A free monthly general-interest magazine for English-speaking locals, distributed in bars, embassies and other anglophone hangouts (www.barcelona-metropolitan.com).

b-guided

Quarterly style magazine in Spanish and English for bars, clubs, shops, restaurants and exhibitions (www.b-guided.com).

Catalonia Today

Lively English-language weekly with a comprehensive round up of local news and cultural events. Run by the publisher of Catalan-language daily *El Punt*. Available from newsstands throughout the city (www.cataloniatoday.cat).

Listings & classifieds

The main papers have daily 'what's on' listings, with entertainment supplements on Fridays (most run TV schedules on Saturdays). For monthly listings, see *Metropolitan* or the handy *Butxaca*, which can be picked up in cultural information centres, such as Palau de la Virreina (*see p321*) on La Rambla; and freebies such as *Mondo Sonoro* (www.mondo-sonoro.com) or *GO* (www.go-mag.com), which can be found in bars and music shops. Of the dailies, *La Vanguardia* has the best classifieds; you can also consult it at www.clasificados.es. www.infojobs.net is a popular resource for job vacancies.

Guía del Ocio

This weekly listings magazine, published Fridays, is available at any kiosk for €1 (www.guia delociobcn.com).

Primeramà

The largest classified-ad publication, is available on Mondays, Wednesdays and Fridays. (www.anuntis.es)

Time Out Barcelona

A new and comprehensive weekly listings magazine that is published in Catalan. There are plans to add a monthly pull-out section in English (www.timeout.cat).

Radio

There are vast numbers of local, regional and national stations, with Catalan having a high profile. Catalunya Mùsica (101.5 FM) is mainly classical and jazz, while Flaix FM (105.7 FM) provides news and music. For something a little more alternative, try Radio Bronka (99 FM) or Radio 3 (98.7 FM), which has a wonderfully varied music policy. You can listen to the BBC World Service on shortwave on 15485, 9410, 12095 and 6195 KHz, depending on the time of day.

Television

The inauguration of two free new channels in 2006, Cuatro and La Sexta, has added a couple of decent American series to TV schedules. The emphasis is on mass entertainment, with tedious variety shows, lame comedians, gossip shows, home-grown sitcoms and trashy American films, peppered with ad breaks. Programme times are unreliable and films are mainly dubbed.

Antena 3

A private channel providing a mixture of chat and American films, as well as popular US programmes such as *The Simpsons* and *South Park*.

BTV

The young staff of the Ajuntament's city channel produce Barcelona's most groundbreaking TV.

Directory

Canal 33

Also regional and in Catalan, with documentaries, sports programmes and round-table discussions.

City TV

A private Catalan channel, cloned from a Toronto city station. The schedules are filled with magazine-style programmes and soft porn.

Cuatro

Owned by pay-TV giant Sogecable, Cuatro shows US and Spanish soaps, such as *House* and *Married with Children*, some sports and the excellent *Las Noticias del Guiñol* (a daily news spoof using puppets).

Digital+

The predominant subscription channel fuses the defunct Canal + and Via Digital, showing films, sport and US series.

La Sexta

La Sexta boasts big sporting events and some decent US shows, such as *The Sopranos*. The picture can be fuzzy; many can't tune in at all.

Tele 5

Also private and part-owned by Silvio Berlusconi. Its main recent attraction has been *Gran Hermano* (*Big Brother*), as well as various celebrity gossip programmes.

TVE1

Spanish state broadcaster 'La Primera' is controlled by the government. Do not expect cutting-edge TV.

TVE2

Also state-run, TVE2, 'La Dos' offers more highbrow fare with some good late-night movies and documentaries.

TV3

Programmes are entirely in Catalan with generally mainstream subject matter. TV3 often has good films shown in the original version.

Satellite & cable

Satellite and cable are becoming increasingly popular in Barcelona. The leader in the market place is Digital+ (*see above*).

Money

Spain's currency is the euro. Each euro (€) is divided into 100 cents (¢), known as *cèntims/céntimos*. Notes come in denominations of €500, €200, €100, €50, €20, €10 and €5. Due to the increasing circulation of counterfeit notes, smaller businesses may be reluctant to accept anything larger than €50.

Banks & currency exchanges

Banks (*bancos*) and savings banks (*caixes d'estalvis/cajas de ahorros*) usually accept euro travellers' cheques for a commission, but they tend to refuse any kind of personal cheque except one issued by that bank. Some bureaux de change (*cambios*) don't charge commission, but rates are worse. Obtaining money through ATMs (which are everywhere) with a debit or credit card is the easiest option, despite the fees often charged.

Bank hours

Banks are normally open between 8.30am and 2pm Mon-Fri. From October to April, most branches also open between 8.30am and 1pm on Saturdays. Hours vary little between banks. Savings banks offer the same exchange facilities as banks and open the same hours; from October to May many are also open late on Thursdays, 4.30-7.45pm.

Out-of-hours banking

Foreign exchange offices at the airport (terminals A and B) are open 7am-11pm daily. Others in the centre open late: some on La Rambla open until midnight, later between July and September. At Sants, change money at La Caixa (8am-8pm daily). At the airport and outside some banks are automatic exchange machines that accept notes in major currencies. The American Express shop offers full AmEx card services, plus currency exchange, money transfers and a travel

agency; Western Union is the quickest (but not the cheapest) way of sending money abroad.

American Express

La Rambla 74, Barri Gòtic (93 342 73 11/www.american express.com). Metro Liceu. **Open** 9am-10.30pm daily. **Map** p345 B5.

Western Union Money Transfer

Loterías Manuel Martín, La Rambla 41, Barri Gòtic (93 412 70 41/www.westernunion.com). Metro Liceu. **Open** 9.30am-10pm daily. **Map** p345 A6.
Other locations Mail Boxes, C/València 214, Eixample (900 63 36 33/93 454 69 83/www.mbe.es); and throughout the city.

Credit & debit cards

Major credit cards are accepted in hotels, shops, restaurants and other places (including metro ticket machines and pay-and-display on-street parking machines). American Express and Diners Club cards are less accepted than MasterCard and Visa. Many debit cards from other European countries can also be used: check with your bank beforehand. You can withdraw cash with major cards from ATMs, and banks will also advance cash against a credit card.

Note: you need photo ID (passport, driving licence or similar) when using a credit or debit card in a shop, but usually not in a restaurant.

Lost/stolen cards

All lines have English-speaking staff and are open 24 hours daily. Maestro do not have a Spanish helpline.

American Express 902 11 11 35.
Diners Club 901 10 10 11.
MasterCard 900 97 12 31.
Visa 900 99 11 24.

Tax

The standard rate for sales tax (IVA) is 16 per cent; this drops to seven per cent in hotels and restaurants, and four per cent on some books. IVA may or may not be included in listed prices at restaurants, and it usually isn't included in rates quoted at hotels. If it's not, the expression *IVA no inclòs/incluido* (sales tax not included) should appear after the price. Beware of this when getting quotes on expensive items. In shops displaying a 'Tax-Free Shopping' sticker, non-EU residents can reclaim tax on large purchases when leaving the country.

Opening times

Most shops open from 9am or 10am to 1pm or 2pm, and then 4pm or 5pm to 8pm or 9pm, Monday to Saturday. Many smaller businesses don't reopen on Saturday afternoons. All-day opening (10am to 8pm or 9pm) is becoming commoner, especially for larger and more central establishments.

Markets open at 7am or 8am; most stalls are shut by 2pm, although many open on Fridays until 8pm. The Ajuntament encourages stallholders at each municipal market to remain open in the afternoons during the rest of the week in an effort to compete with supermarkets. Larger shops are allowed to open on Sundays and on a few holidays, mostly near Christmas.

In summer, many shops and restaurants shut for all or part of August. Some businesses work a shortened day from June to September, from 8am or 9am until 3pm. Most museums close one day each week, usually Mondays.

Police

Barcelona has several police forces: the Guàrdia Urbana (municipal police – navy and pale blue), the Policía Nacional (national police – darker blue uniforms and white shirts, or blue, combat-style gear) and the Mossos d'Esquadra (in a uniform of navy and light blue with red trim). The Mossos is the Catalan government's police force and is taking over from the other two police forces, with the process due to be completed in 2008 (*see p34* **New cops on the block**). But the GU and the PN will keep control of certain matters, like immigration and terrorism, which are dealt with by central government.

The Guàrdia Civil is a paramilitary force with green uniforms, policing highways, customs posts, government buildings and rural areas.

Reporting a crime

If you're robbed or attacked, report the incident as soon as possible at the nearest police station (*comisaría*), or dial 112. In the centre, the most convenient is the 24hr Guàrdia Urbana station (La Rambla 43, Barri Gòtic, 092/93 256 24 30), which often has English-speaking officers on duty; they may transfer you to the Mossos d'Esquadra (C/Nou de la Rambla 76-80, Raval, 088/93 306 23 00) to report the crime formally. To do this, you'll need to make an official statement (*denuncia*). It's highly improbable that you will recover your property, but you need the *denuncia* to make an insurance claim. You can also make this statement over the phone or online (902 10 21 12, www.policia.es); except for crimes involving physical violence, or if the author has been identified. You'll still have to go to the *comisaría* within 72 hours to sign the *denuncia*, but you'll be able to skip some queues.

Postal services

Letters and postcards weighing up to 20g cost 30¢ within Spain; 58¢ to the rest of Europe; 78¢ to the rest of the world – though prices normally rise on 1 January. It's usually easiest to buy stamps at *estancs* (*see below*). Mail sent abroad is slow: five to six working days in Europe, eight to ten to the USA. Postboxes in the street are yellow, sometimes with a white or blue horn insignia. For postal information ring 902 197 197 or go to www.correos.es.

Correu Central

Plaça Antonio López, Barri Gòtic (93 486 80 50). Metro Barceloneta or Jaume I. **Open** 8.30am-9.30pm Mon-Fri; 8.30am-2pm Sat. **Map** p345 D7.
Take a ticket from the machine as you enter and wait your turn. Apart from the typical services, fax-sending and receiving is offered (with the option of courier delivery in Spain, using the Burofax option). To send something express, ask for *urgente*. Some post offices close in August. Many have painfully slow queues. **Other locations** Ronda Universitat 23 and C/Aragó 282, Eixample (both 8.30am-8.30pm Mon-Fri, 9.30am-1pm Sat); and throughout the city.

Estancs/estancos

Government-run tobacco shops, known as an *estanc/estanco* (at times, just *tabac*) and identified by a brown-and-yellow sign, are important institutions. As well as tobacco, they supply postage stamps, public transport *targetes* and phonecards.

Post boxes

A PO box (*apartado postal*) address costs €57.80 annually.

Postal Transfer

C/Ausiàs Marc 13-17, Eixample (93 301 27 32). Metro Urquinaona. **Open** 8.30am-8.30pm Mon-Fri; 9.30am-1pm Sat.
Apart from postal services, there's Western Union money transfer, internet access, cheap international calls, fax, photocopying and banking.

Poste restante

Poste restante letters should be sent to Lista de Correos, 08080 Barcelona, Spain. Pick-up is from the main post office (*see above*); you'll need your passport.

Queuing

Contrary to appearances, Catalans have an advanced queuing culture. They may not stand in an orderly line, but they're normally very aware of when it's their turn, particularly at market stalls. The standard

Directory

drill is to ask when you arrive, *¿Qui es l'últim/la última?* ('Who's last?') and say *jo* ('me') to the next person who asks.

Religion

Anglican: St George's Church

C/Horaci 38, Zona Alta (93 417 88 67/www.st-georges-church. com). FGC Avda Tibidabo. **Main service** 11am Sun.
An Anglican/Episcopalian church with mixed congregation. Activities include the Alpha course (directed at faith-seekers), a women's club, bridge and Sunday school. See website for details.

Catholic mass in English: Parròquia Maria Reina

Carretera d'Esplugues 103, Zona Alta (93 203 41 15). Metro Maria Cristina/bus 22, 63, 75. **Mass** 10.30pm Sun. **Map** p338 A1.

Jewish Orthodox: Sinagoga de Barcelona & Comunitat Israelita de Barcelona

C/Avenir 24, Zona Alta (93 209 31 47/www.cibonline.org). FGC Gràcia. **Prayers** call for times. **Map** p340 F5.

Jewish Reform: Comunitat Jueva Atid de Catalunya

Call for address (93 417 37 04/ www.atid.es). FGC El Putxet. **Prayers** call for times.
You must give notice that you'll be attending this organisation: make sure to email or fax the above number with your passport details by 2pm Friday.

Muslim: Mosque Islamic Cultural Council of Catalunya

C/Tallers 55, ent, 1, Raval (93 301 0831). Metro Catalunya. **Prayers** 2pm daily. Phone for other times. **Map** p342 F10.

Renting a flat

Rental accommodation in Barcelona is pricier than ever. A room in a shared flat costs €350/month plus, while a one-to two-bed apartment in the centre goes for €700/month or more. Standards vary a great deal, so do shop around. Rental agreements generally cover a five-year period, within which the landlord can only raise the rent in line with inflation. Landlords usually ask for a month's rent as a *fiança/fianza* (deposit) and a month's rent in advance; some may also require an employment contract as proof of income. Details of contracts vary wildly: don't sign unless you're confident of your Spanish or Catalan and/or a local lawyer or *gestor* has seen it.

Classified ads in *La Vanguardia* and *Barcelona Metropolitan* (*see p315*) carry apartment ads, as does www.loquo.com (*see p69*). Also useful are *administradores de fincas*: these companies run buildings and sometimes have to find tenants for vacant apartments. www.coleadministradors.com has a list, but bear in mind that its classified ads are often out of date. Try calling instead. Also, while walking, look out for *Es lloga/Se alquila* or *En lloguer/En alquiler* (for rent) signs: you do get lucky. Be cautious of agencies that ask for cash up front for finding you a flat. If you decide to pay, go by recommendation.

Safety & security

Pickpocketing and bag-snatching are epidemic in Barcelona, with tourists a prime target. Be especially careful around the Old City, particularly La Rambla, as well as at stations and on public transport, the airport train being a favourite. However, thieves go anywhere tourists go, including parks, beaches and internet cafés. Most street crime is aimed at the inattentive, and can be avoided by taking precautions:
● Avoid giving invitations: don't keep wallets in accessible pockets, keep your bags closed and in front of you. When you stop, put bags down beside you (or hold them on your lap), where you can see them.
● Don't flash about wads of cash or fancy cameras.
● In busy streets or crowded places, keep an eye on what is happening around you. If you're suspicious of someone, move somewhere else.
● As a rule, Barcelona street thieves tend to use stealth and surprise rather than violence. However, muggings and knife threats do sometimes occur. Avoid deserted streets in the city centre if you're on your own at night, and offer no resistance when threatened.
● Don't carry more money and valuables than you need: use your hotel's safe deposit facilities, and take out travel insurance.

Smoking

For the visitor to Barcelona, it may seem that smoking when and where you want is a given right and, in fact, one effect of the recent tightening of the tobacco law is that there are as many signs telling you that you can smoke, as there are telling you that you can't.

Smoking is banned in banks, shops and offices; while in hotels, and restaurants larger than 100 square metres (1076 square feet), non-smoking zones are required by law. But with tobacco still relatively cheap and socially acceptable, it's common to see small crowds of employees puffing away on the pavement on their lunch breaks; and few cafés and even fewer bars have opted for a strict no-smoking policy, for fear of losing business. In Catalonia, the smoking law applying to the physical separation of smoking and non-smoking areas in larger restaurants has already been relaxed, as many business owners complain of the cost and unfeasibility of restructuring their interiors.

Most hotels have non-smoking rooms or floors; although if you ask for a non-smoking room, some hotels may just give you a room that has had the ashtray removed. Some restaurants and a few, but growing, number of hotels, however, are completely smoke-free. Smoking bans in such places as cinemas, theatres and on public transport are generally widely respected.

Study

Catalonia is generally pro-European, and the vast majority of foreign students who come to Spain under the EU's Erasmus scheme are studying at Catalan universities or colleges. Catalan is usually the language spoken in these universities, although some lecturers are relaxed about the use of Castilian in class for the first few months.

Secretaria General de Joventut - Punt d'Informació Juvenil

C/Calabria 147-C/Rocafort 116, Eixample (reception 93 483 83 83/information 93 483 83 84/ www.gencat.net/joventut). Metro Rocafort. **Open** *Oct-May* 10am-2pm, 4-8pm Mon-Fri. *June-Sept* 10am-2pm, 4.30-8.30pm Mon-Thur, 10am-2pm Fri. Closed 1wk Aug. **Map** p339 D8.
Generalitat-run centre with a number of services: information for young people on travel, work and study.

Accommodation & advice

Barcelona Allotjament

C/Pelai 12, pral B, Eixample (93 268 43 57/www.barcelona-allotjament.com). Metro Catalunya or Universitat. **Open** 10am-2pm, 5-7pm Mon-Thur; 10am-2pm Fri. Closed Aug. **No credit cards**. **Map** p344 A1.
Rooms with local families, in shared student flats and in B&Bs, can be booked through this agency, aimed mainly at students. Rooms in shared apartments cost €300 and up per month, plus a €120 agency fee. It can also rent whole flats.

Borsa Jove d'Habitatge

Plaça Rius i Taulet 3, Gràcia (93 291 43 43/www.habitatgejove. com). Metro Fontana. **Open** *Oct-May* 10am-2pm, 4-8pm Mon-Fri. *June-Sept* 10am-2pm, 4.30-8.30pm Mon-Thur, 10am-2pm Fri. Closed 1wk Aug. **Map** p340 G5.
An accommodation service for 18-35s; it's mostly for whole flats, but there are some single rooms.

Centre d'Informació i Assessorament per a Joves (CIAJ)

C/Sant Oleguer 6-8, Raval (93 442 29 39/www.bcn.cat/ciaj). Metro Liceu or Paral·lel. **Open** *Sept-July* 10am-2pm, 4-8pm Mon-Fri. *Aug* 10am-3pm Mon-Fri. **Map** p342 E11.
Youth information centre run by the city council, with information on work, study, accommodation (classifieds are online, not in the centre itself) and more.

Language classes

If you plan to stay in bilingual Barcelona for a while, you may want (or need) to learn some Catalan. The city is also a popular location for studying Spanish. For full course lists, try the youth information centres above. See www.cervantes.es for schools recommended by Spain's official language institute, the Instituto Cervantes.

Babylon Idiomas

C/Bruc 65, pral 1ª, Eixample (93 488 15 85/www.babylon-idiomas.com). Metro Girona. **Open** 9am-8pm Mon-Fri. **Credit** MC, V. **Map** p344 H8.
Small groups (up to eight people) run at all levels of Spanish in this school, which also has business courses. Staff can arrange accommodation.

Consorci per a la Normalització Lingüística

C/Quintana 11, 1° 1ª, Barri Gòtic (93 412 72 24/www.cpnl.cat). Metro Liceu. **Open** *mid Sept-mid June* 9am-2pm Mon-Fri. *Mid June-mid Sept* 9am-1pm, 4-5.30pm Mon-Thur; 9am-2pm Fri. **No credit cards**. **Map** p345 B5.
The Generalitat organisation for the promotion of the Catalan language has centres around the city offering Catalan courses for non-Spanish speakers at very low prices or even for free (level one). Courses start in

September and February, but the classes are very big and the queues to enrol are very long. There are also free monthly intensive courses and multimedia classes for beginners all year. The CPNL in Plaça Catalunya 9, 2° 1ª (902 07 50 60) specialises in beginners' courses and has a wider timetable. Places are limited to around 23 students per class; call or arrive early when it's time to sign up. **Other locations** C/Mallorca 115, entl 1ª, Eixample (93 451 24 45); and throughout the city.

Escola Oficial d'Idiomes de Barcelona - Drassanes

Avda Drassanes, Raval (93 324 93 30/www.eoibd.es). Metro Drassanes. **Open** *Sept-June* 8.30am-9pm Mon-Fri. **Map** p342 E11.
This state-run school has semi-intensive four-month courses, starting in October and February (enrolment tends to be in either September or January, check the website for details), at all levels in Spanish; and longer courses, usually starting in October, in Catalan, French, German, English and ten other languages. It's cheap and has a good reputation;, but as a result the demand is high and the classes themselves are big. There's also a self-study centre and a good library. There are several other Escolas Oficials in Barcelona where it may be easier to get a place, although they do not offer such a wide range as the one at Drassanes. Call 012 for information or see www.gencat. net/educacio for details.
Other locations Escola Oficial, Avda del Jordà 18, Vall d'Hebrón (93 418 74 85/93 418 68 33); and throughout the city.

Estudios Hispánicos de la Universitat de Barcelona

Gran Via de les Corts Catalanes 585, Eixample (information 93 403 55 19/www.eh.ub.es). Metro Universitat. **Open** Information (Pati de Ciències entrance) *mid June-Aug* 9am-2pm Mon-Fri. *Sept-mid June* 9am-2pm, 4-5.30pm Mon-Thur; 9am-2pm Fri. **Credit** AmEx, DC, MC, V. **Map** p342 F8.
Intensive, fortnight, three-month and year-long Spanish language and culture courses. Enrolment runs year-round.

International House

C/Trafalgar 14, Eixample (93 268 45 11/www.ihes.com/bcn). Metro Urquinaona. **Open** 8am-9pm Mon-Fri; 10am-1.30pm Sat. **Map** p344 E3.

Directory

Intensive Spanish courses all year round. IH is also a leading TEFL teacher training centre, and offers additional courses in Spanish-English translation.

Universities

The Erasmus student-exchange scheme is part of the EU's Socrates programme to help students move between member states. Interested students should contact the Erasmus co-ordinator at their home college. Information is available in Britain from the UK Socrates-Erasmus Council, Rothford, Giles Lane, Canterbury, Kent CT2 7LR (01227762712, www.erasmus. ac.uk). See also europa.eu.int for an overview.

Universitat Autònoma de Barcelona

Campus de Bellaterra (93 581 10 00/information 93 581 11 11/ www.uab.es). FGC or RENFE Universidad Autonoma/by car A58 to Cerdanyola del Valles. **Open** *Sept-July* 10am-1.30pm, 3.30-4.30pm Mon-Fri. *Aug* 10am-1.30pm Mon-Fri.
A 1960s campus at Bellaterra, near Sabadell. Frequent FGC train connections to the centre.

Universitat de Barcelona

Gran Via de les Corts Catalanes 585, Eixample (information 93 403 54 17/www.ub.es). Metro Universitat. **Open** Information 9am-2pm Mon-Fri. Closed 1wk Aug. **Map** p342 F8.
Barcelona's oldest and biggest university. For Spanish courses, *see p319.*

Universitat Pompeu Fabra

Information 93 542 22 28/www.upf. edu. Information points: La Rambla 30-32, Barri Gòtic; C/Ramon Trias Fargas 25-27, Vila Olímpica; Passeig Circumval·lació 8, Born. **Open** *mid June-mid Sept* 9am-8pm Mon-Fri. *Mid Sept-mid June* 9am-9pm Mon-Fri.
There are faculties in various parts of central Barcelona, many of which are in the Old City.

Universitat Ramon Llull

Main offices: C/Claravall 1-3, Zona Alta (902 50 20 50/93 602 22 00/ www.url.es). FGC Avda Tibidabo. **Open** Information 9am-2pm, 4-6.30pm Mon-Fri. Closed 2wks Aug.

A private university bringing together a number of once-separate institutions, including the prestigious ESADE business school (93 280 61 62/93 280 29 95, www.esade.edu).

Telephones

The recent liberalisation of the phone market has led to the dissolution of former state operator Telefónica's monopoly. However, while several new operators have emerged, the market is still very dependent on Telefónica's infrastructure, and rates remain high compared to other European countries.

One of the outcomes of diversification has been the confusion among users, exemplified by the profusion of numbers for directory enquiries. There are now more than 20 numbers (which are operated by various companies) for information; their cost fluctuates wildly. Telefónica itself has several, and is criticised for its advertising of the more expensive ones. It is, however, forced to offer a cheap number (which is free from payphones). Phonecards and phone centres give cheaper call rates, especially for international calls.

Dialling & codes

Normal Spanish phone numbers have nine digits; the area code (93 in the province of Barcelona) must be dialled with all calls, both local and long-distance. Spanish mobile numbers always begin with 6. Numbers starting 900 are freephone lines, while other 90 numbers are special-rate services. Those starting with 80 are high-rate lines and can only be called from within Spain.

International & long-distance calls

To make an international call, dial 00 and then the country code, followed by the area code

(omitting the first zero in UK numbers), and then the number. Country codes are as follows:

Australia 61.
Canada 1.
Irish Republic 353.
New Zealand 64.
South Africa 27.
United Kingdom 44.
USA 1.

To phone Spain from abroad, dial 00, followed by 34, followed by the number.

Mobile phones

The mobile phone, or *móvil*, is omnipresent in Spain. Calls are paid for either through direct debit or by using prepaid phones, topped up with vouchers. Most mobiles from other European countries can be used in Spain, but you may need to set this up before you leave. You may be charged international roaming rates even when making a local call, and you will be charged for incoming calls. Not all US handsets are GSM-compatible; check with your service provider before you leave.

If you're staying more than a few weeks, it may work out cheaper to buy a pay-as-you-go package when you arrive, from places such as FNAC (*see p193*), or buy a local SIMcard for your own phone. Handsets usually include a little credit, which you can then top up (from newsagents, cash machines and *estancs*). Firms include Orange (from cell phone: 1414/ from normal phone: 656 001 470, movil. orange.es), Movistar (1485, www.movistar.es) and Vodafone (607 123 000, www.vodafone.es).

Operator services & useful phone numbers

Operators normally speak Catalan and Spanish only, except for international operators, most of whom speak English.

**General information
(Barcelona)** 010 (8am-10pm
Mon-Sat). From outside
Catalonia, but within Spain,
call 807 117 700.
**International directory
enquiries** 11825.
**International operator for
reverse charge calls** Europe
1008; rest of world 1005.
National directory enquiries
11818 (Telefónica, the cheapest) or
11888 (Yellow Pages, more
expensive, or free on
www.paginasamarillas.com),
among others.
**National operator for reverse
charge calls** 1009. After the
recorded message, press the
asterisk key twice, and then 4.
**Pharmacies, postcodes,
lottery** 098.
Telephone faults service
(Telefónica) 1002.
Time 093.
Wake-up calls 096. After the
message, key in the time at which
you wish to be woken, in the 24hr
clock, in four figures: for example,
0830 for 8.30am, 2030 for 8.30pm.
Weather 807 170 365.

Phone centres

Phone centres (*locutorios*) are
full of small booths where you
can sit down and pay at the
end. They offer cheap calls
and avoid the need for change.
Concentrated particularly in
streets such as C/Sant Pau and
C/Hospital in the Raval, and
along C/Carders-C/Corders in
Sant Pere, they generally offer
other services too, including
international money transfer,
currency exchange
and internet access.
Locutorio *C/Hospital 17, Raval
(93 318 97 39). Metro Liceu.*
Open 10am-10pm daily. **No
credit cards. Map** p344 A2.
Oftelcom *C/Canuda 7, Barri
Gòtic (93 342 73 71). Metro
Catalunya.* **Open** 9am-midnight
daily. **No credit cards.**
Map p344 B2.

Public phones

The most common type of
payphone in Barcelona accepts
coins (5¢ and up), phonecards
and credit cards. There is a

multilingual digital display
(press 'L' to change language)
and written instructions in
English and other languages.
Take plenty of small coins
with you. For the first minute
of a daytime local call, you'll
be charged around 8¢; to a
mobile phone around 13¢; and
to a 902 number around 20¢.
Calls to directory enquiries on
11818 are free from payphones,
but you'll usually have to
insert a coin to make the call
(it will be returned when you
hang up). If you're still in
credit at the end of your call,
you can make further calls by
pushing the 'R' button and
dialling again. Bars and cafés
often have payphones, but
these can be more expensive
than street booths.

Telefónica phonecards
(*targetes telefònica/tarjetas
telefónica*) are sold at
newsstands and *estancs* (*see
p317*). Other cards sold at
phone centres, shops and
newsstands give cheaper
rates on all but local calls.
This latter type of card
contains a toll-free number
to call from any phone.

Time

Local time is one hour ahead
of GMT, six hours ahead of US
Eastern Standard Time and
nine ahead of Pacific Standard
Time. Daylight saving time
runs concurrently with the UK:
clocks go back in October and
forward in March.

Tipping

There are no rules for tipping
in Barcelona, but locals don't
tip much. It's fair to leave five
to ten per cent in restaurants,
but if you think the service
has been bad, don't. People
sometimes leave a little change
in bars. In taxis, tipping is not
standard, but if the fare works
out at a few cents below a euro,
many people round up. It's
usual to tip hotel porters.

Toilets

The problem of people
urinating outside in the
Old City has pressed the
Ajuntament into introducing
more public toilets. There are
24 hour public toilets in Plaça
del Teatre, just off La Rambla,
and more at the top of C/dels
Àngels, opposite the MACBA.
Most of the main railway
stations have clean toilets.
Parks such as Ciutadella and
Güell have a few dotted about,
but you need a 20¢ coin to
use them. The beach at
Barceloneta has six (heavily
in demand) Portaloos; there
are five further up at the beach
at Sant Sebastià, and in season
there are also toilets open
under the boardwalk, along
the beach towards the Port
Olímpic. Most bar and café
owners do not mind if you use
their toilets (you may have to
ask for the key), although some
in the centre and at the beach
are less amenable. Fast-food
restaurants are good standbys.

Toilets are known as *serveis*,
banys or *lavabos* (in Catalan)
or *servicios*, *aseos*, *baños* or
lavabos (in Spanish).

In bars or restaurants, the
ladies' is generally denoted
by a D (*dones/damas*), and
occasionally by an M (*mujeres*)
or S (*señoras*) on the door;
while the men's mostly say
H (*homes/hombres*) or C
(*caballeros*).

Tourist information

The city council (Ajuntament)
and Catalan government
(Generalitat) both run tourist
offices. Information about
what's on can be found in
local papers as well as
listings magazines. See
those listed under Media.

010 phoneline
Open 8am-10pm Mon-Sat.
This city-run information line is
aimed mainly at locals, but it does

an impeccable job of answering all kinds of queries. There are sometimes English-speaking operators available. Call 807 117 700 from outside Catalonia but within Spain.

Centre d'Informació de la Virreina

Palau de la Virreina, La Rambla 99, Barri Gòtic (93 316 10 00/ www.bcn.cat/cultura). Metro Liceu. **Open** 10am-8pm Mon-Sat; 11am-3pm Sun. **Ticket sales** Virreina exhibitions 11am-8pm Tue-Sat; 11am-3pm Sun; timetable varies for other events, generally 10am-7pm Tue-Sat. **Map** p344 B4.
The information office of the city's culture department has details of shows, exhibitions and special events. The bookstore specialises in Barcelona-related items.

Oficines d'Informació Turística

Plaça Catalunya, Eixample (information 807 11 72 22/from outside Spain +34 93 285 38 34/www.bcn.cat/www.barcelonaturisme.com). Metro Catalunya. **Open** *Office* 9am-9pm daily. *Call centre* 9am-9pm Mon-Fri. **Map** p344 C2.
The main office of the city tourist board is underground on the El Corte Inglés/south side of the square: look for the big red signs with 'i' superimposed in white. It has information, money exchange, a shop and a hotel booking service, and sells phonecards and tickets for shows, sights and public transport.
Other locations C/Ciutat 2 (ground floor of Ajuntament), Barri Gòtic; C/Sardenya (opposite the Sagrada Família), Eixample; Plaça Portal Pau (opposite Monument a Colom), Port Vell; Sants station; La Rambla 115, Barri Gòtic; corner of Plaça d'Espanya and Avda Maria Cristina, Eixample; airport.

Palau Robert

Passeig de Gràcia 107, Eixample (93 238 80 91/www.gencat. net/probert). Metro Diagonal. **Open** 10am-7pm Mon-Sat; 10am-2.30pm Sun. **Map** p340 G7.
The Generalitat's centre for tourists is at the junction of Passeig de Gràcia and Avda Diagonal. It has maps and other essentials for Barcelona, but its speciality is a huge range of information in different media for attractions to be found elsewhere in Catalonia. It also sometimes hosts interesting exhibitions on local art, culture, gastronomy and nature.
Other locations Airport terminals A (93 478 47 04) and B (93 478 05 65), open 9am-9pm daily.

Visas & immigration

Spain is one of the European Union countries that's covered by the Schengen Agreement, which led to common visa regulations and limited border controls among member states who were signatories in the agreement. However, neither the UK nor the Republic of Ireland are signatories in this agreement; nationals of those countries will need their passports. Most European Union citizens, as well as Norwegian and Icelandic nationals, only need a national identity card.

Visas are not required for citizens of the United States, Canada, Australia and New Zealand who are arriving for stays of up to 90 days and not for work or study. Citizens of South Africa and other countries need visas to enter Spain; approach Spanish consulates and embassies in other countries for information. Visa regulations do change, so check before leaving home.

Water

Tap water is drinkable in Barcelona, but it tastes of chlorine. Bottled water is what you will be served if you ask for *un aigua/agua* in a bar or restaurant; *fresca* is from the fridge, *natural* is at room temperature. *Agua con gas* is carbonated water.

When to go

Barcelona is usually agreeable year-round, though the humidity in summer can be debilitating, particularly when it's overcast. Many shops, bars and restaurants close (especially during August). Public transport can over compensate for the summer heat, with air-conditioning that is downright bracing.

Climate

Spring in Barcelona is unpredictable: warm, sunny days can alternate with winds and showers. Temperatures in May and June are pretty much perfect; the city is especially lively around 23 June, when locals celebrate the beginning of summer with all kinds of fireworks and fiestas. July and August can be decidedly unpleasant, as the summer heat and humidity kick in and make many locals leave town. Autumn weather is generally warm and fresh, with heavy downpours common around October. Crisp, cool sunshine is normal from December to February. Snow is very rare.

Public holidays

Almost all shops, banks and offices, and many bars and restaurants, close on public holidays (*festius/festivos*), and public transport is limited. Many take long weekends whenever a major holiday comes along. If the holiday coincides with, say, a Tuesday or a Thursday, many people will take the Monday or Friday off: this is what is known as a *pont/puente*. The city's official holidays are as follows:

New Year's Day/Any Nou 1 Jan
Three Kings/Reis Mags 6 Jan
Good Friday/Divendres Sant
Easter Monday/Dilluns de Pasqua
May (Labour) Day/Festa del Treball 1 May
Whitsun/Segona Pascua 31 May
Sant Joan 24 June
Verge de l'Assumpció 15 Aug
Diada de Catalunya 11 Sept
La Mercè 24 Sept
Dia de la Hispanitat 12 Oct
All Saints' Day/Tots Sants 1 Nov
Constitution Day/Día de la Constitución 6 Dec
La Immaculada 8 Dec
Christmas Day/Nadal 25 Dec
Boxing Day/Sant Esteve 26 Dec.

Directory

Working & living

Common recourses for English speakers in Barcelona are to find work in the tourist sector (often seasonal and outside the city), in a downtown bar or teaching English in the numerous language schools. For the latter, it helps to have the TEFL (Teaching English as a Foreign Language) qualifications; these can be gained in reputable institutions in the city as well as in your home country. Bear in mind that teaching work dries up in June until the end of summer, usually September, although it's possible to find intensive teaching courses during July. The amount of jobs in call centres for English speakers and other foreigners has also rocketed of late.

Queries regarding residency and legal requirements for foreigners who are working in Spain can be addressed to the Ministry of Interior's helpline on 900 150 000 (where there are English-speaking operators). Its website (www.mir.es/SGACAVT/extranje/) lays out the regulations in force on these residency matters, but makes for dense reading.

EU citizens

EU citizens living in Spain are exempt from the obligation to own a resident's (*tarjeta de residencia*) but need to have ID or passport from their own country. Students, contracted workers, freelancers, business owners or retired people who have made Spanish social security contributions are entitled to live here and use their own country's ID card or passport for all dealings. However, in order to get a work contract or a resident's bank account, to make tax declarations or for other official bureaucracy, you will need a *Número de Identificación del Extranjero*

(foreigner's identity number), otherwise known as NIE. To do this, head to the Oficina de Comunitarias (see below). To obtain a residency card, you may apply for one at the Delegación de Gobierno's Oficina de Extranjería (see below). First, though, you must get a NIE.

Oficina de Tarjetas Comunitarias

Passeig Joan de Borbó 32, Barceloneta (93 224 06 02/ www.mir.es). **Open** 9am-2pm Mon-Fri. **Map** p342 G13.
Arrive early and queue for your NIE application. Bring your passport along with a photocopy of its main pages and two passport photos. You can download the form at www.mir.es/SGACAVT/modelos/extranjeria/. Then select '*modelos de solicitud*' and then 'EX-14' for the form but you will still have to bring it with you in person. Once you've submitted the paperwork, staff will send your NIE by post within 30-40 days. This is the legal document that backs up your identification number, so keep it safe.

Non-EU citizens

While in Spain on a tourist visa, you are not legally allowed to work. First-time applicants officially need a special visa, obtained from a Spanish consulate in their home country. Even if you are made a job offer while in Spain, you must still make the trip home to apply for this visa. The

process can be lengthy, and not all applications are successful. Armed with this, you can begin the protracted application process for a resident's card and work permit (*permís de treball/permiso de trabajo*) at the Oficina de Extranjería (*see below*). Getting good legal advice is important, given the length of the process and possible rule changes. Note that if you wish to renew or modify your work or residency permit, you can present your documentation at any city post office, rather than queue again.

Oficina de Extranjería

Avda Marquès de l'Argentera 4, sala A, Born (93 482 05 44/information and appointments 93 520 14 10). Metro Barceloneta. **Open** *June-mid Sept* 8am-3pm Mon-Fri. *Mid Sept-May* Phone lines 9am-2pm Mon-Fri. Office 9.30am-5.30pm Mon-Thur; 9am-2pm Fri. **Map** p345 E7.
You will need to submit an application form. Download the form at www.mir.es/SGACAVT/modelos/extranjeria/, selecting '*modelos de solicitud*' and then 'EX-1' for the form. You will also need: a photocopy of your passport; a police certificate from your home country stating you don't have a criminal record (translated into Spanish by a sworn translator; *see p308*); an official medical certificate (obtained on arrival in Spain); three identical passport photographs; documents proving why you are more capable of performing the job than an EU citizen; and proof that you have the qualifications or training required.

Average climate

	Max temp (C°/F°)	Min temp (C°/F°)	Rainfall (mm/in)
Jan	13/56	6/43	44/1.7
Feb	15/59	7/45	36/1.4
Mar	16/61	8/47	48/1.9
Apr	18/64	10/50	51/2
May	21/70	14/57	57/2.2
June	24/76	17/63	38/1.5
July	27/81	20/67	22/0.9
Aug	29/84	20/67	66/2.6
Sept	25/78	18/64	79/3.1
Oct	22/71	14/57	94/3.7
Nov	17/63	9/49	74/2.9
Dec	15/59	7/45	50/2.5

Directory

Spanish Vocabulary

Spanish is generally referred to as *castellano* (Castilian) rather than *español*. Many locals prefer to speak Catalan, but everyone can also speak Spanish. The Spanish familiar form for 'you' – *tú* – is used very freely, but it's safer to use the more formal *usted* with older people and strangers (verbs below are given in the *usted* form). For menu terms, *see p154-55.*

Spanish pronunciation

c before an **i** or an **e** and **z** are like **th** in **thin**
c in all other cases is as in **cat**
g before an **i** or an **e** and **j** are pronounced with a guttural **h**-sound that doesn't exist in English – like **ch** in Scottish 'loch', but much harder;
g in all other cases is as in **get**
h at the beginning of a word is normally silent
ll is pronounced almost like a **y**
ñ is like **ny** in ca**ny**on
a single **r** at the beginning of a word and **rr** elsewhere are heavily rolled

Stress rules

In words ending with a vowel, **n** or **s**, the penultimate syllable is stressed: eg *barato, viven, habitaciones*. In words ending with any other consonant, the last syllable is stressed: eg *exterior, universidad*. An accent marks the stressed syllable in words that depart from these rules: eg *estación, tónica*.

Useful expressions

hello *hola*; **hello** (when answering the phone) *hola, diga*
goodbye/see you later *adiós/hasta luego*

good morning, good day *buenos días*; **good afternoon, good evening** *buenas tardes*; **good evening** (after dark), **good night** *buenas noches*
please *por favor*; **thank you** (very much) *(muchas) gracias*; **you're welcome** *de nada* **do you speak English?** *¿habla inglés?*, **I don't speak Spanish** *no hablo castellano* **I don't understand** *no entiendo* **can you say that to me in Catalan, please?** *¿me lo puede decir en catalán, por favor?*
what's your name? *¿cómo se llama?*
speak more slowly, please *hable más despacio, por favor*; **wait a moment** *espere un momento*
Sir/Mr *señor (sr)*; **Madam/Mrs** *señora (sra)*; **Miss** *señorita (srta)*
excuse me/sorry *perdón*; **excuse me, please** *oiga* (the standard way to attract someone's attention, politely; literally, 'hear me')
OK/fine/(to a waiter) **that's enough** *vale*
where is...? *¿dónde está...?*
why? *¿porqué?*, **when?** *¿cuándo?*, **who?** *¿quién?*, **what?** *¿qué?*, **where?** *¿dónde?*, **how?** *¿cómo?*
who is it? *¿quién es?*, **is/are there any...?** *¿hay...?*
open *abierto*; **closed** *cerrado*; **what time does it open/close?** *¿a qué hora abre/cierra?*
pull (on signs) *tirar*; **push** *empujar*
I would like *quiero*; **how many would you like?** *¿cuántos quiere?*, **how much is it** *¿cuánto es?*
I like *me gusta*; **I don't like** *no me gusta*
good *bueno/a*; **bad** *malo/a*; **well/badly** *bien/mal*; **small** *pequeño/a*; **big** *gran, grande*; **expensive** *caro/a*; **cheap** *barato/a*; **hot** (food, drink) *caliente*; **cold** *frío/a*;
do you have any change? *¿tiene cambio?*
price *precio*; **free** *gratis*; **discount** *descuento*; **bank** *banco*; **to rent** *alquilar*, **(for) rent, rental** *(en) alquiler*; **post office** *correos*; **stamp** *sello*; **postcard** *postal*; **toilet** *los servicios*

Getting around

airport *aeropuerto*; **railway station** *estación de ferrocarril/estación de RENFE* (Spanish railways); **metro station** *estación de metro*
entrance *entrada*; **exit** *salida* **car** *coche*; **bus** *autobús*; **train** *tren* **a ticket** *un billete*; **return** *de ida y vuelta*; **bus stop** *parada de autobus*; **the next stop** *la próxima parada*

excuse me, do you know the way to...? *¿oiga, señor/señora/etc, sabe cómo llegar a...?*
left *izquierda*; **right** *derecha* **here** *aquí*; **there** *allí*; **straight on** *recto*; **to the end of the street** *al final de la calle*; **as far as** *hasta*; **towards** *hacia*; **near** *cerca*; **far** *lejos*

Accommodation

do you have a double/single room for tonight/one week? *¿tiene una habitación doble/para una persona/para esta noche/una semana?* **we have a reservation** *tenemos reserva*; **an inside/outside room** *una habitación interior/exterior* **with/without bathroom** *con/sin baño*; **shower** *ducha*; **double bed** *cama de matrimonio*; **with twin beds** *con dos camas*; **breakfast included** *desayuno incluido*; **air-conditioning** *aire acondicionado*

Time

now *ahora*; **later** *más tarde*; **yesterday** *ayer*, **today** *hoy*; **tomorrow** *mañana*; **tomorrow morning** *mañana por la mañana* **morning** *la mañana*; **midday** *mediodía*; **afternoon/evening** *la tarde*; **night** *la noche*; **late night** (roughly 1-6am) *la madrugada* **at what time...?** *¿a qué hora...?*

Numbers

0 *cero*; **1** *un, uno, una*; **2** *dos*; **3** *tres*; **4** *cuatro*; **5** *cinco*; **6** *seis*; **7** *siete*; **8** *ocho*; **9** *nueve*; **10** *diez*; **11** *once*; **12** *doce*; **13** *trece*; **14** *catorce*; **15** *quince*; **16** *dieciséis*; **17** *diecisiete*; **18** *dieciocho*; **19** *diecinueve*; **20** *veinte*; **21** *veintiuno*; **22** *veintidós*; **30** *treinta*; **40** *cuarenta*; **50** *cincuenta*; **60** *sesenta*; **70** *setenta*; **80** *ochenta*; **90** *noventa*; **100** *cien*; **200** *doscientos*; **1,000** *mil*; **1,000,000** *un millón*

Dates & seasons

Monday *lunes*; **Tuesday** *martes*; **Wednesday** *miércoles*; **Thursday** *jueves*; **Friday** *viernes*; **Saturday** *sábado*; **Sunday** *domingo* **January** *enero*; **February** *febrero*; **March** *marzo*; **April** *abril*; **May** *mayo*; **June** *junio*; **July** *julio*; **August** *agosto*; **September** *septiembre*; **October** *octubre*; **November** *noviembre*; **December** *diciembre* **spring** *primavera*; **summer** *verano*; **autumn/fall** *otoño*; **winter** *invierno*

Directory

Catalan Vocabulary

Over a third of Barcelona residents use Catalan as their predominant everyday language, around 70 per cent speak it fluently, and more than 90 per cent understand it. If you take an interest and learn a few phrases, it is likely to be appreciated.

Catalan phonetics are significantly different from those of Spanish, with a wider range of vowel sounds and soft consonants. Catalans use the familiar (*tu*) rather than the polite (*vostè*) forms of the second person very freely, but for convenience, verbs are given here in the polite form. For menu terms, *see pp154-55*.

Pronunciation

In Catalan, as in French but unlike in Spanish, words are run together, so *si us plau* (please) is more like *sees-plow*.

à at the end of a word (as in Francesc Macià) is an open **a** rather like **ah**, but very clipped
ç, and **c** before an **i** or an **e**, are like a soft **s**, as in **s**it; **c** in all other cases is as in **c**at
e, when unstressed as in *cerveses* (beers), or Jaume I, is a weak sound like cent**re** or comfortable
g before **i** or **e** and **j** are pronounced like the **s** in plea**s**ure; **tg** and **tj** are similar to the **dg** in ba**dg**e
g after an **i** at the end of a word (Pui**g**) is a hard **ch** sound, as in wat**ch**; **g** in all other cases is as in **g**et
h is silent
ll is somewhere between the **y** in **y**es and the **lli** in mi**lli**on
l·l, the most unusual feature of Catalan spelling, has a slightly stronger stress on a single **l** sound, so paral·lel sounds similar to the English parallel
o at the end of a word is like the **u** sound in fl**u**; **ó** at the end of a word is similar to the **o** in tomat**o**; **ò** is like the **o** in h**o**t
r beginning a word and **rr** are heavily rolled; but at the end of many words is almost silent, so ca**rr**er (street) sounds like carr-ay
s at the beginning and end of words and **ss** between vowels are soft, as in **s**it; a single **s** between two vowels is a **z** sound, as in la**z**y

t after **l** or **n** at the end of a word is almost silent
x at the beginning of a word, or after a consonant or the letter **i**, is like the **sh** in **sh**oe, at other times like the English e**x**pert
y after an **n** at the end of a word or in **nys** is not a vowel but adds a nasal stress and a y-sound to the n

Basics

please *si us plau*; **very good/great/OK** *molt bé*
hello *hola*; **goodbye** *adéu*
open *obert*; **closed** *tancat*
entrance *entrada*; **exit** *sortida*
nothing at all *zilch res de res* (said with both s silent)
price *preu*; **free** *gratuit/de franc*; **change, exchange** *canvi*
to rent *llogar*; **(for) rent, rental** *(de) lloguer*

More expressions

hello (when answering the phone) *hola, digui'm*
good morning, good day *bon dia*; **good afternoon, good evening** *bona tarda*; **good night** *bona nit*
thank you (very much) *(moltes) gràcies*; **you're welcome** *de res*
do you speak English? *parla anglés?*; **I'm sorry, I don't speak Catalan** *ho sento, no parlo català*
I don't understand *no entenc*
can you say it to me in Spanish, please? *m'ho pot dir en castellà, si us plau?*
how do you say that in Catalan? *com se diu això en català?*
what's your name? *com se diu?*
Sir/Mr *senyor (sr)*; **Madam/Mrs** *senyora (sra)*; **Miss** *senyoreta (srta)*
excuse me/sorry *perdoni/disculpi*; **excuse me, please** *escolti* (literally, 'listen to me'); **OK/fine** *val/d'acord*
how much is it? *quant és?*
why? *perqué?*; **when?** *quan?*; **who?** *qui?*; **what?** *qué?*; **where?** *on?*; **how?** *com?*; **where is...?** *on és...?*; **who is it?** *qui és?*; **is/are there any...?** *hi ha...?/n'hi ha de...?*
very *molt*; **and** *i* or *o*; **with** *amb*; **without** *sense*; **enough** *prou*
I would like... *vull...* (literally, 'I want'); **how many would you like?** *quants en vol?*; **I don't want** *no vull*; **I like** *m'agrada*; **I don't like** *no m'agrada*
good *bo/bona*; **bad** *dolent/a*; **well/badly** *bé/malament*; **small** *petit/a*; **big** *gran*; **expensive** *car/a*; **cheap** *barat/a*; **hot** (food, drink) *calent/a*; **cold** *fred/a*
something *alguna cosa*; **nothing**

res; **more** *més*; **less** *menys*; **more or less** *més o menys*
toilet *el bany/els serveis/el lavabo*

Getting around

a ticket *un bitllet*; **return** *d'anada i tornada*; **card expired** (on metro) *títol esgotat*
left *esquerra*; **right** *dreta*; **here** *aquí*; **there** *allí*; **straight on** *recte*; **at the corner** *a la cantonada*; **as far as** *fins a*; **towards** *cap a*; **near** *a prop*; **far** *lluny*; **is it far?** *és lluny?*

Time

In Catalan, quarter- and half-hours can be referred to as quarters of the next hour (so, 1.30 is two quarters of 2).

now *ara*; **later** *més tard*; **yesterday** *ahir*; **today** *avui*; **tomorrow** *demà*; **tomorrow morning** *demà pel matí*; **morning** *el matí*; **midday** *migdia*; **afternoon** *la tarda*; **evening** *el vespre*; **night** *la nit*; **late night** (roughly, 1-6am) *la matinada*
at what time...? *a quina hora...?*; **in an hour** *en una hora*; **at 2** *a les dues*; **at 8pm** *a les vuit del vespre*; **at 1.30** *a dos quarts de dues/a la una i mitja*; **at 5.15** *a un quart de sis/a las cinc i quart*; **at 22.30** *a vint-i-dos-trenta*

Numbers

0 *zero*; **1** *u, un, una*; **2** *dos, dues*; **3** *tres*; **4** *quatre*; **5** *cinc*; **6** *sis*; **7** *set*; **8** *vuit*; **9** *nou*; **10** *deu*; **11** *onze*; **12** *dotze*; **13** *tretze*; **14** *catorze*; **15** *quinze*; **16** *setze*; **17** *disset*; **18** *divuit*; **19** *dinou*; **20** *vint*; **21** *vint-i-u*; **22** *vint-i-dos, vint-i-dues*; **30** *trenta*; **40** *quaranta*; **50** *cinquanta*; **60** *seixanta*; **70** *setanta*; **80** *vuitanta*; **90** *noranta*; **100** *cent*; **200** *dos-cents, dues-centes*; **1,000** *mil*; **1,000,000** *un milló*

Dates & seasons

Monday *dilluns*; **Tuesday** *dimarts*; **Wednesday** *dimecres*; **Thursday** *dijous*; **Friday** *divendres*; **Saturday** *dissabte*; **Sunday** *diumenge*
January *gener*; **February** *febrer*; **March** *març*; **April** *abril*; **May** *maig*; **June** *juny*; **July** *juliol*; **August** *agost*; **September** *setembre*; **October** *octobre*; **November** *novembre*; **December** *desembre*
spring *primavera*; **summer** *estiu*; **autumn/fall** *tardor*; **winter** *hivern*

Further Reference

Books

Food & drink

Colman Andrews *Catalan Cuisine* A mine of information on food and much else (also with usable recipes).
Alan Davidson *Tio Pepe Guide to the Seafood of Spain and Portugal* An excellent pocket-sized guide with illustrations of Spain's fishy delights.
Anya von Bremzen *New Spanish Table* A guide to Spanish staples and some entertaining anecdotes.

Guides & walks

J Amelang, X Gil & GW McDonogh *Twelve Walks through Barcelona's Past* Well-thought-out walks by historical theme. Original and better informed than many walking guides.
Xavier Güell *Gaudí Guide* A handy guide, with good background on all the architect's work.
Juliet Pomés Leiz & Ricardo Feriche *Barcelona Design Guide* An eccentrically wide-ranging but engaging listing of everything ever considered 'designer' in BCN.

History, architecture, art & culture

Jimmy Burns *Barça: A People's Passion* The first full-scale history in English of one of the world's most overblown football clubs.
JH Elliott *The Revolt of the Catalans* Fascinating, detailed account of the Guerra dels Segadors and the Catalan revolt of the 1640s.
Felipe Fernández Armesto *Barcelona: A Thousand Years of the City's Past* A solid history.
Ronald Fraser *Blood of Spain* A vivid oral history of the Spanish Civil War and the tensions that preceded it. It is especially good on the events of July 1936 in Barcelona.
John Hooper *The New Spaniards* An incisive and very readable survey of the changes in Spanish society since the death of Franco.
Robert Hughes *Barcelona* The most comprehensive single book about Barcelona: tendentious at times, erratic, but beautifully written, and covering every aspect of the city up to the 1992 Olympics.
Temma Kaplan *Red City, Blue Period: Social Movements in Picasso's Barcelona* An interesting book, tracing the interplay of avant-garde art and avant-garde politics in the 1900s.

George Orwell *Homage to Catalonia* The classic account of Barcelona in revolution, as written by an often bewildered, but always perceptive observer.
Abel Paz *Durruti, The People Armed* A biography of the most legendary of Barcelona's anarchists.
Ignasi Solà-Morales *Fin de Siècle Architecture in Barcelona* Large-scale and wide-ranging description of the city's Modernista heritage.
Colm Tóibín *Homage to Barcelona* Evocative and perceptive journey around the city: good on the booming Barcelona of the 1980s.
Gijs van Hensbergen *Gaudí* A thorough account of the life of the Modernista architect.
Manuel Vázquez Montalbán *Barcelonas* Idiosyncratic but insightful reflections on the city by one of its most prominent modern writers.
Rainer Zerbst *Antoni Gaudí* Lavishly illustrated and comprehensive survey.

Literature

Pere Calders *The Virgin of the Railway and Other Stories* Ironic, engaging, quirky stories by a Catalan writer who spent many years in exile in Mexico.
Victor Català *Solitude* This masterpiece by female novelist Caterina Albert shocked readers in 1905 with its open, modern treatment of female sexuality.
Ildefonso Falcones *Cathedral of the Sea* Hugely popular historical novel, centred on the basilica of Santa Maria del Mar in the Born.
Juan Marsé *The Fallen* Classic novel of survival in Barcelona during the long *posguerra* after the Civil War.
Joanot Martorell & Joan Martí de Gualba *Tirant lo Blanc* The first European prose novel, from 1490: a rambling, bawdy, shaggy-dog story of travels, romances and chivalric adventures.
Eduardo Mendoza *City of Marvels; Year of the Flood* A sweeping saga of the city between its great Exhibitions in 1888 and 1929; and a more recent novel of passions in the city of the 1950s.
Maria-Antònia Oliver *Antipodes; Study in Lilac* Two adventures of Barcelona's first feminist detective.
Mercè Rodoreda *The Time of the Doves; My Cristina and Other Stories* A translation of *Plaça del Diamant*, the most widely read of all Catalan novels; plus a collection of similarly bittersweet short tales.

Carlos Ruiz Zafón *Shadow of the Wind* Required beach reading of recent years; enjoyable neo-Gothic melodrama set in post-war Barcelona.
Manuel Vázquez Montalbán *The Angst-Ridden Executive; An Olympic Death; Southern Seas* Three thrillers starring detective and gourmet Pepe Carvalho.

Music

Angel Molina Leading Barcelona DJ with an international reputation and various remix albums released.
Barcelona Raval Sessions Dance/funk compilation of local artists, famous and unknown, conceived as a soundtrack to the city's most dynamic *barri*.
Lluís Llach An icon of the 1960s and early '70s protest against the Fascist regime combines a melancholic tone with brilliant musicianship. One of the first to experiment with electronic music.
Maria del Mar Bonet Though from Mallorca, del Mar Bonet always sings in Catalan and specialises in her own compositions, North African music and Mallorcan music.
Ojos de Brujo Current darlings of world-music awards everywhere and leading proponents of *rumba catalana* fused with flamenco.
Pep Sala Excellent musician and survivor of the extremely successful Catalan group Sau.

Websites

www.barcelonareporter.com Local news items in English.
www.barcelonarocks.com Music listings and news.
www.barcelonaturisme.com Official tourist authority information.
www.bcn.cat The city council's information-packed website.
www.catalanencyclopaedia.com Comprehensive English-language reference work covering Catalan history, geography and 'who's who'.
www.diaridebarcelona.com Local online newspaper with good English content.
www.lecool.com Excellent weekly round-up of offbeat and interesting cultural events in the city.
www.mobilitat.net Generalitat's website about getting from A to B in Catalonia, by bus, car or train.
www.renfe.es Spanish railways.
www.timeout.com/barcelona The online city guide, with a select monthly agenda.
www.vilaweb.com Catalan web portal and links page; in Catalan.

Index

Advertisers' Index

Please refer to the relevant pages for contact details

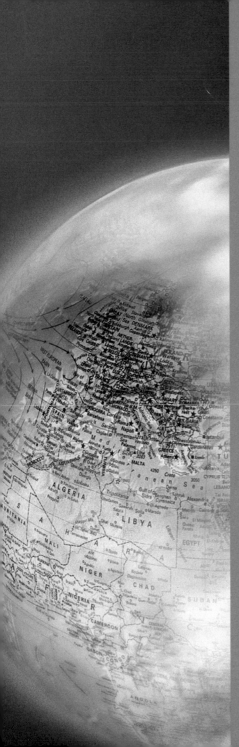

Major sight or landmark	
Hospital or college	
Railway station	
Parks	
River	
Carretera	═══
Main road	
Main road tunnel	- -
Pedestrian road	
Airport	✈
Church	✚
Metro station, FGC station	Ⓜ ⓖ
Area name . . . . EIXAMPLE	

Maps

Barcelona Areas

© Copyright Time Out Group 2008

2 km
1 mile

Parc del Guinardó

HORTA

SANT ANDREU

GUINARDÓ

AVDA DE LA MERIDIANA

Park Güell

LA SAGRERA

C/GUIPÚSCOA

CLOT

GRACIA

Hospital de Sant Pau

POBLENOU

Plaça de les Glòries

GRAN VIA DE LES CORTS CATALANES

RONDA LITORAL

EIXAMPLE (DRETA)

Sagrada Família

VILA OLÍMPICA

RONDA GENERAL MITRE

AVDA DIAGONAL

Parc de la Ciutadella

PORT OLÍMPIC

SANT GERVASI

GRACIA

SANT PERE

BORN

Estació de França

BARCELONETA

PASSEIG DE GRACIA

PASSEIG DE GRACIA

Plaça Catalunya

RAVAL

BARRI GOTIC

PEDRALBES

LES CORTS

C/ARAGÓ

Catedral

LA RAMBLA

PORT VELL

EIXAMPLE (ESQUERRA)

GRAN VIA DE LES CORTS CATALANES

RAVAL

RONDA LITORAL

AVDA JOSEP TARRADELLAS

AVDA PARAL·LEL

POBLE SEC

C/TARRAGONA

Plaça d'Espanya

AVDA DIAGONAL

Estació Barcelona Sants

Estadi Olímpic

MONTJUÏC

SANTS

GRAN VIA DE LES CORTS CATALANES

GRAN VIA CARLES III

Barri Gòtic (pp85-96)
Born & Sant Pere (pp97-103)
Raval (pp104-109)
Barceloneta & Ports (pp110-115)
Montjuïc (pp117-124)
The Eixample (pp125-132)
Gràcia & Other Districts (pp133-143)

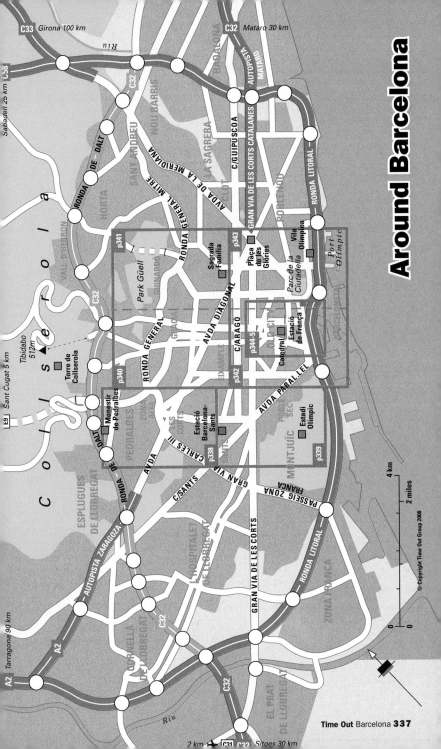

Around Barcelona

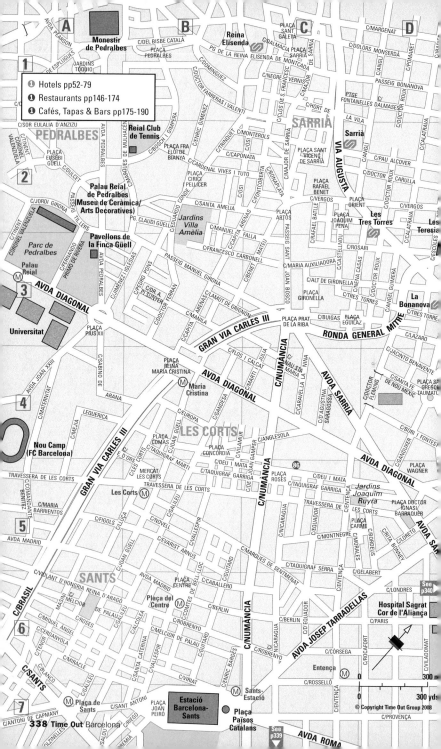

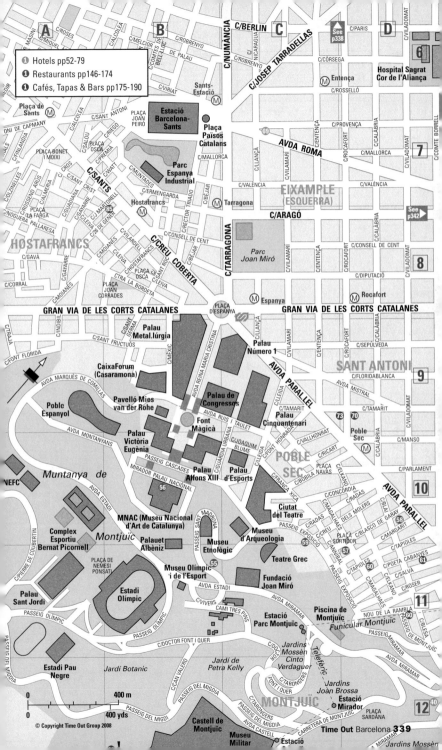

A B C D

1 Hotels pp52-79
1 Restaurants pp146-174
1 Cafés, Tapas & Bars pp175-190

C/ROSES
C/MIQUEL
C/MASSIP
C/MELCIOR
CALOLLEA
C/COMTES DE BELL-LLOC
DE PALAU
C/ROBRENYO
C/BERLIN
C/NUMANCIA
C/NICARAGUA
C/PARIS
C/VILADOMAT
C/JOSEP TARRADELLAS
C/ROBRENYO
C/CÓRSEGA
C/FINLANDIA
C/SANT ANTONI
PLAÇA JOAN PEIRÓ
Estació Barcelona-Sants
Sants-Estació
C/VIRIAT
Plaça Països Catalans
Hospital Sagrat Cor de l'Aliança
6

Plaça de Sants
PLAÇA BONET I MOIXI
Parc Espanya Industrial
C/SANT CRIST
C/CROS
C/GALDU
C/SALOU
PLAÇA OSCA
C/OPRÈMIA
C/MUNTADES
C/SANT ANTONI
Entença
C/PROVENÇA
C/ENTENÇA
C/ROCAFORT
C/CALÀBRIA
C/COMTE BORRELL
C/VILADOMAT
7
AVDA ROMA
C/MALLORCA

C/LLANÇA
C/SANTS
C/VALLESPIR
C/GUADIANA
C/GAYARRE
C/J MARTORELL
C/CALLA DE GENER
C/VILARDELL
C/CANDIANES
Hostafrancs
C/ERMENGARDA
C/REINA MARIA CRISTINA
C/BEJAR
Tarragona
C/VALÈNCIA
C/VILAMARI
C/ENTENÇA
C/ROCAFORT
C/CALÀBRIA
C/VILADOMAT
EIXAMPLE (ESQUERRA)
C/VALÈNCIA

HOSTAFRANCS
C/GÀVA
C/COLZINELLES
C/ROSSEND ARÚS
C/VALLESPIR
C/CALAMERIA
PLAÇA LA FARGA
C/NOGUERA PALLARESA
C/CONSELL DE CENT
C/CREU COBERTA
C/DIRECTOR TRIADÓ
C/ARAGÓ
C/TARRAGONA
Parc Joan Miró
C/CONSELL DE CENT
See p342
8

C/CORRAL
C/CANDIANES
C/CIGARRERS
C/VILADELL
C/HOSTAFRANCS
PLAÇA OSCA
C/SANT ROC
C/LLEIDA
PLAÇA JOAN CORRADES
CTRA LA BORDETA
C/DIPUTACIÓ
C/VILAMARI
Espanya
Rocafort
C/VILADOMAT

GRAN VIA DE LES CORTS CATALANES
PLAÇA D'ESPANYA
GRAN VIA DE LES CORTS CATALANES
9

C/TRAJÀ
C/CINDIOL
Palau Metal.lúrgia
C/SANT GERMÀ
C/SANT FRUCTUÓS
C/MÈXIC
C/LLANÇA
Palau Número 1
C/VILAMARI
C/ENTENÇA
C/ROCAFORT
C/CALÀBRIA
C/SEPÚLVEDA
SANT ANTONI
C/FLORIDABLANCA

C/FONT FLORIDA
AVDA MARQUÈS DE COMILLAS
CaixaForum (Casaramona)
AVDA REINA MARIA CRISTINA
Palau de Congressos
AVDA PARAL·LEL
C/MISTRAL
C/TAMARIT
C/VILADOMAT

Poble Espanyol
Pavelló Mies van der Rohe
AVDA RIUS I TAULET
Font Màgica
Palau Cinquantenari
C/TAMARIT
C/VALLHONRAT
Palau Sec
C/MANSO
C/CALÀBRIA

AVDA MONTANYANS
Palau Victòria Eugènia
AVDA GUÀRDIA URBANA
C/JOAQUIM BLUME
C/FONT HONRADA
C/RICART
POBLE SEC
C/PARLAMENT

Muntanya de
MIRADOR PALAU NACIONAL
PASSEIG CASCADES
Palau Alfons XIII
Palau d'Esports
C/GUÀRDIA URBANA
C/BÒBILA
PLAÇA NAVÀS
C/ELKANO
AVDA PARAL·LEL
10

INEFC
AVDA ESTADI
MNAC (Museu Nacional d'Art de Catalunya)
Montjuïc
Palauet Albéniz
Museu Etnològic
Ciutat del Teatre
Museu d'Arqueologia
Teatre Grec
C/CONCORDIA
C/RADAS
PASSEIG EXPOSICIÓ
C/CREU
PLAÇA SORTIDOR
C/BLASCO DE GARAY
C/MARGARIT
C/TAPIOLES

Complex Esportiu Bernat Picornell
C/PIERRE DE COUBERTIN
PLAÇA DE NEMESI PONSATI
Palau Sant Jordi
Estadi Olímpic
Museu Olímpic i de l'Esport
Fundació Joan Miró
C/VIVERS
AVDA ESTADI
C/TAPIOLES
C/POETA CABANYES
C/SALVA
C/ROSER
11

PASSEIG OLÍMPIC
Estadi Pau Negre
Jardí Botànic
CAMI TRES PINS
C/DOCTOR FONT I QUER
Estació Parc Montjuïc
Jardí de Petra Kelly
Jardins Mossèn Cinto Verdaguer
AVDA MIRAMAR
Piscina de Montjuïc
Funicular Montjuïc
telefèric
NOU DE LA RAMBLA
PASSEIG DE MONTJUÏC
PASSEIG MIRAMAR

PASSEIG DEL MIGDIA
C/CAN VALERO
PASSEIG DEL MIGDIA
C/TARONGERS
MONTJUÏC
Jardins Joan Brossa
Estació Mirador
PLAÇA SARDANA
AVDA MIRAMAR
12

0 ___ 400 m
0 ___ 400 yds
© Copyright Time Out Group 2008
Castell de Montjuïc
Museu Militar
Estació
AVDA CASTELL
CARRETERA DE MONTJUÏC
Jardins Mossèn

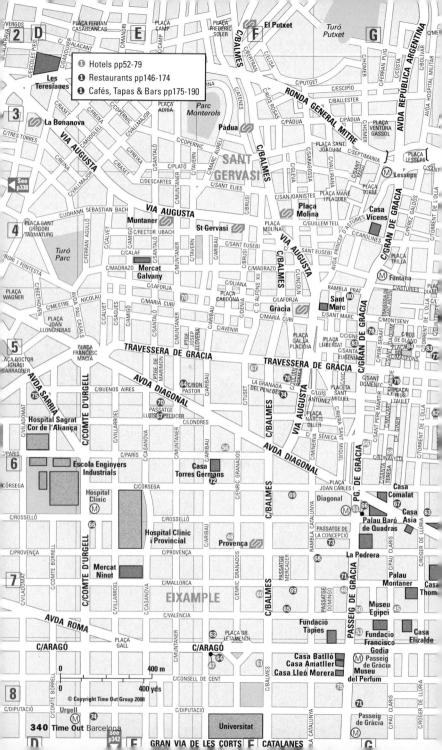

1 Hotels pp52-79
1 Restaurants pp146-174
1 Cafés, Tapas & Bars pp175-190

PLAÇA FERRAN
CASABLANCAS

PLAÇA
CAMP

PLAÇA
FREDERIC
SOLER

El Putxet

Turó
Putxet

G

Les
Teresianes

Parc
Monterols

RONDA GENERAL MITRE

La Bonanova

Pàdua

PLAÇA
ADRIÀ

AVDA REPÚBLICA ARGENTINA

VIA AUGUSTA

PLAÇA VENTURA
GASSOL

PLAÇA SANT
JOAQUIM

VIA AUGUSTA

SANT
GERVASI

C/BALMES

Lesseps

Muntaner

St Gervasi

PLAÇA
MOLINA

Plaça
Molina

Casa
Vicens

GRAN DE GRACIA

PLAÇA SANT
GREGORI
TAUMATURG

Turó
Parc

PLAÇA
WAGNER

PLAÇA
JOAN
LLONGUERAS

Mercat
Galvany

PLAÇA
CARDONA

Gràcia

Sant
Marc

70

Fontana

AVDA SARRIÀ

PLAÇA
FRANCESC
MACIÀ

TRAVESSERA DE GRÀCIA

PLAÇA
GALLA
PLACÍDIA

PLAÇA
LLIBERTAT

83

67

TRAVESSERA DE GRÀCIA

LA GRANADA
DEL PENEDÈS

74

79

77

75

Hospital Sagrat
Cor de l'Aliança

AVDA DIAGONAL

64 C/BON
PASTOR

70

67

56

AVDA DIAGONAL

66

COMTE D'URGELL

Escola Enginyers
Industrials

Casa
Torres Germans

72

PLAÇA
JOAN CARLES I

Diagonal

51

69

Casa
Comalat

67

Casa
Asia

63

Hospital
Clínic

69

Palau Baró
de Quadras

73

66

Hospital Clínic
i Provincial

Provença

48

La Pedrera

Palau
Montaner

Casa
Thom

Mercat
Ninot

EIXAMPLE

80

69

65

71

46

50

45

Museu
Egipci

AVDA ROMA

PLAÇA
GALL

63

PLAÇA DR.
LETAMENDI

Fundació
Tàpies

53

Fundació
Francisco
Godia

Casa
Elizalde

C/ARAGÓ

64

47

61

Casa Batlló
Casa Amatller
Casa Lleó Morera

Passeig
de Gràcia

Museu
del Perfum

75

Urgell

74

© Copyright Time Out Group 2008

Universitat

0 ____ 400 m
0 ____ 400 yds

71

Passeig
de Gràcia

See
p338

See
p342

GRAN VIA DE LES CORTS CATALANES

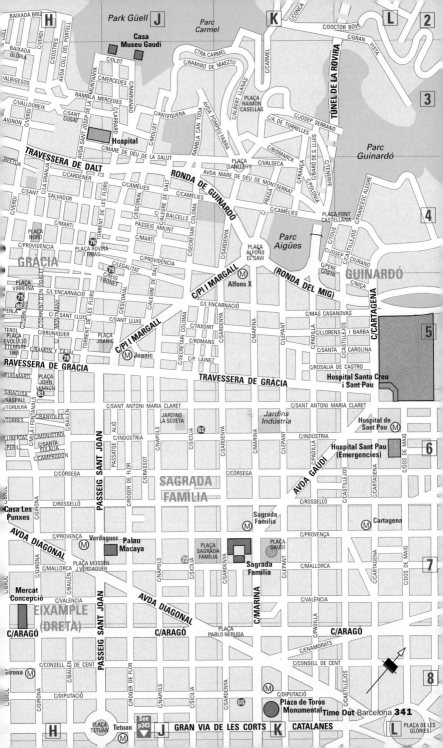

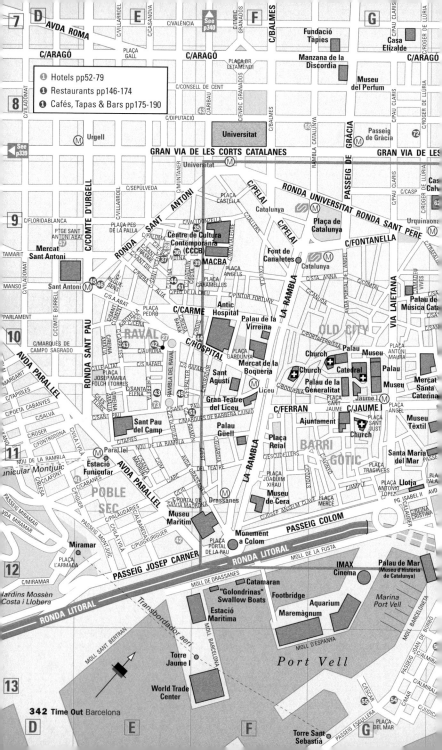

© Copyright Time Out Group 2008

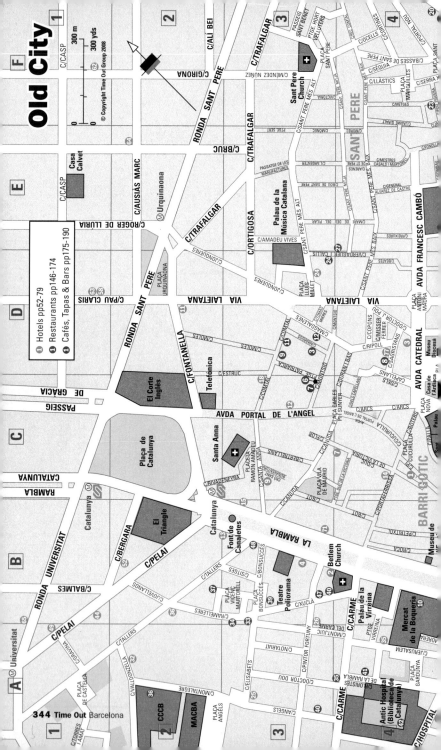

Old City

F E D C B A

1 2 3 4

- 1 Hotels pp52-79
- 1 Restaurants pp146-174
- 1 Cafés, Tapas & Bars pp175-190

300 m
300 yds

© Copyright Time Out Group 2008

C/CASP
C/CASP

Casa Calvet

C/AUSIAS MARC

M Urquinaona

RONDA SANT PERE

C/GIRONA

C/ALI BEI

C/BRUC

C/TRAFALGAR

PASSEIG SANT BENET
PTGE. HORT VELLUTERS
C/OCELLS
C/CORTINES
C/PORTAL NOU

PLAÇA HORT SANT PERE
C/SÈQUIA
C/BASSES DE SANT PERE
PLAÇA SANT PERE

Sant Pere Church

C/MÉNDEZ NÚÑEZ

SANT PERE

C/LLÀSTICS
C/METGES
PLAÇA MARQUILLES
C/SERRA
C/JAUME GIRALT
C/MESTRES CASALS I MARTORELL
C/GENERAL ALVAREZ DE CASTRO
C/FONOLLAR

C/ROGER DE LLÚRIA

C/TRAFALGAR

C/ORTIGOSA

Palau de la Música Catalana

C/AMADEU VIVES

AVDA FRANCESC CAMBÓ

PLAÇA ANTONI MAURA

C/PAU CLARÍS

PLAÇA URQUINAONA

RONDA SANT PERE

VIA LAIETANA

PLAÇA LLUÍS MILLET

AVDA CATEDRAL

PASSEIG DE GRÀCIA

M Catalunya
RAMBLA CATALUNYA

C/FONTANELLA

El Corte Inglés

Telefònica

Plaça de Catalunya

C/BERGARA

El Triangle

C/PELAI

AVDA PORTAL DE L'ANGEL

Santa Anna

PLAÇA RAMON AMADEU

PLAÇA VILA DE MADRID

BARRI GÒTIC

Museu de

RONDA UNIVERSITAT

M Universitat

C/BALMES

C/PELAI

C/TALLERS

Font de Canaletes

LA RAMBLA

Betlem Church

Palau de la Virreina

Mercat de la Boqueria

CCCB

MACBA

Antic Hospital (Biblioteca de Catalunya)

C/CARME

C/HOSPITAL

PLAÇA ANGELS

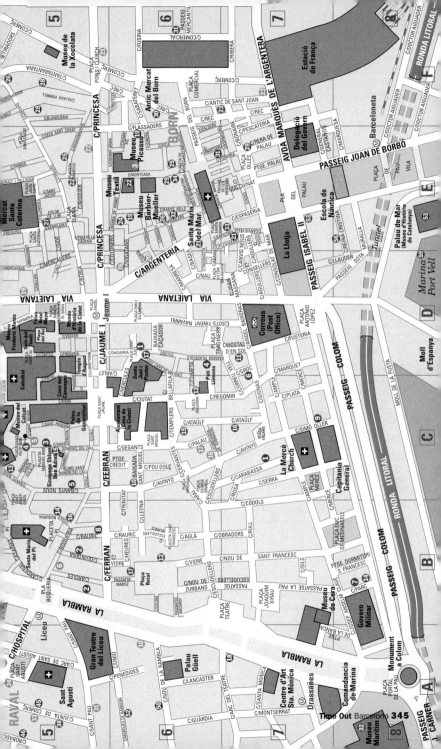

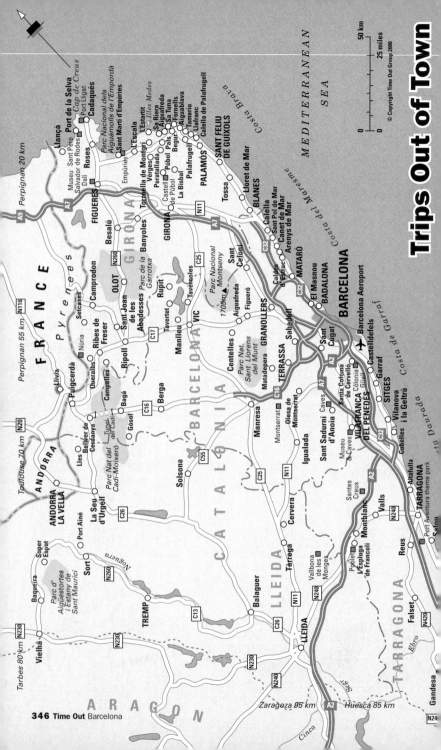

Trips Out of Town

Street Index

Street Index

Pau, Passatge la - p345 B7
Pearson, Avda - p338 A1
Pedralbes, Avda - p338 A1/2/3
Pedralbes, Plaça - p338 B1
Pedro Pons, C. - p338 B3
Pedró, Plaça - p342 E10
Pelai, C. - p342 F9, p344 A1/B1/2
Penedides, C. - p345 A5/6
Pere Costa, C. - p341 K4
Pere IV, C. - p343 K10/L10
Pere Serafí, C. - p340 G5
Pérez Galdós, C. - p340 G4
Perill, C. - p341 H6
Perla, C. - p341 H5
Pes de la Palla, Plaça - p342 E9
Pescateria, C. - p345 E7/F7
Petritxol, C. - p344 B4
Petxina, C. - p345 B5
Peu de la Creu, C. - p342 E10/F10
Pi I Margall, C. - p341 J5/K4/5
Pi, C. - p344 C4, p345 B5
Pi, Plaça - p345 B5
Pi, Passatge - p345 B5
Picasso, Passeig - p343 H10/11
Pierre de Coubertin, C. - p339 A10//11
Pietat, C. - p345 C5
Pintor Fortuny, C. - p342 F10, p344 A3/B3
Piquer, C. - p342 D11/E11
Pius XII, Plaça - p338 A3
Plata, C. - p345 C7
Plató, C. - p340 E3
Plegamans, C. - p345 E6/7
Poeta Boscà, Plaça - p343 H13
Poeta Cabanyes, C. - p339 D11, p342 D11
Polonia, C. - p341 K4
Pomaret, C. - p338 D1
Pompeu Fabra, Avda - p341 J3/K3
Pons I Clerch, Plaça - p345 F5
Portaferrissa, C. - p342 F10/G10, p344 B4/C4
Portal de la Pau, Plaça - p342 F12, p345 A8
Portal de l'Angel, Avda - p342 G9/10, p344 C2/3/4
Portal de Santa Madrona, C. - p342 E11/F11
Portal Nou, C. - p343 H10, p344 F4
Pou de la Cadena, C. - p345 C5
Pou Dolç, C. - p345 C6
Pou Figuera, C. - p344 F4
Praga, C. - p341 K4
Prat de la Riba, Plaça - p338 C3
Premià, C. - p338 A6/B7, p339 A7/B7
Princep d'Astúries, Avda - p340 G4
Princesa, C. - p343 H11, p345 D5/E5/F5
Provença, C. - p338 C7/D7, p340 D7/E7/F7/G7, p341 H7/J7/K7/L7, p339 C7/D7
Providència, C. - p341 H4/J4
Ptge Fontanelles - p338 C1/D1
Puigmartí, C. - p341 H5
Puigxuriguer, C. - p342 E12
Pujades, C. - p343 K10/L10
Pujades, Passeig - p343 J10
Putget, C. - p340 F3/G3
Quintana, C. - p345 B5
Radas, C. - p339 C10/D10
Rafael Batlle, C. - p338 C2/3
Rafael Benet, Plaça - p338 C2
Raimon Casellas, Plaça - p341 K3
Rambla Can Toda - p341 J3
Rambla Catalunya - p340 F6/7/8, p342 F7/8/9, p344 C1
Rambla del Raval - p342 E10/11
Rambla Mercedes - p341 H3/J3
Rambla Prat - p340 G4/5
Ramelleres, C. - p344 B2/3
Ramón de Maeztu, C. - p341 J3/K3
Ramon Amadeu, Placeta - p344 C3
Ramon Berenguer El Gran, Plaça - p345 D5
Ramon Trias Fargas, C. - p343 K11/12
Ramon Turró, C. - p343 K11/L11
Ramon y Cajal, C. - p341 H5
Raset, C. - p340 D3/E3
Raspall, Plaça - p341 H4
Rauric, C. - p345 B5/6
Rec Comtal, C. - p343 H10, p344 F4
Rec, C. - p343 H11, p345 F6/7
Rector Triadó, C. - p339 B7/8
Rector Ubach, C. - p340 E4
Regomir, C. - p345 C6/7
Regomir, Plaça - p345 C6
Reig i Bonet, C. - p341 H4/J5
Reina Amàlia, C. - p342 E10/11
Reina Cristina, C. - p342 G11, p345 E8
Reina Elisenda De Montcada, Passeig de la - p338 B1/C1
Reina Maria Cristina, Avda - p339 B9
Reina Maria Cristina, Plaça - p338 B4
Reina, C. - p340 D3/4

República Argentina, Avda - p340 G2/3
Reque-Sens, C. - p342 E10
Rera de Palau, C. - p345 E7
Revolució Setembre, Plaça 1868 - p341 H5
Ribeira, C. - p343 H11
Ribera, C. - p345 F7
Ribes, C. - p343 J9/K9
Ricart, C. - p339 C10
Riego, C. - p338 A7/B7, p339 A7/B7
Riera Alta, C. - p342 E9/10
Riera Baixa, C. - p342 E10
Riera Sant Miquel, C. - p340 G6
Riereta, C. - p342 E10/11
Ríos Rosas, C. - p340 F3
Ripoll, C. - p344 D4
Rita Bonney, C. - p338 D5
Rius I Taulet, Plaça - p340 G5
Rivadeneyra, C. - p344 C2/3
Robador, C. - p342 F10/11, p345 A5
Robrenyo, C. - p338 B6/C6, p339 B6/C6
Roca, C. - p344 B4
Rocafort, C. - p338 D6/7, p339 D6-9
Roger de Flor, C. - p341 J6/7/8, p343 J7/8/9/10
Roger de Llúria, C. - p340 G6/7/8, p342 G7/8/9
Roig, C. - p342 F10
Roma, Avda - p338 C7, p340 D7/E7, p339 C7/D7, p342 D7/E7
Romans, C. - p341 J5
Ronda de Guinardó - p341 J4/K4
Ronda del Mig - p341 K4/5/L5
Ronda General Mitre - p338 C3/D3, p340 F3/G3
Ronda Litoral - p342 D12/13/E12/F12/G12, p343 H12/J12/K12/L12, p345 A8/B8/C8/D8/E8/F8
Ronda San Pere - p342 G9/H9
Ronda Sant Antoni - p342 E9
Ronda Sant Pau - p342 E10/11
Ronda Sant Pere - p343 H9, p344 D2/E2/F2/3
Ronda.Universitat - p342 F9/G9, p344 A1/B1
Ros de Olano, C. - p340 G5
Rosa Sensat, C. - p343 K11/12
Rosa, C. - p345 C7
Rosalía de Castro, C. - p341 K5/L5
Rosari, C. - p338 C3/D3
Roser, C. - p339 D11, p342 D11
Roses, C. - p338 A6, p339 A6
Roses, Plaça - p338 C5
Rosselló, C. - p338 C6/D6, p340 D6/E6/F6/G6, p341 H6/J6/K6/L6, p339 C6/D7
Rossend Arús, C. - p339 A7/8
Rossic, C. - p345 E6
Rovira i Trias, Plaça - p341 H4
Ruis i Taulet, Avda - p339 B9/C9
Rull, C. - p345 B7
S. Oleguer, C. - p342 Ell
S. Rafael, C. - p342 E10/F10
S. Ramon, C. - p342 E11
S.A.Abat, C. - p342 E10
Sabateret, C. - p345 F6
Sabino de Arana, C. - p338 A3/4
Sagrada Família, Plaça - p341 J7
Sagristans, C. - p344 D4
Sagues, C. - p340 E5
Salou, C. - p338 A7, p339 A7
Salvà, C. - p339 D11, p342 D11
Salvador Espriu, C. - p343 K12/L12
Sancho de Ávila, C. - p343 K10/L10
Sanjoanistes, C. - p340 F4/G4
Sanllehy, Plaça - p341 K4
Sant Agustí Vel, Plaça I - p344 F4
Sant Agustí, Plaça - p345 A5
Sant Antoni Abat, Passatge - p342 D9
Sant Antoni dels Sombrerers, C. - p345 E6
Sant Antoni Maria Claret, C. - p341 J6/K6/L6
Sant Antoni, C. - p338 A7/B7, p339 A7/B7
Sant Antoni, Travessera de - p340 G5
Sant Benet, Passeig - p344 F3
Sant Carles, C. - p343 H13
Sant Climent, C. - p342 E10
Sant Crist, C. - p339 A7
Sant Cugat, C. - p341 H3
Sant Cugat, Plaça - p343 H10, p345 E5
Sant Domènec del Call, C. - p345 C5
Sant Domènec, C. - p340 G5
Sant Elies, C. - p340 F4
Sant Erasme, C. - p342 E9
Sant Eusebi, C. - p340 F4/G4
Sant Felip Neri, Plaça - p345 C5
Sant Francesc, Placeta - p345 B6

Sant Fructuós, C. - p339 A9/B9
Sant Galetà, Plaça - p338 C1
Sant Germa, C. - p339 B9
Sant Gil, C. - p342 E9
Sant Gregori Taumaturg, Plaça - p338 D4, p340 D4
Sant Honorat, C. - p345 C5
Sant Iu, Plaça - p345 D5
Sant Jacint, C. - p345 E5
Sant Jaume, Plaça - p342 G11, p345 C5
Sant Joan Bosc, Passeig o - p338 C2/3
Sant Joan, Passeig - p341 H5/6/7/8, p343 H7/8/9
Sant Joaquim, C. - p340 G5
Sant Joaquim, Plaça - p340 G3
Sant Josep de la Muntanya, Avda - p341 H3
Sant Josep Oriol, Plaça - p345 B5
Sant Just, Plaça - p342 G11, p345 D6
Sant Lluís, C. - p341 H5/J5
Sant Madrona, Passeig - p339 B10/11
Sant Magí, C. - p340 G3/4
Sant Marc, C. - p340 G5
Sant Medir, C. - p339 A6/7
Sant Miquel, Baixada - p345 B6/C6
Sant Miquel, Plaça - p345 C6
Sant Miquel, Placeta - p340 G5
Sant Pau, C. - p342 E11/F11, p345 A5
Sant Pere Màrtir, C. - p340 G5/6
Sant Pere Més Alt, C. - p342 G10/H10, p343 H10, p344 D3/E3/F3
Sant Pere Més Baix, C. - p342 G10/H10, p343 H10, p344 D4/E4/F4
Sant Pere Mitja, C. - p342 G10/H10, p343 H10, p344 E4/F4
Sant Pere, Plaça - p343 H10, p344 F3
Sant Roc, C. - p339 B8
Sant Salvador, C. - p341 H4
Sant Sever, C. - p345 C5
Sant Vicenç De Sarrià, Plaça - p338 C2
Sant Vicenç, C. - p342 E9/10
Santa Amelia, C. - p338 B2
Santa Anna, C. - p344 B3/C3
Santa Carolina, C. - p341 K5/L5
Santa Caterina, C. - p338 B6/7
Santa Caterina, Plaça - p344 F4
Santa Elena, C. - p342 E10
Santa Eugenia, C. - p340 G5
Santa Eulàlia, Baixada - p345 C5
Santa Eulàlia, C. - p341 H6
Santa Fe de Nou Mexic, C. - p338 D4
Santa Madrona, C. - p342 E11
Santa Madrona, C. - p345 E6
Santa Maria, Plaça - p345 E6
Santa Monica, C. - p345 A7
Santa Perpètua, C. - p340 G3/H3, p341 H4
Santa Teresa, C. - p340 G6
Santaló, C. - p340 E3/4/5
Sants, C. - p338 A6/7, p339 A6/7/B7
Saragossa, C. - p340 F34/G4
Sardana - p339 D12
Sardenya, C. - p341 K4/5/6/7/8
Sardenya, C. - p343 K7-11
Sarrià, Avda - p338 C3/4/D4/5, p340 D5/6
Sarrià, Plaça - p338 C1
Seca, C. - p345 E6
Secretari Coloma, C. - p341 J4/5
Sémoleres, C. - p345 E5
Sèneca, C. - p340 F6/G6
Septimania, C. - p340 G3
Sepúlveda, C. - p338 C9/D9, p342 D9/E9
Séquia, C. - p344 F4
Serra Xic, C. - p344 F4
Serra, C. - p345 C7
Sert, Passatge - p344 E3
Seu, Plaça de la - p344 D4
Sicília, C. - p341 J6/7/8, p343 J7/8/9/10
Sidé, C. - p345 D5/E5
Sils, C. - p345 B7
Simó Oller, C. - p345 C7
Siracusa, C. - p341 H6
Sitges, C. - p344 B3
Sol, Plaça - p340 G5
Sombrerers, C. - p345 E6
Sor Eulalia d'Anzizu, C. - p338 A2
Sortidor, Plaça - p339 D10/11
Sostres, C. - p341 H2/3
Sota Muralla, Passeig - p345 D8/E8
Sots-Tinent Navarro, C. - p345 D6/7
Sta Llúcia, C. - p345 C5/D5
Sta. Anna, C. - p340 G5
Tallers, C. - p342 F9, p344 A1/2/B2
Tamarit, C. - p339 C9/D9, p342

D9/E9
Tànger, C. - p343 K9/L9
Tantarantana, C. - p345 F5
Tapies, C. - p342 E11
Tapineria, C. - p345 D5
Tapioles, C. - p339 D10/111, p342 D10/11
Taquigraf Garriga, C. - p338 B5/C5/D5
Taquigraf Martí, C. - p338 B4/5
Taquigraf Serra, C. - p338 C5
Tarongers, C. - p339 C11/12
Tarongeta, C. - p345 D6
Tarragona, C. - p339 C7/8
Tarrós, C. - p345 E5
Tavern, C. - p340 E3/4
Taxdirt, C. - p341 J5/K5
Teatre, Plaça - p345 B6/7
Templers, C. - p345 C6
Tenerife, C. - p341 K3/4
Tenor Masini, C. - p338 A6, p339 A6
Terol, C. - p341 H5
Tetuan, Plaça - p341 H8/J8, p343 H8/J8
Til.Lers, Passeig - p338 A2
Tinent Coronel Valenzuela, C. - p338 A2/3
Tiradors, C. - p345 F5
Tomàs Mieres, C. - p344 D3
Topazi, C. - p340 H4
Tordera - p341 H6
Torn, Plaça - p340 G4
Torrent D'En Vidalet, C. - p341 H5
Torrent de les Flors - p341 H4/5/J4
Torrent de L'Olla, C. - p340 G4/5/6/H4
Torres i Amat, C. - p344 A1
Torres, C. - p341 H6
Torrijos, C. - p341 H5
Tous, C. - p341 K4
Trafalgar, C. - p342 G9/H9, p343 H9/10, p344 E2/3/F3
Traginers, Plaça - p342 G11, p345 D6
Traja, C. - p339 A8/9
Trelawny, C. - p343 J12/13
Tres Torres, C. - p338 C3/D3, p340 D3
Trilla, Plaça - p340 G4
Trinitat, C. - p345 B6/C6
Trinquet, C. - p338 B2
Túnel de la Rovira - p341 K3/4/L2/3
Tuset, C. - p340 F4/5
Unió, C. - p342 F11, p345 A6
Urquinaona, Plaça - p344 D3
València, C. - p340 D7/E7/F7/G7, p341 H7/J7/K7/L7, p339 C7/D7, p342 D7/E7/F7/G7, p343 H7/J7/K7/L7
Valldonzella, C. - p342 E9/F9, p344 A2
Valldoreix, C. - p341 H3
Valespir, C. - p338 B5/6/7
Vallhonrat, C. - p339 C10
Vallirana, C. - p340 G3/4
Vallmajor, C. - p340 D4/E3/4
Valseca, C. - p341 K4
Veguer, C. - p345 D5
Ventura Gassol, Plaça - p340 G3
Verdaguer i Callis, C. - p344 D3/4
Verdi, C. - p341 H2/3/4/5
Vergos, C. - p338 C2/D2, p340 D2
Verònica - p345 C6
Vic, C. - p340 G5
Viceroç Martorell, Plaça - p344 B3
Víctor Balaguer, Plaça - p345 D6/7
Victòria, C. - p344 F3/4
Vidre, C. - p345 B6
Vidrieria, C. - p345 E6/7
Vigatans, C. - p345 D6/E6
Vila de Madrid, Plaça - p344 C3
Vila i Vilà, C. - p342 D11/E11/12
Viladecols, Baixada - p345 D6
Viladomat, C. - p338 D6/7, p340 D5/6/7/8, p339 D6-10, p342 D7/8/9/10
Vilajoiosa, C. - p343 H13
Vilamarí, C. - p339 C7/8/9
Vilamur, C. - p338 B4/5
Vilanova, Avda - p343 J10
Vilardell, C. - p339 B8
Villarroel, C. - p340 E5/6/7/8, p342 E7/8/9
Violant d'Hongria Reina d'Aragó, C. - p338 A6/B6
Virai, C. - p338 B6/7, p339 B6/7
Vireina, Passatge - p344 A4
Vireina, Plaça - p341 H5
Vivers, C. - p339 B11
Wagner, Plaça - p338 D5, p340 D5
Watt, C. - p339 B7
Wellington, C. - p343 J10/11/12
Xuclà, C. - p342 F9/10, p344 B3/4
Zamora, C. - p343 K10/11

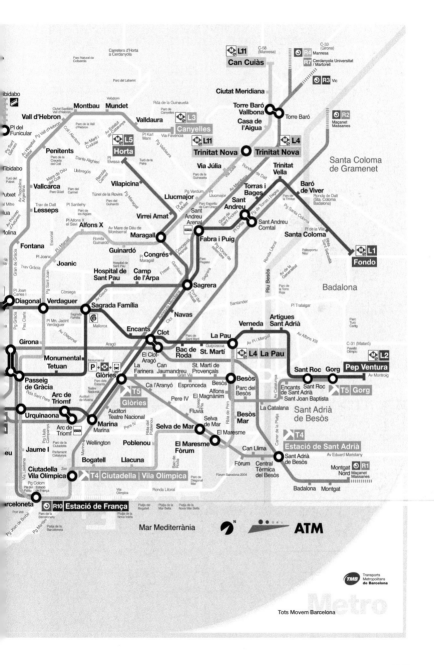

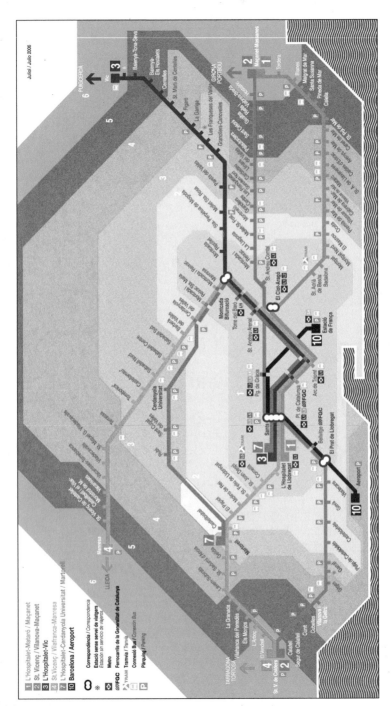